Austrian Review of International and European Law

Austrian Review of International and European Law

VOLUME 28

The titles published in this series are listed at *brill.com/aril*

Austrian Review of International and European Law

VOLUME 28 (2023)

Edited by

Stephan Wittich
Jane A. Hofbauer
Philipp Janig

BRILL | NIJHOFF

LEIDEN | BOSTON

Suggested citation: 28 ARIEL (2023)

Typeface for the Latin, Greek, and Cyrillic scripts: "Brill". See and download: brill.com/brill-typeface.

ISSN 1385-1306
E-ISSN 1573-6512
ISBN 978-90-04-73123-3 (hardback)

This book is printed on acid-free paper and produced in a sustainable manner.

Austrian Review of International and European Law

Manuscripts, editorial communications and book reviews as well as books for review are welcome and may be sent to:

Austrian Review of International and European Law
c/o Section for International Law and International Relations
University of Vienna
Juridicum
Schottenbastei 10-16
A-1010 Vienna
Austria
philipp.janig@univie.ac.at
https://eur-int-comp-law.univie.ac.at/en/ariel-international-law/

Please note that it is the policy of the *Austrian Review* to only consider exclusive submissions for publication!

Editorial

As public international lawyers inclined towards multilateralist approaches, we find that glimmers of hope are few and far between. At the time of writing this editorial, we are witnessing the opening moves of a second Trump administration in the United States, marked by territorial claims being hurled against Greenland, Canada and Panama. All of that unfolds against the backdrop of a new Russian offensive in its ongoing war of aggression against Ukraine. The language accompanying both developments is eerily reminiscent of an imperialist ideology that should have better remained where it belonged – in 19th century textbooks, not contemporary geopolitics.

The attack by Hamas against Israel on 7 October 2023 and the ensuing developments – of particular relevance to the year to which this volume is dedicated – have also placed the 'humanization' of international law under significant strain. While it lies within the nature of lawyers to disaggregate and 'de-politicize' conflict into several distinct exercises of rule-application, it should not go unspoken that modern international law also rests upon an underlying belief in our common humanity. In the last months and years, it all too often seemed that this belief is little more than a thin veneer for many within our 'invisible college' – whether in their disregard for the fate of (civilian) hostages that are being used as bargaining leverage, or for the devasting loss of civilian life in Gaza.

The 'question of Palestine'[1] will also continue to occupy international lawyers and has, *e.g.*, significantly added to the ICJ's docket in recent years: from the Advisory Opinion on *Legal Consequences arising from the Policies and Practices of Israel in the Occupied Palestinian Territory, including East Jerusalem* – already requested in January 2023 – to the allegations of an ongoing genocide and violations of international humanitarian law in Gaza in *South Africa v Israel* and *Nicaragua v Germany*, as well as the most recent request for an Advisory Opinion relating to Israel's ban of UNRWA[2]. The *Situation in the State of Palestine* has also been taken up by the ICC, where we have witnessed a surprising role-reversal by some actors – even more so than in the ICJ context. The issuance of an arrest warrant against Benjamin

---

1 UNGA Res 57/107 (14 February 2003) UN Doc A/RES/57/107.

2 *Obligations of Israel in relation to the Presence and Activities of the United Nations, Other International Organizations and Third States in and in relation to the Occupied Palestinian Territory* (Request for an Advisory Opinion of 19 December 2024).

Netanyahu, in particular, has prompted ostensibly steadfast proponents of an 'international rule of law' to question, or even openly call for the disregard of, the Court's authority. Meanwhile, domestic courts continue to grapple with adjudicating the legality of arms exports to Israel and the curtailment of freedom of expression and assembly in the context of Gaza war-related protests. Worrisome executive overreach – including deportations outside the bounds of the law – poses additional challenges on this front.

There is, however, a small glimmer of hope that emerges from of all of this: the surprising resonance of international law in the public imagination. The oral proceedings on provisional measures in *South Africa v Israel* have especially captured public attention, with the hearings reportedly being broadcasted live in South Africa and elsewhere, and clips being widely shared on social media. Similarly, the subsequent order has sparked public debate on everything from the implications of the exact placement of a comma[3] to the meaning of the 'plausibility' standard in ICJ jurisprudence[4].

The present volume may, hopefully, do its small part in re-affirming the importance of the international legal order. The contributions may broadly be categorized in three groups: the first three addressing various matters of human rights protection, two touching upon questions raised in the context of the ongoing Israel-Palestine conflict and our 'Current Developments' section that is dedicated to various 'Austrian' contributions to international and European law.

The contribution of *Rosana Garciandia* takes note of the recent turn towards inter-state communications before the UN Committee on the Elimination of Racial Discrimination, and the re-examination of its procedural features this may entail. *Garciandia* argues that the perception of treaty bodies and states on the aim of inter-state communications has significantly developed. While initially conceived as being a mechanism for treaty compliance, they now may serve a 'combination of aims' – including dispute settlement and as a strategic instrument in international relations. *Garciandia* concludes that the fulfilment of these complimentary functions may require adapting the procedural features of inter-state communications to provide for sufficient flexibility.

---

3 Patrick Wintour, 'How a single comma is allowing Israel to question ICJ Rafah ruling' (*The Guardian*, 29 May 2024) <www.theguardian.com/global/article/2024/may/29/how-a-single-comma-is-allowing-israel-to-question-icj-rafah-ruling> accessed 1 April 2025.

4 'Former head of ICJ explains ruling on genocide case against Israel brought by S Africa' (*BBC*, 26 April 2024) <www.bbc.com/news/av/world-middle-east-68906919> accessed 1 April 2025.

In her article, *Alrun Cohen* inquires the use of Artificial Intelligence as a counter-terrorism tool from a European human rights perspective, highlighting both potential risks and benefits. In the context of challenges, *Cohen* examines ECtHR case law on the right to privacy (Art 8), non-discrimination (Art 14), the right to an effective remedy (Art 13) and to a fair trial (Art 6). However, she likewise highlights how AI tools can become a boon for counterterrorism, which ultimately operates to safeguard the right to life of (potential) victims. Thus, algorithms may allow authorities to identify patterns and potentially predict terrorist activities, or contribute to the deradicalization of vulnerable persons. *Cohen* concludes that the ECtHR is 'well-equipped to manage' this tension, while also pointing towards ongoing regulatory activities in the field of AI.

The contribution of *György Andrássy* engages in a re-examination of minority rights under Article 27 ICCPR. He argues that the provision necessarily has to give rise to rights for (members of) minorities that go beyond the human rights that everyone enjoys, to not become devoid of purpose. *Andrássy* explains that for religious, linguistic and ethnic minorities that question arises specifically in relation to the freedom of thought, conscience and religion as well as the freedom of expression. However, scholarship has long overlooked these matters. After a detailed discussion of these overlapping entitlements, *Andrássy* argues that the 'true meaning' of Article 27 ICCPR is to entail a 'right to special protection' for historical minorities of each country.

The next two articles both delve deeper into questions that relate to the ongoing Israel-Palestine conflict. In his contribution, *Haris Huremagić* addresses the legal consequences of advisory opinions, specifically against the backdrop of the 2024 Advisory Opinion on the *Occupied Palestinian Territory*. He argues that classical textbooks present us with a 'false dichotomy' between 'binding judgments and non-binding advisory opinions'. In addition to treaty provisions that explicitly provide for the binding force of such opinions, *Huremagić* contends that they can give rise to legal effects *erga omnes* when addressing violations of *jus cogens*. These opinions address obligations that derive from customary international law for the international community as a whole and are as such 'neither strictly binding nor entirely non-binding'. *Huremagić* then turns to the 2024 Advisory Opinion and shows how the reaction of states may support his argument.

Elisabeth Hoffberger-Pippan asks which legal obligations arise for third states when considering arms exports to Israel in the context of the ongoing armed conflict with Hamas. These obligations might stem from both international and European law, and may – of particular importance in the present circumstances – be inferred from current rulings of international courts.

Hoffberger-Pippan then turns to state practice on arms exports to Israel. By focusing on the Netherlands and Germany, she shows how international law finds reflection in decisions of domestic courts, which have to navigate a highly political matter. Even though both countries are bound by the same obligations under international and European law, *Hoffberger-Pippan* highlights the remarkable divergence in judicial oversight. Her contribution closes with a call for a more consistent application across jurisdictions when upholding international obligations.

This year also features a particularly voluminous section on Current Developments, all of which relate to various forms of contributions of Austria to international and European law since 2023.

The contribution by *Isabella E Brunner* provides a personal assessment of the Austrian national position paper on 'Cyber Activities and International Law', which she co-drafted. Published in April 2024, it constitutes part of a broader trend of states clarifying their position on how international law applies in the cyber context and has been lauded as a particularly 'progressive' contribution[5] to that discourse. *Brunner* notes the innovative aspects of the Austrian paper, which also relates to its structure through the use of examples and the highlighting of 'key positions'. The different substantive points of the Austrian position are placed in the broader trend noted above. Most notably, *Brunner* points us toward Austria's unique position of rejecting the notion of 'cyberspace' as a 'new and separate domain' and an entire section being dedicated to 'Diplomatic and Consular Missions, International Organizations and Data Embassies'.

Matthias Radosztics offers insight into an issue that has kept the Office of the Legal Advisor of the Austrian Foreign Ministry occupied ever since the ECtHR handed down its judgment in *Waite and Kennedy* some 25 years ago. As a host of numerous international organizations, Austria is particularly concerned with navigating the tension between their jurisdictional immunities and the employees' right to access to court under Art 6(1) ECHR. This has recently come to the forefront: for the first time ever, the Constitutional Court declared provisions of the OPEC Headquarters Agreement unconstitutional in September 2022, as employees had no access to 'reasonable alternative

---

5 Przemysław Roguski, 'Austria's Progressive Stance on Cyber Operations and International Law' (*Just Security*, 25 June 2024) <www.justsecurity.org/96993/austrias-stance-cyber-operations-international-law/> accessed 26 March 2025.

means' to pursue their rights.[6] As *Radosztics* explains, this has *inter alia* led to amendments to the OPEC Headquarters Agreement, which he complements with a comprehensive survey of dispute settlement mechanisms in Austrian Headquarters Agreements. These efforts were ultimately successful, with the Constitutional Court recently affirming the constitutionality of the new legal framework of OPEC.[7]

The article of *Hannah Grandits* and *Martin Baumgartner* delves deep in what can easily be described as one the most intriguing decisions on international law by an Austrian court. In a judgment of May 2023, the Supreme Court has – for the second time already – weighed in on a long-standing dispute between the Russian Federation and private Ukrainian corporation concerning rights to a real property that was in the ownership of the Soviet Union. *Grandits* and *Baumgartner* critically analyze how the Supreme Court dealt with the various associated issues of international law: from state succession to property, to (regional) customary international law and the persistent objector doctrine, the legal value of *Notes Verbale* of the 'host state', as well as the (non-)opposability of treaties between third states. The Supreme Court ultimately found that the property was co-owned by the Russian Federation and Ukraine, on the basis of two treaties relating to foreign property concluded by the 'successor states' to the Soviet Union in 1991 and 1992. As *Grandits* and *Baumgartner* point out, this could spell more litigation, as the same reasoning would apply to *all* foreign property of the Soviet Union. At any rate, the saga continues before Austrian courts: the Supreme Court has remanded parts of the case back to the lowers courts, to determine whether other states had co-ownership shares in the property.

Last but not least, *Lisa Heschl* examines a recent judgment of the CJEU of October 2024, which was prompted by a preliminary ruling request of the Austrian Supreme Administrative Court. The CJEU was confronted with the Taliban's manifold discriminatory policies towards women – a system that *Heschl* describes as a 'gender apartheid regime'. The Court ultimately considered that in light of this situation, Afghan women and girls were facing an 'act of persecution' within the meaning of Art 9(1.b) Qualificative Directive. *Heschl* highlights that the judgment departs from the CJEU's

---

6 Constitutional Court, Judgment SV 1/2021-23 of 29 September 2022. For an unofficial translation, see Martin Baumgartner, Philipp Janig, Viktoria Ritter, Maximilian Weninger and Stephan Wittich, 'Austrian Judicial Decisions Involving Questions of International Law/Österreichische Judikatur zum Internationalen Recht' (2022) 27 ARIEL 332ff.

7 Constitutional Court, Decision SV 1/2024 of 27 November 2024.

long-standing case law on the requirement to individually assess protection claims, however that it may also be seen as part of a trend towards a gender-sensitive interpretation of EU asylum law.

As always, the volume contains the practice of Austrian courts as well as Austrian diplomatic and parliamentary practice in international law and a book review section.

In 'editorial' news, we are delighted to announce that Philipp Janig – who has long supported us as managing editor – will now on join us as a full co-editor of the ARIEL. *Ad multos annos*! We are also, once again, thankful for the diligent work of our editorial assistant, Maximilian Weninger.

Jane A. Hofbauer, Philipp Janig and *Stephan Wittich*
on behalf of the editorial board

Contents

Austrian Practice in International Law 2023
Österreichische Praxis zum Internationalen Recht 2023

Book Reviews

Articles

Inter-State Communications before United Nations Human Rights Treaty Bodies: Distinctive Features and Evolving Aims

Dr Rosana Garciandia | Senior Lecturer in Public International Law, King's College London, Co-Director of the King's Centre for International Governance and Dispute Resolution, Research Leader at the British Institute of International and Comparative Law

Abstract

In 2018, the United Nations (UN) Committee on the Elimination of Racial Discrimination (CERD Committee) received its first three inter-State communications since the Convention it monitors was adopted in 1965: *Palestine v Israel*, *Qatar v Saudi Arabia* and *Qatar v United Arab Emirates*. These were the first inter-State cases ever initiated before this or any other UN human rights treaty body, activating a mechanism which had laid dormant for decades. In August 2024, the *ad hoc* conciliation commission for *Palestine v Israel* published its final report, marking the first time that an inter-state communication before a UN treaty body reaches its final phase. The awakening of the mechanism has inspired new lines of research, testing the mechanism in the practice of the CERD Committee and triggering analysis of its procedural features in this and other treaties. What remains underexplored is the connection between those features and the aims that States and other actors envisage for the procedure. This article explores that connection and contends that any revision of the features of the mechanism that its use may bring should be informed by its aims, which are multiple and evolving. The article proceeds in three parts. The first part analyses distinctive features of the mechanism. The second part explores the evolution in the aims of inter-State communications in connection with those features. The third part concludes by reflecting on how those connections could inform forthcoming reforms of the mechanism.

Keywords

Inter-state communications – United Nations – human rights treaty bodies – aims – features

Austrian Review of International and European Law **28**: 3-32, 2023.
 | DOI:10.1163/15736512-02801002

I. Introduction

In 2018, the United Nations (UN) Committee on the Elimination of Racial Discrimination (CERD Committee) received its first three inter-state communications since the Convention it monitors was adopted in 1965: *Palestine v Israel, Qatar v Saudi Arabia* and *Qatar v United Arab Emirates*.[1] These were the first inter-state cases ever initiated before this or any other UN human rights treaty body, activating a mechanism which had laid dormant for decades.[2] In August 2024, the *ad hoc* conciliation commission for *Palestine*

[1] The two communications initiated by Qatar were suspended in early 2021 following an agreement between the parties. On 19 January 2022, the CERD Committee decided to terminate the proceeding against Saudi Arabia as neither of the states parties concerned had expressed a wish to continue proceedings. On 26 January 2023, following requests of termination from both states parties, proceedings against the United Arab Emirates were also terminated. For more information, see 'Inter-State Communications: Committee on the Elimination of Racial Discrimination' (*Office of the High Commissioner for Human Rights*) <www.ohchr.org/en/treaty-bodies/cerd/inter-state-communications> accessed 8 April 2024.

[2] Similar mechanisms are available in UN treaties or protocols on civil and political rights (International Covenant on Civil and Political Rights, 16 December 1966, 999 UNTS 171 (ICCPR) Articles 41-42); economic, social and cultural rights (Optional Protocol to the International Covenant on Economic, Social and Cultural Rights, 10 December 2008, 2922 UNTS 29 (OP-ICESCR) Article 10); torture (Convention against Torture and Other Cruel, Inhuman or Degrading Treatment or Punishment, 10 December 1984, 1465 UNTS 85 (CAT) Article 21); the rights of migrant workers (International Convention on the Protection of the Rights of All Migrant Workers and Members of their Families, 18 December 1990, 2220 UNTS 3 (CMW) Article 76 (note, however, that this particular provision has not yet entered into force)); children's rights (Optional Protocol to the Convention on the Rights of the Child on a communications procedure, 19 December 2011, 2983 UNTS 135 Article 12); and enforced disappearances (International Convention for the Protection of All Persons from Enforced Disappearance, 20 December 2006, 2716 UNTS 3 (CED) Article 32). Inter-state procedures are also possible before regional human rights courts. While only a few cases have been heard in the Inter-American (*Nicaragua v Costa Rica*, Interstate Case 01/06, Inter-American Commission on Human Rights Report No 11/07 (8 March 2007); *Franklin Guillermo Aisalla Molina (Ecuador-Colombia)*, Inter-state Petition IP-02, Inter-American Commission on Human Rights Series L/V/II.140 Report No 112/10 (21 October 2010)) and African (*Democratic Republic of Congo v Republics of Burundi, Rwanda, and Uganda*, African Commission on Human and Peoples' Rights, Communication No 227/99 (2003); *Sudan v South Sudan*, African Commission on Human and Peoples' Rights, Communication No 422/12

v Israel published its final report, marking the first time that an inter-state communication before a UN treaty body reaches its final phase.[3] The awakening of the mechanism has inspired new lines of research, testing the mechanism in the practice of the CERD Committee and triggering analysis of its procedural features in this and other treaties.[4] What remains underexplored is the connection between those features and the aims that states and other actors envisage for the procedure.

This article explores that connection and contends that any development or revision of the features of the mechanism that its use may bring should be informed by its aims, which are multiple and evolving. The features of the inter-state communications procedure – *i.e.* the way in which the procedure was designed in the different UN treaties and in subsequent procedural rules – have been associated with the reluctance of states to consent to it,

(2013); *Djibouti v Eritrea*, African Commission on Human and Peoples' Rights, Communication No 478/14 (pending)) systems, inter-state communications have been relatively common before the European Court of Human Rights (ECtHR) (32 cases, including multiple proceedings between *Ukraine v Russia*; *Armenia v Azerbaijan; Azerbaijan v Armenia*). For an analysis of inter-state communications before the ECtHR, see Isabella Risini, *The Inter-State Application under the European Convention on Human Rights: Between Collective Enforcement of Human Rights and International Dispute Settlement* (2018). For an analysis of inter-state communications under the African system, see Frans Viljoen, 'A Procedure Likely to Remain Rare in the African System: An Introduction to Inter-State Communications Under the African Human Rights System' (*Völkerrechtsblog*, 27 April 2021) <https://voelkerrechtsblog.org/a-procedure-likely-to-remain-rare-in-the-african-system/> accessed 8 April 2024.

3 UN Committee on the Elimination of Racial Discrimination, 'Report of the ad hoc Conciliation Commission on the inter-State Communication submitted by the State of Palestine against Israel under Article 11 of the ICERD' (21 August 2024) UN Doc CERD/C/113/3. For an analysis of the *ad hoc* conciliation commission report, see David Keane, 'A Missed Opportunity: The Decision in Palestine v Israel' (EJIL: Talk!, 5 September 2024) <www.ejiltalk.org/a-missed-opportunity-the-decision-in-palestine-v-israel/> accessed 27 September 2024.

4 Jan Eiken and David Keane, 'Towards an Amicable Solution: The Inter-State Communications Procedure under ICERD' (2022) 21 The Law and Practice of International Courts and Tribunals 302; Isabella Risini and Geir Ulfstein, 'Human Rights, State Complaints', in Anne Peters (ed), *Max Planck Encylopedia of Public International Law* (last updated June 2022) <https://opil.ouplaw.com/home/mpil> accessed 8 April 2024; Gay McDougall, 'The International Convention on the Elimination of All Forms of Racial Discrimination' (*United Nations Audiovisual Library of International Law*, February 2021) <https://legal.un.org/avl/pdf/ha/cerd/cerd_e.pdf> accessed 8 April 2024.

both generally and in particular cases.[5] Those features respond partly to what states have traditionally considered to be the aims that the mechanism should serve, namely treaty compliance and the protection of human rights. Importantly, beyond the aims envisaged by states, UN human rights treaty bodies, civil society organisations and other relevant actors have also contributed to an evolution of conceptions as to the aims this mechanism should serve, impacting their approach to its use. In a moment when the limited available inter-state communications practice suggests that more specific rules may be needed and some aspects of the procedure could benefit from reform, such evolution should inform any procedural development or reform.

Methodologically, the analysis is based on desk research, including a review of the relevant academic literature, the work of UN human rights treaty bodies, international and regional courts, and of the *ad hoc* conciliation commission for *Palestine v Israel*, and an analysis of the relevant treaties, including the *travaux préparatoires* and the historical context in which the treaties were negotiated. It also builds on consultation with experts and stakeholders, including states, legal advisers to states, current and former members of UN treaty bodies, civil society organisations, and academics from a variety of disciplines.

The article proceeds in three parts. The first part analyses distinctive features of the mechanism (section II). The second part explores the evolution in the aims of inter-state communications in connection with those features (section III). The third part (section IV) concludes by reflecting on how those connections could inform forthcoming reforms of the mechanism.

II. Distinctive Features of Inter-State Communications

The filing of the three first-ever inter-state communications, all before the CERD Committee in 2018 (*Qatar v Saudi Arabia, Qatar v UAE, Palestine*

---

5 Scott Leckie, 'The Inter-State Complaint Procedure in International Human Rights Law: Hopeful Prospects or Wishful Thinking?' (1988) 10 Human Rights Quarterly 249, 251-253; Christian Tomuschat, 'Lessons Drawn and Upcoming Challenges' in Christian Tomuschat and Marcelo Kohen (eds), *Flexibility in International Dispute Settlement: Conciliation Revisited* (2020) 265, 266; Dai Tamada, 'Inter-State Communication under ICERD: From ad hoc Conciliation to Collective Enforcement' (2021) 12 Journal of International Dispute Settlement 405, 425f; David Keane, 'Mapping the International Convention on the Elimination of All Forms of Racial Discrimination as a Living Instrument' (2020) 20 Human Rights Law Review 236, 266; Arne Vandenbogaerde, *Towards Shared Accountability in International Human Rights Law: Law, Procedures and Principles* (2016) 118.

v Israel), provides an opportunity to examine how the features of the inter-state procedure under Articles 11-13 of the International Convention on the Elimination of Racial Discrimination (ICERD)[6] apply in practice.[7] These cases also sparked discussion of the features of inter-state communications under other treaties.[8]

This section explores four distinctive features of inter-state communications: the voluntary or compulsory nature of the procedure; standing requirements; the conciliatory element incorporated in some treaties; and the use of compromissory clauses connecting inter-state communication procedures with recourse to the International Court of Justice (ICJ). It does so by exploring the practice concerning inter-state communications before the CERD Committee and the ICJ, and observing commonalities with the practice of regional human rights courts.

A. Compulsory v Voluntary Procedures: The ICERD as the Exception

The inter-state procedure established under the ICERD is compulsory in character. Article 11(1) ICERD provides for an 'automatic' inter-state communication procedure.[9] In other words, once states are parties to the treaty, they

6 International Convention on the Elimination of All Forms of Racial Discrimination, 21 December 1965, 660 UNTS 195 (ICERD). For more on the ICERD, see Patrick Thornberry, *The International Convention on the Elimination of All Forms of Racial Discrimination: A Commentary* (2016).

7 Eiken and Keane (n 4) 302.

8 David Keane, 'Towards an "Amicable Solution" in the Universal Human Rights System: Inter-State Communications under the International Convention on the Elimination of Racial Discrimination' (*Völkerrechtsblog*, 28 April 2021) <https://voelkerrechtsblog.org/towards-an-amicable-solution-in-the-universal-human-rights-system/> accessed 8 April 2024; Jorge Contesse, 'Inter-State Cases in Disguise under Inter-American Human Rights Law: Advisory Opinions as Inter-State Disputes' (*Völkerrechtsblog*, 27 April 2021) <https://voelkerrechtsblog.org/de/inter-state-cases-in-disguise-under-inter-american-human-rights-law/> accessed 8 April 2024; Rachel Reilly and Hannah Trout, 'Inter-State Complaints in International Human Rights Law' (*British Institute of International and Comparative Law*, 27 April 2022) <www.biicl.org/documents/153_inter-state_complaints_in_international_human_rights_law_-_event_report.pdf> accessed 8 April 2024.

9 UN Committee on the Elimination of Racial Discrimination, 'Inter-State Communication submitted by the State of Palestine against Israel: Decision on Jurisdiction' (16 June 2021) UN Doc CERD/C/100/5, para 55.

'do not need to give their prior agreement or consent to the Committee for the latter to be seized with an inter-State communication'.[10] The compulsory model is also followed under the European Convention on Human Rights (ECHR) and the African Charter on Human and Peoples' Rights.[11] All other human rights treaties incorporate inter-state communications as a voluntary procedure,[12] meaning that ratifying states retain the power to not opt in to communications and thereby avoid being subjected to the jurisdiction of those bodies. This, however, also means that those states cannot initiate a procedure against other states, as the mechanism is envisaged as reciprocal. Notably, some treaties follow a double opt-in model, requiring the consent of the state not only for initiating the procedure but also for the appointment of the conciliation commission that will hear the communication.[13]

The establishment of voluntary procedures under most UN human rights treaties is consistent with some states' historic reluctance to accept compliance mechanisms envisaged in treaties (both inter-state and individual procedures), which led to a compromise solution reconciling the diverging views.[14] During the negotiation of treaties, many states saw inter-state communications as an unfriendly act,[15] a threat to national sovereignty[16] and the

---

10 *Ibid.*, para 56.

11 Convention for the Protection of Human Rights and Fundamental Freedoms (European Convention on Human Rights, as amended) (ECHR) Article 33; African Charter on Human and Peoples' Rights, 27 June 1981, 1520 UNTS 217 (African Charter) Articles 47-54. Under the African Charter, states may submit communications both to the African Commission and the African Court on Human and Peoples' Rights.

12 Article 41(1) ICCPR; Article 10(1) OP-ICESCR; Article 21(1) CAT; Article 76 CMW; Article 32 CED.

13 Keane, 'Towards an "Amicable Solution" in the Universal Human Rights System' (n 8).

14 Manfred Nowak, 'Comments on the UN High Commissioner's Proposals Aimed at Strengthening the UN Human Rights Treaty Body System' (2013) 31 Netherlands Quarterly of Human Rights 3, 3.

15 For example, during discussions on the draft ICERD, the Iraqi representative claimed that the adoption of an inter-state communication procedure 'might disturb international peace and impair friendly relations between States', with the potential of extending 'the cold war' by interfering in domestic affairs of other states (UN General Assembly Third Committee (20th session) 'Agenda item 58: Draft International Convention on the Elimination of All Forms of Racial Discrimination' (18 November 1965) UN Doc A/C.3/SR.1347, para 7).

16 For example, during negotiations for the ICCPR, those who considered the procedure of the Human Rights Committee contrary to national sovereignty

principle of non-interference,[17] and a tool that could be used with political motivations.[18] Establishing voluntary compliance mechanisms, and therefore giving states the option of not consenting to a specific procedure within a treaty, emphasized the importance of sovereignty, and was thus the preferred formula for most treaties.

But the voluntary formula has led to lower levels of engagement with the procedure in practice. The conventions which adopt a voluntary approach to inter-state communications have seen ratifications of these specific provisions remain rather low,[19] and no cases in the UN system have been initiated to date under a voluntary mechanism. The only voluntary system having received cases is the Inter-American system, where there have been two cases to

---

found that 'no State party should set itself up as a judge of the domestic actions of another (UN General Assembly 'Draft International Covenants on Human Rights: Annotation Prepared by the Secretary-General' (1 July 1955) UN Doc A/2929, 234).

17 For example, during negotiations for the ICCPR, the Ukrainian representative considered that any system other than the reporting system 'would introduce complications into the measures of implementation and ultimately yield negative results' (UN General Assembly Third Committee (21st session) 'Agenda item 62: Draft International Covenants on Human Rights' (7 November 1966) UN Doc A/C.3/SR.1415, para 8). See also UN General Assembly Third Committee (20th session) (n 15) paras 6-7.

18 During discussions on the draft ICERD, the representative of Jordan reacted by acknowledging that 'some Governments would no doubt find it impossible to resist the temptation of using the international machinery for political ends, but that should not prevent the United Nations from seeking to build an international community capable of guaranteeing the principles of human justice and basic rights' (UN General Assembly Third Committee (20th session) (n 15) para 32).

19 For example, of the 173 states parties to the ICCPR, only 50 states have made declarations accepting the competence of the Human Rights Committee in relation to inter-state communications under Article 41 ICCPR. The Inter-American system only sees 11 express declarations of the competence of the Inter-American Commission on Human Rights to receive communications under Article 45 American Convention on Human Rights, and 21 declarations accepting the jurisdiction of the Inter-American Court of Human Rights under Article 62 (American Convention on Human Rights 'Pact of San José, Costa Rica', 22 November 1969, 1144 UNTS 123 (ACHR)). For more information on the ratification of human rights instruments, see 'Status of Ratification Interactive Dashboard' (*Office of the High Commissioner for Human Rights*) <https://indicators.ohchr.org/> accessed 8 April 2024.

date.[20] As Leckie acknowledged decades ago, 'while inherent to a large degree throughout human rights law, the optional nature of this complaint mechanism has and will continue to limit its utilization'.[21]

As mentioned above, the ICERD compulsory model, which remains an exception within the UN human rights system, has resulted in three cases before the CERD Committee. In the view of the CERD Committee, the automatic functionality of its compulsory model 'should indicate, if anything, a stronger desire of the drafters of the Convention to set up protective measures to ensure' treaty compliance.[22] The historical context of the negotiations of the ICERD appears to be one of the main factors influencing the decision to establish a compulsory mechanism.[23] During the Cold War period socialist states were 'strictly opposed to any type of complaints system which they considered as undue interference with State sovereignty'.[24] However, Soviet and other non-aligned states perceived the mechanism as one that could be used as a tool against the West,[25] with non-aligned states being 'primarily interested in combatting colonialism, apartheid and similar forms of racial discrimination'.[26] These elements led to the establishment of a compulsory model, exceptional in the UN human rights system. Turning to current practice, in line with Leckie's observation, the compulsory model has clearly resulted in a higher number of cases. This trend is also observed at the regional level, particularly in the European system, which follows a compulsory model and has been prolific in inter-state cases.[27]

---

20 These are *Nicaragua v Costa Rica* and *Ecuador v Colombia* (see n 2). The Inter-American model allows ad hoc and temporary acceptance of the competence of the Court (Article 45(3) ACHR).

21 Leckie (n 5) 253.

22 'Inter-State communication submitted by the State of Palestine against Israel: Decision on Jurisdiction' (n 9) para 55.

23 Nowak (n 14) 3.

24 *Ibid.*, 3.

25 Thomas Buergenthal, 'The U.N. Human Rights Committee' (2001) 5 Max Planck Yearbook of United Nations Law 341, 342.

26 Nowak (n 14) 3.

27 The African system, also compulsory, has however resulted in a limited number of cases to date. See (n 2).

B. Standing: Who can Initiate an Inter-State Communication Procedure?

UN treaties envisaging inter-state communications require reciprocity;[28] *i.e.*, that both the applicant and respondent states have accepted the competence of the respective treaty body to hear such procedure. As mentioned in the previous section, that consent is given automatically under the ICERD when states ratify the treaty, due to its compulsory model.[29] Under all other UN human rights treaties, which are based on a voluntary model, both the applicant and the respondent state need to have ratified the treaty and consented to the competence of the treaty body.[30]

Apart from reciprocity, there is no requirement for the applicant state to show a connection to a particular identified victim[31] or any direct interest in the human rights violations giving rise to the procedure. This lack of a victimhood requirement for standing before UN treaty bodies is key to the potential of the communication mechanism, as any state party to the treaties can initiate an inter-state procedure against the violating state.

The two applicant states in the three existing cases (Qatar and Palestine) have had a direct interest in initiating proceedings against the respondent states (UAE, Saudi Arabia and Israel). Yet, the possibility of a non-injured state initiating such proceedings on an *erga omnes* or *erga omnes partes* basis is strongly aligned with the idea that the drafters of the treaties had when introducing the inter-state mechanism in the treaty texts: namely, that the procedure should serve the purpose of enforcing the treaties and ultimately preventing human rights violations.[32] *Erga omnes* and *erga omnes partes* procedures (those initiated by states that may not have been directly injured) have great potential when the issue at stake may affect the interpretation or

---

28 See (n 2).

29 In *Palestine v Israel*, the non-recognition of Palestine by Israel as a State was the basis for Israel's non-participation in the conciliation process, and one of the most significant difficulties that the ad hoc conciliation commission had to deal with (see 'Report of the ad hoc Conciliation Commission' (n 3)). Articles 11-13 ICERD (n 6).

30 See (n 2) and (n 12).

31 Malcolm Langford, Cheryl Lorens and Natasha Telson, 'Inter-State Procedure' in Malcolm Langford *et al* (eds), *The Optional Protocol to the International Covenant on Economic, Social and Cultural Rights: A Commentary* (2016) 147, 164 citing Menno Kamminga, *Inter-State Accountability for Violations of Human Rights* (1992).

32 See Section III.A. below.

application of the treaty,[33] or when the human rights obligation is considered owed to the whole international community,[34] justifying what in some international contexts has been called *actio popularis*.[35] Relevant to this point, in its 2024 report, the ad hoc conciliation commission for Palestine v Israel emphasized that eradicating racial discrimination is a shared responsibility of all states parties to the convention, and reminds States parties that under article 2 (1) (b) of the Convention they undertake not to sponsor, defend or support racial discrimination.[36]

C. Conciliation for Human Rights: Compromise, Flexibility and a Non-binding Outcome

One of the features of inter-state communications under some UN treaties is recourse to conciliation or good offices as a way to assist states to come to a friendly resolution. This was emphasized in discussions during the negotiation of various treaties, including the International Covenant on Civil and Political Rights (ICCPR)[37] and the Optional Protocol to the International Covenant on Economic, Social and Cultural Rights.[38] The ICERD puts

---

33 At the ICJ, this premise has led some third party states to initiate cases and others to file declarations of intervention under Article 63 Statute of the International Court of Justice (ICJ Statute). On the standing of not directly injured states in relation to obligations *erga omnes partes*, see Yoshifumi Tanaka, 'The Legal Consequences of Obligations Erga Omnes in International Law' (2021) 68 Netherlands International Law Review 1, 21-22. On third party intervention before the ICJ, see Christine Chinkin, *Third Parties in International Law* (1993) 186-216; Juliette McIntyre, 'Procedural Values in the Intervention Procedure at the International Court of Justice' (2022) 1 Ukrainian Law Review 1. See also (n 103) in this article.

34 See UNGA Res 56/83 'Responsibility of States for internationally wrongful acts' (12 December 2001) UN Doc A/56/83, Article 42.

35 Farid Ahmadov, *The Right of Actio Popularis before International Courts and Tribunals* (2018); François Voeffray, *L'actio popularis ou la défense de l'intérêt collectif devant les juridictions internationales* (2014).

36 See 'Report of the ad hoc Conciliation Commission' (n 3) para 49.

37 UN General Assembly Third Committee (21st session) 'Draft International Covenants on Human Rights: Report of the Third Committee' (13 December 1966) UN Doc A/6546, para 183.

38 The Committee on Economic, Social and Cultural Rights has 'noted that inter-State procedures were invoked only in 'extremely rare' cases and in 'situations of major significance', but 'conceded that should States show an increased

conciliation at the centre of the design of the procedure,[39] and the CERD Committee has emphasized the conciliatory nature of the procedure.[40] For Tomuschat, the CERD Committee procedure comes down to conciliation aimed at providing 'appropriate remedies to the affected persons and at the same time restructur[ing] the relevant domestic mechanisms in view of all similar future disputes'.[41] The 2024 report of the ad hoc conciliation commission for *Palestine v Israel* prioritised the conciliatory process and the importance of finding an amicable solution, even if this emphasis on engagement may have come at the cost of addressing certain points of substance.[42]

The fact that dispute settlement methods are used for human rights issues has been criticised as it will involve 'some kind of compromise',[43] based on the idea that 'respect for human rights by its very essence is non-negotiable'.[44] Yet, there are two characteristics of the dispute settlement methods incorporated into inter-state communications that seem to have much to offer in ensuring the protection of human rights, often requiring states' willingness to cooperate: flexibility on confidentiality and transparency, and the non-binding nature of the outcome.

Conciliation or good offices are characterized by giving the parties significant leeway to define, with the support of the conciliation commission or body, the specific procedural rules that best fit their interests, and to find the right balance for the parties between confidentiality and transparency.[45] States' preference for a specific level of confidentiality or transparency can change

---

willingness to use inter-State procedures in the future, such a mechanism could be an attractive means of resolving such disputes' (Langford (n 31) 163).

39 Articles 11-13 ICERD (n 6).

40 'Inter-State communication submitted by the State of Palestine against Israel: Decision on Jurisdiction' (n 9) para 58.

41 Tomuschat (n 5) 266.

42 See Keane, 'A Missed Opportunity' (n 3).

43 Peter H Kooijmans, 'Inter-State Dispute Settlement in the Field of Human Rights' (1990) 3(3) Leiden Journal of International Law 87, 90.

44 *Ibid.*, 90.

45 The successful conciliation between Australia and Timor Leste under the UN Convention on the Law of the Sea provides an example of the potential of this flexibility, which states appreciate: see *Timor Sea Conciliation (Timor-Leste v Australia)* (Report and Recommendations of the Compulsory Conciliation Commission between Timor-Leste and Australia on the Timor Sea of 9 May 2018) PCA Case No 2016-10.

based on the interests at stake and the relationship between the parties;[46] the specific arrangement on this may be established together by the parties and the relevant body in the course of proceedings, not necessarily at the outset.[47] It is one of the many factors influencing states' approach to dispute settlement choices.[48] With this in mind, it is noteworthy that the preference for more confidentiality, which some experts have long called for,[49] has consolidated in the recent practice of the CERD Committee. In *Palestine v Israel*, it was established that the discussions of the Committee need to be held behind closed doors.[50] This trend may influence states' perception of this procedure in general and in specific cases.[51]

Turning to the second characteristic: the outcome of the conciliation procedure is a report by the conciliation commission containing non-binding recommendations for the parties. The non-binding nature of those recommendations may be considered to potentially discourage states from becoming involved in the process. This view is strengthened when looking at the significantly higher number of inter-state cases under the ECHR,[52] which envisages an inter-state procedure resulting in a binding judgment by

---

46 Loretta Malintoppi, 'Methods of Dispute Resolution in Inter-state Litigation: When States Go to Arbitration Rather Than Adjudication' (2006) 5 The Law and Practice of International Courts and Tribunals 133.

47 *Timor Sea Conciliation*, Commission Report and Recommendations (n 45) paras 60-61.

48 Malintoppi (n 46). See also Serena Forlati, 'Confidentiality of Conciliation Proceedings and Their Outcome. A Reflection in Light of the Experience of the Timor-Leste/Australia Conciliation Commission' in Christian Tomuschat and Marcelo Kohen (eds), *Flexibility in International Dispute Settlement: Conciliation Revisited* (2020) 181.

49 In the early 1990s, Kooijmans considered plausible the contention that confidential negotiations would work better than public exposure, given the sensitive issues at stake (Kooijmans (n 43) 88).

50 See UN Committee on the Elimination of Racial Discrimination, 'Rules of Procedure of the ad hoc Conciliation Commission on the Interstate Communication Submitted by the State of Palestine against Israel under Article 11 International Convention on the Elimination of All Forms of Racial Discrimination' (25 April 2022), Rules 12 and 16.

51 Shirley V Scott, 'Litigation Versus Dispute Resolution Through Political Processes' in Natalie Klein (ed), *Litigating International Law Disputes: Weighing the Options* (2014) 24. See also, for a similar argument in arbitration proceedings, Malintoppi (n 46) 140-141.

52 More than 30 cases: see (n 2).

the European Court on Human Rights (ECtHR).[53] However, the fundamental question is whether or not the non-binding recommendations produced by a conciliation commission are likely to be followed, as recommendations can in some cases be far more effective than formally binding decisions.[54] In addition, other UN bodies, including treaty bodies and the ICJ, may engage with the recommendations adopted by the conciliation commission, contributing to bringing the parties a step closer to compliance.[55] Assuming that the parties engage in the conciliation process in good faith in a genuine attempt to reach a common ground solution,[56] the non-binding nature of a conciliation commission's recommendations may not be as strong a determinant. States may even find this flexibility appealing, which may influence their consent to the mechanism in general and in specific cases.

Interestingly, under Article 39 ECHR, friendly settlement resulting in a non-binding outcome is also a possibility that the ECtHR may offer. Although not widely used to date,[57] a broader use of friendly settlement by the ECtHR

53 Article 33 ECHR.

54 On compliance with soft law, see Jonathan L Charney, 'Commentary: Compliance with International Soft Law' in Dinah Shelton (ed), *Commitment and Compliance: The Role of Non-Binding Norms in the International Legal System* (2003) 115-117, and the book more broadly.

55 Although not following the decision of a conciliation commission, an illustration of this possible engagement is the ICJ judgment on preliminary objections in Qatar v UAE (*Application of the International Convention on the Elimination of All Forms of Racial Discrimination (Qatar v United Arab Emirates)* (Preliminary Objections) [2021] ICJ 71 (Judgment of 4 February), where the Court notes the CERD communication (paras 31 and 33) and explains that it can look at the practice of treaty bodies and regional human rights courts (paras 77, 100 and 101).

56 As was the case in *Timor Sea v Australia*, see *Timor Sea Conciliation*, Commission Report and Recommendations (n 45); Elizabeth Exposto, 'The Timor Sea Conciliation and Treaty: Timor-Leste's Perspective' (2019) 36 Australian Yearbook of International Law 43, 54f.

57 The few examples include *France, Norway, Denmark, Sweden and Netherlands v Turkey*, ECommHR Application No 9940/82 – 9944/82, Decision of 7 December 1983 and *Denmark v Turkey*, ECtHR, Application No 34382/97, Judgment of 5 April 2000. An analysis of the potential of friendly settlement can be found in Nicola Wenzel, 'Rethinking Friendly Settlements under the European Convention on Human Rights: Why We Should Design a New Friendly Settlement Procedure for Inter-State Cases' (*Völkerrechtsblog*, 28 April 2021) <https://voelkerrechtsblog.org/rethinking-friendly-settlements-under-the-echr/> accessed 8 April 2024; Helen Keller and Réka Piskóty, 'Friendly Settlements as the Sleeping Beauty in Inter-State Cases: Opportunities and Risks for the European Court of Human

or an ad hoc commission – the so called 'sleeping beauty' of this framework[58] – could have the potential to shift this model closer to the conciliatory model that the CERD Committee has adopted.

D. Inter-State Communications and Compromissory Clauses: ICERD and the ICJ

The decision of states on whether to engage in inter-state communications under the ICERD may be influenced by the compromissory clause under Article 22 ICERD, which allows them to refer an inter-state case to the ICJ if it has not been settled by negotiation or other envisaged procedures, although this is a heavily reserved provision, with 25 states having made a reservation on it, which limits its potential to states parties to the treaty not having made such reservation.[59] Other UN human rights treaties that include compromissory clauses do not refer to inter-state communication procedures in their respective provisions, as the procedure is either voluntary in nature or non-existent.[60] The ICJ has interpreted Article 22 ICERD in two cases,

Rights' (*Völkerrechtsblog*, 28 April 2021) <https://voelkerrechtsblog.org/friendly-settlements-as-the-sleeping-beauty-in-inter-state-cases/> accessed 8 April 2024.

58 Keller and Piskóty (n 57).

59 The following states have made reservations on this provision: Afghanistan, Bahrain, China, Cuba, Egypt, Equatorial Guinea, India, Indonesia, Iraq, Israel, Kuwait, Lebanon, Libya, Madagascar, Morocco, Mozambique, Nepal, Saudi Arabia, Singapore, Syria, Thailand, Turkey, USA, Vietnam, and Yemen. In 2018, Qatar instituted proceedings before the ICJ against the United Arab Emirates under Article 22 ICERD, with the Court delivering its preliminary objections judgment in 2021 (*Application of the International Convention on the Elimination of All Forms of Racial Discrimination (Qatar v United Arab Emirates)* (Preliminary Objections) [2021] ICJ Rep 71 (Judgment of 4 February)). More recently, Armenia instituted proceedings against Azerbaijan also under Article 22 ICERD, with the Court's delivering its first order on provisional measures in December 2021 (*Application of the International Convention on the Elimination of All Forms of Racial Discrimination (Armenia v Azerbaijan)* (Request for the Indication of Provisional Measures) [2021] ICJ 361 (Order of 7 December)).

60 Article 30 CAT; Article 92 CMW; Article 42 CED; Convention on the Elimination of All Forms of Discrimination Against Women, 1 March 1980, 1249 UNTS 13, Article 29.

in a way that will likely determine the use that states make of inter-state communications: *Georgia v Russia*[61] and *Ukraine v Russia*.[62]

In 2008, the Republic of Georgia brought a case against Russia before the ICJ under Article 22 ICERD, alleging racial discrimination against ethnic Georgians in South Ossetia and Abkhazia, amounting to violations of Articles 2, 3, 4, 5 and 6 ICERD.[63] It was the first case basing jurisdiction of the ICJ on Article 22 ICERD.[64] Indeed, Georgia based its argument on the ICJ's jurisdiction exclusively on ICERD's compromissory clause. One of the preliminary objections raised by Russia concerned the conditions to be met under Article 22 before seising the Court; *i.e.*, having recourse to negotiations or to the 'procedures expressly provided for in this convention'.[65] In addressing the objection, the Court focused on whether Georgia had engaged in negotiations, given that no other ICERD mechanism had been relied upon. It concluded that the requirement had not been satisfied as no negotiations had been initiated to address the dispute.[66] However, no clarification was provided on whether the inter-state communication procedure under Articles 11-13 ICERD was a cumulative or alternative requirement, as the Court considered that, given the circumstances, it did 'not need to examine' this point.[67]

In 2017, Ukraine initiated proceedings against Russia before the ICJ, based partly on the ICERD, in light of the disputes between Crimean Tatars and ethnic Ukrainians in Crimea.[68] In this case, the Court clarified that bringing the matter to the CERD Committee through an inter-state communication

---

61 *Application of the International Convention on the Elimination of All Forms of Racial Discrimination (Georgia v Russian Federation)* (Preliminary Objections) [2011] ICJ 70 (Judgment of 1 April).

62 *Application of the International Convention for the Suppression of the Financing of Terrorism and of the International Convention on the Elimination of All Forms of Racial Discrimination (Ukraine v Russian Federation)* (Preliminary Objections) [2019] ICJ 558 (Judgment of 8 November).

63 *Georgia v Russian Federation* (n 61). See also Sandy Ghandhi, 'International Court of Justice: *Application of the International Convention on the Elimination of All Forms of Racial Discrimination (Georgia v Russian Federation)* Provisional Measures Order of 15 October 2008' (2009) 58 ICLQ 713, 716.

64 Risini and Ulfstein (n 4).

65 Article 22 ICERD (n 6).

66 *Georgia v Russian Federation* (n 61) paras 141, 184.

67 *Ibid.*, para 183.

68 *Ukraine v Russian Federation* (n 62).

procedure under Articles 11-13 ICERD was not a precondition for it to have jurisdiction over the case.[69]

The Court considered, exploring the features of the inter-state communications procedure under Articles 11-13 ICERD, that 'the objective of the CERD Committee procedure is for the States concerned to reach an agreed settlement of their dispute'.[70] On that basis, it established that:

> 'negotiation' and the 'procedures expressly provided for in [the] Convention' are two means to achieve the same objective, namely to settle a dispute by agreement. Both negotiation and the CERD Committee procedure rest on the States parties' willingness to seek an agreed settlement of their dispute.[71]

In the view of the Court, 'it would not be reasonable to require States parties which have already failed to reach an agreed settlement through negotiations to engage in an additional set of negotiations' under Articles 11-13.[72] It thus found that the requirements under Article 22 ICERD were alternative.[73]

Subsequent cases may provide further opportunities for the Court to revisit or reemphasize this position.[74] In any case, the clarification by the ICJ in

---

[69] *Ibid.*, para 60.

[70] *Ibid.*, para 109.

[71] *Ibid.*, para 110.

[72] *Ibid.*, para 110.

[73] *Ibid.*, para 113.

[74] Interestingly, in 2018, Qatar initiated proceedings before the ICJ against the United Arab Emirates under Article 22 ICERD, in parallel to the inter-state communication it initiated before the CERD Committee. On 4 February 2021, the Court concluded the dispute fell outside its jurisdiction *ratione materiae* (according to the first preliminary objection): see *Qatar v United Arab Emirates* (n 59). One of the preliminary objections raised by the United Arab Emirates related to the interpretation of Article 22 ICERD; however, the Court did not clarify that point. Proceedings initiated recently by Armenia and Azerbaijan against each other before the ICJ *(Armenia v Azerbaijan* (n 59); *Application of the International Convention on the Elimination of All Forms of Racial Discrimination (Azerbaijan v Armenia)* (Request for the Indication of Provisional Measures) [2021] ICJ 405 (Order of 7 December)) offer further opportunities for the Court to revisit this matter. The ICJ has acknowledged it has *prima facie* jurisdiction and adopted provisional measures in both cases. For a critical analysis of the use of compromissory clauses, see Filippo Fontanelli, 'The Disputes Between Armenia and Azerbaijan: The CERD Compromissory Clause as a One-way Ticket to Hague' (*EJIL: Talk!*, 11 November 2021) <www.ejiltalk.org/the-disputes-between-armenia-and-azerbaijan-the-cerd-compromissory-clause-as-a-one-way-ticket-to-hague/> accessed 8 April 2024.

Ukraine v Russia that the preconditions in Article 22 ICERD are alternative is likely to have an impact on states' decision to engage with inter-state communications. Now that it has been established that an inter-state communication is not necessarily a requirement for ICJ jurisdiction, states may have less incentive to initiate this procedure before the CERD Committee.

III. The Aims of Inter-State Communications: From Treaty Compliance to a Combination of Aims

The features analysed in section II respond partly to what states have traditionally considered should be the aims of inter-state communications: treaty compliance and the protection of human rights. The work of UN human rights treaty bodies and civil society organisations has led to an evolution of views as to the aims that this mechanism should serve. This section presents the aims of inter-state communications as multiple and evolving, in connection with the features discussed in the previous section.

If UN human rights treaty bodies develop further or more detailed rules on inter-state communication procedures (*e.g.* on levels of confidentiality or on collective procedures), and as states make decisions about whether to use these procedures or not, such decisions will consciously or unconsciously be connected to those actors' perceptions of the aims of the mechanism, and to the way in which those aims interplay and evolve. Now that an inter-state case, *Palestine v Israel*, has achieved its final phase and discussions may arise about pros and cons of this mechanism, newly perceived aims may shape the features of inter-state communications in specific ways.

A. The Traditional Aims: Treaty Compliance and the Protection of Human Rights

States have traditionally understood inter-state communications as an instrument for treaty compliance. During negotiations of human rights treaties, many delegations put emphasis on the potential of the mechanism for treaty compliance. For example, during the drafting of the ICCPR, some states considered inter-state complaints as a system that would safeguard the provisions of the Covenant,[75] representing an 'additional possibility of

---

[75] UN General Assembly, 'Draft International Covenants on Human Rights: Annotation Prepared by the Secretary-General' (n 16) 235.

securing compliance'.[76] Treaty compliance continues to be recognised as the main aim of inter-state communications to date. As mentioned, in its decision on jurisdiction in *Palestine v Israel*, the CERD Committee saw the 'automatic' inter-state communication procedure under Article 11(1) ICERD as indicative of a 'stronger desire of the drafters [...] to set up protective measures to ensure that the provisions of the Convention are adequately observed and complied with by all States parties'.[77]

Connected to treaty compliance, states, UN bodies and other actors perceive inter-state communications as an instrument for protecting human rights or preventing human rights violations.[78] In 2004, the Human Rights Committee addressed the issue of the use of inter-state communications in its General Comment 31. Taking as a starting point states' obligation under the UN Charter to 'promote universal respect for, and observance of, human rights and fundamental freedoms', as well as the 'contractual dimension' of the ICCPR, the Committee reminded 'States parties of the desirability of making the declaration contemplated in article 41',[79] which envisages inter-state communications. The Committee emphasized the provision's 'potential value', and that calling attention to possible breaches by other states parties 'should, far from being regarded as an unfriendly act, be considered as a reflection of legitimate community interest'.[80] It did, however, also acknowledge that inter-state communications 'should be seen as supplementary to, not diminishing of, States Parties' interest in each other's discharge of their obligations'.[81] The references in the report of the *ad hoc* conciliation commission for *Palestine v Israel* to obligations of the parties and obligations of third parties are consistent with an understanding of inter-state communications as an instrument for protecting human rights and preventing human rights violations.[82]

Some of the features of inter-state communications analysed in section II are strongly aligned with the traditional aims of treaty compliance and

---

76 UN General Assembly Third Committee (21st session) (n 17) para 3.

77 'Inter-State communication submitted by the State of Palestine against Israel: Decision on Jurisdiction' (n 9) para 55.

78 McDougall (n 4).

79 UN Human Rights Committee, 'General Comment No 31 [80]: The Nature of the General Legal Obligation Imposed on States Parties to the Covenant' (26 May 2004) UN Doc CCPR/C/21/Rev.1/Add.13, para 2.

80 *Ibid.*, para 2.

81 *Ibid.*

82 See 'Report of the ad hoc Conciliation Commission' (n 3).

human rights protection. The voluntary nature of most procedures reflects the resistance of many states to binding accountability processes that was common at the time the treaties were drafted, in line with these more traditional views that the aim of the mechanism should be focused on treaty compliance. The reciprocity and lack of victimhood entrench well with the vision of inter-state communications as a tool for ensuring treaty compliance. Compromissory clauses like the one included in Article 22 ICERD can also be seen as consistent with these aims of the mechanism, as recourse to the ICJ is an additional way to ensure treaty compliance. This is particularly the case now that the ICJ has clarified that the initiation of an inter-state communication procedure is not a requirement for the invocation of the ICJ's jurisdiction under Article 22. However, other features and their evolution through the work of treaty bodies are best explained in light of a combination of the multiple and evolving aims of the mechanism, discussed in sections II.B and II.C below.

B. Dispute Settlement as an Aim: The Conciliatory CERD Approach

The analysis of the *travaux préparatoires* and the three inter-state cases before the CERD Committee points towards dispute settlement as another aim of the mechanism. Inter-state communications may settle a specific dispute related to human rights or contribute to the settlement of a broader dispute.

The fact that inter-state communications envisage dispute settlement methods in its procedure, such as conciliation or good offices, read alongside the explicit references to dispute settlement in some cases, is indicative of its perception as a dispute settlement mechanism.[83] During the drafting process of the CAT, the Chairman-Rapporteur suggested alternative implementation provisions 'in an effort to reconcile the divergent views expressed by members of the Working Group'.[84] Interestingly, his suggested Article 20(2) provided that 'the existence of a dispute shall particularly be recognised' where an inter-state communication is filed.[85] In the ICERD, although Article 11(2)

---

[83] Vandenbogaerde (n 5) 118.

[84] United Nations Economic and Social Council, 'Report of the Working Group on a Draft Convention Against Torture and Other Cruel, Inhuman or Degrading Treatment or Punishment' (5 March 1982) UN Doc E/CN.4/1982/L.40, para 52.

[85] *Ibid.*, Annex III (Implementation provisions suggested by the Chairman-Rapporteur as a possible alternative to the draft articles 17-34, contained in document E/CN.4/1493 (1982) UN Doc E/CN.4/1982/WG.2/WP.6) p. 2.

refers to a 'matter' and not to a dispute or case, Articles 12 and 13 expressly refer to a dispute.[86] In addition, in its decision on jurisdiction in Palestine v Israel, the CERD Committee noted that 'the inter-State mechanism under the Convention provides a unique instrument to settle inter-State disputes'.[87] In Ukraine v Russia, the ICJ also referred to inter-state communications before the CERD Committee as a means to achieve the objective of settling 'a dispute by agreement'.[88] The 2024 report of the *ad hoc* conciliation commission for *Palestine v Israel* has confirmed that the aim of the process is to seek an amicable solution.[89]

The work of the CERD Committee has made a further contribution in shaping contemporary understandings of the aims of this mechanism. In its decision on jurisdiction in *Palestine v Israel*, the Committee observed the ICERD inter-state communication procedure's 'special nature, which is conciliatory, as opposed to adversarial',[90] and 'is aimed at ensuring the collective good of all States parties'.[91] To this end, it added, it should be 'implemented in a manner that is practical, constructive and effective'.[92]

The work of the CERD Committee interpreting and facilitating the conciliation process envisaged in the ICERD inter-state communication procedure in these three cases has contributed to a perception of the mechanism as one aimed at settling a dispute, or at settling the human rights dimension of a broader dispute, in a peaceful and amicable way. Together with the more traditional aims, this aim should inform how the features of the mechanism are shaped. Taking transparency as an example, as explained in section II.B in relation to the preference for more confidentiality, the CERD Committee opted for discussions behind closed doors in *Palestine v Israel*.[93] While it

86 David Keane, 'ICERD and Palestine's Inter-State Complaint' (*EJIL: Talk!*, 30 April 2018) <www.ejiltalk.org/icerd-and-palestines-inter-state-complaint/> accessed 8 April 2024.

87 Inter-State communication submitted by the State of Palestine against Israel: Decision on Jurisdiction' (n 9) para 58 (emphasis added).

88 *Ukraine v Russian Federation* (n 62) para 110.

89 See (n 3).

90 Inter-State communication submitted by the State of Palestine against Israel: Decision on Jurisdiction' (n 9) para 58.

91 *Ibid.*, para 59.

92 *Ibid.*, para 67.

93 UN Committee on the Elimination of Racial Discrimination, 'Rules of Procedure of the ad hoc Conciliation Commission on the Interstate Communication Submitted by the State of Palestine against Israel' (n 50) Rules 12 and 16.

has been argued that 'it seems very difficult to freeze a dispute for the sake of a confidential procedure in the modern world of global information',[94] in the aforementioned decision, the CERD Committee appeared to favour dispute settlement as an aim over treaty compliance. Other committees could use this precedent to analyse which aim they would like to prioritise in this regard, although in some instances there may be limitations as to how public the process can be.[95]

Similarly, informed by this perceived aim in conjunction with others, states may be more likely to engage with inter-state communications and embark on a conciliation process resulting in non-binding recommendations by an ad hoc conciliation commission if they see the human rights issue as part of a dispute with another state, rather than as an issue of treaty compliance – the latter of which they could find more appealing options for resolving. States' perspectives in this regard could be influenced by the decisions of treaty bodies on the appointment of members of conciliation commissions, or on other aspects of the conciliation process that can be more or less judicialized.

C. Inter-State Communications as a Strategic Instrument in International Relations

The analysis of statements of several actors in the international sphere referring to inter-state communications point towards two additional aims: i) providing an avenue for state responsibility; and ii) allowing states to 'signal' themselves; *i.e.*, to appear internationally or domestically as an active agent tackling human rights violations, as a 'good citizen', or conversely, as an active agent targeting another state as a 'bad citizen'.

There is a contemporary interest in inter-state communications as an avenue for holding states responsible for human rights violations, especially amongst human rights activists and civil society organisations. However, the language used in the discussions at the time of the negotiation of the treaties was much more focused on ensuring treaty compliance or the friendly settlement of disputes. State responsibility is inevitably linked to non-compliance as the consequence of breaching an international obligation, albeit explicit

---

94 Emmanuel Decaux, 'The Potential for Inter-State Conciliation within the Framework of the UN Treaties for the Protection of Human Rights' in Christian Tomuschat and Marcelo Kohen (eds), *Flexibility in International Dispute Settlement: Conciliation Revisited* (2020) 39, 80.

95 Under Article 41(1)(d) ICCPR, there is a mandate for confidentiality when examining communications.

reference to state responsibility in the genesis of the treaties is very limited. During the negotiation of the ICERD, the Swedish representative made mention to responsibility, but was referring to the protection of 'human rights and individual freedoms by placing on the international community the responsibility for ensuring that those rights and freedoms were respected'.[96] During the drafting process of the Optional Protocol to the Convention on the Rights of the Child, it was highlighted that inter-state communication procedures would be 'part of a continuum of accountability mechanisms, starting at the community level and comprising national justice systems, ombudspersons offices and regional mechanisms'.[97]

The development of the contemporary rules of state responsibility, set out by the International Law Commission, has contributed significantly to a more explicit use of the notion. The exercise consolidated a set of rules, which also apply to human rights,[98] and may add new perspectives for inter-state communications. However, some practical questions arise when considering the potential of inter-state communications as a mechanism for state responsibility, for example, the suitability of UN treaty bodies for qualifying damages or of a conciliation commission for quantifying damages.[99] Yet, an argument can be made in favour of using inter-state communication procedures as an avenue to hold states accountable for human rights violations, in conjunction with other aims. As Leckie explains, 'some form of international accountability or review must exist so that states parties can contribute to the realization of the guarantees provided in international instruments'.[100]

Some of the features of the procedure under the ICERD studied in section II are well suited to an inter-state mechanism which includes state

96 UN General Assembly Third Committee (20th session) (n 15) para 27.

97 UN Human Rights Council, 'Report of the Open-ended Working Group to Explore the Possibility of Elaborating an Optional Protocol to the Convention on the Rights of the Child to Provide a Communications Procedure' (21 January 2010) UN Doc A/HRC/13/43, para 19.

98 The perception that human rights were a self-standing regime to which the law of state responsibility and notions such as attribution or circumstances precluding wrongfulness would not apply, in accordance with the *lex specialis* principle, faded away as the debate on fragmentation in this area was overcome: see Mads Andenas and Eirik Bjorge (eds), *A Farewell to Fragmentation: Reassertion and Convergence in International Law* (2015).

99 The broader project of which this article forms a part 'explores these questions'. For more information and findings of the project, see the special issue of the International Human Rights Law Review, see Rosana Garciandia and Jean-Pierre Gauci, 'Editorial Note' (2024) 13(1) International Human Rights Law Review 1.

100 Leckie (n 5) 257.

responsibility as one of its multiple aims, along with treaty compliance. The compulsory nature of the ICERD mechanism is one such feature, as the drafters envisaged the prohibition of racial discrimination as a rule that required special protection, very much influenced by the historical context of treaty negotiations. The compromissory clause (Article 22 ICERD) is also relevant, as it situates inter-state communications in the broader net of mechanisms that can ensure state responsibility. Even the non-binding nature of conciliation commission recommendations may be a valid way to ensure state responsibility (see section II.C), as in some cases non-binding outcomes can be more effective than binding ones.

The other possible aim is allowing states to 'signal' themselves in the international sphere, as active agents addressing human rights violations. States could use inter-state communications, not only for treaty compliance purposes or to settle a dispute, but also as a strategic instrument in international relations. This can be the case for states initiating an inter-state procedure, for states engaging in a procedure initiated against them, and for third states, which could eventually be given the option of issuing a collective inter-state communication in support of an injured state.[101]

In line with the Human Rights Committee's description of the mechanism as 'a reflection of legitimate community interest',[102] states parties not directly affected by a human rights violation may decide to initiate proceedings against another state (*erga omnes* or *erga omnes partes* obligations). They could also consider joining forces with other states (affected or non-affected) to initiate collective proceedings against one or various injuring states. Although not explicitly envisaged in UN treaties and protocols, the possibility of a group of states initiating a communication procedure before a UN treaty body against another state could add a collective dimension to the potential of inter-state communications, following similar trends already seen in international litigation.[103] Collective cases (including joinder of proceedings, third party

101 The project (n 99) also explores the potential and challenges of collective inter-state communications in further detail.

102 UN Human Rights Committee, 'General Comment No 31' (n 79) para 2.

103 Two litigation strategies have resulted in a strong sense of collective response. First, the strategy followed by the Gambia against Myanmar before the ICJ, initiating a case for Myanmar's violations of the human rights of the Muslim Rohingya population without being directly affected (*Application of the Convention on the Prevention and Punishment of the Crime of Genocide (The Gambia v Myanmar)* (Preliminary Objections) [2022] ICJ 477 (Judgment of 22 July) paras 107-108, 112). This initiative, which follows on from *Belgium v Senegal*, is based on the violations of *erga omnes partes* obligations (see Yoshifumi Tanaka, 'The

Legal Consequences of Obligations Erga Omnes in International Law' (2021) 68 Netherlands International Law Review 1, 21-22) and has been relied on most recently in the joint application by Canada and the Netherlands against Syria under the Convention against Torture and the application by South Africa against Israel under the Genocide Convention (*Application of the Convention against Torture and Other Cruel, Inhuman or Degrading Treatment or Punishment (Canada and the Netherlands v Syrian Arab Republic)* (Application Instituting Proceedings) <www.icj-cij.org/sites/default/files/case-related/188/188-20230608-APP-01-00-EN.pdf> accessed 20 February 2024, para 7; *Application of the Convention on the Prevention and Punishment of the Crime of Genocide in the Gaza Strip (South Africa v Israel)* (Application Instituting Proceedings) <www.icj-cij.org/sites/default/files/case-related/192/192-20231228-app-01-00-en.pdf> accessed 20 February 2024, paras 13, 16, 131-133). The Court has accepted the *erga omnes partes* argument for *prima facie* standing in its orders for provisional measures in both cases (*Application of the Convention against Torture and Other Cruel, Inhuman or Degrading Treatment or Punishment (Canada and the Netherlands v Syrian Arab Republic)* (Request for the Indication of Provisional Measures) General List No 188 [2023] ICJ 1 (Order of 16 November), paras 50-51, 57; *Application of the Convention on the Prevention and Punishment of the Crime of Genocide in the Gaza Strip (South Africa v Israel)* (Request for the Indication of Provisional Measures) General List No 192 [2024] ICJ 1 (Order of 26 January), paras 33f).

Second, massive third-party intervention has resulted in the recent cases between Ukraine and Russia before the ICJ and ECtHR. At the ICJ, 32 states intervened at the preliminary objection stage of proceedings, of which 23 (at the time of writing) have affirmed declarations at the merits stage (*Allegations of Genocide under the Convention on the Prevention and Punishment of the Crime of Genocide (Ukraine v Russian Federation)* ICJ Press Release 2024/59 <www.icj-cij.org/sites/default/files/case-related/182/182-20240806-pre-01-00-en.pdf> accessed 8 August 2024). Meanwhile, 26 states are noted to be intervening in the ECtHR case (European Court of Human Rights, 'Update on the third-party intervention requests granted in Inter-State case *Ukraine and the Netherlands v. Russia*' (ECHR 082 2023, 17 March 2023)). This renewed interest in interventions has led scholars to analyse the pros and cons of third-party intervention and its potential as a tool for *actio popularis* (see Brian McGarry, 'Obligations Erga Omnes (Partes) and the Participation of Third States in Inter-State Litigation' (2023) 22 The Law and Practice of International Courts and Tribunals 273; Brian McGarry, 'A Rush to Judgement? The Wobbly Bridge from Judicial Standing to Intervention in ICJ Proceedings' (2023) 100 QIL, Zoom-in 5; Kyra Wigard, Ori Pomson, and Juliette McIntyre, 'Keeping score: an empirical analysis of the interventions in Ukraine v Russia' (2023) Journal of International Dispute Settlement 1. The Court also recently unanimously decided that the declarations filed by Canada, Denmark, France, Germany, the Netherlands, and the United Kingdom (jointly) and the Maldives (individually) under Article 63 ICJ Statute are admissible *(Application of the Convention on the Prevention and Punishment of the Crime of Genocide* intervention, and advisory opinions) before the ICJ[104] and ECtHR[105] are an interesting precedent to consider, as is the collective nature of inter-state procedures before the International Tribunal on the Law of the Sea (ITLOS)[106],

(The Gambia v Myanmar) (Admissibility of the Declarations of Intervention: Order) General List No 178 [2024] ICJ 1 (Order of 3 July) para 49). Intervention has also been a relevant topic in *South Africa v Israel*. Nicaragua has filed an application for permission to intervene under Article 62 ICJ Statute; Colombia, Libya, Mexico, Spain, and Turkey have each filed declarations of intervention under Article 63 ICJ Statute; and Palestine has filed an application for permission to intervene and a declaration of intervention under Articles 62 and 63 ICJ Statute respectively (Application for Permission to Intervene by the Government of the Republic of Nicaragua, 23 January 2024 <www.icj-cij.org/sites/default/files/case-related/192/192-20240123-int-01-00-en.pdf> accessed 8 August 2024; Declaration of Intervention by the Republic of Colombia, 5 April 2024 <www.icj-cij.org/sites/default/files/case-related/192/192-20240405-int-01-00-en.pdf> accessed 8 August 2024; Declaration of Intervention of the State of Libya, 10 May 2024 <www.icj-cij.org/sites/default/files/case-related/192/192-20240510-int-01-00-en.pdf> accessed 8 August 2024; Declaration of Intervention by the United Mexican States, 24 May 2024 <www.icj-cij.org/sites/default/files/case-related/192/192-20240524-int-01-00-en.pdf> accessed 8 August 2024; Declaration of Intervention of Spain, 28 June 2024 <www.icj-cij.org/sites/default/files/case-related/192/192-20240628-int-01-00-en.pdf> accessed 8 August 2024; Declaration of Intervention by the Republic of Türkiye, 7 August 2024 <www.icj-cij.org/sites/default/files/case-related/192/192-20240807-int-01-00-en.pdf> accessed 8 August 2024; Request for Intervention and Declaration of Intervention of Palestine, 3 June 2024 <www.icj-cij.org/sites/default/files/case-related/192/192-20240603-int-01-00-en.pdf> accessed 8 August 2024). Separately, Germany has also announced that it intends to intervene in the South Africa case (see Stefan Talmon, 'Germany Rushes to Declare Intention to Intervene in the Genocide Case brought by South Africa Against Israel Before the International Court of Justice' (*German Practice in International Law*, 15 January 2024) <https://gpil.jura.uni-bonn.de/2024/01/germany-rushes-to-declare-intention-to-intervene-in-the-genocide-case-brought-by-south-africa-against-israel-before-the-international-court-of-justice/> accessed 20 February 2024).

104 Wigard, Pomson, and McIntyre (n 103) 7-13.

105 *Denmark, Norway, Sweden and the Netherlands v Greece (I)*, ECommHR, Application No 3321/67-3323/67, 3344/67 (25 March 1968); *Denmark, France, Norway, Sweden and the Netherlands v Turkey* (n 54); *Ukraine and the Netherlands v Russian Federation* Application No 8019/16, 43800/14 and 28525/20 (ECtHR, 13 March 2014).

106 See Michael Wood and Eran Sthoeger, 'Third-Party Intervention and Involvement in Inter-State Arbitration' in Helene Ruiz Fabri *et al* (eds), *A Bridge over Troubled Waters: Dispute Resolution in the Law of International Watercourses and the Law of the Sea* (2020) 64-66.

arbitral tribunals (*e.g.* the International Centre for Settlement of Investment Disputes (ICSID)), or under the International Labour Organization (ILO) Constitution.[107]

Collective inter-state communications could have the potential of reducing the confrontational barrier for states to take action. As Leckie explains in relation to one of the ECtHR collective inter-state cases, 'it appears that if there had not been a collective effort by the five states acting together the complaint may never have been filed'.[108] Beyond that, collective inter-state communications would allow states to signal themselves as supporting the injured state or to signal that the behaviour of the targeted state is subject to widespread condemnation. States initiating a collective communication would take up a dual role, that of litigant and of 'master of the treaty', partaking in its authentic interpretation.[109] Acknowledging 'signalling' as a possible aim for inter-state communications, in connection with the more traditional aims, could inspire a shift towards more *actio popularis* cases before UN treaty bodies. This would allow states to channel their sovereign voices in processes aimed at treaty compliance and state responsibility, through a mechanism that is lawful, respectful and provides space for constructive resolution of the situation.[110] The publicity associated with *actio popularis* would require higher levels of transparency than those ideal for dispute settlement, a conflicting element that would have to be carefully balanced.

---

[107] Of the 14 complaint proceedings that have resulted in the establishment of Commissions of Inquiry pursuant to the ILO Constitution, the complaints against Belarus (2003), Haiti (1983), Greece (1968), Myanmar (1996), Nicaragua (1987), Poland (1982), Romania (1989), Venezuela (2015) and Zimbabwe (2010) were filed by more than one workers' or employers' delegate of the International Labour Conference.

[108] Leckie (n 5) 295.

[109] See contributions of Nicolas Angelet and Alina Miron to the panel 'The Role of the ICJ in State Intervention by Non-Parties to a Dispute' at the 2021 International Law Weekend, hosted by the American Branch of the International Law Association on 29-30 October 2021.

[110] Rosana Garciandia, Jean-Pierre Gauci, 'Inter-State Communications Before UN Human Rights Treaty Bodies: Testing the Waters for Collective Communications' (forthcoming).

IV. Evolving Aims and Features: Influencing Reform

Based on the above analysis, this article concludes that as perceptions of the aims of inter-state communications held by different actors evolve, the connection between features and aims provides an insightful tool for considering the design of further rules or potential reforms of the mechanism.

Traditionally, states have perceived inter-state communications as an unfriendly act used primarily for treaty compliance purposes on a rather exceptional basis. As treaties and protocols have subsequently been ratified, states have been reluctant to accept the competence of committees to receive and consider inter-state communications, in a similar manner to their reluctance to accept individual communication procedures.[111] Schabas explains this and the underuse of the mechanism partly as a consequence of the burden that the submission of an inter-state complaint places on political and diplomatic relations, which has led governments to 'resort to this tool in only extreme situations'.[112] Before the three abovementioned ICERD cases were initiated in 2018, the Human Rights Committee and the CERD Committee had asked a few states whether they were considering initiating inter-state communication procedures, but none ever materialised.[113]

As this article contends, the perceptions states and treaty bodies have of inter-state communications has evolved over time. While previously seen merely as mechanisms for treaty compliance, there is potential for inter-state communications to fulfil a variety of different and sometimes complementary functions (*e.g.* dispute settlement, state responsibility or international 'signalling'). The awakening of the dormant ICERD mechanism with the three cases before the CERD Committee has led experts to explore the potential of such processes in other areas of human rights law, opening the door to a less sceptical approach to inter-state communications and their potential. However, these three cases remain exceptional, and wider use may require revisiting some of the procedural features of the mechanism,

---

111 See, for example, Thornberry (n 6) 42.

112 William Schabas, *U.N. International Covenant on Civil and Political Rights: Nowak's CCPR Commentary* (2019) 917. This had already been anticipated in discussions leading to the adoption of the ICCPR and other treaties. The Canadian representative, Ronald Macdonald, emphasized that '[t]he major difficulty, however, was that it might not be used as often as it could be since friends did not like to tangle in public, while rivals were only too frequently tempted to do so' (UN General Assembly Third Committee (21st session) (n 17) para 3).

113 Manfred Nowak, *U.N. Covenant on Civil and Political Rights: CCPR Commentary* (2005); Leckie (n 5) 253; Reilly and Trout (n 8).

as well as states' perceptions of their nature and utility, in connection with their perceived aims.[114]

As discussed in section III, the combination of traditional and newly perceived aims may shape the features of inter-state communications in specific ways, as we chart unexplored territory where new rules of procedure are likely to be required. Exploring those possible new rules through the lens of the multiple and evolving aims of inter-state communications may shed light on the best possible design of such rules.

Acknowledging dispute settlement as an aim of the mechanism, the evolution towards its use as conciliatory could bring higher levels of flexibility in relation to confidentiality or transparency. Specific arrangements on confidentiality may be established in ad hoc rules by a conciliation commission dealing with a specific case, and therefore on a case-by-case basis. Higher levels of confidentiality may provide an environment more suitable for states to settle their disputes through diplomatic means. A purely confidential model would best serve the aim of dispute settlement, but it may be weaker as a method for ensuring treaty compliance, state responsibility, or signalling, where more publicity would be desired. Now that inter-state communications may become a more regular element of the human rights landscape, limiting confidentiality to specific parts of the procedure would ensure the balancing of the various potential aims of the mechanism.

If international 'signalling' consolidates as a trend in inter-state communications, following the trends observed in international litigation, collective inter-state communications could see the light of day. Although, as Tomuschat has emphasized, it is early 'to forecast their outcomes',[115] decisions on the three inter-state cases under the ICERD so far have provided interesting insight into the Committee's views as to the aims and potential of the mechanism.

Putting those developments into perspective in light of the work on other fronts in international human rights law and dispute resolution, the future appears uncertain in terms of states' engagement with inter-state communications. What does appear clear is that the features of inter-state communications will evolve hand in hand with the aim(s) of the mechanism. This evolution will, in turn, make states more open to engaging with inter-state communications, as a mechanism that can achieve multiple goals through a variety of distinctive features.

114 Another element that may require consideration if the inter-state mechanism were to become more widely used are the limited resources that UN treaty bodies face in the fulfilment of their functions.

115 Tomuschat (n 5) 265.

Acknowledgements

Thanks to Dr Jean-Pierre Gauci and Professor Philippa Webb for all the insightful conversations and for their feedback on previous versions of this article. Thanks to King's College London and its Centre for International Governance and Dispute Resolution (CIGAD) and to the British Institute of International and Comparative Law (BIICL) for their support to this research project. Thanks to the project's research assistants for their excellent work.

Artificial Intelligence in Counterterrorism and Human Rights

Alrun Cohen | Senior Legal Counsel, alrun.cohen@gmail.com

Abstract

With the rise of elusive 'lone wolf' terrorists, public authorities increasingly turn to artificial intelligence (AI), algorithm-driven tools, and biometric systems to detect individuals at risk of radicalization. These technologies, from facial recognition to predictive analytics, offer powerful capabilities to identify potential threats and terrorism patterns, protecting public safety. Yet, their deployment raises human rights concerns. Balancing counterterrorism efforts to protect citizens with the human rights of suspects, in particular the rights to privacy, effective remedy, fair trial, and non-discrimination, requires careful scrutiny. This article examines both the risks and benefits of AI and biometrics through the lens of the European Court of Human Rights.

Keywords

Human Rights – Artificial Intelligence – Terrorism – Data Protection – Effective Remedy – Fair Trial – Non-Discrimination – Transparency

I. Introduction

Dynamics of terrorism have significantly evolved, changing the rate and scope of attacks. The UN Office of Counter-Terrorism highlights the growing concern over the misuse of digital technologies for committing, recruiting for, funding, or planning attacks.[1] Terrorism is not only perpetrated by organisations but also by individuals who act independently. The rise of online media has fuelled the 'lone wolf' phenomenon. Research indicates that lone actors are more likely to be radicalized and plan their attacks online compared to group actors.[2] For instance, Anders Breivik, who carried out the 2011

---

1 Office of Counter-Terrorism, 'Cybersecurity' <www.un.org/counterterrorism/cybersecurity> accessed 1 August 2024.

2 Jonathan Kenyon, Jens F Binder and Christopher Baker-Beall, 'An Analysis of Terrorist Attack Perpetrators in England and Wales: Comparing Lone Actors, Lone Dyads, and Group Actors' (2024) 1 Journal of Threat Assessment and

Austrian Review of International and European Law **28**: 33-60, 2023.
 | DOI:10.1163/15736512-02801003

Norway attacks that killed 77 people, had been indoctrinated through internet forums, where he also disseminated his far-right ideology, acquired chemicals, and planned his attack.[3] Similarly, Dzhokhar and Tamerlan Tsarnaev, who carried out the bombing attack at the Boston Marathon in 2013, are seen as 'self-taught', 'unaffiliated with any particular terrorist group' and heavily influenced by jihadist[4] online propaganda.[5] As lone actors are hard to flag with traditional methods, authorities increasingly rely on AI, algorithm-based tools, and biometric technologies to identify potential threats.

Against this backdrop, the article examines the emerging practices of predictive intelligence and biometrics in detecting terrorist threats considering the case law of the European Court of Human Rights (ECtHR). The analysis centers on the most common violations of rights enshrined in the European Convention on Human Rights (ECHR), including the right to respect for private and family life (Article 8), the right to an effective remedy (Article 14), the right to a fair trial (Article 6) and the prohibition of discrimination (Article 9). At the same time, the article explores how the use of AI can strengthen these same rights (Chapter IV). This legal analysis forms the foundation for proposals to balance the risks and benefits associated with the use of AI in counterterrorism (Chapter V). The proposals are deduced

Management 1, 17; Jonathan Kenyon, Jens F Binder and Christopher Baker-Beall, 'Online Radicalization: Profile and Risk Analysis of Individuals Convicted of Extremist Offences' (2022) 28 Legal and Criminological Psychology 1, 8. The study found that individuals with strong mental illness or personality disorders were significantly more prevalent in the Internet group than in the Hybrid and Face-to-face groups. However, those who radicalized both online and offline were most likely to commit an attack; see also Boaz Ganor, 'Understanding the Motivations of "Lone Wolf" Terrorists: The "Bathtub" Model' (2021) 15(2) Perspectives on Terrorism 23, 23.

3 Izak Krzysztof, 'Anders Behring Breivik. A Case Study of a Far-Right Terrorist – A Lone Wolf' (2023) 3 Terroryzm Part I, 280, 288, 291 and Part II, 410, 420; Gabriel Weimann, 'Lone Wolves in Cyberspace' (2012) 3(2) Journal of Terrorism Research 75, 76.

4 A recent study found that among 143 self-radicalized attackers, 48% were Islamist extremists and 41% were extreme right-wing. The data covered reports from October 2010 to December 2021: Kenyon, Binder and Baker-Beall (n 2) 9.

5 Michael Cooper, Michael S Schmidt and Eric Schmitt, 'Boston Suspects Are Seen as Self-Taught and Fueled by Web' (*The New York Times*, 23 April 2013) <www.nytimes.com/2013/04/24/us/boston-marathon-bombing-developments.html> accessed 25 May 2024; Clint Watts, 'Detecting the Radicalization and Recruitment of the Boston Bombers' (*Foreign Policy Research Institute*, 26 April 2013) <www.fpri.org/2013/04/detecting-the-radicalization-and-recruitment-of-the-boston-bombers/> accessed 25 May 2024.

from the case law, studies, and literature, and consider the AI Act 2024 of the European Union[6], the AI Convention 2024 of the Council of Europe[7] and the UNESCO Recommendation on the Ethics of Artificial Intelligence 2023[8]. The key findings conclude the article (Chapter VI).

II. Premises

For the scope of this legal analysis, 'algorithm'[9] is defined as a set of instructions executed when triggered, whereas 'AI' refers to a group of algorithms capable of learning and creating new algorithms based on new data, described as 'intelligence'.[10] Thus, AI is a machine-based system that infers from its input how to generate outputs such as predictions, content, recommendations, or decisions that may influence environments (AI Convention 2024, Article 2).

Building on this, predictive intelligence[11] enables the automated analysis of data such as age, residence, education, health, and social connections to identify suspects and patterns, and to predict the location and timing

---

6 Regulation (EU) 2024/1689 of the European Parliament and of the Council of 13 June 2024 laying down harmonised rules on artificial intelligence and amending Regulations (EC) No 300/2008, (EU) No 167/2013, (EU) No 168/2013, (EU) 2018/858, (EU) 2018/1139 and (EU) 2019/2144 and Directives 2014/90/EU, (EU) 2016/797 and (EU) 2020/1828 (Artificial Intelligence Act) [2024] OJ L 2024/1689 (hereinafter referred to as 'AI Act').

7 Council of Europe Framework Convention on Artificial Intelligence and Human Rights, Democracy and the Rule of Law <https://rm.coe.int/1680afae3c> accessed 1 August 2024 (hereinafter referred to as 'AI Convention 2024').

8 UNESCO, 'Recommendation on the Ethics of Artificial Intelligence' (adopted on 23 November 2021) <https://unesdoc.unesco.org/ark:/48223/pf0000381137> accessed 25 May 2024.

9 The author acknowledges that multiple complex interlinked algorithms and AI systems exist. For the purposes of this legal analysis and due to word constraints, the simple terms 'algorithm' an 'AI' will be used, sometimes also simultaneously.

10 Victoria Ibold, 'Künstliche Intelligenz im Sicherheitsrecht – Begründungsgebot quo vadis?' (2024) Zeitschrift für das gesamte Sicherheitsrecht 10, 12f; Reinhard Klaushofer, 'Die menschenrechtliche Dimension Künstlicher Intelligenz' (2019) 74(3) Zeitschrift für öffentliches Recht 399, 407.

11 Kathleen McKendrick, 'Artificial Intelligence Prediction and Counterterrorism' (August 2019) The Royal Institute of International Affairs Research Paper, at 8 <www.chathamhouse.org/sites/default/files/2019-08-07-AICounterterrorism.pdf> accessed 1 August 2024.

of attacks.[12] It can measure an individual's risks and prepare decisions. A growing area of predictive intelligence involves online networks, where lone wolves are often radicalized and share knowledge through social media.[13] Automated algorithms can entice individuals by showing them content that aligns with their existing views, making it harder for them to consider other perspectives. This can reinforce extremist beliefs and limit exposure to diverse ideas.[14] However, algorithms can also be used to deradicalize online users by providing a 'positive' narrative (see Chapter IV.D). Similarly, algorithm-based and AI systems can scan social networks by analysing sentiments towards keywords linked to terrorism, such as 'bomb', 'ISIS', 'Hamas' or 'Hezbollah' to detect potential risks.[15]

AI is often combined with biometric methods, which measure human characteristics. The General Data Protection Regulation (GDPR) defines in Article 4(14) biometric data as personal data related to physical, physiological, or behavioural traits that allow unique identification of a person.[16] This includes measurements of the face, eye movement, iris scans, body shape, voice, prosody, gait, posture, blood pressure, fingerprints, DNA, and

---

12 Maggie Gray and Amy Ertan, 'Artificial Intelligence and Autonomy in the Military: An Overview of NATO Member States' Strategies and Deployment' (2021) 19 <https://ccdcoe.org/uploads/2021/12/Strategies_and_Deployment_A4.pdf> accessed 1 August 2024; Islamic Military Counter Terrorism Coalition, 'Artificial Intelligence and Counterterrorism: Limitations, Opportunities and Risks' (January 2020) Special Reports No 9, at 3 <https://imctc.org/en/eLibrary/INTReports/Documents/Report-Issu-09-EN.pdf> accessed 1 August 2024.

13 Manfredi Pozzoli, 'Violent Assemblages: Rethinking Screens, Media, and Lone Wolf Terrorism' (*Global Network on Extremism & Technology*, 13 April 2023) <https://gnet-research.org/2023/04/13/violent-assemblages-rethinking-screens-media-and-lone-wolf-terrorism/> accessed 25 May 2024.

14 Jonathan Kenyon, Jens F Binder and Christopher Baker-Beall, 'Terrorism and the Internet: How Dangerous is Online Radicalization?' (2022) 13:997390 Frontiers in Psychology <www.ncbi.nlm.nih.gov/pmc/articles/PMC9606324/> accessed 1 August 2023.

15 Scott A Robbins, 'Machine Learning and Counter-Terrorism: Ethics, Efficacy, and Meaningful Human Control' (Doctoral thesis, Delft University of Technology 2021) 28; Sofea Azrina Azizan and Izatdin Abdul Aziz Aziz, 'Terrorism Detection Based on Sentiment Analysis Using Machine Learning' (2017) 12(3) Journal of Engineering and Applied Sciences 691, 692.

16 Regulation (EU) 2016/679 of the Parliament and of the Council of 27 April 2016 on the protection of natural persons with regard to the processing of personal data and on the free movement of such data, and repealing Directive 95/46/EC [2016] OJ L119/1.

heartbeat patterns ('heart print').[17] Biometrics are highly sensitive as a person can change their name, but not their DNA. Historically, biometric data has been misused by authoritarian regimes (*e.g.*, the Nazi regime) to 'determine' ethnicity.[18] Also nowadays, using AI on marginalized groups based on characteristics such as gender or ethnicity is increasingly exacerbating inequalities due to biased data and flawed models.

The EU's 2024 AI Act classifies biometrics as 'high-risk AI systems' (Article 6 Section 2, Annex III), but permits their use for labelling or filtering lawfully acquired biometric datasets, like images, or categorizing biometric data for law enforcement purposes (Article 5 Section 1 lit g).[19] It prohibits using AI to predict someone's likelihood of committing a crime based solely on profiling, unless it supports a human assessment based on verifiable facts (Article 5 Section 1 lit d). However, the AI Act does not apply to AI used for national security purposes (Article 2 Section 3), which includes counterterrorism. National security remains in the responsibility of member states (Article 4 Section 2 TEU), allowing the use of real-time biometrics like face recognition for the prevention of threats to life like terrorist attacks and the localisation or identification of suspects (Article 5 Section 1 lit h). Similarly, the GDPR does not apply to data processing by authorities for preventing, investigating, detecting, or prosecuting criminal offenses and safeguarding 'public security' (Article 2 Section 2 lit d). And the AI Convention 2024 is also not mandatory in the fields of national security.(Article 3 Section 2).[20] Due to the absence of a clear mandatory set of rules, the ECtHR's case law remains highly relevant.[21]

17 UNICRI and UNCCT, 'Algorithms and Terrorism: The Malicious Use of Artificial Intelligence for Terrorist Purposes' (2021) 34 <https://unicri.it/sites/default/files/2021-06/Malicious%20Use%20of%20AI%20-%20UNCCT-UNICRI%20Report_Web.pdf> accessed 19 August 2024; Robbins (n 15) 26f.

18 Krisztina Huszti-Orbán and Fionnuala Ní Aoláin, 'Use of Biometric Data to Identify Terrorists: Best Practice or Risky Business?' (2020) 6 <www.ohchr.org/sites/default/files/Documents/Issues/Terrorism/biometricsreport.pdf> accessed 1 August 2024.

19 AI Act 2024 (n 6).

20 AI Convention 2024 (n 7).

21 For brevity, the European Court of Human Rights will hereafter be also referred to as 'the Court'.

III. Challenges for Human Rights

Terrorism has always had a 'twofold effect' on human rights law:[22] On the one hand, states parties to the ECHR are obliged to protect the right to life and integrity of their citizens (Article 2 ECHR). This includes taking preventive measures[23] to safeguard individuals whose lives are at risk due to criminal acts.[24] This responsibility becomes even more crucial when a whole society faces threats,[25] especially such as those posed by terrorism.[26] On the other hand, states must also protect the human and fundamental rights of potential suspects and perpetrators. When evaluating the legitimate aim of intervening in other human rights, the state's obligation under Article 2 ECHR must be taken into account. The use of algorithms and AI in this context has raised concerns about privacy rights, biases and discrimination and fair remedies as well as accountability, particularly in light of the 'black box' issue.

A. Right to Respect for Private Life (Article 8 ECHR)

1. Scope

Article 8(1) ECHR guarantees to everyone 'the right to respect for his private and family life, his home and his correspondence.' The protection of personal data is of fundamental importance to a person's enjoyment of their rights guaranteed by Article 8.[27] 'Personal data' is understood as any unique

---

22 Ralph Janik, 'Terrorism' in Christina Binder, Manfred Nowak, Jane A Hofbauer and Philipp Janig (eds), *Elgar Encyclopedia of Human Rights*, vol 4 (2022) para 7.

23 *Tagayeva and Others v Russia*, ECtHR, Application No 26562/07 and 6 others, Judgment of 18 September 2017, para 491.

24 *Osman v The United Kingdom*, ECtHR, Application No 87/1997/871/1083, Judgment of 28 October 1998, para 115; *Paul and Audrey Edwards v The United Kingdom*, ECtHR, Application No 46477/99, Judgment of 14 June 2002, para 54.

25 *Mastromatteo v Italy*, ECtHR (GC), Application No 37703/97, Judgment of 24 October 2002, para 69; *Choreftakis and Choreftaki v Greece*, ECtHR, Application No 46846/08, Judgment of 17 January 2012, paras 48-49.

26 *Tagayeva and Others v Russia* (n 20) para 482.

27 ECtHR, 'Guide on Article 8 of the European Convention on Human Rights' (9 April 2024) para 227 <https://ks.echr.coe.int/documents/d/echr-ks/guide_art_8_eng> accessed 26 August 2024.

'information relating to an identified or identifiable individual'.[28] Therefore, Article 8 protects various kinds of data, including data with an identifiable IP address,[29] surveillance camera footage[30] or GPS data indicating someone's whereabouts.[31] It becomes highly sensitive, when the data reveals a person's ethnicity, bearing in mind the rapid developments in the field of genetics and Information Technology (IT).[32] This concerns biometrics such as cellular samples, fingerprints, DNA and voice samples.[33] The storage of data on someone's political affiliations or activity[34] and intimate data revealing a person's health information[35] are protected in the same way.

The ECtHR emphasized that insufficient consideration of modern technology's complexity can lead to unjustified violations of the right to privacy and that ensuring proportionality and effective safeguards is crucial to its protection.[36] Consequently, the right to privacy can be violated by a variety of measures, may it be targeted or bulk surveillance, intercepting one's correspondence, collecting, or retaining personal or biometrical data.[37] The Court found violations of Article 8 often regarding means of secret surveil-

---

28 *Amann v Switzerland*, ECtHR, Application No 27798/95, Judgment of 16 February 2000, para 65.

29 *Benedik v Slovenia*, ECtHR, Application No 62357/14, Judgment of 24 July 2018, paras 108-109.

30 *Antović and Mirković v Montenegro*, ECtHR, Application No 70838/13, Judgment of 28 February 2018.

31 *Uzun v Germany*, ECtHR, Application No 35623/05, Judgment of 2 December 2010.

32 *S and Marper v The United Kingdom*, ECtHR (GC), Application Nos 30562/04 and 30566/04, Judgment of 4 December 2008, para 71.

33 *Ibid.*, paras 70-77; *Aycaguer v France*, ECtHR, Application No 8806/12, Judgment of 22 June 2017, para 45; *Trajkovski and Chipovski v North Macedonia*, ECtHR, Application Nos 53205/13 and 63320/13, Judgment of 13 June 2020, para 40; *Gaughran v the United Kingdom*, ECtHR, Application No 45245/15, Judgment of 13 June 2020, para 63.

34 *Rotaru v Romania*, ECtHR (GC), Application No 28341/95, Judgment of 4 May 2000, paras 43-44; Catt v The United Kingdom, ECtHR, Application No 43514/15, Judgment of 24 January 2019, paras 112 and 123.

35 *Mockutė v Lithuania*, ECtHR, Application No 66490/09, Judgment of 27 February 2018, paras 93-95.

36 *Gaughran v The United Kingdom*, ECtHR, Application No 45245/15, Judgment of 13 June 2020, paras 86 and 96-98.

37 Janik (n 22) para 33.

lance, *e.g.* phone interception.[38] In many cases though, a violation was not caused by the data-related action, but the lack of effective guarantees against arbitrariness and abuse.[39] Safeguards and remedies include notification and access to one's data as well as remedies to correct or delete data.[40]

2. The Legal Interference

a. … is in Accordance with the Law

The interference must be 'in accordance with the law'. The measure must have a basis in the domestic law and be compatible with the rule of law. The law must be accessible to the person concerned and foreseeable as to its effects.[41] However, 'foreseeability' in the context of secret surveillance cannot mean that concerned persons are able to foresee when authorities are likely to observe them, otherwise they may adapt their conduct accordingly.[42] Rather, it requires the domestic law to be sufficiently clear to give citizens an adequate indication of the conditions under which public authorities are empowered

---

38 *Kennedy v The United Kingdom*, ECtHR, Application No 26839/05, Judgment of 18 May 2010; *Klass and Others v Germany*, ECtHR, Application No 5029/71, Judgment of 6 September 1978; *Centrum för Rättvisa v Sweden*, ECtHR (GC), Application No 35252/08, Judgment of 25 May 2021; *Big Brother Watch and Others v The United Kingdom*, ECtHR (GC), Application No 58170/13, Judgment of 25 May 2021.

39 *Klass and Others v Germany* (n 38) paras 365-374; *Big Brother Watch and Others v The United Kingdom* (n 38); *Zakharov v Russia*, ECtHR (GC), Application No 47143/06, Judgment of 4 December 2015, para 231ff.

40 European Union Agency for Fundamental Rights, 'Surveillance by Intelligence Services: Fundamental Rights Safeguards and Remedies in the EU, Volume II: Field Perspectives and Legal Updates' (2017) 114, 123ff <https://fra.europa.eu/sites/default/files/fra_uploads/fra-2017-surveillance-intelligence-services-vol-2_en.pdf> accessed 19 August 2024; Eleni Kosta, 'Algorithmic State Surveillance: Challenging the Notion of Agency in Human Rights' (2022) 16(1) Regulation & Governance 212, 217.

41 *Zakharov v Russia* (n 39) para 228; *Rotaru v Romania* (n 34) para 52; S and *Marper v The United Kingdom* (n 32) para 95; *Kennedy v The United Kingdom* (n 38) para 151 f.

42 *Zakharov v Russia* (n 39) para 229.

to resort to any such measures.[43] In addition, the law must indicate the scope of any discretion conferred to the authorities and the manner of its exercise with clarity to provide for adequate protection against arbitrary abuse.[44] Accordingly, in *Centrum för Rättvisa v Sweden*[45] the Grand Chamber found that Sweden violated Article 8 based on three arguments: 1) the absence of a clear law on the deletion of non-personal data, 2) the absence of a requirement to consider privacy interests when deciding to transmit intelligence material to third (foreign) parties and 3) the absence of an *ex post facto* review.

b. … Pursues a Legitimate Aim

The measure must serve a legitimate aim in terms of Article 8(2) with the most relevant aim being national security. Using surveillance measures to protect foreign, defence, and security policies, and to identify threats, is legitimate.[46]

For example, storing private data in a secret police register for vetting candidates aims to protect national security.[47] Similarly, GPS surveillance to investigate an attempted murder claimed by a terrorist group and to prevent future bomb attacks serves national security and victim protection.[48] Even the prevention of future attacks and identifying future offenders[49] justify setting up databases and collecting personal information about convicted persons and suspects, with the crime's seriousness playing a significant role.[50] This interest may outweigh individual data protection.[51]

---

43 *Big Brother Watch and Others v The United Kingdom* (n 38) para 333; *Centrum för Rättvisa v Sweden* (n 38) para 247; *Huvig v France*, ECtHR, Application No 11105/84, Judgment of 24 April 1990, para 29; *Weber and Saravia v Germany*, ECtHR (GC), Application No 54934/00, Judgment of 29 June 2006, para 93.

44 *Big Brother Watch and Others v The United Kingdom* (n 38) para 230.

45 *Centrum för Rättvisa v Sweden* (n 38) paras 369-377.

46 *Ibid.*, para 279.

47 *Leander v Sweden*, ECtHR, Application No 9248/81, Judgment of 26 March 1987, para 49.

48 *Uzun v Germany* (n 31) para 78.

49 *S and Marper v The United Kingdom* (n 32) para 100.

50 Gardel v France, ECtHR, Application No 16428/05, Judgment of 17 March 2010, para 63; *MB v France*, ECtHR, Application No 22115/06, Judgment of 10 May 2010, para 54.

51 *S and Marper v The United Kingdom* (n 32) paras 101 and 104.

c. … is Necessary in a Democratic Society

The interference must be necessary in a democratic society, meet a 'pressing social need' and be 'proportionate to the legitimate aim pursued'.[52] Secret surveillance is accepted only if strictly necessary to protect democratic institutions, with adequate safeguards against abuse.[53] Data retention may be essential at first, but it can become unnecessary over time or for specific types of data. Therefore, for instance, indefinite retention of fingerprints, cellular samples, and DNA profiles of (not convicted) suspects breaches Article 8, regardless of the offense's seriousness or the suspects' age.[54] However, retaining photos taken during an investigation may remain necessary after the arrest to prevent future crimes.[55] The case law shows how data retention practices must be carefully evaluated to balance individual rights with the necessity of preserving information for public safety and crime prevention.

d. … is Effective

The Court acknowledged that modern telecommunications necessitate adapting investigative tools, including AI.[56] Authorities must act fast when an attack risk becomes known. Therefore, authorities need immediate knowledge about suspects, allowing them to secretly collect and rapidly analyse data to be effective, for which AI and algorithm-based systems have become indispensable.

e. … is Proportionate

The proportionality criterion requires balancing state interests in national security and anti-terrorism with the severity of interference in suspects' private lives. This balance depends on data quality and system accuracy;

---

52 *Vicent Del Campo v Spain*, ECtHR, Application No 5527/13, Judgment of 6 November 2018, para 46.

53 *Klass and Others v Germany* (n 38) para 42; *Big Brother Watch and Others v The United Kingdom* (n 38) para 334, *Zakharov v Russia* (n 39) para 236; *Kennedy v The United Kingdom* (n 38) para 155; *Centrum för Rättvisa v Sweden* (n 38) para 248; *Huvig v France* (n 43) para 29.

54 *S and Marper v The United Kingdom* (n 32) paras 145-125.

55 *Suprunenko v Russia*, ECtHR, Application No 8630/11, Judgment of 19 June 2018 paras 63-65.

56 *Breyer v Germany*, ECtHR, Application No 50001/12, Judgment of 30 January 2020, para 88.

a higher false accusation rate in an AI system reduces its proportionality.[57] ECtHR case law shows a flexible system, considering factors like retention duration, data type and sensitivity, access limitations to special authorities, offence seriousness, the suspect's age, and safeguards against abuse.

Data should be retained only as long as necessary,[58] with greater scrutiny for sensitive personal data.[59] For example, GPS data is less intrusive than visual or acoustical surveillance,[60] while DNA samples require higher protection due to their sensitive nature, leading the Court in *Marper v UK* to identify a violation of Article 8 due to the indefinite retention of such data.[61]

The Court found a forty-year retention period for non-severe offences problematic, with deletion rights only for non-convicted persons.[62] Even a six-year retention in an extremism database without safeguards[63] or a one-year retention without review[64] can constitute a violation of Article 8. In *P.N. v Germany,*[65] a five-year retention for identifying repeat offenders was no violation due to individualized verification and the guaranteed review. Likewise, bulk surveillance does not automatically violate Article 8.[66] Clear procedural rules are crucial safeguards against arbitrariness, specifying legal measures and the targeted individuals, setting duration limits, restricting their use to the determined purpose, determining the possibility to transmit data to other entities and stipulating rules for deletion.[67]

---

57 McKendrick (n 11) 25.

58 *S and Marper v The United Kingdom* (n 32) para 116ff; P*eruzzo and Martens v Germany*, ECtHR, Application Nos 7841/08 and 57900/12, Decision of 4 June 2013, para 46.

59 *Z v Finland*, ECtHR, Application No 22009/93, Judgment of 25 February 1997, para 96.

60 *Uzun v Germany* (n 31) para 52.

61 *S and Marper v The United Kingdom* (n 32) paras 73, 103-104 and 113.

62 *M.K v France*, ECtHR, Application No 19522/09, Judgment of 18 April 2013, paras 44f.

63 *Catt v the United Kingdom* (n 34) paras 120-122.

64 *Centrum för Rättvisa v Sweden* (n 38) paras 354 and 357ff.

65 *P.N. v Germany*, ECtHR, Application No 74440/17, Judgment of 11 June 2020, paras 87-90.

66 *Big Brother Watch and Others v The United Kingdom* (n 38) paras 322-323; *Centrum för Rättvisa v Sweden* (n 38) para 261.

67 *Zakharov v Russia* (n 39) paras 30-234; *Big Brother Watch and Others v The United Kingdom* (n 38) para 498.

Key safeguards include prior judicial authorization and judicial review to assess the rationale behind retention and ensure independence, impartiality, and due process.[68] Individuals should have the right to request deletion of their data. In addition, an independent Ombudsperson, separate from the executive, serves as a safeguard against abuse, especially regarding secret surveillance, where the individual is unaware of the monitoring and review is required without their intervention.[69] Once a notification no longer jeopardizes the measure, the person must be informed to enable adequate remedies.

To conclude, the duration of the retention, the intrusiveness of the data, the seriousness of the offense, existing safeguards, in particular the right to review are pivotal considerations in assessing a violation. The potential for misuse is inherent in covert AI surveillance granting access to personal data.

B. No Unreasonable Distinction (Article 14 in conjunction with Article 8 ECHR)

Article 14 of the Convention mandates that rights and freedoms be enjoyed without discrimination based on sex, race, national, or social origin. Avoiding discrimination is a priority for institutions combating terrorism. The OSCE 'participating States unequivocally reject the association of terrorism with any particular race, nationality or religion.'[70] At the same time, this also means that justified distinctions are permissible if supported by reliable data, ensuring transparency and accessibility, especially regarding beliefs and ideologies. If the data indicates a higher risk from fundamentalist groups (*e.g.*, Islamist extremists), it is justified to monitor them more closely.

However, automated systems relying on inaccurate evidence risk more errors than human judgment.[71] Decisions based on biased AI systems can be discriminatory, creating feedback loops that perpetuate past biases and target

---

68 *Zakharov v Russia* (n 39) paras 233, 249 and 275; *S and Marper v The United Kingdom* (n 32) para 119; *Rotaru v Romania* (n 32) para 59; *Kennedy v The United Kingdom* (n 38) para 127; *Uzun v Germany* (n 31) para 56; *Klass and Others v Germany* (n 38) para 55.

69 *Guðmundur Andri Ástráðsson v Iceland*, ECtHR (GC), Application No 26374/18, Judgment of 1 December 2020, paras 152-153 and 246; *Reczkowicz v Poland*, ECtHR, Application No 43447/19, Judgment of 22 July 2021, para 223; *Zakharov v Russia* (n 39) para 233.

70 OSCE, 'Countering Terrorism' <www.osce.org/countering-terrorism> accessed 26 May 2024.

71 Robbins (n 15) 9f.

marginalized groups.[72] This issue is sensitive, especially with historically biased criminal justice data, creating a cycle and resembling confirmation bias, seeking evidence that aligns with their existing hypotheses.[73] Thereby, especially AI systems can increase surveillance and misidentification of minority groups, particularly through facial recognition. This profiling fosters mistrust and alienation, potentially driving some individuals towards radicalization as resistance.

In addition, facial recognition systems are often biased due to underrepresentation of marginalized groups in their training data. This leads to higher rates of misidentification for people of colour, women, and other marginalized individuals.[74] As a result, innocent people from these groups are more likely to be wrongly labelled as criminals, perpetuating discrimination, and systematic inequality.

Therefore, protecting the right to non-discrimination requires state actors to ensure the high quality of data feeding AI systems.[75] Data must be inclusive of all social classes, ethnicities, and population groups, as poor or biased data inevitably perpetuates prejudices, potentially leading to discriminatory outcomes.[76] Thus, it seems important that methods and assessments to prevent discrimination are implemented already at the data collection stage and not just when the algorithm or AI system is in use.

---

72 David Leslie, Christopher Burr, Mhairi Aitken, Josh Cowls, Mike Katell and Morgan Briggs, 'Artificial Intelligence, Human Rights, Democracy, and the Rule of Law: A Primer' (2021) 17 <https://edoc.coe.int/en/artificial-intelligence/10206-artificial-intelligence-human-rights-democracy-and-the-rule-of-law-a-primer.html> accessed 1 August 2024.

73 Ibold (n 10) 13; Robbins (n 15) 10.

74 Sidney Perkowitz, 'The Bias in the Machine: Facial Recognition Technology and Racial Disparities' (5 February 2021) MIT Case Studies in Social and Ethical Responsibilities of Computing <https://mit-serc.pubpub.org/pub/bias-in-machine/release/1> accessed 1 August 2024.

75 Janneke Gerards, 'The Fundamental Rights Challenges of Algorithms' (2019) 37(3) Netherlands Quarterly of Human Rights 205, 208; UNESCO Recommendation on the Ethics of AI (n 8).

76 Klaushofer (n 10) 421; Österreichischer Rat für Robotik und Künstliche Intelligenz, 'Die Zukunft Österreichs mit Robotik und Künstlicher Intelligenz positiv gestalten' (November 2018) 48 <www.bmk.gv.at/themen/innovation/publikationen/forschungspolitik/ki/whitepaper.html> accessed 19 August 2024; Independent High-Level Expert Group on Artificial Intelligence, 'A Definition of AI: Main Capabilities and Disciplines' (2019) 5 <https://ec.europa.eu/newsroom/dae/document.cfm?doc_id=56341> accessed 1 August 2024.

C. Effective Remedy (Article 13 in conjunction with Article 8 ECHR)

Article 13 ECHR protects the right to an 'effective remedy before a national authority notwithstanding that the violation has been committed by persons acting in an official capacity'. This means that Article 13 provides individuals with a right to an effective remedy against the court as well as a police officer who used AI to detain a person. Both control mechanisms, *i.e.* independent authorities overseeing surveillance activities, as well as easy and transparent access to effective remedies for the persons concerned play a relevant role here.

1. Independent and Binding

A national authority under Article 13 can be an independent judicial or quasi-judicial (administrative) body or a tribunal.[77] The main guarantee is its institutional independence from the executive, including the appointment processes of judges, term duration for members and safeguards against external pressures.[78] They must also be impartial, adequately resourced, accountable, and subject to public scrutiny themselves.[79] The authority shall be transparent by providing reports about their activities. Contrary to the ECtHR case law, it had been shown that some oversight bodies heavily depend on the executive.[80] Further, the competence to issue binding decisions is a key element of an effective remedy. This should include the right to order the termination of the monitoring, to obtain the destruction of the stored data and to award the data owner appropriate compensation.

---

[77] *Leander v Sweden* (n 47) para 65; *Segerstedt-Wiberg and Others v Sweden*, ECtHR, Application No 62332/00, Judgment of 6 June 2006, para 117.

[78] *Big Brother Watch and Others v The United Kingdom* (n 38) para 359; *Guðmundur Andri Ástráðsson v Iceland* (n 69) paras 152-153 and 246; *Dolińska-Ficek and Ozimek v Poland*, ECtHR, Application Nos 49868/19 and 57511/19, Judgment of 8 November 2021, para 279.

[79] *Szabo and Vissy v Hungary*, ECtHR, Application No 37138/14, Judgment of 12 January 2016, para 82; UNGA Res 71/199, 'The Right to Privacy in the Digital Age' (19 December 2016) UN Doc A/RES/71/199, para 5(d).

[80] European Union Agency for Fundamental Rights (n 40) 11.

2. Transparency v 'Black Box'

The remedy must be accessible and capable of directly remedying the substantive issues.[81] This is an issue, when the decisions are not made or even controlled by humans, but generated automatically.[82] Most AI systems are unexplainable due to their hidden layers and complex architectures, often involving billions of parameters, making them impossible to analyse and understand.[83] Suspects might not even know they have been identified by AI or an algorithm, but even if so, the decision making process is not disclosed to them; it stays a 'black box'.[84] Without appropriate information, they cannot understand the reasoning, let alone challenge the algorithm and identify gaps in the decision making process.[85]

The ECtHR's case law is distinctive in this matter. In the context of secret surveillance, the Court accepts that the remedy has to be only as effective as it can be.[86] This can be shown on the example of the notification: A targeted person does not have to be notified, if a notification could jeopardize the secret surveillance.[87] However, after notification of the measure, the individual must be enabled to remedy the measure within a reasonable time.[88] Rights and

---

81 *Hasan and Chaush v Bulgaria*, ECtHR (GC), Application No 30985/96, Judgment of 26 October 2000, para 100.

82 Verónica Dahl, 'Summary of the Panel Discussion "Algorithms' Impact on Human Behaviour"' in Emilia Gómez (ed), Assessing the Impact of Machine Intelligence on Human Behaviour: An Interdisciplinary Endeavour (2018) 31; Molavi Ramak, 'Künstliche Intelligenz – Entwicklung, Herausforderungen, Regulierung' (2018) 26(1) Journal für Rechtspolitik 9, 11.

83 Althaf Marsoof, Andrés Luco, Harry Tan and Shafiq Joty, 'Content-filtering AI Systems – Limitations, Challenges and Regulatory Approaches' (2023) 32(1) Information & Communications Technology Law, 64, 84.

84 Ibold (n 10) 13 f; Janneke Gerards and Raphaële Xenidis, 'Algorithmic Discrimination in Europe: Challenges and Opportunities for Gender Equality and Non-discrimination Law' (2020) 10 <https://op.europa.eu/en/publication-detail/-/publication/082f1dbc-821d-11eb-9ac9-01aa75ed71a1> accessed 1 August 2024; Robbins (n 15) 84; Andrés Páez, 'Negligent Algorithmic Discrimination' (2021) 84(3) Law and Contemporary Problems 19, 24, 27; Human Rights Council, 'The Right to Privacy in the Digital Age: Report of the United Nations High Commissioner for Human Rights' (2021) UN Doc A/HRC/48/31, paras 20 and 56.

85 Ibold (n 10) 10, 15.

86 *Klass and Others v Germany* (n 38) paras 78-79.

87 *Ibid.*, paras 58 and 71; *Leander v Sweden* (n 47) paras 66 and 78-84.

88 *Zakharov v Russia* (n 39) para 287; see also Kosta (n 40) 212-224, 217.

information must be presented to targeted persons in a clear, understandable, and easily accessible way, so they are able to determine which information is essential to exercise their rights.[89] They must get access to the data, be able to rectify and delete the data and seek a judicial review as to whether the measures complied with the law.

D. Fair Trial (Article 6 ECHR)

1. Access and Judicial Review

When data storage decisions are based solely on algorithms or AI without judicial review, the lack of a public hearing is problematic. Excluding the public entirely, even for the protection of classified information, is insufficient.[90] Some degree of public access must be ensured while maintaining the confidentiality of sensitive data.[91] In addition, Article 6 requires courts to provide reasoned decisions, demonstrating that parties' arguments were heard and enabling proper exercise of the right to appeal.[92]

However, a lack of public hearing and reasoning can be remedied by providing a public hearing at the appeal stage, if the Court of Appeal has full jurisdiction to review the merits of the case.[93] The review should consider factors like the subject matter of the initial decision by the court of first

---

[89] Balázs Gáti, 'Data Protection Aspects of the Use of Facial Recognition Systems for Law Enforcement' in Dimitrije Ćeranić, Svjetlana Ivanović, Radislav Lale and Samir Aličić (eds), Collection of Papers "Law Between Creation and Interpretation", vol III (2023) 306, 322.

[90] *Vasilev v Bulgaria*, ECtHR, Application No 7610/15, Judgment of 16 November 2021, paras 106-111; regarding special circumstances: *Kennedy v The United Kingdom* (n 38) para 188.

[91] *Vasilev v Bulgaria* (n 90) paras 106 and 116-118.

[92] *Hirvisaari v Finland*, ECtHR, Application No 49684/99, Judgment of 27 September 2001, para 30; *Suominen v Finland*, ECtHR, Application No 37801/97, Judgment of 1 July 2003, paras 36-37; *García Ruiz v Spain*, ECtHR, Application No 30544/96, Judgment of 21 January 1999, para 26.

[93] *Ramos Nunes de Carvalho e Sá v Portugal*, ECtHR (GC), Application Nos 55391/13, 57728/13 and 74041/13, Judgment of 6 November 2018, para 192; Le Compte Van Leuven and De Meyere v Belgium, ECtHR, Application Nos 6878/75 and 7238/75, Judgment of 18 October 1982, para 60; *Albert and Le Compte v Belgium*, ECtHR, Application Nos 7299/75 and 7496/76, Judgment of 24 October 1983, para 36.

instance, the manner in which it was rendered, and the dispute's substance, including the grounds for appeal.[94]

2. Presumption of Innocence

Article 6 (2) ensures the presumption of innocence, meaning any doubt should favour the defendant.[95] Including data in databases raises a risk of stigmatization. This risk increases when decisions rely more on algorithms and less on human oversight. For example, in the Netherlands, AI systems have flagged peaceful protesters as potential threats, leading to unnecessary surveillance and data retention, violating their rights to privacy and freedom of assembly.[96] Retaining individuals' private data should not imply suspicion. To uphold the presumption of innocence, the law must differentiate between various groups. For instance, data on suspects should not be stored as long as data on convicted individuals.[97] Protecting the presumption of innocence is crucial, particularly in the context of data retention. The potential for stigmatization is high when data is algorithmically managed. There is an interconnection with the risk of discrimation. Therefore, it is essential to implement legal safeguards, especially human oversight.

IV. Chances for Human Rights

Beyond the outlined risks, AI also offers benefits both for the rights of suspects and the protection of citizens. AI can handle vast amounts of data that humans cannot efficiently analyse, leading to more accurate and precise pre-selection.[98] This technology helps identify patterns, increases accuracy,

---

94 *Denisov v Ukraine*, ECtHR (GC), Application No 76639/11, Judgment of 25 September 2018, para 67; *Oleksandr Volkov v Ukraine*, ECtHR, Application No 21722/11, Judgment of 9 January 2013, paras 108 and 123.

95 *Barberà, Messegué and Jabardo v Spain*, ECtHR, Application No 10590/83, Judgment of 6 December 1988, para 77.

96 Amnesty International, 'The Netherlands: Police Violate Rights of Peaceful Protesters' (31 May 2023) <www.amnesty.org/en/latest/news/2023/05/the-netherlands-police-violate-rights-of-peaceful-protesters/> accessed 26 May 2024.

97 *S and Marper v The United Kingdom* (n 32) para 122.

98 Human Rights Council (n 84) para 13; Damien Van Puyvelde, Stephen Coulthart and Shahriar M Hossain, 'Beyond the Buzzword: Big Data and National Security Decision-Making' (2017) 93(6) International Affairs 1397, 1398.

and ensures that decisions about interferences are justified. Additionally, AI has the potential to rationally evaluate the effectiveness of surveillance models and correct biased decision-making, making the process fairer and more objective. Eventually, it also plays an important role for deradicalisation.

A. Resources: Large Amounts of Data

The smaller the number of profiles analysed by public authorities, the less precise the analyses. Algorithms and AI address this by rapidly collecting and filtering vast amount of data, enabling pre-decisions and improving classification and understanding of groupings.[99] This targeted resource use enhances investigative quality. For instance, a study group used AI to collect 3.1 million tweets mentioning ISIS in some form, authored by more than 250 000 users within two months to analyse historic timelines of users supporting or opposing ISIS.[100] Similarly, the British Home Office states to have used an algorithm to detect 94% of ISIS propaganda videos with a 99.995% accuracy rate.[101]

B. Insights: Revealing Patterns of Terrorists

AI surpasses human investigators in detecting patterns within terrorist groups by systematically filtering data and unveiling valuable insights into group behaviour and developments. Researchers have applied AI including Social-Network-Analysis algorithms to 'better understand the roots of this organization [ISIS] and its supporters'.[102] AI can also predict fragmentations within terrorist groups like ISIL and Al-Qaida and understand how and why they split.[103] By classifying current supporters, the system was able to predict individuals likely to support these groups in the future.[104]

---

99 McKendrick (n 11) 17.

100 Walid Magdy, Kareem Darwish and Ingmar Weber, '#FailedRevolutions: Using Twitter to Study the Antecedents of ISIS Support' (2016) 21(2) First Monday <https://arxiv.org/pdf/1503.02401.pdf>.

101 Robbins (n 15) 29.

102 Magdy, Darwish and Weber (n 100).

103 UNICRI and UNCCT, 'Countering Terrorism Online with Artificial Intelligence: An Overview for Law Enforcement and Counter-Terrorism Agencies in South Asia and South-East Asia' (2021) 25 <www.un.org/counterterrorism/sites/www.un.org.counterterrorism/files/countering-terrorism-online-with-ai-uncct-unicri-report-web.pdf> accessed 1 August 2024.

104 Magdy, Darwish and Weber (n 100).

At the same time, AI reveals characteristics of lone-wolf terrorists, identifying similarities, variances, and correlations within the social milieu. It analyses the impact of various (counter-)strategies on terrorist behaviour, aiding early detection of group patterns and lone-wolf characteristics. Thus, they contribute to the early detection of terrorist group patterns as well as lone-wolf terrorist characteristics. This enhances citizen protection against terror acts while also reducing false suspicions of innocent people. Improved knowledge of terrorist profiles sharpens AI systems, increasing accuracy in pre-decisions about potential suspects and aligning classifications more closely with actual threats.

C. Predictability: Increase Success in Preventing Terrorism

AI systems excel at predicting both group behaviours and lone-wolf terrorists, particularly in online communication and social media.[105] Since extremist communities communicate largely online, AI can analyse these channels to detect radicalization levels, anticipate new movements, and predict acute threats such as attacks.[106] These systems interpret daily online interactions and assess risk levels, enabling law enforcement to prevent potential attacks.[107] Operating at high speed, AI provides accurate alerts to authorities. For example, *INSIKT* Intelligence's program analyses the network structure of terrorist groups.[108] It uses machine learning models to detect threats on the Internet. As the models process more data, they become increasingly accurate, effectively reducing the likelihood of attacks.

D. Deradicalization: Early Detection of Persons Susceptible to Radicalization

Effective AI systems can identify individuals vulnerable to radicalization early and assist in their deradicalization. Traditional methods struggle to detect such persons, but techniques like Natural Language Processing (NLP) can identify keywords, narratives and patterns indicating radicalization on

---

105 McKendrick (n 11) 18 f.

106 Neil F Johnson *et al*, 'New Online Ecology of Adversarial Aggregates: ISIS and Beyond' (2016) 352(6292) Science 1459.

107 UNICRI and UNCCT (n 103) 38.

108 See <www.firstlinepractitioners.com/fr/provider/insikt-intelligence> accessed 12 August 2024.

social media accounts.[109] Some tools even detect suicide risks and mental health problems, vulnerabilities, and as they evolve, they can also assess vulnerability to violent extremist ideologies. For example, the 'Redirect Method' identifies vulnerable persons before they fall prey to extremist lethal ideologies. This 'open-source methodology' uses targeted advertising to connect people searching for harmful content with positive, alternative messages.[110] It targets users of websites related to terrorist propaganda and redirects them to websites with counter-narratives. For instance, the program detects users searching for ISIS videos on YouTube and redirects them to educational sites about radicalization dangers. [111] Trustworthy AI systems can intervene early and prevent young people from being seduced by extremist ideologies.

E. Privacy: Anonymization

Predictive models can be based on databases from online sources that sufficiently anonymize their users, or the data can be pseudonymized in advance. Therefore, it can be used to identify patterns and predict future terrorist behaviour while maintaining privacy protections.

F. Accuracy: Higher Justification for an Interference

The ECtHR has not set a specific legal standard for AI accuracy, but several AI features can enhance decision-making: The 'Recall' method measures how often a model correctly identifies an event or person, while the 'Precision' method tracks the number of false alarms.[112] These functions surpass human accuracy, improving both counterterrorism effectiveness and privacy protection. They can also assess whether a measure is proportional by comparing it to the threat level indicated by data stored in the system. Higher accuracy improves both counterterrorism effectiveness and privacy protection.

---

[109] UNICRI and UNCCT (n 103) 24.

[110] Monshoot, 'The Redirect Method' <www.redirectmethod.org> accessed 1 August 2024.

[111] UNICRI and UNCCT (n 103) 26.

[112] McKendrick (n 11) 26.

G. Transparency: Revealing and Explaining the Decision

Human decisions are often complex, influenced by biases, and not always well-justified. The complexity increases when algorithms are involved in decision-making. For people to accept algorithmic decisions, such as being placed on a no-fly list by an algorithm, the reasoning behind these decisions must be clear.[113] Achieving this clarity involves explaining the algorithm's and AI's decision-making process in simple terms without compromising the secrecy of investigative work. Additionally, human oversight is necessary to provide an accountable rationale for decisions.[114] To ensure transparency, we can use qualitative and quantitative technical standards. Key features include predictability, which assesses how easily outcomes can be anticipated, and explainability, which measures how well the decision-making process can be explained.[115] Both predictability and explainability can improve with each decision made by the system. AI has the potential to mitigate human bias in decision making by revealing and minimizing discriminatory patterns, provided the data is selected not arbitrarily, but carefully.[116] Moreover, systems can be trained to evaluate their own errors transparently and without emotional bias, making the decision-making process more transparent than human decisions.

V. Proposals

A. Foundational Principles

Based on the ECHR, the analysis of the ECtHR's case law about human rights restrictions, on the one hand, and the opportunities offered by AI systems on the other hand, this section attempts to align both sides and elaborate proposals. Any proposal needs a foundation.

The UNESCO Recommendation on Ethics of AI and the AI Convention 2024 (even though not mandatory for national security) provide for a fabulous foundation for any use of AI in light of human right's protection. Both

---

113 Robbins (n 15) 84; Ramak (n 82) 10

114 Robbins (n 15) 84.

115 Andrew Tutt, 'An FDA for Algorithms' (2017) 69(1) Administrative Law Review 83, 102.

116 Gerards and Xenidis (n 84) 122.

emphasize the value of human dignity, being the 'foundation for the universal, indivisible, inalienable, interdependent and interrelated system of human rights and fundamental freedoms'.[117] Article 7 of the AI Convention 2024 obliges each Party to adopt measures to respect human dignity. Additionally, the UNESCO Recommendation's core principles (page 20ff) and the AI Convention's main provisions (Articles 8 to 21) deserve proper recognition. Due to their significant similarities, they will be combined and presented in alignment with the structure of the UNESCO Recommendation:

1. AI use must be proportionate and do no harm;
2. AI systems must be safe and secure, thus assessed and tested under supervision;
3. Fairness and non-discrimination should ensure that AI benefits are accessible to all and AI actors should avoid perpetuating biased applications;
4. An assessment of AI's human, social, cultural, economic, and environmental impact shall improve sustainability;
5. Ensuring data protection and governance;
6. Human and public oversight is inevitable;
7. AI systems must be transparent, explainable and reliable;
8. Responsibility and accountability must be inherent to each stage of the AI lifecycle (see also Article 9 of the AI Convention 2024);
9. Public awareness should be promoted through accessible education;
10. AI regulations must respect both international law and stakeholder interests;
11. States must adopt measures for the identification, assessment, prevention, and mitigation of risks and must guarantee accessible and effective remedies for human rights violations and for procedural safeguards in accordance with international and domestic law.

Furthermore, the AI Act 2024 provides for a risk classification of AI systems, that can – regardless of its scope – help national courts and stakeholders to understand risks related to AI and promote recommendations for their

---

[117] UNESCO Recommendation on the Ethics of AI (n 8) 18.

assessments. The EU AI Act categorizes four risk levels, all of which can have touchpoints in the surveillance of individual terrorist suspects:[118]

1. Unacceptable Risk: Banned systems, including those for manipulation, exploiting vulnerabilities, social scoring, systems that create biometric categorizations for race, political views and such, as well as real-time biometric identification in public spaces.
2. High Risk: Subject to strict regulations, these include AI in critical infrastructure, education, employment, law enforcement, migration, profiling, and the use in the judicial system. They must meet standards for data governance, transparency, and human oversight.
3. Limited Risk: Systems like chatbots that require transparency, informing users they are interacting with AI.
4. Minimal Risk: Systems such as spam filters that face no specific regulations but should adhere to general principles like fairness.

In addition, the European Declaration on Digital Rights and Principles for the Digital Decade and the High-Level Expert Group on Artificial Intelligence (AI HLEG) developed ethical guidelines.[119] They identified three elements of Trustworthy AI to be considered also by national courts when assessing the lawfulness of AI systems. AI should be:

1. lawful, ensuring compliance with all applicable laws and regulations,
2. ethical, ensuring adherence to ethical principles and values and
3. robust, both from a technical and social perspective to ensure that, even with good intentions, AI systems do not cause any unintentional harm.

---

[118] See Articles 5 and 6 of the AI Act 2024 (n 6); Latham & Watkins LLP, 'EU AI Act: Navigating a Brave New World' (July 2024) <www.lw.com/admin/upload/SiteAttachments/EU-AI-Act-Navigating-a-Brave-New-World.pdf> accessed 1 August 2024.

[119] Independent High-Level Expert Group on Artificial Intelligence, 'Ethics Guidelines for Trustworthy AI' (2019) 35 <https://ec.europa.eu/newsroom/dae/document.cfm?doc_id=60419> accessed 1 August 2024.

Thus, AI should be lawful, transparent, explainable, fair and respecting human and fundamental rights.[120] Based on this foundation, the following measures are proposed.

B. International Standards

A determined legal framework is essential for defining the competences of intelligence and law enforcement agencies and implementing safeguards against abuse. The intersection of transparency, decision-making causalities, and biases creates a complex landscape that requires careful navigation. Current regulations, like the GDPR, AI Act, and AI Convention, do not fully cover counterterrorism purposes, leaving a gap in clear guidelines. Nevertheless, these existing frameworks, along with the European Court of Human Rights' case law, the European Declaration on Digital Rights and Principles for the Digital Decade, and the Ethics Guidelines for Trustworthy AI from the High-Level Expert Group on AI, offer valuable foundations for developing comprehensive mandatory regulations. These elements can help ensure that intelligence services operate within a pre-defined, transparent, accountable, and ethically sound framework, balancing national security with the legal certainty and the protection of fundamental rights.

C. Special Authority

There is a lack of a centralized international authority for setting minimum standards, especially in handling secrecy, privacy protection, and anti-discrimination. While this calls for an international solution, in the meantime, a specialized body with independent experts, particularly in criminal intelligence, counterterrorism and human rights could collaborate with authorities to fill this gap. Additionally, an ombudsperson should oversee secret surveillance measures.

D. Interdisciplinary Teams

Addressing new forms of terrorism requires interdisciplinary work among experts in several areas such as law, psychology, security, communications, and computer science. Comprehensive knowledge of AI systems, their use, and their risks, is essential at all levels, from production to authorization, assessments, and review. Moreover, human rights training is recommended

---

[120] Marsoof, Luco, Tan and Joty (n 83) 85.

to ensure awareness of biases, transparency, and accountability in decision-making, particularly for stakeholders involved in counterterrorism.

E. Shifting the Burden of Proof

Predictability and explainability are crucial features of AI systems. They should provide clear, simple explanations without compromising investigations.[121] If someone wants to challenge an algorithm-based decision before the court, the lack of transparency makes it difficult to prove biases. This could be adressed by shifting the burden of proof from the plaintiff (individual) to the defendant (state). Alternatively, prima facie evidence could rely on probability and plausibility, where showing another system with a clear, unbiased dataset would not yield the same result.

The AI Act mandates that high-risk AI systems be designed for sufficient transparency, allowing developers to interpret and appropriately use the system's output (Article 13). These systems should come with instructions on accuracy and metrics and be overseen by natural persons (Article 14), ensuring understanding of capabilities and limitations, monitoring operations, avoiding over-reliance, interpreting outputs correctly, and intervening when necessary.

F. Making Humans Responsible

Humans should retain the final decision-making authority or a 'veto' over AI decisions, particularly in critical cases. In other cases, safeguards must ensure that AI provides transparent and reasonable explanations. Human intervention is crucial to prevent discriminatory outcomes, such as those often associated with facial recognition.[122] While the AI Act proposes human verification of AI decisions, this does not apply to high-risk AI systems used in law enforcement (Article 14). This exclusion warrants critical review, as the use of AI in law enforcement can significantly impact individuals. Ensuring human oversight in these high-stakes situations protects fundamental rights and the rule of law.

G. Obliging Private Businesses

The private sector plays a big role in AI development. Law enforcement agencies rely on companies which provide financial resources, technical

121 European Union Agency for Fundamental Rights (n 40) 13.

122 Gáti (n 89) 309, 316.

expertise, and rapid AI advancements. Concerns about the fairness of commercially developed algorithms for public use highlight the need for assessing their human rights compatibility. Systems become better accountable by involving various stakeholders including Human Rights experts, AI experts, and academia before AI systems get used. A step ahead, each developer of AI should be mandated to receive human rights and ethical training.[123] The Hiroshima Process Guidance promotes valuable principles, AI developers should follow.[124] Despite not being directly subject to human rights obligations, companies should comply with soft laws.

And, eventually, public authorities should be required to use only systems which comply with human rights standards, in this way, companies would be indirectly bound to meet human rights standards if they want to stay in the market. Companies could obtain a ‚human rights certificate' for their developed systems by meeting the necessary criteria.

Additionally, in the context of the business sector, a critical look should be also taken at the (legal) responsibilities of social media, where radicalization often begins in an open space.

VI. Summary

Modern terrorism has evolved, with attackers often acting as 'lone wolves' radicalized online. The subsequent increasing use of AI and biometrics to detect threats raises human and fundamental rights concerns. Therefore, it is crucial to balance counterterrorism efforts with the protection of human rights.

AI and biometric technologies impact various rights under the ECHR, including privacy (Article 8), non-discrimination (Article 14), effective remedy (Article 13), and fair trial (Article 6). Ensuring proportionality, necessity, and adequate safeguards is crucial to protect these rights. ECtHR case law mandates that Article 8 ECHR infringements must be based on clear, accessible, and foreseeable legal grounds, and must pursue legitimate

---

123 CERD Committee, 'General Recommendation No 36 on Preventing and Combating Racial Profiling by Law Enforcement Officials' (17 December 2020) UN Doc CERD/C/GC/36, para 43; Independent High-Level Expert Group on AI (n 119) 3.

124 European Commission, Hiroshima Process International Guiding Principles for Organizations Developing Advanced AI system (30 October 2023) <https://digital-strategy.ec.europa.eu/en/library/hiroshima-process-international-guiding-principles-advanced-ai-system> accessed 20 May 2024.

aims, such as national security. Violations often arise from inadequate safeguards, highlighting the need for precise legal criteria, limited data use, specific access, and judicial pre-authorization- and review. Similarly, effective remedies under Article 13 ECHR and a fair trial under Article 6 ECHR require procedural guarantees, especially for data collected through secret surveillance. This includes transparency in AI reasoning and judicial review. To avoid discrimination under Article 14 ECHR, high-quality data, bias checks, human oversight, and accountability are essential.

At the same time, AI offers benefits for counterterrorism, such as handling large datasets, identifying patterns and predicting terrorist activities. By evaluating and correcting biases, AI can enhance both counterterrorism effectiveness as well as human rights protection, reducing discriminatory decisions, improving accuracy in pre-selection, and offering more transparent outcomes. AI also contributes to deradicalization by filtering vulnerable persons from social media and redirecting them to positive narratives.

Eventually, the analysis has shown that the ECHR and the case law of the ECtHR are well-equipped to manage the tension between counterterrorism efforts and new technologies while safeguarding human rights. Nevertheless, there have been calls for the need for cross-border regulations in this area. Current legal frameworks, such as the GDPR, AI Act, and AI Convention, do not fully address the use of AI in counterterrorism, creating a regulatory gap. The article suggests leveraging these frameworks, alongside ECtHR case law, to develop mandatory legal and ethical regulations for AI use in counterterrorism. It proposes establishing a specialized authority with independent experts as well as interdisciplinary teams trained in human rights, overseeing AI systems from development to implementation. AI-supported decisions should be well-reasoned, allowing individuals to challenge them in court. To address transparency issues ('how did the algorithm decide?'), shifting the burden of proof in court proceedings from the plaintiff (individual) to the defendant (state) is recommended. In addition, human oversight is crucial to mitigate biases and discrimination with AI systems. Eventually, by mandating public authorities to purchase and use only AI systems that have been proven to uphold human rights, private businesses are indirectly compelled to adhere to human rights standards (‚human rights certificate').

Acknowledgments

Alrun Cohen previously worked as an attorney and as research assistant and lecturer at the University of Vienna. This article is based on the author's Master's Thesis

'Artificial Intelligence and Counterterrorism – Challenges and Chances for Human Rights', completed in the Human Rights Master of Laws (LL.M.) postgraduate program at the University of Vienna and the Ludwig Boltzmann Institute of Fundamental and Human Rights, and awarded by the Dr. Maria Schaumayer Foundation in 2024. In preparing this work, Alrun Cohen extends her heartfelt thanks to her supervisor, Ralph Janik, for his supportive guidance during the thesis, and to her dear friend, Ido Lurie, for his insightful feedback, which enhanced the clarity of key passages.

The Real Meaning of Article 27 ICCPR and the Deeper Understanding of Overlapping Human Rights Its Exploration Requires

György Andrássy | Professor Emeritus at the Faculty of Law, University of Pécs, Hungary, andrassy.gyorgy@ajk.pte.hu

Abstract

Although Article 27 of the International Covenant on Civil and Political Rights (ICCPR) is the cornerstone of international minority protection, its meaning remains unclear. This paper explores the real meaning of the Article, relying mainly on the interpretation of the Human Rights Committee (HRCttee). According to the HRCttee, the rights under Article 27 are 'distinct from and additional to' all universal individual rights under the ICCPR. Obviously, the rights of religious minorities are primarily additional to freedom of conscience and religion, the right of linguistic minorities to freedom of language use derived by the HRCttee from freedom of expression, and the right of ethnic minorities to cultural freedom (also derived from freedom of expression). However, the application of these three (primarily) private-life freedoms in the spheres of public life, presents significant problems: the great number of languages, religions and cultures seems to make a reasonable application of non-discrimination in these spheres impossible (as this would *e.g.* require states to officialise everyone's language in each country). However, the paper demonstrates that human rights are (also) divided by territory and that the sub-rights of the three freedoms relating to public life (*e.g.* official language rights) entitle everyone, but in only one country. As a result, a reasonable application of non-discrimination becomes possible even regarding these sub-rights. The paper then clarifies where different individuals have the said public life sub-rights and finally explores the real meaning of Article 27 minority rights in terms of material equality. Nevertheless, an important conclusion is that the minority question under Article 27 is largely a human rights question.

Keywords

International minority protection – Human Rights Committee – freedom of language – religion and culture – territorial classification of human rights – real – material or positive equality.

Austrian Review of International and European Law **28**: 61-94, 2023.
 | DOI:10.1163/15736512-02801004

I. Introduction

The adoption of the International Covenant on Civil and Political Rights (ICCPR) in 1966 and its entry into force in 1976[1] gave new impetus to the study of the minority question. However, Article 27 has turned out to be unclear. As Tomuschat wrote in 1983, 'one may easily agree that Art. 27 is a rather succinct provision which raises more problems than it really resolves'.[2]

The vague wording of Article 27 ICCPR and the connected issues of its implementation caused worry in the United Nations (UN) Sub-Commission on the Prevention of Discrimination and Protection of Minorities (Sub-Commission) and therefore Francesco Capotorti, a member of the Sub-Commission, was appointed as Special Rapporteur on the issue in 1971.[3] In his final study, Capotorti presented the problem of the meaning of Article 27 mainly as the problem of the implications of the rights under the Article. Namely, he emphasized that the principles enunciated in the provision are an established fact, but that '[a]ll their *implications* must also be understood'.[4] He added that this understanding 'will be a lengthy process and should be started at once'.[5]

Accordingly, he himself made an effort to clarify some of those implications,[6] but also recommended the preparation of a UN declaration on the rights of members of minority groups, arguing that 'the principles set forth in article 27 [...] are not applied in all countries' – thus, '[t]he essential requirement is to throw light on the various *implications* of article 27'.[7]

---

1 International Covenant on Civil and Political Rights, 16 December 1966, 999 UNTS 171 (ICCPR).

2 Christian Tomuschat, 'Protection of Minorities under Article 27 of the International Covenant on Civil and Political Rights' in Rudolf Bernhardt (ed), *Völkerrecht als Rechtsordnung Internationale Gerichtsbarkeit Menschenrechte, Festschrift für Hermann Mosler* (1983) 949, 950.

3 Francesco Capotorti, 'Study on the Rights of Persons Belonging to Ethnic, Religious and Linguistic Minorities' (1979) UN Doc ECN.4Sub.2384Rev.1-EN, Annex I, para 1.

4 *Ibid* (emphasis added).

5 *Ibid.*

6 *Ibid.*, para 386. However, he pointed out that the implications of freedom of thought, conscience and religion and of the religious minority right under Article 27 'cannot be clearly separated, even though from the logical point of view they appear distinct.'.

7 *Ibid.*, para 617 (emphasis added).

The Capotorti study had significant impact on commentators and the competent organs of the UN, which accepted the idea to prepare a declaration on the rights under Article 27. However, even though the drafting of this Declaration started quickly, it took until 1992 for it to be adopted by the UN General Assembly (UNGA). Hence, although the text of the Declaration was 'inspired by'[8] Article 27, it actually represented 'a continuation and a new beginning'.[9] Nevertheless, the UN Minority Declaration explored certain implications of Article 27 rights and the UN Working Group on Minorities – within a kind of monitoring mechanism[10] of this otherwise non-binding instrument – even adopted a Commentary on the Declaration.

In the meantime, the UN Human Rights Committee (HRCttee) elaborated the main elements of its own interpretation of the rights under Article 27 and emphasized that these rights are 'distinct from and additional to' all universal human rights recognized in the ICCPR.[11]

At the regional level, mainly in Europe, numerous binding and non-binding instruments have been adopted relating to minority issues and most of them rely, directly or indirectly, on Article 27 rights. These include, *inter alia*, the Framework Convention for the Protection of National Minorities (Framework Convention), the Helsinki Final Act of the Conference on Security and Cooperation in Europe, as well as the recommendations and guidelines of the OSCE (Organization for Security and Co-operation in Europe) High

8 UNGA Res 47/135, Declaration on the Rights of Persons Belonging to National or Ethnic, Religious and Linguistic Minorities (18 December 1992) UN Doc A/RES/47/135, fourth preambular paragraph.

9 Patrick Thornberry, 'The UN Declaration on the Rights of Persons Belonging to National or Ethnic, Religious and Linguistic Minorities: Background, Analysis, Observations, and an Update' in Alan Phillips and Allan Rosas (eds), *Universal Minority Rights* (1995) 13, 37.

10 Alan Phillips, 'Promoting and Implementing the UN Declaration: An MRG Perspective' in Alan Phillips and Allan Rosas (eds), *Universal Minority Rights* (1995) 135, 135, 139-140, 146-150.

11 UN Human Rights Committee, 'CCPR General Comment No. 23: Article 27 (Rights of Minorities)' (8 April 1994) UN Doc CCPR/C/21/Rev.1/Add.5, para 1.

Commissioner on National Minorities.[12] The European Community and the European Union also took certain steps regarding the issue.[13]

While Article 27 ICCPR is thus the cornerstone of international minority protection and is 'the only treaty provision'[14] that is 'explicitly directed at the protection of minorities in a universal human rights instrument',[15] its real meaning is still vague. However, it seems that the results so far achieved in clarifying this meaning provide sufficient basis for further progress.

This contribution argues that the real meaning of Article 27 has only been partially explored, that the 'real' meaning can and should be explored, and that the exploration of this real – but mainly implicit – meaning necessarily entails the exploration of the full meaning of those universal human rights which have the closest relationship with the three Article 27 minority rights. Accordingly, the study undertakes to explore the real meaning of Article 27 and the full meaning of Articles 18 and 19 ICCPR as they relate to Article 27 rights.

To this end, the underlying thought is the fundamental realization of Capotorti, Thornberry and the HRCttee that the three Article 27 minority rights are (as the HRCttee states) 'distinct from and additional to'[16] all universal human rights recognized in the ICCPR. It is also important that Capotorti, Thornberry and the HRCttee identified the most relevant of those rights – *i.e.*

---

12 Framework Convention for the Protection of National Minorities, 1 February 1995, 2151 UNTS 243; Conference on Security and Co-operation Final Act, Helsinki (1975) <www.osce.org/files/f/documents/5/c/39501.pdf>; Among the recommendations and guidelines of the OSCE High Commissioner on National Minorities see, *e.g.*, The Hague Recommendations Regarding the Education Rights of National Minorities (1996) <www.osce.org/files/f/documents/e/2/32180_0.pdf>; The Oslo Recommendations Regarding the Linguistic Rights of National Minorities (1998) <www.osce.org/files/f/documents/8/1/67531.pdf>; The Tallinn Guidelines on National Minorities and the Media in the Digital Age (2019) <www.osce.org/files/OSCE-Tallinn-guidelines-online%203.pdf>; Recommendations on the Effective Participation of National Minorities in Social and Economic life (2023) <www.osce.org/files/f/documents/2/3/553783.pdf>.

13 See, *e.g.*, the Arfe resolution of the European Parliament, Doc 1-965/80, OJ C287 1981, 106; the Kuijpers resolution of the European Parliament, Doc A2-0150/87, OJ C 318, 144; and the Killilea resolution of the European Parliament, Doc A3-0042/1994, OJ C 061, 110.

14 William A Schabas, *UN Covenant on Civil and Political Rights: Nowak's CCPR Commentary* (2019) 797.

15 *Ibid.*

16 UN Human Rights Committee, General Comment 23 (n 11) para 1.

those contained in Article 18 and 19 of the ICCPR – and took some initial steps to interpret the relationship between them and the rights under Article 27. In this way (from a methodological point of view), they established a unique research (and legislative) project, which however remained unfinished and regarding certain aspects in a very initial phase. This contribution thus intends to continue and (in essence) complete this research project.

The contribution contains relatively few references, mainly because it follows a rather untrodden path: in recent decades Article 27 is no longer as central to minority rights research and discourse as it was before and the question at the heart of this contribution has almost sunk into oblivion.[17]

---

[17] For example, Roddley states that the religious right under Article 27 (and the corresponding Article 2(1) provision of the UN Minority Declaration) arguably '[a]dds little to Article 18', but he does not specify this 'little' addition and the importance of the issue of additionality as such. It is true that the HRCttee adopted the General Comment on Article 27 only after the completion of Rodley's paper (as is mentioned in the 'Afterword'), but Roddley does not refer even to Thornberry's standpoint, see Nigel S Roddley, 'Conceptual Problems in the Protection of Minorities: International Legal Developments' (1995) 17 Human Rights Quarterly 48, 53 and 71. Furthermore, an overview of the meaning of Article 27 mentions the implications of the Article only concerning the UN Minority Declaration, without referring to the importance of the issue, *e.g.*, in the Capotorti study, see Moira Paz, 'The Failed Promise of Language Rights: A Critique of the International Language Rights Regime' (2013) 54 Harvard International Law Journal 157, 170-177. Similarly, Barten notes (referring to the HRCttee's General Comment 23 at para 1) that Article 27 'is a supplementary article and does not replace the other articles of the ICCPR.', but then she pays little attention to the issue of implications (or more forceful content) of the Article, see Ulrike Barten, 'Article 27 ICCPR: A First Point of Reference' in Ugo Caruso and Rainer Hofmann (eds), *The United Nations Declaration on Minorities* (2015) 47. In the second edition of his commentary on the ICCPR, Nowak still writes (referring to HRCttee General Comment 23 at para 5.3.) that the '"right of individuals belonging to a linguistic minority to use their language among themselves, in private or in public, is distinct from other language rights protected under the Covenant," in particular freedom of expression under Art. 19,' and then notes that 'no further indication was given as to how Art. 27 goes beyond Art. 19.', see Manfred Nowak, *UN Covenant on Civil and Political Rights: CCPR Commentary* (2005) 660, fn 143. Though Nowak's latter observation is essential, it is already missing from the third edition of the Commentary, see Schabas (n 14). Of course, the issue of how Article 27 rights go beyond other rights under the ICCPR is touched upon in various contexts, especially regarding Article 26 in Nowak's commentary; for example, a rather comprehensive interpretation of this relationship is given under the title 'Limitations' in both the second and the third editions, but no reference is made to para 1 of General Comment 23 of the

Therefore, recent literature only rarely touches upon the question and if it does so, then mainly regarding, *e.g.*, the concept of 'minority' in general or the concept of 'old' and 'new' minorities.[18]

HRCttee, see Nowak, *ibid.* 667 and Schabas (n 14) 833. Similarly, Taylor, in the section entitled 'Interaction between Article 27 and other Covenant Provisions' of his Commentary on the ICCPR, does not mention that according to the HRCttee, Article 27 rights are 'distinct from and additional to' all universal rights under the Covenant. Nevertheless, in connection with religious minorities he states that '[u]nlike the rights of members of ethnic minorities "to enjoy their own culture", or of linguistic minorities to "use their own language", which have no direct counterpart in other Covenant provisions, the right to profess and practise one's own religion is particularly closely aligned with the right in Article 18 "either individually or in community with others [...] to manifest his religion or belief in worship, observance, practise and teaching'. While the author of this contribution agrees with that assessment, Taylor specifies the differences between this 'Article 27 right' and its 'Article 18 analogue' and he again does not even mention that according to the HRCttee, this Article 27 right is not only 'distinct from,' but also 'additional to' the religious right in question under Article 18. See Paul M Taylor, *A Commentary on the International Covenant on Civil and Political Rights* (2020) 789, 804. Finally, it is worth quoting Schabas in connection with the case law of the HRCttee: '[i]n practice, Art. 27 has proven to be of rather limited importance in terms of protecting minorities. The case law of the Human Rights Committee tends to confirm that most if not all of the rights that members of minorities can exercise under Art. 27 can be enforced through other provisions of the Covenant, notably Art. 26.', see Schabas (n 14) 798. The present author would argue that this is partly because even the HRCttee has not shed light on what Article 27 rights add to the other rights in the ICCPR, especially to the freedoms recognized in Articles 18 and 19.

18 *Cf. e.g.* Jennifer Jackson-Preece, 'Beyond the (Non) Definition of Minority' (February 2014) ECMI Brief # 30, 3-18 <www.files.ethz.ch/isn/177881/issue%20brief%20nr.30.pdf> accessed 29 October 2024; Taylor (n 17) 795-806; Hurst Hannum, 'The Concept and Definition of Minorities' in Marc Weller (ed), *Universal Minority Rights. A Commentary on the Jurisprudence of International Courts and Treaty Bodies* (2007). There Hannum *inter alia* notes that the HRCttee in its General Comment on Article 27 does not refer to the *travaux préparatoires* of the ICCPR and that there is a difference between the concept of minorities in the latter and the former, see *ibid*, 49, 60. In connection with the Thematic Commentary No 4 of the Advisory Committee on the Framework Convention, Pentassuglia states that 'Although the Advisory Committee has consistently supported the idea of a broader application of this treaty, a large number of the current states parties that have taken a stance on this matter (*at least* more than half of the current treaty membership) has equally consistently held on to a more restrictive understanding of the concept of "national minority."', see Gaetano Pentassuglia, 'Introduction: The Unpacking of Ethno-Cultural Diversity' in Gatetano Pentassuglia (ed), *Ethno-Cultural Diversity and Human Rights.*

This contribution seeks to elaborate on the most important features of the real meaning of Article 27, without being able to provide a full and detailed account of all its aspects. Throughout the study it will however become gradually clear how the exploration of the real meaning of Article 27 contributes to a deeper understanding of numerous human rights recognized in the main instruments of the International Bill of Human Rights.

The study is divided into nine Sections. Following the short historical overview above (I), Section II presents the problem of the real meaning of Article 27 in more detail. Sections III-VII interpret the freedoms enshrined in Articles 18 and 19 both in isolation and in conjunction with Article 27 rights and step by step addresses their content related to language, religion and culture. Based on the results obtained, Section VIII briefly defines the real meaning of Article 27. Section IX draws some conclusions.

II. The Fundamental Thesis of the HRCttee and the Research Perspective that Follows From it

Article 27 ICCPR reads:

> In those States in which ethnic, religious or linguistic minorities exist, persons belonging to such minorities shall not be denied the right, in community with the other members of their group, to enjoy their own culture, to profess and practise their own religion, or to use their own language.[19]

Challenges and Critiques (2018) 17. Medda-Windischer writes that 'what distinguishes all minority groups is that they manifest, albeit implicitly, a desire to maintain a collective identity which differs from a dominant culture. Culture in this context is [...] a sense of communal self-identity that pervades almost every aspect of life, including work and economic activity.', see Roberta Medda-Windischer, 'Old and New Minorities: Diversity Governance and Social Cohesion from the Perspective of Minority Rights' (2017) 11 Acta Univ. Sapientiae, European and Regional Studies 25, 39. It is also worth noting that according to Paz, the HRCttee 'has never once found an Article 27 breach in relation to language violations in the functions surveyed.', see Paz (n 17) 165. Another remarkable observation is that more than half of the communications based on Article 27 and decided on the merits by the HRCttee originated from persons belonging to indigenous peoples, *cf.* Annelies Verstichel, 'Recent Developments in the UN Human Rights Committee's Approach to Minorities, with a Focus of Effective Participation' (2005) 12 International Journal on Minority and Group Rights 25, 31. Schabas also points out that '[m]uch of the case law under Art. 27 has concerned the rights of indigenous peoples.', see Schabas (n 14) 801.

19 ICCPR (n 1) Article 27.

The HRCttee has stated in relation thereto that:

> this article establishes and recognizes a right which is conferred on individuals belonging to minority groups and which is *distinct* from, and *additional* to, all the other rights which, as individuals in common with everyone else, they are already entitled to enjoy under the Covenant.[20]

As stated above, this is an extremely important observation which however has not (yet) received the attention it deserves. What makes it so meaningful is that it generally clarifies the relationship between Article 27 rights and other rights recognized under the ICCPR. In this respect the HRCttee points out that Article 27 rights have sometimes been confused with the rights under Articles 1 and 26 and with the duties of states under Article 2(1) ICCPR.[21]

The HRCttee's thesis is logical: if Article 27 minority rights are not distinct from and additional to all universal individual human rights under the ICCPR, then they become redundant, as individuals belonging to ethnic, religious and linguistic minorities would already enjoy these rights as universal human rights. Therefore, understanding the full meaning of those universal rights under the ICCPR that are closely related to Article 27 rights is necessary to understand the real meaning of Article 27 rights. With some diplomatic elegance, already Capotorti raised this issue:

> There is indubitably a particularly close relationship between article 18 of the International Covenant on Civil and Political Rights, regarding freedom of thought, conscience and religion, and article 27 in so far as it concerns religious minorities; there is even reason to wonder whether, viewed in this light, it may not duplicate what is stated in article 18.[22]

Thornberry pointed out this problem more sharply: 'Article 27 must oblige the State to provide something more than is provided by Article 18; otherwise Article 27 is redundant'.[23] Furthermore, Thornberry raised the problem in connection with the other two Article 27 rights too:

> unless Article 27 is given a more forceful content, it adds nothing to the Covenant. Freedom of thought, conscience and religion is already protected

---

20 UN Human Rights Committee, General Comment 23 (n 11) para 1 (emphasis added).

21 *Ibid.*, at paras 2-4.

22 Capotorti (n 3) para 227.

23 Patrick Thornberry, *International Law and the Rights of Minorities* (1991) 193.

by Article 18, and there is also, for example, as far as language and culture are concerned, the provision on freedom of expression in Article 19.[24]

It is worth noting however, that in a certain respect, Article 27 rights undoubtedly add *something* to the ICCPR, through its explicit (literal) recognition of what is in part recognized only implicitly in Articles 18 and 19, especially in the context of linguistic and cultural rights. The notable difference is of course that while Articles 18 and 19 recognize the rights in question as universal rights, Article 27 recognizes them as minority rights. On the other hand, the minority character of Article 27 rights also adds something to the ICCPR: it is precisely why these rights must have 'a more forceful content', a content which is 'distinct from and additional to' the content of all universal rights under the ICCPR.

Let us now return to the HRCttee's principal thesis, according to which Article 27 rights are 'distinct from and additional to' all universal rights under the ICCPR. In this regard, the main difficulty lies in the fact that the HRCttee has not, beyond the thesis, devoted much attention to the issue either in its General Comment on Article 27 or in its General Comments on Articles 18 and 19.[25] For example, the HRCttee notes that the minority language right under Article 27 'should be distinguished from the general right to freedom of expression protected under article 19',[26] but remains silent on how the minority language right under Article 27 is additional to the general language right under Article 19. This omission is problematic, not only because the HRCttee ought to clarify the point in light of its own thesis. In general, if acknowledged experts express the view that the literal meaning of Article 27 rights may be redundant, and the HRCttee as a treaty body is expected to eliminate possible redundancies in the ICCPR by interpretation (an expectation that also follows from the principle of *ut res magis valeat quam pereat*), then it ought to consider the issue thoroughly. That being said, the HRCttee has provided an extremely important partial exploration of the meaning of Article 19 regarding language rights in the *Ballantyne* case (which will be discussed briefly below).

---

24 *Ibid.*, 180.

25 See UN Human Rights Committee, General Comment 23 (n 11) para 5.3; UN Human Rights Committee, 'CCPR General Comment No. 22: Article 18 (Freedom of Thought, Conscience or Religion)' (30 July 1993) UN Doc CCPR/C/21/Rev.1/Add.4, paras 2, 5 and 9; UN Human Rights Committee, 'General Comment No. 34 Article 19: Freedom of Opinion and Expression' (12 September 2011) UN Doc CCPR/C/GC/34, paras 4, 12, 14, 18, 28 and 33.

26 UN Human Rights Committee, General Comment 23 (n 11) para 5.3.

In conclusion, the real meaning of Article 27 rights can be approached in three ways (which overlap to a certain degree):

(1.) by exploring all implications of Article 27 rights;

(2.) by exploring the full meaning of at least Articles 18 and 19 rights in the context of their relationship with Article 27 minority rights;

(3.) through a combination of (1.) and (2.).

This contribution mainly focuses on the second path, which primarily is based on logical and, to a certain extent, grammatical, systematic and historical interpretation. This is complemented by some normative arguments.

III. Towards the Real Meaning of Article 27 through the Lens of Articles 18 and 19

When it comes to the relationship between freedom of opinion and expression (Article 19) and the linguistic minority right under Article 27, the first difficulty is that the wording of Article 19 does not even contain the word 'language'. At the same time, Article 19(2) recognizes freedom of expression, including in oral and written speech. The question *in which language* one may express something orally and in writing was addressed by the HRCttee in the *Ballantyne* case:

> A State may choose one or more official languages, but it may not exclude, outside the spheres of public life, the freedom to express oneself in a language of one's choice.[27]

Thus, the HRCttee discovered a linguistic freedom for all in Article 19, which, I think, ought to be called the 'freedom of language'.

First of all, 'the freedom to express oneself in a language of one's choice'[28] means the freedom to choose the language to be used. However, since this freedom has no time limit, anyone can decide to use their language whenever possible and to insist on and maintain this language throughout their life. In addition, anyone can decide to use another language at any time according to their own abilities, potentially resulting in a change of their language or that of their descendants. Such a language shift often occurs amongst different

---

27 *Ballantyne et al v Canada*, Human Rights Committee, Communication Nos 385/1989/Rev.1, 359/1989, Decision of 31 March 1993, para 11.4.

28 *Ibid.*

generations of immigrants and less frequently among persons belonging to historical and/or national minorities. Thus, the linguistic freedom the HRCttee derived from freedom of expression includes the freedom to maintain or to change one's own language. Regarding the latter, Article 5 of the Framework Convention sets out that

> the Parties shall refrain from policies or practices aimed at assimilation of persons belonging to national minorities *against their will* and shall protect these persons from any action aimed at such assimilation.[29]

Accordingly, the persons concerned have the right to change their own language voluntarily; furthermore, pursuant to Article 5(1) of the Framework Convention they must also have the right or at least the opportunity to maintain their own language. All of this indicates that the freedom to use one's own and any other language implies the freedom to maintain and to change one's own language. Thus, everyone has the right to use any language on the one hand, and everyone has the right to maintain and to change her/his own language, on the other. Therefore, the most appropriate term for this bundle of rights may be the 'freedom of language'.

For example, pursuant to Article 18(1) ICCPR, the freedom of thought, conscience and religion includes also two freedoms: (1.) 'freedom to have or to adopt a religion or belief of his choice'[30] and (2.) 'freedom [...] to manifest his religion or belief in worship, observance, practice and teaching'. Thus, the internal freedom and the external freedom are two aspects of the freedom of conscience and religion as a joint name. Therefore, the internal and the external aspects of the linguistic freedom derived (partly by the HRCttee) from Article 19 may likewise be jointly called the 'freedom of language'.[31]

29 Framework Convention for the Protection of National Minorities (n 12) Article 5 (emphasis added). Already in 1990, a similar provision was already included in para 32 of the Document of the Copenhagen Meeting of the Conference on the Human Dimension of the CSCE/OSCE <www.osce.org/files/f/documents/9/c/14304.pdf> accessed 29 October 2024.

30 I note that according to the HRCttee, this component of the freedom of conscience and religion includes 'the freedom to choose a religion or belief, including the right to replace one's current religion or belief with another or to adopt atheistic views, as well as to retain one's religion or belief'. UN Human Rights Committee, General Comment 22 (n 25) para 5.

31 The terms 'freedom of language' and 'linguistic freedom' are rarely used. For some examples (and their interpretation) in the jurisprudence of the former European Commission of Human Rights and the European Court of Human Rights, see György Andrássy, 'Freedom of Language as a Partly Territorial Right of Everyone

It is therefore remarkable that Article 18 of the Constitution of Switzerland reads: '*La liberté de la langue est garantie.*'[32]

Let us now return to the language right contained in Article 27; the HRCttee asserted that it

> should be distinguished from the general right to freedom of expression protected under article 19. The latter right is available to all persons, irrespective of whether they belong to minorities or not.[33]

However, as noted, the HRCttee has explained that Article 27 rights are not only *distinct from* but also *additional to* all universal human rights. Nevertheless, the HRCttee does not mention how the minority language right under Article 27 is additional to the language right under Article 19.

Moreover, it appears that the normative content of the language right under Article 19 goes beyond the Article 27 minority language right. While the HRCttee considers that Article 19 includes the right of everyone to use their own and any other language of their choice (outside the spheres of public life), the wording of Article 27 is limited to grant persons belonging to linguistic minorities the right to use their own language. But no matter how important the right to use their own language is for the persons belonging to linguistic minorities, this right is less than what they enjoy with everyone else under Article 19. Consequently, in order to be 'additional' to the freedom of language under Article 19, the language right recognized in Article 27 must include a much more forceful (implicit) content. Yet, the HRCttee does not address this issue at all.

Similar considerations apply to the Article 27 minority cultural right. As we have seen, Thornberry argued that freedom of expression under Article 19 makes this minority right also redundant, unless the minority right is

---

and the Issue of Minority Language Rights' (2021) 14 Foreign Policy Review 28, 33-37 and 45. Xabier Arzoz also uses the term 'freedom of language', with his understanding of the freedom (as a private life freedom) being very similar to the one espoused in this contribution. However, in other respects his standpoint is rather different. Xabier Arzoz, 'The Nature of Language Rights' (2007) 6 Journal on Ethnopolitics and Minority Issues in Europe 1, 7, 20-21, 25-27; Xabier Arzoz, 'Language Rights as Legal Norms' (2009) 15 European Public Law 541, 547, 560, 567-68.

32 Constitution fédérale de la Confédération Suisse, see <www.fedlex.admin.ch/eli/cc/1999/404/fr> accessed 29 October 2024 ('The freedom of language is guaranteed.' translation by the author).

33 UN Human Rights Committee, General Comment 23 (n 11) para 5.3.

given a more forceful content. However, Thornberry has not specified this proposition.

The cultural right inherent in freedom of expression should likewise be referred to as 'freedom of culture'. First, freedom of expression obviously includes everyone's freedom to cultural expression, *i.e.* everyone's freedom to express and enjoy their own culture and to express and enjoy any other culture of their choice. Second, it is reasonable to assume that everyone is also entitled to freedom of cultural expression 'outside the spheres of public life', just as everyone is entitled to freedom of language 'outside the spheres of public life'. Third, the freedom of cultural expression has likewise no time limit and therefore includes the freedom to preserve as well as to change one's own culture or, in other words, to choose one's own culture. On that basis – and in light of the considerations above why the linguistic freedom inherent in Article 19 should be called 'freedom of language' – the freedom to cultural expression inherent in Article 19 should similarly be referred to as 'freedom of culture'.

This is further supported by the fact that it is customary to derive cultural freedoms (*e.g.* freedom of art and freedom of literature) from freedom of expression.[34] Therefore, it is reasonable to assume that freedom of expression includes a more comprehensive freedom as well, *i.e.* the freedom of culture. More importantly, the HRCttee holds that freedom of expression includes, *inter alia* 'cultural and artistic expression'[35] which may be the *freedom* of cultural and artistic expression or freedom of culture and art.

The meaning of 'cultural and artistic expression' can also be approached from the provision under Article 15(1)(a) of the International Covenant on Economic, Social and Cultural Rights (ICESCR), which provides for 'the right of everyone: (a) to take part in cultural life'. With regard to the present context, the Committee on Economic, Social and Cultural Rights (CESCR) considered that '[t]he right to take part in cultural life can be characterized as a freedom'.[36] In terms of normative content, (in the understanding of

---

34 Frederick Schauer, *Free Speech: A Philosophical Enquiry* (1982) 109-112; András Koltay, *A szólásszabadság alapvonalai* [Outlines of Freedom of Speech] (2009) 157-58 and 187-89; Decision of the Constitutional Court of Hungary, 30/1992. (V. 26) AB határozat, III./2.1.

35 UN Human Rights Committee, General Comment 34 (n 25) para 11.

36 UN Committee on Economic, Social and Cultural Rights, 'General Comment No. 21: Right of Everyone to Take Part in Cultural Life (Art. 15, para. 1 (a) of the International Covenant on Economic, Social and Cultural Rights)' UN Doc E/C.12/GC/21, para 6.

the CESCR[37]) the freedom under Article 15(1)(a) ICESCR is essentially synonymous with the freedom of culture as described above.

Moreover, the fact that the CESCR considers the right 'to take part in cultural life' to be a freedom makes it even more plausible that the 'cultural and artistic expression' – derived by the HRCttee from an explicit freedom (*i.e.* the freedom of expression) – constitutes a freedom as well, namely the freedom of cultural or artistic expression or, in short, freedom of culture and art. This supports referring to the cultural right implicit in freedom of expression as the right to freedom of culture. Following this, the HRCttee's interpretation of the cultural right inherent in freedom of expression under Article 19 ICCPR and the CESCR's interpretation of the right of everyone to take part in cultural right under Article 15(1)(a) ICESCR appear to reinforce each other.

Still, an objection can also be raised at this point: if freedom of expression under Article 19 ICCPR entails the core or even entire normative content of the cultural right under Article 15(1)(a) ICESCR, does not the former make the latter redundant? In my opinion, this is not the case. Within the ICCPR, there are large overlaps between certain universal rights. This includes overlaps between *e.g.* freedom of opinion and expression and freedom of thought, conscience and religion and the more specific freedom, *i.e.* freedom of conscience and religion[38] is not considered redundant. Furthermore, even if a universal right would *implicitly* include essentially the entire content of another, more specific and *explicitly* recognized universal right, it is probable that the latter would not be considered redundant either. While the former right could be conceived as *lex generalis*, the latter could be conceived as *lex specialis*, and that what the former recognizes only implicitly, the latter recognizes expressly. This also applies to the relationship between the freedom of opinion and expression under Article 19 ICCPR and the cultural freedom under Article 15(1)(a) ICESCR (notwithstanding the differences in state parties).

Now let us compare the literal meaning of the minority cultural right under Article 27 ICCPR and everyone's freedom of culture extracted from Article 19 ICCPR. What we find is that Article 19 gives everyone the right to express and enjoy their own and any other culture (at least outside the spheres of public life), while the wording of Article 27 only grants persons belonging to ethnic minorities the right to enjoy (and express) their own

---

37 *Ibid.*, in particular, paras 6-43 and especially paras 6 and 15(a).

38 However, if we consider the relationship between freedom of thought and freedom of opinion, not the latter but the former proves to be more comprehensive.

culture. Therefore, the normative content of the freedom of culture under Article 19 appears to go beyond the minority cultural right under Article 27, rather than the other way around. Therefore, for the minority right under Article 27 to be 'additional to' the universal cultural freedom inherent in Article 19 (as the HRCttee holds with reasons), then it must have a much more forceful (implicit) content than what it explicitly stated in its wording.

The third minority right in Article 27 is the right of persons belonging to religious minorities to profess and practise their own religion. As Capotorti and Thornberry pointed out, this right must be compared primarily with freedom of thought, conscience and religion under Article 18 ICCPR. While the HRCttee did not make this comparison in its General Comment on Article 27 or on Article 18[39], it appears certain that the result would largely be the same as in the previous two cases. In other words, a purely literal meaning of the religious minority right under Article 27 would be redundant in light of the freedom of conscience and religion for all in Article 18. Thus, for the religious right under Article 27 to complement the Article 18 freedom, it must have a more forceful but implicit content.

We have therefore arrived at three universal freedoms: freedom of language, freedom of culture and freedom of conscience and religion. While the first two are less well known,[40] the third is a classic freedom. All three freedoms are primarily private life freedoms, covering the private life in a broad sense and include a large part of religious, spiritual, cultural, and economic life. This is clear from the text of Article 18, which recognizes freedom of thought, conscience, and religion but also from the HRCttee's statement, according to which '[a] State may choose one or more official languages, but it may not exclude, outside the spheres of public life, the freedom to express oneself in a language of one's choice.'[41]

---

39 The HRCttee's only reference to the need for such a comparison: 'information as to respect for the rights of religious minorities under article 27 is necessary for the Committee to assess the extent to which the freedom of thought, conscience, religion and belief is implemented by States parties.', see UN Human Rights Committee, General Comment 22 (n 25) para 9.

40 Freedom of language is well-known in Switzerland because of its constitutional recognition. *Cf.* Bernhard Ehrenzeller, Benjamin Schindler, Rainer J Schweizer and Klaus A Vallender (eds), *Die Schweizerische Bundesverfassung, St. Galler Kommentar* (2014) 445-459.

41 *Ballantyne et al v Canada* (n 27) para 11.4.

IV. The Three Freedoms and the Spheres of Public Life – The Official Language Problem

In connection with all three freedoms, hard questions arise in the spheres of public life. The most serious one affects the freedom of language. This follows from the need of the institution of the official (or state or national) language: even those states whose laws are silent on this issue have at least one official language, since the state machinery operates in only one or a few languages, which then must be considered the official language(s).

The concept of an official language includes a tacit obligation for individuals: in principle, everyone must use this language in all spheres of official language use. However, if the law obliges someone to do something, it also entitles them to that same behaviour. Therefore, the concept of an official language also includes a tacit or implicit right, an official language right: in principle, everyone living or staying in a country has the right to use the official language(s) of the country in all spheres of official language use.

However, even if there are many persons whose own language is identical with the official language (or one of them) in a country, there are also people for whom that is not the case. While the former have the (implicit) right under domestic law to use their own language as the/an official language, the latter do not which seems to be discrimination on the ground of language.[42] Furthermore, most researchers think that this discrimination could be eliminated in only two ways: either by officializing in each country the own language of everyone in the country, or by officializing in each country an entirely alien language (*e.g.* Latin or Esperanto).[43] The first solution seems to be reasonable in that a lot of people understand and speak only their own

---

42 This problem is well-known but is usually presented in the way that those, whose own language is the same as the official language in a country enjoy various advantages over those, whose own language is different from the official language, *cf.*, *e.g.*, Thornberry (n 23) 199-200. However, in my view, the problem is not only about advantages, but implicit human rights. For more details see György Andrássy, *Nyelvi jogok* [Language Rights] (1998) 31-44.

43 Pool provides an overview of a long debate and describes the outcome in this way (but not exactly in this terminology). He refers to, *e.g.*, the standpoint of Bruno de Witte, who 'while insisting that equality under the law would require governments to "use as many languages as are spoken by the target public," says services may be denied in some languages "on the basis of administrative or judicial efficiency. It is clear, for example that a single user cannot demand an additional official language, but a group consisting of about half the population can legitimately do so"', see Jonathan Pool, 'The Official Language Problem' (1991) 85 American Political Science Review 495, 495-97.

language[44] and even the vast majority of those who speak and understand (an)other language(s), understand and speak their own language best, they use it most frequently and most willingly and they identify with this language.[45] Nevertheless, most researchers consider the first solution also to be impractical (for good reason), because it would require officializing a lot of languages in all countries. Thus, it appears that there cannot be any 'elegant' or theoretically impeccable solution.[46] De Varennes presents the problem as follows:

> The state machinery must function in a language, or at most in a few languages, for most of its communication, work and service activities, making it impossible not to make any distinction as to language. Therefore, a government is obliged to favour a particular language or a limited number of languages. This creates a distinction: by limiting itself to a single language, the state is involved in a difference or distinction of treatment [...]. It must [...] be emphasized that this is an unavoidable situation, since no state has the resources to provide all of its services in every language spoken within its jurisdiction.[47]

The problem seems to be even more serious because in principle native speakers of any language can visit all countries, and thus a stable regulation could only be if all the languages spoken by mankind as own languages would

---

44 For certain philosophical aspects of the issue of own language and justification of freedom of language (regarding Locke, Green and Rawls), see, *e.g.*, György Andrássy, 'Freedom of Language: A Universal Human Right to Be Recognised' (2012) 19 International Journal on Minority and Group Rights 195, 202-207; on the same issues regarding J S Mill and the European Charter for Regional or Minority Languages, see György Andrássy and Márk Vogl, 'Article 1c. Non-territorial languages' in Alba N López, Eduardo J Ruiz Vieytez and Iñigo U Libarona (eds), *Shaping Language Rights: Commentary on the European Charter for Regional and Minority Languages in Light of the Committee of Experts' Evaluation* (2012) 79, 108-109 and 115-117.

45 On the concept of mother tongue and own language see, *e.g.*, Tove Skutnabb-Kangas, *Linguistic Genocide in Education or Worldwide Diversity and Human Rights?* (2000) 105-108; Tove Skutnabb-Kangas and Teresa L McCarty, 'Key Concepts in Bilingual Education: Ideological, Historical, Epistemological and Empirical Foundations' in Jim Cummins and Nancy Hornberger (eds), *Encyclopedia of Language and Education* (2008) 5, 1, 7.

46 Pool (n 43) 495; Will Kymlicka and Alan Patten, 'Language Rights and Political Theory' (2003) 23 Annual Review of Applied Linguistics 3, 11.

47 Fernand de Varennes, *Language, Minorities and Human Rights* (1996) 80 and 88.

be made official in every country.[48] However, the current number of such languages is around 7,000 and it is impossible for any country to have 7,000 official languages. It is true, on the other hand, that most of these languages have a very small native language community,[49] and a great number of these languages do not have a written form or script and therefore they could play only a limited role as official languages. Nevertheless, even 500-600 official languages per country would still be unrealistic.

Therefore, even though it seems that the official language problem cannot be solved flawlessly, the author of this study holds that efforts need to be made to mitigate linguistic inequality, differential treatment, and discrimination to the point where this is still reasonably possible. It is worth mentioning that in the context of the minority issue Thornberry drew a similar conclusion:

> From the point of view of the minority, however, the selection of a particular language as official may place members of the minority at a disadvantage; it would seem incumbent upon the State to ensure that this disadvantage is, as far as possible, eliminated.[50]

For the purpose of mitigating (or, as far as possible, eliminating) inequality, differential treatment and discrimination, this contribution suggests a method in accordance with existing state practice.[51] The starting points for the method are that practically all states make the language of the linguistic majority official, with certain states making one or more minority languages official as well, and that states choose one or more official languages from among the languages traditionally or historically spoken in their territory.[52]

Furthermore, several states do not grant official language status to any of their historical minority languages but make it possible for native speakers of these languages to use their language orally and in writing in certain official matters. This indicates that the distinction between 'old' and 'new' linguistic and ethnic minorities is widely accepted and not only among legislators. For example, Kymlicka holds that it is not

> unjust that the American government (and other Western democracies) have decided not to give immigrants the legal status and resources needed

---

48 Andrássy (n 44) 223 (and footnote 58 on that page).

49 Ethnologue <www.ethnologue.com/> accessed 29 October 2024.

50 Thornberry (n 23) 199-200.

51 For an earlier version of the method, see Andrássy (n 44) 225-226.

52 Colonisation made the issue more complicated but the attitude of choosing the official language(s) from historical languages seems to have remained.

> to become national minorities [...] For example, if a group of Americans decide to emigrate to Sweden, they have no right that the Swedish government provide them with institutions of self-government or public services in their mother tongue [...] Similarly, Swedish immigrants to America have no basis for claiming the language rights or self-government rights needed to recreate their societal culture.[53]

Thus, the reasonable solution would be that domestic legislators should first exclude languages that are not used in the country from the list of potential official languages (because this would not actually affect the speakers of these languages). In a second step, domestic legislators should exclude the languages of those persons who stay only temporarily in the country (*e.g.* tourists, guest workers, investors), since they would only be temporarily deprived of their official language rights, and they are able to foresee this and can make decisions on that basis.

Accordingly, domestic legislators should make official the languages of those who live in the country. However, these persons may still speak too many languages. Therefore, as a third step legislators may exclude the languages of immigrants, as their decision to immigrate to the host country also is made in light of the non-official status of their language, which they voluntarily accept.

Consequently, legislators should recognize the historical languages of their countries as official languages and, accordingly, those persons should have official language rights in a given country, whose own language is identical with a historical language of that country.[54]

This solution appears reasonable and just, even though it seems to eliminate linguistic inequality, differential treatment, and discrimination only between the speakers of historical majority and historical minority languages in any given state. However, every language that is used as a mother tongue or as a first language is a historical language somewhere in the world and, therefore, every such language ought to be official in at least one state. Accordingly, everyone should be entitled to official language rights in some country.

In other words, it seems that even the elimination of discrimination regarding the institution of the official language is possible. The remaining

---

53 Will Kymlicka, *Multicultural Citizenship* (1995) 95-96.

54 Andrássy (n 44) 225-26. My considerations are similar to Kymlicka's and (as Patten notes) such considerations are 'familiar even from everyday discourse', see Alan Patten 'Who Should Have Official Language Rights?' (2000) 200 Supreme Court Law Review 101, 105. In this paper Patten also provides a good summary of Kymlicka's considerations and his 'consent theory', see *ibid.*, 105-107.

problem is that this kind of elimination of discrimination seems to be in contradiction with the prevailing understanding of human rights and human rights law, which considers human rights as rights of everyone everywhere. Nevertheless, the results obtained above actually anticipates what the next Section will prove. Both kinds of reasoning strengthen each other.

V. The Decisive Realization: Human Rights are (Also) Divided by Territory

In the narrower legal context of the ICCPR, the official language problem can be described as follows. First, it is a fact, that every state party has at least one official language and some of the state parties have two, three or even more. Accordingly, in a state party the first language speakers of the/an official language have the implicit right to use their own language as the/an official language of this state. Second, the HRCttee holds that Article 26 ICCPR 'prohibits discrimination in law or in fact in any field regulated or protected by public authorities.'[55] and thus the prohibition also applies to regulations and practices regarding official languages and their use in the state parties. Third, therefore, the state parties could comply with the requirement of the general principle of non-discrimination only if they would make official the first languages of all persons living or staying in their territory. However, taking into consideration, *e.g.*, tourists, immigrants or diplomats, this would result in an absurd number of official languages.

The official language problem is not the only serious problem regarding the general principle of non-discrimination. It is therefore understandable that the HRCttee has developed a general standpoint in these issues:

> Finally, the Committee observes that not every differentiation of treatment will constitute discrimination, if the criteria for such differentiation are reasonable and objective and if the aim is to achieve a purpose which is legitimate under the Covenant.[56]

However, it is clear that in those fields where the principle of non-discrimination applies (in the understanding of the HRCttee), 'every differentiation of treatment' should *prima facie* be considered discrimination. Accordingly, the first interpretative task is to find reasonable ways to eliminate or at

---

[55] UN Human Rights Committee, 'CCPR General Comment No. 18: Non-discrimination' (10 November 1989) UN Doc U.N. Doc. HRI/GEN/1/Rev.1, para 12.

[56] *Ibid.*, para 13.

least mitigate discrimination in these cases. The above-presented method was created precisely for this purpose, and as we have seen, its application reasonably mitigates and in a certain context eliminates discrimination related to the otherwise hard case, the official language problem. However, as we have also seen, part of the problem remains. The author of this contribution found the key to a reasonable solution to this part of the problem with the help of Article 21 of the Universal Declaration of Human Rights (UDHR) which reads:

> 1. Everyone has the right to take part in the government of his country, directly or through freely chosen representatives.
> 2. Everyone has the equal access to public service in his country. […][57]

According to the clauses 'of his country' and 'in his country' in these paragraphs, everyone has the rights recognized by them only 'of his country' or 'in his country' (this is also true of everyone's right to vote and to be elected under paragraph 3, since these rights only specify the right under paragraph 1). However, if there exists such a category of human rights (although it is generally held that human rights are everyone's rights everywhere), then official language rights could classify as such rights, since in this case much fewer languages would have to be made official in each country and thus the way would be open towards a much more satisfactory solution to the official language problem. Furthermore, if official language rights are really such rights, *i.e.* they entitle everyone but not everywhere, this reinforces the results elaborated on above in section IV.

That being said, it is really a prevailing tenet in the philosophy/theory of human rights and in the understanding of international human rights law that human rights are rights of everyone everywhere.[58] The relevant provision of the ICCPR is Article 2(1):

---

[57] UNGA Res 217 A (III) 'Universal Declaration of Human Rights' (10 December 1948) UN Doc A/810 (UDHR).

[58] An example from philosophy: '[…] *human* rights are rights possessed by all human beings (at all times and in all places), simply in virtue of their humanity.', see John Simmons, 'Human Rights and World Citizenship: The Universality of Human Rights in Kant and Locke' in John Simmons, *Justification and Legitimacy. Essays on Rights and Obligations* (2001) 185 (emphasis added). Furthermore, according to a former UN High Commissioner for Human Rights, human rights 'are the inalienable entitlements of all people, at all times, and in all places', see Zeid Ra'ad Al Hussein, 'Introduction: Universal Declaration of Human Rights' (2015) <www.un.org/en/udhrbook/foreword.shtml> accessed 9 October 2024.

> Each State Party to the present Covenant undertakes to respect and to ensure to all individuals within its territory and subject to its jurisdiction the rights recognized in this Covenant, without distinction of any kind, such as race, colour, sex, language, religion [...].[59]

Thus, in principle, all the rights under the ICCPR entitle everyone in the territory of each state party (and potentially everywhere in the world). At the same time, as we have seen, Article 21 of the UDHR recognizes certain rights that are rights of everyone but not everywhere. Maybe such rights are exceptions, but even if so, official language rights are also such rights (*i.e.* rights that everyone has but not everywhere) as in this case the principles of non-discrimination and equal treatment would not require to officialise everyone's language in every country.

The importance of this realization can be illustrated with an example: let us assume that all human rights are rights of everyone everywhere, and therefore, approximately 600 languages ought to be made official in each country. However, if there are human rights under the ICCPR that are rights of everyone but not everywhere, and official language rights are such rights, then it is sufficient that the language of each human is made official in only one country in the world. And since the number of states today is around 200, each state would only have to make an average of three languages official, which would mean that on average two hundred times fewer languages would have to be made official.

Three official languages per country is no longer unreasonable and impractical: Switzerland, for example, has three main official languages. On the other hand, the distribution of languages between countries is uneven and this causes difficulties; furthermore, we have already seen two other problems above: first, that most living languages have a very small native language community and second, that in most cases these languages do not have a written form or script. However, all three (and further) difficulties can be remedied, at least partly, by exploiting the flexibility of the institution of the official language and by other auxiliary solutions.[60]

---

59 ICCPR (n 1) Article 2(1).

60 States often complain that the implementation of language rights entail costs that they are unable and unwilling to fully bear. However, the fact is that as long as linguistic diversity exists, the translation of information between languages always involves cost. The question is therefore not how the costs can be eliminated, but who bears them or who should bear them and in what proportion. On the other hand, public expenditure can be significantly reduced, for example by employing persons for public service positions who speak both the majority and the given

Finally, it is essential to stress that all of this is not only about numbers: the right to equal protection of the law and the principles of non-discrimination and equal treatment can only be applied regarding the institution of official language reasonably, *i.e.* without absurd results, if official language rights are rights that everyone has but not everywhere. After all, it seems that this discovery is the key to a third solution to the official language problem: a solution that is reasonable and feasible, or 'elegant'.

What makes this result problematic, however, is that Article 25 ICCPR recognizes the same three rights as Article 21 UDHR, albeit in different wording, and the prevailing interpretation of the three rights relies on Article 25 ICCPR. Accordingly, Article 25 rights are not universal human rights but only citizen's rights.[61] However, they are also rights that entitle potentially everyone (pursuant to Article 24 ICCPR every child has the right to acquire a nationality), and every person has these Article 25 rights in only those countries of which they are citizens. In other words, Article 25 rights are also territorial rights.[62] Furthermore, the political rights under the UDHR and the ICCPR are not exceptions to human rights that everyone has everywhere, but they belong to a different category of human rights.[63]

Finally, in terms of territory, human rights (under the International Bill of Human Rights) are divided into three groups of rights: 1. non-territorial rights, that everyone has everywhere; 2. territorial rights, that everyone has but not everywhere; 3. partly territorial rights (or mixed rights) that everyone partially has everywhere, partially not.

---

minority language. In this respect, instructive examples are, inter alia the Constitution of India and the language law of the European Union. *Cf.* Constitution of India, Arts. 343-351. <https://cdnbbsr.s3waas.gov.in/s380537a945c7aaa788c-cfcdf1b99b5d8f/uploads/2023/05/2023050195.pdf>.

61 UN Human Right Committee, 'CCPR General Comment No. 15: The Position of Aliens under the Covenant' (11 April 1986) UN Doc HRI/GEN/1/Rev.1, para 2; Nowak (n 17) 576; Sarah Joseph, Jenny Schultz and Melissa Castan, *The International Covenant on Civil and Political Rights, Cases, Materials, and Commentary* (2003) 496. While stating that Article 25 rights 'apply only to citizens', Taylor quotes the relevant part from Article 2 (1) in footnote, but he makes no comment on the contradiction between the two sentences. Taylor (n 17) 693.

62 For more details see György Andrássy, 'Non-Territorial, Territorial and Mixed Human Rights: A New Classification' (2021) 28 European Public Law 325, 328-333.

63 *Ibid.*, 346.

Overall, the exploration of the territorial distribution of human rights recognized in international human rights law provides a sound basis for a reasonable solution to the official language problem in several countries.

The present contribution has dealt with freedom of language and official language rights. There is a close relationship between them: both freedom of language as a private life freedom and official language rights as public life rights have the 'own language' as a fundamental element. Therefore, official language rights belong to freedom of language, they are special sub-rights of freedom of language in the spheres of public life.

As was shown above, freedom of language as a private life freedom derives from freedom of expression, but freedom of expression applies to everyone 'regardless of frontiers'. Consequently, freedom of language as a private life freedom is a non-territorial right. In contrast, official language rights, as we have seen, are territorial rights. Therefore, freedom of language in a broad sense belongs to the group of partly territorial rights.

VI. Territorial Sub-Rights of Freedom of Religion as well as Freedom of Culture

Several commentators think that in the spheres of public life there is a sharp contradiction between the status of languages and religions, arguing that '[g]overnments can simply ignore [...] religions' by separating the church and the state, 'but must *use*, and thus *choose*, languages',[64] that is, while efficient neutrality is possible regarding religion, such a neutrality is impossible concerning language in the spheres of public life. However, let us see the HRCttee's standpoint in connection with religions:

> The fact that a religion is recognized as a state religion or that it is established as official or traditional or that its followers comprise the majority of the population, shall not result in any impairment of the enjoyment of any of the right under the Covenant, including articles 18 and 27, nor in any discrimination against adherents of other religions or non-believers. In particular, certain measures discriminating against the latter, such as measures restricting eligibility for government service to members of the predominant religion or giving economic privileges to them or imposing special restrictions on the practice of other faiths, are not in accordance with the prohibition of discrimination based on religion or belief and the

64 Pool (n 43) 496 (emphasis in the original).

> guarantee of equal protection under article 26. [...] If a set of belief is treated as official ideology in constitutions, statues, proclamations of ruling parties, etc., or in actual practice, this shall not result in any impairment of the freedoms under article 18 or any other rights under the Covenant nor in any discrimination against persons who do not accept the official ideology or who oppose it.[65]

Furthermore, the HRCttee states the following:

> [A]rticle 18.4. permits public school instruction in subjects such as the general history of religions and ethics if it is given in a neutral and objective way [...]. The Committee notes that public education that includes instruction in a particular religion or belief is inconsistent with article 18.4 unless provision is made for non-discriminatory exemptions or alternatives that would accommodate the wishes of parents or guardians.[66]

Nevertheless, the existence of a state religion (or an institutionalized non-religious belief) in a country seems to be more problematic than the HRCttee suggests. The reason is that those persons whose own religion is identical with the/a state religion, have the (implicit) right to believe in their own religion (or conviction) as a state religion and practise or manifest this belief or conviction as state religion, while those, whose own religion is not identical with the/a state religion, do not have these (implicit) rights. And it seems that even the separation of the state and religion, the church or non-religious belief does not eliminate this inequality in rights, different treatment, and discrimination completely.

The remaining problems relate mainly to the overlap between religious and state holidays/celebrations, time calculation, as well as to the issue of state support of church institutions, especially church schools, and, most importantly, to the religious and ideological neutrality of public education.[67] Thus, even after church (religion)-state separation, some people still have certain special rights: they have the (implicit) right to celebrate some of the

---

65 UN Human Rights Committee, General Comment 22 (n 25) paras 9-10.

66 *Ibid.*, para 6.

67 Balázs Schanda, 'A gondolat, a lelkiismeret és a vallás szabadsága' [Freedom of Thought, Conscience and Religion] (2018) <https://ijoten.hu/szocikk/a-gondolat-a-lelkiismeret-es-a-vallas-szabadsaga> accessed 29 October 2024. Péter Paczolay, 'A lelkiismereti és vallásszabadság' [Freedom of Conscience and Religion] in Gábor Halmai and Gábor Tóth (eds), *Emberi jogok* [Human Rights] (2003) 527, 543, 549-552, 558-575.

holidays of their own religion (or non-religious belief) even as official state holidays, to enjoy the day of rest of their religion (or non-religious belief) even as a public day of rest, and to be able to consider the time calculation of their religion (or non-religious belief) even as the official time calculation. The problems are similar in relation to the neutrality of public education.

Nevertheless, all these problems can only be serious if we consider everyone's (implicit) religious human rights non-territorial in the spheres of public life. However, since there are territorial human rights as well, the rights in question are also such rights: rights of everyone but only in one country in the world. Because in this case, the number of religions (and non-religious beliefs) to be considered on a country level is reduced to such an extent that equal protection, equal treatment, non-discrimination, and neutrality can almost completely be secured in many countries.

As far as freedom of culture is concerned, similar conclusions can be drawn regarding the national culture (or national cultures). The freedom of conscience and religion as well as the freedom of culture constitute non-territorial private life freedoms. These freedoms are closely related to the religious and cultural rights respectively that everyone has in the spheres of public life (in one of the countries of the world), in that the latter rights are in fact (implicit) sub-rights of the broadly understood freedom of conscience and religion and freedom of culture. Therefore, in broader understanding, the freedom of conscience and religion as well as freedom of culture constitute partly territorial rights.

VII. Where do Individuals Have Linguistic, Religious and Cultural Public Life Sub-Rights?

The question now is where do different individuals have the public life (implicit) sub-rights of freedom of language, freedom of conscience and religion, as well as of freedom of culture? Regarding sub-rights of freedom of language, this has already been answered above, before addressing the territorial division of human rights: domestic legislators ought to officialise the historical language(s) of the territory of their states. The preparatory work of the UDHR and the ICCPR also confirm this result. While drafting of the UDHR, there were heated debates on language rights, especially in the context of minorities. For example, the Brazilian delegate de Athayde argued that

> [i]f foreigners were able to use their mother tongue in the schools, before the courts and in various other circumstances, immigrants would have no interest in learning Portuguese and in becoming assimilated as rapidly as possible into the Brazilian population.[68]

The Australian delegate Watt stated:

> [t]he European countries were rightly concerned with guaranteeing the protection of minorities. That problem, however, was unknown in Australia and in Latin-American countries, where the issue was one of assimilation and not of protection of minorities.[69]

He also stressed that 'Australia would not be able to admit as a fundamental right the use before a tribunal of any language other than the national language.'[70] On the other hand, the Belgian delegate Dehousse ascertained:

> [t]he problem of minorities [...] was distinct from that of immigration. The immigrant went to establish himself in a foreign country and it was natural that he should submit to the laws of the country that received him; minorities, on the other hand, were historically constituted groups, settled in one or more determined territories.[71]

Finally, the British delegate Davies summarized the debate as follows:

> As the United States representative had aptly remarked, it had not been possible to effect a compromise in a single article between the views of the New World which wished to assimilate immigrants and those of the Old World in which racial minorities existed.[72]

It is clear that the delegates represented different views, but they agreed that while protection of minorities was desirable in Europe since European countries had 'racial' or 'ethnic' minorities, in the 'New World', where immigrants comprised minorities, such protection was not justified. However, if the delegates agreed that immigrants and their descendants did not have the right to use their own language before the courts and other authorities and

---

68 UNGA, Hundred and Sixty-First Meeting. Draft international declaration of human rights (E/800) (27 November 1948) Doc. A/C.3/SR.161, 721.

69 *Ibid.*, 725.

70 *Ibid.*, 726.

71 *Ibid.*, 724-725.

72 *Ibid.*, 731.

did not have the right to educate their children in their minority languages in the receiving countries, then they could have been even less supportive of making official the languages of immigrants in these countries. In accordance with this, neither the states of the 'Old World', nor the 'New World' made the languages of immigrants official, nor do they make them official today: their official language or languages are chosen from among the languages traditionally spoken in their territory, *i.e.* among their historical languages[73] and this is also approved by experts.[74]

In the end, the drafting of the UDHR did not produce any minority provision in the final text, but the General Assembly adopted a resolution entitled Fate of Minorities, which set out, *inter alia* that 'the United Nations cannot remain indifferent to the fate of minorities'.[75]

These debates on minorities between the states of the 'Old' and the 'New World' resurfaced during the drafting of the ICCPR. The final proposal of the Sub-Commission received strong support in the Commission on Human Rights but before it was adopted, the Chilean delegate Diaz Casanueva stated that:

> It should also consider whether it might not be preferable to limit such a provision to those States with well-established *historical* minorities [...] It was with that last consideration in mind that he had submitted an amendment (E/CN.4/L.261) to the sub-commission's text.[76]

The protocol of the meeting contains a further reference to this issue:

> Mr. Diaz Casanueva (Chile) pointed out that neither the French, nor the English text of his amendment (E/CN.4/L.261), both of which had now been distributed, contained the word "historical", which was included into his original Spanish text.[77]

---

73 Colonial past modifies this somewhat, but it does not seem to change the basic attitude of former colonies.

74 Patten (n 54) 101-115.

75 UNGA Res 217 (III) (16 December 1948) UN Doc A/Res/217(III), 77.

76 United Nations Economic and Social Council, 'Commission on Human Rights. Ninth Session. Summary Record of the Three Hundred and Seventieth Meeting' (3 October 1953) UN Doc E/CN.4/SR.370.5, 11 (emphasis added).

77 *Ibid.*

At the next meeting Casanueva modified his amendment to read as follows: 'In those States, in which ethnic, religious or linguistic minorities exist'[78], and this text became the first clause of the Sub-commission's proposal which was ultimately adopted as Article 27 of the ICCPR.

That persons belonging to historical national, ethnic, religious, and linguistic minorities have stronger rights in their country than persons belonging to non-historical, or immigrant minorities in this country was also highlighted by the Commentary of the Working Group on Minorities to the UN Minority Declaration in 2005:

> Those who have been established for a long time on the territory may have stronger rights than those who have recently arrived. The best approach appears to be to avoid making an absolute distinction between "new" and "old" by excluding the former and including the latter, but to recognize that in the application of the Declaration, the "old" minorities have stronger entitlements than the "new".[79]

In summary, there exists extensive regulation and/or practice in countries around the world, according to which persons belonging to traditional, historical ethnic (or national), religious and linguistic minorities do have stronger cultural, religious and linguistic rights, than persons belonging to non-historical or (in most cases) immigrant minorities.[80] Furthermore, since we have already shown above that public life sub-rights of freedom of language are territorial, more precisely that they entitle everyone but in only

---

78 United Nations Economic and Social Council, 'Commission on Human Rights. Ninth Session. Summary Record of the Three Hundred and Seventy-First Meeting' (4 May 1953) UN Doc E/CN.4/SR.371, 4.

79 United Nations Economic and Social Council, 'Commission on Human Rights. Commentary of the Working Group on Minorities to the United Nations Declaration on the Rights of Persons Belonging to National or Ethnic, Religious and Linguistic Minorities' (4 April 2005) UN Doc E/CN.4/Sub.2/AC.5/2005/2, paras 10 and 11; for more details see, *e.g.*, Asbjorn Eide, 'An Overview of the UN Declaration and Major Issues Involved' in Ugo Caruso and Rainer Hofmann (eds), *The United Nations Declaration on Minorities* (2015) 66, 81; Asbjorn Eide, *Minority Governance in and beyond Europe* (2014) 23-38.

80 However, in recent years, a process has started which points in the direction of loosening this dichotomy. See, *e.g.*, Advisory Committee on the Framework Convention, Thematic Commentary No. 4 (27 May 2016) para 31 <https://rm.coe.int/CoERMPublicCommonSearchServices/DisplayDCTMContent?documentId=09000016806a4811> accessed 29 October 2024. For a scholarly observation, see, *e.g.*, Pentassuglia (n 18) 17.

one country, then we can define where different persons have these public life sub-rights or official language rights.

Most persons have the right to use their language as an official language in the country in which their language is a historical language and they live as members of the linguistic community which traditionally speaks the language in this country, or they live elsewhere (for example as immigrants), but originate from the linguistic community in question and they have not changed their language. This applies both to persons belonging to the linguistic majority and the linguistic minorities of the given country. In contrast, those persons who live as immigrants or descendants of immigrants in their new country where they or their ancestors have changed their language to that of the official language of the new country have official language rights in the receiving country.

Considering that we have shown above that the public life sub-rights of freedom of conscience and religion, as well of freedom of culture are also territorial and they entitle everyone in only one country, considerations and observations on the public life sub-rights of freedom of language apply – *mutatis mutandis* – to these other public life sub-rights as well.

Therefore, all persons belonging to a historical cultural, religious (or non-religious) and linguistic community of a given country are fully entitled to freedom of culture, freedom of conscience and religion as well as to freedom of language (whether these persons belong to the respective majority or minority group). In contrast, immigrants and their descendants, if they have not changed their culture, religion (or non-theistic belief) and/or their language, are only entitled to the private-life freedoms. Although this appears to be discrimination in the host state, it is not, in fact, because the public life sub-rights in question are territorial rights and accordingly the persons concerned are also fully entitled to these rights but not in the host state, but in their country of origin. Therefore, in connection with the territorial classification of human rights it is justified to introduce the concept of *real* and *apparent* discrimination.

VIII. The True Meaning of the Three Minority Rights under Article 27

As mentioned above, the HRCttee holds that Article 27 rights are 'distinct from and additional to' all universal human rights recognized in the ICCPR. This of course applies to freedom of language, freedom of culture, and freedom of conscience and religion, too. Accordingly, the Article 27 minority right regarding language has a more forceful content than freedom of language, the Article 27 minority right regarding culture has a more forceful content than freedom of culture, and the Article 27 minority right regarding religion has a more forceful content than freedom of conscience and religion.

However, if Article 27 minority rights are distinct from and additional to all individual human rights under the ICCPR, and they entitle only persons belonging to historical linguistic, ethnic (cultural) and religious minorities, then these minority rights necessarily secure favourable differential treatment, favourable distinction and favourable additional rights for persons belonging to the said minorities. Therefore, the question arises: how can these minority rights be justified?

The prevailing view has been that a distinction must be made between equality in law and real equality or equality in fact (or, in other words, between legal and material or negative and positive equality), and that minority rights must secure not equality in law but real equality or equality in fact.[81] The drafters of the ICCPR also based the recognition of the rights under Article 27 on this distinction:

> It was agreed that, while article 2, paragraph 1, and article 24 of the draft covenant on civil and political rights[[82]] contained a general prohibition of discrimination, differential treatment might be granted to minorities in order to ensure them real equality of status with the other elements of the population.[83]

This suggests that equality in law is not sufficient to eliminate certain unjust inequalities that adversely afflict persons belonging to historical linguistic, ethnic, and religious minorities. Therefore, these inequalities should also be eliminated, *i.e.* real equality ought to be established. The inequalities in question undoubtedly originate from the minority existence of the members of the said minorities and, more specifically, from the fact that the minority groups they belong to are smaller than that of the corresponding historical

---

81 See, *e.g.*, David Hunter Miller, *The Drafting of the Covenant*, vol II (1928) 91; *Minority Schools in Albania* [1935] PCIJ Series A/B No 64 (Advisory Opinion of 14 January) 17; Pablo de Azcárate, *League of Nations and National Minorities: An Experiment* (1945) 21-24 and 59-60.

82 Article 24 became Article 26 in the final text.

83 UNGA, 'Draft International Covenants on Human Rights: Annotation' (1 July 1955) UN Doc A/2929, para 183; For a partial understanding of 'real equality' or 'de facto equality', see Barten (n 17) 54-56.

linguistic, ethnic, and religious majority groups. In this way, the mentioned inequalities are especially related to the weaker and more vulnerable position, lower prestige and smaller survival chances of the historical minority languages, cultures and religions.

Accordingly, the true content of the three minority rights under Article 27 is likely to be, in general, that persons belonging to historical linguistic, ethnic or religious minorities of each country have the right to special protection for their historical language, culture or religion, a protection that is additional to or exceeds the protection provided by the entirety of freedom of language, freedom of culture and freedom of conscience and religion and ensures elimination (or at least a proper compensation) of the weaker and vulnerable position, lower prestige and lower survival chances of the said minority languages, cultures and religions.

Nevertheless, this result may need to be supplemented. Insofar as there are new linguistic, ethnic, and religious minorities, the question arises whether their members also have certain minority rights under Article 27. I am inclined to think that they do, in addition to their existing private life sub-rights, as discussed above. Thus, they should have the right to adequate assistance for acquiring the basic knowledge of the language of the historical linguistic majority or that of a historical linguistic minority of the host country, and they also have the right to adequate assistance for acquiring certain knowledge about the historical cultures and historical religions of the host country. Accordingly, it seems that the distinction made by the prevailing view between old and new minorities,[84] also appears in the real content of the three minority rights under Article 27. Nevertheless, it may be questioned whether the three minority rights of persons belonging to the new minorities derive from Article 27, since pursuant to the wording of Article 27, the rights of persons belonging to linguistic, ethnic, or religious minorities refer to their own language, their own culture, and their own religion and not to other languages, cultures, and religions. In any case, it is certain that the proper meaning of Article 27 includes, first and foremost the three minority rights of persons belonging to old, historical linguistic, ethnic, and religious minorities.

IX. Conclusion

As indicated already in the heading of this article, the exploration of the real meaning of Article 27 of the ICCPR entails a deeper understanding of several

[84] The best example in international law is the European Charter for Regional or Minority Languages.

human rights. This has already become partially apparent in the discussions above. Primarily, it has turned out that while Article 27 rights are distinct from and additional to all universal human rights under the ICCPR, the most important of these rights, *i.e.* freedom of language, freedom of culture, and freedom of conscience and religion, are only in part recognized explicitly in the ICCPR and by the HRCttee. This incomplete recognition is a serious human rights shortcoming. Besides, it has become clear, that the HRCttee's interpretation of some other human rights, such as freedom of opinion and expression, political rights, the right to education (neutrality of public education) must (also) be supplemented and to a certain extent revised.

The results from above also allow for additional conclusions. For example, attention needs to be paid to the new concepts of real and apparent discrimination, since this issue arises regarding all territorial and partly territorial rights, *i.e.* around 40 per cent of human rights. It is also worth noting that the full meaning of freedom of language, freedom of culture, freedom of conscience and religion, and the real meaning of Article 27 rights are likely to contribute to refining the concept of linguistic, cultural, and religious diversity within international human rights law.

Finally, the fact that the ICCPR and the HRCttee do not recognize explicitly the public life sub-rights of freedom of language, freedom of culture and freedom of conscience and religion affects everyone, but differently. For illustration, let us take the language question. First, persons belonging to immigrant linguistic minorities (if they or their ancestors have not changed their language) do not suffer from the lack of the explicit recognition of public life sub-rights of freedom of language because they do not have these sub-rights in the host country. Second, persons belonging to historical linguistic majorities also do not suffer from the lack of the explicit recognition of these public life sub-rights because their language is the/an official language in their country and therefore, they enjoy these sub-rights pursuant to domestic law. However, persons belonging to historical linguistic minorities, who are also entitled to these public life sub-rights of freedom of language, do not usually enjoy them pursuant to domestic law and therefore, they suffer greatly from the lack of the explicit recognition by the ICCPR and the HRCttee of these sub-rights. This is a serious problem, even more so because most of these persons would presumably be satisfied with the enjoyment of the full content of freedom of language and would not even claim minority language rights. In any case, it is certain that the minority question (and not only the minority language question) under Article 27 of the ICCPR is largely a human rights issue.

The Many Worlds of Advisory Opinions – About Recent Practice, Compliance and False Dichotomies

Haris Huremagić | PhD Candidate at the Geneva Graduate Institute, haris.huremagic@graduateinstitute.ch

Abstract

While advisory opinions are legally not binding by virtue of the Statute of the International Court of Justice (ICJ), a closer look at practice reveals that most advisory opinions prompt states and international organizations to conform their acts to them. This is particularly evident in situations of serious *ius cogens* violations, where advisory opinions can trigger legal effects *erga omnes*. For instance, the recent advisory opinion on *Legal Consequences arising from the Policies and Practices of Israel in Occupied Palestinian Territory, including East Jerusalem,* found serious *ius cogens* violations and has induced 'third' states and international organizations to the underlying conflict to comply with their obligations under customary international law. Hence, the distinction between binding judgments and non-binding advisory opinions is a false dichotomy. Depending on the circumstances, advisory opinions can be either binding or non-binding, occasionally both at the same time, and in most instances, advisory opinions are neither binding nor non-binding.

Keywords

International Court of Justice, advisory opinion, proceedings, compliance, community interests, public interest, peremptory norms, *ius cogens*, *erga omnes*, Israel, Palestine

I. Introduction

In classical textbooks the world appears neatly ordered and relatively uncomplicated. Physics textbooks often present a picture where, for instance, the theory of gravity explains the world around us with remarkable precision, where Newton's laws of motion remain universally applicable, and where the fundamental problem of reconciling gravity with quantum mechanics is largely absent.[1] By the same token, yet with less importance and implications, international law textbooks are occasionally not less inaccurate in describing

1 See *e.g.*, Jearl Walker, *Halliday & Resnick: Fundamentals of Physics*, vol I (2022).

 | DOI:10.1163/15736512-02801005

the 'real world' of international law. In this regard, it is common to divide the jurisdiction of the International Court of Justice (ICJ) by distinguishing between its contentious and advisory functions. Pursuant to conventional wisdom, the ICJ renders decisions in contentious cases which are binding upon the parties, while its advisory opinions are non-binding.[2] A closer look at relevant practice, however, suggests that this distinction between binding decisions and non-binding advisory opinions is a false dichotomy.

Although the Statute of the ICJ (ICJ Statute) grants binding force exclusively to its 'decisions'[3], several international treaties occasionally provide for advisory opinions to carry binding effect, for example the Constitution of the International Labour Organization.[4] In some instances, advisory opinions have set the law, for instance, in relation to the admissibility of treaty reservations.[5] In other instances, advisory opinions were even treated as *res iudicata* by international courts and tribunals.[6] When advisory opinions were concerned with a dispute pending between two entities, they have in most instances been 'complied' with by the respective state or international organization.[7]

---

2 See *e.g.*, Malcolm Shaw, *International Law* (2022) 2297, 2340-2341.

3 Statute of the International Court of Justice, 26 June 1945, XV UNCIO 355, Article 59.

4 Constitution of the International Labour Organization, 1 April 1919, 15 UNTS 40, Article 37(2); see also Convention on the Privileges and Immunities of the United Nations, 13 February 1946, 1 UNTS 15, Article VIII, Section 30; Agreement on the Privileges and Immunities of the International Atomic Energy Agency, 1 July 1959, 374 UNTS 5334, Article X, Section 34.

5 See *Reservations to the Convention on the Prevention and Punishment of the Crime of Genocide* [1951] ICJ 15, 23-24 (Advisory Opinion of 28 May); Vienna Convention on the Law of Treaties, 22 May 1969, 1155 UNTS 331, Article 19.

6 See *e.g., Dispute concerning delimitation of the maritime boundary between Mauritius and Maldives in the Indian Ocean (Mauritius/Maldives)* (Preliminary Objections) [2021] ITLOS 17, paras 205-206 (Judgment of 28 January); Case C-104/16 P *Council v Front Polisario* [2016] ECLI:EU:C:2016:973, paras 88-92.

7 See *e.g.*, *Reparation for Injuries Suffered in the Service of the United Nations* [1949] ICJ 174, 187-88 (Advisory Opinion of 11 April); Government of Israel, 'Letter dated 14 June 1950 from the Minister for Foreign Affairs of the Government of Israel to the Secretary-General Concerning a Claim for Damage Caused to the United Nations by the Assassination of Count Folke Bernadotte and a Reply Thereto from the Secretary-General' <https://documents.un.org/doc/undoc/gen/nl5/015/06/pdf/nl501506.pdf> accessed 21 November 2024; *Legal Consequences of the Separation of the Chagos Archipelago from Mauritius in 1965* [2019] ICJ 95, para 183 (Advisory Opinion of 25 February); UK Government, 'UK

The many worlds of advisory opinions attest to their flexibility, and extraordinary ability to advance matters in the common interest. When advisory opinions deal with situations involving *ius cogens* norms, they can unfold legal effects *erga omnes*, and hence require actions by all states and international organizations.[8] This article seeks to explore the recent practice and compliance with such 'collective' obligations outlined in the advisory opinions of the International Court of Justice (ICJ). Firstly, the legal effects of advisory opinions will be discussed in more detail. Secondly, this article will look into the practice and compliance relating to the most recent advisory opinion regarding the continuous occupation by Israel of the Palestinian territories[9], followed by a conclusion.

II. The Legal Effects of Advisory Opinions

The starting point for discussing the legal effects of advisory opinions is naturally the ICJ Statute. While the Statute does not expressly address the binding force of advisory opinions, Article 59 foresees that 'decisions' are binding between the parties and for the particular case only. In this regard, since advisory opinions do not constitute 'decisions' and generally do not settle disputes, it can be deduced that they are formally not legally binding by virtue of the ICJ Statute.[10] Since there are no formal parties in advisory proceedings, it is in principle only the requesting organ which could be bound by the opinion pursuant to the ICJ Statute.

Some scholars contend that advisory opinions are indeed binding upon the requesting organ in certain circumstances.[11] This view is based on the initial

and Mauritius joint statement, 3 October 2024', Press Release, 3 October 2024 <https://www.gov.uk/government/news/uk-mauritius-deal-to-protect-national-security-safeguarding-the-operation-of-strategic-military-base> accessed 21 November 2024.

8 See, *e.g.*, *Legal Consequences arising from the Policies and Practices of Israel in the Occupied Palestinian Territory, including East Jerusalem* [2024] <https://icj-cij.org/sites/default/files/case-related/186/186-20240719-adv-01-00-en.pdf> accessed 21 November 2024, para 285 (Advisory Opinion of 19 July).

9 *Policies and Practices of Israel* (n 8).

10 *Interpretation of Peace Treaties* [1950] ICJ 65, 71 (Advisory Opinion of 30 March).

11 See, *e.g.*, Georges Abi-Saab, *Les exceptions préliminaires dans la procédure de la Cour internationale* (1967) 75-83; Robert Kolb, *The Elgar Companion to the International Court of Justice* (2014) 278.

reasons of the drafters for including an advisory function in the ICJ Statute. In this regard, Robert Kolb mentions two main purposes of the advisory function of the ICJ and its predecessor, the Permanent Court of International Justice (PCIJ). Firstly, it was anticipated that the Council and the Assembly of the League of Nations (LoN), as political bodies with limited legal expertise and resources, would handle primarily political disputes but with legal aspects. To clarify these legal issues, the PCIJ would issue advisory opinions.[12] Secondly, it was expected that the LoN, as a new international organization, would face uncertainties regarding the Covenant's interpretation, the powers of its organs, member rights, and other procedural issues. In this regard, the PCIJ was seen as a logical source for guidance through its advisory opinions.[13]

Considering this, some scholars argue that, while the requesting organ could choose to solve the underlying dispute primarily by political rather than legal means, insofar as it pursues legal solutions, it is bound by the ICJ's legal views as expressed in the advisory opinion.[14] However, in reality it seems difficult to distinguish the 'legal' from the 'political means' since the former, as the normative framework, will inform 'political means' and set the general direction and aims. In any case, this is to some extent supported by the ICJ's latest advisory opinion, where it stated that 'it is for the General Assembly and the Security Council to consider what further action is required to put an end to the illegal presence of Israel, taking into account the present Advisory Opinion.'[15] Indeed, in nearly all cases, the requesting organ will 'comply', meaning it will act in accordance with the advisory opinion — such as by adopting resolutions or creating institutions to give effect to it.[16] An example of this is the establishment of a register of damage caused by the construction of the wall, by the UN General Assembly (UNGA) in the aftermath of the *Wall* advisory opinion.[17] Interestingly, the UNGA stated that it did so in

---

12 Kolb (n 11) 258.

13 *Ibid.*, 259.

14 See, *e.g.*, Kolb (n 11) 278; Abi-Saab (n 11) 75-83.

15 *Policies and Practices of Israel* (n 8) para 281.

16 See Laurence Boisson de Chazournes and Antonella Angelini, 'After "The Court Rose": The Rise of Diplomatic Means to Implement the Pronouncements of the International Court of Justice' (2012) 11 The Law & Practice of International Courts and Tribunals 1, 33 *et seq.*

17 United Nations Register of Damage Caused by the Construction of the Wall in the Occupied Palestinian Territory, established by UNGA Res ES-10/17 (15 December 2006) UN Doc A/RES/ES-10/17.

compliance with the advisory opinion's 'dispositif'[18], a term exclusively used to describe the operative part of a judgment, to which *res iudicata* attaches.[19]

In any case, when it comes to 'internal disputes' regarding the application or interpretation of the UN Charter, the advisory opinions of the ICJ have been complied with.[20] For instance, in *Certain Expenses*, the ICJ decided by relying on the implied powers doctrine that the expenditure for peacekeeping operations are 'expenses of the Organization' pursuant to Article 17(2) of the UN Charter, which has since then been a settled matter.[21] It is indeed unlikely that any organ of the UN could disregard an advisory opinion on such 'constitutional' matters without causing an institutional and political crisis. In most cases, the requesting organ's own interests will induce compliance with the advisory opinion.[22] Thus, even if such advisory opinions are formally not vested with binding force by the ICJ Statute, they are factually binding.

Often advisory opinions emerge in the contexts of bi- or multilateral disputes and can affect the interests of 'third' states and international organizations. For instance, advisory opinions occasionally deal with pending disputes between the UN and a member state. In these circumstances, advisory proceedings function as a dispute settlement mechanism with *de facto* parties by circumventing the jurisdictional constraints of the ICJ, which formally only settles disputes between states.[23] For example, the *Applicability of the Obligation to Arbitrate* concerned a dispute between the US and UN under the UN Headquarters Agreement regarding the US prohibiting the Palestine Liberation Organization (PLO) to maintain offices within US jurisdiction including its permanent mission to the UN.[24] During the advisory proceedings,

---

18 *Ibid.*, Preambular Paragraph 5.

19 See Article 95(1) of the Rules of Court; while, pursuant to Article 107, the final paragraph of an advisory opinion is referred to as 'the reply to the question'.

20 See, *e.g.*, *Competence of Assembly regarding admission to the United Nations* [1950] ICJ 4 (Advisory Opinion of 3 March); and, *e.g.*, UN, 'About Membership' <https://www.un.org/en/about-us/about-un-membership> accessed 22 November 2024.

21 *Certain Expenses of the United Nations (Article 17, paragraph 2, of the Charter)* [1962] ICJ 151, 179-80 (Advisory Opinion of 20 July); and see, *e.g.*, UN, 'Fifth Committee Approves $5.59 Billion Budget for 14 Peacekeeping Operations', Press Release, 21 June 2024 <https://press.un.org/en/2024/gaab4463.doc.htm> accessed 22 November 2024; see also *Reparation for Injuries* (n 7).

22 Boisson de Chazournes and Angelini (n 16) 33.

23 ICJ Statute, Article 34(1).

24 *Applicability of the Obligation to Arbitrate under Section 21 of the United Nations Headquarters Agreement of 26 June 1947* [1988] ICJ 12 (Advisory Opinion of 26 April).

the ICJ even briefly mentioned the possibility of provisional measures.[25] In such instances, where advisory opinions substitute contentious proceedings, separate agreements between the factual parties stipulate that the advisory opinion shall have binding force between them.[26] Thus, advisory opinions become binding by virtue of the respective treaty rather than by the ICJ Statute pursuant to which they are not binding.[27]

In many cases, advisory opinions are embedded in broader bi- and multilateral disputes, and, while sometimes being reduced to abstract legal questions, directly affect the interests of 'third' states and international organizations.[28] In *Western Sahara*, for instance, which concerned a dispute regarding the sovereignty over the territory of Western Sahara, the ICJ recognized that it concerned a pending dispute between Morocco and Spain, the then administering power of the territory in question, and allowed the appointment of a judge *ad hoc* on behalf of Morocco.[29] Also in such circumstances, states do, in many cases, 'comply' with advisory opinions.[30] For instance, Mauritius and the UK recently reached a (so far political) agreement recognizing Mauritius' sovereignty over the Chagos Archipelago, following the ICJ's advisory

---

25 *Applicability of the Obligation to Arbitrate under Section 21 of the United Nations Headquarters Agreement of 26 June 1947* [1988] ICJ 3, 4 (Order of 9 March); see generally on this topic, Haris Huremagić, 'UNRWA, Gaza and the Recent Request for an Advisory Opinion - Could the ICJ Indicate Provisional Measures? (*völkerrechtsblog*, 23 January 2025) <https://voelkerrechtsblog.org/unrwa-gaza-and-the-recent-request-for-an-advisory-opinion/> accessed 23 January 2025.

26 See, *e.g.*, Convention on the Privileges and Immunities of the United Nations (n 4); see also Agreement regarding the Headquarters of the United Nations, 26 June 1947, 12 UNTS 147, Article 21(b), where the advisory opinion while binding functions as a 'preliminary reference ruling' similar to such instruments before the Court of Justice of the EU.

27 A point made by many scholars, *e.g.*, Robert Kolb, *The International Court of Justice* (2014) 1187-1188; see also *Judgments of the Administrative Tribunal of the ILO upon Complaints Made against UNESCO* [1956] ICJ 77, 84 (Advisory Opinion of 23 October).

28 See, *e.g.*, *Reparation for Injuries* (n 7); *International Status of South-West Africa* [1950] ICJ 128 (Advisory Opinion of 11 July); *Legal Consequences of the Construction of a Wall in the Occupied Palestinian Territory* [2004] ICJ 136 (Advisory Opinion of 9 July); *Chagos* (n 7); *Policies and Practices of Israel* (n 8).

29 *Western Sahara* [1975] ICJ 6, 8 (Order of 22 May 1975).

30 See, *e.g.*, *Chagos* (n 7); *Reparation for Injuries* (n 7).

opinion that the UK's continued administration of the territory, separated from Mauritius in 1965, is unlawful and must end, with the archipelago returned to Mauritius.[31]

Yet, there are also notable examples of 'non-compliance'. While the narrow scope of the questions and the ICJ's answers make assessing Morocco's 'compliance' with the *Western Sahara* advisory opinion a matter of interpretation, the *Wall* advisory opinion stands out as a clear example of 'non-compliance.'[32] Yet, although Israel has not 'complied', the Israeli Supreme Court stated that the advisory opinion should be given 'full appropriate weight'[33] and agreed with the legal reasoning of the *Wall* advisory opinion. However, it disagreed with the advisory opinion's conclusion, arguing that the ICJ lacked sufficient factual context to reach its opinion.[34] In any case, 'non-compliance' with advisory opinions does not go unaddressed, as states and international organizations, such as international courts[35], frequently regard these opinions as authoritative statements of the law and consistently call on the relevant state to comply.[36] In this regard, already a PCIJ committee observed that 'where there are in fact contending parties, the difference between contentious cases

---

31 See *Chagos* (n 7) and UK and Mauritius joint statement (n 7); however, this agreement has recently been reopened for negotiations, see Yasine Mohabuth, 'New Mauritian PM sends fresh Chagos proposals to UK' (*BBC*, 17 December 2024) <https://www.bbc.com/news/articles/cm2ekk2pv1no> accessed 2 January 2025.

32 See, *e.g.*, *Policies and Practices of Israel* (n 8) para 67; UNGA Res 77/247 (9 January 2023) UN Doc A/RES/77/247, para 11; International Commission of Jurists, 'Israel: Ensure Full Compliance with the International Covenant on Civil and Political Rights', Legal Briefing, June 2020 <https://www.icj.org/wp-content/uploads/2020/06/Israel-ICCPR-compliance-Advocacy-Analysis-Brief-2020-ENG.pdf> accessed 22 November 2024.

33 HCJ 7957/04 *Mara'abe et al. v The Prime Minister of Israel et al.* (2005) 60(2) PD 477, para 56.

34 See *ibid.*, paras 56-74.

35 See, *e.g.*, *Delimitation of the maritime boundary between Mauritius and Maldives* (n 6) paras 202-203.

36 See, *e.g.*, UNGA Res 77/247 (n 32); UNGA Res ES-10/24 (19 September 2024) UN Doc A/RES/ES-10/24; Government of Slovenia, 'Slovenia welcomes the Advisory opinion issued by ICJ', Press Release, 19 July 2024 <https://www.gov.si/en/news/2024-07-19-slovenia-welcomes-the-advisory-opinion-issued-by-icj-on-legal-consequences-arising-from-the-policies-and-practices-of-israel-in-the-occupied-palestinian-territory-including-east-jerusalem/> accessed 21 November 2024.

and advisory cases is only nominal' and that 'the view that advisory opinions are not binding is more theoretical than real.'[37]

Additionally, advisory opinions have regularly been used for the enforcement and promotion of community interests. Without discussing this notion in more depth[38], it is sufficient to note that advisory opinions have addressed matters that, owing to the character of the rights implicated, concerned the international community as a whole. This is particularly true in the context of de-colonization and/or when *ius cogens* (peremptory) norms, particularly the right to self-determination, were involved.[39] In these cases, the ICJ stipulated the obligations upon the international community not to recognize as lawful, not to render aid or assistance, and to cooperate to bring to an end a situation created by a serious *ius cogens* violation.[40]

These obligations derive from customary international law and are, as such, codified in Article 41 of the ILC Articles on State Responsibility (ASR).[41] They are triggered once a state seriously breached a *ius cogens* norm, *i.e.* once it breached such a norm in a gross or systematic manner.[42] Yet, the ICJ has consistently emphasized in its advisory opinions that the obligations under Article 41 ASR stem from the *erga omnes* character of the obligations breached in the specific situations rather than from the notion of *ius cogens* norms.[43] This view, in the author's opinion, has been aptly scrutinized by individual members of the ICJ in their separate opinions and declarations.[44]

---

37 'Report of the Committee appointed on September 2nd, 1927' in PCIJ, *Fourth Annual Report of the Permanent Court of Justice (June 15th, 1927-June 15th, 1928)*, PCIJ Series E No. 4, 76.

38 For a discussion of the notion of 'community interests' see, *e.g.*, Sarah Thin, 'Community Interest and the International Public Legal Order' (2021) 68 Netherlands International Law Review 35-59.

39 See *Legal Consequences for States of the Continued Presence of South Africa in Namibia (South West Africa) notwithstanding Security Council Resolution 276 (1970)* [1971] ICJ 16 (Advisory Opinion of 21 June); *Wall* (n 28); *Chagos* (n 7); *Policies and Practices of Israel* (n 8).

40 See, *e.g.*, *Namibia* (n 39) para 133; *Wall* (n 28) para 163; *Chagos* (n 7) para 183; *Policies and Practices of Israel* (n 8) para 285.

41 UNGA Res 56/83 'Responsibility of States for internationally wrongful acts' (12 December 2001) UN Doc A/56/83, Article 41.

42 *Ibid.*, Article 40.

43 See, *e.g.*, *Wall* (n 28) paras 154-160; *Chagos* (n 7) para 180; *Policies and Practices of Israel* (n 8) paras 273-279.

44 See, *e.g.*, *Wall* (n 28), Separate Opinion of Judge Higgins, paras 37-40; *Policies and Practices of Israel* (n 8), Declaration of Judge Tladi, paras 28-35.

While avoiding further speculation, it appears that the ICJ is either grappling with some ambiguity or attempting to convey a deeper message – one that has yet to be fully understood.

While in all situations subject to advisory proceedings before the ICJ, instances of serious breaches of *ius cogens* norms were rather clear-cut, such a finding before an international court, whether in advisory or contentious proceedings, would make it all the more unattainable for a state to credibly assert a different view. Recent advisory proceedings have demonstrated that a significant number of states and international organizations actively participate to express their views[45], which are carefully considered by 15 judges during thorough deliberations. In this regard, scholars regularly point out that the ICJ approaches advisory proceedings with the same rigour as with contentious cases, and hence 'both are authoritative judicial statements deciding questions that have been submitted to the Court.'[46] Consequently, it would be difficult to assign substantial weight to the views of individual states, which disagree with the conclusions of an advisory opinion of the ICJ.

Put simply, when the ICJ identifies a serious violation of a *ius cogens* norm and reminds states of their obligations codified in Article 41 ASR, it creates a near-irrebuttable presumption that a situation has arisen where each state is bound by the resulting 'collective' obligation under customary international law not to render aid or assistance, and to cooperate to bring to an end a situation created by a such a serious *ius cogens* violation. In this context, an advisory opinion can thus trigger legal effects *erga omnes.* This is also confirmed by practice, since, for instance, the UNGA regularly '[c]alls upon all States Members of the United Nations to comply with their legal obligations as mentioned in the advisory opinion'.[47] States have demonstrated considerable practice in adhering to their 'collective' obligations as outlined in advisory opinions—a topic explored further in the next

---

45 See, *e.g.*, *Policies and Practices of Israel* (n 8) where, for instance, 57 states and international organizations filed written statements, see ICJ Press Release No. 2023/43, 7 August 2023; in *Obligations of States in respect of Climate Change* more than 90 states and international organizations have participated in the proceedings, see Press Release No. 2024/31, 12 April 2024.

46 Abi-Saab (n 11) 75; see also Jane A Hofbauer, 'Not Just a Participation Trophy? Advancing Public Interests through Advisory Opinions at the International Court of Justice' (2023) 22 The Law and Practice of International Courts and Tribunals 234, 239-242.

47 UNGA Res ES-10/15 (2 August 2004) UN Doc A/RES/ES-10/15, para 3; see also, *e.g.*, UNGA Res 73/295 (24 May 2019) UN Doc A/RES/73/295, para 5; UNGA Res ES-10/24 (n 36) para 4.

section. In conclusion, when addressing grave breaches of *ius cogens* norms, advisory opinions occupy a unique position: they are neither strictly binding nor entirely non-binding for the international community as a whole. Thus, they hold the authority to generate legal effects *erga omnes*.

III. Compliance with the Advisory Opinion on the *Legal Consequences arising from the Policies and Practices of Israel in Occupied Palestinian Territory, including East Jerusalem*

A. The Advisory Opinion, Other Obligations and the Issue of Compliance

On 19 January 2023 the UNGA submitted a request for an advisory opinion to the ICJ containing two questions. Firstly, the ICJ was asked to consider the legal consequences arising from Israel's ongoing violation of the Palestinian people's right to self-determination, including, for instance, by its prolonged occupation, settlement activities, and annexation of Palestinian territory occupied since 1967. Secondly, the ICJ was asked to examine how Israel's policies and practices impact the legal status of the occupation and to determine the resulting legal obligations for all states and the United Nations.[48]

The ICJ determined that Israel's continued presence in the Occupied Palestinian Territory (OPT) is unlawful, while referring to Israel's policies of settlement expansion, annexation, and other measures and legislation in violation of international humanitarian and human rights law.[49] In this context, the ICJ found violations of several *ius cogens* norms, including Article 3 of the Convention on the Elimination of Racial Discrimination[50] (prohibition of racial segregation and apartheid)[51], and the Palestinian people's right to self-determination.[52] Consequently, the ICJ concluded that Israel is under an obligation to end its unlawful presence in the OPT as quickly as possible.[53]

48 UNGA Res 77/247 (9 January 2023) UN Doc A/RES/77/247, para 18.

49 *Policies and Practices of Israel* (n 8) para 285.

50 Convention on the Elimination of All Forms of Racial Discrimination, 7 March 1966, 660 UNTS 195.

51 *Policies and Practices of Israel* (n 8) para 229.

52 *Ibid.*, paras 252-258.

53 *Ibid.*, para 285.

Furthermore, it emphasized that all states and international organizations must refrain from recognizing as lawful the situation resulting from Israel's unlawful presence and that all states are prohibited from rendering any aid or assistance to maintain this situation.[54]

In response to the advisory opinion, many states called on Israel as well as on all states to comply with the obligations stipulated therein.[55] The European Union (EU) reacted by stating the 'ICJ Advisory Opinion will need to be analysed more thoroughly, including in view of its implications for EU policy.'[56] Additionally, the UNGA adopted Resolution ES-10/24 calling upon 'all States to comply with their obligations under international law, inter alia, as reflected in the advisory opinion, including their obligation [...] [n]ot to recognize as legal the situation arising from the unlawful presence of Israel in the Occupied Palestinian Territory,' and '[n]ot to render aid or assistance in maintaining the situation [...].'[57]

---

54 *Ibid.*

55 See, *e.g.*, Press Release of Slovenia (n 36); Ministry of Foreign Affairs of Spain, Press Statement 037, 19 July 2024 <www.exteriores.gob.es/en/Comunicacion/Comunicados/Paginas/2024_COMUNICADOS/20240719_COMU037.aspx> accessed 28 November 2024; Ministry of Foreign Affairs of Iceland (@MFAIceland), 'The ICJ's advisory opinion is clear…' X, 20 July 2024 <https://x.com/MFAIceland/status/1814619004482244966> accessed 28 November 2024; Department of Foreign Affairs of Ireland, 'Statement by the Tánaiste on the ICJ Advisory Opinion', Press Release, 19 July 2024 <https://www.gov.ie/en/press-release/651e6-statement-by-tanaiste-on-the-icj-advisory-opinion/> accessed 28 November 2024; Permanent Mission of Liechtenstein to the UN (@LiechtensteinUN), 'LI welcomes today's @CIJ_ICJ's Advisory Opinion' X, 19 July 2024 <https://x.com/LiechtensteinUN/status/1814319081857622368> accessed 28 November 2024; Minister of Foreign Affairs of Norway (@EspenBarthEided), 'The ICJ is crystal clear…' X, 19 July 2024 <https://x.com/MalaysiaMFA/status/1814481537347530839> accessed 28 November 2024; <https://x.com/EspenBarthEide/status/1814319638945071597> accessed 28 November 2024; Ministry of Foreign Affairs of Malaysia (@MalaysianMFA), 'Press Release…' X, 20 July 2024.

56 European External Action Service, 'Israel/Palestine: Statement by the High Representative on the Advisory Opinion of the International Court of Justice', 20 July 2024 <https://www.eeas.europa.eu/eeas/israelpalestine-statement-high-representative-advisory-opinion-international-court-justice_en> accessed 28 November 2024.

57 UNGA Res ES-10/24 (n 36) para 4.

During the debate in the 10th emergency special session of the UNGA, the vast majority of states stressed that Israel and all other states must 'comply'[58], 'implement'[59], or 'give effect'[60] to the advisory opinion. Moreover, most states that abstained from voting on Resolution ES-10/24 clarified that their decision was not due to disagreement with the advisory opinion, but rather because they believed the UNGA resolution went beyond the scope of the opinion.[61] In other words, the authority of the ICJ's advisory opinion was not contested by any state, apart from Israel, Hungary, Fiji, Papua New Guinea and the United States.[62] While the US criticized the 'breadth' of the advisory opinion, it also underscored that Israel's settlement activities are inconsistent with international law.[63] Fiji and Papua New Guinea emphasized the 'level of dissenting and separate opinions' raising 'the specter of the credibility of the Advisory Opinion'.[64]

Yet, whether and to which extent recent practice of states in relation to the conflict in Israel and the OPT can be traced back to the *Policies and*

---

[58] UNGA, 10th Emergency Special Session, 53rd Plenary Meeting (17 September 2024), item 5: Draft resolution A/ES-10/L.31/Rev.1:, *e.g.*, Statement of Norway; Statement of Djibouti; Statement of South Africa; all available at <https://www.un.org/en/ga/sessions/emergency10th.shtml> accessed 28 November 2024.

[59] *Ibid.*, *e.g.*, Statement of Bangladesh; Statement of Guyana; Statement of Malta.

[60] *Ibid.*, *e.g.*, Statement of Luxembourg; Statement of Sierra Leone; Statement of St. Vincent and Grenadines.

[61] *Ibid.*, *e.g.*, Explanation of Vote of Australia; Explanation of Vote of Austria; Explanation of Vote of Bulgaria; Explanation of Vote of Germany; Explanation of Vote of the United Kingdom; Explanation of Vote of the Netherlands.

[62] See Jeremy Sharon, 'World Court: Israeli presence in East Jerusalem, West Bank is illegal and must end' (*The Times of Israel*, 19 July 2024) <https://www.timesofisrael.com/world-court-israeli-presence-in-east-jerusalem-west-bank-is-illegal-and-must-end/> accessed 2 December 2024; Magyarország kormánya (Government of Hungary), Press Release, 19 July 2024 <https://kormany.hu/hirek/magyarorszag-kormanya-nem-ert-egyet-a-nemzetkozi-birosag-2024-julius-19-en-hagaban-kozzetett-tanacsadoi-velemenyeben-foglalt-megallapitasokkal> accessed 2 December 2024; Statement of Fiji (n 58) and Explanation of Vote of Papua New Guinea (n 58).

[63] See Kanishka Singh, 'US criticizes ICJ opinion on Israeli occupation of Palestinian territories' (*Reuters*, 20 July 2024) <https://www.reuters.com/world/us-criticizes-icj-opinion-israeli-occupation-palestinian-territories-2024-07-20/> accessed 2 December 2024.

[64] Explanation of Vote of Papua New Guinea (n 58); see also Statement of Fiji (n 58).

Practices of Israel advisory opinion is hard to ascertain. Firstly, states often adopt certain measures out of extra-legal reasons. Secondly, a multitude of legal obligations from different sources might apply to a specific situation and require the adoption or omission of similar measures. Therefore, the legal regime that primarily induces states to adopt or omit certain measures can typically be inferred from the context, unless explicitly stated; in some cases, it might never be definitively determined.

For instance, the advisory opinion was issued after the underlying situation had significantly worsened on and in the aftermath of 7 October 2023. Thus, the ICJ had indicated provisional measures in several orders in the related contentious case between South Africa and Israel under the Convention on the Prevention and Punishment of the Crime of Genocide (Genocide Convention).[65] In its Order of 26 January 2024, the ICJ confirmed *inter alia* that it had *prima facie* jurisdiction and that 'at least some of the rights claimed by South Africa and for which it is seeking protection are plausible', such as 'the right of the Palestinians in Gaza to be protected from acts of genocide [...]'.[66] Additionally, on 1 March 2024, Nicaragua initiated proceedings against Germany before the ICJ alleging that Germany *inter alia* breached 'the obligation to facilitate and cooperate in bringing about the Palestinian People's right to self-determination, by providing aid and particularly military equipment to Israel that is used to deny this right of self-determination.'[67] The ICJ stated in its Order on provisional measures that it 'remains deeply concerned about the catastrophic living conditions of the Palestinians in the Gaza Strip'[68] and considered 'it particularly important to remind all States of their international obligations relating to the transfer of arms to parties to an armed conflict [...]'.[69] Moreover, the Human Rights Council in its resolution of 5 April 2024 recognized 'the grave violations of multiple peremptory norms by Israel' and called upon 'all States to ensure that their arms exports do not

---

65 See *Application of the Convention on the Prevention and Punishment of the Crime of Genocide in the Gaza Strip (South Africa v Israel)* Order of 26 January 2024, Order of 28 March 2024, Order of 24 May 2024, all available at <https://icj-cij.org/case/192/orders> accessed 29 November 2024.

66 *South Africa v Israel* (Order of 26 January 2024) (n 66) para 54.

67 *Alleged Breaches of Certain International Obligations in respect of the Occupied Palestinian Territory (Nicaragua v Germany),* Order of 30 April 2024, para 2 <https://www.icj-cij.org/sites/default/files/case-related/193/193-20240430-ord-01-00-en.pdf> accessed 29 November 2024.

68 *Ibid.*, para 22.

69 *Ibid.*, para 24.

contribute to or benefit from this unlawful situation'.[70] On 10 May 2024, the United States, the largest supplier of weapons to Israel, released its first report under National Security Memorandum 20.[71] The report evaluated the conduct of Israel and other foreign government recipients of US arms, concluding that it is 'reasonable to assess' that Israel used US-supplied weapons in violation of international humanitarian law.[72] Finally, on 20 May 2024, the Prosecutor of the ICC requested arrest warrants *inter alia* for Benjamin Netanyahu and Yoav Gallant citing reasonable grounds to believe they were criminally responsible for war crimes and crimes against humanity.[73] Thus, by mid-2024 sufficient evidence, judicial and other pronouncements were available that attested to a clear risk of violations of human rights and international humanitarian law, as well as serious violations of multiple *ius cogens* norms.

These circumstances triggered several obligations in relation to the situation in Israel and the OPT. For instance, pursuant to common Article 1 of the Geneva Conventions[74] all states are under an obligation 'to respect and to ensure respect' for the Geneva Conventions, meaning every state party 'whether or not it is a party to a specific conflict, is under an obligation to ensure that the requirements of the instruments in question are complied

---

70 Human Rights Council Resolution 55/28 (5 April 2024) UN Doc A/HRC/RES/55/28, para 13.

71 'National Security Memorandum on Safeguards and Accountability with Respect to Transferred Defense Articles and Defense Services', see for more information <https://www.whitehouse.gov/briefing-room/presidential-actions/2024/02/08/national-security-memorandum-on-safeguards-and-accountability-with-respect-to-transferred-defense-articles-and-defense-services/> accessed 1 December 2024.

72 See John Ramming Chappell, 'Key Takeaways from Biden Administration Report on Israeli Use of US Weapons' (*Just Security*, 11 May 2024) <https://www.justsecurity.org/95583/israel-weapons-hamas-us-report-takeaways/> accessed 1 December 2024.

73 ICC, 'Statement of ICC Prosecutor Karim A.A. Khan KC: Applications for arrest warrants in the situation in the State of Palestine' (20 May 2024) <https://www.icc-cpi.int/news/statement-icc-prosecutor-karim-aa-khan-kc-applications-arrest-warrants-situation-state> accessed 1 December 2024; on 21 November 2024, ICC Pre-Trial Chamber I issued the requested arrest warrants, see ICC Press Release of 21 November 2024 <https://www.icc-cpi.int/news/situation-state-palestine-icc-pre-trial-chamber-i-rejects-state-israels-challenges> accessed 1 December 2024.

74 *E.g.*, Geneva Convention relative to the Protection of Civilian Persons in Time of War (Geneva Convention IV), 12 August 1949, 75 UNTS 287, Article 1.

with.'[75] Moreover, state parties to the Arms Trade Treaty are under the obligation not to authorize any transfer of conventional arms if they know that 'that the arms or items would be used in the commission of genocide, crimes against humanity, grave breaches of the Geneva Conventions of 1949 [...]'[76], or if, after conducting an export assessment, there is an overriding risk that the arms 'could be used to commit or facilitate' a serious violation of international humanitarian or human rights law.[77] EU member states are also required by Article 2 of the EU Council Common Position 2008/944/CFSP to deny export licenses for military technology and equipment if there is a 'clear risk' that military technology or equipment might be used *inter alia* 'in the commission of serious violations of international humanitarian law.'[78]

The *Policies and Practices of Israel* advisory opinion, issued on 19 July 2024, therefore did not emerge in isolation; rather, it added another layer to the dense framework of norms governing, for example, the transfer of weapons to Israel. This opinion also represents an important judicial statement on serious violations of *ius cogens* norms, which further reinforced the customary 'collective' obligation as codified in Article 41 ASR, an obligation that had arguably already been triggered by mid-2024. These obligations overlap, as the transfer of weapons can also constitute aid or assistance in the maintenance of a situation created by serious violations of *ius cogens*, including the right to self-determination. While it may be difficult to pinpoint the exact legal regime that primarily induced states' decisions to adopt or omit certain measures, this is ultimately of secondary importance. What matters most is that states fulfil their international obligations, for instance as outlined in advisory opinions, regardless of their motivations.

---

75 *Nicaragua v Germany* (n 67) para 23; see also *Wall* (n 28) para 158; although the question of whether common Article 1 of the Geneva Conventions has an 'external' dimension is disputed, see, *e.g.*, Lawrence Hill-Cawthorne, 'Common Article 1 of the Geneva Conventions and the Method of Treaty Interpretation' (2023) 72 International & Comparative Law Quarterly 869-908.

76 Arms Trade Treaty, adopted 2 April 2013, 3013 UNTS 269, Article 6(3); see also Akshaya Kumar, 'Continued Arm Exports to Israel in the Face of Constructive Notice' (*Lawfare*, 25 June 2024) <https://www.lawfaremedia.org/article/continued-arms-exports-to-israel-in-the-face-of-constructive-notice> accessed 2 January 2025, arguing that 'constructive knowledge' is sufficient under the Arms Trade Treaty.

77 *Ibid.*, Article 7; see also *Nicaragua v Germany* (n 67) para 16.

78 Council Common Position 2008/944/CFSP of 8 December 2008 defining common rules governing control of exports of military technology and equipment [2008] OJ L335/99, Article 2(2)(c); see also *Nicaragua v Germany* (n 67) para 16.

B. Recent Practice and Compliance

The recent practice connected to the *Policies and Practices of Israel* advisory opinion of the ICJ and generally the situation in Israel and the OPT can be broadly divided into three categories. One category concerns measures related to the transfer of arms, another encompasses broader international trade measures, and the third pertains to restrictive measures against individual persons or entities in connection with extremist settler violence. All these measures could in principle have been taken in compliance with the 'collective' obligation under Article 41 ASR, as reflected in the advisory opinion.

With regard to extremist settler violence,[79] Australia,[80] Canada,[81] the EU,[82] the UK,[83] and the United States[84] had adopted first sanctions against individual extremist settlers or entities prior to the issuance of the advisory opinion, but reinforced measures afterwards.[85] However, in his first day in office, US

---

79 See also *Policies and Practices of Israel* (n 8) paras 148-155.

80 Australian Ministry of Foreign Affairs, 'Human Rights Sanctions in response to Israeli settler violence in the West Bank', 25 July 2024 <https://www.foreign-minister.gov.au/minister/penny-wong/media-release/human-rights-sanctions-response-israeli-settler-violence-west-bank> accessed 14 December 2024.

81 'Special Economic Measures (Extremist Settler Violence) Regulations: SOR/2024-91', 16 May 2024, Canada Gazette, Part II, Volume 158, Number 12.

82 Council Decision (CFSP) 2024/1967 of 15 July 2024 amending Decision (CFSP) 2020/1999 concerning restrictive measures against serious human rights violations and abuses [2024] <https://eur-lex.europa.eu/legal-content/EN/TXT/HTML/?uri=OJ:L_202401967> accessed 14 December 2024; 'Council Implementing Regulation (EU) 2024/1960 of 15 July 2024 implementing Regulation (EU) 2020/1998 concerning restrictive measures against serious human rights violations and abuses' (2024) <https://eur-lex.europa.eu/legal-content/EN/TXT/HTML/?uri=OJ:L_202401960> accessed 14 December 2024.

83 UK Government, 'UK sanctions extremist settlers in the West Bank', Press Release, 12 February 2024 <https://www.gov.uk/government/news/uk-sanctions-extremist-settlers-in-the-west-bank> accessed 14 December 2024.

84 Executive Order 14115 of February 1, 2024, 'Imposing Certain Sanctions on Persons Undermining Peace, Security, and Stability in the West Bank' Federal Register Vol. 89, No. 24, 7605.

85 See, *e.g.*, 'Regulations Amending the Special Economic Measures (Extremist Settler Violence) Regulations: SOR/2024-179', 17 September 2024, Canada Gazette, Part II, Volume 158, Number 21; UK Government, 'New UK sanctions target illegal outposts and organisations supporting extremist Israeli settlers in the West Bank', Press Release, 15 October 2024 <https://www.gov.uk/government/news/new-uk-sanctions-target-illegal-outposts-and-organisations-supporting-ex-

President Trump revoked US sanctions against extremist settlers.[86] In some jurisdictions,[87] targeted sanctions against extremist settlers were expressly taken on the basis of UN Security Council resolution 1373 (2001), adopted in the aftermath of 9/11 and obliging states to suppress terrorism by implementing targeted financial sanctions.[88] Similarly, most states that stopped arms exports to Israel did so before the advisory opinion was issued,[89] while several domestic court cases on this matter are still pending.[90] However, in the advisory opinion's aftermath, the UK suspended around 30 export licenses, referring to 'a clear risk that items exported to Israel under these 30 licences might be used in serious violations of IHL.'[91]

---

tremist-israeli-settlers-in-the-west-bank> accessed 14 December 2024; US Department of State, 'Sanctioning Additional Violent Israeli Individuals and Entities', 18 November 2024 <https://www.state.gov/sanctioning-additional-violent-israeli-individuals-and-entities/> accessed 14 December 2024.

86 The White House, 'Initial Rescissions of Harmful Executive Orders and Actions', 20 January 2025 <https://www.whitehouse.gov/presidential-actions/2025/01/initial-rescissions-of-harmful-executive-orders-and-actions/> accessed 23 January 2025.

87 See, *e.g.*, Australian Government, 'Consolidated List', 9 December 2024 <https://www.dfat.gov.au/international-relations/security/sanctions/consolidated-list> accessed 14 December 2024.

88 UNSC Res 1373 (28 September 2001) UN Doc S/RES/1373.

89 See, *e.g.*, Ministry of Foreign Affairs of Spain, 'Comunicado sobre la venta de armamento a Israel', Comunicado 06, 12 February 2024 <https://www.exteriores.gob.es/es/Comunicacion/Comunicados/Paginas/2024_COMUNICADOS/20240212_COMU006.aspx> accessed 2 December 2024; Alessandro Farrugia, 'Il ministro Tajani: "Non diamo armi a Tel Aviv, Schlein è male informata. Navi italiane nel Mar Rosso"' (*Quotidiano Nazionale*, 19 January 2024) <https://www.quotidiano.net/esteri/tajani-non-diamo-armi-a-israele-schlein-navi-italiane-mar-rosso-3ee0532b> accessed 2 December 2024.

90 See Jacques Hartmann, Lea Köhne and Vincent Widdig, 'Arms Exports and Access to Justice: Enforcing International Law through Domestic Courts' (*EJIL:Talk!*, 25 October 2024) <https://www.ejiltalk.org/arms-exports-and-access-to-justice-enforcing-international-law-through-domestic-courts/> accessed 2 December 2024.

91 Government of the UK, 'UK suspends around 30 arms export licences to Israel for use in Gaza over International Humanitarian Law concerns', Press Release, 2 September 2024 <https://www.gov.uk/government/news/uk-suspends-around-30-arms-export-licences-to-israel-for-use-in-gaza-over-international-humanitarian-law-concerns> accessed 2 December 2024.

Moreover, decisions on whether to allow or deny the transit of arms through a state's territory are made regularly, but these decisions are usually not made public. Depending on the governing instrument, states are required to deny transit if there is knowledge or a 'clear risk' that the arms could be used in the commission of serious violations of international humanitarian law.[92] However, how states evaluate such risks remains unclear. It is likely that the recent advisory opinion has influenced these assessments, especially as it forms part of a broader series of judicial statements concerning Israel's actions, which makes it increasingly difficult for states to justify taking a different approach. On 24 August 2024, for instance, Namibia denied port access to the German-owned cargo vessel MV Kathrin, since it was 'carrying weapons intended for Israel.'[93] The Minister of Justice, Yvonne Dausab, explained that Namibia was complying with the obligation 'not to support or be complicit in Israeli war crimes, crimes against humanity, genocide, as well as its unlawful occupation of Palestine' *inter alia* 'under the Genocide Convention' but also 'as articulated in the recent advisory opinion by the International Court of Justice'.[94] The vessel was also denied port access by Angola, Slovenia, Malta and Montenegro.[95] Similarly, Spain recently refused entry to two vessels under the US flag transporting arms to Israel,[96] as part of a broader policy not to authorize access to any ships carrying weapons for Israel.[97] Interestingly, individuals have also 'enforced' obligations when

---

92 See, *e.g.*, Council Common Position (n 78) Article 2(2)(c); Arms Trade Treaty (n 76) Article 6(3).

93 See Eveline de Klerk, 'Namibia blocks Israeli weapon-carrying vessel' (*New Era*, 27 August 2024) <https://neweralive.na/namibia-blocks-israeli-weapon-carrying-vessel> accessed 2 December 2024.

94 *Ibid.*

95 See European Legal Support Center, 'Emergency motion against the delivery of explosives carried by the German ship MV Kathrin to Israel', Press Release, 30 October 2024 <https://elsc.support/news/emergency-motion-against-the-delivery-of-explosives-from-the-german-ship-mv-kathrin-to-israel> accessed 3 December 2024.

96 'Danish Maersk container ship denied docking at Spanish port over arms to Israel' (*The Local*, 10 November 2024) <https://www.thelocal.dk/20241110/danish-maersk-container-ship-denied-docking-at-spanish-port-over-arms-to-israel> accessed 3 December 2024.

97 'Spain will not authorise calling of ships carrying weapons for Israel' (*Reuters*, 17 May 2024) <https://www.reuters.com/world/europe/spain-will-not-authorise-calling-ships-carrying-weapons-israel-2024-05-17/> accessed 3 December 2024.

in their opinion states were failing to do so, such as Greek dockworkers at the Port of Piraeus who blocked the loading of a container of ammunition destined for Israel in protest against the war in Gaza.[98]

With regard to broader trade related measures, the ICJ clarified in its advisory opinion that states have *inter alia* 'the duty of distinguishing dealings with Israel between its own territory and the Occupied Palestinian Territory', which encompasses the obligation to 'abstain from entering into economic or trade dealings with Israel concerning the Occupied Palestinian Territory' and 'to take steps to prevent trade or investment relations that assist in the maintenance of the illegal situation created by Israel in the Occupied Palestinian Territory.'[99] In this regard, the Government of Ireland has, in direct response to the *Policies and Practices of Israel* advisory opinion, announced its intention to adopt the 'Occupied Territories Bill'[100] that would make it an offence to import or sell goods or services originating from settlements or to extract resources from the OPT.[101] The bill was initially introduced in 2018, but then deemed contrary to EU law. The Government argues, however, that '[t]he advisory opinion has changed the legal context for the Control of Economic Activity (Occupied Territories) Bill 2018', and while trade matters remain an exclusive EU competence, 'if the EU does not take measures to limit or prevent trade with the settlements, there are exceptional grounds in EU law that could allow a member state to take measures itself.'[102] However, in a recent case in the Netherlands, Al-Haq and nine other civil society organizations filed a civil case against the state, seeking bans on military

---

98 'Greek Piraeus port dockers block ammunition cargo destined for Israel' (*Reuters*, 18 October 2024) <https://www.reuters.com/world/greek-piraeus-port-dockers-block-ammunition-cargo-destined-israel-2024-10-18/> accessed 3 December 2024.

99 *Policies and Practices of Israel* (n 8) para 278.

100 Department of Foreign Affairs of Ireland, 'Statement by Tánaiste Micheál Martin on the Occupied Territories Bill', Press Release, 22 October 2024 <https://www.gov.ie/en/press-release/dad83-statement-by-tanaiste-micheal-martin-on-the-occupied-territories-bill/> accessed 4 December 2024.

101 'Control of Economic Activity (Occupied Territories) Bill 2018', Articles 6-9, draft text available at <https://www.oireachtas.ie/en/bills/bill/2018/6/> accessed 4 December 2024.

102 Minister for Foreign Affairs of Ireland, 'Select Committee on Foreign Affairs and Defence debate - Tuesday, 5 Nov 2024; Control of Economic Activity (Occupied Territories) Bill 2018: Discussion' <https://www.oireachtas.ie/en/debates/debate/select_committee_on_foreign_affairs_and_defence/2024-11-05/5/> accessed 4 December 2024.

exports, cooperation with Israel, and Dutch trade or investment tied to Israeli settlements in the OPT, citing the ICJ's advisory opinion. The District Court of The Hague rejected all claims, and in relation to trade measures referred to the Netherlands' long-standing 'discouragement policy', the ongoing evaluation of trade measures, and the state's discretion over foreign policy decisions. In this regard, the District Court held that the Netherlands' current trade policy with Israel and the OPT is not 'clearly unlawful'.[103]

Moreover, the Norwegian government, citing the ICJ's advisory opinion, issued an advice to Norwegian companies 'not to engage in business cooperation or trade that serves to perpetuate Israel's illegal presence in Palestine – *i.e.* in the West Bank, including East Jerusalem, and Gaza.'[104] Additionally, on 3 December 2024, the Norwegian sovereign wealth fund ('Government Pension Fund Global') announced its decision to divest from Israel's largest telecommunication group 'Bezeq', which is providing services to settlements, due to 'an unacceptable risk that the company contributes to serious violations of the rights of individuals in situations of war and conflict [...].'[105] Similarly, a bill was recently introduced in the Senate of Australia in direct response to the advisory opinion and expressly relying on the 'collective' obligation of Article 41 ASR.[106] It is aimed at prohibiting investments of the Australian sovereign wealth fund ('Future Fund') in illegal Israeli settlements or in companies that invest in such settlements.[107]

The EU already distinguishes between Israel and the OPT in its trade relations, as the EU-Israel Association Agreement excludes products from

---

[103] The Hague District Court, Judgment of 13 December 2024, Case No C/09/673870/ KG ZA 24-948, ECLI:NL:RBDHA:2024:20828, paras 4.29-4.35.

[104] Ministry of Foreign Affairs of Norway, 'Do not engage in trade and business cooperation that serves to perpetuate Israel's occupation of Palestine', Press Release, 22 October 2024 <https://www.regjeringen.no/en/aktuelt/do-not-engage-in-trade-and-business-cooperation-that-serves-to-perpetuate-israels-occupation-of-palestine/id3061358/> accessed 4 December 2024.

[105] Norges Bank, 'Decisions on exclusion and observation', Press Release, 3 December 2024 <https://www.nbim.no/en/the-fund/news-list/2024/decisions-on-exclusion-and-observation2/> accessed 4 December 2024.

[106] 'Treasury Laws Amendment (Divesting from Illegal Israeli Settlements) Bill 2024', Explanatory Memorandum, 28 November 2024 <https://www.aph.gov.au/Parliamentary_Business/Bills_Legislation/Bills_Search_Results/Result?bId=s1440> accessed 14 December 2024.

[107] *Ibid.*

Israeli settlements, meaning they do not benefit from preferential tariffs.[108] However, the EU still permits trade with settlement-originating goods, provided they are labelled accordingly, in line with the 2005 EU-Israel Technical Arrangement.[109] On 17 October 2024, 30 members of the European Parliament argued that this approach 'does not comply with the obligations laid out by the ICJ', which they claim require a complete ban on trade with settlement-originating goods. They questioned whether the European Commission intends 'to comply with its obligations under international law and urgently ban all trade with the illegal Israeli settlements'.[110] The Commission merely responded that 'Member States will discuss further in the relevant Council preparatory bodies the impact of the Advisory Opinion on EU positions and policies.'[111] In an internal legal analysis addressed to then EU High Representative Josep Borrell, Frank Hoffmeister, the Chief Legal Officer of the European External Action Service, contended that the ICJ's advisory opinion does not require a ban on importing goods from settlements.[112] While this interpretation of the advisory opinion is rather questionable[113], the memorandum emphasizes that the opinion 'clarifies international obligations binding on Israel as occupying power of the Occupied Palestinian Territory;

---

108 Euro-Mediterranean Agreement establishing an association between the European Communities and their Member States, of the one part, and the State of Israel, of the other part (2000) OJ L147/3, Protocol 4, Article 2; see also European Commission, 'Israel' <https://policy.trade.ec.europa.eu/eu-trade-relationships-country-and-region/countries-and-regions/israel_en> accessed 4 December 2024.

109 European Commission, 'EU-Israel Technical Arrangement' <https://taxation-customs.ec.europa.eu/eu-israel-technical-arrangement_en> accessed 4 December 2024.

110 'Implementation of the ICJ advisory opinion as regards EU trade with illegal Israeli settlements', Parliamentary question E-002150/2024, 17 October 2024 <https://www.europarl.europa.eu/doceo/document/E-10-2024-002150_EN.html> accessed 5 December 2024.

111 Rules of Procedure of the European Parliament, Rule 144; see also Parliamentary question (n 110).

112 See Arthur Neslen, 'EU "Bending" Rules to Allow Trade With Israeli Settlements, Leaked Analysis Shows' (*The Intercept*, 23 October 2024) <https://theintercept.com/2024/10/23/eu-israel-settlements-trade-gaza/> accessed 3 December 2024.

113 See, *e.g.*, Yussef Al Tamimi, 'Implications of the ICJ Advisory Opinion for the EU-Israel Association Agreement' (*EJIL:Talk!*, 30 July 2024) <https://www.ejiltalk.org/implications-of-the-icj-advisory-opinion-for-the-eu-israel-association-agreement/> accessed 3 December 2024.

the fact that the opinion itself is advisory in nature does not change the nature of Israel's legal obligations.'[114]

Therefore, the ICJ's recent advisory opinion on Israel's policies and practices in the OPT underscores the broader implications of such opinions. It shows how advisory opinions can trigger legal effects *erga omnes*, reinforcing the 'collective' obligations of states not to recognize, aid, or assist in the maintenance of situations created by serious violations of *ius cogens* norms. The response of states to advisory opinions demonstrates how the issue of 'compliance' is not solely dictated by the formal legal status of advisory opinions but is often driven by their persuasive authority, the weight of international consensus, and the broader legal and political context. Thus, advisory opinions, as judicial statements that are neither binding nor non-binding, play a useful and pragmatic role in enhancing the compliance with the 'collective obligations' as codified in Article 41 ASR.

IV. Conclusion

Advisory opinions are often characterized as non-binding, yet in practice, they can have varying legal effects. Depending on the circumstances, advisory opinions may either be binding or non-binding. When states or international organizations conclude separate agreements to recognize an advisory opinion as legally binding, those advisory opinions are binding and non-binding at the same time. However, in most instances, the authority attributed to advisory opinions blurs this distinction: advisory opinions are in reality neither binding nor non-binding. They occupy a space where the dichotomy between binding and non-binding loses its relevance, or, in other words, reveals its falsity. This is because, despite their lack of formal binding force, states and international organizations have in practice acted in conformity with advisory opinions. Thus, in reality, they also influence and guide the behaviour of states and international organizations.

This is particularly true in situations of serious *ius cogens* violations, where advisory opinions, through their persuasive force and authoritative standing, can clarify the facts and legal implications and help all states assess their 'collective' obligations in order to bring such situations to an end. In this way, advisory opinions effectively contribute to the promotion and enforcement of community interests in connection with the 'collective'

[114] Reprinted in Neslen (n 112).

obligations of Article 41 ASR. At the same time, notable examples of 'non-compliance' demonstrate the limitations of advisory opinions, particularly when the interests of individual states take precedence over the protection of community interests. While the practice of states in response to the most recent advisory opinion on Israel's presence, policies and practices in the OPT attests to the persuasive and authoritative weight of advisory opinions, the reaction of certain states has also underscored a worrying trend: the application of international law in a selective manner.

Obligations for Third States in the War between Israel and Hamas: To Deliver or Not to Deliver

Elisabeth Hoffberger-Pippan | Senior Researcher at Peace Research Institute Frankfurt (PRIF)

Abstract

This article examines the legal obligations of third states regarding arms deliveries to Israel in the context of the ongoing armed conflict with Hamas. Special emphasis will be placed on the respective national practices, with a particular focus on the Netherlands and Germany. The legal avenues available to challenge export licenses vary significantly across jurisdictions, with some countries imposing considerably greater procedural hurdles than others. Another critical issue is the reluctance of national courts to intervene in export licensing decisions. This hesitancy stems from the fact that such decisions are deeply intertwined with security policy considerations and are primarily regarded as matters of political discretion. A coherent export control practice that aligns with international law is therefore urgently needed.

Keywords

International humanitarian law – human rights – arms exports – state practice – separation of powers – International Court of Justice – International Criminal Court

I. Introduction

When the terrorist group Hamas attacked Israel on 7 October 2023, the world was shocked by the scale of the atrocity and the brutality of the attackers. Over 250 people were taken hostage and more than 1,200 people died in the attack, most of them Israeli citizens, but also foreign nationals. The full extent of the atrocities only became apparent in the course of the investigation.[1] In a video shown to journalists, it became clear that hundreds of people had been brutally

---

1 Daniel Byman *et al*, 'Hamas's October 7 Attack: Visualizing the Data' (*Center for Strategic and International Studies*, 19 December 2023) <https://www.csis.org/analysis/hamass-october-7-attack-visualizing-data> accessed 30 December 2024.

Austrian Review of International and European Law **28**: 119-154, 2023.
 | DOI:10.1163/15736512-02801006

massacred.[2] The attack in question was the largest attack on Jews since the Holocaust.[3] It was only a few weeks before Israel, invoking its inherent right to self-defense[4], carried out massive military strikes against Hamas in the Gaza Strip, one of the world's most densely populated areas.[5] While the military operations initially concentrated on the North, it was not long before the first air strikes also began in the South. The civilian population has undoubtedly suffered greatly as a result of this armed conflict. The humanitarian situation in the Gaza Strip has increasingly deteriorated.[6] Calls for a ceasefire grew louder and louder over time, especially as the massive air strikes on hospitals

---

2 Joel Gunter, 'Israel shows Hamas bodycam attack footage to journalists' (*BBC*, 23 October 2023) <https://www.bbc.com/news/world-middle-east-67198270> accessed 30 December 2024.

3 Jamie Dettmer, 'How the Holocaust shapes Israel's war in Gaza' (*Politico*, 2 February 2024) <https://www.politico.eu/article/how-the-holocaust-shapes-israels-war-in-gaza/> accessed 30 December 2024.

4 Elaborating on the question of whether Israel had a legitimate right to defend itself pursuant to Article 51 UN Charter would exceed the scope of this article. Suffice it to say that there is an ongoing debate as to whether Israel was entitled to invoke Article 51 UN Charter. At least some legal commentators argue that the Gaza Strip was still occupied by Israel when the latter began its military invasion in response to the terror attacks by Hamas. See, for example, Ralph Wilde, 'Israel's War in Gaza is Not a Valid Act of Self-defence in International Law' (*Opinio Juris*, 9 November 2023) <https://opiniojuris.org/2023/11/09/israels-war-in-gaza-is-not-a-valid-act-of-self-defence-in-international-law/> accessed 30 December 2024. As regards the question of whether the Gaza Strip was occupied territory at the time of Israel's invasion see also Report of the Panel of Experts in International Law: Convened the Prosecutor of the International Criminal Court (20 May 2024) <https://www.icc-cpi.int/sites/default/files/2024-05/240520-panel-report-eng.pdf> accessed 30 December 2024.

5 *Cf.* Mahar Nassar, 'The Gaza Strip – why the history of the densely populated enclave is key to understanding the current conflict' (*The Conversation*, 10 October 2023) <https://theconversation.com/the-gaza-strip-why-the-history-of-the-densely-populated-enclave-is-key-to-understanding-the-current-conflict-215306> accessed 30 December 2024.

6 For recent information on the humanitarian situation see United Nations Office for the Coordination of Humanitarian Affairs (OCHA), 'Humanitarian Situation Update – Gaza Strip' <https://www.unocha.org/publications/report/occupied-palestinian-territory/humanitarian-situation-update-203-gaza-strip#:~:text=Humanitarian%20Developments,also%20continue%20to%20be%20reported> accessed 30 December 2024.

and schools put the civilian population in ever greater danger.[7] At the same time, border closures made it increasingly difficult to get humanitarian aid to the civilian population.[8] Accusations that Israel was and still is violating international humanitarian law (IHL) or even committing war crimes and genocide with its military actions in the Gaza Strip has significantly increased in the past months. Notwithstanding, in an effort of collective self-defense against the non-state actor Hamas, numerous states have supported Israel with weapons and weapons components. This, in turn, provoked significant criticism. At numerous demonstrations across the globe, people have called for an arms embargo against Israel, as the continued use of weapons in the Gaza Strip exacerbates the challenges faced by the civilian population and further contributes to Israel's violation of international law.[9] In light of the catastrophic situation in the Gaza Strip paired with continued allegations that Israel was and still is committing serious violations of IHL or even war crimes, numerous states – for both political and legal reasons – have severely restricted or even completely stopped supplying arms to Israel, although it is not yet possible at this point to say conclusively whether and which specific norms of international law have been violated by Israel and its defence forces.[10] On 15 January 2025, Israel and Hamas, with the mediation and diplomatic support of the United States of America, Egypt, and Qatar, reached a ceasefire agreement that took effect on 19 January 2025. The agreement includes a six-week cessation of hostilities, the release of Israeli hostages in exchange for Palestinian prisoners, and a commitment to the reconstruction

---

7 Calls for a ceasefire have, finally, made it to the UN Security Council (SC). See, for example, UN Security Council Resolution 2728 (2024) 25 March 2024. In the Resolution the SC demands a ceasefire for the month of Ramadan. See also UN Security Council Resolution 2735 (2024) 10 June 2024. In the Resolution, the SC welcomes the ceasefire proposal of 31 May between Israel and Hamas.

8 United Nations Press Release, 'Humanitarian Situation in Gaza "a Moral Stain on Us All", Secretary-General Tells Security Council, Stressing International Law Must Be Respected by All' SG/SM/22310, 17 July 2024.

9 *Cf.* Middle East Monitor, 'Church group calls for German to impose arms embargo on Israel over Gaza' (19 December 2024) <https://www.middleeastmonitor.com/20241219-church-group-calls-for-german-to-impose-arms-embargo-on-israel-over-gaza/> accessed 30 December 2024.

10 Law No 185 of 9 July 1990, published in the Official Gazette No 163 of 14 July 1990. For the new implementing regulation for this law, see Ministerial Decree No 19 of 7 January 2013.

of the Gaza Strip over the next three to five years.[11] At the time of writing, whether the ceasefire agreement is successful and whether it has an impact on arms deliveries remains to be seen.

In light of these developments, this article seeks to illuminate state practice regarding the delivery of arms or arms components to Israel. Particular attention will be devoted to the Netherlands and Germany, as court rulings have already been issued in both countries where applicants have sought the revocation of export licenses or even the cessation of all arms deliveries and shipments of arms components to Israel. The comparison of these court decisions is particularly valuable for gaining insights into the application and implementation of international legal norms that generally restrict or impose conditions on arms exports to a belligerent state. For the sake of completeness, however, the practice of other states should also be examined, either because court proceedings have already taken place in this context as well, or because a state has notably opposed arms exports or the transfer of arms components to Israel, citing Israel's violations of international law.

The structure of this article is as follows. Chapter II provides a concise analysis of the provisions of international law that have been the subject of relevant national court proceedings in either Germany or the Netherlands or in both countries. As will be demonstrated, numerous provisions of international law place restrictions on the supply of weapons or weapons components to a belligerent state. However, the precise interpretation and application of these international legal norms are often contested, both in state practice and within academic discourse. This results in a lack of legal clarity, which undermines the effective implementation of international law in this context. Chapter III focuses on actual state practice. Before delving into the practices of the Netherlands and Germany – specifically examining key court decisions – this chapter will also offer a brief overview of the state practice of other states. In this context, statements by state representatives and decisions by national parliaments are considered as evidence of state practice, alongside recent judicial rulings. Chapter IV addresses the primary challenges associated with the application and enforcement of international legal norms at the national level, particularly in cases where such norms might prohibit or at least restrict the export of arms or arms components. One of the most

11 See US Embassy in Israel, Statement from Former President Joe Biden (15 January 2025) <https://il.usembassy.gov/statement-from-president-joe-biden/> accessed 10 February 2025; 'Key events that led to Israel-Hamas ceasefire deal in Gaza' (*BBC*, 19 January 2025) <https://www.bbc.com/news/articles/cvg4ryde7q5o> accessed 10 February 2025.

significant challenges is the Janus-faced nature of export licenses. On the one hand, they represent political decisions made by the respective federal government or relevant ministries. On the other hand, both international and national law impose constraints on political decision-makers, thereby influencing the scope of political discretion. When courts rule on export licenses, the judiciary intervenes – at least to some extent – in the executive's decision-making powers.

II. Weapon Deliveries to Israel: What Does International Law Say?

Before undertaking an in-depth analysis of state practice regarding the delivery of arms or arms components, it is essential to examine the key norms of international law that bind states in determining whether, and under what parameters, arms or components thereof may be supplied to a country engaged in armed conflict. The range of potentially applicable international legal norms is evidently broad. The following chapter will focus on those norms that have been the subject of national judicial proceedings, particularly in the Netherlands and Germany. These include Common Article 1 of the Geneva Conventions[12] (GC), the Arms Trade Treaty[13] (ATT), the EU Common Position on Arms Exports[14], and – at least indirectly – decisions of the International Court of Justice (ICJ) and the International Criminal

12 Geneva Convention (I) for the Amelioration of the Condition of the Wounded and Sick in Armed Forces in the Field, 12 August 1949, 75 UNTS 31; Geneva Convention (II) for the Amelioration of the Condition of Wounded, Sick and Shipwrecked Members of Armed Forces at Sea, 12 August 1949, 75 UNTS 85; Geneva Convention (III) relative to the Treatment of Prisoners of War, 12 August 1949, 75 UNTS 135; Geneva Convention (IV) relative to the Protection of Civilian Persons in Time of War, 12 August 1949, 75 UNTS 287; Protocol additional to the Geneva Conventions of 12 August 1949, and relating to the protection of victims of international armed conflicts (Protocol I), 8 June 1977, 1125 UNTS 3 (AP I GC).

13 Arms Trade Treaty, 2 April 2013, 3013 UNTS 269 (ATT).

14 European Council Common Position 2008/944/CFSP of 8 December 2008 defining common rules governing control of exports of military technology and equipment, L 335/99, 13 December 2008.

Court (ICC), respectively.[15] For the sake of completeness, it should also be noted that the United Nations General Assembly (UNGA),[16] the UN Human Rights Council[17] (HRC) and even the United Nations Security Council,[18] have issued resolutions urging both parties to the conflict – Israel on one side and Hamas on the other – to cease hostilities. The HRC has even called on arms-supplying states to restrict or even suspend the supply of arms or arms components if 'there are reasonable grounds to suspect that such goods, technologies or weapons might be used to violate or abuse human rights'.[19]

---

15 *Application of the Convention on the Prevention and Punishment of the Crime of Genocide in the Gaza Strip (South Africa v Israel)* Application Instituting Proceedings, 29 December 2023 ICJ [2023] General List No 192; *Legal Consequences Arising from the Policies and Practices of Israel in the Occupied Palestinian Territory, including East Jerusalem* [2024] <https://icj-cij.org/sites/default/files/case-related/186/186-20240719-adv-01-00-en.pdf> accessed 10 February 2025 (Advisory Opinion of 19 July 2024); International Criminal Court, Press Release, 'Situation in the State of Palestine: ICC Pre-Trial Chamber I rejects the State of Israel's challenges to jurisdiction and issues warrants of arrest for Benjamin Netanyahu and Yoav Gallant' (the actual arrest warrants are still classified as 'secret') (21 November 2024) <https://www.icc-cpi.int/news/situation-state-palestine-icc-pre-trial-chamber-i-rejects-state-israels-challenges> accessed 30 December 2024.

16 UNGA, 'Demand for ceasefire in Gaza: Draft Resolution' (5 December 2024) UN Doc A/ES-10/L.33; UNGA Res ES-10/22, 'Protection of civilians and upholding legal and humanitarian obligations' (19 December 2023) UN Doc A/RES/ES-10/22.

17 Human Rights Council, 'Human rights situation in the Occupied Palestinian Territory, including East Jerusalem, and the obligation to ensure accountability and justice: Draft Resolution' A/HRC/55/L.30, 26 March 2024.

18 UNSC Res 2728 (25 March 2024) UN Doc S/RES/2728; UNSC Res 2735 (10 June 2024) UN Doc S/RES/2735. For a detailed overview of various attempts of agreeing on a ceasefire between Israel and Hamas see Maya Nicholson, 'Tracking the U.S. Position on Gaza Through UN Security Council Resolutions' (*Lawfare*, 30 July 2024) <https://www.lawfaremedia.org/article/tracking-the-u.s.-position-on-gaza-through-un-security-council-resolutions> accessed 30 December 2024.

19 Human Rights Council, 'Human rights situation in the Occupied Palestinian Territory, including East Jerusalem, and the obligation to ensure accountability and justice: Draft Resolution' (n 17) para 13.

A. Common Article 1 of the 1949 Geneva Conventions

Common Article 1 of the GC is identical across all four Conventions and imposes an obligation on the High Contracting Parties to 'respect and ensure respect for the present Convention in all circumstances'. By the same token, Additional Protocols I[20] and III[21] to the GC employ the same terminology.[22] Furthermore, according to the study of the International Committee of the Red Cross on customary international humanitarian law, Common Article 1 is reflective of customary law.[23] Common Article 1 has been invoked as a legal foundation for potentially prohibiting third states from supplying weapons and weapons components to Israel.[24] However, certain scholarly contributions argue that Common Article 1 does not impose specific obligations on third states to reassess their export control practices.[25] At the same time, it remains uncertain whether the mere risk of an infringement is sufficient or whether an actual infringement must have been committed by the recipient state. Both

---

20 Protocol additional to the Geneva Conventions of 12 August 1949, and relating to the protection of victims of international armed conflicts (AP I GC) (n 12).

21 Protocol additional to the Geneva Conventions of 12 August 1949, and relating to the adoption of an additional distinctive emblem, 8 December 2005, 2404 UNTS 261 (AP III GC).

22 Article 1 para 1 AP I GC (n 12); Article 1 para 1 AP III GC (n 21).

23 International Committee of the Red Cross, International Humanitarian Law Database, Rule 139 'Respect for International Humanitarian Law' <https://ihl-databases.icrc.org/en/customary-ihl/v1/rule139#Fn_DD225D4C_00007> accessed 30 December 2024. The ICJ also supports this view. See *Armed Activities on the Territory of the Congo (Democratic Republic of the Congo v Uganda)* (Request for the Indication of Provisional Measures) [2000] ICJ 111 (Order of 1 July 2000) para 47.

24 See *e.g.*, Rechtbank Den Haag, Zaaknummer C/09/673870/ KG ZA 24-948 [13 December 2024] ECLI:NL:RBDHA:2024:20828, para 4.10 (unfortunately, the judgment is only available in Dutch).

25 Michael N Schmitt and Sean Watts, 'Common Article 1 of the 1949 Geneva Conventions' (*Lieber Institute Westpoint Articles of War*, 12 April 2024) <https://lieber.westpoint.edu/common-article-1-1949-geneva-conventions/> accessed 30 December 2024. For further details on Common Article 1 see Michael N Schmitt and Sean Watts, 'Common Article 1 and the Duty to "Ensure Respect"' [2020] 96 *International Law Studies* 675, 679. Nevertheless, these authors seem to represent a minority position.

the ICJ[26] and certain voices in the literature[27] are of the opinion that concrete obligations for third countries can arise from Common Article 1. By the same token, the Dutch Court of Appeal in the Hague in its decision[28] of 12 February 2024, officially acknowledged an external dimension of Common Article 1, and emphasized that a clear risk of serious violations of IHL, among others, suffices to trigger the obligation for states exporting weapons and weapons components to revoke (or at least reassess) their export licenses.[29]

B. The Arms Trade Treaty

The ATT, adopted in 2013,[30] is an international agreement that aims to regulate international trade in conventional arms and prevent their diversion

---

26 *Legal Consequences of the Construction of a Wall in the Occupied Palestinian Territory* [2004] ICJ 136, paras 158-159 (Advisory Opinion of 9 July).

27 Milanovic (n 25); Marco Sassòli, 'State Responsibility for Violations of International Humanitarian Law' (2002) 84 International Review of the Red Cross 401. Conversely, other authors argue that Common Article 1 does not impose a specific obligation on third states. This latter group primarily references the *travaux préparatoires* of the GC, asserting that these appear to 'militate against acceptance of an external compliance dimension of the obligation to ensure respect'. See *e.g.*, Robin Geiss, 'The Obligation to Respect and to Ensure Respect for the Conventions' in Andrew Clapham, Paola Gaeta and Marco Sassòli (eds) *The 1949 Geneva Conventions: A Commentary* (2015) 111 – 134, at 129. See also, ICRC Commentary to Geneva Convention I of 2016, para 120 <https://ihl-databases.icrc.org/en/ihl-treaties/gci-1949/article-1/commentary/2016?activeTab=> accessed 30 December 2024; Emily Crawford and Alison Pert, *International Humanitarian Law* (2020) 271; Marko Milanovic, 'Common Article 1 Does Prohibit Complicity in IHL Violations, Through Arms Transfers or Otherwise' (*EJIL Talk!*, 15 April 2024) <https://www.ejiltalk.org/common-article-1-does-prohibit-complicity-in-ihl-violations-through-arms-transfers-or-otherwise/> accessed 30 December 2024.

28 Gerechtshof Den Haag, Zaaknummer 200.336.130/01 [12 February 2024] ECLI:NL:GHDHA:2024:191, paras 3.12 and 5.25.

29 Johanna Trittenbach, Jessica Dorsey and Otto Spijkers, 'Dutch Appeals Court Blocks Deliveries of F-35 Parts to Israel: Overview, Analysis and Initial Reflections' (*Opinio Juris*, 15 February 2024) <https://opiniojuris.org/2024/02/15/dutch-appeals-court-blocks-deliveries-of-f-35-parts-to-israel-overview-analysis-and-initial-reflections/> accessed 30 December 2024.

30 A total of 116 states have ratified the Arms Trade Treaty (ATT), including nearly all states that supply weapons or weapons components to Israel. While the United States and Israel have not ratified the treaty, they have signed it, thereby committing themselves not to undermine its objective and purpose. See UN

to unlawful activities. The ATT imposes specific legal obligations on states regarding arms transfers, particularly concerning the sale of weapons to countries where there is a risk of human rights violations or violations of international humanitarian law. One of the most central provisions of the ATT is the requirement for exporting states to assess the potential risks associated with arms transfers. Article 6 para 3 ATT[31] explicitly prohibits states from authorizing exports if they have knowledge that the arms or items would be used to commit genocide, crimes against humanity, or grave breaches of the GC of 1949. This obligation compels states to conduct thorough risk assessments before any arms transfer, ensuring that their decisions align with international legal standards.[32] Under Article 7 para 1 lit b i and ii ATT,[33] on the other hand, exporting states are required to undertake an extensive risk assessment to determine whether the arms or items could be used to commit or facilitate serious violations of human rights or humanitarian law. This includes evaluating the recipient country's track record on human rights and the likelihood that the arms or items might be used in conflicts where they could exacerbate violence. States must also consider the broader context,

---

Treaties Database, Arms Trade Treaty <https://treaties.un.org/pages/ViewDetails.aspx?src=TREATY&mtdsg_no=XXVI-8&chapter=26> accessed 30 December 2024. See also Article 18 Vienna Convention on the Law of Treaties. Vienna Convention on the Law of Treaties, 23 May 1969, 1155 UNTS 331 (VCLT).

31 'A State Party shall not authorize any transfer of conventional arms covered under Article 2 (1) or of items covered under Article 3 or Article 4, if it has knowledge at the time of authorization that the arms or items would be used in the commission of genocide, crimes against humanity, grave breaches of the Geneva Conventions of 1949, attacks directed against civilian objects or civilians protected as such, or other war crimes as defined by international agreements to which it is a Party.'

32 *Cf.* Stuart Casey-Maslen and Gilles Giacca, 'Article 6: Prohibitions' in Stuart Casey-Maslen *et al* (eds), *The Arms Trade Treaty: A Commentary* (2016) 178ff.

33 'If the export is not prohibited under Article 6, each exporting State Party, prior to authorization of the export of conventional arms covered under Article 2 (1) or of items covered under Article 3 or Article 4, under its jurisdiction and pursuant to its national control system, shall, in an objective and non-discriminatory manner, taking into account relevant factors, including information provided by the importing State in accordance with Article 8 (1), assess the potential that the conventional arms or items: […] (b) could be used to: (i) commit or facilitate a serious violation of international humanitarian law; (ii) commit or facilitate a serious violation of international human rights law'.

including the potential for arms diversion and the capacity of the recipient state to control the weapons effectively.[34]

C. The EU Common Position on Arms Exports

The EU Common Position on Arms Exports,[35] established in 2008, was notably referenced in Dutch court proceedings aimed at blocking the issuance of export licenses for weapons and weapon components destined for Israel. According to Article 1 of the EU Common Position, '[e]ach Member State shall assess the export licence applications made to it for items on the EU Common Military List mentioned in Article 12 on a case-by-case basis against the criteria of Article 2'. Article 2 of the Common Position lists criteria to be taken into account when issuing export licenses, including '[r]espect for the international obligations and commitments of Member States, in particular the sanctions adopted by the UN Security Council or the European Union, agreements on non-proliferation and other subjects, as well as other international obligations'. Under Article 2 para 2 lit c member states shall 'deny an export licence if there is a clear risk that the military technology or equipment to be exported might be used in the commission of serious violations of international humanitarian law'. The EU Common Position is legally binding,[36] a fact that has been affirmed by various courts.[37] And yet, the issue of its primacy over national law and its direct applicability in

---

34 See also Moritz Rhades, 'Waffenlieferungen als Staatsräson?' (*Verfassungsblog*, 14 March 2024) <https://verfassungsblog.de/waffenlieferungen-als-staatsrason/> accessed 30 December 2024.

35 European Council Common Position 2008/944/CFSP (n 14).

36 The Common Position is a decision pursuant to Article 25 lit b ii TEU (Treaty on European Union) in conjunction with Article 29 TEU. Decisions are legally binding in accordance with Article 288 IV TFEU (Treaty on the Functioning of the European Union). See Treaty on European Union, C 202/3, 7 June 2016 (TEU); Treaty on the Functioning of the European Union, C 326/47, 26 October 2012 (TFEU).

37 Gerechtshof Den Haag, 12 February 2024 (n 28) para 5.32; Rechtbank Den Haag, 13 December 2024 (n 24) para 4.11; Verwaltungsgericht Berlin, 4 L 44/24 [10 June 2024] ECLI:DE:VGBE:2024:0610.4L44.24.00, paras 10-13; Verwaltungsgericht Frankfurt, 5 L 2333/24.F [11 September 2024] ECLI:DE:VGFFM:2024:0911.5L 2333.24.F.00; Verwaltungsgericht Frankfurt, 5 L 3799/24.F [16 December 2024] ECLI:DE:VGFFM:2024:1216.5L3799.24.F.00, para 16.

national court proceedings remains unresolved.[38] The Dutch Court of Appeal, for example, has classified the EU Common Position as directly applicable at the national level[39] but whether other EU member states will ascribe to the EU Common Position a similar effect or normative force depends, of course, on their respective constitutional traditions and cannot be definitively determined at this stage.

D. The Role of the International Courts and Tribunals

Alongside international treaties and EU law, domestic court proceedings in the Netherlands and Germany respectively also made reference to decisions rendered by the ICJ and the ICC to identify potentially binding obligations for states engaged in the provision of arms or components thereof. Three decisions were of particular relevance. First, the ICJ, in the case of *South Africa v Israel*, imposed provisional measures against Israel, which may also have implications for states involved in supplying arms or arms components.[40] Additionally, in July 2024, the ICJ delivered an Advisory Opinion on the legal status of Palestine, which could similarly influence the actions of arms-supplying states.[41] Lastly, in October 2024, the ICC issued arrest warrants for the sitting Israeli Prime Minister, Benjamin Netanyahu, the former Israeli Defense Minister, Yoav Gallant, and former Hamas senior member Mohammed Diab Ibrahim Al-Masri.[42] These arrest warrants could also affect export control policies and licensing decisions of states supplying arms or components thereof to Israel.

---

[38] See for example, Aurel Sari, 'Article 29' in Hermann Josef-Blanke and Stelio Mangiameli (eds) *The Treaty on European Union (TEU): A Commentary* (2013) 1017-1039; Elfriede Regelsberger and Dieter Kugelmann, 'Artikel 25' in Rudolf Streinz (ed) *EUV/AEUV* (2018) mn 5.

[39] Gerechtshof Den Haag, 12 February 2024 (n 28) para 5.32; see also Trittenbach, Dorsey and Spijkers (n 29).

[40] *Application of the Convention on the Prevention and Punishment of the Crime of Genocide in the Gaza Strip (South Africa v Israel)* [2024] ICJ (Order of 26 January) available at <https://www.icj-cij.org/sites/default/files/case-related/192/192-20240126-ord-01-00-en.pdf> accessed 30 December 2024.

[41] *Legal Consequences Arising from the Policies and Practices of Israel in the Occupied Palestinian Territory, Including East Jerusalem* (n 15).

[42] International Criminal Court, Press release (n 15).

1. *South Africa v Israel* – Request for Provisional Measures

On 29 December 2023, South Africa initiated proceedings against Israel before the ICJ.[43] South Africa's request basically centres on allegations that Israel, through its conduct in the Gaza Strip, has been violating the Genocide Convention[44] and that 'it has engaged in, is engaging in and risks further engaging in genocidal acts against the Palestinian people in Gaza'.[45] Shortly after the proceedings commenced, the Court indicated a number of provisional measures including that

> [t]he State of Israel shall, in accordance with its obligations under the Convention on the Prevention and Punishment of the Crime of Genocide, in relation to Palestinians in Gaza, take all measures within its power to prevent the commission of all acts within the scope of Article II of this Convention.[46]

Decisions of the ICJ on provisional measures are legally binding upon the parties to the proceedings.[47] Accordingly, the Court's order on provisional measures in *South Africa v Israel* is legally binding upon Israel. Third states, however, have not been explicitly addressed[48] by the Court and are thus – *prima facie* – not obliged to comply with the Court's order. However, the specific treaty in question and the relevant norms contained therein must also

---

43 *Application of the Convention on the Prevention and Punishment of the Crime of Genocide in the Gaza Strip (South Africa v Israel)* (n 40).

44 Convention on the Prevention and Punishment of the Crime of Genocide, 9 December 1948, 78 UNTS 277.

45 Luciano Pezzano, 'The Obligation to Prevent Genocide in South Africa v. Israel: Finally a Duty with Global Scope?' (*EJIL Talk!*, 4 January 2024) <https://www.ejiltalk.org/the-obligation-to-prevent-genocide-in-south-africa-v-israel-finally-a-duty-with-global-scope/> accessed 30 December 2024.

46 *Application of the Convention on the Prevention and Punishment of the Crime of Genocide in the Gaza Strip (South Africa v Israel)* (n 40).

47 *Ibid.*, para 83. See also *Allegations of Genocide under the Convention on the Prevention and Punishment of the Crime of Genocide (Ukraine v Russian Federation)* (Provisional Measures) [2022] ICJ 211, para 84 (Order of 16 March). In the LaGrand case, the ICJ for the first time confirmed that orders on provisional measures have binding effect. See *LaGrand (Germany v the United States of America)* [2001] ICJ 466, para 109 (Judgment of 27 June).

48 This would – technically speaking – also not be possible as they are not parties to the dispute.

undergo thorough analysis in order to determine whether states supplying arms or components thereof to Israel have a legal duty to reconsider or even revoke their export licenses. With respect to Common Article I in conjunction with Articles II and III of the Genocide Convention, there appears to be some support for adopting such an interpretation. In its Order, the ICJ characterized the prohibition of genocide – including the duties to prevent and punish – as an *erga omnes partes* obligation.[49] Arguably, the obligation to prevent and punish genocide obligates third states to reassess or revoke their export licenses when there is a clear risk of serious violations of IHL, among others. It is important to note that the Court employed relatively vague language in its Order concerning the genocide accusation raised by South Africa. For instance, the Court stated that

> [i]n the Court's view, the facts and circumstances mentioned above are sufficient to conclude that at least some of the rights claimed by South Africa and for which it is seeking protection are plausible. This is the case with respect to the right of the Palestinians in Gaza to be protected from acts of genocide and related prohibited acts identified in Article III, and the right of South Africa to seek Israel's compliance with the latter's obligations under the Convention.[50]

Article III, however, also obliges the parties to prevent genocide and allows for the imposition of provisional measures on this basis. That being said, the terminology employed by the ICJ does not necessarily imply that Israel is currently committing or has committed genocide.[51]

Against this background, the role of the Court's Order in the District Court proceedings of the Hague (which was decided on 13 December 2024) was mainly indirect.[52] While cited by the applicants, the Court itself simply acknowledged the existence of the ICJ's decision without, however, delving further into its legal doctrinal implications.

---

[49] *Application of the Convention on the Prevention and Punishment of the Crime of Genocide in the Gaza Strip (South Africa v Israel)* (n 40) para 33.

[50] *Ibid.*, para 54.

[51] *Cf.* Christian Walter, 'Warum Deutschland vor dem IGH dem von Südafrika gegen Israel erhobenen Vorwurf des Völkermords entgegentreten sollte' (*Völkerrechtsblog*, 11 January 2024) <https://verfassungsblog.de/warum-deutschland-vor-dem-igh-dem-von-sudafrika-gegen-israel-erhobenen-vorwurf-des-volkermords-entgegentreten-sollte/> accessed 30 December 2024.

[52] Rechtbank Den Haag, 13 December 2024 (n 24).

In Germany, the Sahra Wagenknecht Alliance (Bündnis Sahra Wagenknecht), a political party, submitted a parliamentary inquiry to the German Federal Government on 7 March 2024, referencing the ICJ's Order. The central question posed was whether the German government intended to halt the supply of weapons and weapons components to Israel in light of the ICJ ruling.[53] The German government responded as follows:

> The Federal Government decides on the granting of licenses for arms exports to Israel on a case-by-case basis and in the light of the situation after careful consideration, taking into account foreign and security policy considerations in accordance with the legal and political requirements, including consideration of obligations under international law.[54]

As the example of Germany in particular illustrates, states supplying weapons or weapons components to Israel have exercised relative caution in their interpretation and application of the ICJ's Order. In principle, Orders of the Court apply only *inter partes*, and even though the prohibition of genocide under international law arguably extends to states supplying weapons or weapons components to Israel, these states appear to fulfil their international legal duties by conducting regular assessments of the overall situation up to and including the withdrawal of permits already granted or the non-approval of new applications.

2. *Nicaragua v Germany* – Pending Proceedings in front of International Court of Justice

On 1 March 2024, Nicaragua instituted proceedings against Germany before the ICJ.[55] Nicaragua has argued that Germany, *inter alia*, is in violation of

---

[53] Deutscher Bundestag, Kleine Anfrage der Abgeordneten Sevim Dağdelen, Dr. Sahra Wagenknecht, Ali Al-Dailami, Klaus Ernst, Andrej Hunko, Christian Leye, Amira Mohamed Ali, Żaklin Nastić, Jessica Tatti, Alexander Ulrich und der Gruppe BSW, Drucksache 20/10579, para 11, 7 March 2024 <https://dserver.bundestag.de/btd/20/105/2010579.pdf> accessed 30 December 2024.

[54] Deutscher Bundestag, Antwort der Bundesregierung auf die Kleine Anfrage der Abgeordneten Sevim Dağdelen, Dr. Sahra Wagenknecht, Ali Al-Dailami, weiterer Abgeordneter und der Gruppe BSW, Drucksache 20/10806, para 11, 22 March 2024 <https://dserver.bundestag.de/btd/20/108/2010806.pdf> accessed 30 December 2024 (translation by the author).

[55] *Alleged Breaches of Certain International Obligations in respect of the Occupied Palestinian Territory (Nicaragua v Germany)* Application Instituting Proceedings, 1 March 2024, para 1.

Article 1 of the Genocide Convention by 'not only failing to prevent the ongoing genocide but by providing aid, including military equipment, to Israel that would be used in the commission of genocide, by Israel [...]'.[56] Furthermore, Nicaragua has submitted that Germany has violated Article 1 of the Fourth GC as well as 'intransgressible principles of humanitarian law', by, among others, providing (military) aid to Israel 'that would be used in the commission of genocide, crimes against humanity, grave breaches of the Geneva Conventions of 1949, attacks directed against civilian objects or civilians protected as such, or other war crimes, in violation of its duties under the 1949 Geneva Conventions and customary international law'.[57] In view of these allegations, Nicaragua requested the Court to indicate, among others, the following provisional measures: The Court should oblige Germany to cease all aid, particularly in the form of military equipment, to Israel with immediate effect. At the same time, the Court should oblige Germany to ensure that the weapons already supplied to Israel would not be used to violate international law.[58] In its Order on the request for provisional measures, the ICJ remained relatively brief and essentially limited itself to the following points: Since November 2023, there has been a significant decline in arms deliveries and military equipment for which an export license was required. In October 2023, the total value of weapons and military equipment amounted to 200 million euros, but this figure fell to 24 million euros in November 2023. In March 2024, this figure then amounted to one million euros. Germany also claimed that only four weapons licenses had been issued since 7 October 2023: two for training ammunition, one for propellant charges for test purposes and one for the export of 3,000 portable anti-tank weapons. Israel approached Germany in 2023 and requested the provision of tank ammunition, but the German government has not yet made a decision on this. Similarly, according to Germany, the decision as to whether Germany will

56 *Ibid.*, para 67.

57 *Ibid.* Other accusations concern obligations under humanitarian law (as opposed to 'intransgressible principles of humanitarian law'), 'conventional and customary law obligations including the obligation to facilitate and cooperate in bringing about the Palestinian People's right to self-determination, by providing aid and particularly military equipment to Israel that is used to deny this right of self-determination and moreover helps to maintain and impose an apartheid regime. Nicaragua's concerns were sharpened once again due to the constantly worsening situation in the Gaza Strip'.

58 *Ibid.*, paras 68-74.

provide Israel with a submarine is still open.[59] In view of these aspects, the Court came to the conclusion that it was not necessary to indicate provisional measures which would have obliged Germany, *inter alia*, to cease its export practice (both of arms, arms components and other military equipment).[60] It appears that the Court is satisfied with Germany's increasing restrictions on arms deliveries to Israel. The weapons or weapon components supplied to Israel seem to have been used either for testing purposes or had only limited military effectiveness. In the ICJ's view, this suggests that the imposition of provisional measures is not necessary.

The decision of the ICJ has played a role in proceedings before the Berlin Administrative Court.[61] In its ruling, the Court mainly reflected the position the ICJ had already taken:

> The change in the respondent's licensing practice from spring 2024 at the latest is precisely a reaction to the events and thus proves that the fears expressed by the applicants are by no means necessarily to be expected. This is also supported by the decision of the International Court of Justice (ICJ) in the case *Nicaragua v. Germany* of April 30, 2024.[62]

The applicants partially withdrew their request on their own initiative. The Administrative Court dismissed the application for interim relief concerning the remaining claims.[63] The applicants subsequently appealed this decision; however, the Higher Administrative Court rejected the appeal in an order issued on 8 August 2024.[64]

---

59 *Alleged Breaches of Certain International Obligations in respect of the Occupied Palestinian Territory (Nicaragua v Germany)* [2024] ICJ para 18 (Order of 19 July).

60 *Ibid.*, para 20.

61 Verwaltungsgericht Berlin, 10 June 2024 (n 37) para 14.

62 *Ibid.* (translation by the author).

63 *Ibid.*

64 Oberverwaltungsgericht Berlin-Brandenburg 1 S 46/24 [8 August 2024] ECLI:DE:OVGBEBB:2024:0808.OVG1S46.24.00.

3. *Legal Consequences Arising from Policies and Practices of Israel in the Occupied Palestinian Territory, Including East Jerusalem* – ICJ Advisory Opinion of 19 July 2024

The ICJ's advisory opinion[65] on the legal status of the occupied Palestinian territories has also played a role in at least one instance: the judgment of the Dutch District Court of The Hague from 13 December 2024.[66] In its advisory opinion, the ICJ, *inter alia*, determined that Israel's occupation of the Palestinian territories, including East Jerusalem, is unlawful and must be brought to an end.[67] In regard to legal consequences for all states, the Court emphasized in particular that

> all States are under an obligation not to recognize as legal the situation arising from the unlawful presence of Israel in the Occupied Palestinian Territory. They are also under an obligation not to render aid or assistance in maintaining the situation created by Israel's illegal presence in the Occupied Palestinian Territory. It is for all States, while respecting the Charter of the United Nations and international law, to ensure that any impediment resulting from the illegal presence of Israel in the Occupied Palestinian Territory to the exercise of the Palestinian people of its right to self-determination is brought to an end. In addition, all the States parties to the Fourth Geneva Convention have the obligation, while respecting the Charter of the United Nations and international law, to ensure compliance by Israel with international humanitarian law as embodied in that Convention.[68]

The Court, however, refrained from asserting that third states – for example, through revised arms export practices – are obligated to contribute to the cessation of this unlawful situation. Nevertheless, in the case decided by the Dutch District Court, the applicants advanced precisely such an interpretation.[69] The temporal scope of the advisory opinion notably did not extend to

---

65 *Legal Consequences Arising from Policies and Practices of Israel in the Occupied Palestinian Territory, Including East Jerusalem* (n 15).

66 Rechtbank Den Haag, 13 December 2024 (n 24).

67 *Legal Consequences Arising from Policies and Practices of Israel in the Occupied Palestinian Territory, Including East Jerusalem* (n 15) para 285.

68 *Ibid.*, para 279.

69 For a more in-depth analysis see Marten Zwanenburg and Johanna Trittenbach, 'Dutch District Court Judgment on Military Support to and Trade with Israel' (*Lieber Institute Westpoint Articles of War*, 23 December 2024)

the events unfolding after 7 October 2023.[70] Nevertheless, it provides for a general obligation of all states not to render aid or assistance in maintaining the situation created by Israel's illegal presence which arguably includes also arms exports (even if not expressly mentioned). In the case decided by the Dutch District Court, the applicants advanced precisely such an interpretation. The Court, however, refrained from further discussing the ICJ's advisory opinion.

4. Arrest Warrants against Benjamin Netanjahu and Yoav Galant – International Criminal Court

On 21 November 2024, the ICC issued arrest warrants against the incumbent Israeli Prime Minister Benjamin Netanyahu, former Defence Minister Yoav Galant as well as against the – presumably deceased – Hamas operative Mohammed Diab Ibrahim Al-Masri.[71] Also these played a (limited) role in the case decided by the District Court of The Hague in its judgment of 13 December 2024.[72] The primary argument advanced by the applicants was that the arrest warrants issued by the ICC, along with the substantial suspicion that both the incumbent Israeli Prime Minister and the former Israeli Defence Minister had engaged in conduct potentially constituting violations of international criminal law – whether as individuals, accomplices, or military commanders – obligated the Netherlands to completely cease arms exports for the future.[73] In its dismissal of claims, the Dutch court, however, again did not provide further details regarding the arrest warrants.

In December 2024, during interim relief proceedings before the Frankfurt Administrative Court, the applicants also invoked the ICC arrest warrants to support their argument that Germany's supply of weapons and weapon

---

<https://lieber.westpoint.edu/dutch-district-court-judgment-military-support-trade-israel/> accessed 30 December 2024.

70 *Legal Consequences Arising from Policies and Practices of Israel in the Occupied Palestinian Territory, Including East Jerusalem* (n 15) para 81.

71 International Criminal Court, Press release, 'Situation in the State of Palestine: ICC Pre-Trial Chamber I issues warrant of arrest for Mohammed Diab Ibrahim Al-Masri (Deif)' (21 November 2024) <https://www.icc-cpi.int/news/situation-state-palestine-icc-pre-trial-chamber-i-issues-warrant-arrest-mohammed-diab-ibrahim> accessed 30 December 2024.

72 Rechtbank Den Haag, 13 December 2024 (n 24) para 2.8; Zwanenburg and Trittenbach (n 69).

73 *Cf.* Zwanenburg and Trittenbach (n 69).

components to Israel constituted a violation of international law.[74] In this context, the Administrative Court stated the following:

> In addition to the previous court's statements, the issuance of arrest warrants by the International Criminal Court against Israeli Prime Minister Benjamin Netanyahu and former Defense Minister Yoav Galant on 21 November 2024 in particular cannot lead to a change in the approval situation. This is a circumstance that must be taken into account by the defendant as part of the balancing of interests but does not give the applicant direct authority to file an application.[75]

The Administrative Court Frankfurt dismissed the application on the grounds that foreign trade law does not have a third-party effect that protects individuals. The court noted that neither the right to life nor the right to physical integrity is explicitly listed as a restricted fundamental right in the Foreign Trade and Payments Act.[76]

Overall, it can be concluded that international law encompasses a broad range of relevant treaties and similar instruments, all of which have the potential to constrain state behaviour when determining whether to supply weapons or weapons components to a belligerent state. Additionally, international courts play a role in this context – both the ICJ and the ICC have issued decisions that exert at least an indirect influence on the question of whether states continue to authorize such supplies to Israel.

III. State Practice: Identifying Commonalities and Inconsistencies

Following an in-depth examination of the relevant international legal framework concerning the legality of arms deliveries to Israel, the subsequent chapter will conduct a detailed analysis of associated state practice. Admittedly, it is virtually impossible to comprehensively outline all state practice in this context. Instead, a concise overview of general trends regarding export control licenses for military equipment to Israel will be presented.

74 Verwaltungsgericht Frankfurt, 16 December 2024 (n 37) para 4.

75 *Ibid.*, para 22 (translation by the author).

76 Verwaltungsgericht Frankfurt, 16 December 2024 (n 37). See also Foreign Trade and Payments Act (FTPA) of 6 June 2013 (Federal Law Gazette I p 1482), as last amended by Article 1 of the Act of 23 May 2022 (Federal Law Gazette I p 754).

This will be followed by a focused comparison of the export control practices of the Netherlands and Germany. This comparative approach is particularly fitting, as these two states exemplify strikingly divergent practices and legal frameworks governing arms exports despite both being EU members and in principle being bound by the same international treaties.

A. General Overview of State Practice concerning Arms Transfer to Israel

The concern that Israel violates international law through its military intervention in the Gaza Strip is shared by a relatively large number of states. According to official sources, Spain, for example, has not sent any weapons or weapons components to Israel since the attack by Hamas on 7 October 2023. The Spanish government under Pedro Sánchez (who himself belongs to the Social Democratic Party) is one of the countries that has criticized Israel the most for its military intervention in the Gaza Strip. In May 2024, the government even decided to no longer allow ships transporting weapons or weapons components destined for Israel to dock in Spanish ports.[77] Italy also announced relatively soon after the start of hostilities by Israel that it would no longer supply arms to Israel. Italian law[78] prohibits the supply of weapons to countries in armed conflict. Unlike the Spanish government, the Italian government under Georgia Meloni has pledged its complete solidarity and support for Israel. However, due to the still existing and relatively strict domestic export control regulations, Italy was unable to issue further export licenses for weapons and weapons components. The Italian government is now working on a revision of the Italian export control laws, which in turn has met with criticism from many sides, as export control runs the risk of becoming too political and non-transparent, legal protection options would be

[77] Zain Hussain, 'How top arms exporters have responded to the war in Gaza' (*SIPRI*, 3 October 2024) <https://www.sipri.org/commentary/topical-backgrounder/2024/how-top-arms-exporters-have-responded-war-gaza> accessed 30 December 2024. Laura Kayali, 'Spanish PM Sánchez urges countries to stop selling arms to Israel' (*Politico*, 11 October 2024) <https://www.politico.eu/article/spanish-pm-sanchez-urges-countries-to-stop-selling-arms-to-israel/> accessed 30 December 2024.

[78] 'Italy arms exports to Israel continued despite block, minister says' (*Reuters*, 14 March 2024) <https://www.reuters.com/world/europe/italy-arms-exports-israel-continued-despite-block-minister-says-2024-03-14/> accessed 30 December 2024.

reduced and access to courts would be made more difficult for those affected.[79] Canada also announced that it would no longer supply weapons to Israel from January 2024. The decision was made by means of a non-binding vote in the House of Commons. The vote was initiated by the New Democratic Party, which supports Justin Trudeau's minority government in principle, but has expressed increasing concern about the humanitarian situation in the Gaza Strip.[80] Belgium also spoke out very early on in favour of stopping arms deliveries to Israel. It campaigned for an EU-wide ban on arms deliveries to Israel, but this was ultimately not adopted. Finally, on 6 October 2024, French President Emanuel Macron called to halt all weapon deliveries to Israel if they were intended to be used in the Gaza Strip.[81]

In addition to these political decisions, there are already a number of domestic court decisions dealing with the question of the legality of arms deliveries or the delivery of arms components to Israel. In the UK, for example, the two human rights organizations Global Legal Action Network (GLAN) and Al-Haq have made use of their right to have export licences reviewed through the courts and called for a legal review of export licences to Israel on 18 December 2023.[82] This request was rejected on 19 February 2024.[83] The applicants requested an oral hearing to explain the situation in

---

79 Giulia Carbonaro, 'Italy's government is trying to make exporting arms easier, but activists say it'd be a disaster' (*Euronews*, 11 October 2023) <https://www.euronews.com/2023/10/11/italys-government-is-trying-to-make-exporting-arms-easier-but-activists-say-itd-be-a-disas> accessed 30 December 2024; Francesco Vignarca, 'Italy: Amending current law to facilitate arms exports' (*Vignarca*, 28 February 2024) <https://www.vignarca.net/2024/02/italy-amending-current-law-to-facilitate-arms-exports/> accessed 30 December 2024.

80 Michael T Klare, 'Canada and UK Restrict Arms Sales to Israel Over Gaza War' (*Arms Control Today*, October 2024) <https://www.armscontrol.org/act/2024-10/news/canada-and-uk-restrict-arms-sales-israel-over-gaza-war> accessed 30 December 2024.

81 Ruth Comerford, Macron calls to halt arms deliveries to Israel in Gaza war' (*BBC*, 6 October 2024) <https://www.bbc.com/news/articles/cjr3zd4d8y5o> accessed 30 December 2024.

82 See Part 54 of the Civil Procedure Rules (CPR). The Civil Procedure Rules 1998 No 3132 (L. 17). There was a major amendment to these rules in 2024. The amendment has entered into force in October 2024. See the Civil Procedure (Amendment No 3) Rules 2024 No 839 (L. 11).

83 High Court of Justice, King's Bench Division, Administrative Court, The King on the Application of Al Haq and Secretary of State for Business and Trade and BAE Systems PLC, notification of the Judge's decision on the application for permission to apply for judicial review (CPR 54.11, 54.12), AC-2023-LON-003634.

more detail with the final hearing to be set for mid-2025.[84] At this stage, it is not yet possible to determine how the court will decide, however, in the past, there have indeed already been court decisions that have at least had an impact on approved export licenses. In 2019, for example, the UK Court of Appeal ruled that the export decisions regarding arms exports to Saudia Arabia had to be reviewed again by the responsible minister given the mounting evidence of severe humanitarian law and human rights violations and given the historical record of past violations by Saudia Arabia.[85] Furthermore, the Court stated that it was 'irrational and therefore unlawful' for the Secretary of State for International Trade 'to have granted licences for the export of arms to Saudi Arabia for use in Yemen without making any assessment as to whether violations of International Humanitarian Law had taken place'.[86] A new application for judicial review by the Campaign Against Arms Trade (CAAT) was rejected by the High Court of Justice handing down the request on 6 June 2023.[87] The Court opined that 'the then Secretary of State for International Trade was not acting irrationally in their decision to license arms sales to the Saudi-led Coalition'.[88] At this point, it should be noted that the Labor government has decided to suspend arms deliveries to Israel. Although only 30 of the total of 350 licenses are affected by this decision, it nevertheless shows that some reconsideration has taken place within the British government (not least due to the recent change of government).[89]

---

84 See Global Legal Action Network (GLAN), 'UK Weapons Sales to Israel' <https://www.glanlaw.org/israel-weapons-sales> accessed 30 December 2024).

85 Court of Appeal (Civil Division) on Appeal from the High Court of Justice, Queen's Bench decision, The Queen (on the application of Campaign Against Arms Trade), the Secretary of State for International Trade and Amnesty International, Human Rights Watch and Rights Watch UK, and Oxfam International, Case No T3/2017/2079, 20 June 2019.

86 High Court of Justice, King's Bench Division (n 83) para 40.

87 Campaign against Arms Trade, 'Arms Trade Campaigners Defiant after Disappointing High Court Judgment over Saudia Arabia Arms Sales' (CAAT, 6 June 2023) <https://caat.org.uk/news/arms-trade-campaigners-defiant-after-disappointing-high-court-judgment-over-saudi-arabia-arms-sales/> accessed 30 December 2024.

88 High Court of Justice, King's Bench Division, Administrative Court, Divisional Court, The King on the Application of Campaign Against Arms Trade and Secretary of State for International Trade and Mwtana for Human Rights and Oxfam, 6 June 2023, Case No CO/3579/2020.

89 The Economist, 'Britain's ban on arms sales to Israel combines politics and legalism' 5 September 2024, 26 accessed 30 December 2024.

Proceedings have also taken place in the United States of America in view of the US government's continuing arms deliveries to Israel.[90] However, the US District Court ultimately came to the conclusion that it had no jurisdiction, as the issue in question was not a legal one but a purely political one.[91] Legal proceedings have also been initiated in Canada and in Denmark, but these proceedings have not yet been concluded at the time of writing.[92]

B. Zooming In: The Netherlands

In recent months, Dutch courts have made several significant rulings regarding the export of weapons to Israel, which have brought the ethical and legal implications of such exports to the forefront. A broad distinction can be drawn between two judgments, both rendered by the District Court of The Hague. The first judgment,[93] issued on 15 December 2023, addresses whether an export license granted in 2016 for components of the F-35 fighter aircraft destined for Israel – an indefinite license in its original form – violates international law in light of the changed circumstances in Israel. The second judgment,[94] dated 13 December 2024, concerns a more general petition by the applicants seeking a prohibition on all future arms deliveries, the supply

90 See the full text of the complaint, Attorneys for Plaintiffs Defense for Children International – Palestine et al-, United States District Court for the Northern District of California, Case No 3:23-cv-5829, 13 November 2023. The Court's jurisdiction is based on 28 US Code §§ 1331 and 1350 as well as 18 USC §1091 and § 2201 *et seq.*

91 United States District Court, Northern District of California, Order Granting Motion to Dismiss and Denying Motion for Preliminary Injunction, Case No 23-cv-05829-JSW, 31 January 2024.

92 Federal Court of Canada, Hammam Farah, Hiba Farah, Ayman Oweida, XY, Canadian Lawyers for International Human Rights, Al-Haq-Law in the Service of Man vs. Minister of Foreign Affairs and Attorney General of Canada, Notice of Application to Federal Court for Judicial Review, Court File No T-473-24, 5 March 2024 <https://claihr.ca/wp-content/uploads/2024/03/2024.03.05-ISSUED-Notice-of-Application-for-Judicial-Review-_-Federal-Court.pdf> accessed 30 December 2024; Amnesty International Press Release, 'NGOs sue the Danish state to stop arms exports to Israel' <https://amnesty.dk/ngoer-sagsoger-den-danske-stat-for-at-stoppe-vabeneksport-til-israel/#eng> accessed 30 December 2024.

93 Rechtbank Den Haag, C/09/657026, KG ZA 23-991 ECLI:NL:GHDHA:2024:191 [15 December 2023] (unfortunately, the judgment is only available in Dutch).

94 Rechtbank Den Haag, 13 December 2024 (n 24).

of arms components, and any trade with companies operating in the occupied Palestinian territories. Both judgments will be briefly summarized below, followed by a detailed analysis of their principal findings.

1. Judgment of 15 December 2023 by the District Court of the Hague

On 15 December 2023, the Dutch District Court of The Hague delivered its summary judgment on the question of whether the Dutch Government, by granting export licenses for *inter alia* parts of the F-35 fighter jet, violated international law, most notably humanitarian and human rights law.[95] The proceedings were initiated by a group of NGOs including Oxfam Novib, PAX, and The Rights Forum. In its judgment, the court noted that Common Article 1 of the Geneva Conventions of 1949, the Genocide Convention and customary international law oblige states to ensure that other states comply with international law, in this case particularly international humanitarian law and the Genocide Convention. In doing so, they must make a certain effort. However, it is up to the state in question to decide how or what efforts it makes.[96] The applicants appealed against this decision.

In a landmark decision on 12 February 2024, the Court of Appeal ruled that the Netherlands was in breach of international law by continuing to export parts of the F-35 fighter jet to Israel.[97] The Dutch government initially issued a general export license.[98] This included transits of US arms exports to third countries (with transit through the Netherlands), a general export license for parts and components of the F-35 Lightning II fighter aircraft manufactured in the Netherlands, and a general export license for weapons or weapons components to European and equivalent countries other than Israel.[99] The permit has no end date but Article 8 of the export license stipulates that the permit may no longer be used if foreign policy or security considerations prohibited the continued use of the permit.[100] In light of the devastating effects of the Israeli military intervention in the Gaza Strip, the Minister for

95 Rechtbank Den Haag, 15 December 2023 (n 93).

96 *Ibid.*, paras 4.13-4.14 (translation by the author).

97 Gerechtshof Den Haag, 12 February 2024 (n 28).

98 Regeling Algemene Vergunning NL009, geraadpleegd op 05-10-2024, available at <https://wetten.overheid.nl/BWBR0038437/2021-07-31> accessed 30 November 2024.

99 For further details see Trittenbach, Dorsey and Spijkers (n 29).

100 See Regeling Algemene Vergunning NL009 (n 98).

Foreign Trade and Development Cooperation carried out a subsequent review of the export license, but ultimately came to the conclusion that it did not need to be withdrawn or at least restricted. The Court of Appeal, however, took a different view and found that the Minister would have been obliged to revoke the license. The applicable law on the basis of which the Minister should have come to this conclusion was, on the one hand, the EU Common Position, and the ATT and Common Article 1 of the Geneva Conventions on the other. As the Court reasoned, these were directly applicable due to two specific provisions, namely Articles 11(3) and 5(4) of the Strategic Goods Decree,[101] which provides that exports are to be suspended if they violate international law. However, even if this represented a significant victory for the applicants, the proceedings in question are far from concluded and are presently under consideration by the Supreme Court.

2. Judgment of 13 December 2024 by the District Court of The Hague

The judgment rendered by the Dutch Court of Appeal, as outlined above, is not only still pending in front of the Supreme Court, but there has also been a more recent, almost diametrically opposed, judgment by the District Court of The Hague in December 2024. On 13 December 2024, the District Court of the Hague dismissed a lawsuit filed by Al-Haq and nine other civil society organizations against the Dutch government.[102] The plaintiffs sought to compel the Netherlands to cease all military exports in form of a blanket ban for all future export decisions and to completely cease any cooperation with Israel as well as to prohibit trade with companies operating in Israeli settlements within the Occupied Palestinian Territory (OPT). They submitted that the Dutch government's policies violated international law by facilitating alleged Israeli transgressions against Palestinians and that this in turn, 'constitutes a tort under Dutch civil law'.[103] The District Court rejected these claims, emphasizing the Dutch state's general discretion in foreign and defence policy matters. It noted that the government was obligated to assess arms exports on a case-by-case basis, ensuring compliance with international regulations and

---

101 Decree of 3 February 2015 amending the Strategic Goods Decree in connection with the implementation of the Arms Trade Treaty concluded in New York on 2 April 2013 (Trb. 2013, 143), available at <https://www.eerstekamer.nl/behandeling/20150225/publicatie_inwerkingtreding> accessed 30 November 2024..

102 Rechtbank Den Haag, 13 December 2024 (n 24).

103 Zwanenburg and Trittenbach (n 69).

evaluating potential risks of misuse in violation of international humanitarian law.[104] The Netherlands was found to meet this obligation, as there also had been instances where export licenses were denied due to such concerns. However, an automatic ban on all future arms deliveries or deliveries of arms components – even in view of the precarious humanitarian situation in the Gaza Strip – was not tenable for the court.[105] Regarding trade with companies in Israeli settlements, the District Court highlighted the Dutch government's 'discouragement policy', which informs businesses about the illegal status of the occupied territories to prevent inadvertent involvement in human rights violations. The Court therefore concluded that the state's current trade policy was not manifestly unlawful and declined to impose a total ban on trade contacts with Israel.[106] This judgment is distinct from the one of February 2024, where the Hague Court of Appeal ordered the Dutch government to halt these exports, citing a 'clear risk' of the parts being used in ways that could violate international law. However, the case from 2023 was also different in that it involved a specific export license that did not have an end date.[107]

In summary, the District Court of The Hague upheld the Dutch government's discretion in matters of foreign policy and arms exports, provided that individual export decisions comply with international obligations. The Court's ruling underscores the importance of case-by-case assessments over blanket bans in the context of international arms trade. However, some aspects are worth noting. While the Dutch Court of Appeal in its 2023 decision dealt extensively with the applicability and normative force of common Article 1 of the GC and its effects on third states,[108] the District Court of the Hague did not mention common Article 1 at all. This aspect alone is objectionable due to the need for legal clarity.

C. Zooming In: Germany

Since the attack by the terrorist group Hamas and Israel's military intervention in the Gaza Strip, Germany has been confronted with several legal proceedings. Several NGOs, including the Berlin-based European Center for Constitutional and Human Rights (ECCHR), tried to fight German export

[104] Rechtbank Den Haag, 13 December 2024 (n 24) para 4.14.

[105] *Ibid.*

[106] *Ibid.*, paras 4.31 and 4.33.

[107] Zwanenburg and Trittenbach (n 69).

[108] Gerechtshof Den Haag, 12 February 2024 (n 28) para 5.25.

licenses through judicial means. However, this sometimes seems difficult, not least due to German domestic law and constitutionally protected principles.

1. Decision by the Administrative Court Berlin of 10 June 2024

On 11 April 2024, the ECCHR filed an urgent motion for legal protection in the name of five Palestinian nationals to stop further war weapons export licenses to Israel at the Administrative Court Berlin.[109] The request for provisional measures included past, current, and future exports of weapons or weapons components. However, on 10 June 2024, the Court rejected the motion.[110]

Before the legal opinion of the Administrative Court Berlin can be discussed in more detail, it is worth taking a look at the legal basis on which the application for provisional measures is based. In the present proceedings, the applicants are seeking a temporary injunction to restrain an administrative act – the granting of an export license for the delivery of weapons or weapons components to Israel.[111] In accordance with Article 26 para 2 of the German Constitution or Basic Law (in German: *Grundgesetz*), '[w]eapons designed for warfare may be manufactured, transported or marketed only with the permission of the Federal Government. Details shall be regulated by a federal law'.[112] The respective federal law is the War Weapons Control Act[113]

---

109 For more information see ECCHR, 'No German weapons to Israel' <https://www.ecchr.eu/en/case/no-german-weapons-to-israel/> accessed 30 December 2024.

110 Verwaltungsgericht Berlin, 10 June 2024 (n 37).

111 § 123 Verwaltungsgerichtsordnung (VwGO). Verwaltungsgerichtsordnung in der Fassung der Bekanntmachung vom 19. März 1991 (BGBl. I S. 686), die zuletzt durch Artikel 5 des Gesetzes vom 24. Oktober 2024 (BGBl. 2024 I Nr. 328) geändert worden ist. Neugefasst durch Bek. v. 19.3.1991 I 686; zuletzt geändert durch Art. 5 G v. 24.10.2024 I Nr. 328 (§ Section 123 of the Code of Administrative Court Procedure (VwGO). Administrative Court Code in the version published on March 19, 1991 (BGBl. I p. 686), last amended by Article 5 of the Act of October 24, 2024 (BGBl. 2024 I No. 328). Revised by promulgation of 19.3.1991 I 686; last amended by Art. 5 G of 24.10.2024 I No. 328) (translation by the author).

112 Grundgesetz für die Bundesrepublik Deutschland in der im Bundesgesetzblatt Teil III, Gliederungsnummer 100-1, veröffentlichten bereinigten Fassung, das zuletzt durch Artikel 1 des Gesetzes vom 19. Dezember 2022 (BGBl. I S. 2478) geändert worden ist, zuletzt geändert durch Art. 1 G v. 19.12.2022 I 2478.

113 Gesetz über die Kontrolle von Kriegswaffen in der Fassung der Bekanntmachung vom 22. November 1990 (BGBl. I S. 2506), das zuletzt durch Artikel 25

(WWCA) (in German: *Kriegswaffenkontrollgesetz*). According to Article 6 para 3 No 2 WWCA, a licence shall be denied if 'there is a reason to assume that the granting of a licence would violate the international obligations of the Federal Republic of Germany or endanger their fulfilment'.[114] Article 6 para 3 No 2 WWCA thus represents the link between the German legal system and its obligations under international law.

Based on this legal framework, the Administrative Court Berlin rejected the application for provisional measures.[115] It might have also been decisive that the German government had not issued any export licenses for weapons of war to be used on the Gaza Strip since the beginning of 2024. With regard to export licenses that had already been issued and those that will be issued in the future, the Administrative Court stated that it was not in a position to impose provisional measures with regard to future export licenses since the German legal system does not provide for purely preventive provisional measures. At least this is implicit in the Court's conclusions. The imposition of provisional measures with regard to future arms deliveries would only be possible if the authorization of arms exports is sufficiently probable and if this authorization would constitute a violation of Germany's obligations under international law.[116] With regard to past approvals for arms deliveries (*i.e.* those that took place before the Israeli military intervention in response to the Hamas attack on 7 October 2023). The Court underscored that no export licenses for weapons of war or their components had been issued since the spring of 2024. In its view, this served as evidence that the German Federal Government was continuously assessing the situation on the ground, as well

---

des Gesetzes vom 19. Dezember 2022 (BGBl. I S. 2606) geändert worden ist Neugefasst durch Bek. v. 22.11.1990 I 2506; zuletzt geändert durch Art. 25 G v. 19.12.2022 I 2606 (Act on the Control of War Weapons in the version published on November 22, 1990 (Federal Law Gazette I p. 2506), last amended by Article 25 of the Act of December 19, 2022 (Federal Law Gazette I p. 2606). New version published on November 22, 1990 I 2506; last amended by Article 25 of the Act of December 19, 2022 I 2606 (translation by the author).

114 Translation by the author.

115 For more details see also Lea Köhne and Vincent Widdig, 'A quest for transparency in arms exports: The Berlin administrative court's stance on exports of arms to Israel' (*EJIL Talk!*, 3 July 2024) <https://www.ejiltalk.org/a-quest-for-transparency-in-arms-exports-the-berlin-administrative-courts-stance-on-exports-of-arms-to-israel/> accessed 30 December 2024.

116 Verwaltungsgericht Berlin, 10 June 2024 (n 37) para 11.

as the security policy and international law implications, and was therefore not acting unlawfully.[117]

2. Decision by the Administrative Court Frankfurt of 11 September 2024

On 15 July 2024, five Palestinians from the Gaza Strip filed an application for interim relief with the Administrative Court of Frankfurt am Main. In contrast to the proceedings before the Berlin Administrative Court, the applicants did not only invoke an interest in legal protection in general to be derived from the relevant legal provisions.[118] Rather, they also emphasized that their constitutionally protected right to life within the meaning of Article 2 para 2 No 1 Basic Law was endangered by the arms deliveries in question here.[119] Another difference to the Berlin procedure relates to the distinct legal basis. While the applicants before the Berlin Administrative Court invoked the WWCA,[120] the Foreign Trade and Payments Act[121] (FTPA) (in German *Außenwirtschaftsgesetz*) was the basis for the proceedings before the Frankfurt Administrative Court.[122] While the WWCA regulates exports of weapons *per se*, the Foreign Trade and Payments Act covers 'everything

---

117 *Ibid.*, para 14.

118 Verwaltungsgericht Frankfurt, 16 December 2024 (n 37).

119 Kristoffer Burck and Vera Strobel, 'A Hands-Off Approach to International Law: The Frankfurt Administrative Court's Stance on Arms Exports to Israel' (*EJIL Talk!*, 26 September 2024) <https://www.ejiltalk.org/german-arms-exports-to-israel-the-frankfurt-administrative-court-takes-a-hands-off-approach-to-international-law/> accessed 30 December 2024; see also Max Kolter, 'Verwaltungsgericht will sich nicht in Außenpolitik einmischen' (*Legal Tribune Online*, 16 September 2024) <https://www.lto.de/recht/hintergruende/h/vg-frankfurt-51233324f-waffen-export-genehmigung-staatsraeson-israel-gaza> accessed 30 December 2024.

120 Act on the Control of War Weapons in the version published on 22 November 1990 (Federal Law Gazette I p. 2506) (translation by the author).

121 FTPA (n 76). See also special ordinance of the Federal Ministry for Economic Affairs and Climate Action (BMWK) on fees for individually attributable public services in its area of responsibility and that of the Federal Office for Economic Affairs and Export Control (BAFA) for war weapons control, export control and investment screening (Special Ordinance of BMWK and BAFA on fees for War Weapons Control, Export Control and Investment Control – BMWKBGebKAIV), 16 September 2023, FNA 202-5-24, Federal Law Gazette I 2023 No 248.

122 Burck and Strobel (n 119).

except weapons of war'.[123] This includes military equipment (such as night vision devices), but also certain ammunition and even software. According to Article 4 para 2 No 4 of the FTPA, '[i]n foreign trade and payments transactions, legal transactions and actions can be restricted and obligations to act can also be imposed by ordinance, in order to implement international agreements which, the legislative bodies have approved in the form of a Federal act'.[124] As in the proceedings before the Berlin Administrative Court, the applicants filed an application for provisional measures in accordance with Section 80 of the Administrative Court Act.[125] While the applicants in the proceedings before the Berlin Administrative Court relied on violations of international law, the applicants before the Frankfurt Administrative Court based their special interest in the granting of interim relief on their constitutionally guaranteed right to life. However, the Frankfurt Administrative Court rejected the applicants' entitlement to file an application arguing that there was no need for legal protection

3. Decision by the Administrative Court Berlin of 2 December 2024

Despite the precarious humanitarian situation in the Gaza Strip, German Chancellor Olaf Scholz announced the authorization of the delivery of additional weapons to Israel on 10 October 2024. It is noteworthy that Germany had not granted any export licenses for arms deliveries to Israel between March 2024 and August 2024. However, as of October 2024, this policy of restraint and licensing practice is set to change.[126] In light of this, several NGOs initiated legal proceedings against the Federal Chancellor's announced decision, seeking a judicial ruling that would compel the Federal Government to prohibit the authorization of weapons or weapons components to Israel in accordance with Article 6 para 3 No 2 of the WWCA.[127] This request thus aims to *preemptively* deny an impending licenses. Simultaneously, however, the applicants have also petitioned for the revocation of licenses already granted

[123] *Ibid.*

[124] Translation by the author.

[125] Verwaltungsgericht Frankfurt, 11 September 2024 (n 37).

[126] 'Scholz kündigt weitere Waffenlieferungen an Israel an' (*Zeit Online*, 10 October 2024) <https://www.zeit.de/news/2024-10/10/scholz-kuendigt-weitere-waffenlieferungen-an-israel-an> accessed 30 December 2024.

[127] Verwaltungsgericht Berlin, 4 L 801/24, ECLI:DE:VGBE:2024:1202.4L801.24.00 [2 December 2024].

since 21 August 2024, particularly the authorization for the supply of tank ammunition.[128] The court first noted that the applicant's request was essentially identical to the matter already decided by the Berlin Administrative Court in its ruling of 10 June 2024.[129] Although the proceedings concerned a specific commitment by the German Federal Chancellor, the court determined that the applicants lacked a 'qualified need for legal protection for the granting of preventive interim legal protection'.[130]

4. Decision by the Frankfurt Administrative Court of 16 December 2024

A further rejection of a request for urgent measures in relation to arms exports to Israel was delivered by the Administrative Court of Frankfurt am Main at the end of 2024.[131] In these proceedings, the applicants contended that the Foreign Trade and Payments Act incorporated a dimension of third-party protection. They argued that both the European Convention on Human Rights (ECHR)[132] and the Genocide Convention conferred upon the Act a protective effect that specifically safeguards the rights of Palestinians residing in Gaza.[133] Moreover, as the scope of the ECHR was not geographically confined to its member states, Germany was also obligated to protect the applicants in situations where actions by other states infringed upon fundamental rights. By approving the export of arms, the applicants argued that Germany was complicit in a violation of Article 2 of the ECHR. Additionally, given the prolonged violations of international law by the Israeli military in Gaza, the respondent's mere appeals to Israel to adhere to international legal standards were argued to be insufficient to effectively or adequately protect the applicant's right to life, as guaranteed under Article 2 para 2 of the Basic Law

---

128 *Ibid.*, paras 5-6.

129 *Ibid.*, para 9.

130 *Ibid.*, para 10 (translation by the author).

131 Verwaltungsgericht Frankfurt, 11 September 2024 (n 37).

132 Convention for the Protection of Human Rights and Fundamental Freedoms, 4 November 1950, 213 UNTS 221.

133 Verwaltungsgericht Frankfurt, 11 September 2024 (n 37) para 4; see also Max Kolter, 'VG Frankfurt stoppt Rüstungsexporte nach Israel nicht' (*Legal Tribune Online*, 17 December 2024) <https://www.lto.de/recht/hintergruende/h/vg-frankfurt-51379924f-eilantrag-ecchr-waffenexporte-ruestungsexporte-beschluss> accessed 30 December 2024.

and Article 2 para 1 of the ECHR.[134] In these proceedings, as in the earlier ones, the Administrative Court Frankfurt rejected the argument that the FTPA carried an individual protective effect. Instead, the Court emphasized that while Germany was bound by the international legal framework, no direct legal entitlement could be derived from it – not even on the basis of the ECHR or the right to life as enshrined in Article 2 of the German Basic Law. The Court further stated that decisions regarding export licenses are predominantly political in nature, and refrained from pre-empting such decisions in the spirit of judicial self-restraint or attributing to them an individual protective dimension.[135]

D. State Practice Compared

Both the Netherlands and Germany regard Israel as an important geopolitical partner.[136] In the case of Germany, its historical context and the declaration that the protection of Israel constitutes a *raison d'état* (Staatsräson) are additional factors that were considered – at least by the Administrative Court Frankfurt – when evaluating the permissibility of supplying weapons or weapons components to Israel.[137] Nevertheless, it should not be overlooked that the concept of *raison d'état* is a purely political one. From a legal-dogmatic perspective, such political principles should not, in fact, be incorporated into the final legal assessment when interpreting the ATT and the EU Common Position.[138] Despite the precarious humanitarian situation in the Gaza Strip and the mounting suspicions that Israeli forces have committed war crimes there, both countries have continued to supply weapons to Israel, albeit to a

134 Verwaltungsgericht Frankfurt, 11 September 2024 (n 37) para 4.

135 *Ibid.*, paras 20-23.

136 For more information on the relationship between the Netherlands and Israel and Germany and Israel respectively see, *e.g.*, Hussain (n 77). For more information on Germany see Peace Report 2024, 'A Rudderless World' <https://www.friedensgutachten.de/en> accessed 30 December 2024.

137 *Cf.* Verwaltungsgericht Frankfurt, 11 September 2024 (n 37) para 24.

138 Germany, for example, has reconsidered and even reduced arms exports to Israel but Germany does not accuse Israel of serious violations of IHL. Rather, it insists that a complete arms embargo would go too far. Riham Alkoussa, 'Germany has stopped approving war weapons exports to Israel, source says' (*Reuters*, 19 September 2024) <https://www.reuters.com/world/germany-has-stopped-approving-war-weapons-exports-israel-source-says-2024-09-18/> accessed 30 December 2024.

limited extent.[139] This underscores the significance of the judicial decisions rendered in these two countries. Two key aspects are particularly relevant in this context: individuals' access to justice in challenging export licenses and their corresponding interest in legal protection, as well as the scope of judicial review. Export licenses are fundamentally a matter of political discretion, where judicial oversight is inherently limited to safeguard the principle of the separation of powers –an aspect explicitly enshrined, at least in the German Constitution. This limitation is especially pronounced when it comes to legal challenges against *future* export decisions.

1. Access to Legal Remedies and the Existence of a Qualified Need for Legal Protection

In Germany, individuals face (and even more so interest groups) significant challenges in seeking legal remedies against export control decisions related to arms exports, primarily governed by the FTPA and the WWCA. Under the FTPA, decisions regarding the export of military goods are often made with considerable discretion by the federal government and relevant authorities. These decisions are typically not subject to public scrutiny, limiting the ability of affected individuals or organizations to challenge them. Furthermore, the FTPA lacks provisions for individuals to contest decisions, creating a gap in legal protection for those who may be adversely affected by arms exports.[140] Similarly, the WWCA governs the export of war weapons, imposing strict regulations. However, it also offers limited avenues for legal recourse. While it provides a framework for the licensing of arms exports, individuals cannot directly appeal export licensing decisions.[141] Although there is no formal legal avenue to directly challenge export licenses, administrative action – including export licenses – may be subject to judicial review under German administrative law through a request for interim legal protection. However, it should not be overlooked that, although legal protection options exist in principle, these administrative acts do not have a third-party effect. Demonstrating direct involvement is both difficult and rare. The core issue

---

139 *Ibid.*; allegedly, the Netherlands have tried to bypass the court order not to send components for the F-35 fighter jet to Israel. See NL Times, 'Dutch gov't looking for ways to continue delivering F-35 parts to Israel after court ban' (15 March 2024) <https://nltimes.nl/2024/03/15/dutch-govt-looking-ways-continue-delivering-f-35-parts-israel-court-ban> accessed 30 December 2024.

140 Burck and Strobel (n 119).

141 *Ibid.*

lies in the fact that it is particularly challenging –especially with regard to future export approvals – to substantiate a corresponding legitimate interest in legal protection. In the proceedings before the Administrative Court Berlin, which rejected the applicant's motion in its decision of 2 December 2024, the court concluded that, particularly in the context of arms deliveries to Israel, it is not possible to determine with sufficient precision whether and to what extent weapons supplied by Germany would infringe upon the applicant's rights.[142] This line of reasoning is particularly problematic in the context of future export licenses and armed conflicts, which are inherently characterized by a lack of transparency, operational ambiguity, and, at times, chaotic conditions, making it unrealistic to expect that one could determine in advance whether the supplied weapons would be used in violations of IHL or human rights law. This leaves only the possibility of retrospective legal recourse. However, in the specific context of armed conflict, such recourse may already come too late to preserve human life. Therefore, there is a pressing need for reforms to – potentially – allow individuals to fight export licenses even before they are being issued. This would at least make sense where individuals have knowledge about the issuance of future export licenses and where they can prove that they have a legitimate and qualified interest in legal protection.[143] In the Netherlands, there is also a legal possibility to fight export licenses – at least those that have already been issued – *e.g.* by way of tort action. The legal basis for this is paragraph 6:162 of the Dutch Civil Code which, in contrast to Germany, also allows for class action.[144] The fundamental issue, therefore, is not the theoretical absence of legal avenues to contest export licenses in court. Rather, it often concerns the lack of a sufficiently substantiated need for legal protection. While the Dutch court acknowledged that the applicants had a legitimate and qualified interest in legal protection in the case concerning the export license for components of the F-35 fighter aircraft, the Court argued that the applicants did not have a legitimate and qualified interest in legal protection in the case of December 2024.[145] This is precisely because those proceedings addressed future and even potential (*i.e.*, not yet foreseeable) arms deliveries or the provision of weapons.

142 Verwaltungsgericht Berlin, 2 December 2024 (n 127) para 10.

143 *Ibid.*

144 6:162 Burgerlijk Wetboek, Geraadpleegd op 04-02-2025, Geldend van 01-09-2017 t/m 30-06-2018 (in English: 6:162 Civil Code, Accessed 04-02-2025, Valid from 01-09-2017 to 30-06-2018) (translation by the author).

145 Rechtbank Den Haag, 15 December 2023 (n 93)

2. Challenging Export Licences in Judicial Proceedings – Politics before law?

Another noteworthy aspect is how the courts in both countries dealt with the area of tension between politics and law. Both the Administrative Court Frankfurt and the Administrative Court Berlin emphasized that the issuance of export licenses constitutes a political decision, warranting judicial self-restraint on the part of the courts.[146] German courts limited their judicial review – partly due to the principle of separation of powers – to the question of whether export licenses were issued arbitrarily.[147] Another issue is that the applicants in various proceedings before German courts primarily sought to prevent future arms deliveries or the transfer of arms components to Israel. However, the German legal system, in accordance with the principle of the separation of powers, only provides for judicial oversight of administrative actions in a retrospective manner. In this context, the Berlin Administrative Court stated:

> The Administrative Court Code is designed for the provision of subsequent legal protection, as effective legal protection (Art. 19 para. 4 sentence 1 GG) can, in principle, be adequately ensured through subsequent – if necessary, also interim – legal protection. Moreover, subsequent legal protection better upholds the constitutionally enshrined principle of the separation of powers, as preventive legal protection generally imposes greater restrictions on the executive's scope of action within the legal framework.[148]

Nonetheless, the Administrative Court emphasized that the determination of whether interim legal protection may also be granted as a preventive measure must be made on a case-by-case basis, requiring an individual assessment of the relevant circumstances.[149] It remains doubtful, however, whether a reconsideration of this approach can be expected in German legal practice. In contrast, the Dutch Court in its decision from December 2024 drew the boundary of judicial review authority at the point where, in the view of the

146 Verwaltungsgericht Frankfurt, 11 September 2024 (n 37) para 13; Verwaltungsgericht Berlin, 10 June 2024 (n 37) para 4. The Verwaltungsgericht Berlin even referenced the constitutionally recognized principle of separation of powers. See Article 20 para 2 German Basic Law.

147 See Verwaltungsgericht Berlin, 10 June 2024 (n 37).

148 Verwaltungsgericht Berlin, 2 December 2024 (n 127) para 10 (translation by the author).

149 *Ibid.*

applicants, export licenses are to be categorically and universally denied.[150] Ultimately, this does not imply that law must yield to politics. Rather, in both countries, a balance must be struck between these two spheres of action.

IV. Conclusion

The armed conflict between Israel and Hamas has posed profound challenges to the international community as a whole. This is particularly true for states that have previously supplied weapons or weapon components to Israel or were, at a minimum, in a position to do so. However, in light of the extensive nature of Israeli operations in the Gaza Strip, the immense suffering of the Palestinian civilian population, and allegations of violations of international humanitarian law and the commission of war crimes, many states have re-evaluated their licensing practices.

The granting of export licences for arms deliveries and components is far from a straightforward matter, as it operates within the complex intersection of law and politics. Nonetheless, numerous states took early action to halt arms shipments and the supply of weapon components to Israel. The comparison of state practice, particularly between the Netherlands and Germany, underscores the challenges of effectively enforcing international legal norms in the realm of arms transfers. While the Netherlands offers more robust avenues for judicial scrutiny and individual appeal, Germany's approach places greater emphasis on political discretion. However, despite significant differences in legal frameworks and access to remedies, both countries grapple with the tension between politics and law, underscoring the inherent tension between judicial oversight and executive authority in export licensing decisions. These cases reveal that international law remains a crucial yet contested benchmark for regulating arms exports to belligerent states, especially in contexts where violations of humanitarian law are alleged.

Ultimately, the findings of this article call for a more consistent application of international legal standards across jurisdictions. Strengthening judicial mechanisms and ensuring greater transparency in arms export processes are vital steps toward reconciling the demands of law with the realities of geopolitics. Only through such measures can states uphold their international obligations while addressing the humanitarian and legal challenges posed by arms transfers to conflict zones.

---

[150] Rechtbank Den Haag, 13 December 2024 (n 24).

Current Developments

The Austrian Position Paper on Cyber Activities and International Law – A Commentary

Isabella E Brunner | Postdoctoral Researcher at The Hague Program on International Cybersecurity, Faculty Governance and Global Affairs, Leiden University, i.brunner@fgga.leidenuniv.nl

Abstract

Recently, Austria joined the ever-increasing number of states who have published their national positions on how international law applies to cyber activities. This commentary addresses some remarkable aspects of the position, which includes Austria's views on 'cyberspace' itself, cyber espionage, attribution, collective countermeasures, preventive cyber measures, privileges and immunities of international organizations and diplomatic and consular missions, as well as International Criminal Law.

Keywords

Cyber activities – state practice and *opinio juris* – cyberspace – cyber espionage – state responsibility – attribution – countermeasures – privileges and immunities – international criminal law

I. Introduction

In April 2024, Austria published its national position paper on 'Cyber Activities and International Law'.[1] With that, it joined a continuously growing number of states who wish to clarify their national views on how international law applies to the cyber context (at the time of writing, around 30 national positions were already published).

[1] Austria, 'Position Paper of the Republic of Austria: Cyber Activities and International Law' (April 2024), <https://docs-library.unoda.org/Open-Ended_Working_Group_on_Information_and_Communication_Technologies_-_(2021)/Austrian_Position_Paper_-_Cyber_Activities_and_International_Law_(Final_23.04.2024).pdf> last accessed 7 January 2025.

Austrian Review of International and European Law **28**: 157-172, 2023.
 | DOI:10.1163/15736512-02801007

Since 2018, states – largely those from the Global North – have been publishing these views,[2] in an attempt to strengthen their argument that existing international law applies to the cyber context. These positions mainly seek to enlighten readers how international law applies and weaken the argument by some states (including the Russian Federation) that a new treaty on state conduct in cyberspace is necessary.[3] The national positions are also important, as they reflect states' own views on international law in the cyber context. While the Tallinn Manual processes – under the auspices of NATO, which led to the publication of two manuals (a third one is currently in progress[4]) written by an international group of (academic) experts laying out how international law applies to the cyber context[5] – are great initiatives, ultimately international law is made by states. Thus, these national positions are highly valuable additions to the debate in practice.

The Austrian position paper is 22 pages long and has 14 sections. While not entirely unique in its approach, it nonetheless contains some noteworthy aspects which will be explained in more detail in this article. This includes, amongst other things, Austria's view on 'cyberspace' more broadly, its views on cyber espionage, its approach with regard to collective countermeasures, as well as its views on privileges and immunities of international organizations and diplomatic and consular missions (the first state to address this topic). It

2 Yohannes Eyenew Ayalew and Yuval Shany, 'The 2024 AU Common Position on the Application of International Law in the Cyberspace: Some Implications for the Development of Digital Human Rights' (EJIL:Talk!, 15 November 2024) <www.ejiltalk.org/the-2024-au-common-position-on-the-application-of-international-law-in-the-cyberspace-some-implications-for-the-development-of-digital-human-rights/> last accessed 7 January 2025.

3 The Russian Federation has been pushing the idea of a UN-wide treaty on 'information security' for several years now. Most recently, on 3 December 2024, it re-published its updated concept for a treaty, with six co-sponsors, see Russian Federation, 'Updated Concept of the Convention of the United Nations on Ensuring International Information Security: Proposal of the Russian Federation' (3 December 2024) <https://docs-library.unoda.org/Open-Ended_Working_Group_on_Information_and_Communication_Technologies_-_(2021)/ENG_Concept_of_convention_on_ensuring_international_information_security.pdf> last accessed 7 January 2025.

4 NATO CCDCOE, 'CCDCOE to Host the Tallinn Manual 3.0 Process' (2020) <https://ccdcoe.org/news/2020/ccdcoe-to-host-the-tallinn-manual-3-0-process/> last accessed 7 January 2025.

5 Michael N Schmitt, *Tallinn Manual on the International Law Applicable to Cyber Warfare* (2013); Michael N Schmitt and Liis Vihul (eds), *Tallinn Manual 2.0 on the International Law Applicable to Cyber Operations* (2017).

should be noted that the present author had the honour to draft the position paper; however, views expressed in this commentary are entirely the author's.

II. Austria's Use of Examples and Key Positions

Structure-wise, an interesting, and indeed quite unique, aspect of the Austrian position paper is that it makes ample use of examples on how traditional rules of international law apply to the cyber context. The examples help better understand the often quite technical and theoretical aspects of such positions and enables readers to better grasp incidents when such rules might be broken in the cyber context. While other national positions have at times made use of scenarios to illustrate their point,[6] these are relatively rare. The use of such examples is also a commitment to demystify the rules of international law more generally, which are often held to be quite complex – especially among non-lawyers who have to deal with these issues in political discussions. For instance, since 2019, it has been repeatedly noted during the sessions of the UN Open-Ended Working Groups on Cyber Issues that the development of scenarios would help diplomats better understand how international law applies to the cyber context.[7]

In addition, key positions throughout the position paper – put into a rectangular frame on top of each section – outline the most important points of each thematic issue. That way, the reader gets a better grasp of what the priorities of Austria are. Austria may have drawn inspiration from the Norwegian position paper here, as the latter contains 'key messages' throughout the text, which also highlight the most important points and views.[8]

---

6 See *e.g.*, Australia's quite elaborate use of scenarios in its national position, UNGA, 'Official compendium of voluntary national contributions on the subject of how international law applies to the use of information and communications technologies by States submitted by participating governmental experts in the Group of Governmental Experts on Advancing Responsible State Behaviour in Cyberspace in the Context of International Security Established Pursuant to General Assembly Resolution 73/266' (13 July 2021) UN Doc A/76/136*, 3ff.

7 Notes of the sessions are with the present author.

8 Vibeke Musæus, 'Norway's Position Paper on International Law in Cyberspace' (2023) 92 Nordic Journal of International Law 470.

III. Austria's Position on 'Cyberspace'

One uniqueness of the Austrian position paper already becomes apparent in its title: 'Cyber Activities and International Law'. This is a slight divergence from other positions, which tend to refer to 'cyberspace' when discussing international law's application (or applicability) to the cyber context.[9] The position, in its section on General Remarks, clarifies the choice of its title, and its views on this issue more broadly, by noting:

> All references to 'cyberspace' have been deliberately omitted in view of the fact that all cyber activities do not take place in a separate 'virtual space', but in the real world.[10]

This is a particularly unique position, as especially Western countries (including most importantly NATO members) like to refer to 'cyberspace' as a new and separate 'domain' next to air, land, and sea.[11] The Austrian position paper counters this assumption, and there might be various reasons for that, which include the following.

---

9 See, *inter alia*, Canada, 'International Law Applicable in Cyberspace' <www.international.gc.ca/world-monde/issues_development-enjeux_developpement/peace_security-paix_securite/cyberspace_law-cyberespace_droit.aspx?lang=eng> last accessed 7 January 2025; Costa Rica, 'Costa Rica's Position on the Application of International Law in Cyberspace' <https://docs-library.unoda.org/Open-Ended_Working_Group_on_Information_and_Communication_Technologies_-_(2021)/Costa_Rica_-_Position_Paper_-_International_Law_in_Cyberspace.pdf> last accessed 7 January 2025; Germany, 'On the Application of International Law in Cyberspace' <www.auswaertiges-amt.de/resource/blob/2446304/32e7b2498e10b74fb17204c54665bdf0/on-the-application-of-international-law-in-cyberspace-data.pdf> last accessed 7 January 2025; The Netherlands, 'Appendix: International law in cyberspace' <https://www.government.nl/binaries/government/documenten/parliamentary-documents/2019/09/26/letter-to-the-parliament-on-the-international-legal-order-in-cyberspace/international-law-in-the-cyberdomain-netherlands.pdf> last accessed 7 January 2025; Switzerland, 'Switzerland's position paper on the application of international law in cyberspace' <https://www.eda.admin.ch/content/dam/eda/en/documents/aussenpolitik/voelkerrecht/20210527-Schweiz-Annex-UN-GGE-Cybersecurity-2019-2021_EN.pdf> last accessed 7 January 2025.

10 Position Paper (n 1) 3.

11 See, *inter alia*, NATO CCDCOE, 'NATO Recognises Cyberspace as a "Domain of Operations" at Warsaw Summit', <https://ccdcoe.org/incyder-articles/nato-recognises-cyberspace-as-a-domain-of-operations-at-warsaw-summit/> last accessed 7 January 2025.

As Austria explicitly points out, the reference to 'cyberspace' suggests a 'virtual space' with no actual attachment to the 'real world'. In the present author's opinion, Austria is correct in this assumption. As William Gibson, who has largely been held to be the author of the term 'cyberspace' – at least what we understand of it today (there are views that the term was coined already earlier[12]) – has said:

> All I knew about the word 'cyberspace' when I coined it, was that it seemed like an effective buzzword. It seemed evocative and essentially meaningless. It was suggestive of something, but had no real semantic meaning, even for me, as I saw it emerge on the page.[13]

Figure 1: ChatGPT's rendering of an image of 'cyberspace'. The description accompanying the image was: 'a high-tech visual representation of cyberspace, showing interconnected digital pathways and holographic data streams.'

---

[12] Talita Dias and Antonio Coco, *Cyber Due Diligence in International Law* (2022) 32f.

[13] William Gibson in the documentary, 'No Maps for These Territories' in 2000.

When thinking about the term 'cyberspace', often a space, similar to outer space, comes to mind, which seems largely detached from our 'offline' world, suggesting that 'cyberspace' is an entirely separate sphere. In fact, when the present author asked ChatGPT, a large language model, to create an image of 'cyberspace' it rendered an image depicted in Figure 1. The image shows a grid (which suggests to represent a network) floating in something that looks like the universe. It certainly does not show the cable infrastructure necessary to connect computers with each other, or servers located on physical territory (on Earth), or even satellite infrastructure (in outer space) enabling internet connectivity.

In contrast, what the Austrian position seeks to show is that cyber activities make use of a realm of physical infrastructure: the 'cyberspace' is in fact a combination of cables, servers, computers and other hardware that together enables us to connect with each other online. This necessary attachment to physical infrastructure shows that, as such, cyberspace is, in fact, not a space detached from our 'offline world', but a space which is very much rooted within our physical world, and capable of being touched and interacted with.[14] It is thus not a lawless space but can be regulated – also under international law.

While, arguably, the reference to 'cyber activities' is equally elusive, use of the word 'activities' demonstrates more clearly that international law can regulate specific acts conducted by states or non-state actors attributable to them, and that many activities, if not all, can be controlled through law.

IV. Cyber Espionage as a Violation of State Sovereignty

Another noteworthy pronouncement is Austria's opinion that cyber espionage activities can, under certain circumstances, violate a state's sovereignty.[15] Apart from Austria, there are five other states who have spoken out about the issue of cyber espionage. These are Brazil, Canada, Costa Rica, New Zealand, and Norway.[16] While Canada, New Zealand, and Norway note that

---

14 *Cf.* also Dias and Coco (n 12) 10, who note that '"cyberspace" is not a separate domain, but a set of digital technologies that pervade all traditional domains of land, air, sea and outer space'.

15 Position Paper (n 1) 4.

16 UNGA, 'Official compendium of voluntary national contributions on the subject of how international law applies to the use of information and communications technologies by states' (n 6) 18 (Brazil); Canada, 'International Law Applicable in

cyber espionage does not constitute a violation of international law,[17] Austria, Brazil, and Costa Rica provide a more nuanced opinion about cyber espionage and how it relates to the rule of sovereignty.[18]

Austria appears to accept the violation of a state's sovereignty through cyber espionage activities if it leads to a similar result as a cyber operation that leads to a temporary loss of functionality or temporary loss of access to essential governmental services.[19] This view can be explained by the fact that the paper notes that limited 'intrusions leading to [...] the temporary loss of functionality of critical infrastructure within a state or a cyber activity that temporarily prevents access to essential governmental services' may violate a state's sovereignty, and then immediately notes that '[s]imilarly, cyber espionage activities, including industrial espionage against corporations, within a state's territory may also violate the state's sovereignty.'[20] The example provided in the paper further clarifies:

> State A initiates a cyber espionage activity against the Foreign Ministry of state B for the purpose of obtaining illegal access to the internal communication and information system. When state B discovers that its system is compromised, it is required to conduct a total shutdown of the system and temporarily establish an alternative while the IT system is cleaned and restored. Such a cyber activity would constitute a violation of state B's sovereignty.[21]

Cyberspace' (n 9) para 19; Costa Rica, 'Costa Rica's Position on the Application of International Law in Cyberspace' (n 9) para 22; New Zealand, 'The Application of International Law to State Activity in Cyberspace' (December 2020) <www.dpmc.govt.nz/publications/application-international-law-state-activity-cyberspace> last accessed 7 January 2025, para 14; Musæus (n 8) 477, footnote 15.

17 Canada, 'International Law Applicable in Cyberspace' (n 9) para 19; New Zealand, 'The Application of International Law to State Activity in Cyberspace' (n 16) para 14; Musæus (n 8) 477, footnote 15.

18 Position Paper (n 1) 4f; UNGA, 'Official compendium of voluntary national contributions on the subject of how international law applies to the use of information and communications technologies by states' (n 6) 18 (Brazil); Costa Rica, 'Costa Rica's Position on the Application of International Law in Cyberspace' (n 9) para 22.

19 Position Paper (n 1) 4; the latter would, in the present author's view, arguably automatically lead to a loss of the former, as a loss of access would mean that the infrastructure would not function properly.

20 *Ibid.*, 4.

21 *Ibid.*, 5.

The example provided shows a similar result (if not identical) of a temporary loss of functionality (*i.e.* loss of access), namely the necessary total shutdown of the computer system. With this example, Austria shines light on the highly problematic elements of cyber espionage, that, once a cyber espionage activity has been discovered, a state will have to take any feasible measures to end the activity and to secure their systems. Moreover, while it may become apparent that a hostile cyber activity eventually constitutes cyber espionage (and thus, in the eyes of some states, is lawful), this activity could also be considered so-called 'pre-positioning'[22] or the preparatory steps to other hostile, more disruptive acts. However, even if the cyber activity was merely an act of espionage, especially when it affected a ministry such as the ministry of foreign affairs, the consequences can still be severe. In particular, as demonstrated in the example in the position paper, a detection could potentially mean having to shut down governmental servers temporarily, which would result in the ministry not functioning properly for some time. That pure espionage activities can cause potential devastating harm is also demonstrated by China's hack of the US Office of Personnel Management in 2015, where Chinese state officials were able to steal sensitive data of US government personnel, including top secret information about US intelligence staff.[23] The damage done through this and other hacks by the Chinese was estimated to take the US decades to undo,[24] and – in the case of the intelligence officials – might not be mended at all.

Given that, so far, states have either not directly made statements on espionage, or, to the contrary, have noted that cyber espionage activities *per se* do not violate international law, the Austrian position is quite a bold move. Although Austria certainly stops short of saying that acts of cyber espionage always violate international law, it still has opened the possibility that some of them, especially when linked to a temporary loss of functionality or access

22 Pre-positioning can be defined as 'the process by which computer code is installed on the network or system of a rival state, to allow for future hostile cyber activity if required', see Juliet Skingsley, 'Cyber-Rattling: Can "Pre-Positioning" in Cyberspace Amount to a Threat of the Use of Force Under Article 2(4) of the United Nations Charter?' (2024) 11 Journal on the Use of Force and International Law 50, 50.

23 Brendan I Koerner, 'Inside the Cyberattack that Shocked the US Government' (*Wired,* 23 October 2016) <www.wired.com/2016/10/inside-cyberattack-shocked-us-government/> last accessed 7 January 2025.

24 Garrett M Graff, 'China's Hacking Spree Will Have a Decades-Long Fallout' (*Wired,* 11 February 2020) <www.wired.com/story/china-equifax-anthem-marriott-opm-hacks-data/> last accessed 7 January 2025.

to governmental systems (or having similar effects), have the potential to violate a state's sovereignty.

Reasons for Austria's clear stance on this issue may include its considerably smaller size in population, and thus its reduced geopolitical relevance (*i.e.* its actions are arguably not put under the same scrutiny as are, for instance, the actions of the US, China or Russia), as well as it being a strong proponent of the rule of law. Yet, with openly positioning itself this way, Austria may also risk isolating itself from other, like-minded, states who wish to leave this issue in a legal 'grey zone'.

Nonetheless, it is undoubtedly commendable that Austria addresses the growing problem of lack of regulation in this field and, as noted above, the potential harm cyber espionage incidents are capable of causing.

V. State Responsibility

On state responsibility, there are three issues which are particularly interesting: First, Austria's explicit reference to the 'effective control' standard required for attribution of non-state actors to a state. Second, Austria's views on collective countermeasures, and third, Austria's views on preventive cyber measures.

A. Austria and the 'Effective Control' Attribution Standard

Austria is also (unlike many other states) very clear on the legal attribution of cyber activities conducted by non-state actors to a state. While the attribution of cyber activities by state organs to the state is straightforward,[25] there has been a long-standing debate which activities conducted by non-state actors shall be attributable to the state and which standard of control should be applied, both in and outside the cyber context. The cyber context has exacerbated the issue of attribution, as some states are held to largely sanction non-state actors' cyber activities against other states.[26] This has led some

---

25 According to Article 4 ILC Articles on Responsibility of States for Internationally Wrongful Acts, '[t]he conduct of any State organ shall be considered an act of that State under international law', ILC, 'Draft Articles on Responsibility of States for Internationally Wrongful Acts, with Commentaries' (2001) UN Doc A/56/10, at 26, 40.

26 *Cf.* Tim Maurer, *Cyber Mercenaries: The State, Hackers, and Power* (2017) in particular at 123ff.

commentators to argue for the lowering of the threshold of control required to attribute non-state actors to the state.[27]

Austria is remarkably clear that the control standard required remains 'effective control', also in the cyber context. It thus aligns itself with the International Court of Justice's (ICJ) view on this matter more generally (outside of the cyber context), and rejects the propositions made by some academics to lower the threshold to 'overall control' or an even lower threshold.

In short, although the ICJ, in the *Nicaragua* case, found that 'effective control', *i.e.* control over each and every act of a non-state actor, is required for that act to be attributable to a state,[28] the International Criminal Tribunal for the Former Yugoslavia (ICTY) in the *Tadić* case suggested that, at least for organized and hierarchically structured groups, an 'overall control' standard, *i.e.* a lower-level standard would suffice.[29] Although after that, the ICJ, in the *Bosnian Genocide* case, rejected this view and clarified once more that 'effective control' would be required,[30] this debate opened up questions whether 'effective control' might be too stringent of a standard.

With its clear endorsement of the 'effective control' standard, Austria joins four other states who have made similarly clear references.[31] In contrast, no

---

[27] See, *inter alia*, Scott J Shackelford, 'From Nuclear War to Net War: Analogizing Cyberattacks in International Law' (2009) 27 Berkeley Journal of International Law 191, 233ff; David J Ryan *et al*, 'International Cyberlaw: A Normative Approach' (2011) 42 Georgetown Journal of International Law 1161, 1187f; Nicholas Tsagourias and Michael Farrell, 'Cyber Attribution: Technical and Legal Approaches and Challenges' (2020) 31 European Journal of International Law 941, 962ff; Nicholas Tsagourias, 'Cyber Attacks, Self-Defense and the Problem of Attribution' (2012) 17 Journal of Conflict and Security Law 229, 238ff; Peter Margulies, 'Sovereignty and Cyberattacks: Technology's Challenge to the Law of State Responsibility' (2013) 14 Melbourne Journal of International Law 496.

[28] *Military and Paramilitary Activities in and Against Nicaragua (Nicaragua v United States of America)* (Merits) [1986] ICJ 14, para 115 (Judgment of 27 June).

[29] ICTY, *Prosecutor v Duško Tadić*, IT-94-1-A, Appeals Chamber, Judgement, 15 July 1999, para 120.

[30] *Application of the Convention on the Prevention and Punishment of the Crime of Genocide (Bosnia and Herzegovina v Serbia and Montenegro)* (Merits) [2007] ICJ 43, paras 402-407 (Judgment of 26 February).

[31] These are Brazil, Ireland, the Netherlands, and Norway, see UNGA, 'Official compendium of voluntary national contributions on the subject of how international law applies to the use of information and communications technologies by states' (n 6) p 21 (Brazil); Ireland, 'Position Paper on the Application of International Law in Cyberspace' (July 2023) <www.dfa.ie/media/dfa/ourrolepolicies/interna-

state has yet explicitly suggested the lowering of the threshold, despite some states using particularly ambiguous wording. Nonetheless, this suggests that there is currently no interest in the lowering of this particular standard of control, which aligns with the ICJ's view that acts of non-state actors should only be attributed to the state in the most exceptional circumstances.[32] It also makes sense, as states clearly do not wish to broaden their responsibility for acts over which they did not necessarily have specific control. Austria's clarification helps further solidify this view.

B. Austria and Collective Countermeasures

As for collective countermeasures, Austria is part of the more 'progressive' camp of states who have spoken out in favour of the possibility to take collective countermeasures under very strict conditions. Austria notes as follows:

> Austria holds the view that states may also take collective countermeasures against a state that breaches an obligation *erga omnes,* i.e. an obligation owed to the international community as a whole [...], e.g. against a state that commits acts of aggression or genocide, especially if the directly injured state has requested the assistance of other states. Cyber activities would rarely breach such an obligation. However, a public cyber campaign attributable to a state that calls for acts of violence against a national, ethnical, racial or religious group with the intention to destroy this group, could amount to public incitement to commit genocide in violation of Art. III(c) of the Genocide Convention. However, in such cases, the principle of proportionality [...] poses significant limitations to the exercise of collective countermeasures and must at all times be taken into account.[33]

With this view, Austria joins six other states (Costa Rica, Denmark, Estonia, Ireland, New Zealand, and Poland) who have spoken out positively about the possibility to take some sort of measures, either collectively, or on behalf of another state. On the contrary, two states, Canada and France, have negated this possibility, at least for now. As to those seven states open to collective countermeasures, there are two distinct camps, however. There are those

tionallaw/Ireland---National-Position-Paper.pdf> last accessed 7 January 2025, at 5-6, para 22; The Netherlands, 'Appendix to the Letter to the Parliament on the International Legal Order in Cyberspace: International Law in Cyberspace' (n 9) at 6; Musæus (n 8) 482.

32 *Bosnian Genocide* (n 30) para 406.

33 Position Paper (n 1) at 9.

states which find that countermeasures could be taken in aid of another state, no matter the breach of the obligation, versus those states which only see the possibility of taking collective countermeasures in case of a breach of an *erga omnes* obligation. Austria belongs to the latter of the two camps.[34]

C. Austria and Preventive Cyber Measures

Lastly, Austria, very briefly, addresses the issue of what it terms 'preventive cyber measures'. It notes:

> Preventive cyber measures, prior to the commission of an internationally wrongful act conducted by or attributable to a state, such as exploiting vulnerabilities in other states' ICT networks and placing 'logic bombs' therein, cannot be justified under the law of state responsibility.[35]

This position aligns with the requirements stipulated in the ILC Articles on Responsibility of States for Internationally Wrongful Acts that countermeasures may only be used to induce a state to cease its wrongful conduct.[36] This means that any measures taken before that latter state has committed an internationally wrongful act are strictly unlawful. This position appears to speak strongly against suggestions made by other states, in particular the United States of America that, in the cyber context, states should be able to take 'proactive' defensive measures such as hacking an adversarial state's computer systems in order to prevent those adversaries from hacking your systems first.[37]

---

[34] On collective cyber countermeasures, see, *inter alia,* Samuli Haataja, 'Cyber Operations and Collective Countermeasures under International Law' (2020) 25 Journal of Conflict & Security Law 33; Jeff Kosseff, 'Collective Countermeasures in Cyberspace' (2020) 10 Notre Dame Journal of International & Comparative Law 18; Isabella Brunner, '1998: UNGA Resolution 53/70 "Developments in the Field of Information and Telecommunications in the Context of International Security" and Its Influence on the International Rule of Law in Cyberspace' (2020) 23 Austrian Review of International and European Law 183, 198.

[35] Position Paper (n 1) at 9.

[36] ILC Articles on State Responsibility (n 25) Commentary to Chapter II, at 128, para 1.

[37] See, *e.g.*, the United States' 'Defend Forward' strategy, first elaborated in its 2018 Cyber strategy, United States Department of Defense, 'Cyber Strategy: Summary' (2018) <https://media.defense.gov/2018/Sep/18/2002041658/-1/-1/1/cyber_strategy_summary_final.pdf> last accessed 7 January 2025, at 1.

VI. Diplomatic and Consular Missions, International Organizations and Data Embassies

Austria is the first state to have a section dedicated entirely to the privileges and immunities of diplomatic and consular missions, as well as international organizations (IOs) in the context of cyber activities. This is highly commendable, as this area of international law has, so far, been largely overlooked by academics and states alike. Nonetheless, with an ever-increasing number of cyber operations being conducted against both diplomatic missions as well as IOs,[38] it becomes more and more important to understand how existing rules apply to the cyber context in this area.

The Austrian position makes clear that Information and Communications Technology (ICT) infrastructure on the premises of diplomatic and consular missions, as well as IOs, enjoys inviolability. This is very much in line with the provisions of the Vienna Convention on Diplomatic Relations (VCDR) as well as the Vienna Convention on Consular Relations (VCCR), and respective headquarters agreements.

It is commendable that Austria also includes a reference to states' positive duties with respect to both diplomatic and consular missions, as well as IOs. With respect to diplomatic and consular missions, Austria notes:

> The receiving state has the duty to take all appropriate steps to protect the mission against any intrusion or damage and to prevent any disturbance of the peace of the mission or impairment of its dignity. Thus, a state that becomes aware of a malicious cyber activity against a diplomatic or consular mission in its territory, has to take all appropriate steps to protect the mission from such an activity.[39]

---

38 This includes, *inter alia,* the alleged hack of the US ambassador to China Nicholas Burns by China, or the hacks against the ICRC or the ICC in recent years. See Dustin Volz and Warren P Strobel, 'U.S. Ambassador to China Hacked in China-Linked Spying Operation' (*The Wall Street Journal,* 20 July 2023) <www.wsj.com/articles/u-s-ambassador-to-china-hacked-in-china-linked-spying-operation-f03de3e4?mod=latest_headlines> last accessed 7 January 2025; International Committee of the Red Cross, 'Cyber Attack on ICRC: What We Know' (*ICRC,*16 February 2022) <www.icrc.org/en/document/cyber-attack-icrc-what-we-know> last accessed 7 January 2025; International Criminal Court, 'Measures Taken Following the Unprecedented Cyber-Attack on the ICC' (*ICC,* 20 October 2023) <www.icc-cpi.int/news/measures-taken-following-unprecedented-cyber-attack-icc> last accessed 7 January 2025.

39 Position Paper (n 1) 15.

Similarly, with respect to IOs, Austria notes:

> Host states [...] have a duty to protect the premises of the IO from outside disturbances or unauthorized entry. Thus, if a state becomes aware of a malicious cyber activity against an IO situated on its territory, it has to take all appropriate steps to protect the IO from such an activity. In this regard, Austria is working closely with IOs situated on its territory.[40]

This particular reference to states' positive duties is important, as not much information about the extent of this duty in the cyber context is publicly available. Austria's position at least highlights that once a state has become aware of an activity, it would have to take appropriate steps to protect the IO. Austria's position also makes clear that cooperation between the IO and the host state is important, implying it wishes to uphold respect for the IO's privileges and immunities.

VII. International Criminal Law

Finally, Austria's view on international criminal law is also noteworthy. Again, Austria is the first state to specifically address international criminal law in its position. The applicability of international criminal law to cyber activities has been previously addressed by some academics, and there has been an initiative led by Liechtenstein, and co-sponsored by Austria and other states, bringing together experts on international law, to shed light on this issue.[41] Austria being part of this initiative may explain this particular reference to international criminal law in the position paper. The topic has gained renewed attention when the Chief Prosecutor of the International Criminal Court (ICC), Karim Khan, published an article in *Foreign Policy* on the topic, making clear pronouncements that cyber operations have the potential to fall under the jurisdiction of the court.[42] The Prosecutor has also

---

40 *Ibid.*

41 See Permanent Mission of Liechtenstein to the United Nations, 'The Council of Advisers' Report on the Application of the Rome Statute of the International Criminal Court to Cyberwarfare' (August 2021) <www.ila-americanbranch.org/wp-content/uploads/2022/10/The-Council-of-Advisers-Report-on-the-Application-of-the-Rome-Statute-of-the-International-Criminal-Court-to-Cyberwarfare.pdf> last accessed 7 January 2025.

42 Karim AA Khan KC, 'Technology Will Not Exceed Our Humanity' in Foreign Policy Analytics, 'Digital Frontlines' (Fall 2023) 50f <https://digitalfrontlines.io/

taken concrete steps to follow up on this topic, and convened a conference at the beginning of 2024 on this matter.[43] The outcome of the conference, which examined the practical implications of cyber operations conducted to commit serious offences under the Rome Statute, would inform the Prosecutor's new 'policy on cyber-enabled crimes',[44] but is yet to be released.

While strengthening the view that international criminal law is applicable to cyber activities, Austria also provides an important caveat, noting that '[w]hile cyber activities are in principle capable of amounting to international crimes, in practice, most cyber activities will not reach this threshold.'[45] This is important to clarify that cyber activities tend to constitute activities below the threshold of the use of force, and to prevent any escalatory measures.

VIII. Conclusion

Overall, the position paper provides a great insight into how Austria views the application of international law to cyber activities. It adds additional food for thought to the existing position papers and thus helps clarify further how international law applies to the cyber context. Hopefully, it also encourages other states to come forward with their own views, to help strengthen the international rules-based order.

Acknowledgments

The author would like to thank Jane A Hofbauer and Maximilian Weninger for helpful comments on earlier works of this article.

---

wp-content/uploads/sites/8/2023/08/digital-front-lines-report-FP-analytics-microsoft-2023.pdf> last accessed 7 January 2025.

43 International Criminal Court, 'Statement by ICC Prosecutor Karim A.A. Khan KC on Conference Addressing Cyber-Enabled Crimes through the Rome Statute System' (22 January 2024) <www.icc-cpi.int/news/statement-icc-prosecutor-karim-aa-khan-kc-conference-addressing-cyber-enabled-crimes-through> last accessed 7 January 2025.

44 *Ibid.*

45 Position Paper (n 1) 20.

The Protection of the Right to a Fair Trial in Austrian Headquarters Agreements Over Time

Matthias Radosztics | Head of Unit for Multilateral International Law Issues in the Office of the Legal Advisor, Federal Ministry of European and International Affairs, Republic of Austria

Abstract

This article analyses headquarters agreements with international organizations based in Austria with a focus on the settlement of labour disputes between the organizations and their employees in light of the jurisprudence of the European Court of Human Rights (ECtHR) and the Austrian Constitutional Court. It will use the *Waite and Kennedy* judgment of the ECtHR and the OPEC-case of the Austrian Constitutional Court as starting points and demonstrate that even though headquarters agreements generally differ from one another in certain aspects, there has been a uniform development when it comes to ensuring the right to a fair trial in line with Article 6 of the European Convention on Human Rights.

Keywords

Immunity from jurisdiction of international organizations – headquarters agreements – Austria as a host country to international organizations – right to a fair trial – access to courts – settlement of labour disputes with international organizations

I. Setting the Scene: The Case Law of the European Court of Human Rights

The European Court of Human Rights (ECtHR) has over the years delivered several judgments dealing with labour disputes of international organizations with their employees, setting the standard for their jurisdictional immunities in Europe. This started with its landmark judgment in *Waite and Kennedy v Germany*, in which the ECtHR was concerned with the permissibility of Germany granting immunities to the European Space Agency (ESA).[1] It

[1] *Waite and Kennedy v Germany*, ECtHR (GC), Application No 26083/94, Judgment of 18 February 1999, para 59 *et seq.*

 | DOI:10.1163/15736512-02801008

considered that such immunities of international organizations constituted a restriction to the right of access to justice under Article 6(1) of the European Convention of Human Rights (ECHR). However, that right was not absolute and restrictions to that right could be permissible, insofar as they were proportionate. The Court confirmed that the granting of privileges and immunities to international organizations was an indispensable means for ensuring the proper functioning of such organizations, free from unilateral influence of individual governments. As a 'material factor' to determine the proportionality of such a restriction under Article 6(1) ECHR, the Court assessed whether individuals had 'reasonable alternative means to protect effectively their rights under the Convention'.[2] It had to be assured that the limitations applied did not restrict nor reduce the access to justice left to the individual in such a way or to such an extent that the very essence of the right to a fair trial was impaired.[3] In the given case, the ESA Appeals Board amounted to an adequate alternative remedy for labour disputes.[4] Moreover, the ECtHR found that it would be wrong to interpret Article 6(1) of the ECHR in a way that national law had to be applied in labour law disputes with international organizations, as this would 'thwart the proper functioning of international organizations and run counter to the current trend towards extending and strengthening international cooperation'.[5] These principles were also applied in its simultaneous judgment in *Beer and Regan v Germany*, which likewise concerned the ESA.[6]

This jurisprudence was confirmed on several subsequent occasions. In the case *Gasparini v Italy and Belgium*, the ECtHR invoked several of its previous judgments and reiterated that the parties to the ECHR were not prohibited from transferring sovereign rights to international organizations. However, they could not thereby discharge their obligations under the ECHR. As long as it could be assumed that the international organization in question protected fundamental rights in a comparable (and not necessarily identical) manner, there was a presumption that the state was not in breach of its obligations under the ECHR while fulfilling its obligations arising from its membership of the international organization in question. However, such a presumption

---

2 *Ibid.*, para 68.

3 *Ibid.*, para 59.

4 *Ibid.*, paras 69-71.

5 *Ibid.*, para 72.

6 *Beer and Regan v Germany*, ECtHR (GC), Application No 28934/95, Judgment of 18 February 1999, para 58 *et seq*.

could be rebutted if, in the light of the circumstances of the specific case, the protection of fundamental rights had to be regarded as manifestly deficient. The Court continued that the scrutiny to determine whether the proceedings before the dispute settlement mechanism of an international organization were 'manifestly deficient', would necessarily be less extensive than its scrutiny under Article 6 in respect of domestic proceedings in States that were parties to the ECHR. In the case at hand, the lack of publicity alone did not undermine the fairness of the proceedings as a whole.[7]

In its judgment in the case *Klausecker v Germany* the ECtHR confirmed that access to the ILO Administrative Tribunal (ILOAT), which was provided for in the case of labour law disputes at the European Patent Office (EPO), was in conformity with the ECHR.[8] It held that it

> does not see any reason to consider, in the light of the elements brought before it by the applicant, that since the transfer by Germany of its sovereign powers to the EPO the rights guaranteed by the Convention would generally not receive within the EPO an 'equivalent protection' to that secured by the Convention system.[9]

The judgments of the ECtHR leave no doubt that, to comply with Article 6 ECHR, employees of international organizations must have access to an independent and impartial dispute settlement mechanism in case of labour disputes. Host countries of international organizations are therefore obliged to either anchor such mechanisms in the headquarter agreements or ensure that the organizations adopt their own internal regulations. The design of these mechanisms is, however, left to the discretion of the organizations, as long as the mechanisms fulfil certain core criteria of the right to a fair trial.

II. The Power to Make Internal Regulations

In light of the *Waite and Kennedy* jurisprudence, international organizations, as a rule, either submit themselves to existing international tribunals (such as

---

7 *Gasparini v Italy and Belgium*, ECtHR, Application No 10750/03, Decision of 12 May 2009; see also *Bosphorus Hava Yolları Turizm ve Ticaret Anonim Şirketi v Ireland*, ECtHR (GC), Application No 45036/98, Judgment of 30 June 2005, para 152 *et seq.*

8 *Klausecker v Germany*, ECtHR, Application No 415/07, Decision of 6 January 2015, para 62 *et seq.*

9 *Ibid.*, para 101.

ILOAT) or set up their own dispute settlement mechanisms for labour disputes with their employees. The competence to create their own mechanisms emanates from the power of international organizations to make regulations within their headquarters seats. If such regulations exist, national law, insofar as it is inconsistent with a regulation of the international organization in question, is inapplicable within the headquarters seat of the organization.

The competence to make regulations is often spelled out explicitly in headquarters agreements. In Austria, such provisions can, for example, be found in Article III Section 16 of the Headquarters Agreement Regarding the Seat of the United Nations in Vienna,[10] Article III Section 6 of the Headquarters Agreement with the OSCE[11] or Article 4 of the Headquarters Agreement with the OPEC Fund for International Development.[12] However, even in absence of a specific treaty provision to this effect, this competence is generally recognized without exception by host countries of international organizations as being an implied statutory competence of the organization (emanating from the so-called implied powers doctrine[13]). If international organizations had to submit themselves to the law of the host country regarding their internal affairs, they would not be able to fulfil their tasks with the necessary independence.

The power of organizations to make their own regulations may even derive from customary international law.[14] One of the oldest relevant examples is

---

[10] Agreement between the Republic of Austria and the United Nations regarding the seat of the United Nations in Vienna, 29 November 1995, 34923 UNTS 254, Federal Law Gazette III No 99/1998.

[11] Agreement between the Republic of Austria and the Organization for Security and Co-Operation in Europe (OSCE) Regarding the Headquarters of the Organization for Security and Co-Operation in Europe, 14 June 2017, Federal Law Gazette III No 84/2018.

[12] Agreement between the Republic of Austria and the Organization of the Petroleum Exporting Countries Regarding the Headquarters of the Petroleum Exporting Countries, 18 February 1974, Federal Law Gazette No 382/1974.

[13] *Reparation for Injuries Suffered in the Service of the United Nations* [1949] ICJ 1949, 14 (Advisory Opinion of 11 April); *Certain Expenses of the United Nations (Article 17, paragraph 2, of the Charter)* [1962] ICJ 1962, 32 (Advisory Opinion of 20 July); Ignaz Seidl-Hohenveldern, Gerhard Loibl, *Das Recht der internationalen Organisationen einschließlich der supranationalen Gemeinschaften* (1992) paras 1517 *et seq*.

[14] Thomas A Mensah, 'Headquarters Agreements and the Law of International Organizations' in Holger Hestermeyer *et al* (eds), *Coexistence, Cooperation and Solidarity: Liber Amicorum Rüdiger Wolfrum*, Vol 2 (2012) 1463, 1470.

the International Labour Organization (ILO), which has applied its own personnel statutes without objection of its host country Switzerland since 1919. Likewise, Switzerland accepted the internal labour law of the GATT Secretariat in Geneva without a headquarters agreement or a statute based on international law. It was not until 18 August 1977 that Switzerland and the GATT Secretariat reached an agreement on the applicability of the 1946 Convention on Privileges and Immunities of the United Nations.[15]

Those statutes were also repeatedly reviewed by international administrative courts in the context of internal labour dispute. As early as 1929, in the case of *di Palma Castiglione v International Labour Office*[16] the Administrative Tribunal of the League of Nations recognized the ability of intergovernmental institutions to issue internal regulations:

> The Administration is at liberty to establish for its staff such regulations as it may see fit, provided that it does not in any way infringe the acquired rights of any staff member.[17]

In 1957, the Administrative Tribunal of the International Labour Organization (ILO) confirmed in the *Waghorn* case that it was bound in the exercise of its jurisdiction by the internal regulations of the organization and not by national law.[18]

In the same vein, neither the Protocol on the Privileges and Immunities of the EU[19] nor the 1946 Agreement on the Privileges and Immunities of the United Nations Organization between the Swiss Federal Council and the Secretary-General of the United Nations Organization[20] contain provisions that the EU or the United Nations may issue their own labour law regulations.

---

15 Wolfgang Benedek, *Die Rechtsordnung des GATT aus völkerrechtlicher Sicht* (1990) 267.

16 In re *Di Palma Castiglione v International Labour Organization* [1929] League of Nations Administrative Tribunal Judgement No 1 of 15 January 1929, 2.

17 *Ibid.*, 2. See also Pierre Klein, 'International Organizations or Institutions, Internal Law and Rules' in Anne Peters (ed), *Max Planck Encyclopaedia of Public International Law* (February 2019) para 2 <https://opil.ouplaw.com/>.

18 In re *Waghorn* [1957] ILO Administrative Tribunal, Judgement No 28 of 12 July 1957, 3.

19 Protocol on the Privileges and Immunities of the EU [2012] OJ C 326/1 (consolidated text).

20 Agreement on the Privileges and Immunities of the United Nations Organization between the Swiss Federal Council and the Secretary-General of the United Nations Organization, 19 April 1946, AS 1956 1092.

It is, however, undisputed that the two organizations are authorised to do so and, consequently, they have made use of this right (see Official Journal of the European Union No L 56 of 4 March 1968 or resolution A/RES/63/253 of 17 March 2009 by the General Assembly of the United Nations).

More recently, the Austrian Constitutional Court itself, in the context of the IAEA, held that '[t]he enforcement of labour law provisions constitutes a core element of the immunity of International Organizations'.[21] It is therefore undisputed that international organizations have the right to adopt their own internal rules for the settlement of labour disputes without interference of the host country. In the case of Austria, this right is generally reflected in headquarters agreements by (1) a provision that allows the international organization to adopt its own regulations that are applicable within its seat and/or (2) a provision that obliges the organization to create an independent dispute settlement mechanism for labour disputes. It must be noted, however, that these provisions cannot be found in every single headquarters agreement that the Republic of Austria has concluded.

III. The 2021 Ruling of the Austrian Constitutional Court in the OPEC Case

In April 2021, a former employee of OPEC filed an application with the Austrian Constitutional Court pursuant to Art 140a of the Federal Constitutional Law (*B-VG*), requesting the Court to declare several provisions in the OPEC Headquarters Agreement (OPEC-HA) unconstitutional, in particular those on jurisdictional immunities.[22] The underlying proceedings concerned a labour

---

21 Constitutional Court, Judgment SV2/2015 of 25 February 2016, for an unofficial translation see Jane A Hofbauer, Philipp Janig, Michael J Moffatt and Stephan Wittich, 'Austrian Judicial Decisions Involving Questions of International Law/ Österreichische Judikatur zum Internationalen Recht' (2016) 21 ARIEL 198ff.

22 Constitutional Court, Judgment SV 1/2021-23 of 29 September 2022. For an unofficial translation, see Martin Baumgartner, Philipp Janig, Viktoria Ritter, Maximilian Weninger and Stephan Wittich, 'Austrian Judicial Decisions Involving Questions of International Law/Österreichische Judikatur zum Internationalen Recht' (2025) 27 ARIEL 332ff. For discussions of the case, see *OPEC Immunity Case, Anonymous v Organization of Petroleum Exporting Countries and Austria (joining)*, Decision on the constitutionality of treaties, SV 1/2021-23; ILDC 3402 (AT 2022), 29 September 2022, Austria; Philipp Janig, 'X v. OPEC. Judgment No. SV 1/2021 (SV 1/2021-23). ECLI:AT:VFGH:2022:SV1.2021' (2024) 118 American Journal of International Law 331-337.

law dispute (unjustified termination of employment) between OPEC and the former employee, which could not be dealt with by Austrian civil courts (in this instance the Vienna Labour and Social Court) due to OPEC's immunity from Austrian jurisdiction.

The applicant considered that this dismissal violated his constitutionally guaranteed rights under the ECHR, as he was denied access to Austrian civil courts.

The applicant requested the partial repeal of Article 4 (1) OPEC-HA on OPEC's power to adopt its own internal regulations, Article 5 (1) and (2) OPEC-HA on the inviolability of the seat of the organization, Article 9 OPEC-HA on its immunity from Austrian jurisdiction and Article 10 OPEC-HA on the inviolability of OPEC's property.[23] In his view, these provisions contradicted Article 6(1) ECHR (right to a fair trial), Article 13 ECHR (right to an effective remedy) and Article 1 of the First Additional Protocol to the ECHR (protection of property). More specifically, with regard to Article 6 ECHR, he argued that OPEC's internal organizational law did not provide for an appropriate alternative dispute resolution mechanism in line with the *Waite and Kennedy* jurisprudence of the ECtHR. OPEC only allowed complaints to be addressed to the Secretary General, who had decided on his dismissal in the first place. In addition, this complaint mechanism was only available to current employees and not to former employees.

The Constitutional Court declared the application in part inadmissible, insofar as it challenged Article 4(1) and Article 10 OPEC-HA. It considered that these provisions were not relevant to resolve the underlying dispute before the labour court, meaning that the application was too broad in this respect. However, it declared the application admissible insofar as it concerned the jurisdictional immunities (Art 9 OPEC-HA) and inviolability of the seat (Art 5 OPEC-HA), which was 'inextricably linked' to Article 9.

On the merits, the Constitutional Court confirmed that Article 6(1) ECHR includes a right of access to an independent and impartial tribunal established by law, which also applied to labour disputes with an international organization. According to the case law of the ECtHR, this right could be subject to restrictions, but such restrictions were only permissible if they pursued a legitimate aim and if there was a reasonable relationship of proportionality between the means employed and the aim sought. The Constitutional Court continued that, according to the ECtHR, the proportionality of restricting

23 Agreement between the Republic of Austria and the Organization of the Petroleum Exporting Countries Regarding the Headquarters of the Petroleum Exporting Countries (n 12).

access to a court in the context of the immunity of international organizations depended essentially on the availability of an adequate alternative legal remedy,[24] which offered equivalent, but not necessarily identical, legal protection,[25] such as the possibility of appeal to the Administrative Tribunal of the International Labour Organization or arbitration proceedings.[26]

The Constitutional Court confirmed that Article 9 OPEC-HA pursued the goal of ensuring that OPEC could function free from unilateral interference by the host state, which constituted a legitimate objective within the meaning of the case law of the ECtHR. However, as long as the Headquarters Agreement could not guarantee that an appropriate mechanism for the settlement of labour disputes was in place that safeguarded the rights of employees (which was not the case with OPEC), it could not be assumed that the restricted access to the courts in labour disputes was proportionate.

As a result, the Constitutional Court declared Article 5(1) and (2) and Article 9 OPEC-HA to be in violation of Article 6(1) ECHR and thus unconstitutional. However, it decided that these provisions were to remain applicable until 30 September 2024, giving the Austrian Federal Government the possibility to rectify the situation.

IV. Amendment of the OPEC Headquarters Agreement

Following the judgment of the Constitutional Court, the Austrian Federal Ministry for European and International Affairs entered into negotiations with OPEC, the outcome of which was an Amendment Protocol, which – after parliamentary approval – entered into force on 1 June 2024.[27] The Protocol amends Article 5 and Article 9 OPEC-HA, which the Constitutional Court had declared unconstitutional. The new provisions contain an obligation under international law for OPEC to introduce an ECHR-compliant mechanism of legal protection for labour disputes with its current and former employees.

24 *Waite and Kennedy* (n 1).

25 See *Boivin v 34 Member States of the Council of Europe*, ECtHR, Application No 73250/01, Decision of 9 September 2008.

26 See *Klausecker* (n 8).

27 Protocol between the Republic of Austria and the Organization of the Petroleum Exporting Countries (OPEC) Amending the Agreement between the Republic of Austria and the Organization of the Petroleum Exporting Countries Regarding the Headquarters of the Petroleum Exporting Countries, 16 January 2024, Federal Law Gazette III No 88/2024.

The new version of Article 5 reads as follows:

> (1) The headquarters seat shall be inviolable. No officer or official of the Republic of Austria, or other person exercising any public authority within the Republic of Austria shall enter the headquarters seat to perform any duties therein except with the consent of, and under conditions approved by, the Secretary General. The consent of the Secretary General may, however, be assumed in case of fire and other disaster requiring prompt protective action.
>
> (2) The service of legal process, including the seizure of private property, shall not take place within the headquarters seat except with the express consent of, and under the conditions approved by, the Secretary General.
>
> (3) This article shall apply subject to the provisions of Article 9.

The new version of Article 5 OPEC-HA retained paragraphs 1 and 2 as before, which stipulate that the seat of OPEC enjoys inviolability. Austrian officials can only enter the OPEC premises with the express consent of the Secretary General of the Organization, in order to carry out official acts there. This also applies to acts of enforcement.

However, a new paragraph 3 was added, stipulating that the provisions of Article 5 apply 'subject to' the new Article 9 and its obligation to create an independent and impartial dispute resolution mechanism (see below). The wording of this new paragraph creates a limitation of OPEC's inviolability. In practical terms this means that the service of court documents to OPEC in labour disputes is possible, in case the obligations contained in the new Article 9 are not entirely fulfilled.

The new version of Article 9 OPEC-HA reads as follows:

> (1) OPEC and its property, wherever located and by whomsoever held, shall have immunity from every form of legal process, except:
>
> a. in so far as in any particular case OPEC shall have expressly waived its immunity. It is, however, understood that no waiver of immunity shall extend to any measure of execution.
>
> b. in the case of civil action brought by a third party for damages in connection with the operation of motor vehicles on OPEC's behalf in Austria.
>
> (2) Employment disputes between OPEC and its staff or former staff members shall be settled by an independent and impartial dispute resolution mechanism pursuant to OPEC's internal regulations that protects the rights of its staff or former staff members. The decisions issued by this mechanism shall be final and binding for the parties.

The new Article 9 OPEC-HA in principle confirms the jurisdictional immunity of OPEC.[28] Its paragraph 2 stipulates that employment disputes with current and former staff members shall be settled in accordance with the internal regulations of the organization, as is customary in other comparable international organizations. However, OPEC is expressly obliged to ensure that the dispute resolution mechanism, which protects the rights of current and former staff members, is independent and impartial. The explanatory notes to the government bill clarify that this provision was introduced in light of Article 6(1) of the ECHR, meaning that the dispute settlement mechanism established by OPEC must meet the criteria of the right to a fair trial.[29]

Meanwhile, on 27/28 October 2022, OPEC amended the OPEC Staff Regulations to establish an Appeals Committee as an independent and impartial body to review appeals filed by a staff member or a former staff member in employment disputes arising from decisions taken by the Secretary General of the organization.[30] Both, the Appeals Committee and the changes to the OPEC-HA were subsequently confirmed to be in line with Article 6(1) of the ECHR by the Constitutional Court in a later case brought before the Court.[31]

V. Dispute Settlement Mechanisms in Austrian Headquarters Agreements

The new formulation of the OPEC Headquarters Agreement cited above is in line with other Austrian headquarters agreements. Especially more recent agreements typically contain provisions that oblige international organizations to guarantee access to an independent and impartial dispute settlement mechanism, without specifying how this mechanism should look like, as this would interfere into the organization's competence to adopt its own rules and regulations that are applicable within its seat. In practice, individual Headquarters Agreements may foresee that international organizations are subject to the Austrian Labour Courts (such as the Permanent Secretariat

---

28 In addition, the new sub-paragraph in Article 9(1)(b) creates a true exception to the immunity of OPEC.

29 Explanatory Notes, 2413 der Beilagen XXVII. GP, 1 <https://www.parlament.gv.at/dokument/XXVII/I/2413/fname_1605318.pdf> accessed 24 January 2025.

30 Organization of the Petroleum Exporting Countries, 'About the Committee' <https://www.opec.org/opec_web/en/7195.htm> accessed 24 January 2025.

31 Constitutional Court, Decision SV 1/2024 of 27 November 2024.

of the Alpine Convention[32]). However, international organizations usually accept the jurisdiction of independent international tribunals, such as ILOAT or arbitration, or – in many cases – create their own structures.

Already many 'older' headquarters agreements contain clauses on dispute resolution that are modelled after Art VIII Sec 29 of the 1946 Convention on the Privileges and Immunities of the United Nations.[33] This was the case, for example, for the Headquarters Agreement between the Republic of Austria and the International Atomic Energy Agency.[34] Section 50 of this Agreement reads as follows:

> The IAEA shall make provision for the appropriate methods of settlement of
>
> a) Disputes arising out of contracts and disputes of private law character to which the IAEA is a party; and
>
> b) Disputes involving an official of the IAEA who, by reason of his official position, enjoys immunity, if such immunity has not been waived by the IAEA.

Section 34 of the Headquarters Agreement between the Republic of Austria and the United Nations Industrial Development Organization,[35] which has in the meantime been replaced by a new headquarters agreement, contained a similar clause.

However, the practice to include a provision on the settlement of labour disputes into the headquarters agreements was not followed in every case. Examples for the lack of such provisions could be found in the Headquarters Agreement between the Republic of Austria and OPEC[36] or the Headquarters

---

32 See Art 5(1)(d) Agreement between the Republic of Austria and the Permanent Secretariat of the Convention on the Protection of the Alps concerning its Seat, 13 January 2004, Federal Law Gazette No III 5/2004.

33 Convention on the Privileges and Immunities of the United Nations, 13 February 1946, 90 UNTS 327.

34 Agreement between the Republic of Austria and the International Atomic Energy Agency regarding the Headquarters of the International Atomic Energy Agency, 11 December 1957, Federal Law Gazette III No 82/1958.

35 Agreement between the Republic of Austria and the United Nations regarding the Headquarters of the United Nations industrial Development Organization, 13 April 1967, Federal Law Gazette III No 245/1967.

36 Agreement between the Republic of Austria and the Organization of the Petroleum Exporting Countries Regarding the Headquarters of the Petroleum Exporting Countries (n 12).

Agreement between the Republic of Austria and the OPEC Fund for International Development,[37] both of which have been amended in the meantime. The Headquarters Agreement between the Republic of Austria and the Joint Vienna Institute, dating back to 1997, contains exceptions from the Institute's immunity from jurisdiction and enforcement in Article 5, but no provision on the independent settlement of labour disputes with its employees[38]

Moving ahead in time, the Headquarters Agreement Regarding the Seat of the United Nations in Vienna[39] as well as the new Headquarters Agreement with UNIDO[40], both contain – like their predecessors – dispute settlement clauses similar to the one of the IAEA, with the slight difference that they also include experts on mission.

In the aftermath of the ECtHR's judgment in *Waite and Kennedy*, the practice on the settlement of labour disputes in Austrian Headquarters Agreements remained inconsistent for some time. The Headquarters Agreements with the International Centre for Migration Policy Development (ICMPD),[41] the International Commission for the Protection of the Danube River,[42] the International Organization for Migration (IOM)[43] and the International Bank

---

37 Agreement between the Republic of Austria and the OPEC Fund for International Development Regarding the Headquarters of the Fund, 21 April 1981, Federal Law Gazette III No 248/1982.

38 Agreement between the Republic of Austria and the Joint Vienna Institute regarding the Headquarters of the Joint Vienna Institute, 6 March 1997, Federal Law Gazette III No 187/1997.

39 Agreement between the Republic of Austria and the United Nations Regarding the Seat of the United Nations in Vienna (n 10).

40 Agreement between the Republic of Austria and the United Nations Industrial Development Organization Regarding the Headquarters of the United Nations Industrial Development Organization, 29 November 1995, Federal Law Gazette III No 100/1998.

41 Agreement between the Republic of Austria and the International Centre for Migration Policy Development (ICMPD) Regarding the Headquarters of the International Centre for Migration Policy Development, 8 September 1999, Federal Law Gazette III No 145/2000.

42 Agreement between the Republic of Austria and the International Commission for the Protection of the Danube River Regarding the Headquarters of International Commission for the Protection of the Danube River, 14 December 2000, Federal Law Gazette III No 227/2001.

43 Agreement between the Republic of Austria and the International Organization for Migration Regarding the Legal Status of the Organization in Austria and the Headquarters of its Offices in Vienna, 27 December 2013, Federal Law Gazette III No 115/2014.

for Reconstruction and Development, the International Finance Corporation and the Multilateral Investment Guarantee Agency[44] contain exceptions from the immunity from jurisdiction and enforcement, but no provision on the independent settlement of labour disputes with its employees.

Contrary to those agreements, the Headquarters Agreement with the Energy Community contains the following provision in Article 5(4), which explicitly covers labour disputes:

> With regard to any dispute between the Energy Community and a private party, including any of the Officials of the Secretariat as defined in Article 1 (d) of this Agreement, the Energy Community agrees that these shall be finally settled by a tribunal composed of a single arbitrator appointed by the Secretary General of the Permanent Court of Arbitration, Peace Palace, Carnegieplein 2, 2517 KJ The Hague, The Netherlands, in accordance with the relevant Optional Rules for Arbitration involving international organizations and private parties. The tribunal shall decide a dispute in accordance with such rules of law as may be agreed by the parties. In the absence of such agreement, the tribunal shall apply such rules of international law and general principles of law as may be applicable. Matters concerning the interpretation of the Treaty establishing the Energy Community and its appendices shall not be within the competence of the tribunal.[45]

Similarly, the Headquarters Agreement with the International Anti-Corruption Academy (IACA) contains a clause on arbitration in case of disputes between the Academy and private parties in Article 5(4).[46]

The Headquarters Agreement with the OSCE on the other hand contains a provision similar to the one in the UN Headquarters Agreements in Section 36 (b), according to which the OSCE shall make provisions for appropriate methods for the settlement of disputes involving an official of or expert on

---

44 Agreement between the Republic of Austria and the International Bank for Reconstruction and Development, the International Finance Corporation and the Multilateral Investment Guarantee Agency Regarding the Establishment of Liaison Offices in Vienna, 21 July 2010, Federal Law Gazette III No 23/2011.

45 Agreement between the Republic of Austria and the Energy Community Regarding the Seat of the Secretariat of the Energy Community, 29 May 2007, Federal Law Gazette III No 87/2007.

46 Agreement between the Republic of Austria and the International Anti-Corruption Academy (IACA) Regarding the Seat of the International Anti-Corruption Academy in Austria, 10 October 2011, Federal Law Gazette III No 100/2012.

mission for the OSCE who, by reason of his or her official position, enjoys immunity, if such immunity has not been waived.[47]

The new Austrian Headquarters Law[48] from 1 May 2021, which replaced the Law on Privileges and Immunities of International Organizations of 1977,[49] was a milestone. As was the case with the old law of 1977, it lists various privileges and immunities and authorizes the Federal Government to adopt ordinances or conclude treaties under international law with a simplified parliamentary approval procedure to award these privileges and immunities to international organizations. However, as under the prior legislation, headquarters agreements do not necessarily have to be based on this law. In case they go beyond what is permissible within the framework of the Headquarters Law, they may be adopted under the 'regular' process foreseen for treaties that modify or complement existing law, according to Article 50 of the Federal Constitutional Law (*B-VG*), requiring full parliamentary approval. Nevertheless, the Headquarters Law can, like its predecessor, be regarded as best practice in Austria when it comes to privileges and immunities of international organizations.

Since the adoption of the Headquarters Law, all new headquarters agreements concluded by Austria were based on this law and adopted with a simplified parliamentary procedure. Existing Headquarters Agreements, on the other hand, that had previously been adopted under Article 50 of the Federal Constitutional Law with full parliamentary approval, had to be amended according to the same procedure (such as the OPEC-HA).

Section 10(3) of the new Headquarters Law provides for an explicit obligation for the respect of human rights in headquarters agreements, particularly when it comes to legal protection mechanisms:

> Privileges and immunities under §§ 11 to 14 may only be granted in accordance with international standards and to the extent that this does not contradict Austria's obligations under international and human rights law.

---

[47] Agreement between the Republic of Austria and the Organization for Security and Co-Operation in Europe (OSCE) Regarding the Headquarters of the Organization for Security and Co-Operation in Europe, 14 June 2017, Federal Law Gazette III No 84/2018.

[48] Headquarters Law, 25 March 2021, Federal Law Gazette I No 54/2021. For an unofficial English translation see <www.ris.bka.gv.at/Dokumente/Erv/ERV_2021_1_54/ERV_2021_1_54.pdf> accessed 24 January 2025.

[49] Law on Privileges and Immunities of International Organizations, 29 December 1977, Federal Law Gazette I No 677/1977.

> To this end, when granting privileges and immunities, particular attention shall be paid to the existence of effective legal protection mechanisms.[50]

Moreover, Section 11(4) recognizes the right of international organizations to adopt their own internal regulations:

> International Organizations and funds established by them may be granted the following privileges and immunities:
>
> […]
>
> 4. authority to issue internal regulations for the seat, providing that these do not conflict with the appropriate application of Austrian health and fire protection regulations[51]

As a result, the newest generation of headquarters agreements – concluded after the enactment of the new Headquarters Law – contain explicit clauses for the protection of the right to a fair trial for the employees of the respective organizations. For instance, Article 5(4) in the Headquarters Agreement with NATO *inter alia* provides that

> [e]mployment disputes between the Organization and its employees shall be settled by an effective dispute resolution mechanism that protects the rights of the employees pursuant to the Organization's internal regulations.[52]

The explanatory notes of the government bill seeking parliamentary approval for this agreement make it clear that this provision requires a settlement mechanism in line with the standards of the ECHR:

> According to paragraph 4, a dispute involving the Liaison Office and a private party shall be settled by arbitration, unless another dispute settlement mechanism has been agreed with the private party or the dispute concerns labour disputes. The latter shall be settled in accordance with the internal rules of the organization, as is customary in other comparable international organizations. NATO is explicitly obliged to ensure that this is an effective dispute resolution mechanism that protects the rights of employees. This provision is included in the Agreement for the purposes of compatibility

---

50 Headquarters Law (n 48).

51 *Ibid.*

52 Agreement between the Austrian Federal Government and the North Atlantic Treaty Organization (NATO) on the Legal Status of the Liaison Office in Vienna, 10 May 2021, Federal Law Gazette III No 197/2021.

> with Art. 6 (right to a fair trial) of the Convention for the Protection of Human Rights and Fundamental Freedoms (ECHR) […].[53]

The Amendment Protocol for the OPEC Fund for International Development (OFID) Headquarters Agreement introduced a similar provision into Article 9(2) of the OFID Headquarters Agreement.[54] The Headquarters Agreement with the International Vaccine Institute goes one step further and in Article 5(3) specifically requires a dispute settlement mechanism in accordance with the ECHR:

> Employment disputes between the Institute and its employees shall be settled by an effective dispute resolution mechanism that protects the rights of the employees in accordance with the European Convention on Human Rights, pursuant to the Institute's internal regulations.[55]

A provision with the same wording can be found in the Headquarters Agreement with the Permanent Court of Arbitration.[56]

It has to be noted, however, that in order to fulfil Article 6 ECHR, the obligation to establish an impartial and independent settlement mechanism for labour disputes does not necessarily have to be contained in the headquarters agreement. It may be created by any means possible, such as, for example, in the organization's statutes or internal staff regulations. However, the inclusion into a headquarters agreement, which creates obligations under international law, offers a greater degree of certainty, both for the individuals concerned as well as for the host country, which is itself bound by the ECHR.

---

53 Explanatory Notes, Federal Law Gazette III No 197/2021 <www.bundeskanzleramt.gv.at/dam/jcr:9993816e-fccd-41f0-bfbd-f1d37cc35517/10_6_erlaeu.pdf> accessed 24 January 2025 (translation by the author).

54 Protocol between the Republic of Austria and the OPEC Fund for International Development amending the Agreement between the Republic of Austria and the OPEC Fund for International Development Regarding the Headquarters of the Fund, 9 October 2019, Federal Law Gazette III No 94/2020.

55 Agreement between the Austrian Federal Government and the International Vaccine Institute on the Legal Status of the International Vaccine Institute in Austria, 14 December 2022, Federal Law Gazette III No 54/2023.

56 Agreement between the Austrian Federal Government and the Permanent Court of Arbitration on the Legal Status of the Permanent Court of Arbitration in Austria, 22 December 2022, Federal Law Gazette III No 57/2023.

VI. Conclusion

The analysis of different Austrian headquarters agreements over time shows a clear trend of incorporating the right to a fair trial according to Article 6 of the ECHR into these agreements in line with the jurisprudence of the ECtHR and the Austrian Constitutional Court. It is, however, usually left to the organization's internal decision what the dispute settlement mechanism should look like. This, together with the judgment of the Constitutional Court, has led to a better protection for employees of international organizations in Austria and a strengthening of their human rights.

State Succession in Respect of Foreign Property of the Former Soviet Union: A Discussion of Recent Case Law of the Austrian Supreme Court from an International Law Perspective

Hannah Grandits | Researcher and Lecturer, Department of European, International and Comparative Law, University of Vienna, hannah.grandits@unvie.ac.at

Martin Baumgartner | Researcher and Lecturer, Department of European, International and Comparative Law, University of Vienna, martin.baumgartner@univie.ac.at

Abstract

The end of the Soviet Union continues to present courts with difficult questions of international law. In particular, the succession to foreign property of the former Soviet Union remains highly controversial. In a dispute over a plot of land in Vienna, the Austrian Supreme Court in its judgment 10 Ob 9/23f ruled that both Ukraine and Russia gained co-ownership of the property and continue the legal status of the Soviet Union with regard to assets located outside its (former) borders. The Austrian Supreme Court's judgment is significant because the law of state succession is characterised by uncertainty due to scarce practice. This article takes a critical look at the Supreme Court's findings concerning the legal fate of the former Soviet Union's foreign property. It addresses four questions that were not fully answered in the Supreme Court's judgment but may be important for authorities and courts in countries where other assets of the former Soviet Union are located and where similar disputes may arise. The article discusses (1) whether Russia's payment of the former Soviet Union's external debts had consequences for the ownership of Soviet foreign assets, (2) whether the practice of states where the foreign assets are situated can contribute to the formation of customary international law, (3) whether it is possible that one successor state (in this case Ukraine) can be classified as a *persistent objector* and thus not have the rules of customary international law on state succession applicable between other successor states applied to it, and (4) why the interpretation of the relevant treaties between the successor states pursuant to the Vienna Convention on the Law of Treaties (VCLT) leads to the result that the contracting states have acquired co-ownership of foreign property.

Austrian Review of International and European Law **28**: 191-224, 2023.

 | DOI:10.1163/15736512-02801009

Keywords

Foreign property – real estate ownership – co-ownership – persistent objector – debt – Soviet Union – state succession – state succession in respect of foreign property – treaty law – treaty interpretation – customary international law – judgment 10 Ob 9/23f

I. Introduction

In its judgment 10 Ob 9/23f of 16 May 2023, the Austrian Supreme Court dealt with the succession of states in respect of property located abroad. This issue has received little attention so far.[1] The dispute between the Russian Federation and a Ukrainian company concerned a plot of land in Vienna that had been acquired by the Soviet Union in the mid-1970s. The dispute stems from the fact that Russia and Ukraine have still not managed to reach an agreement on the allocation of specific assets of the former Soviet Union to one state or the other.

In its judgment, the Supreme Court primarily dealt with treaties concluded by Russia, Ukraine and other former Soviet republics in the early 1990s. Based on these treaties, the Supreme Court ruled that both Ukraine and Russia, as co-owners, continue the legal status of the Soviet Union in respect of property located outside the borders of the former Soviet Union. The judgment of the Supreme Court has shown that difficult questions on the legal fate of the property of the former Soviet Union do not solely concern the two states that are directly affected (*i.e.* Russia and Ukraine). The 'collapse' of the former Soviet Union may present courts and authorities in every state where former Soviet property is located with difficult questions of international law – even more than 30 years after the end of the Soviet Union. Given that there is still no agreement between Ukraine and Russia regarding the allocation of property, similar disputes are bound to arise in the future.

The Supreme Court considered four legal questions which merit further analysis:

(1) How does the payment of the former Soviet Union's external debt affect the ownership of Soviet property that is located abroad?

(2) What relevance does the practice of the former Soviet republics and of the states where the property is located have for the formation of customary international law?

---

1 See below Martin Baumgartner, Philipp Janig, Viktoria Ritter, Maximilian Weninger and Stephan Wittich, 'Austrian Judicial Decisions Involving Questions of International Law/Österreichische Judikatur zum Internationalen Recht' at page 264.

(3) Is Ukraine a *persistent objector*? Can there even be a *persistent objector* in the present case? If yes, can Ukraine evade the rules of customary international law on state succession that apply between the remaining successor states?

(4) Does the interpretation of the treaties that were concluded by the successor states lead to the conclusion that the parties to the treaty acquire co-ownership of the property located abroad?

Section II will introduce the reader to the judgment of the Supreme Court in 10 Ob 9/23f and its background. Section III then turns to the treaties on which the Supreme Court's judgment is based. The relevant treaties link the payment of external debts to the apportionment of assets located abroad.[2] However, the Supreme Court deemed the question of which state paid the debts of the former Soviet Union to be irrelevant. Section III therefore deals with the legal consequences of the payment of external debts by Russia.

Although the Supreme Court's judgment is based on treaties, it also addresses questions of customary international law: for example the possibility that subsequent customary international law overrides the provisions of the treaties.[3] Section IV and Section V therefore deal with aspects of the judgment that concern questions of customary international law. Section IV deals with the difficult question of what significance the practice of the states where the property is located can have for the classification of a case of state succession and for the ownership of property located within the territory of these states.

The Supreme Court formulated an exception to the rule of the *persistent objector* in international law.[4] Section V argues that the Supreme Court's statements concerning the *persistent objector* are incorrect. The Supreme Court assumes requirements that have only very rarely been advocated in the literature and have not yet been used by any international court or tribunal.

---

2 See, for example, Article 3 of the Treaty on the Legal Succession in respect of the External Public Debt and Assets of the USSR, 4 December 1991, 2380 UNTS 95. On the question of succession in respect of debts, see for example August Reinisch and Gerhard Hafner, *Staatensukzession und Schuldenübernahme beim "Zerfall" der Sowjetunion* (1995) or Ernst Feilchenfeld, *Public Debts and State Succession* (1931).

3 On this possibility, see for example Rebecca Crootof, 'Change Without Consent: How Customary International Law Modifies Treaties' (2016) 41 Yale Journal of International Law 237.

4 On the legal concept of the persistent objector, see James Green, *The Persistent Objector Rule in International Law* (2016).

Finally, the article focuses on the two treaties on which the Supreme Court's judgment is based. The relevant treaty provisions are formulated rather vaguely. They do not expressly state that the contracting parties acquire co-ownership of any specific asset by virtue of the conclusion of the treaties. Section VI therefore examines the question if the Supreme Court could have interpreted the treaties differently.

Despite its criticism, the article ultimately agrees with the Supreme Court's conclusion: Russia is not the sole owner of the foreign property of the former Soviet Union.

II. The Supreme Court's Judgment 10 Ob 9/23f

It might appear strange that a Ukrainian company and the Russian Federation are involved in a legal dispute over a plot of land in Vienna that used to belong to the Soviet Union, given that the 'collapse' of the Soviet Union happened more than 30 years ago. The reason for the dispute is that Russia and Ukraine have not managed to reach a final agreement on the allocation of property that is located outside the former Soviet Union's borders. In the early 1990s, most of the former Soviet republics, including Russia and Ukraine, concluded multilateral treaties on the division of property located abroad and the division of external public debt according to certain percentages. According to these agreements, all successor states should be entitled to a certain share of property situated abroad. However, there is no agreement on the allocation of specific assets to one state or another.

The root of the legal dispute lies in differing views on the effects of the 'collapse' of the Soviet Union: the two treaties on the distribution of property situated abroad refer to all former Soviet republics as 'states-successors'. They thus suggest that the Soviet Union ceased to exist, which is why the external assets must be divided among its successors.[5] This is contrary to Russia's intention to continue the legal personality of the Soviet Union and thus to

[5] Treaty on the Legal Succession in respect of the External Public Debt and Assets of the USSR (n 2) and Agreement on the Division of all Property of the former USSR abroad, 6 July 1992, 2380 UNTS 69. The 1991 Treaty states this quite clearly. According to its Article 1(e), a successor state is a state that has 'replaced' another state in case of state succession. Article 2 then states that all treaty parties, including Russia and Ukraine, are considered 'states-successors' of the USSR, *i.e.* collectively replacing it.

be the sole owner of all its property that is located abroad.[6] This intention also found explicit expression in a constitutional amendment in 2020, which inserted a new provision, stating that Russia would be the legal successor to the 'assets of the USSR outside the territory of the Russian Federation'.[7] This claim is opposed by Ukraine because it has not received a complete inventory or precise information from Russia on the Soviet Union's property abroad and is therefore unable to verify the value of assets and liabilities.[8] For this reason, Ukraine also refused to ratify the so-called 'zero option' agreement offered by Russia. This agreement would have stipulated that Russia were to take over all of the Soviet Union's property abroad, but in return would have to service all of the USSR's external debts.[9] Russia succeeded in concluding such 'zero option' agreements with the other former Soviet republics. The result of these agreements was that Russia's share of the Soviet Union's

---

6 The presidential decree of 8 February 1993, stated that the Russian Federation, as the 'continuator state' of the USSR takes over all rights to the movable and immovable property of the former USSR located abroad. See Theodor Schweisfurth, 'Ausgewählte Fragen der Staatensukzession im Kontext der Auflösung der UdSSR' (1994) 32 Archiv des Völkerrechts 99, 121. The Russian Foreign Minister Andrei Kozyrev explained as early as 1992 that 'successor states are all those states that have emerged in place of the past state. [...] But being a continuator state means that the connection to the outside world has passed to Russia. In this way we have inherited the Soviet Union's seat on the Security Council – this demonstrates our role as a great power.', see Rossiyskaya Gazeta of 21 November 1992, cited in Reinisch and Hafner (n 2) 5. On Russia's claim to continuity and the term 'continuator state', see also August Reinisch, Ignaz Seidl-Hohenveldern, Waldemar Hummer and Heribert Köck, 'Die Staaten' in August Reinisch (ed), *Österreichisches Handbuch des Völkerrechts* (6th edn, 2021) MN 892ff. On Russia's intention to be a 'continuator state' to the USSR, see also Zhenis Kembayev, 'Probleme der Rechtsnachfolge von der Sowjetunion auf die Russische Föderation' (2008) 46 Archiv des Völkerrechts 106, 122ff: Russia referred to itself as 'continuator' in communications with third states and in unilateral declarations.

7 Art 67(1) Constitution of the Russian Federation, amended by the federal constitutional law No. 1-FKZ of 14 March 2020.

8 Theodor Schweisfurth in Ulrich Fastenrath, Theodor Schweisfurth and Carsten Thomas Ebenroth, *Das Recht der Staatensukzession* (1996) 49, 216f. See also Alexey Uvarov, 'The heavy legacy of the Soviet regime' (*Riddle*, 29 November 2022) <https://ridl.io/the-heavy-legacy-of-the-soviet-regime/> accessed 7 November 2024.

9 This bilateral agreement between Russia and Ukraine was signed on 9 December 1994 but never ratified.

property abroad increased by the share of those states that it concluded such agreements with.[10]

The dispute before the Supreme Court reflects the contradiction between the solution found in the multilateral treaties of 1991 and 1992, and Russia's opinion that, as the continuator state of the Soviet Union, it would take over all property that is located abroad.

After the end of the Soviet Union, a Soviet state-owned company ('SDP'), which had used the property in Vienna for decades, was transformed into a joint stock company under Ukrainian law ('UDP', the defendant). The UDP continued to use the property in Vienna for its main representation in Austria. The plaintiff, the Russian Federation, argued that it was the sole owner of the property (and had been entered in the land register as such) and that the Ukrainian company was using the property without legal title. It thus requested that the Ukrainian company vacate the property. The UDP argued that Russia lacked legal standing and that the land register did not reflect the true legal situation because Russia had not become the sole owner of the property after the end of the Soviet Union.[11]

The Supreme Court relied on treaties that provided for the division of the property located abroad and the division of the external debts of the former Soviet Union, which Russia, Ukraine and other successor states had concluded in 1991 and 1992: The Treaty on the Legal Succession in respect of the External Public Debt and Assets of the USSR and the Agreement on the Division of all Property of the former USSR abroad.[12] According to these treaties, Russia was to receive 61.34% of the assets and Ukraine 16.37%. The Supreme Court found that Russia could thus not continue the legal position of the Soviet Union alone. Instead, Ukraine and the Russian Federation became co-owners of the property.[13] As Russia had not become the sole owner after the end of the Soviet Union, Russia could not demand the handover of the plot of land. For such a request to be valid, it would have to be made by all co-owners of the property collectively.[14]

It is remarkable that the Supreme Court came to the conclusion that the property was co-owned by the so-called 'successor states' of the Soviet Union

[10] Austrian Supreme Court, 16 May 2023, 10 Ob 9/23f, para 44.

[11] Supreme Court (n 10) paras 1-4.

[12] Treaty on the Legal Succession in respect of the External Public Debt and Assets of the USSR (n 2) and Agreement on the Division of all Property of the former USSR abroad (n 5).

[13] Supreme Court (n 10) paras 54, 62.

[14] *Ibid.*, para 69.

(*i.e.* by the states that were referred to as 'successor states'/'states-successors' in the multilateral treaties of 1991 and 1992: Russia, Ukraine and other former Soviet republics) without addressing the question of whether the end of the Soviet Union should be categorized as a complete dismemberment (*dismembratio*) or as a sequence of separations under international law (scholars have expressed different views about the so-called 'collapse' or 'dissolution' of the USSR[15]). As the Supreme Court's judgment is based on treaties, it considered the legal categorization of the 'dissolution' of the USSR as ultimately irrelevant. The categorization of the respective type of state succession would have been a relevant preliminary question if the affected states had not reached a final and conclusive agreement on the legal effects of the end of the Soviet Union on property located abroad. As the Supreme Court emphasized:

> In the case of the events that took place in the former USSR, from the perspective of international law, there were reasons that spoke in favour of both the assumption that the Russian Federation continued the previous state and that the USSR ceased to exist through dismemberment [...]. The classification of these events and the related question of whether the Russian Federation generally [...] continued the identity of the former state and whether this was accepted by the community of states is not decisive here because this case only concerns the effects of these events with regard to the property located abroad and these effects were subject to separate bilateral and multilateral agreements between the parties involved.[16]

Thus, the Supreme Court did not have to deal with the question whether –according to customary law – the assets abroad remain property of the continuing state and the successor states if the events were to be qualified as separations. This question is also controversial in international law.[17] Russia's

---

15 See, for example, the different opinions of Schweisfurth (n 6) (who assumes a complete dismemberment) and Kembayev (n 6) 113 and Reinisch, Seidl-Hohenveldern, Hummer and Köck (n 6) MN 845 (according to these authors, the 'collapse' of the Soviet Union constitutes a separation). The occasional use of the terms 'dissolution' or 'collapse' (of the Soviet Union) in this text does not imply a legal classification. We use the terms 'complete dismemberment' (*dismembratio*) and separation to distinguish between different types of state succession.

16 Supreme Court (n 10) para 33, see also para 38.

17 See, for example, Andreas Zimmermann and James Devaney, 'State Succession in Matters Other than Treaties' in Anne Peters (ed), *Max Planck Encyclopedia of Public International Law* (2018) para 18 <https://opil.ouplaw.com/>.

opinion of being a 'continuator state' to the Soviet Union also played no role in the resolution of the legal dispute before the Supreme Court.[18]

The Supreme Court further held that it was irrelevant whether Russia had paid the external debts that would have been attributable to Ukraine according to the quota foreseen in the treaties.[19]

As a result of these specific treaty provisions, it was unnecessary to resort to customary international law to assess the legal effects of the collapse of the Soviet Union on the property located abroad. Nevertheless, the judgment contains some interesting statements on questions of customary international law, as the Supreme Court sought to determine if the treaty rules could have been amended by subsequent custom (the court inquired into the 'existence of a state practice according to which the property located abroad should (only) accrue to the Russian Federation [...]').[20] Here, the Supreme Court considered *Notes Verbales* of the Austrian Federal Ministry for Foreign Affairs. These stated that according to current state practice and customary international law, Russia had become the sole owner of the property abroad of the former Soviet Union. Numerous other European states shared this opinion.[21] However, the Supreme Court found it doubtful whether the Austrian *Notes Verbales* and comparable statements of other European states constituted relevant state practice. In addition, the state practice of the 'specially affected states', *i.e.* the successor states to the Soviet Union, pointed in the opposite direction. The Supreme Court found that the Austrian *Notes Verbales* did not constitute relevant state practice.[22]

Moreover, even if the existing practice provided for the sole ownership of Russia, the Supreme Court considered that Ukraine would not be bound by it. It found Ukraine to be a persistent objector because it had persistently objected to such a rule.[23] In this context, the Supreme Court also formulated a specific prerequisite for the application of the persistent objector rule: the development of a new rule of customary international law (that is rejected by the persistent objector) must not be 'almost uniformly supported by the rest of the international community'.[24] The Supreme Court only referred to a single textbook in support of its assertion that the persistent objection would

18 Supreme Court (n 10) para 56.

19 *Ibid.*, para 57.

20 *Ibid.*, paras 46ff, para 50.

21 *Ibid.*, para 46.

22 *Ibid.*, para 50.

23 *Ibid.*, para 51.

24 *Ibid.*, para 53, see also para 31.

lose its effect in such a case.[25] Despite assuming this additional prerequisite, the Supreme Court ultimately qualified Ukraine as a persistent objector.

The judgment 10 Ob 9/23f is significant because it contains detailed elaborations on different questions of state succession resulting from the collapse of the former Soviet Union. Prior jurisprudence of the Supreme Court and of other domestic courts concerning property of the former USSR mainly dealt with land register issues because the Russian Federation requested to be entered into the land registers of various states instead of the USSR.[26] In Denmark, for example, the courts accepted the Russian Federation's request to be entered in the land register instead of the Soviet Union.[27] The High Court of Justice in London also confirmed the entry of the Russian Federation as the sole owner in the land register, but decided that the Russian Federation could not dispose of the respective property alone until an agreement had been reached with Ukraine.[28] The Regional Court of Berlin, on the other hand, rejected the Russian Federation's request to be entered in the land register, arguing that there had been no transfer of ownership to the Russian Federation alone.[29] In 2004, the Supreme Court had already rejected applications by both the Russian Federation and the current defendant, the Ukrainian company, to amend the land register. The Supreme Court held that the solution to the problem of succession to the property of the Soviet Union was not apparent and that it was not possible to determine complex questions of customary international law in land register proceedings.[30]

In contrast, the present judgment had to assess the legal consequences of the 'dissolution' of the Soviet Union for property located abroad under public international law. It thus deals with the question which state or which states have acquired ownership of property located in Vienna that used to belong to the Soviet Union.

---

25 Namely a textbook by a German professor for public law and international law, see Matthias Herdegen, *Völkerrecht* (21st edn, 2022) § 16 MN 24.

26 See Theodor Schweisfurth, 'Immobiliareigentum der UdSSR in Deutschland: Völkerrechtliche und grundbuchrechtliche Fragen der Staatensukzession' (1998) Zeitschrift für Vermögens- und Immobilienrecht 57.

27 Supreme Court Denmark, Ukraine v Registration Judges in Lyngby (Gentofte) and Copenhagen, U.2007.1533H, reported in ILDC 3259 (DK 2007) 22 March 2007.

28 See Uvarov (n 8).

29 Regional Court Berlin, Decision of 14 November 1995.

30 Austrian Supreme Court, 9 November 2004, 5 Ob 152/04w; Austrian Supreme Court, 9 November 2004, 5 Ob 238/04t.

III. The (Ir)Relevance of the External Debt

The Supreme Court decided the dispute on the basis of treaties that contain specific rules on the succession to property located abroad. It referred to the Agreement on the Division of all Property of the former USSR Abroad of 6 July 1992[31] and the Treaty on the Legal Succession in respect of the External Public Debt and Assets of the USSR of 4 December 1991[32]. These treaties divide the external assets and debts of the USSR according to certain percentage shares and connect these two matters.

However, the Supreme Court held that it was irrelevant that the Russian Federation had in fact paid the external debts that were attributable to Ukraine according to the treaties.[33] The following section discusses whether the *de facto* assumption of the debts by Russia could have had an impact on the ownership of property located abroad. This might be relevant for two reasons: firstly, the treaties cited by the Supreme Court explicitly link the payment of the external debts to the property rights. Thus, the payment of the external debts may be understood as a condition for the succession to the property located abroad. Secondly, the fact that these payments were accepted by the creditor states could be interpreted as relevant state practice, indicating that Russia is a continuator state and not a mere successor state.

The Preamble to the 1991 Treaty on the Legal Succession in respect of the External Public Debt and Assets of the USSR emphasizes the link between the proportional payment of the external debt of the USSR and the states' rights to the property located abroad. Its Article 3 also stipulates that the parties are under an obligation to participate in the liquidation of the external debt and: '*if the above commitment is met*, [the Parties] shall undertake to guarantee the right of property for any of the Parties with respect to its allocated share in the assets of the USSR'[34]. Thus, the obligation to pay the agreed share of the external debts is a prerequisite for the right of each party to take ownership in accordance with the agreed percentage share to which it is entitled.[35]

---

31 Agreement on the Division of all Property of the former USSR abroad (n 5).

32 Treaty on the Legal Succession in respect of the External Public Debt and Assets of the USSR (n 2).

33 Supreme Court (n 10) para 57.

34 Article 3, Treaty on the Legal Succession in respect of the External Public Debt and Assets of the USSR (n 2) (emphasis added).

35 Schweisfurth (n 26) 60.

Similarly, Article 1(3) of the 1992 Agreement on the Division of all Property of the former USSR abroad states that the parties

> shall be guided by the principle of interdependence between the obligation to participate in liquidation and bearing costs of service of the state external debt of the former USSR in the shares established in the above scale, and the possibility to exercise the property right of each of the Parties for its due share of all property of the former USSR abroad.[36]

However, the preamble to this agreement also refers to the 'right of each party to possess, use and dispose of its fair fixed part of the property of the former USSR abroad that belongs to it' (*i.e.* this right apparently already existed at the time of the conclusion of the agreement).

Although some of the treaty provisions seem contradictory, it appears that the state parties' intention was to link the external debts to the external assets. The provisions seek a fair balance between the division of assets and the payment of debts and therefore provide that assets and debts should be divided according to the same percentages. This equitable division of assets and debts also follows the approach foreseen in Article 41 of the 1983 Vienna Convention on Succession of States in respect of State Property, Archives and Debts, which also emphasizes the equitable distribution of debts and property.[37]

---

36 Agreement on the Division of all Property of the former USSR abroad (n 5) Article 1(3).

37 Article 41, Vienna Convention on Succession of States in Respect of State Property, Archives and Debts, 8 April 1983 (not in force); United Nations Conference on Succession of States in Respect of State Property, Archives and Debts Official Records Vol 2: 'the State debt of the predecessor State shall pass to the successor States in equitable proportions, taking into account, in particular, the property, rights and interests which pass to the successor States in relation to that State debt'. The guidelines of the Institut de Droit International on State succession in Matters of Property and Debts, La Succession d'Etats en matière de biens et de dettes, Vancouver, 26 August 2001, also link the division of the property located abroad to the payment of external debts. See, for example, Article 9: 'a correlation should be ensured between the proportion of such property, rights and interests on the one hand, and State debts on the other'. See also Martti Koskenniemi and Jan Klabbers, 'Succession in Respect of State Property, Archives and Debts, and Nationality' in CoE ad hoc Committee of Legal Advisers on Public International Law, *Preliminary Draft Report on the Pilot Project of the Council of Europe on State Practice Regarding State Succession and Issues of Recognition* (1998) 50: 'Debts and assets are but two sides of the same coin'.

Scholars have also stressed the connection between the external debts and the property located abroad.[38] Some have even argued that the treaties of 1991 and 1992 have lost their relevance because the external debts were not divided in accordance with the treaty provisions but were paid by Russia alone.[39]

However, Russia paid the Ukrainian share of the external debt on its own initiative and without Ukraine's consent. In a Memorandum of Understanding from October 1991, the Soviet Union and its republics agreed to joint and several liability towards foreign creditors.[40] In the event of a successor state's default, the creditor states could therefore turn to Russia. Ukraine, however, wanted to pay its share of the debt independently of Russia. In an attempt to prevent Russia from assuming all the debts and assets of the former Soviet Union, Ukraine offered to pay part of the Soviet Union's debt as provided for in the treaties. Simultaneously, it called upon the creditor states (and the states in which the property was located) to suspend Russian use of the former Soviet Union's property until all former Soviet republics reached an agreement on the actual allocation of that property.[41] However, the creditor states refused to agree to an independent servicing of Ukraine's share of the debt and rejected its proposals.[42] In January 1993, Russia and Ukraine once again agreed that both states should contribute to the servicing of external debts.[43] However, Ukraine's payment of its share of the debt was ultimately frustrated by Russia's payment of the entire debt.[44]

The payment of external debts by Russia was contrary to the approach foreseen in the treaties of 1991 and 1992, and was made without prior consent of Ukraine. Therefore, it cannot extinguish Ukraine's claim to its share of the property located abroad. A state cannot unilaterally change rights and obligations contained in a treaty (in this case by settling the debt), especially since the treaty provisions require an agreement between the parties to the

---

38 See for example Koskenniemi and Klabbers (n 37) 50f.

39 Ole Terkelsen on Ukraine v Registration Judges in Lyngby (Gentofte) and Copenhagen, Appeal Decision, U.2007.1533H, 22 March 2007, see ILDC 3259 (DK 2007) A5.

40 Paul Williams and Jennifer Harris, 'State Succession to Debts and Assets: The Modern Law and Policy' (2001) 42 Harvard International Law Journal 355, 378, referring to the appeal of the Prime Minister of Ukraine Vitold P Fokin on 29 January 1992.

41 *Ibid.*

42 Williams and Harris (n 40) 378.

43 See Schweisfurth (n 6) 123.

44 See Uvarov (n 8).

treaty on the actual allocation of assets. This is also explicitly stated in Article 14 of the 1991 Treaty on the Legal Succession in respect of the External Public Debt and Assets of the USSR, which prohibits parties from taking unilateral actions that would 'deprive this treaty of its subject without coordinating their actions with all the Parties'. However, this is exactly what Russia did by paying Ukraine's share of the external debt without Ukraine's consent.[45]

Irrespective of the treaties, the payment of debts also constitutes state practice that might contribute to the formation of customary international law. It is not only Russia's practice that matters here, but also the state practice of the creditor states, which rejected repayment by Ukraine and instead had all debts paid by Russia.[46] In addition to bilateral agreements on the payment of debts, negotiations also took place with states of the Paris Club of creditors, which agreed to Russia repaying all external debts.[47] This state practice indicates that the creditor states accepted Russia as the sole successor to the external debts and assets of the former Soviet Union.

It is questionable whether this state practice was initially accompanied by the necessary *opinio iuris* which is required for the formation of customary international law: the creditor states had a practical interest in negotiating with Russia because Russia was an economically potent debtor, whereas the other former Soviet republics would probably not have been able to service their share of the debt anyway.[48]

However, certain statements and documents, such as the *Note Verbale* of the Austrian Federal Ministry for Foreign Affairs from 2008 or similar statements from other European states may be evidence of *opinio iuris*.[49] In

---

45 Russia could also not argue that the payment of the debt caused a fundamental change of circumstances pursuant to Article 62 of the Vienna Convention on the Law of Treaties. Termination of a treaty is not possible if the fundamental change of circumstances is the result of a breach of the treaty (Article 14 of the 1991 Treaty) by the party invoking Article 62. Article 62(2)(b), Vienna Convention on the Law of Treaties, 23 May 1969, 1155 UNTS 331 (VCLT).

46 Hubert Beemelmans, 'State Succession in International Law: Remarks on Recent Theory and State Practice' (1997) 15 Boston University International Law Journal 71, 115.

47 *Ibid.*

48 Stefan Oeter, 'State Succession and the Struggle over Equity: Some Observations on the Laws of State Succession with Respect to State Property and Debts in Cases of Separation and Dissolution of States' (1995) 38 German Yearbook of International Law 73, 78.

49 'This assessment [that the Russian Federation is to be regarded as the sole owner of all properties of the former USSR in third states], which deviates from the

these notes and declarations, Russia was recognized as the sole owner of all properties of the former Soviet Union that are located outside its borders. As the Supreme Court correctly emphasized, such *Notes Verbales* are not binding.[50] However, in conjunction with the aforementioned state practice, they may constitute evidence of customary international law.

In the *Note Verbale*, the Austrian Foreign Ministry based its legal opinion on the full repayment of the former USSR's external debts by Russia. According to the *Note Verbale*, this legal opinion 'deviated from the previous legal situation and its legal assessment within Austria' – Austria's legal opinion until the early 2000s was that the 'division of the assets of the former USSR requires a mutual agreement by its territorial successors.'[51]

The payment of the external debts by Russia can therefore be considered to have changed the Austrian *opinio iuris*. It might thus be argued that by paying the external debts and by the creditor states accepting that payment, Russia had acquired ownership of all properties located abroad. This argument is however not compatible with the treaties of 1991 and 1992 and would allow the conclusion that the creditor states could influence the succession in respect of property merely by either accepting the debt repayment or refraining from doing so. Particularly in view of Ukraine's willingness towards the creditors to pay its share of the external debts, this argument must be rejected.

IV. State Practice of the Former Soviet republics and State Practice of Countries in which the Property is Located (State Practice After 1992)

The succession with regard to the external property led to additional state practice, subsequent to the 1991 and 1992 treaties. Two questions arise here. The first question is whether the treaty provisions of 1991 and 1992 could be amended by subsequent treaties. In this case, it is not the legal relationship between Russia and the other successor states that is relevant but only the relationship between Russia and Ukraine. Russia was able to conclude

previous legal situation and its legal assessment within Austria, is now also shared by the Federal Ministry for European and International Affairs.' *Note Verbale*, Austrian Federal Ministry for Foreign Affairs, dated 7 August 2008, GZ: BMeiA-RU.8.19.01/0022-I.2/2008.

50 Supreme Court (n 10) para 58.

51 *Ibid.*

so-called 'zero option agreements' with most of the other successor states.[52] According to these agreements, the respective treaty partner transferred its share of the external assets of the former Soviet Union to Russia and was simultaneously released from its obligation to repay its share of the external debt. Thus, between Russia and the states that agreed to enter into the zero option agreements, all shares of external debts and assets were transferred to Russia.[53] This made it possible for Russia to accumulate the debts and assets of the former Soviet Union. The new bilateral agreements between the respective states replaced the conflicting provisions of the 1991 and 1992 treaties.[54] Thus, Russia's share increased by the share of the other states. If Russia had succeeded in concluding such zero option agreements with all parties to the 1991 and 1992 treaties, the new agreements would have effectively replaced the 1991 and 1992 treaties as *leges posteriores*. However, this did not happen because Ukraine refused to conclude the zero-option agreement with Russia.[55] Thus, there is no apparent reason why the 1991 and 1992 treaties should not apply between Russia and Ukraine.

The second question concerns the legal effects of state practice subsequent to the treaties on their operation, and for customary international law on state succession more generally. The Supreme Court correctly observed that subsequent customary international law cannot amend the treaties and affect the rights that were granted to Ukraine therein, if that customary law does not apply to Ukraine in the first place.[56] However, we argue that state practice can help to clarify the consequences of the dissolution of the USSR on property located abroad. The legal consequences of state succession arise at the time when the state succession in question takes place. Thus, international law that is formed subsequently can no longer change the legal consequences of that particular instance of state succession. However, subsequent state practice can *clarify* whether the dissolution of the USSR was a complete dismemberment (*i.e.* that the USSR ceased to exist) or a separation of the Soviet republics from the USSR, which was continued by the Russian Federation, and therefore continued ownership of the external assets. Insofar as the interpretation of the treaties of 1991 and 1992 does not lead to the conclusion that co-ownership

---

52 For example, the Agreement on Succession in Respect of the External Public Debt and Assets of the Former USSR between Russia and Turkmenistan of 31 July 1992.

53 Supreme Court (n 10) para 43.

54 Article 30 para 3 and para 4(a) VCLT (n 45).

55 Supreme Court (n 10) para 44.

56 *Ibid.*, paras 51ff.

of the properties is already created by the treaties themselves (see Section VI. below), the classification of the type of state succession as a preliminary question can have a considerable impact on the succession with regard to property of the former Soviet Union.

In its analysis, the Supreme Court focused on state practice of the former Soviet republics, as they were specially affected by the succession.[57] In fact, when identifying customary law, the practice of the specially affected states must be taken into account.[58] While this requirement should not be overemphasized as states that are not specially affected can also contribute to the formation of customary international law,[59] the question arises as to why other states (*i.e.* states that are not successor states of the Soviet Union) should not also be specially affected. Both the states where foreign property is located as well as the creditor states of the former USSR are also affected by state succession in respect of external assets and debts. To identify customary law, the practice of those states can therefore not be ignored.

The Supreme Court considered that the reason why the successor states of the USSR thought it necessary to conclude bilateral zero-option agreements with the Russian Federation was that they initially operated under the presumption that the property of the USSR should pass to all of them: if the entire foreign property of the former USSR had already accrued to Russia beforehand (because of its status as a 'continuator state'), the zero-option agreements with the successor states would not have been necessary.[60] This view is persuasive and might be correct, but it is not necessarily the only possible explanation why they concluded the zero-option agreements. Another reason why states enter into agreements is that they want to clarify and specify (or codify) existing rules of customary international law.[61] The International Court of Justice (ICJ) has already held that the conclusion of an agreement can speak both in favour of and against the existence of an identical rule of customary international law.[62]

---

57 *Ibid.*, para 50.

58 *North Sea Continental Shelf (Federal Republic of Germany/Netherlands)* [1969] ICJ 3, para 74 (Judgment of 20 February): '[...] State practice, including that of States whose interests are *specially affected*' (emphasis by the authors).

59 ILC, *Draft Conclusions on the Identification of Customary International Law, with Commentaries* (2018) Conclusion 8, para 4.

60 Supreme Court (n 10) para 50.

61 See, for example, Yoram Dinstein, *The Interaction between Customary International Law and Treaties* (2006) 346ff.

62 *Ahmadou Sadio Diallo (Republic of Guinea v Democratic Republic of the Congo)* [2007] ICJ 582, para 90 (Judgment of 24 May).

However, in the case of the zero-option agreements, some former Soviet republics were pressured by Russia to agree[63] or were unable to refuse their consent due to their political or financial situation.[64] Thus, it is difficult to prove the *opinio iuris* that is necessary for the identification of customary law. In fact, it is difficult to draw any conclusion (in favour of or against the existence of a norm of customary international law) from the existence of the zero-option agreements.

Stronger evidence against Russia being the sole successor to all external debts and assets (apart from the treaties of 1991 and 1992) can be derived from various declarations made at the beginning of the 1990s. In these declarations, all Soviet republics were designated as successors with regard to external debts and assets and the declarations also confirmed the proportional division of assets and debts (see also section VI.).[65] Paradoxically, the existence of the zero-option agreements might even weaken the view that, according to customary international law, Russia is the sole successor with regard to property situated abroad: the behaviour of states after the conclusion of these agreements is now not (primarily) based on customary law, but on the zero-option agreements that clearly regulate the succession with regard to property abroad. *Opinio iuris* is therefore more difficult to prove.[66]

The reaction of other states, such as creditor states or states where external assets are situated, could thus be more instructive. State practice can take a variety of forms and may include diplomatic correspondence, various legislative and administrative acts or decisions of national courts.[67] The Supreme Court itself considered that the *Notes Verbales* of the Austrian Foreign Ministry, which assumed a complete transfer of ownership from the USSR to Russia, can be part of state practice.[68] Moreover, domestic court decisions such as that of the Danish Supreme Court from 2007[69] can also constitute relevant state practice and contribute to the formation or clarification of customary international law. However, the majority of state practice results (at least

---

63 Schweisfurth (n 8) 152f.

64 Oeter (n 48) 82f.

65 For further examples, see Schweisfurth (n 26) 60.

66 Dinstein (n 61) 376.

67 ILC, *Draft Conclusions* (n 59) Conclusion 6.

68 Supreme Court (n 10) paras 46f, 53.

69 Supreme Court Denmark (n 27). In this decision, the Supreme Court of Denmark held that Denmark had recognized that Russia had taken over all rights and obligations relating to real estate in Denmark and that the required grounds for the requested title corrections to the land registry were therefore fulfilled.

implicitly) from the fact that the creditor states treated Russia as the sole debtor of all Soviet debts (see section III).

Even if the practice of the states where the property of the former Soviet Union is located, in conjunction with that of Russia and the majority of the Soviet successor states, is regarded as sufficient to establish a rule of customary international law that provides that Russia alone should succeed to the external debts and assets of the former Soviet Union, this rule would not be applicable if Ukraine had objected to this rule of customary international law while it was in the process of formation. This was argued by the defendant in the proceedings. The possibility of a *persistent objection* will be addressed in section V.

V. The Supreme Court's Statements regarding the Persistent Objector Rule

The Supreme Court ultimately did not have to examine the applicable customary international law in detail, as it decided the dispute on the basis of the treaties of 1991 and 1992, and because it applied the *persistent objector* rule. According to this rule, an emerging norm of customary international law cannot bind a state that has persistently objected to this rule while it was in the process of formation.[70] The Supreme Court considered that Ukraine would not be bound by a rule providing for the sole ownership of Russia as Ukraine was a *persistent objector*.[71]

Although it was not relevant for the application of the persistent objector rule in this context, the Supreme Court referred to the German professor Matthias Herdegen who argued that '[t]he persistent objection loses its effect if the formation of a new rule is almost uniformly supported by the community of states'.[72] However, this argument has no basis in international law.[73]

---

[70] Bruno Simma and Stephan Wittich, 'Das Völkergewohnheitsrecht' in August Reinisch (ed), *Österreichisches Handbuch des Völkerrechts* (6th edn, 2021) MN 175.

[71] Supreme Court (n 10) para 51.

[72] Supreme Court (n 10) para 31. With reference to Herdegen (n 25) § 16 MN 24.

[73] However, Jonathan Charney, to whom Herdegen refers, argues that a persistent objector can only exist in the case of particular customary international law, and that a state cannot evade a rule of general customary international law by persistent objection. Jonathan Charney, 'The Persistent Objector Rule and the Development of Customary International Law' (1986) BYIL 56.

In fact, an emerging rule must be supported by state practice that is 'extensive and virtually uniform' to become customary international law.[74] A persistent objection cannot prevent the emergence of such a rule, but it can prevent a state from being bound by it. The Supreme Court should therefore not have relied on Herdegen's opinion that a persistent objection is ineffective if the formation of a norm is almost uniformly supported by the community of states. While it might indeed be difficult for states to maintain their objections in the face of overwhelming state practice,[75] this is not due to the rule suggested by Herdegen, but because of practical considerations and the pressure exerted by the international community on the persistent objector: for example, several states gave up their initial objections to the formation of new customary rules on the breadth of the territorial sea because maintaining their objections would have resulted in serious disadvantages for these states,[76] and China struggled to remain a persistent objector with regard to the restrictive approach on state immunity.[77]

The *ratio* behind the persistent objector rule is to balance different interests in the process of the formation of customary international law: on the one hand, the protest of a single state should not prevent the formation of a new norm of customary international law (after all, the formation of customary international law does not depend on the consensus of all states). On the other hand, it should be possible for an individual state to avoid being bound by any norm by means of a particularly qualified protest.[78] The balance inherent in

---

74 *North Sea Continental Shelf* (n 58) para 74: 'State practice [...] should have been both extensive and virtually uniform.'

75 See for example Green (n 4) 225ff.

76 See Olufemi Elias, 'Persistent Objector' in Wolfrum (ed), Max Planck Encyclopedia of Public International Law (2006) para 4f. The United Kingdom initially insisted on a breadth of 3 miles but abandoned this position in favour of the 12 mile rule advocated by the majority of states, because opposition to the new rule only brought practical disadvantages to the United Kingdom.

77 'China has also been a persistent objector to the restrictive immunity approach. As with the Soviet Union, China has struggled to have its exempt position respected in foreign courts [...] there are signs that China too is beginning to abandon its objections and reluctantly accept restrictive immunity [...]. The objections of China have therefore similarly been cited as an indication of the difficulty (or impossibility) of effectively maintaining persistent objector status.' Green (n 4) 234f. China has indeed changed its state immunity law in January 2024.

78 Prosper Weil, 'Towards Relative Normativity in International Law?' (1983) 77 AJIL 413, 433f.

the persistent objector rule would be disturbed if the 'almost uniform' support by the community of states could render a persistent objection ineffective.

While the persistent objector rule is rarely applied in practice and there are high hurdles to its application,[79] it is also not entirely clear whether it is relevant in the present case. For state succession in respect of the assets of the former USSR, it is unlikely that the treaties of 1991 and 1992 could have been amended by subsequent (regional) customary international law. Ukraine's resistance makes this unlikely for two reasons: firstly, in order for a treaty to be modified by subsequent customary international law, all treaty parties must participate in the formation of the new rule of customary international law.[80] Moreover, a treaty cannot be modified by the practice of states that are not even parties to the treaty (such as practice of states in which the foreign property is located). Secondly, a rule of regional customary international law according to which Russia is to be the sole owner of the assets located abroad cannot be formed due to the resistance of Ukraine. If there is even one state that opposes the creation of a norm of regional customary regional international law, such a norm cannot be created in the first place.[81]

Rather, the crucial point is whether the 'dissolution' of the Soviet Union is to be categorized either as a complete dismemberment or as a separation according to the pre-existing rules of customary international law on state succession. The subsequent state practice of all states (*i.e.* the successor state as well as the practice of the states where the property is located) can provide clarity here.[82] However, it is questionable whether this categorization constitutes newly emerging customary international law that a state can evade as a persistent objector.[83] This would only be the case if one assumes that the question of state succession with regard to the assets of the former Soviet Union cannot be solved on the basis of the international law existing in 1991 and the rules for complete dismemberment and separation. Only if

79 Green (n 4) 2, 225ff.

80 See Irina Buga, *Modification of Treaties by Subsequent Practice* (2018).

81 Simma and Wittich (n 70) MN 185: Due to their narrow scope of application, particular/regional norms of customary law must not merely be recognized 'generally' by a majority, but rather by all states within the region that are to be bound by them.

82 See also *Legal Consequences of the Separation of the Chagos Archipelago from Mauritius in 1965* [2019] ICJ 95, para 104 (Advisory Opinion of 25 February).

83 A state must raise its objections while a norm of customary international law is still in the process of formation. A later protest would be ineffective. Elias (n 76) para 15.

one considers the state practice with regard to the foreign property of the Soviet Union as contributing to the formation of a newly emerging norm of (general) customary international that applies to the Soviet Union and later similar cases of state succession, could Ukraine be considered a persistent objector. In view of the extremely inconsistent state practice this is however more than questionable.

The Supreme Court does not distinguish these different questions. If a dispute can be decided on the basis of the treaties alone (see section VI below), there is no need to determine the existence of customary international law anyway. If not, however, and if customary international law became relevant for deciding cases involving the succession with regard to property located abroad, there would be no way around a detailed analysis of these questions.

VI. Interpretation of the 1991 and 1992 Treaties

A. Why do Courts in Countries in Which the Property is Located Refer to the 1991 and 1992 Treaties?

The Supreme Court decided that it was not necessary to qualify the 'dissolution' of the Soviet Union as a particular type of succession,[84] because the

[84] The categorization of a specific type of state succession under international law – in particular the question whether it is a complete dismemberment or a separation – has fundamental consequences for the property located abroad. A state succession can lead to a change of ownership with regard to a state's assets located in third countries. However, this is not always the case. It depends on whether there is a state that continues the legal personality of the predecessor state, or whether this predecessor state has ceased to exist, and various successor states have taken its place. However, the legal categorization of the break-up of the Soviet Union is controversial: on the one hand, it is argued that the Soviet Union has 'ceased to exist'. In this case, there would be a complete dismemberment of the Soviet Union with several new states taking its place. All former Soviet republics (including Russia) would therefore be 'successor states' (see for example Schweisfurth (n 6)). On the other hand, it has also been argued that the break-up of the Soviet Union was a separation of the Soviet republics from the USSR, whose legal personality Russia continues to this day (see, for example, Kembayev (n 6) 113. Reinisch, Seidl-Hohenveldern, Hummer and Köck (n 6) MN 845). There seems to be general agreement that in case of complete dismemberment of a state, its property located abroad should be divided among the successor states. In contrast, there is no clear rule in customary international law for the case of separation. The Vienna Convention on Succession of States in respect

states that were directly affected (Russia, Ukraine and other successor states) had concluded treaties on the succession in respect of property located abroad. The Agreement on the Division of all Property of the former USSR abroad of 6 July 1992[85] specified the provisions of the Treaty on the Legal Succession in respect of the External Public Debt and Assets of the USSR of 4 December 1991,[86] which divided the external debts and assets among the former Soviet republics according to certain percentages.

The Supreme Court engaged with the question of why these treaties had legal relevance before Austrian courts, given that Austria was not a treaty party and the treaties as such could thus not be binding for Austria (*pacta tertiis nec nocent nec prosunt*). It referred to these treaties because it regarded them as an expression of the choice made by the states that were directly affected by the legal consequences of state succession and therefore decided that they were relevant under customary international law.[87] Treaties concluded between states that are directly affected by a state succession provide courts and authorities in states where the property is located with the most important means for clarifying questions of state succession in respect of this property.

The Supreme Court thus presumed the existence of a norm of customary international law which provides that agreements on the consequences of state succession should have priority:

> The states have considerable discretion in choosing the legal consequences of state succession and assets are therefore often divided by treaty. Even if treaties do not have direct legal effects for other subjects of international law that are not party to the treaty, they may be an expression of an agreement by the states that are affected by the dissolution process on the

of State Property, Archives and Debts (n 37) is silent on this matter. One could therefore conclude *e contrario* that under general customary international law, all immovable property located abroad should remain with the 'rump state' (*i.e.* the smaller but still existing predecessor state). However, there are also good arguments that speak in favour of an apportionment of the property among the separating state and the continuing rump state: Andreas Zimmermann and James Devaney, for example, argue that since the law of state succession is governed by the principle of equity, there should be a division of the property located abroad in the case of separation. Zimmermann and Devaney (n 17) para 18.

85 Treaty on the Legal Succession in respect of the External Public Debt and Assets of the USSR (n 2).

86 Agreement on the Division of all Property of the former USSR abroad (n 5).

87 Supreme Court (n 10) para 32.

legal consequences of state succession and are therefore relevant under customary international law'.[88]

The Vienna Convention on Succession of States in Respect of State Property, Archives and Debts[89] also stipulates that agreements between the states that are directly affected take precedence (see in particular Articles 17(1) and 18(1)).[90] Thus, insofar as a rule of customary international law on the priority of such agreements exists, the two treaties of 1991 and 1992 are (indirectly) relevant for Austrian courts. These courts have an obligation under customary international law to take the treaty provisions into account when they decide on the consequences of state succession for property located in Austria. The approach taken by the Supreme Court is also in accordance with the argument that there exists a general duty under customary international law that obliges states not to frustrate the implementation of treaties concluded between other states. States must therefore respect any agreements of the successor states on the division of the assets of the predecessor state.[91]

Scholars have proposed various other justifications for the bindingness of treaties, which were concluded by the states that are directly affected by the state succession, for courts and authorities in the states where the property is located.[92] In some cases, however, the binding nature of such agreements for the states where the property is located has also been rejected.[93]

---

88 *Ibid.*

89 Vienna Convention on Succession of States in Respect of State Property, Archives and Debts (n 37).

90 Article 17.1 and Article 18.1 contain provisions '[...] unless the predecessor State and the successor State otherwise agree' and '[...] unless the successor States concerned otherwise agree' respectively.

91 Ian Sinclair, *The Vienna Convention on the Law of Treaties* (1984) 99.

92 See, for example, the somewhat divergent view of Brigitte Stern, *La succession d'États* (1996) 262 Recueil des Cours 9, 169: Although she also refers to customary international law to justify the effect of treaties for states where the property is located, she argues that such treaties are only binding for the courts and authorities in these states if they 'implement' the solutions prescribed by customary international law. Treaties between successor states are binding for these states because they are bound by customary international law in the first place. If the treaties deviate from the (very general) rules of customary international law on state succession in respect of property, they are not binding for the states where the property is located.

93 'Such an agreement is *res inter alios acta* in relation to third States [...] third States in whose territory property covered by State succession is situated are not

B. Interpretation of the Treaties

In the Treaty on the Legal Succession in respect of the External Public Debt and Assets of the USSR of 4 December 1991, all former Soviet republics are equally referred to as 'states-successors' (Article 2). Whether Russia should otherwise be considered as the 'continuator state' of the Soviet Union was therefore irrelevant for the Supreme Court:

> whether the Russian Federation generally [...] continued the identity of the previous state and whether this was accepted by the community of states [...] is not decisive here because this case only concerns the effects of these events with regard to the property located abroad and these effects were subject to separate bilateral and multilateral agreements between the parties involved.[94]

Therefore, the court does not have to consider questions of customary international law if the parties have reached a final and conclusive agreement on the succession to the property located abroad.[95] It is thus crucial whether the treaties already provide a basis for the transfer of the property of the former Soviet Union to the treaty parties. According to the Supreme Court, the transfer of ownership to the treaty parties 'results from the clear Art. 1 para. 2' of the 1992 Agreement on the Division of all Property of the former USSR abroad.[96]

In contrast to what the Supreme Court suggests, Article 1(2) does not explicitly state that all successor states are to become co-owners of each individual property object located abroad. It rather provides that the property of the former USSR is divided and transferred to the parties in accordance with their fixed shares. The Supreme Court assumed that the transfer of property to the successor states occurred directly through the 1992 Agreement. This assumption is persuasive as the authentic Russian text of Article 1(2)

---

required to take action in pursuance of such agreements'. Opinion No 12 of the Badinter Commission, cited in Vladimir-Djuro Degan, 'State Succession' (1993) 4 Finnish Yearbook of International Law 130, 187.

94 Supreme Court (n 10) para 33. See also *ibid.*, para 38: 'irrespective of the categorization of the 'break-up' of the USSR under international law, the property of the former USSR should not belong to the Russian Federation alone', according to the treaties.

95 On the relationship between treaties and customary international law and explaining that the rules of customary law may be useful to fill in possible lacunae in the treaty, see Dinstein (n 61) 404ff.

96 Supreme Court (n 10) para 38.

is formulated in the present tense which is why the agreement of 1992 itself can provide a basis for the transfer of the property to the parties.[97] Thus, the transfer of ownership does not depend on the conclusion of 'separate agreements' which are mentioned in Article 4.[98] Article 4 provides that allotment in kind shall be carried out on the basis of separate agreements (such a separate agreement regarding the allocation of property in kind has of course not been reached between Russia and Ukraine[99]). Article 1(2), read in context of Article 4, could have been interpreted differently, *i.e.* that the treaty itself merely expresses the intention to conclude agreements on the transfer of ownership at a later date. However, even if the process of the division of the property is clearly not completed with the conclusion of the 1992 agreement, it is nevertheless unlikely that the transfer of ownership should only take place with the conclusion of the separate agreements. Because of the formulation of Article 1(2) in the authentic Russian version, the better argument is that the 1992 agreement is already the legal basis for the transfer of ownership of the property located abroad. To support this conclusion, the Supreme Court also emphasized Article 3. According to this provision, the agreement gives each party the right to possess, use and dispose of its 'owned' share of all property of the former USSR.[100] This does not necessarily mean that the treaty parties become co-owners of each individual property abroad. The rights to possession, usage, and disposal refer to the (abstract) share of the

---

97 According to the wording of the (original) Russian text of the treaty. Interestingly, there are also translations in the United Nations Treaty Series that might suggest a transfer of ownership at a later date, for example the French version: 'Les propriétés susmentionnées *feront* l'objet d'une division et *deviendront* la propriété des Parties conformément au barème suivant de parts fixées des actifs de l'ex-URSS' (emphasis added); see also the English version: 'The above-mentioned property *shall* be subject to division and become property of the parties [...]' (emphasis added). See 2380 UNTS 76 (English), 80 (French).

98 These 'separate agreements' on the allocation of specific property objects give the parties the right to own, use and dispose of foreign assets independently (Article 4).

99 In the case of Yugoslavia, for example, all successor states reached a multilateral agreement on the allocation in kind of the property located abroad. They agreed on the allocation of certain properties to the various successor states. The allocation of the individual properties was then offset against the agreed percentage shares of the successor states. See Mirjam Skrk, Ana Petric and Marko Rakovec, 'The Agreement on Succession Issues and Some Dilemmas Regarding Its Implementation' (2015) 75 Zbornik znanstvenih razprav 213, 227ff.

100 Supreme Court (n 10) para 39.

entire property.[101] However, Article 1(2) and Article 3 together indicate that co-ownership already arises on the basis of the 1992 agreement.

In any case, the 1991 Treaty on the Legal Succession in respect of the External Public Debt and Assets of the USSR and the 1992 Agreement on the Division of all Property of the former USSR abroad lay the foundation for a distribution of property located abroad and stipulate that each party is entitled to a share of all the property located in any state outside the former USSR.[102] The treaty provisions are not always clear, and are (perhaps intentionally) formulated in a very general and vague manner.[103] However, as they allow the interpretation that the 1992 agreement already gives rise to co-ownership of all parties – the Supreme Court also based its decision on an article by Theodor Schweisfurth, who argues that this is the case[104] – it constitutes a final and conclusive agreement on the succession to the property located abroad, and there is no need to resort to customary international law. Customary international law would only play a role if the 1992 agreement did not establish co-ownership of the treaty parties (although this has also been argued, see below).

It is not always easy to say whether a rule has achieved the status of customary international law in the area of state succession. Thus, the problem is that there may not be clear rules of customary international law that can be used as 'fallback' if the treaty parties have not clearly and conclusively articulated their will regarding a specific issue.[105] It is therefore difficult to say what would happen if a court found that the treaties of 1991 and 1992 do

---

101 Theodor Schweisfurth interprets the share mentioned in Article 3 as an abstract share. See Schweisfurth (n 8). Since Article 3 gives the parties the right to dispose of their abstract share of property, it could be seen as a basis for the 'zero option agreements' which transferred parties' shares to Russia.

102 See the division according to certain percentages in Article 4 of the 1991 Treaty on the Legal Succession in respect of the External Debt and Assets of the USSR (n 2) and Article 1 of the 1992 Agreement on the Division of all Property of the former Soviet Union abroad (n 5).

103 Article 3 of the 1992 Agreement on the Division of all Property of the former Soviet Union abroad (n 5) reads: 'Each Party has the right to independently possess, use and dispose of its owned (or that was passed into the ownership of each Party) fixed share of all property of the former USSR, as well as the right to have its allotment in kind. Possibility of division in kind of the property of the former USSR abroad shall be carried out taking into account the normal operation of property objects.'

104 Schweisfurth (n 26) 57.

105 Zimmermann and Devaney (n 17) para 49.

not provide for the transfer of ownership and that such a transfer could only occur through the division of the property in kind (via 'separate agreements'). In that case, the property would probably have to remain with the state that continues the legal personality of the Soviet Union until the division in kind is completed. However, this would presuppose that the 'dissolution' of the Soviet Union was a series of separations of the Soviet republics, that Russia remained as a 'rump state' or 'continuator state' that continues the identity of the Soviet Union and that in such a case the property located abroad remains (at least initially) with the rump state.[106]

While Theodor Schweisfurth assumes a complete dismemberment of the Soviet Union and co-ownership of the successor states,[107] other authors have argued the opposite: that the break-up of the Soviet Union was a separation and that the rump state (*i.e.* Russia) remains the sole owner until a concrete agreement between the rump state and the successor states on the division of the property is reached (see also the guidelines on state succession in matters of property and debts of the *Institut de Droit International*[108]). Such an agreement must be proven to the courts of the state where the property is located.[109] According to Hubert Beemelmans, this agreement cannot merely consist of treaties that broadly regulate the division of the property according to certain percentages. He argues that if the division of property is to be implemented in two stages – first in an agreement on the 'overall'

106 On this preliminary question, see (n 84).

107 Schweisfurth (n 26) 63f.

108 According to Article 19(4) of the Guidelines on State Succession in matters of property and debts of the Institut de Droit International, immovable state property remains in principle with the continuing state. However, the successor states have the right to an equitable apportionment of the property. At first glance, this provision probably appears quite contradictory. It provides that in the event of separation, the property situated abroad initially remains with the continuing state (predecessor state), but the successor states are entitled to a division of these assets (*i.e.* the continuator state would be under an obligation to negotiate an agreement on the division with the successor states). Until this division, the property would however remain with the rump state. See Institut de Droit International, La Succession d'Etats en matière de biens et de dettes, Vancouver, 26 August 2001, Article 19(4): 'En cas de cession et de sécession (continuité de l'Etat prédécesseur), les biens immobiliers d'Etat de l'Etat prédécesseur situés en dehors de son territoire restent, en principe, sa propriété. Toutefois les Etats successeurs ont droit à une répartition équitable de ces biens.'

109 Hubert Beemelmans, 'Die Staatennachfolge in Staatsvermögen in Drittstaaten, Auslandsschulden, gebietsbezogene rechtliche Regelungen und Staatsangehörigkeit – eine Problemskizze' (1995) 41 Osteuropa Recht 73, 83.

division of the property according to certain percentages and then in a further agreement on the specific allocation of the individual property objects – the latter agreement should be decisive for the transfer of ownership.[110]

There are different arguments that speak against Bemelmans' claim that only the specific allocation of the property objects by separate agreements establishes the ownership of the successor states and that Russia remains the owner of the immovable property as a 'rump' or 'continuator state' until such a concrete allocation of the property is completed. In particular, it must be taken into consideration that the break-up of the Soviet Union was not a typical case of separation. Early declarations and treaties by Russia, Ukraine and the other successor states imply that the Soviet Union ceased to exist and that its property rights were extinguished as well, as in the case of complete dismemberment. The Alma-Ata Declaration of 21 December 1991 stated: 'With the formation of the Commonwealth of Independent States the USSR ceases to exist'.[111] The 1992 Agreement on the Division of all Property of the former USSR abroad also refers to the 'termination of existence of the USSR as a state-subject of international law' and the 1991 Treaty on the Legal Succession in respect of the External Public Debt and Assets of the USSR refers to all signatories equally as 'states-successors' (including Russia).[112] Moreover, the treaties are guided by Article 18(1)(b) of the Vienna Convention on Succession of States in respect of State Property, Archives and Debts, which applies in case of complete dismemberment of a state. Article 18(1)(b) provides that immovable property located abroad shall pass to all successor states 'in equitable proportions'.

---

110 *Ibid.*, 83. Allocation means that the states agree on who is to receive which specific property object, taking into account their respective shares. However, the states could also agree that co-ownership should arise with regard to specific property objects. A different interpretation of the provisions of the 1992 treaty would speak in favour of this outcome (the English and French translations of the 1992 treaty would speak in favour of such an interpretation because they are arguably more future-oriented).

111 Alma-Ata Declaration, 21 December 1991.

112 Treaty on the Legal Succession in respect of the External Debt and Assets of the USSR (n 2) Article 2.

C. What if the Treaties Provide no Conclusive Answer to the Question of Ownership of the Property of the Former Soviet Union? Deciding the Dispute on the Basis of Customary International Law

The legal fate of the property located abroad is decided in the moment of state succession (although changes may occur later, for example through the conclusion of bilateral or multilateral treaties).[113] In case of complete dismemberment, the property is divided and passes to the successor states in accordance with customary international law.[114]

Russia is now generally regarded as a 'continuator' of the Soviet Union, which would speak in favour of a separation. However, Brigitte Stern argues that Russia was not always a continuator state but rather just one successor state among many before it 'transformed' into a continuator state.[115] Thus, the break-up of the Soviet Union was no ordinary case of separation because it was not clear from the beginning that Russia would continue the identity of the USSR. Instead, at the time of the dissolution of the Soviet Union, its property rights were extinguished, and the successor states became owners of the property in its stead. Even though the international community ultimately regarded Russia as continuator of the Soviet Union, many third countries initially assumed that the property located abroad would be subject to partition. This changed over time and Russia was recognized by many states as the sole owner of the property of the former USSR (see section III). Although recognition by third states can be important in order to clarify whether a state is a continuator state or a 'normal' successor state, the fate of the property located abroad

---

[113] See Steven Wheatley, 'Revisiting the Doctrine of Intertemporal Law' (2021) 41 Oxford Journal of Legal Studies 484, 487; and the principle from the *Island of Palmas case* (*Netherlands v USA*) (1928) 2 RIAA 829, 845: 'a juridical fact must be appreciated in the light of the law contemporary with it, and not of the law in force at the time when a dispute in regard to it arises or falls to be settled'.

[114] See, for example, Zimmermann and Devaney (n 17) and the section 'Current Customary Law with regard to State Succession concerning Property and Debts', para 11ff, para 18 and the Vienna Convention on Succession of States in respect of State Property, Archives and Debts (n 37) Article 18 para 1 lit b.

[115] Stern (n 92) 388ff, 404ff: 'Différents textes ont prévu une répartition équitable conforme à l'article 18 de la Convention de 1983, concernant les cas de dissolution, ce qui confirme qu'au départ la Russie se considérait bien comme un Etat successeur parmi d'autres, sauf en ce qui concernait son statut au Conseil de sécurité de l'ONU'.

should not be determined exclusively by the subjective reactions of the states where the property is located, but (also) by objective factors at the time of state succession.[116]

The circumstances of the dissolution of the Soviet Union speak against Russia retaining all of the USSR's property abroad due to its role as the 'continuator state' of the USSR. Instead, the property located abroad was subject to division among all successor states (including Russia) at the time when the Soviet Union dissolved. This is also supported by the fact that the Treaty on the Legal Succession in respect of the External Public Debt and Assets of the USSR of 4 December 1991 provided for the division of the Soviet Union's property abroad even before the Soviet Union was formally dissolved.

Even if the 1991 Treaty and the 1992 Agreement on the Division of all Property of the former USSR abroad do not explicitly state that the treaty parties should become co-owners of the property located abroad until they manage to reach an agreement on the allocation of the property, customary international law might provide for co-ownership as well. Some authors argue that customary international law provides for co-ownership in such situations.[117] The Vienna Convention on Succession of States in respect of State Property, Archives and Debts does not specify which rights the successor states may exercise until they agree on the allocation of the property located abroad. However, the guidelines of the *Institut de Droit International*[118]

---

116 Rein Mullerson, 'The continuity and succession of states by reference to former USSR and Yugoslavia' (1993) 42 International and Comparative Law Quarterly 473, 476: 'To determine whether, from the point of view of international law, there was a dismemberment of the Soviet Union (so that it has ceased to exist and there are only successor States) or whether one of the former Soviet republics continues its existence, it is necessary to take into account objective as well as subjective factors.' On the importance of the subjective element, see however James Crawford, *The Creation of States in International Law* (1979) 406: 'Where there are substantial changes in the entity concerned, continuity might depend upon recognition [...]'.

117 See, for example, Konrad G Bühler, 'Casenote: Two Recent Austrian Supreme Court Decisions on State Succession from an International Law Perspective' (1997) 2 ARIEL 213, 233ff, 237: '[C]o-successor States [...] form a *communio incidens* under international law with respect to jointly inherited property pending a determination of their respective shares and a distribution or partition among them', or Beemelmans (n 109) 80, referring to the case of total dismemberment. On *communio incidens*, see also the decision of the Austrian Supreme Court, 17 December 1996, 4 Ob 2304/96v.

118 Institut de Droit International, La Succession d'Etats en matière de biens et de dettes (n 108).

stipulate that the successor states are co-owners pending a partition of the property among them, provided that the property is not allocated to a specific state: 'les Etats concernés devraient être considérés comme formant, dès le début de la procédure de répartition, une indivision (*communio incidens*)'.[119]

VII. Conclusion

The judgment of the Supreme Court shows that the end of the Soviet Union continues to present courts with difficult questions of international law and that the succession to foreign property of the former Soviet Union remains highly controversial. The court relied on treaties concluded by the former Soviet Republics in the early 1990s and thus managed to solve the dispute without addressing the question of whether the end of the Soviet Union should be categorized as a complete dismemberment (*dismembratio*) or as a sequence of separations under international law.

However, a court that draws on these treaties (*i.e.* on the Agreement on the Division of all Property of the former USSR abroad of 6 July 1992 and the Treaty on the Legal Succession in respect of the External Public Debt and Assets of the USSR of 4 December 1991) to determine the succession in respect of the property located abroad should not completely ignore the *de facto* assumption of external debts by Russia. The treaties expressly link the payment of external debts with the ownership of property located abroad. The payment of debts may even be understood as a condition for succession to the property. However, Russia paid the external debts on its own initiative and without Ukraine's consent. It could therefore not eliminate Ukraine's claim to its share of the property. A state cannot unilaterally change rights and obligations contained in a treaty. The 1991 treaty even explicitly protects the parties against unilateral actions by one treaty party that would deprive the others of their rights. The fact that the creditor states rejected Ukraine's offer to pay its share of the debts, and only accepted payment of debts by Russia does not impact Ukraine's rights either because the creditor states cannot influence state succession by either accepting debt repayment or refusing to do so.

However, the practice of the states where the property is located resulted precisely from the fact that they treated Russia as the sole debtor of all Soviet

---

[119] *Ibid.*, Article 10(2): '[T]he States concerned should be deemed to own the assets and be liable for the debts in common (*communio incidens*) from the outset of the apportionment procedure.'

debts. Of course, the practice of these states (such as the *Notes Verbales* of the Austrian Foreign Ministry cited by the Supreme Court) cannot amend the 1991 and 1992 treaties. However, the practice of third states might help to clarify whether the 'dissolution' of the Soviet Union was a complete dismemberment (and the USSR ceased to exist) or a series of separations of the Soviet republics from the USSR, whose legal identity was continued by the Russian Federation. The categorization of the respective type of state succession would be a relevant preliminary question if a court concluded that the treaties do not constitute a final and conclusive agreement on the legal effects of the dissolution of the Soviet Union on property located abroad.

However, the circumstances of the dissolution of the Soviet Union speak against the idea that Russia alone should take over all external debts and assets. Not only the treaties of 1991 and 1992, but also various declarations by the former Soviet republics in the early 1990s referred to all Soviet republics equally as successors to external debts and assets and confirmed the proportional division. According to these treaties and declarations, the Soviet Union ceased to exist as a subject of international law. Even though the international community ultimately accepted Russia's claim to continue the identity of the Soviet Union, many third countries initially assumed that the property located abroad would be subject to a division. This changed over time and Russia was recognized by many states as the sole owner of the property of the former USSR. The states where the property is located changed their legal opinion primarily because of the repayment of debts by Russia. This inconsistency however shows that the 'dissolution' of the Soviet Union was no ordinary separation which makes it unlikely that the Russian Federation became the sole owner of the property located abroad. Instead, at the time of the dissolution of the Soviet Union, its property rights were extinguished, and the successor states became owners of the property in its stead. Subsequent recognition by third states can be important to clarify whether a state is a 'continuator' state or a mere successor state. However, the determination of the type of state succession and the fate of the property abroad cannot be based solely on the subjective reactions of third states (which are influenced by factual circumstances such as the assumption of debt) but must also be assessed according to objective factors at the time of state succession.

It is therefore unclear why the Supreme Court applied the persistent objector rule. For the question of state succession to the property of the former USSR, it is less decisive whether the treaties from 1991 and 1992 could have been amended by subsequent (regional) customary international law. In view of Ukraine's resistance, this is unthinkable anyway. A treaty can only be modified by subsequent customary international law if all treaty parties participate in its formation. Rather, the crucial point is whether the dissolution of the Soviet Union is to be considered as a complete dismemberment or as a separation according to the pre-existing rules of customary international law on state succession. However, it is questionable whether this categorization constitutes newly emerging customary international law that a state can evade as a persistent objector. Only if one considers the state practice regarding the foreign property of the Soviet Union as contributing to the formation of a newly emerging norm of general customary international that applies to the Soviet Union and subsequent similar cases of state succession, could Ukraine be considered a persistent objector. In view of the extremely inconsistent state practice this is more than questionable.

The Supreme Court also referred to a legal opinion according to which the persistent objection loses its effect if the formation of a new rule is almost uniformly supported by the rest of the community of states. This argument has no basis in international law. In fact, an emerging rule must be supported by state practice that is 'widespread and almost uniform' to become customary international law. A persistent objection cannot prevent the emergence of such a rule, but it can prevent a state from being bound by it. Courts should not assume that there exists a requirement that a persistent objection may not be directed against a norm that is almost uniformly supported by the community of states. If there is an overwhelming state practice, it might indeed be difficult for states to maintain their objections. However, this is due to practical considerations and the pressure that the international community regularly exerts on the persistent objector. The balance inherent in the persistent objector rule would be disturbed if the 'almost uniform' support by the community of states could render a persistent objection ineffective.

The classification of the type of state succession under general customary international is irrelevant if the parties have reached a final and conclusive agreement on the succession to the property located abroad. Thus, it is crucial whether the treaties alone provide a basis for the transfer of the property of the former Soviet Union to the treaty parties or whether they only provide for the division in principle. The 1991 and 1992 treaties do not explicitly state that that all contracting parties become co-owners of each individual property object abroad. The key question is thus whether the transfer of ownership occurs directly through the treaties or if the transfer of ownership depends on the conclusion of 'separate agreements' concerning the allocation of the property. The wording of the 1992 treaty and the circumstances of the 'dissolution' of the Soviet Union support the former interpretation. However, it has also been argued that only the second step, the conclusion of specific agreements on individual property objects, leads to a transfer of ownership.

While we agree with the decision of the Supreme Court that Ukraine and Russia are co-owners of the property, this article has argued that the court should have explained why the payment of debts by Russia was irrelevant. Moreover, the Supreme Court should have discussed the interpretation of the 1991 and 1992 treaties in more depth. The Supreme Court's arguments regarding customary international law and the persistent objector rule could have been more precise.

Co-ownership might also create considerable practical difficulties – not only in Austria – but also in other states where property is located. Of course, the judgment of the Supreme Court is not binding for courts in other countries. However, the Russian aggression in Ukraine makes it perhaps more likely that proceedings in other countries to clarify the ownership of former Soviet assets will be initiated. Following the Supreme Court's determination of co-ownership, the case was referred back to the court of first instance. Russia's request would have to include all co-owners. The Supreme Court left open the possibility that other states apart from Russia and Ukraine could also be co-owners of the property in question. It remains to be seen how the Russian Federation will deal with this dilemma and whether it will explicitly recognize Ukraine's succession to the property abroad by naming it as a co-owner.

Acknowledgments

We thank Jane A Hofbauer, Philipp Janig, Benjamin Letzler, Rebecca McMenamin, Michael Waibel, Maximilian Weninger, Anna Zimmermann and the participants of the 6th Munich Public International Law Early Career Researcher Forum for helpful comments.

The Individual Assessment of Protection Claims by Afghan Women and Girls: Note on CJEU C-608/22

Lisa Heschl | Post-Doctoral Scientist, European Training and Research Centre for Human Rights and Democracy, University of Graz, Austria, lisa.heschl@uni-graz.at

Abstract

One of the guiding principles of European asylum law is to assess protection claims individually, taking into account both the objective situation in a country of origin and subjective circumstances on the side of the applicant. In C-608/22, the Court of Justice of the European Union got the opportunity to interpret Article 4(3) Qualification Directive and the requirements for the individual assessments of protection claims by Afghan women and girls. With its finding that 'gender' and 'nationality' are sufficient grounds to establish refugee status, the Court has not only departed from its settled case law but has also sparked immediate criticism for limiting member states discretion in assessing asylum applications. This contribution aims to embed the findings in C-608/22 in the wider efforts of the Court to adopt a gender-sensitive interpretation of EU asylum law arguing that the judgment is a consequential development of the Court's case law on protecting the rights of women applying for asylum in the EU.

Keywords

Refugee status – Afghan women and girls – member of a particular social group – individual assessment – Article 4(3) Qualification Directive – gender-sensitive interpretation EU law

I. Introduction

In September 2022, the Austrian Supreme Administrative Court (VwGH) referred a request for a preliminary ruling to the Court of Justice of the European Union (CJEU) to clarify important interpretative questions regarding the application of the Qualification Directive (QD) to the situation of Afghan women and girls. In particular, the referring court wanted to know whether the accumulation of the numerous human rights restrictions and violations

Austrian Review of International and European Law **28**: 225-242, 2023.
 | DOI:10.1163/15736512-02801010

women and girls in Afghanistan are facing[1] amount to an act of persecution required by Article 9(1.b) QD as constitutive element for refugee status. Secondly, the court sought guidance on the question whether 'gender' and 'nationality' may be considered a sufficient basis for recognizing Afghan women and girls without further assessment of the individual circumstances of their applications.[2] As a last episode in a series of cases related to gender related aspects of EU asylum law,[3] the CJEU finally issued its judgment in

---

1 See, *e.g.*, EUAA, 'Country Guidance Afghanistan' (*EUAA* 2024) <https://euaa.europa.eu/publications/country-guidance-afghanistan-may-2024> accessed 7 March 2025; EUAA, 'Afghanistan – Country Focus' (*EUAA* 2024) <https://euaa.europa.eu/publications/afghanistan-country-focus-0> accessed 7 March 2025.

2 Case C-608/22 *Bundesamt für Fremdenwesen und Asyl and Others (Femmes afghanes)* [2024] ECLI:EU:C:2024:828 (hereinafter *Afghan Women and Girls*). The two questions referred read: '1) Is the accumulation of measures taken, supported or tolerated in a State by a de facto government actor and consisting, in particular, of the fact that women: – are denied participation in political office and political decision-making processes; – are provided with no legal means to be able to obtain protection from gender-based and domestic violence; – are generally at risk of forced marriages; even though they have been prohibited by the de facto government actor, women are not afforded effective protection against forced marriages and such marriages are sometimes performed with the participation of de facto government actors in the knowledge that it is a forced marriage; – are not allowed to engage in gainful employment or are allowed to do so only to a limited extent, mainly at home; – have difficulties in accessing health facilities; – are fully or largely denied access to education (for example by allowing girls only a primary school education); – are not allowed to be or move about in public without being accompanied by a man (who must be of a certain family relationship) or, at most, are permitted to do so only a certain distance from home; – must completely cover their bodies and veil their faces in public; – may not take part in any sports as referred to in Article 9(1)(b) of Directive 2011/95/EU (1) of the European Parliament and of the Council of 13 December 2011 on standards for the qualification of third-country nationals or stateless persons as beneficiaries of international protection, for a uniform status for refugees or for persons eligible for subsidiary protection, and for the content of the protection granted (recast), to be regarded as sufficiently severe as to affect a woman in a similar manner as described in Article 9(1)(a) of that directive? 2) Is it sufficient, for the granting of asylum status, that a woman is affected by those measures in the country of origin merely on the basis of her gender, or is it necessary to assess a woman's individual situation in order to determine whether she is affected by those measures — to be considered in their entirety — within the meaning of Article 9(1)(b) of Directive 2011/95/EU?'.

3 In January 2024, the Grand Chamber of the CJEU in a preliminary ruling requested by the Sofia Administrative Court in 2021, already held that women

October 2024.[4] The Court's response to the first question that the structural discrimination and the widespread violation of human rights of women and girls in their cumulation amount to persecution in the sense of Article 9(1.b), was rather uncontested. Yet, its findings regarding the second question to interpret Article 4(3) QD in a way that for assessing protection claims by Afghan women and girls factors other than nationality and gender must not be taken into account by national authorities, sparked immediate criticism among policy makers and political commentators. In particular, the judgment was perceived as unduly infringing the rights of member states to assess each claim individually taking into account not only objective situations in the country of origin but also individual circumstances of the applicant, *i.e.* whether the latter is individually persecuted. According to critiques, the quasi group-recognition of all Afghan women and girls put forward by the Court would contradict member states efforts to curb irregular migration.[5]

The judgment and the criticism have to be embedded within two parallel but harshly diverging developments regarding the situation in Afghanistan and Afghan asylum seekers. On the one hand, national asylum authorities and courts have increasingly begun to re-evaluate the situation for male Afghan protection seekers. Despite the international recognition of the severe

---

in general and women facing domestic violence or refusing forced marriage in the country of origin in particular, may qualify as a protected social group under Article 10 QD (Case C-621/21 *WS (Femmes victimes de violences domestiques)* [2024] ECLI:EU:C:2024:47)). In June 2024 in C-646/21 the CJEU found, that women, including minors, who share as a common characteristic the fact that they genuinely came to identify with the fundamental value of equality between women and men during their stay in a member state, can be regarded as belonging to a particular social group (Case C646/21 *K, L v Staatssecretaris van Justitie en Veiligheid* [2024] ECLI:EU:C:2024:487).

4 *Afghan Women and Girls*, Case C-608/22 (Summary of the request for a preliminary ruling pursuant to Article 98(1) of the Rules of Procedure of the Court of Justice, 22 September 2022).

5 For instance, the Austrian Ministry of Interior immediately declared that Austria will keep the practice of assessing individual circumstances of each case. See, *e.g.*, 'EuGH-Urteil zu Afghaninnen: Österreich bleibt bei Einzelfallprüfungen' (*Der Standard*, 7 October 2024) <www.derstandard.at/story/3000000239761/eugh-urteil-zu-afghaninnen-oesterreich-bleibt-bei-einzelfallpruefungen> accessed 10 March 2025; 'Nach dem EuGH-Urteil zu Afghaninnen: Experten fordern „Korrektur“ der Judikatur' (7 October 2024) <www.diepresse.com/18941091/nach-dem-eugh-urteil-zu-afghaninnen-experten-fordern-korrektur-der-judikatur> accessed 10 March 2025.

general humanitarian and human rights situation in the country,[6] 23 515 return decisions following negative decisions were issued in the EU for male Afghans in 2023.[7] While so far, returns to Afghanistan are still legally and factually impeded by *non-refoulement* obligations[8] and the non-recognition of the Taliban regime, there is a clear tendency in political debates to allow for returns to Afghanistan at least for certain groups such as criminals.[9] On the other hand, the precarious situation of Afghan women and the consequential eradication of their rights by the Taliban remains widely recognized resulting in the adoption of updated asylum guidelines and practices[10] and efforts to hold the Taliban legally accountable for the atrocities committed.[11] While the Court's findings in the *Afghan Women and Girls* case are a reflection of the latter developments, the reactions to the judgment and the accusation that it would open the door for an abuse of national asylum procedures seem to be caught in between.

In this light, this contribution aims to add to the debate by providing an analysis of the procedural aspects of the judgment focusing on the finding of

---

6 UN Secretary General (UNSG), 'The Situation in Afghanistan and its Implications for International Peace and Security' (13 June 2024) UN Doc A/78/914-S/2024/469; UNHCR, 'Guidance Note on the International Protection Needs of People fleeing Afghanistan' (February 2023) <www.refworld.org/docid/63e0cb714.html> accessed 10 March 2025.

7 Eurostat, 'Third Country Nationals Ordered to Leave by Citizenship, Age and Sex' (2023) <https://ec.europa.eu/eurostat/databrowser/view/migr_eiord1__custom_9989775/default/table?lang=en> accessed 10 March 2025.

8 Compare particularly Art 5 Directive 2008/115/EC providing that member states have to take *non-refoulement* obligations into account when returning a person to a country.

9 See, *e.g.*, Daniel Thym, 'Zur Debatte über Abschiebungen nach Afghanistan und Syrien – Einzelfallprüfung statt „Alles oder nichts"' (*Verfassungsblog*, 10 June 2024) <https://verfassungsblog.de/abschiebung-afghanistan-syrien-rechtlich/> accessed 7 March 2025.

10 *E.g.*, Emma Wilbur, 'Denmark, Sweden Offer Protection to All Women, Girls from Afghanistan' (*Human Rights Watch*, 9 February 2023) <www.hrw.org/news/2023/02/09/denmark-sweden-offer-protection-all-women-girls-afghanistan>; Finish Immigration Service, 'Refugee Status to Afghan Women and Girls' (15 February 2023) <https://migri.fi/en/-/refugee-status-to-afghan-women-and-girls> both accessed 7 March 2025.

11 *E.g.* Kyra Wigard, 'A Groundbreaking Move: Challenging Gender Persecution in Afghanistan at the ICJ' (*EJIL:Talk* 2024) <www.ejiltalk.org/a-groundbreaking-move-challenging-gender-persecution-in-afghanistan-at-the-icj/> accessed 7 March 2025.

the Court that in the assessment of cases of Afghan women and girls national authorities must not take any factors into account other than their nationality and gender.[12] To contextualise this finding, the contribution will start with an analysis of the Court's recent efforts to recognize gender and sex as grounds for persecution acknowledging that women can form a particular social group (Part II). While questions related to the grounds of persecution have not been part of the *Afghan Women and Girls* case, the Court's approach is still important to consider as the findings in the case at hand are clearly linked to the Court's previous case law. Part III will analyse subsequently how the Court departed from its established case law regarding the requirements for individual assessments in asylum procedures. While previously the Court has underlined the importance of individual assessments of objective and subjective circumstances in asylum determination procedures, the severity of the situation in Afghanistan together with its recent approach to a gender-sensitive interpretation of EU asylum law seems to have opened the path at the Court to accept a *de facto* group recognition of Afghan women and girls. Subsequently, Part IV will draw some conclusions and aims to classify the finding of the Court in its wider approach to enhance protection of female protection seekers under EU asylum law while embedding the criticism raised in these efforts.

II. Gender Based Persecution of Women and Girls: A Pretext

The question whether gender and nationality are sufficiently decisive factors for assessing protection claims by Afghan women and girls is separated but still inherently connected to the question how gender can be linked to persecution as required by the Geneva Refugee Convention (GRC) and Article 10 QD.[13]

In its recent case law, the CJEU provided important clarifications on the recognition of women acknowledging that women may be persecuted only because of their gender and as particular social group. In *WS (Femmes victimes de violences domestiques),*[14] the Court relying on UNHCR Guidelines

---

12 For a more detailed analysis of the CJEU's findings regarding the interpretation of Article 9(1.b) QD, see Lisa Heschl, 'Developing the Human Rights-Based Approach to Persecution Further? The CJEU's Approach in the Afghan Women and Girls Case' (2025) 27 European Journal of Migration and Law 94.

13 Article 10 QD links an act of persecution with a specific ground mirroring the requirements of Article 1 (A.2) GRC.

14 *WS (Femmes victimes de violences domestiques)* (n 3).

and other international and regional rights norms,[15] adopted a rather broad approach in interpreting the two cumulative requirements for establishing a particular social group holding that

> women, as a whole, may be regarded as belonging to a 'particular social group', within the meaning of Article 10(1)(d) of Directive 2011/95, where it is established that, in their country of origin, they are, on account of their gender, exposed to physical or mental violence, including sexual violence and domestic violence.[16]

It continues that

> women who refuse forced marriages, where such a practice may be regarded as a social norm within their society, or who transgress such a norm by ending that marriage, may be regarded as belonging to a social group with a distinct identity in their country of origin if, on account of that behaviour, they are stigmatised and exposed to the disapproval of their surrounding society resulting in their social exclusion or acts of violence.[17]

Yet, the Court reiterates that membership of a particular social group does not establish whether a group member has a well-established fear of persecution. In order to determine whether a woman relying on the membership of a particular social group ground has well-founded fear of persecution, the Court requests member states to carry out an individualised assessment carried out with vigilance and care taking into account *inter alia* the

> position of women before the law, their political rights, their social and economic rights, the cultural and social mores of the country and consequences for non-adherence, the prevalence of such harmful traditional practices, the incidence and forms of reported violence against women, the protection available to them, any penalties imposed on those who perpetrate

---

15 In particular the CEDAW and the Istanbul Convention. For further information hereon see Gesa Kübek and Jonas Bornemann, 'International Law as a Trailblazer for a Gender-Sensitive Refugee System in the EU. The Court of Justice's Ruling in Case C-621/21, Women who are Victims of Domestic Violence' (*European-LawBlog*, 29 January 2024) <www.europeanlawblog.eu/pub/oa98cmvt/release/1> accessed 7 March 2025.

16 *WS (Femmes victimes de violences domestiques)* (n 3) para 57.

17 *Ibid.*, para 58.

the violence, and the risks that a woman might face on her return to her country of origin after making such a claim.[18]

Furthermore, the Court determined that the requisite nexus between persecution by a non-state actor and a particular social group is established in two scenarios: either when the act of persecution occurs on that basis, irrespective of whether the failure by the state to protect women was motivated by that basis; or when the failure of the state to protect was motivated by that basis, even if the mistreatment by non-state actors itself was not.[19]

The question whether Afghan women and girls form a particular social group has neither been raised by the referring court nor have the AG or CJEU referred to it. Still, arguably, the findings of the Grand Chamber in *WS (Femmes victimes de violences domestiques)* are applicable to Afghanistan, a society in which gender-based violence is clearly rampant. When it comes to the recognition of Afghan women and girls, following the recommendations by UNHCR[20] and the European Union Agency for Asylum (EUAA)[21], several member states have, acknowledged that gender and sex are sufficient grounds for persecution in the aftermath of the Taliban take-over in 2021. Sweden, in December 2022 recognized that the degradation of Afghan women and girls amounts to persecution because of gender granting refugee status and a resident permit on this basis;[22] in December 2022, the Finish Immigration Service updated its guidelines regarding asylum applications submitted by people from Afghanistan granting refugee status to all women and girls;[23] in February 2023, Denmark's Refugee Appeals Board announced that refugee status would be granted to all women and girls from Afghanistan based solely on their gender;[24] and finally, in July 2024, France's National Court of Asylum (CNDA) recognized that all Afghan women and girls are eligible for refugee status.[25]

---

18 *Ibid.*, para 61.

19 *Ibid.*, para 67.

20 UNHCR, Guidance Note on the International Protection Needs of People Fleeing Afghanistan (n 6).

21 EUAA, Country Guidance Afghanistan (n 1).

22 See Wilbur (n 10).

23 See Finish Immigration Service (n 10).

24 See Wilbur (n 10).

25 See as CNDA, 'La Cour reconnait l'appartenance de l'ensemble des femmes afghanes à un groupe social susceptible d'être protégé comme réfugié' (CNDA

But already before 2021, national courts have recognized the specific situation of Afghan women and girls. The Austrian Supreme Administrative Court in its reference for a preliminary ruling, referred to early case law relating to the situation of Afghan women and girls under the former rule of the Taliban (prior to 2001), where it was recognized that for the purpose of granting refugee status it was sufficient that the person concerned was affected by the measures in question solely on the basis of being a women irrespective of disproportionate consequences in the case of failure with rules and measures that were considered to amount to persecution.[26] After 2001 and the changing circumstances, the lines of argumentation in Afghan women and girls cases changed as the overall situation has been perceived to have changed for Afghan women and girls.

Accordingly, and in line with the general tendency to narrow the category of women as particular social group, national courts adopted the view that the inherent characteristic 'sex or gender' have to be combined with some additional characteristics relevant for Afghan women and girls to be recognized as distinct by the surrounding society.[27] These cases relate more to the individual risk of the applicants to be persecuted often connected to forced marriage, domestic violence, and the so called 'westernization' or adoption of 'western values' by Afghan women and girls. The need to add a specifying factor to gender in order to establish a grounds for persecution is reflective of the so called 'floodgate' argument. According to the latter, the refugee definition would lose its individual character if sex or gender was recognized as basis for a particular social group because of the resulting large numbers of women swamping countries with female applicants.[28] As discrimination of and violence against women are endemic and universal, a specific category of women as specific group is too large and ambitious as millions or more women could present themselves as refugees circumventing

11 July 2024) https://www.cnda.fr/decisions-de-justice/dernieres-decisions/la-cour-reconnait-l-appartenance-de-l-ensemble-des-femmes-afghanes-a-un-groupe-social-susceptible-d-etre-protege-comme-refugie2 accessed 24 March 2025.

26 *Afghan Women and Girls,* Summary of the request (n 4) para 14.

27 See EASO, 'Guidance on Membership of a Particular Social Group' (*EUAA* 2020) https://euaa.europa.eu/sites/default/files/EASO-Guidance-on%20MPSG-EN.pdf accessed 10 March 2025.

28 See for example Nahla Valji, Lee Ann de la Hunt and Helen Moffett, 'Where are the Women? Gender Discrimination in Refugee Policies and Practices' (2003) 55 Agenda: Empowering Women for Gender Equity, Women. The Invisible Refugees 61, 68.

the narrow procedures designed to determine who is a *bona fides* refugee and who is simply dissatisfied with the social and economic situation in the country of origin.[29]

In *WS (Femmes victimes de violences domestiques)* the Court has clearly took a stand for the irrelevance of the size of a group to prevent the qualification of women as a whole as particular social group. In the same light, in *Afghan Women and Girls* the CJEU acknowledged that women and girls in Afghanistan are persecuted merely because of their gender.[30] Giving the Court's finding that the Taliban have established a regime of 'gender segregation and oppression'[31] this recognition does not seem to be particularly surprising. Yet, it is exactly this pre-text, the recognition that women and girls form a particular social group and are therefore persecuted that played into the development of the Court's reasoning in the answer to the second question. Given that the Court acknowledged that the situation in Afghanistan *per se* amounts to the persecution of women and girls as particular social group,[32] it seems to be consequential to argue that national authorities can actually deviate from the assessment of personal circumstances other than gender and nationality, granting refugee protection without Afghan women and girls having to show that they are personally targeted by the Taliban.

III. The Assessment of Personal Circumstances in Asylum Claims: Article 4(3) QD and the CJEU's Gender-Sensitive Interpretation

In its submission, the referring Austrian Court expressed doubt that all women and girls in Afghanistan are individually concerned to a comparable level by

---

[29] See Peter C Godfrey, 'Defining the Social Group in Asylum Proceedings: The Expansion of the Social Group to Include a Broader Class of Refugees' (1994) 3 Journal of Law and Policy 257, 280-281.

[30] The measures imposed by the Taliban which are applied deliberately and systematically 'blatantly and relentlessly deny Afghan women fundamental rights related to human dignity on account of their gender.' *Afghan women and girls* (n 2) para 44.

[31] Case C-608/22 *Afghan Women and Girls* (Opinion) [2023] ECLI:EU:C:2023:856, para 56.

[32] The findings of the Court related to the question whether the general discrimination of women and girls amount to persecution according to Article 9(1.b) QD suggests its recognition of Afghan women and girls as particular social group.

the measures and policies of the Taliban questioning that the cumulation of measures and human rights violations would reach the severity required under Article 9(1.b) QD for all of them.[33] The underlying assumption is that not all Afghan women and girls must oppose the Taliban regime and the social, moral and religious norms governing the lives of Afghans these days must not necessarily considered by all Afghan women as restricting their dignity or but rather as certain dogmas. Furthermore, one could argue that policies by the Taliban regarding access to education have lesser impact on grown already educated women than on girls; not all women want to engage in the political sphere and become politically active; and already married women do not have to fear to be forcibly married. In this light, despite the prevailing structural discrimination and the generalised violation of the rights of women, gender and nationality must not be taken as sole factors for substantiating protection claims as it would allow also those seeking asylum out of, *e.g.*, economic reason immediate protection.

In principle, under international refugee law – which does not regulate status determination procedures as such – it is well established that in order to assess a protection claim different factors pertaining to both the situation in the country of origin and the personal circumstances of the applicant have to be taken into account by the competent deciding authority.[34] Importantly in this regard, individual assessments of personal circumstances should not only be evaluated from a state perspective. Instead, from the perspective of the applicants, the importance of individual assessments of claims and the obligation that individual circumstances are taken into account have to be also considered from a human rights perspective as confirmed by the European Court on Human Rights (ECtHR) in its case law. In *M.A. v Denmark* the Court found that Denmark has neglected its obligations under the Convention when relying on a general rule while failing to conduct an individualised assessment of a claim in an application for temporary or subsidiary protection.[35] Similarly,

33 *Afghan Women and Girls* (n 4) para 34.

34 See, *e.g.*, UNHCR, 'Handbook on Handbook on Procedures and Criteria for Determining Refugee Status under the 1951 Convention and the 1967 Protocol relating to the Status of Refugees' (2019) paras 189ff.

35 *M.A.* concerned the rejection of a family reunification request by a Syrian national who has been granted temporary protection in Denmark in 2015. His application was rejected based on a general rule in the Danish Alien Act that beneficiaries of temporary protection in Denmark are different from beneficiaries of refugee status can only request family reunification after a three-year period. The Court found that this general rule did *inter alia* not strike 'a fair balance between, on the one hand, the applicant's interest in being reunited with his wife in Denmark

in *Hoti v Croatia* the Court found that Croatia has violated Article 8 ECHR in not taking the personal circumstances and private life situation of the applicant into account when refusing to extent his residence permit.[36] These judgments can clearly be considered as solicitations to states to ensure that all claims are individually assessed and not assessed under inelastic general rules based on general assumptions.

Yet, there might be circumstances and situations of displacement allowing for assessments focusing on objective situations with individual situations to be subordinated. At the international level such *prima facie* recognition[37] has in particular been promoted in the context of large-scale displacement and arrivals but UNHCR has also recognized the appropriateness of such an approach 'in relation to groups of similarly situated individuals whose arrival is not on a large-scale, but who share a readily apparent common risk of harm'.[38] With regard to the characteristics shared by similarly situated individuals UNCHR enumerates ethnicity, place of former habitual residences religion, gender, political background or age, or a combination thereof, as factors exposing them to the same risk.[39] *Prima facie* recognition is, thus, essentially 'a collective form of status determination that presumes that each individual member of a particular group qualifies for refugee status based on objective information on the circumstances causing flight.'[40] Again, such a form of recognition of refugee status serves a twofold purpose: While it ensures that national asylum procedures are relieved, it also ensures immediate

and, on the other, the interest of the community as a whole to control immigration' and that there would have been an obligation to individually assess the waiting period of three years in light of the personal circumstances of the applicant in order that Art 8 ECHR would be respected. See *M.A. v Denmark*, ECtHR (GC), Application No 6697/18, Judgment of 9 July 2021, paras 193-194. For a more detailed analysis of the judgment see Thomas Gammeltoft-Hansen, Mikael Rask Madsen and Henrik Palmer Olsen, 'The Limits of Indirect Deterrence of Asylum Seekers' (*Verfassungsblog*, 2021) <https://verfassungsblog.de/the-limits-of-indirect-deterrence-of-asylum-seekers/> accessed 10 March 2025.

36 *Hoti v Croatia*, ECtHR, Application No 63311/14, Judgment of 26 April 2024, paras 134, 140, 143.

37 UNHCR, 'Guidelines on International Protection No. 11: Prima Facie Recognition of Refugee Status' (2015), para 1.

38 *Ibid.*, para 9

39 *Ibid.*, para 10.

40 Marjoleine Zieck, 'Introductory Notes to Guidelines on International Protection No. 11: Prima Facie Recognition of Refugee Status (UNHCR)' (2025) 54 International Legal Materials 1115, 1115.

and effective protection for those whose need of protection can be based on the objective circumstances in a country of origin.

Legal foundations and contours of such a practice, however, still seem to be rather opaque[41] and at odds with the individualised procedures known to the CEAS[42] even though member state practice with regard to Afghan women and girls suggests differently as for instance certain members states such as Sweden and Denmark, have already recognized Afghan women and girls without an individual assessment of their situation. Most explicitly, the Swedish Migration Agency concluded that the requirement for an assessment of individual circumstances should be abolished in cases involving Afghan women and girls.[43] These national practices seemed to be in tension with the approach prescribed by the QD and the approach taken by the CJEU regarding the individual assessment of asylum claims reiterating only recently the necessity for an individualised assessment of an applicant's claim.[44]

---

41 See as well Türkan Ertuna Lagrand and Salvo Nicolosi, 'Rethinking Gender-Based Asylum: A Look at the Advocate General's Opinion on Women Fleeing the Taliban' (*EU Law Analysis*, 21 November 2023) <http://eulawanalysis.blogspot.com/2023/11/rethinking-gender-based-asylum-look-at.html> accessed 10 March 2025.

42 At this point it should be noticed that the new Crisis Regulation (Preamble 54-56, Article 14) foresees the possibility of *prima facie* recognition of international protection in cases when objective circumstances suggest that applications for international protection from groups of applicants from a specific country of origin are well-founded. Regulation (EU) 2024/1359 of the European Parliament and of the Council of 14 May 2024 addressing situations of crisis and force majeure in the field of migration and asylum and amending Regulation (EU) 2021/1147. The possibility of *prima facie* recognition is also discussed in the context of the expiring Temporary Protection Directive (TPD) as an approach to ensure that after its expiration national asylum systems would not become potentially overwhelmed by applications by Ukrainians. See, *e.g.*, Meltem Ineli Ciğer, 'When Temporary Protection Ends: Longer-term Solutions for Refugees from Ukraine' (*European Policy Analysis*, September 2023) <www.sieps.se/globalassets/publikationer/2023/2023_11epa.pdf accessed> 10 March 2025.

43 See Swedish Refugee Law Centre, 'Country Report: Differential Treatment of Specific Nationalities in the Procedure – Sweden' (*ECRE*, 10 July 2024) <https://asylumineurope.org/reports/country/sweden/asylum-procedure/differential-treatment-specific-nationalities-procedure/> accessed 10 March 2025. The position is not available anymore at the Swedish Migration Agency's website.

44 *WS (Femmes victimes de violences domestiques)* (n 3) para 60. Asylum determination procedures 'must be individual in character and be carried out on a case-by-case basis with vigilance and care, solely on the basis of a specific

Article 4(3) QD defines that asylum determination procedures should be carried out on an individual case-by-case basis with vigilance and care with the national authority assessing the specific circumstances of the given case in order to determine whether the established facts and circumstances are such a threat that a person because of her individual situation experiences reasonable fear of persecution.[45] In this assessment the deciding authority has to take into account different factors including *inter alia* country of origin information (*lit* a), documentation and statements by the applicant (*lit* b), and the individual position and the personal circumstances of the applicant (*lit* c). Accordingly, the CJEU has acknowledged that it is

> settled case-law that every decision on whether to grant refugee status or subsidiary protection status must be based on an individual assessment [...], which aims to determine whether, in the light of the applicant's personal circumstances, the conditions for granting such a status are satisfied.[46]

However, while Article 4(3) QD describes the means for assessing claims, it does not prescribe how to weight or hierarchise these factors for the decision. It is up to the national asylum authorities to decide whether they grant more importance to the individual position and the personal circumstances of the applicant or to the general circumstances in the country of origin. The margin of appreciation granted to member states in Article 3 QD to introduce or retain more favourable standards for determining who qualifies for protection and for determining the latter content as long as those standards are compatible with the Directive, has been acknowledged by the CJEU in its case law. For instance, in *Ahmedbekova*[47], it recognized that

evaluation of the facts and circumstances, in accordance with the rules set out not only in paragraph 3 but also in paragraph 4 of that article [Art 4 QD], in order to determine whether the established facts and circumstances constitute such a threat that the person concerned may reasonably fear, in the light of his or her individual situation, that he or she will in fact be the victim of acts of persecution if he or she were to return to his or her country of origin.'

45 See to that effect *ibid.*; *K, L v Staatssecretaris van Justitie en Veiligheid* (n 3) para 59.

46 Case C652/16 *Ahmedbekova* [2018] EU:C:2018:801, para 48. See as well Case C-199/12 to C-201/12 *X and Others* [2013] EU:C:2013:720, para 73; Case C-473/16 *F* [2018] EU:C:2018:36, para 41; and Case C-238/19 *Military Service and Asylum* [2020] EU:C:2020:945, para 23.

47 *Ahmedbekova* (n 46).

> more favourable standards referred to in Article 3 [QD] may, inter alia, consist in relaxing the conditions under which a third-country national or stateless person can enjoy refugee or subsidiary protection status.[48]

When it comes to the margin of discretion regarding the assessment of asylum applications, the Court in *A and others*[49], a case concerning the sexual orientation of the applicant, stated that even though Article 4 QD is applicable to all asylum determination procedures irrespective of the claimed grounds for persecution, it is for the national competent authorities

> to modify their methods of assessing statements and documentary or other evidence having regard to the specific features of each category of application for asylum, in observance of the rights guaranteed by the Charter.[50]

In the past the CJEU has already acknowledged that under certain circumstances the objective situation in a country can outweigh the individual concern criterion. In *Elgafaji*[51], a case concerning the scope of subsidiary protection according to Article 15 QD, it established the 'exceptional objectivity' test acknowledging that under certain circumstances the situation in a country due to the degree of indiscriminate violence in the event of an armed conflict could be so severe that solely the presence of a civilian in the country or region would substantiate a real risk of becoming subject to a serious threat.[52] While the national competent authority in those cases has to assess the objective side, *i.e.* the situation in the country of origin and the level of indiscriminate violence, the applicant must not show that he or she is specifically targeted by reason of factors particular to his or her personal circumstances. Instead,

> the more the applicant is able to show that he is specifically affected by reason of factors particular to his personal circumstances, the lower the level of indiscriminate violence required for him to be eligible for subsidiary protection.[53]

---

48 *Ibid.*, para 70.

49 Case C-148/13 *A and Others* [2024] ECLI:EU:C:2014:2406.

50 *Ibid.*, para 54.

51 Case C-465/07 *Elgafaji* [2009] ECLI:EU:C:2009:94.

52 *Ibid.*, paras 35, 37-38.

53 *Ibid.*, para 39.

Already in his opinion in the *Afghan Women and Girls* case, AG de la Tour acknowledged the specific characteristics of applications by Afghan women and girls that would allow to focus on the general objective circumstances in the country of origin rather than on the individual characteristics of the singular application.[54] The level of discrimination Afghan women and girls are facing, the specific objective circumstances, not only create a general need of protection but also require specific and gender sensitive modes of assessment.[55] Following the AG's opinion, in its judgment the CJEU first, made reference to the need of gathering country information explicitly focusing on the situation of Afghan women and girls. It reiterated that member states are required by Article 10(3.b) Procedures Directive (PD)[56] to take into account and provide deciding authorities with precise and up-to date information provided by the EUAA and UNHCR about the situation in a country.[57] In order to assess the situation of Afghan women and girls in line with the UNHCR Guidelines concerning gender-related persecution, the competent national authorities must, thus, gather country of origin information truly reflective of the situation in the country of origin having relevance for the examination of applications made by women.[58] Having said that, the Court in a second step, turned to the margin of appreciation member states have according to Article 3 QD to adopt more favourable standards. Again, heavily relying on the findings by the EUAA and UNHCR, the Court acknowledged that 'there is a presumption of recognition of refugee status for Afghan women and girls, given the acts of persecution carried out against them by the Taliban solely on account of their gender.'[59] Accordingly, the Court found, that because of the margin of discretion granted to member states under Article 3 QD, competent authorities, once the nationality and gender of the applicant are established, are entitled

> to consider that it is currently unnecessary to establish, in the individual assessment of the situation of an application for international protection,

---

54 *Afghan Women and Girls* (n 2) para 72.

55 *Ibid.*, para 54.

56 Directive 2013/32/EU of the European Parliament and of the Council of 26 June 2013 on common procedures for granting and withdrawing international protection (recast) [2013] OJ L 180.

57 *Afghan Women and Girls* (n 2) para 52.

58 *Ibid.*, para 53.

59 *Ibid.*, para 56.

> that there is a risk that she will actually and specifically be subject to acts of persecution if she returns to her country of origin.[60]

The Court clearly placed, thus, an obligation on states to ensure that their methods of assessment are gender sensitive taking into account the specific situation of women and girls in Afghanistan. In its conclusion, and against the background that the Taliban regime has been described as 'being unlike any other'[61], it interpreted Article 4(3) QD as not requiring competent authorities to take factors other than 'gender' and 'nationality' into account when assessing applications by Afghan women and girls.[62] The Court, thus, acknowledged that asylum claims by Afghan women and girls should be assessed with the presumption that their claims are well-founded and opened the path for member states to apply accelerated procedures as Afghan women and girls must not show that due to their personal situation they face a personal risk of persecution.

IV. Conclusions

While reliable data is missing, estimates suggest that roughly 20 million women and girls are daily victims of the gender apartheid regime established by the Taliban.[63] For those women and girls, the judgment by the CJEU is a recognition of the hardships they are facing. At the same time, the Court's interpretation of Article 4(3) QD and the finding that nationality and gender are sufficient for granting protection with no need to assess personal circumstances of applicants further, opens the door for member states to apply accelerated procedures for Afghan women and girls easing tensions between state practice and EU asylum legislation. However, importantly, the Court found that Article 4(3) QD allows for such an interpretation but did not find that member states violate EU law if continuing to take individual circumstances into account when assessing claims by Afghan women and girls. Yet, it is quite questionable how additional considerations of personal circumstances would relate to the general assumption of persecution of Afghan women and girls as established by the Court in response to the first

---

60 *Afghan Women and Girls* (n 2) para 57.

61 *Ibid.*, para 73.

62 *Ibid.*, para 58.

63 CIA, 'The World Factbook' (*CIA*, 2025) <www.cia.gov/the-world-factbook/countries/afghanistan/#people-and-society> accessed 11 March 2025.

question referred. Indeed, authorities are still allowed to take into account personal circumstances. In such a case, national authorities would, however, still have to consider the findings by the Court that the general situation in Afghanistan and the violations of the rights of women and girls in their cumulative effect amount to persecution in the sense of Article 9(1.a) QD. In the past, as has been pointed out, in the case of Afghan women in order to establish a well-founded fear of persecution additional characteristics such as the adoption of 'western' values have been required as addition to inherent characteristics as 'sex or gender'. In light of the findings by the Court on the application of Article 9 (1.b) QD on the situation in Afghanistan, when upholding the individualisation of asylum claims by Afghan women and girl, it would be, thus, on the national authorities to argue why the overall assumption that protection claims by Afghan women and girls are well-founded would not apply in an individual case.

While the Court departed from its settled case law on individual assessments, its approach shows sensitiveness to state practices on the assessment of asylum applications in specific contexts. In this regard, it is nothing new that certain objectively established situations in a country of origin subordinated the assessment of individual circumstances to factors such as nationality or ethnicity. For instance, even though the practice has changed over the years, the granting of refugee status to Syrian men between age 18 and 42 fleeing forced conscription was in Germany between 2015 and 2016 mainly based on the establishment of their ethnicity, age, and sex.[64] Furthermore, the whole temporary protection scheme invoked for Ukrainians through the activation of Directive 2001/55/EC[65] is largely based on the criterion of nationality as decisive factor.[66] The Court has been very clear, that the situation of women

64 Terese Fachinger, Paula Hoffmeyer-Zlotnik and Marlene Stiller, 'Country Report Germany: Differential Treatment of Specific Nationalities in the Procedure' (*ECRE*, 10 July 2024) <https://asylumineurope.org/reports/country/germany/asylum-procedure/differential-treatment-specific-nationalities-procedure/> accessed 10 March 2025.

65 Council Directive 2001/55/EC of 20 July 2001 on minimum standards for giving temporary protection in the event of a mass influx of displaced persons and on measures promoting a balance of efforts between Member States in receiving such persons and bearing the consequences thereof [2001] OJ L 212.

66 The TPD foresees as well that temporary protection also applies to nationals of a third country (other than Ukraine) and stateless people who were residing in Ukraine before 24 February 2022 with a permanent Ukrainian residence permit, who cannot safely return to their country of origin. See Art 2 Council Implementing Decision (EU) 2022/382 of 4 March 2022 establishing the existence of a

and girls and the eradication of their rights by the Taliban is unlike anything seen before. Because of this situation, a required context-sensitive and gendered interpretation of EU asylum law has been put forward by the Court. Additionally, as has already been described, after the take-over by the Taliban several member states have amended their guidelines on the assessment of asylum applications by Afghan women and girls, acknowledging that the latter should be recognized on the basis of their gender and nationality without further need to assess individual circumstances. The findings essentially reconcile, thus, current state practices with EU law.

It is notably in this regard, that the Court interpreted EU asylum rules systematically in light of international human rights law, such as the Convention on the Elimination of All Forms of Discrimination against Women (CEDAW) and the Council of Europe Convention on Preventing and Combating Violence against Women and Domestic Violence (Istanbul Convention) as well as UNCHR and EUAA's guidelines underscoring the importance of the progressive and harmonized interpretation of EU asylum law in light of international human rights. The judgment, thus, allows member states to apply a pragmatic and harmonized approach to the protection of Afghan women and girls ensuring that they receive protection as victims of systematic oppression. The latter has been widely recognized, and it is beyond doubt that the situation of Afghan women and girls is not going to improve as long as the Taliban regime is in power. With the judgment in the *Afghan Women and Girls* case, the Court has done its bit to ensure that EU asylum law is interpreted in line with human rights standards putting the women and girls from Afghanistan at the centre of its analysis rather than unsubstantiated fears of a perceived loss of control over irregular migration.

mass influx of displaced persons from Ukraine within the meaning of Article 5 of Directive 2001/55/EC and having the effect of introducing temporary protection.

Austrian Practice in International Law 2023

Österreichische Praxis zum Internationalen Recht 2023

Edited by
Gerhard Hafner and *Stephan Wittich*

Structure

AA. International law in general/Völkerrecht – allgemein

I. Nature, basis, purpose/Natur, Grundlage, Funktionen

1. In general/Allgemeines
2. *Ius cogens*
3. Soft law

II. History/Geschichte

BB. Sources of international law/Völkerrechtsquellen

I. Treaties/Verträge

II. Custom/Völkergewohnheitsrecht

III. General principles of law/Allgemeine Rechtsgrundsätze

IV. Judicial decisions/Gerichtsentscheidungen

V. Opinions of writers/Lehrmeinungen

VI. Equity/Billigkeit

VII. Unilateral acts, including acts and decisions of international organisations and conferences/Einseitige Akte, einschließlich der Akte und Beschlüsse von internationalen Organisationen und Konferenzen

VIII. Comity/Courtoisie (*comitas gentium*)

IX. Codification and progressive development/Kodifikation und progressive Weiterentwicklung

CC. The law of treaties/Recht der Verträge

I. Conclusion and entry into force of treaties/Abschluss und Inkrafttreten völkerrechtlicher Verträge

1. Conclusion/Abschluss
2. Reservations and declarations/Vorbehalte und Erklärungen
3. Provisional application and entry into force/Vorläufige Anwendung und Inkrafttreten

II. Observance, application and interpretation of treaties/ Einhaltung, Anwendung und Auslegung von Verträgen

1. Observance of treaties/Einhaltung von Verträgen
2. Application of treaties/Anwendung von Verträgen

Austrian Review of International and European Law **28**: 243-258, 2023.
 | DOI:10.1163/15736512-02801011

3. Interpretation of treaties/Auslegung von Verträgen
4. Treaties and third states/(Verträge und) Drittstaaten

III. Amendment and modification of treaties/Änderung und Modifikation von Verträgen

IV. Invalidity, termination and suspension of operation of treaties/Ungültigkeit, Beendigung und Suspendierung von Verträgen

1. General rules/Allgemeine Bestimmungen
2. Invalidity/Ungültigkeit
3. Termination and suspension of operation including denunciation and withdrawal/Beendigung und Suspendierung von Verträgen, einschließlich der Kündigung von Verträgen und des Rücktritts vom Vertrag
4. Procedure/Verfahren
5. Consequences of invalidity, termination or suspension of operation/Folgen der Ungültigkeit, Beendigung oder Suspendierung von Verträgen

V. Depositaries, notifications, corrections and registration/ Depositär, Notifikationen, Berichtigungen und Registrierung

VI. Consensual arrangements, other than in treaty-form/ Willensübereinkünfte in anderer Form

DD. Relationship between international law and internal law/Völkerrecht und innerstaatliches Recht

I. In general/Allgemeines

II. Application and implementation of international law in internal law/Innerstaatliche Anwendung und Durchführung des Völkerrechts

III. Remedies under internal law for violations of international law/Innerstaatliche Rechtsmittel bei Völkerrechtsverletzungen

EE. Subjects of International law/Völkerrechtssubjekte

I. States/Staaten

1. Status and powers/Status und Befugnisse

a. Personality/Rechtspersönlichkeit
b. Sovereignty and independence/Souveränität und Unabhängigkeit
c. Non-intervention/Interventionsverbot
d. Domestic jurisdiction/Vorbehaltener Wirkungsbereich
e. Equality of states/Gleichheit
f. State immunity/Staatenimmunität

g. Other powers, including treaty-making powers/Andere Befugnisse, einschließlich der Vertragsabschlussbefugnis

2. Recognition/Anerkennung

a. Recognition of states/Anerkennung von Staaten
b. Recognition of governments/Anerkennung von Regierungen
c. Types of recognition/Arten der Anerkennung

aa. *de facto\de jure*
bb. conditional\unconditional/bedingt\unbedingt

d. Acts of recognition/Anerkennungsakte
aa. implied\express/stillschweigend\ausdrücklich
bb. collective\unilateral/kollektiv\einseitig

e. Effects of recognition/Wirkungen der Anerkennung
f. Non-recognition and its effects/Nicht-Anerkennung und deren Wirkungen
g. Withdrawal of recognition/Rücknahme der Anerkennung

3. Types of states/Arten von Staaten

a. Unitary states, federal states and confederations/ Einheitsstaaten, Bundesstaaten und Staatenbünde
b. Personal unions, real unions/Personalunionen, Realunionen
c. States under protection/Protektorate

4. Formation, continuity, succession and extinction of states/Entstehung von Staaten, Kontinuität, Staatennachfolge und Untergang von Staaten

a. Conditions for statehood/Elemente der Staatlichkeit
b. Formation/Bildung von Staaten
c. Identity, continuity/Identität, Kontinuität
d. Extinctions/Untergang von Staaten

aa. Cases of state succession/Fälle der Staatennachfolge

i. Union, with or without demise of former state/Zusammenschluss unter Auslöschung oder Fortbestand eines bisherigen Staates
ii. Separation/Abspaltung
iii. Newly independent states

bb. Effects of state succession/Rechtliche Folgen der Staatennachfolge

i. Territory and other areas under national jurisdiction/Staatsgebiet und andere der Jurisdiktion unterstehende Gebiete
ii. Nationality/Staatsangehörigkeit
iii. Succession in respect of treaties/Staatennachfolge in Verträge
iv. Archives/Archive
v. Debts/Schulden

vi. Property/Staatsvermögen
vii. Responsibility/Staatenverantwortlichkeit
viii. Other rights and obligations/Sonstige Rechte und Pflichten

5. Self-determination/Selbstbestimmung

II. International organisations/Internationale Organisationen

1. In general/Allgemeines

a. Status and Powers/Status und Befugnisse

aa. Personality/Rechtspersönlichkeit
bb. Powers, including treaty-making power/Befugnisse einschließlich der Vertragsabschlussbefugnis
cc. Privileges and immunities of the organisation/Privilegien und Immunitäten der Organisation

b. Participation of states in international organisations and in their activities/Mitgliedschaft in internationalen Organisationen, Teilnahme an ihren Aktivitäten

aa. Admission/Zulassung
bb. Suspension, withdrawal, expulsion/Suspension der Mitgliedschaft, Austritt, Ausschluss
cc. Obligations of membership/Verpflichtungen aus der Mitgliedschaft
dd. Representation of states, including privileges and immunities/Vertretung der Staaten, einschließlich ihrer Privilegien und Immunitäten

c. Legal effect of acts of international organisations/Rechtswirkung von Akten internationaler Organisationen
d. Personnel of international organisations, including their privileges and immunities/Bedienstete internationaler Organisationen, einschließlich ihrer Privilegien und Immunitäten
e. Responsibility of international organisations (see MM.)/Verantwortlichkeit internationaler Organisationen (siehe MM.)
f. Succession of international organisations/Nachfolge internationaler Organisationen

2. Particular types/Arten internationaler Organisationen

a. Universal organisations/Universelle Organisationen
b. Regional organisations/Regionalorganisationen
c. Organisations constituting integrated (*e.g.*, economic) communities/Internationale Gemeinschaften (z.B. wirtschaftlicher Natur)
d. Other types of organisations/Andere Arten von Organisationen

III. Other subjects of international law and entities and groups/Andere Völkerrechtssubjekte, Einheiten und Gruppen

1. Insurgents/Insurgenten
2. Belligerents/Kriegsführende
3. The Holy See/Der Heilige Stuhl
4. Mandated and trust territories/Treuhand- und Mandatsgebiete
5. Dependent territories/Abhängige Gebiete
6. Special regimes/Besondere Regime
7. Others (indigenous people, minorities, national liberation movements, etc.)/Sonstige (indigene Völker, Minderheiten, Nationale Befreiungsbewegungen)

FF. The position of the individual (including the corporation) in international law/Die Stellung der Einzelperson (einschließlich der juristischen Person) im Völkerrecht

I. Nationality/Staatsangehörigkeit

II. Diplomatic and consular protection (see MM.)/Diplomatischer und konsularischer Schutz (siehe MM.)

III. Aliens or non-nationals/Fremde

IV. Members of minorities/Angehörige von Minderheiten

V. Stateless persons/Staatenlose

VI. Refugees/Flüchtlinge

VII. Immigration and emigration, extradition, expulsion, asylum/ Einwanderung und Auswanderung, Auslieferung, Ausweisung, Asyl

1. Immigration and emigration/Einwanderung, Auswanderung
2. Extradition/Auslieferung
3. Expulsion/Ausweisung
4. Asylum/Asyl

VIII. Human rights and fundamental freedoms/Menschenrechte und Grundfreiheiten

IX. Expropriation/Enteignung

X. Crimes under international law/Völkerrechtliche Verbrechen

XI. Criminal responsibility of the individual (see MM.)/Strafrechtliche Verantwortlichkeit des Einzelmenschen (siehe MM.)

GG. Organs of the state and their legal status/Die Staatsorgane und ihr rechtlicher Status

I. Head of state/Das Staatsoberhaupt

II. Minister/Minister

III. Other organs of the state/Andere Staatsorgane

IV. Diplomatic missions and their members/Diplomatische Vertretungen und ihre Mitglieder

V. Consulates and their members/Konsulate und ihre Mitglieder

VI. Special missions/Spezialmissionen

VII. Trade delegations, information centres, etc./Handelsvertretungen, Informationseinrichtungen etc.

VIII. Armed forces/Streitkräfte

IX. Protecting powers/Schutzmächte

HH. Jurisdiction of the state/Jurisdiktion (Hoheitsgewalt)

I. Basis of jurisdiction/Grundlage der Jurisdiktion

1. Territorial principle/Territorialitätsprinzip
2. Personal principle/Personalitätsprinzip
3. Protective principle/Schutzprinzip
4. Universality principle/Universalitätsprinzip
5. Other principles/Andere Grundlagen

II. Types of jurisdiction/Arten der Jurisdiktion

1. Jurisdiction to prescribe/Legislative Jurisdiktion
2. Jurisdiction to adjudicate/Urteilsjurisdiktion
3. Jurisdiction to enforce/Durchsetzungsjurisdiktion

III. Extra-territorial exercise of jurisdiction/Extraterritoriale Ausübung von Hoheitsgewalt

1. General/Im allgemeinen
2 Consular jurisdiction/Konsularjurisdiktion
3. Jurisdiction over military personnel abroad/Jurisdiktion über im Ausland stationiertes Militärpersonal
4. Others (artificial islands, *terra nullius*, etc.)/Sonstiges (künstliche Inseln, *terra nullius* etc.)

IV. Limitations upon jurisdiction (servitudes, leases, etc.)/ Einschränkungen der Hoheitsgewalt (Servituten, ähnliche Gebrauchsrechte)

V. Concurrent jurisdiction/Konkurrierende Jurisdiktion

II. State territory/Das Staatsgebiet

I. Territory/Das Gebiet

1. Elements of territory/Gebietsteile
   a. Land, internal waters, rivers, lakes and land-locked seas (see also JJ. and KK.)/Land, Binnengewässer, Flüsse, Seen und Binnenmeere (siehe auch JJ. Und KK.)
   b. Sub-soil/Unterirdisches Gebiet
   c. Territorial sea (see KK.)/Küstenmeer (siehe KK.)
   d. Airspace (see LL.)/Luftraum (siehe LL.)
2. Good neighborliness/Gute Nachbarschaft

II. Boundaries and frontiers/Grenzen

1. Delimitation/Delimitation
2. Demarcation/Demarkation
3. Stability/Stabilität

III. Acquisition and transfer of territory/Gebietserwerb und Gebietsübertragung

1. Acquisition/Gebietserwerb
2. Transfer/Gebietsübertragung

JJ. International watercourses/Internationale Gewässer

I. Rivers and Lakes/Flüsse und Seen

1. Definiton/Definition
2. Navigation/Schiffahrt
3. Irrigation/Bewässerung
4. Uses for other purposes/Sonstige Nutzungen
5. Protection of the environment/Umweltschutz
6. Institutional aspects/Institutionelle Aspekte

II. Subterranean waters/Grundwasser

III. Canals/Kanäle

KK. Seas/Meere

I. Internal waters, including ports and bays/Innere Gewässer, Hafenanlagen, Buchten

II. The territorial sea/Das Küstenmeer

III. Straits/Meerengen

IV. Archipelagic waters/Archipelagische Gewässer

V. Contiguous zone/Anschlusszone

VI. Exclusive economic zone, exclusive fisheries zone/Ausschließliche Wirtschaftszone, ausschließliche Fischereizone

VII. Continental shelf/Festlandsockel

VIII. High seas/Die Hohe See

1. Freedom of the sea/Grundsatz der Meeresfreiheit
2. Hot pursuit/Nachteile
3. Visit and search/Durchsuchung
4. Piracy/Piraterie
5. Conservation of living resources/Bewahrung der lebenden Ressourcen

IX. Islands, rocks and low-tide elevations/Inseln, Felsen, trocken-fallende Erhebungen

X. Enclosed and semi-enclosed seas/Eingeschlossene und halbeingeschlossene Meere

XI. International sea-bed area/Internationaler Meeresboden

XII. Land locked and geographically-disadvantaged states/Binnenstaaten und geographisch benachteiligte Staaten

XIII. Protection of the maritime environment/Schutz der Meeresumwelt

XIV. Maritime scientific research/Wissenschaftliche Meeresforschung

XV. Cables and pipelines/Kabel, Rohrleitungen

XVI. Artificial islands, installations and structures/Künstliche Inseln, Anlagen und Bauwerke

XVII. Tunnels/Tunnels

XVIII. Vessels/Schiffe

1. Legal regime/Recht der Schiffahrt

   a. Warships/Kriegsschiffe
   b. Public vessels other than warships/Andere Staatsschiffe
   c. Merchant ships/Handelsschiffe

2. Nationality/Nationalität von Schiffen
3. Jurisdiction over vessels/Jurisdiktion über Schiffe

   a. Flagstate/Flaggenstaat
   b. Coastal state/Küstenstaat
   c. Port state/Hafenstaat
   d. Other exercise of jurisdiction/Sonstige Ausübung der Jurisdiktion

LL. Air Space, outer space and Antarctica/Luftraum, Weltraum, Antarktis

I. Air Space/Luftraum

1. Legal status/Rechtsstellung
2. Uses/Nutzungen
3. Legal regime of aircraft/Rechtlicher Status des Luftfahrzeuges

II. Outer space/Weltraum

1. Legal status/Rechtsstellung
2. Uses/Nutzungen
3. Legal regime of spacecraft/Rechtlicher Status des Weltraumobjektes

III. Antarctica/Die Antarktis

1. Legal status/Rechtsstellung
2. Uses/Nutzungen

MM. International responsibility/Völkerrechtliche Verantwortlichkeit

I. General conception/Konzept der völkerrechtlichen Verantwortlichkeit

II. General issues of responsibility/Allgemeines zur völkerrechtlichen Verantwortlichkeit

1. The elements of responsibility (*e.g.*, unlawfulness of the act, attribution to the state)/Die Elemente der Staatenverantwortlichkeit (z.B. unerlaubter Akt, Zurechenbarkeit)
2. Circumstances excluding responsibility (self-defence, necessity, reprisals)/Ausschluss der Verantwortlichkeit (Selbstverteidigung, Notstand, Repressalien)
3. Procedure/Verfahren
   a. Diplomatic protection/Diplomatischer Schutz
      aa. Nationality of claims/Nationalität der Ansprüche
      bb. Exhaustion of local remedies/Ausschöpfung der innerstaatlichen Rechtsmittel
   b. Consular protection/Konsularischer Schutz
   c. Peaceful settlement (see NN.)/Friedliche Streitbeilegung (siehe NN.)
4. Consequences of responsibility (*restitutio in integrum*, damages satisfaction, guarantees)/Folgen der völkerrechtlichen Verantwortlichkeit (restitutio in integrum, Schadenersatz, Genugtuung, Sicherheitsleistungen)

III. Responsible entities/Träger der Verantwortlichkeit

1. States/Staaten
2. International organisations/Internationale Organisationen
3. Entities other than states and international organisations/Andere Einheiten
4. Individuals and groups of individuals, including corporations/ Individuen und Gruppen einschließlich juristischer Personen

NN. Pacific settlement of disputes/Friedliche Streitbeilegung

I. The concept of an international dispute/ Vorliegen eines internationalen Streites

II. Means of settlement/Methoden zur Streitbeilegung

1. Negotiations and consultations/Verhandlungen und Konsultationen
2. Good offices/Die Guten Dienste
3. Enquiry and fact-finding/Untersuchung
4. Mediation/Vermittlung
5. Conciliation/Vergleich
6. Arbitration/Schiedsgerichtsbarkeit
   a. Arbitral tribunals and commissions/Schiedsgerichte und -kommissionen
   b. Permanent Court of Arbitration/Ständiger Schiedshof
7. Judicial settlement/Gerichtliche Streitbeilegung
   a. International Court of Justice/Der Internationale Gerichtshof
   b. Courts or tribunals, other than the ICJ/Sonstige Gerichte und Gerichtshöfe
8. Settlement within international organisations/Streitbeilegung innerhalb der internationalen Organisationen
   a. United Nations/Vereinte Nationen
   b. Organisations other than the United Nations/Andere Organisationen
9. Other means of settlement/Sonstige Methoden der Streitbeilegung

OO. Coercive measures short of the use of force/Zwangsmaßnahmen unter der Schwelle der Gewaltanwendung

I. Unilateral acts/Einseitige Akte

1. Retorsion/Retorsion
2. Countermeasures/Gegenmaßnahmen
3. Pacific blockade/Friedliche Blockade
4. Intervention (see also EE.)/Intervention (siehe auch EE.)
5. Other unilateral acts/Andere einseitige Akte

II. Collective measures/Kollektivmaßnahmen

1. United Nations/Vereinte Nationen
2. Collective measures outside the United Nations/ Kollektivmaßnahmen außerhalb der Vereinten Nationen

PP. Use of force/Gewaltanwendung

I. Prohibition of use of force/Gewaltverbot

II. Legitimate use of force/Rechtmäßiger Gewaltgebrauch

1. Self-defense/Selbstverteidigung
2. Collective measures/Kollektivmaßnahmen

    a. United Nations/Vereinte Nationen
    b. Outside the United Nations/Außerhalb der Vereinten Nationen

3. Others/Sonstiges

III. Disarmament and arms control/Abrüstung und Rüstungskontrolle

QQ. The law of armed conflict and international humanitarian law/Recht des bewaffneten Konfliktes und internationales humanitäres Recht

I. International armed conflict/Der internationale bewaffnete Konflikt

1. Definition/Definition
2. The laws of international armed conflict/Das Recht des internationalen bewaffneten Konflikts

    a. Sources/Rechtsquellen
    b. The commencement of international armed conflict and its effects (*e.g.*, diplomatic and consular relations, treaties, private property, nationality, trading with the enemy, *locus standi personae in judicio*)/Der Beginn des internationalen bewaffneten Konfliktes und seine Rechtsfolgen (z.B. diplomatische und konsularische Beziehungen, Verträge, Privateigentum, Staatsangehörigkeit, Feindhandel, *locus standi personae in judicio*)
    c. Land warfare/Landkrieg
    d. Sea warfare/Seekrieg
    e. Air warfare/Luftkrieg
    f. Distinction between combatants and non-combatants/Kombattanten – Nicht-Kombattanten
    g. International humanitarian law (droit humanitaire international)/Internationales humanitäres Recht
    h. Belligerent occupation/Kriegerische Besetzung
    i. Conventional, nuclear, bacteriological and chemical weapons/ Konventionelle, nukleare, bakteriologische und chemische Waffen

j. Treaty relations between combatants (cartels, armistices etc.)/Vertragliche Beziehungen zwischen den Kombattanten (Absprachen, Waffenstillstände)
k. Termination of international armed conflict, treaties of peace/Beendigung des internationalen bewaffneten Konfliktes, Friedensverträge

3. Reparations/Reparationen

II. Non-international armed conflict/Nicht-internationaler bewaffneter Konflikt

RR. Neutrality, non-belligerency/Neutralität, Nicht-Kriegführung

I. The laws of neutrality/Neutralitätsrecht

1. Land warfare/Landkrieg
2. Sea warfare/Seekrieg
3. Air warfare/Luftkrieg

II. Permanent neutrality/Dauernde Neutralität

III. Neutrality in the light of the Charter of the United Nations/ Neutralität im Licht der Satzung der Vereinten Nationen

IV. Policy of neutrality and non-alignment/Neutralitätspolitik, Bündnisfreiheit

V. Non-belligerency/Nicht-Kriegführung

SS. Legal aspects of international relations and cooperation in particular matters/Rechtliche Aspekte der internationalen Beziehungen und Zusammenarbeit in bestimmten Bereichen

I. General economic and financial matters/Wirtschaftliche und Finanzwirtschaftliche Angelegenheiten

1. Trade/Handel
2. Loans/Kredite
3. Investments/Investitionen
4. Taxes/Steuern
5. Monetary matters/Monetäre Angelegenheiten
6. Development/Entwicklung

II. Transport and communications/Transport, Kommunikation

III. Environment/Umwelt

IV. Natural Resources/Natürliche Ressourcen

V. Technology/Technologie

VI. Social and health matters/Soziale und gesundheitliche Angelegenheiten

VII. Cultural matters/Kulturelle Angelegenheiten

VIII. Legal matters (*e.g.*, judicial assistance and crime control etc.)/Rechtliche Angelegenheiten (z.B. Rechtshilfe und Verbrechensbekämpfung etc.)

IX. Military and security matters/Militärische Angelegenheiten, Sicherheitsangelegenheiten

PART I – Austrian Judicial Decisions Involving Questions of International Law/Österreichische Judikatur zum Internationalen Recht

Martin Baumgartner | Researcher and lecturer, Section for International Law and International Relations, University of Vienna

Philipp Janig | Researcher and lecturer, Section for International Law and International Human Rights Law, University of the Bundeswehr Munich, and editor

Viktoria Ritter | Environmental Lawyer, Ökobüro – Alliance of the Austrian Environmental Movement

Maximilian Weninger | Researcher and lecturer, Section for International Law and International Relations, University of Vienna

Stephan Wittich | Professor, Section for International Law and International Relations, University of Vienna, and editor

Index of Judgments and Decisions*

BB. Sources of international law/Völkerrechtsquellen

II. – See *EE.I.4.d.bb.vi.; SS.VIII.*

CC. The law of treaties/Recht der Verträge

II.4. – See *EE.I.4.d.bb.vi.*

DD. Relationship between international law and internal law/Völkerrecht und innerstaatliches Recht

I. – See *EE.I.4.d.bb.vi.; SS.VIII.*

---

* The digest covers the period from 1 January 2023 to 31 December 2023. German originals of the decisions may be found in full text at <www.ris.bka.gv.at/Judikatur/>, by selecting the respective court (with '*Justiz*' covering decisions by the Supreme Court and the lower civil and criminal courts), entering the case number into the box '*Geschäftszahl*' and selecting '*Entscheidungstexte (TE)*' for the full text.

Austrian Review of International and European Law **28**: 259-338, 2023
 | DOI:10.1163/15736512-02801012

BB. Sources of international law/Völkerrechtsquellen

II. Custom/Völkergewohnheitsrecht

See *EE.I.4.d.bb.vi.; SS.VIII.*

CC. The law of treaties/Recht der Verträge

II. Observance, application and interpretation of treaties/ Einhaltung, Anwendung und Auslegung von Verträgen

4. Treaties and third states/(Verträge und) Drittstaaten

See *EE.I.4.d.bb.vi.*

DD. Relationship between international law and internal law/ Völkerrecht und innerstaatliches Recht

II. Application and implementation of international law in internal law/Innerstaatliche Anwendung und Durchführung des Völkerrechts

See *EE.I.4.d.bb.vi.; SS.VIII.*

EE. Subjects of International law/Völkerrechtssubjekte

I. States/Staaten

4. Formation, continuity, succession and extinction of states/Entstehung von Staaten, Kontinuität, Staatennachfolge und Untergang von Staaten

d. Extinctions/Untergang von Staaten

bb. Effects of state succession/Rechtliche Folgen der Staatennachfolge

vi. Property/Staatsvermögen

EE.I.4.d.bb.vi.

Supreme Court, Judgment 10 Ob 9/23f of 16 May 2023, ECLI:AT:OGH0002:2023:0100OB00009.23F.0516.000

Oberster Gerichtshof, Entscheidung 10 Ob 9/23f vom 16. Mai 2023, ECLI:AT:OGH0002:2023:0100OB00009.23F.0516.000

Keywords

State succession into property – 'dissolution' of the USSR – customary international law – state practice – *opinio juris* – persistent objector – treaty interpretation – 1991 Treaty on the Legal Succession in Respect of the External Public Debt and Assets of the USSR – 1992 Agreement on the Division of all Property of the former USSR abroad – treaty effects on third states – ownership share of Ukraine in Soviet real property located in Austria

Staatennachfolge in Vermögen – „Auflösung" der UdSSR – Völkergewohnheitsrecht – Staatenpraxis – Rechtsüberzeugung (*opinio juris*) – *persistent objector* – Vertragsinterpretation – 1991 Vertrag über die Rechtsnachfolge in bezug auf die staatlichen Auslandsschulden und die Aktiva der Union der SSR – 1992 Abkommen über die Aufteilung sämtlichen Eigentums der ehemaligen Union der SSR im Ausland – Drittwirkung von Verträgen – Miteigentümerschaft der Ukraine hinsichtlich sowjetischen Grundeigentums in Österreich

Facts and procedural history (summary)

The plaintiff, the Russian Federation, demanded that the defendant, a Ukrainian stock company (the 'UDP'), vacate and handover a property situated in Vienna. *In eventu,* the plaintiff demanded the vacation of the property *per se* (without a handover to the Russian Federation). That request was based on the land registry, according to which the plaintiff was registered as the owner of the property, which for decades had been in continuous use by the UDP or its legal predecessor, a state-owned shipping company.

In 1974, the Soviet Embassy in Austria concluded a contract to buy property in Vienna to establish representative offices of the Soviet shipping company (the 'SDP') in Austria. The SDP had been founded by Soviet authorities in 1944. When the Soviet Union collapsed, the shipping company became a Ukrainian state-owned company that was subsequently turned into a stock company (the 'UDP'). Ukraine held 100 per cent of the shares. The UDP developed into a private stock company and continued using the premises in Vienna for its representation in Austria.

Under Soviet law, state-owned companies could not own property. The property held by them was owned by the state. Therefore, also the SDP and the premises in Vienna were owned by the Soviet Union until its collapse. The Russian Federation argued that it became the owner of the premises thereafter and that the UDP had no right to use them. The UDP argued that the Russian Federation had no standing to bring the claim, because the Russian Federation did not become the sole owner of the premises in Vienna after the collapse of the Soviet Union. Consequently, it lacked consent of the other successor states to bring a claim against UDP. Moreover, they argued that UDP itself acquired ownership of the property, which it derived from Ukraine, whose ownership was derived from the SDP.

The present judgment stems from the second time the dispute came before the Austrian Supreme Court. In the first round of proceedings, the lower courts granted the request of Russia to vacate the premises. They found that Russia succeeded the Soviet Union and could therefore bring the claim against UDP. In its first decision, the Supreme Court set these decisions aside due to the lower courts' incorrect assessment of questions of Austrian law and remitted the matter back to the court of first instance. The Supreme Court did not apply public international law.

In the second round of proceedings, the court of first instance rejected the Russian Federation's claim to vacate the property. It held that the core of the dispute between the Russian Federation and UDP was an international dispute between two subjects of international law: the Russian Federation and Ukraine. This dispute had to be settled before international dispute settlement bodies. As the SDP used the property in Vienna for its activities and was later transformed into a Ukrainian state-owned company, the property was allocated to Ukraine. Russia's request could therefore not succeed. The court of first instance based its decision on an interpretation of the *uti possidetis* principle. On that basis, following an instance of state succession, property in foreign countries in possession of a state should remain with this state until international dispute settlement proceedings eventually lead to a different allocation of the premises.

The court of second instance confirmed this decision, explaining that there was a 'legal limbo', because the question of ownership had not been determined in international dispute settlement proceedings. Therefore, it rejected Russia's claim to vacate the property. Russia as well as UDP appealed the decision to the Supreme Court.

The Supreme Court held (in excerpts):

Decision

The documents submitted with the plaintiff's appeal and the defendant's response to the appeal are rejected.

Both appeals are upheld in part.

The contested decision is amended so that it reads – including the confirmed and amended parts – as a partial judgment:

'1. The interlocutory application of the defendant for a declaratory judgment that the plaintiff is not the owner of the property register number * is rejected.

2. It is established that the plaintiff is not the sole owner of the property register number *.

3. The claim that the defendant is obliged to hand over the property register number * vacated, to the plaintiff within 14 days is dismissed.

4. The decision on costs is reserved for the final decision.'

In all other respects, in particular with regard to the additional claim that the defendant is obliged to vacate the property register number * *per se*, the decisions of the lower courts are set aside. To this extent, the case is referred back to the court of first instance for a new decision after supplementary proceedings.

[…]

Legal findings:

[…]

[19] 2.1. Pursuant to Art 9(2) of the Federal Constitutional Law (*B-VG*), the generally recognised rules of international law are deemed to be part of federal law, which in any case includes customary international law (Reinisch, *Handbuch des Völkerrechts*[6] [2021] MN 221 f; Grabenwarter/Frank, *B-VG* Art 9 MN 2; Muzak, *B-VG*[6] Art 9 MN 1).

[20] 2.2 The application of customary international law is thus the application of domestic law. The application and interpretation of international law can therefore constitute a legal question of considerable importance within the meaning of Sec 502 Code of Civil Procedure (*ZPO*) (Lovrek in Fasching/Konecny[3] IV/1 § 502 ZPO MN 69). The case law cited by the court of appeal, according to which the Supreme Court is not called upon to ensure the uniformity or further development of foreign law or to develop guidelines for its correct understanding, concerns the application of foreign law (RS0042948), for which a guiding function is assigned to other (judicial) bodies. It does not concern the application of international law.

[21] 2.1. In fact, there is no case law of the highest courts about the treatment of foreign property of the former USSR in Austria and the related questions of international law. The appeals are therefore admissible.

[22] 3. Both appeals are based on the question of who is entitled to ownership of the property at issue. In the appeal proceedings it is no longer disputed that until 1991, the USSR was in any case the owner. There is disagreement regarding

the question of how the 'disintegration' of the USSR affected the ownership of the property in question, or more precisely: which state (or states) is (are) to be regarded as the owner of the property since then. Questions of international law play an essential role here. Although the Supreme Court addressed these questions in the decisions cited in its first decision to set aside the former judgments of the courts of lower instances (10 Ob 19/18v [paras 2.2, 2.3 and 2.6]), it did not have to answer them there.

[23] 3.1 As already stated by the Supreme Court in the first round of proceedings (10 Ob 19/18v [para 5.2]), international law – which is invoked by both parties – is to be determined *ex officio* (Hoyer, on 5 Ob 152/04w and 5 Ob 238/04t, ZfRV 2005, 78). For the determination of international law, recourse can be had to the cooperation of the parties or to an expert opinion pursuant to Sec 4 Private International Law Act (*IPRG*), especially since facts can also play an essential role for the resolution of questions of international (customary) law. However, this is merely an aid to ascertaining the basis that is necessary for the resolution of the legal questions (in this case questions of international law). These legal questions are then to be resolved independently by the court, so that the court is not bound by the expert opinion, which is also what Sec 4 Private International Law Act (*IPRG*) provides (7 Ob 14/98d; Neumayr in *KBB*[6] § 4 IPRG MN 1; Verschraegen in Rummel, *ABGB*[3] § 4 IPRG MN 2).

[24] 3.2. The lower courts based the rejection of all claims on the consideration that the proceedings were based on a dispute under international law between two states, over which they had no authority to decide. Because of the necessary dispute resolution procedure under international law, the courts found that there was a legal limbo, so that the claims had to be rejected. This cannot be accepted, because those subjects of international law who would be obliged to settle their dispute under international law according to this interpretation of the law are not involved in the present proceedings.

[25] The legal opinion expressed by the expert during the proceedings in the first instance is, moreover, based on the 'further development' of the *uti possidetis*-principle. However, this principle concerns the determination of state borders (Herdegen, *Völkerrecht*[21] [2022] § 4 MN 11; Reinisch, *Handbuch des Völkerrechts*[6] [2021] MN 679; Epping in Ipsen, *Völkerrecht*[7] [2018] § 7 MN 11) and there is no territorial dispute at issue here: it is undisputed that the property at issue is located on the territory of the Republic of Austria. There are also no indications in international law scholarship or practice that this principle would be applied with regard to disputes concerning the continuation of or succession to legal positions concerning foreign property as advocated by the expert.

[26] It is therefore not apparent on what grounds of international law the Austrian courts should be precluded from assessing the preliminary question under inter-

national law as to which state or states are entitled to ownership of the foreign assets of the former USSR.

[27] Another question is whether the Russian Federation and Ukraine would be obliged to settle disputes between each other in a certain form and would, for example, have to conduct proceedings before an arbitral tribunal. However, a legal dispute between these states is not to be decided here, so that it does not need to be discussed further.

[28] 3.3. Since the question of international legal personality and its continuity after processes of disintegration or after a possible succession of states with regard to state property (between Austria and the states concerned) is not regulated by international treaty law, this question is governed by customary international law (Doehring, *Völkerrecht*[2] [2004] MN 168). The Vienna Convention on Succession of States in respect of State Property, Archives and Debts of 8 April 1983, which sought to codify such customary international law, has not yet entered into force.

[29] 3.4. In the prevailing international law doctrine, customary international law emerges when there is a practice that is generally recognised as law, *i.e.* supported by a belief of legal obligation (*opinio iuris*) (Herdegen, *Völkerrecht*[21] [2022] § 16 MN 1; Reinisch, *Handbuch des Völkerrechts*[6] [2021] MN 163; Vitzthum in Vitzthum/Proelß, *Völkerrecht*[8] [2019] Section 1 MN 131; Dörr in Ipsen, *Völkerrecht*[7] [2018] § 19 MN 2; Fischer/Köck, *Völkerrecht*[6] [2004] MN 160).

[30] In detail, much is disputed. However, it is recognised that customary law, which is not of a peremptory nature, can also be replaced or amended by newly emerging norms (Herdegen, *Völkerrecht*[21] [2022] § 16 MN 25; Reinisch, *Handbuch des Völkerrechts*[6] [2021] MN 202; Vitzthum in Vitzthum/Proelß, *Völkerrecht*[8] [2019] Section 1 MN 136; Doehring, *Völkerrecht*[2] [2004] MN 295). The newly created norm of customary international law can be universal, general or regional, depending on its personal scope (Reinisch, *Handbuch des Völkerrechts*[6] [2021] MN 202).

[31] Based on a decision of the ICJ in the so-called *Fisheries* Case, it is moreover – also in scholarship – accepted as given that a state can exempt itself from the application of a new (non-peremptory) norm of customary rule by persistent objection during the norm's formation. Although the state cannot prevent the emergence of the norm of customary international law, it can prevent itself from being bound by it ('persistent objector'). Other states cannot hold the norm against it (ICJ, 18 December 1951, ICJ Reports 1951, 116 [131]; Herdegen, *Völkerrecht*[21] [2022] § 16 MN 22; Reinisch, *Handbuch des Völkerrechts*[6] [2021] MN 175; Vitzthum in Vitzthum/Proelß, *Völkerrecht*[8] [2019] Section 1 MN 133; Dörr in Ipsen, *Völkerrecht*[7] [2018] § 19 MN 28 f). However, in case of claims for special treatment, the persistent objection loses its effect if the development

of a new customary rule is almost uniformly supported by the community of states (Herdegen, *Völkerrecht*[21] [2022] § 16 MN 24).

[32] 3.5. As the different qualification of disintegration processes in the past shows, the reaction of the community of states plays an important role (Herdegen, *Völkerrecht*[21] [2022] § 8 MN 25; Reinisch, *Handbuch des Völkerrechts*[6] [2021] MN 846; Epping in Ipsen, *Völkerrecht*[7] [2018] § 7 MN 204). However, the respective states concerned have considerable discretion in choosing the legal consequences of state succession (Herdegen, *Völkerrecht*[21] [2022] § 8 MN 25; Reinisch, *Handbuch des Völkerrechts*[6] [2021] MN 848; Epping in Ipsen, *Völkerrecht*[7] [2018] § 7 MN 205), so that assets are often divided by treaty (Reinisch, *Handbuch des Völkerrechts*[6] [2021] MN 864). Even if treaties under international law do not have any direct legal effects for other subjects of international law who are not treaty parties, these treaties can therefore be an expression of the legal consequences of state succession as chosen by the states affected by disintegration processes and be relevant under customary international law.

[33] 3.6 In the case of the events in the former USSR, there are arguments that speak in favour of Russia continuing the legal personality of the USSR as well as for the disappearance of the USSR by dissolution (Kau in Vitzthum/Proelß, *Völkerrecht*[8] [2019] Section 3 MN 185; see also Reinisch, *Handbuch des Völkerrechts*[6] [2021] MN 893 f; Epping in Ipsen, *Völkerrecht*[7] [2018] § 7 MN 210). The qualification of these events and the related question of whether the Russian Federation generally (for example also with regard to international treaties or membership of the United Nations) continued the identity of the previous state, and whether this was accepted by the community of states (*cf* Reinisch, *Handbuch des Völkerrechts*[6] [2021] MN 894, according to which the other successor states, however, assumed certain rights and obligations as partial legal successors), is not decisive here, as this case only concerns the effects of these events with regard to the foreign assets of the USSR and these effects were regulated by the states involved through bilateral and multilateral agreements.

[34] 3.7 The Russian Federation entered into international treaty arrangements with the other states to regulate the treatment of foreign assets and debts of the former USSR. These agreements provided for the division of the foreign assets and debts – on a multilateral and bilateral basis.

[35] 3.7.1 The basis for this division was created by the 'Treaty on the Legal Succession in Respect of the External Public Debt and Assets of the USSR' of 4 December 1991 (submitted in the proceedings at first instance in German translation), which was signed (not by all successor states, but) by the Russian Federation and Ukraine. According to the preamble of this treaty, 'it is impossible to guarantee the liquidation of the external debt of the USSR unless matters of

the division of the USSR assets are settled' and 'the principles of international law and the provisions of the Vienna (1983) Convention on Succession of States in Respect of State Property, Archives and Debts' were taken into account. According to Art 1, the assets of the USSR are defined for the purposes of this treaty as (*inter alia*) the immovable and movable state property of the USSR outside the state borders of its territory. Art 2 names as successor states of the USSR, *inter alia*, the Russian Federation and Ukraine. According to Art 3(1) of the treaty, the parties undertake (subject to the concurrent agreement to bear proportionately the foreign debt) to guarantee the right of ownership for each party to a certain percentage of the assets of the USSR to which each party is entitled. Art 4 determines these percentages (Russian Federation 61.34%, Ukraine 16.37%). For all questions connected with the implementation of this treaty, an Intergovernmental Council supervising debt service and assets usage was established, which is composed of authorised representatives of the successor states (Art 7).

[36] 3.7.2 In the 'Agreement of the Heads of State of the Commonwealth of Independent States on property of the former USSR abroad' of 30 December 1991, all eleven CIS states agreed 'that each of them has the right for a corresponding fixed fair share in the property of the former USSR abroad, and shall promote the realization of this right' (Schweisfurth, *Ausgewählte Fragen der Staatensukzession im Kontext der Auflösung der UdSSR*, ArchVR 1994, 99 [120]).

[37] 3.7.3 This agreement was followed by the 'Agreement on the division of all property of the former USSR abroad' of 6 July 1992 (submitted in the first instance proceedings in German translation), which was signed by all successor states of the USSR with the exception of Azerbaijan and Georgia (Schweisfurth, *Immobiliareigentum der UdSSR in Deutschland*, VIZ 1998, 57 [60]). The preamble explicitly refers to the Treaty of 4 December 1991 and the Agreement of 30 December 1991. The object of the Agreement 'is the movable and immovable property' of the USSR outside the state borders (Art 1(1)). This property is subject to division and 'becomes property of the Parties' (Art 1(2)), according to a fixed percentage as in the agreement of 4 December 1991. The respective share refers to all property in each specific country (Art 1(4)). Each side has the right to independent possession, use and disposal of the fixed share of the entire property of the USSR to which it is entitled and the right to distribution in kind (Art 3), which should take place on the basis of separate agreements between the parties (Art 4). A Commission on succession was entrusted with the settlement of all questions connected with the realisation of this agreement (Art 6). An arbitral tribunal was to have jurisdiction over disputes concerning the interpretation and application of this Agreement (Art 7).

[38] 3.8 From this it is evident that – irrespective of the assessment of the 'disintegration' of the USSR under international law or the succession in treaties under international law – the foreign property of the former USSR was not to belong to the Russian Federation alone, even according to the clear intention of the Russian Federation itself. At the latest with the Agreement of 6 July 1992, which according to its preamble intended to cover the legal succession to the foreign property in accordance with the Treaty of 4 December 1991 and the Agreement of 30 December 1991, the property was transferred to the states bound by this Agreement at the fixed percentages according to the clear Art 1(2). The parties do not claim that this agreement did not become effective as an international treaty and there are no indications of this in the file (this would also be contrary to the existing literature on international law). The agreement does not focus on whether the foreign assets were last transferred or allocated to a specific enterprise (domiciled in a participating state). Nor can any other restriction of the effects agreed therein be inferred from the Agreement, so that the states concerned entered into the legal position of the USSR with regard to foreign property of the former USSR, including the property in question. Thus, the states became *pro rata* (co-)owners of the foreign property (Schweisfurth, VIZ 1998, 57 [63]).

[39] The fact that a division of the property in kind was reserved for further regulations (Art 4) and that the agreement entrusted a commission with the further regulation of questions of the realisation of the agreement (Art 6) does not prevent these legal effects, especially since on the basis of the agreement each party was already entitled to independent possession, use and disposal of the fixed share (Art 3).

[40] With regard to the property at issue here, the Agreement between the Russian Federation and Ukraine on the Mutual Recognition of Rights and the Regulation of Property Relations of 15 January 1993 does not change anything, so that the question of whether this agreement has been ratified is not relevant. According to its Art 1, this agreement would only concern the recognition of property located on the territories of the Parties and expressly excludes the assets specified in the agreement of 4 December 1991. The property in question, however, was state property of the USSR, which is subject to the agreement of 4 December 1991, and would therefore not be covered by the agreement of 15 January 1993. A distinction between the administrative assets ('state property') and the 'financial assets' not directly required for the fulfilment of governmental tasks – as advocated by the defendant (see also para 4.1.2. below) – cannot be derived from any of the aforementioned treaties or agreements. The Vienna Convention on Succession of States in respect of State Property, Archives and Debts of 1983, which according to some preambles of the above-mentioned

treaties or agreements was expressly taken into account, also does not recognise such a distinction (Kau in Vitzthum/Proelß, *Völkerrecht*[8] [2019] Section 3 MN 197; Epping in Ipsen, *Völkerrecht*[7] [2018] § 7 MN 217).

[41] 3.9 The fact that the existing rules under international treaty law were amended by (new) treaties between the states involved is not alleged by the parties to these proceedings and is not otherwise to be inferred from the file. However, the following events occurred, the effects of which must be examined under international law.

[42] 3.9.1 Presumably because the negotiations of the Commission mandated by the Agreement of 6 July 1992 (Art 6) proved difficult and because it did not succeed in the concrete division of the foreign assets, the Commission's activities were discontinued and it was decided to resolve the outstanding questions at the bilateral level (Schweisfurth, ArchVR 1994, 99 [121]). However, this was only partially successful. Probably in order to end the state of limbo regarding the foreign property of the former USSR (Schweisfurth, VIZ 1998, 57 [61]; Schweisfurth, ArchVR 1994, 99 [121]), the Russian Federation, by presidential decree of 8 February 1993, took over the property of the former USSR 'as continuator state of the USSR'. This included all rights to the movable and immovable property of the former USSR located abroad, as well as the fulfilment of all obligations connected with the use of this property. At the same time, the government of the Russian Federation was to decide bilaterally all questions connected with the implementation of the Agreement of 30 December 1991 (Schweisfurth, VIZ 1998, 57 [61]).

[43] 3.9.2 In the course of 1993, agreements were then signed with all other successor states with the exception of Ukraine, so that the respective shares in the foreign assets were transferred to the Russian Federation (either definitively against the assumption of the foreign debts by the Russian Federation or at least provisionally until further arrangements were made) (Kembayev, *Probleme der Rechtsnachfolge von der Sowjetunion auf die Russische Föderation*, ArchVR 2008, 106 [125]; Schweisfurth, VIZ 1998, 57 [61]).

[44] 3.9.3 Ukraine, however, consistently objected to the transfer of all foreign assets and the position of the Russian Federation and refused a corresponding allocation of assets and liabilities to the Russian Federation (Kembayev, ArchVR 2008, 106 [125]), even though it could not service the share of existing foreign debts at the time (Kembayev, ArchVR 2008, 106 [126]). The Russian Federation and the Ukraine signed a bilateral agreement on 9 December 1994, which, however, was not ratified by the Ukrainian parliament (Kembayev, ArchVR 2008, 106 [126]), because it apparently wanted to check for a potential surplus of assets over liabilities (*cf* Schweisfurth, VIZ 1998, 57 [62]).

[45] 3.9.4 This dispute between the Russian Federation and Ukraine concerning the foreign assets continued thereafter (Schweisfurth, VIZ 1998, 57 [62]; Schweisfurth, ArchVR 1994, 99 [121 f]).

[46] 3.9.5 In a *note verbale* of 7 August 2008, the Austrian Federal Ministry for European and International Affairs, GZ BMeiA RU.8.19.01/0022-I.2/2008 declared with reference to the decisions of the Supreme Court in 5 Ob 152/04w and 5 Ob 238/04t, that on the basis of current state practice and the customary international law created by it, the Russian Federation was now also to be regarded as the owner of the properties currently still appearing in the Austrian land register as property of the USSR. Moreover, on the basis of the developments in international law in recent years, which had recognised the complete identity of the Russian Federation with the former USSR, the previously unclear ownership of the Russian Federation of the properties, which were still owned by the USSR according to the Austrian land register, was now clarified. Thus, the Federal Ministry for European and International Affairs advocated for a corresponding correction of the land register.

[47] In a second *note verbale* of 2 October 2008, GZ BMeiA RU.8.19.01/0035-I.2/2008, the Federal Ministry for European and International Affairs supplemented the above-mentioned note verbale and listed those States which, in its opinion, agreed that the Russian Federation took over ownership from the USSR (Denmark, Germany, Finland, Greece, Ireland, Italy, Luxembourg, Netherlands, Portugal, Sweden, Slovenia, Czech Republic, Hungary, United Kingdom) or in which this question did not arise (*e.g.* due to the lack of properties of the former USSR) (Estonia, France, Latvia, Lithuania, Malta).

[48] 3.10. As explained, state practice plays an important role for the assessment of customary international law, and customary law that is not of a peremptory nature can also be abrogated or amended.

[49] Since the present case only concerns the treatment of foreign property, only state practice in this respect is relevant; state practice regarding state succession in respect of international treaties or the position in international organizations is therefore not relevant.

[50] However, the existence of state practice, according to which the foreign property of the former USSR should (only) accrue to the Russian Federation, is already questionable. Such a (concrete) practice cannot be inferred from the expert opinions. According to the *notes verbales* from 2008, some (European) states may have acted in this sense. In contrast, the behaviour of the states specially affected – the successor states of the USSR, which transferred their shares in the foreign assets to the Russian Federation in exchange for the assumption of the foreign debts by the Russian Federation even after the presidential decree

of 8 February 1993 – indicates a contrary behaviour, as their behaviour would otherwise be inexplicable. As explained, the fact that other states or individual decisions of the International Court of Justice have recognized the Russian Federation as a 'continuator state' in international treaty law or membership of the United Nations is not of relevance for this case. A practice generally recognised as law, *i.e.* supported by a sense of legal obligation, is therefore not evident.

[51] However, even if one were to assume that such a practice existed and, moreover, that the treaties could be changed by a subsequent state practice and customary international law (Doehring, *Völkerrecht*^{2} [2004] MN 295), it must be taken into account that Ukraine also (continued to) persistently object to this state practice, which is not even disputed by the plaintiff in the appeal proceedings.

[52] 3.10.1. The Presidential Decree of 8 February 1993, in which the Russian Federation declared that it would take over the foreign property in its entirety as continuator state of the USSR, itself mentions the Agreement of 30 December 1991 (according to which each participating state had the right to a corresponding fixed and equitable share of the foreign property of the former USSR) and requires the government of the Russian Federation to decide the related questions in bilateral agreements. It is therefore already questionable whether it is guided by sufficient intention to (unilaterally) change the arrangements made so far. In any case, Ukraine persistently objected to the position of the Russian Federation (Kembayev, ArchVR 2008, 106 [125]). The Presidential Decree was thus a unilateral domestic act without any effects under international law (Schweisfurth, VIZ 1998, 57 [62]; unclear – but in the obvious assumption that no protest had been lodged – Schweisfurth, ArchVR 1994, 99 [121]).

[53] 3.10.2 The *notes verbales* of the Federal Ministry for European and International Affairs from 2008 could in principle be part of a state practice which can lead to the formation of customary international law (amending existing customary international law). However, Ukraine continued to persistently object to any such state practice (*cf* the evidence in the file and *e.g.* the article of 1 June 2010 'Ukraine besteht auf Anteil an UdSSR-Vermögen' (Ukraine insists on share in USSR assets) [available at https://p.dw.com/p/NdoP], the article 'A pause in talks on Soviet property' in The Ukrainian Weekly of 6 February 2011 [available at www.ukrweekly.com/archive/pdf3/2011/The_Ukrainian_Weekly_2011-06.pdf]) or the article by Alexey Uvarov of 29 November 2022 on ridl.io [available at ridl.io/the-heavy-legacy-of-the-soviet-regime]. An effect under international law *vis-à-vis* Ukraine is therefore out of the question. There are no indications that the conduct of the Russian Federation with regard to foreign assets of the USSR was almost uniformly supported by the rest of the community of states, which could lead to the persistent objector also being bound by customary international

law despite its persistent objection (Herdegen, *Völkerrecht*[21] [2022] § 16 MN 24). This is also not asserted in the appeal proceedings.

[54] 4. For these reasons, on the basis of the above-mentioned treaties and agreements, the legal status of the USSR with regard to the ownership of the foreign assets was (ultimately) continued (at least) by the Russian Federation and Ukraine (also Schweisfurth, VIZ 1998, 57 [63 and 64]). Whether and on what basis of circumstances other states also entered into this legal status (and still hold this legal status) is not to be examined due to the lack of corresponding submissions by the parties (*cf* on the possible relevance paras 6.3. and 7.1. below). On the other hand, the concrete extent to which the respective states continue the legal status of the USSR is irrelevant, because the answer to the legal questions at issue does not depend on the respective extent of the co-ownership share.

[55] In addition, the following should be stated in response to the respective positions of the parties in the appeal proceedings:

[56] 4.1.1 The plaintiff does not deal in detail with the international treaties and agreements described and the effects that can be derived from them, but essentially relies on the widely and repeatedly presented assertion that the 'disintegration' of the USSR is not to be regarded as *dismembratio*, but rather that the Russian Federation is to be regarded as identical with the USSR ('continuator state'). However, the qualification of the events according to general customary international law is not of decisive importance due to the agreements between the states concerned that specifically concern foreign property, so that there are no secondary deficiencies in the findings in this respect.

[57] The relevance of the question of whether the Russian Federation (also) assumed and paid the foreign debts that were allocated to Ukraine according to the apportionment percentages is not apparent. Insofar as the plaintiff derives its relevance from the *notes verbales* from 2008 (because the legal opinion expressed therein is based on the complete payment of the foreign debts of the former USSR), the reason for the declaration by the Ministry is not relevant. In any case, it does not have effects under international law (above para 3.10.2.). In this respect, too, the basis for the finding is therefore not deficient.

[58] The plaintiff in its appeal does not argue that the courts are formally bound by the Federal Ministry of European and Foreign Affairs' *notes verbales*. The existence of a unilateral act in the form of a recognition under international law that binds all organs of a state cannot be derived from the content of these *notes verbales*. They merely communicate (altered) assessments under international law, so that they do not express a willingness on Austria's part to be bound by international law, which is necessary for the creation of obligations. There is therefore no '*de facto* binding force' of these *notes verbales*.

[59] 4.1.2 The deficiency of the appeal proceedings alleged by the defendant was examined; it is not present (Sec 510(3) Code of Civil Procedure (*ZPO*)).

[60] In the appeal, the defendant argues that the property in question should not be regarded as 'genuine' foreign property because it had served a company which had its registered office in Ukraine. As such, it had become property of Ukraine in its entirety in accordance with the Agreement of 15 January 1993. As explained above (para 3.8.), this agreement excludes from its scope of application those assets of the USSR which are specified in the agreement of 4 December 1991. However, this agreement designates as assets the 'immovable and movable state property' of the USSR outside the state borders of its territory (Art 1(2)). According to the law of the USSR (determined in the present proceedings by means of an expert opinion), which is not disputed by the defendant, the property in dispute was also included. The restriction advocated by the defendant only to such property of the USSR which is not allocated to a specific company cannot be inferred from the agreement of 4 December 1991.

[61] Even considerations of equity according to Art 18(1)(b) of the Vienna Convention on Succession of States in respect of State Property, Archives and Debts of 1983 do not lead to the sole ownership of Ukraine, because the participating states made arrangements in treaties which take precedence over the customary international law codified in the Convention (*cf* also Art 14(1), Art 15(4), Art 17(1) and Art 18(1) of the Convention).

[62] 4.2. As an interim result, it can therefore be stated that because of the continuation of the ownership position of the former USSR on a *pro rata* basis as agreed in the 1991 treaty, the Russian Federation and Ukraine are (in any case) co-owners of the property in dispute.

[63] 4.3 The defendant did not challenge the assessment of the court of first instance that the SDP had not acquired ownership either through construction or in any other way, that no legal relationship such as a trust or tenancy agreement could have existed between the USSR and the SDP and that the defendant was not entitled to compensation for the counterclaims raised in the appeal. It did not raise these issues further in the appeal proceedings either, so that they do not need to be addressed further.

[64] 5. For the interlocutory applications for a declaratory judgment filed by the defendant, the following follows:

[65] 5.1. Based on this result, the rejection of the defendant's interim application for a declaratory judgment that the plaintiff is not the owner of the property must be confirmed, because the latter must in any case be regarded as the (co-)owner.

[66] However, since she is not the sole owner, the alternative interim application is justified. According to case law, such a determination is permissible (RS0010338); it does not decide on a (legal) fact, but clarifies legal relationships between the parties (10 Ob 36/16s [para 4.2]).

[67] Since the further interim application for a declaratory judgment was filed in the alternative, it is therefore no longer to be decided.

6. With regard to the claim it therefore follows:

[68] 6.1. Each partner in a community has the right to take the legal remedies necessary to safeguard the overall right, which are necessary to safeguard their ownership interest; the opposing party cannot plead in such an action that the plaintiff alone is not authorized to assert these claims (RS0013417; see also RS0013226). The plaintiff's right to bring an action is therefore established.

[69] 6.2. However, it does not follow from the plaintiff's entitlement to bring an action for eviction that the vacated property must also be handed over to her alone in all cases. This would require a legal title on her part, which is neither claimed nor otherwise evident here, as the plaintiff based her request solely on her sole ownership. In the absence of such a special legal title, the co-owners as a whole are entitled, which is why all co-owners would have to be named as entitled parties in the request for transfer (RS0013226 [T4]). Since the plaintiff is not the sole owner of the property, she cannot demand the requested transfer to herself. The rejection of the plaintiff's main claim by the lower courts must therefore be confirmed.

[70] 6.3 The plaintiff also recognized this problem and alternatively filed a request for eviction *per se*. According to established case law, however, such a request is precluded by the fact that the eviction within the meaning of Sec 349 Enforcement Code (*EO*) cannot be separated from the handover of the vacated property to the creditor (RS0013226 [T2]).

[71] However, a dismissal of the contingent claim cannot be considered at this stage because the plaintiff has clearly overlooked this legal situation and it has not yet been discussed with her. She must therefore first be given the opportunity to submit factual submissions on any other existing beneficiaries (in addition to the Russian Federation and Ukraine) and to modify the contingent claim accordingly (see 10 Ob 53/08d). For this purpose, the decisions of the lower courts, insofar as they concern the contingent claim, must be set aside.

[72] 7.1. In the continued proceedings, a corresponding discussion will therefore have to take place regarding the overall beneficiaries and the formulation of the contingent claim, and on the basis of any factual submissions made by the plaintiff regarding the existing beneficiaries, the court of first instance will

have to make findings as to which states – if applicable, beyond the Russian Federation and Ukraine – are to be regarded as (co-)owners of the property in dispute. Depending on a modification of the claim by the plaintiff, it must then be examined whether all materially entitled persons are named therein, in which case the claim can be granted. If not all entitled persons are named, this claim will also have to be dismissed.

[…]

II. International organisations/Internationale Organisationen

1. In general/Allgemeines

c. Legal effect of acts of international organisations/ Rechtswirkung von Akten internationaler Organisationen

EE.II.1.c.

Supreme Administrative Court, Judgment Ro 2022/21/0002 of 30 November 2023, ECLI:AT:VWGH:2023:RO2022210002.J00

Verwaltungsgerichtshof, Erkenntnis Ro 2022/21/0002 vom 30. November 2023, ECLI:AT:VWGH:2023:RO2022210002.J00

Keywords

Expulsion – sanctions – United Nations Security Council (UNSC) – Art 25 UN Charter – Art 41 UN Charter – UNSC resolutions under Chapter VII – UNSC Resolution 2397 (2017) – EU Common Foreign and Security Policy (CFSP) – legal effects of a UNSC resolution on CFSP decisions by the EU – human rights exceptions to sanctions

Ausweisung – Sanktionen – Sicherheitsrat der Vereinten Nationen – Art 25 UN Charta – Art 41 UN Charta – Resolutionen des Sicherheitsrats der Vereinten Nationen unter Kapitel 7 – UN Sicherheitsratsresolution 2397 (2017) – Gemeinsame Außen- und Sicherheitspolitik (GASP) – Rechtliche Folgen von Resolutionen des UN-Sicherheitsrats auf die GASP – Menschenrechtliche Ausnahmen von Sanktionen

Facts and procedural history (summary)

The co-participant is a national of the Democratic People's Republic of Korea (DPRK; also 'North Korea'). He has lived in Austria since 1996, with interruptions in the periods from 2000 to 2002 and 2012 to 2015, when he was in 'North Korea'. He worked in Austria in various functions for the International

Taekwon-Do Federation, namely as 'Treasurer' from 1996 to 2000, as Secretary General from 2002 to 2012 and as President since 2015. In this function, the co-participant earns a monthly net income of around EUR 2000. During his stay in Austria, the co-participant has held various residence permits, most recently a 'Red-White-Red Card Plus' valid until 6 February 2022 that was issued to him on 6 February 2019.

By decision dated 3 March 2020, the Federal Office for Immigration and Asylum issued a return decision against the co-participant. This decision was based on Sec 52(4) No 1 Aliens Police Act (*FPG*) arguing that a ground for refusal became apparent later, in conjunction with Sec 9 Federal Office for Immigration and Asylum Procedures Act (*BFA-VG*) based on considerations of the private and family life of the co-participant. The Federal Office for Immigration and Asylum determined pursuant to Sec 52(9) Aliens Police Act (*FPG*) that the deportation of the co-participant to the DPRK was permissible.

The Federal Office for Immigration and Asylum justified the permissibility of the return decision by stating that Austria was obliged under 'international and European law' to refrain from issuing work permits to persons with North Korean citizenship and to return such persons with a work permit to the DPRK 'in compliance with human rights' on the basis of resolutions of the United Nations Security Council and the Council of the European Union within the framework of the Common Foreign and Security Policy (CFSP). Disregarding these international obligations would have a 'massive impact on Austria's credibility under the rule of law and would significantly damage Austria's reputation in the European and international community of states'. The requirement of Sec 11(2) No 5 Settlement and Residence Act (*NAG*), according to which a residence permit may only be issued to a foreigner if 'the relations of the Republic of Austria with another state or another subject of international law are not significantly impaired', is therefore not fulfilled. As part of the balancing of interests in accordance with Sec 9 Federal Office for Immigration and Asylum Procedures Act (*BFA-VG*), the Federal Office for Immigration and Asylum acknowledged that the co-participant held a respected position as 'president of a worldwide sports association' and had always behaved in a 'law-abiding' manner. It also assumed that the return decision constituted an interference with private and family life 'worthy of protection'. However, considering the last stay in Austria of only around four years, it concluded with more detailed reasons that the particularly high public interest in terminating the stay outweighed the interests of the co-participant in remaining in Austria. This was due to the sanctions to be implemented against 'North Korea'. Furthermore, the deportation of the co-participant to the DPRK, given that he belonged to the 'pro-government elite' of his country, was permissible against the background of Art 2 and 3 ECHR.

The co-participant lodged an appeal against this decision on 28 May 2020. The Federal Administrative Court granted the appeal lodged by the co-participant in a decision of 16 February 2022 and revoked the contested decision without substitution. The facts were undisputed, as set out above. In its legal assessment, the Federal Administrative Court took account of Council Decision 2016/849 of 27 May 2016 (as amended by Council Decision [CFSP] 2018/293 of 26 February 2018) on restrictive measures against the DPRK. Its Art 26a(4) and (5) prohibits the renewal of work permits for DPRK nationals and, under certain conditions, requires their return to the DPRK by 21 December 2019 at the latest. However, the Federal Administrative Court held that it was not directly applicable to the co-participant due to a lack of direct effect. Council Regulation (EU) 2017/1509 of 30 August 2017 concerning restrictive measures against the DPRK (also in its amended version) does not provide for an obligation not to renew work permits or enforce return decisions for DPRK nationals. Furthermore, the Austrian Sanctions Act 2010 does not contain any requirements or other provisions in this regard that are applicable to the co-participant. There is thus no legal basis for the assumption that the grounds for refusal of a residence permit under Sec 11(2) No 5 Settlement and Residence Act (*NAG*) are fulfilled. An impairment of relations with another state or subject of international law within the meaning of the aforementioned provision was 'therefore' out of the question. As a result, the Federal Administrative Court held that there is no ground for refusal of a residence permit. Therefore, the requirements for a return decision pursuant to Sec 52(4) Aliens Police Act (*FPG*) are not met. Consequently, the court found that the contested decision should be annulled (in its entirety) without substitution.

The Federal Administrative Court declared the appeal to the Supreme Administrative Court admissible pursuant to Art 133(4) Federal Constitutional Law (*B-VG*). There was a lack of case law from the Supreme Administrative Court on Sec 11(2) No 5 Settlement and Residence Act (*NAG*) and consequently also on the question of the circumstances under which the relations of the Republic of Austria with another state or subject of international law are significantly impaired.

The present appeal by the Federal Office for Immigration and Asylum is directed against this decision.

The Supreme Administrative Court held (in excerpts):

The contested decision is overturned due to the illegality of its content.

Considerations:

[…]

[12] In support of its admissibility, the appeal agrees with the reasoning of the Federal Administrative Court and argues in summary that there is a lack of case

law from the Supreme Administrative Court on the question of whether UN Security Council resolutions and EU Council decisions on restrictive measures within the framework of the CFSP, specifically paragraph 8 of Resolution 2397 (2017) and Art 26a(5) of Decision (CFSP) 2016/849, could, without further implementation, lead to a residence permit being issued contrary to such a regulation that significantly impairs the relations of the Republic of Austria with other states or subjects of international law and, consequently, that the grounds for refusal under Sec 11(2) No 5 of the Settlement and Residence Act (*NAG*) are given. For this reason, the appeal proves to be admissible; it is also justified.

[...]

[15] As the residence permit last issued to the co-participant was still valid at the time of the Federal Office for Immigration and Asylum decision of 3 March 2020 was issued, the Federal Office for Immigration and Asylum rightly used Sec 52(4) No 1 of the Settlement and Residence Act (*NAG*) as the relevant legal basis. In this regard, the Federal Administrative Court also argued in the contested decision that the extension of this residence permit had taken place on 6 February 2019 and thus at a time when Art 26a of Decision (CFSP) 2016/849 in the version relevant here had already been published in the Official Journal of the European Union on 27 February 2018, so that there was no reason for refusal within the meaning of Sec 52(4) No 1 Settlement and Residence Act (*NAG*) that had subsequently occurred or subsequently became known.

[16] This is true in principle regarding the time at which the official decision was issued. However, when the contested decision of 16 February 2022 was issued, the validity of the residence permit issued to the co-participant had already expired and he had applied for renewal in due time, which had the effect of perpetuating the co-participant's lawful residence in accordance with Sec 24(1) third sentence Settlement and Residence Act (*NAG*). The Federal Administrative Court therefore had to examine at the relevant time of issuing its decision whether the conditions for issuing a return decision pursuant to Sec 52(4) No 4 Aliens Police Act (*FPG*) were met (for the distinction between the two facts, see for example Supreme Administrative Court of 19 August 2021, Ra 2021/21/0031, para 19/20, with further references). This is what the Federal Administrative Court ultimately did – without going beyond the scope of the appellate proceedings (return decision pursuant to Sec 52 Aliens Police Act (*FPG*) including ancillary rulings) – with the assessment it made on the merits, according to which, in its opinion, the grounds for refusal of Sec 11(2) No 5 Settlement and Residence Act (*NAG*) invoked by the Federal Office for Immigration and Asylum do not preclude the granting of a further residence permit to the co-participant.

[17] In this assessment, however, the Federal Administrative Court initially disregarded the fact that the amendment to Decision (CFSP) 2016/849 by Council Decision (CFSP) 2018/293 of 26 February 2018, which added Art 26a(5), which it primarily considered to be decisive, is based on the United Nations Security Council Resolution of 22 December 2017, 2397 [2017].

[18] In this resolution, the UN Security Council expressed its concern that, despite the adoption of an earlier resolution prohibiting member states from issuing work permits to DPRK nationals (paragraph 17 of resolution 2375 [2017]), North Korean nationals continue to work in other states to generate 'export earnings', which the DPRK uses to support its banned nuclear and ballistic missile programmes. Therefore, where relevant, it was decided that UN Member States shall repatriate to the DPRK all DPRK nationals who earn income on the territory of a Member State immediately, but no later than 24 months from the date of adoption of this resolution, unless the Member State determines that the repatriation of a DPRK national is prohibited under applicable domestic law and applicable international law, including international refugee law and international human rights law (see paragraph 8 of resolution 2397 [2017]). In adopting this resolution, the UN Security Council acted in accordance with Chapter VII of the United Nations Charter (UN Charter) and took measures pursuant to Art 41 thereof, which are binding on the Member States of the United Nations, including the Republic of Austria, pursuant to Art 25 and Art 48(2) of the UN Charter.

[19] Largely identical in content to paragraph 8 of UN Security Council Resolution 2397 (2017), Art 26a(5) of EU Council Decision (CFSP) 2016/849 stipulates that the Member States must take immediate action, but no later than 21 December 2019, shall ensure the return of all DPRK nationals who earn income within the jurisdiction of the Member States, unless a Member State determines that the return of a DPRK national is prohibited by applicable national or international law, including international refugee law and international human rights law.

[20] In addition, Art 26a(4) of this Decision (CFSP) 2016/849 (added by Decision (CFSP) 2017/1860 of 16 October 2017) provides that, in order to stop transfers to the DPRK (in support of prohibited North Korean programmes), Member States shall not renew work permits for DPRK nationals present on their respective territories, except for refugees and other beneficiaries of international protection, subject to applicable national legal requirements and procedures.

[21] However, this obligation has no independent relevance insofar as it is given effect by the subsequent measure to repatriate all DPRK nationals earning an income in the Member States. Conversely, Art 26a(5) of the aforementioned decision no longer applies if no income is earned as a result of the non-renewal of a work permit.

[22] According to Art 29 of the Treaty on European Union (TEU), Member States 'shall ensure' that their 'national policies' are consistent with Council decisions adopted in the framework of the CFSP which define the Union's position on a particular issue. Such Council decisions under the CFSP concerning restrictive measures against individuals oblige the Member States to take corresponding legislative and administrative measures (see *Schmalenbach* in Jaeger/Stöger (eds), EUV/AEUV, Art 29 EUV, MN 7/9).

[23] Contrary to the opinion of the Federal Administrative Court, it is irrelevant in this context that Council Regulation (EU) 2017/1509 of 30 August 2017 concerning restrictive measures against the DPRK does not refer to the measures to be taken by the Member States pursuant to the aforementioned Art 26a of Decision (CFSP) 2016/849. According to Art 1 of that regulation, it only contains obligations for nationals of the Member States and for legal persons, entities and bodies established or operating under their law.

[24] The requirements of para 8 of UN Security Council Resolution 2397 [2017] set out in MN 18 above and the requirements of Decision (CFSP) 2016/849 set out in MN 19 and 20 above are therefore binding on the Republic of Austria under international and EU law on the basis of Art 41 in conjunction with Art 25 and Art 48(2) of the UN Charter and Art 29 TEU and oblige it to take appropriate measures against North Korean nationals. However, contrary to the legal opinion expressed in the response to the appeal, it is not relevant whether the income earned by a DPRK national is used to support prohibited programmes in 'North Korea', given the clear wording in this respect.

[25] Against this background, Sec 52(4) Aliens Police Act (*FPG*) in conjunction with Sec 11(2) No 5 Settlement and Residence Act (*NAG*) was initially rightly considered as the domestic legal basis for issuing a return decision against the co-participant who is legally resident in the federal territory as a national of the DPRK. According to Sec 11(2) No 5 Settlement and Residence Act (*NAG*), a residence permit may only be issued to a foreigner if 'the relations of the Republic of Austria with another state or another subject of international law are not significantly impaired'. However, such a significant impairment of international relations is quite conceivable – irrespective of a domestic act of implementation – if the Republic of Austria does not fulfil the obligation under international and EU law described above not to extend a 'work permit' (which goes hand in hand with the extension of a 'Red-White-Red Card Plus' residence title last issued to the co-participant in accordance with Sec 8(1) No 2 Settlement and Residence Act (*NAG*) in conjunction with Sec 17 No 1 of the Act Governing the Employment of Foreign Nationals (*AuslBG*) under national law) or to 'repatriate' or 'return' nationals of the DPRK by 21 December 2019 at the latest (*cf* the fact that a 'residence permit' issued contrary to the require-

ments of a UN Security Council resolution under Chapter VII of the UN Charter may be likely to impair the Republic of Austria's relations with the 'community of states as a whole' and thus also with another state, Supreme Administrative Court of 19 September 1996, 94/18/0925). The Federal Administrative Court failed to recognise this and, in this respect, the Federal Office for Immigration and Asylum's appeal is to be followed.

[26] However, both the obligations under paragraph 8 of Resolution 2397 [2017] and those under Art 26a(5) of Decision (CFSP) 2016/849, to which the Federal Office for Immigration and Asylum exclusively refers in the appeal in this case, are subject to conflicting national law and contradictory international 'human rights norms'. With regard to the obligation to return DPRK nationals working in a Member State, both paragraph 8 of Resolution 2397 [2017] and Art 26a(5) of Decision (CFSP) 2016/849 stipulate that this obligation does not exist if this is prohibited under applicable national law or applicable international law, including international refugee law and international human rights law.

[27] From this point of view, Sec 11(3) Settlement and Residence Act (*NAG*), according to which a residence permit can be issued (among other things) despite the absence of a requirement pursuant to paragraph 2 No 5 if this is necessary to maintain private and family life within the meaning of Art 8 ECHR, and Sec 9(1) Federal Office for Immigration and Asylum Procedures Act (*BFA-VG*), according to which the issuing of (*inter alia*) a return decision in accordance with Sec 52 Aliens Police Act (*FPG*), which interferes with the private or family life of the foreigner, is only permissible if this is urgently required to achieve the objectives stated in Art 8(2) ECHR.

[28] Therefore, if Art 8 ECHR precludes the refusal of a residence permit or even the issuing of a return decision against the co-participant, the Republic of Austria is not obliged to do so from the outset.

[29] On the basis of a different legal opinion, the Federal Administrative Court failed to carry out the assessment required under Art 8 ECHR based on the criteria set out in Sec 11(3) Settlement and Residence Act (*NAG*) and Sec 9(2) Federal Office for Immigration and Asylum Procedures Act (*BFA-VG*). In the assessment to be carried out in the proceedings to be continued – after the oral hearing expressly requested in the complaint and required in the specific case – the strong ties of the co-participant to Austria described at the beginning will have to be taken into account and weighed against the public interests in terminating the co-participant's stay arising from the obligations under international law. In this context, the Federal Administrative Court will also have to take into account that the assumption made by the Federal Office for Immigration and Asylum within the framework of the legal assessment regarding the existence

of the requirements under Sec 11(2) No 5 Settlement and Residence Act (*NAG*) (see para 4 above) is not yet based on any comprehensible factual basis and is therefore a mere presumption with regard to the case of the co-participant to be assessed in the present case.

[30] For the reasons outlined above, the Federal Administrative Court's decision has been unlawful, which is why it must be annulled pursuant to Sec 42(2) No 1 Administrative Court Act (*VwGG*).

FF. The position of the individual (including the corporation) in international law/Die Stellung der Einzelperson (einschließlich der juristischen Person) im Völkerrecht

VI. Refugees/Flüchtlinge

See also *FF. VIII.-4*

FF. VI.

Supreme Administrative Court, Judgment Ra 2021/20/0246 of 15 March 2023, ECLI:AT:VWGH:2023:RA2021200246.L00

Verwaltungsgerichtshof, Erkenntnis Ra 2021/20/0246 vom 15. März 2023, ECLI:AT:VWGH:2023:RA2021200246.L00

Keywords

1951 Refugee Convention – Art 33(2) 1951 Refugee Convention – European Convention on Human Rights (ECHR) – Art 2 ECHR – Art 3 ECHR – Charter of Fundamental Rights of the EU (CFR) – *non-refoulement* – withdrawal of international protection after a crime – balancing of interests

Genfer Flüchtlingskonvention (GFK) – Art 33 Abs 2 GFK – Europäische Menschenrechtskonvention (EMRK) – Art 2 EMRK – Art 3 EMRK – Charta der Grundrechte der Europäischen Union (GRC) – non-refoulement – Entzug des Flüchtlingsstatus – Interessensabwägung

Facts and procedural history (summary)

In 2015, the individual concerned (the co-participant in the present proceedings) was granted asylum status in Austria, under the assumption that he was stateless and of Palestinian descent. The Federal Office for Immigration and Asylum also found that the co-participant was subject to individual persecution, since he had been kidnapped in Syria. During his residence in Austria, he became delinquent and was convicted of several crimes and sentenced to one year and three months in prison. The co-participant proceeded to commit several additional crimes. As a result, the Federal Office for Immigration and Asylum, in September 2019, decide that he was no longer considered to hold refugee status under Sec 7(4) Asylum Act 2005 (*AsylG*). Moreover, the Office decided that he was neither to be granted subsidiary protection status and nor an official residence permit for reasons worthy of consideration. In addition, the Office issued a return decision, which, however, stated that the return or deportation of the co-participant to Syria was not permissible, due to the risk of the co-participant becoming subject to forced recruitment in Syria.

The co-participant appealed this decision before the Federal Administrative Court, which upheld the appeal. It found that not all four conditions for a revocation of his protection status were fulfilled: while he had committed a particularly serious crime, had been legally convicted of it and was a danger to the public, the Court concluded that the public interest in terminating his residence did not outweigh his interest in being protected. In the context of this weighing of interests, the Federal Administrative Court considered that the reprehensibility of a crime and the potential danger of the individual had to be weighed against the extent and nature of the measures threatening the refugee, including potential torture or inhumane treatment. Therefore, the exception clause of Art 33(2) of the 1951 Refugee Convention had to be interpreted strictly.

The Federal Office for Immigration and Asylum appealed this decision before the Supreme Administrative Court, arguing that the weighing of interests carried out by the Federal Administrative Court was not necessary for protection against deportation. It argued that the co-participant had national protection against deportation in the form of a legally enforceable finding that deportation is not permissible, if there is a prohibition of refoulement. The origin of the previous case law also lies in a time before the entry into force of Community and Union law on asylum matters. An examination of the grounds for exclusion contained in the relevant directives – namely Directive 2011/95/EU and the previously applicable Directive 2004/83/EC – shows that the aim of these provisions is to maintain the credibility of the protection system provided for by the directives in accordance with the 1951 Refugee Convention. In the appeal proceedings before the Supreme Administrative Court, the Court submitted a preliminary rulings request to the CJEU pursuant to Art 267 TFEU. In response to these questions, the CJEU stated that when considering the revocation of refugee status under Art 14(4)(b) of Directive 2011/95/EU, authorities must determine whether withdrawing the status is proportionate, based on the threat the individual poses to society. However, there is no need to weigh public interest in their deportation against their personal interest in maintaining international protection, especially concerning potential risks in the home country. The CJEU stated that under Art

5 of Directive 2008/115/EC, an expulsion order cannot be issued if it is clear that the individual cannot be deported due to the principle of non-refoulement, meaning they cannot be returned to a country where they would face persecution or serious harm. Against this background, the Supreme Administrative Court issued its decision.

The Supreme Administrative Court held (in excerpts)

[…]

Decision

The contested decision is annulled on grounds of unlawfulness of its content, insofar as it annulled points I. and II. of the decision of the Federal Office for Immigration and Asylum of 24 September 2019, 1047761604-180476727, without replacement.

Otherwise, the appeal is dismissed as unfounded.

Reasoning

[…]

[62] It should be noted at the outset that the ground for exclusion contained in Sec 6 (1) No 4 Asylum Act 2005 (*AsylG*), correlates with the ground stated in Art 14 (4)(b) of the Status Directive. Upon the existence of the ground for exclusion, the application for international protection with regard to the granting of the status of a person entitled to asylum pursuant to Sec 6(2) Asylum Act 2005 (*AsylG*) can be rejected without further examination and, pursuant to Sec 7(1)(1) Asylum Act 2005 (*AsylG*), the status of a person entitled to asylum is to be withdrawn *ex officio* by means of an official decision. Accordingly, a refugee may be deprived of the status granted to him by a government or administrative authority, a court or a quasi-judicial authority, or its extension may be refused, if the foreigner constitutes a danger to the community of the Member State because he has been convicted of a particularly serious crime (Art 14(4) Qualification Directive). In such a case, the Member States may also decide not to grant a refugee status where such a decide has not yet been taken (Art 14(5) Qualification Directive).

[…]

[84] The cases in which Member States may withdraw refugee status, as listed in Art 14(4) of the Qualification Directive, are essentially the same as those in which Member States may refuse a refugee under Art 21(2) of that Directive and Art 33(2) 1951 Refugee Convention.

[85] However, whereas a refugee can no longer claim the principle of non-refoulement in such cases to a country where his life or freedom is threatened

under Art 33(2) 1951 Refugee Convention, Art 21(2) of the Qualification Directive must be interpreted and applied in accordance with the rights enshrined in the EU Charter of Fundamental Rights, in particular Arts 4 and 19(2), according to which torture and inhuman or degrading punishments and treatments are unconditionally prohibited, regardless of the behaviour of the person concerned, as is deportation to a state in which a person is at serious risk of such treatment. Therefore, Member States may not remove, expel or extradite an alien if there are substantial grounds for believing that he or she would face a real risk of being subjected to treatment prohibited by Arts 4 and 19(2) EU Charter of Fundamental Rights in the country of destination.

[86] Thus, where the refoulement of a refugee falling within one of the categories referred to in Art 14(4) and Art 21(2) of the Qualification Directive would expose him to a real risk of a violation of his fundamental rights as enshrined in Arts 4 and 19(2) EU Charter of Fundamental Rights, the Member State concerned cannot derogate from the principle of non-refoulement under Art 33(2) 1951 Refugee Convention.

[87] However, in so far as Art 14(4) of the Qualification Directive provides that Member States may withdraw 'refugee status' within the meaning of that directive in the cases specified therein, whereas Art 33(2) 1951 Refugee Convention permits the return of a refugee in such a situation to a State where his life or freedom would be threatened, EU law provides for more extensive international protection of the refugees concerned than that guaranteed by the 1951 Refugee Convention.

[88] Thus, under EU law, the competent authority may be authorised to withdraw the refugee status granted to a third-country national, in accordance with Art 14(4)(b) of Directive 2011/95, but it does not necessarily have the power to remove that person to his country of origin.

[89] From a procedural point of view, such a removal would also require the adoption of a return decision in accordance with the substantive and procedural safeguards laid down in Directive 2008/115, which, *inter alia*, provides, in Art 5, that the Member States are to respect the principle of non-refoulement when implementing that directive.

[90] Thus, the withdrawal of refugee status under Art 14(4) Qualification Directive does not require a decision to be taken on the separate issue of whether that person may be removed to his country of origin.

[91] Therefore, the consequences for the third-country national or for the general public of the Member State in which he is staying of a possible return to his country of origin are not to be taken into account when the decision to revoke

the refugee status is taken, but, if applicable, if the competent authority intends to issue a return decision against that third-country national (see on all this CJEU of 6 July 2023, C-663/21, paras 35 to 42).

[92] Unlike the previous case law, a weighing of interests in such a way that the reprehensibility of a crime and the potential danger to the general public are to be weighed against the asylum seeker's interests in protection, including the extent and nature of the measures threatening him in his country of origin, is therefore no longer to take place in the future.

[93] *In summary, the following criteria arise for the assessment under Sec 6(1)(4) Asylum Act 2005 (AsylG), taking into account the EU law requirements of Art 14(4)(b) Status Directive:*

[94] The foreigner must have been convicted of a crime within the meaning of Sec 17 Criminal Code (*StGB*). The offence on which the conviction is based must be one that, in view of its specific characteristics, is of exceptional gravity in that it is one of the offences that most seriously undermines the legal order of the society concerned. These include, for example, homicide, rape, child abuse, arson, trafficking in narcotics and addictive substances, armed robbery, violation of the sexual integrity of children and crimes committed for terrorist reasons. When assessing whether the offence for which a third-country national has been convicted is of exceptional severity, all the special circumstances of the individual case must be taken into account, in particular the penalty imposed and generally foreseen for that offence, the nature of the offence, the aggravating and mitigating consideration of the type and extent of the damage caused by the offence, as well as the procedure for punishing the offence – for example, whether, with regard to an offence, the conduct of the main criminal proceedings has been entrusted to a court with a jury (Sec 31(2) Code of Criminal Procedure (*StPO*)) even if the penalty is lower. Since the offence for which the foreigner was convicted must, in itself, demonstrate the degree of severity mentioned, it is not permissible to affirm this degree of severity by cumulating various offences, none of which constitutes a particularly severe offence as such.

[95] When assessing whether the foreigner 'because of this criminal conduct represents a danger for the community', it is necessary to examine whether the foreigner concerned represents a genuine, present and sufficiently serious threat affecting one of the fundamental interests of the society of the Member State in which he is present. In doing so, the case law of the Supreme Administrative Court on the identical standard contained in Sec 67(1) second sentence Aliens Police Act (*FPG*) can be referred to, observing the further requirements of Sec 6(1)(4) Asylum Act 2005 (*AsylG*) (such as the mandatory requirement of a conviction for a crime within the meaning of Sec 17 Criminal Code (*StGB*)) as well as the

other requirements of Art 14(4)(b) of the Qualification Directive. In the context of the assessment of risk, an assessment must be made on the basis of concrete findings regarding the relevant circumstances as to whether and with regard to which circumstances the assumption of risk is justified. The focus should not be on the mere fact of the foreigner's conviction, but on the nature and severity of the underlying offence and on the personality profile that emerges from it. For a comprehensible risk assessment, it is not sufficient to merely cite the court, the dates of the judgment, the relevant penal provisions and the penalty imposed. Depending on the individual case, it may also not be sufficient to simply describe the actions as expressed in the judgment of the criminal court, but it may be necessary to make further findings in order to be able to carry out the assessment of risk in a manner that complies with the law. The fact that the third-country national concerned has been convicted of a particularly serious offence is, however, of particular importance. Depending on the circumstances under which the offence was committed, this may help to prove the existence of a genuine and significant threat to a fundamental interest of the general public. The foreign national's criminal record should not automatically be taken as proof that the required level of risk exists. The longer the period since the final conviction for a particularly serious offence, the more the developments after the commission of such an offence must be taken into account in the examination of whether a real and substantial danger exists at the time the decision is made.

[96] It must also be examined whether the withdrawal of asylum status must be regarded as proportionate in relation to the danger posed by the foreigner. In the weighing up, account must be taken, on the one hand, of the danger posed by the foreigner to the community and, on the other hand, of the effects of the loss of the rights associated with the status of a person entitled to asylum. It shall also be examined whether the purpose of withdrawing the status of being entitled to asylum can also be achieved by measures that are less detrimental to the foreigner and that are aimed at effectively establishing the protection of the general public of the member state in which the foreigner concerned is staying. In doing so, other measures ordered by courts or authorities against the foreigner that pursue this purpose shall also be taken into account. The consequences that an alien would face if returned to his or her country of origin, and in particular the fact that deportation to the country of origin is not permitted for the reasons stated in Art 50(1) or (2) Aliens Police Act (*FPG*) […].

[97] *Regarding the issue of a return decision in the case of the inadmissibility of deportation for an indefinite period*

[98] Sec 8(1) Asylum Act 2005 (*AsylG*) provides that whenever the status of a person entitled to asylum is not granted or is withdrawn, it must be examined whether a return, removal or deportation of the foreigner to his country of

origin would result in a real risk of a violation of Art 2 ECHR, Art 3 ECHR or of Additional Protocol No 6 or No 13 to the Convention, or would entail for him as a civilian a serious threat to his life or person by reason of indiscriminate violence in the context of an international or internal armed conflict.

[99] If such a danger exists and if the foreign national does not have an internal flight alternative within the meaning of Sec 11 Asylum Act 2005 (*AsylG*) (Sec 8(3) Asylum Act 2005 (*AsylG*)), the foreign national is in principle to be granted subsidiary protection status under Sec 8(1) of the Asylum Act 2005 (*AsylG*).

[…]

[102] However, the foreigner is not to be granted subsidiary protection status despite the existence of such a danger if one of the reasons of Sec 9(2) Asylum Act 2005 (*AsylG*) applies. In such a case, the rejection of the application for granting the status of a person eligible for subsidiary protection or the *ex officio* pronouncement of non-granting of the status of a person eligible for subsidiary protection pursuant to Art 8(3a) Asylum Act 2005 (*AsylG*) as well as the withdrawal of the status of a person eligible for subsidiary protection status pursuant to Art 9(2) Asylum Act 2005 (*AsylG*) with the enactment of a measure terminating residence and the determination that a rejection, return or deportation of the foreigner to his country of origin is inadmissible because this would mean a real risk of a violation of Art 2 ECHR, Art 3 ECHR or Additional Protocol No 6 or No 13 to the Convention, or would expose him or her as a civilian to a serious threat to life or personal safety by reason of indiscriminate violence in the context of an international or internal armed conflict.

[103] In its judgment of 6 July 2023, C-663/21, on the EU law requirements of the Return Directive, the CJEU ruled that a Member State may not deport an illegally staying third-country national without a return decision having first been issued against that third-country national in compliance with the substantive and procedural safeguards introduced by that directive (para 48).

[104] Art 5 of the Return Directive, which constitutes a general rule applicable to the Member States when implementing that directive, also requires the competent national authority to respect, at every stage of the return procedure, the principle of non-refoulement, which is guaranteed as a fundamental right in Art 18 EU Charter of Fundamental Rights in conjunction with Art 33 1951 Refugee Convention and in Art 19(2) EU Charter of Fundamental Rights. This applies (*inter alia*) where that authority intends, after hearing the person concerned, to issue a return decision against him (para 49 of the judgment C-663/21).

[105] On this basis, the CJEU concluded in the judgment of 6 July 2023, C-663/21, that Art 5 of the Return Directive precludes the issuing of a return

decision against a third-country national if it is established that his or her removal to the intended country of destination is precluded for an indefinite period of time under the principle of non-refoulement (second point of decision of that judgment).

[106] *Assessment in the light of the requirements of European Union law*

[107] The unambiguous wording of Sec 8(3a) as well as Sec 9(2) Asylum Act 2005 (*AsylG*), according to which the rejection of an application, the non-recognition of the status of a person entitled to subsidiary protection or the withdrawal of this status pursuant to one of these provisions is to be combined with the adoption of a measure terminating residence, cannot be interpreted in a manner that is compatible with EU law. On the contrary, the cited EU law requirements demand that in such a situation a return decision is not issued […].

[108] Inconsistent national law that is in conflict with directly applicable EU law in a specific constellation is superseded for that constellation. The superseding effect of EU law means that the national statutory provision remains applicable in the form in which it no longer conflicts with EU law. The displacement only reaches the extent that is just enough to bring about a situation that is in conformity with EU law […].

[109] In view of the primacy of EU law, it is therefore necessary in the future to review the second sentence of Sec 8(3a) and the second sentence of Sec 9(2) of the Asylum Act 2005 (*AsylG*), which order, which provides that the rejection of an application, the non-granting of subsidiary protection status or the withdrawal of such status in accordance with these provisions is to be combined with the adoption of a measure terminating residence, is to be disapplied in order to establish a legal situation that complies with EU law.

[110] However, in such a case, any pronouncements that are legally dependent on the adoption of the measure terminating residence must also be omitted.

[111] The only thing that has to be done is to make the determination provided for in these provisions – which does not conflict with the requirements of Union law – that the foreigner may not be expelled, returned or deported to his country of origin, as this would pose a real risk of a violation of Art 2 ECHR , Art 3 ECHR or Additional Protocol No 6 or No 13 to the Convention, or if it would expose him/her as a civilian to a serious threat to life or personal safety as a result of indiscriminate violence in the context of an international or internal armed conflict.

[112] The fact that this (further) decision to be taken on the basis of Sec 8(3a) Asylum Act 2005 (*AsylG*) and Sec 9(2) Asylum Act 2005 (*AsylG*) […] from

the issuing of a return decision would not be separable […], is no longer to be assumed against this background.

[…]

Result

[123] The impugned decision was to be set aside on the grounds of unlawfulness of its content pursuant to Sec 42(2) No 1 Administrative Court Act (*VwGG*) to the extent that the appeal brought by the co-respondent was allowed and the official removed the official pronouncements by which his asylum status had been withdrawn and it had been established that he was no longer entitled to refugee status by operation of law and that he had not been granted subsidiary protection status. Otherwise, the appeal was to be dismissed as unfounded […].

VII. Immigration and emigration, extradition, expulsion, asylum/Einwanderung und Auswanderung, Auslieferung, Ausweisung, Asyl

3. Expulsion/Ausweisung

See also *EE.II.1.c.*

FF.VII.3.

Supreme Court, Judgment 13 Os 77/23g of 20 September 2023, ECLI:AT:OGH0002:2023:0130OS00077.23G.0920.000

Oberster Gerichtshof, Entscheidung 13 Os 77/23g vom 20. September 2023, ECLI:AT:OGH0002:2023:0130OS00077.23G.0920.000

Keywords

Extradition – European Convention on Extradition – applicable law in extradition proceedings – Art 22 European Convention on Extradition – principle of speciality – Art 14 European Convention on Extradition – Art 3 Fourth Add Protocol European Convention on Extradition – consent of the individual concerned to extradition – Arts 4, 5(a) Third Add Protocol European Convention on Extradition

Auslieferung – Europäisches Auslieferungsübereinkommen (EuAlÜbk) – Anwendbares Recht in Auslieferungsverfahren – Art 22 EuAlÜbk –Prinzip der Spezialität – Art 14 EuAlÜbk – Art 3 Viertes Zusatzprotokoll zum Europäischen Auslieferungsübereinkommen – Zustimmung des Individuums zur Auslieferung – Art 4, 5(a) Drittes Zusatzprotokoll zum Europäischen Auslieferungsübereinkommen

Facts and procedural history (summary)

The Republic of Serbia sought the extradition of the individual *J* for prosecution. The Regional Court Klagenfurt considered the case as AZ 8 HR 45/23s. During the hearing on 13 April 2023, the individual agreed to be extradited without formal proceedings, pertaining to the offenses mentioned in the extradition request, which were detailed in the indictments from the District Prosecutor's Office in Vrsac dated 7 July 2020 and 28 May 2020. On 13 April 2023, the Regional Court Klagenfurt decided that the extradition was only permissible concerning the facts described in the indictment from 7 July 2020. The court emphasized that the extradition was subject to the 'principle of speciality' and rejected the prosecution's request to also allow extradition for the offense described in the 28 May 2020 indictment.

The Klagenfurt Public Prosecutor's Office appealed this decision. The Higher Regional Court Graz partially granted the appeal by removing the stipulation that the extradition was subject to the 'principle of speciality'. However, the court of appeal dismissed the remainder of the appeal. In particular, it upheld the decision that extradition for the offense described in the 28 May 2020 indictment was impermissible, as the requirement for dual criminality under Art 2 of the European Convention on Extradition was not met.

Furthermore, the Higher Regional Court Graz ruled that the principle of speciality under Art 14 European Convention on Extradition did not apply. This was due to the consent given by the person concerned (Art 4 of the Third Add Protocol European Convention on Extradition in conjunction with Austria's reservation to Art 5(a) Third Add Protocol European Convention on Extradition). Therefore, the assumption of speciality concerning the facts described in the 7 July 2020 indictment was deemed incorrect.

The Procurator General's Office appealed the decision of the Higher Regional Court of Graz and asked the Supreme Court to annul the decision.

The Supreme Court held (in excerpts):

Decision

In the extradition case of * J*, AZ 8 HR 45/23s of the Regional Court Klagenfurt, the decision of the Higher Regional Court Graz as the court of appeal of 24 May 2023 violates Sec 23(1) of the Extradition and Mutual Assistance Act (*ARHG*) and Art 14 European Convention on Extradition (as amended by Art 3 of the Fourth Add Protocol European Convention on Extradition).

[...]

Legal findings:

[5] As the General Procurator's Office correctly points out in its appeal for annulment, the decision of the Higher Regional Court of Graz is not in accordance with the law:

[6] The European Convention on Extradition, Federal Law Gazette No 1969/320, as complemented by the Second (Federal Law Gazette No 1983/297), the Third (Federal Law Gazette III No 2015/70) and the Fourth (Federal Law Gazette III No 2016/42) Additional Protocol, applies in relation to Serbia.

[7] Pursuant to Art 12(1) of the Third Add Protocol European Convention on Extradition and Art 7(1) of the Fourth Add Protocol European Convention on Extradition, the European Convention on Extradition shall apply *mutatis mutandis* insofar as it is compatible with the provisions of the additional protocols. According to Art 22 of the European Convention on Extradition, unless otherwise provided for in this Convention, the law of the requested state applies exclusively to the extradition proceedings, thus (for the present case) the Extradition and Mutual Assistance Act (*ARHG*) (*cf* Sec 1 Extradition and Mutual Assistance Act (*ARHG*)) and – subsidiary to this – the Code of Criminal Procedure (*StPO*) (Sec 9 Extradition and Mutual Assistance Act (*ARHG*)) apply *mutatis mutandis*.

[8] Sec 31 Extradition and Mutual Assistance Act (*ARHG*) governs the (formal) procedure on the permissibility of extradition. In extradition law, the generally recognised rule of international law is the principle of speciality (for the present case) enshrined in Art 3 Fourth Add Protocol European Convention on Extradition (previously Art 14 of the European Convention on Extradition) and Sec 23 Extradition and Mutual Assistance Act (*ARHG*). It is intended to ensure that the extradited person is prosecuted by the requesting state exclusively for the offence(s) for which the requested state has granted extradition or for which it has consented to prosecution after the extradition has been carried out (*Göth-Flemmich/Riffel* in WK[2] ARHG § 23 MN 1 f and § 40 MN 1 as well as 12 Os 61/23x [para 11] with further references).

[9] In accordance with this principle, extradition is generally only permissible if compliance with it is ensured (Sec 23(1) Extradition and Mutual Assistance Act (*ARHG*)).

[10] No speciality obligation exists (in addition to other exceptions provided for in Sec 23(3) No 1 and 2 Extradition and Mutual Assistance Act (*ARHG*)) in the case of so-called simplified extradition pursuant to Sec 32 Extradition and Mutual Assistance Act (*ARHG*) (*Göth-Flemmich/Riffel* in WK[2] ARHG § 32 MN 6):

[11] If a person concerned – as in this case according to the factual assumptions of the Higher Regional Court (BS 2) * J* – validly agrees to extradition on

the basis of a foreign request for extradition and is to be handed over without formal extradition proceedings (Sec 32(1) Extradition and Mutual Assistance Act (*ARHG*)), the court must submit the files directly to the Federal Ministry of Justice (Sec 32(4) Extradition and Mutual Assistance Act (*ARHG*)). In such a case, no decision on the permissibility of the extradition pursuant to Sec 31 (in conjunction with Sec 33) Extradition and Mutual Assistance Act (*ARHG*) is to be made (*Göth-Flemmich/Riffel* in WK[2] ARHG § 32 MN 8).

[12] The Extradition and Mutual Assistance Act (*ARHG*) does not provide for an (isolated) waiver of compliance with speciality by the person concerned. However, in view of the obligation to provide information stipulated in Sec 32(2) Extradition and Mutual Assistance Act (*ARHG*), it can be inferred from Sec 32 Extradition and Mutual Assistance Act (*ARHG*) that in the event of a simplified extradition – which is dependent on the person's legally valid consent in accordance with Sec 32(1) Extradition and Mutual Assistance Act (*ARHG*) – the person concerned is not entitled to the protection under Sec 23 (1) and (2) Extradition and Mutual Assistance Act (*ARHG*) or (for the present case) Art 14 of the European Convention on Extradition (as amended by Art 3 of the Fourth Add Protocol European Convention on Extradition) (*cf* also Sec 23(3) No 3 Extradition and Mutual Assistance Act (*ARHG*); on the whole, however, again *Göth-Flemmich/Riffel* in WK[2] ARHG § 23 MN 1 and § 32 MN 6 as well as the explanatory remarks to the government bill (*ErläutRV 374 BlgNR 25. GP 3*), according to which the consent of the person concerned to simplified extradition under the Extradition and Mutual Assistance Act (*ARHG*) 'automatically' includes the waiver of the principle of speciality).

[13] However, valid consent given by the person concerned in accordance with Sec 32(1) Extradition and Mutual Assistance Act (*ARHG*) does not in every case necessitate a procedure in accordance with Sec 32(4), 34(3) first sentence Extradition and Mutual Assistance Act (*ARHG*). The admissibility requirements under Sec 10 to 22 Extradition and Mutual Assistance Act (*ARHG*) must also be met for simplified extradition. If there are doubts (Sec 34 (3) second sentence Extradition and Mutual Assistance Act (*ARHG*)) about the permissibility of the extradition, formal extradition proceedings must be carried out in accordance with Sec 31, 33 and 34 Extradition and Mutual Assistance Act (*ARHG*) (12 Os 61/23x [para 14]; *Göth-Flemmich/Riffel* in WK[2] ARHG § 32 MN 5).

[14] If the court takes a formal decision on the permissibility of the extradition – as in this case due to such concerns – despite the consent of the person concerned to an extradition in simplified proceedings, it must also examine the admissibility requirements of Sec 23 Extradition and Mutual Assistance Act (*ARHG*). The Federal Minister of Justice then authorises the extradition (if she does not refuse

it in accordance with Sec 34(1) Extradition and Mutual Assistance Act (*ARHG*)) subject to speciality (again *Göth-Flemmich/Riffel* in WK[2] ARHG § 32 MN 8).

[15] In other words, the consent of the person concerned to their transfer in simplified proceedings (Sec 32(1) Extradition and Mutual Assistance Act (*ARHG*)) does not in itself lead to the loss of protection by the principle of speciality pursuant to Sec 32 Extradition and Mutual Assistance Act (*ARHG*). In addition, it is necessary that (in actual fact) no decision is taken on the permissibility of the extradition pursuant to Sec 31 Extradition and Mutual Assistance Act (*ARHG*).

[16] The Third Add Protocol European Convention on Extradition (*cf* Göth-*Flemmich/Riffel* in WK[2] ARHG § 32 MN 9) – contrary to the opinion of the court of appeal – does not provide otherwise:

[17] The obligation (under international law) to extradite under the simplified procedure pursuant to Art 1 of this Additional Protocol requires the consent not only of the person concerned, but also of the requested state (arg 'and') (which is implicitly granted by a simplified extradition [see *Schwaighofer*, Auslieferung und Internationales Strafrecht 165 and 187 as well as RIS Justiz RS0073377]; on the possibility of refusing this consent, see *Riegel/Trautmann* in *Schomburg/Lagodny*, Internationale Rechtshilfe in Strafsachen[6] 3. ZP EuAlÜbk Kurzübersicht MN 6 and Art 1 MN 1, furthermore Art 6 MN 2 and Art 7 of the Third Add Protocol European Convention on Extradition, which explicitly consider the [exceptional] case that the requested party decides against the application of the simplified procedure although the person concerned has consented).

[18] On this basis, in accordance with Art 4 of the Third Add Protocol European Convention on Extradition in conjunction with the declaration made by Austria when depositing the instrument of ratification of Art 5 lit a of the Third Add Protocol European Convention on Extradition (according to which 'Art 14 of the Convention shall not apply if the extradited person consents to his extradition in accordance with Art 4 of this Protocol', Federal Law Gazette III No 2015/70), the consent of the person concerned (Art 4 of the Third Add Protocol European Convention on Extradition, Sec 32(1) Extradition and Mutual Assistance Act (*ARHG*)) is a necessary but not sufficient condition for the loss of speciality protection under this Additional Protocol. If – as is the case here – formal extradition proceedings are initiated (Sec 31, 33 f Extradition and Mutual Assistance Act (*ARHG*)), the additional requirement of Austria's consent to extradition in simplified proceedings is not met (see *ErläutRV 374 BlgNR 25. GP 2 f* and 12 Os 61/23x [para 12]).

[19] The reasoning of the Higher Regional Court's decision – which expresses a contrary legal opinion – therefore violates Sec 23 (1) Extradition and Mutual Assi-

stance Act (*ARHG*) and Art 14 European Convention on Extradition (as amended by Art 3 of the Fourth Add Protocol European Convention on Extradition).

[20] There are no further legal consequences than the declaration of this violation of the law, given that it does not operate to the disadvantage of the person concerned in this case (Sec 292 penultimate sentence of the Code of Criminal Procedure (*StPO*)).

[21] The statement (made by the Regional Court and overturned by the Higher Regional Court) that extradition is 'associated with speciality effect', is merely declaratory in nature (so that even its omission cannot bind the Federal Minister of Justice in the extradition decision to be made pursuant to Sec 34 Extradition and Mutual Assistance Act (*ARHG*) in the sense of assuming a lack of speciality protection [for the distinction between the court's decision-making competence and that of the Federal Minister of Justice in extradition proceedings under the Extradition and Mutual Assistance Act (*ARHG*), see 13 Os 27/15t, 30/15h and – foundational – 14 Os 8/02, RIS Justiz RS0116270]). An appeal (only) directed against this would have had to be rejected for this reason alone (see RIS Justiz RS0109708).

VIII. Human rights and fundamental freedoms/ Menschenrechte und Grundfreiheiten

See also *FF.VI.*

FF.VIII.-1

Constitutional Court, Judgment G 297/2022-24 of 15 March 2023, ECLI:AT: VFGH:2023:G297.2022

Verfassungsgerichtshof, Erkenntnis G 279/2922-24 vom 15. März 2023, ECLI:AT: VFGH:2023:G297.2022

Keywords

European Convention on Human Rights (ECHR) – right to freedom of expression – Art 10 ECHR – Art 8 ECHR – right of reply – publication of a counter statement – financial risk as a violation of Arts 8 and 10 ECHR

Europäische Menschenrechtskonvention (EMRK) – Meinungsäußerungsfreiheit – Art 10 EMRK – Art 8 EMRK – Recht auf Gegendarstellung – Veröffentlichung einer Gegenäußerung – Kostenrisiko als Verletzung der Art 8 und 10 EMRK

Facts and procedural history (summary)

On 22 and 23 October 2019, a periodical published an article in print and online about the high personnel costs that would arise in connection with the enforcement of the smoking ban in the hospitality industry, which the applicant (a politician) had supported. In response, the applicant, basing itself on Sec 12 Media Act (*MedienG*), requested that the media owners published counter statements, stating that the allegations were incorrect or misleadingly incomplete. The media owners did not proceed to publish those statements.

The applicant then filed a request with the Regional Criminal Court Vienna to order the media owners to publish the counter statements, which the Court granted. The media owners filed an appeal with the Higher Regional Court Vienna against that decision, which had no suspensive effect according to Sec 15(5) Media Act (*MedienG*). The media owners thus published the counter statements, as ordered by the Regional Criminal Court Vienna.

The Higher Regional Court Vienna upheld the appeal, since the counter statements lacked the necessary adversarial form that was required by the Media Act (*MedienG*). In addition, the applicant was ordered to pay the media owners a fee pursuant to Sec 17(5) Media Act (*MedienG*) for the publication of the unlawfully obtained counter statements, as well as for the publication of excerpts of the appeal judgment.

The media owners then requested the Regional Criminal Court Vienna (as the court of first instance) to determine that fee, which it set at EUR 236,051.27 by decision of 31 December 2022.

The applicant filed an appeal against this decision and, on that occasion, also submitted a request for judicial review of the law with the Constitutional Court. The applicant in essence argued that they carried a serious financial risk due to the obligation to pay a fee for the counter statement following the appeals judgment, which violated Arts 8 and 10 ECHR.

The Constitutional Court held (in excerpts)

[…]

Decision

I. 1. Sec 17(5) of the Federal Act on the Press and other Media of 12 June 1981 (Media Act (*MedienG*)), Federal Law Gazette No 314/1981, as amended by Federal Law Gazette No 20/1993, is repealed as unconstitutional.

2. The repeal takes effect on 30 June 2024.

3. Earlier statutory provisions shall not re-enter into force.

[…]

Reasons for decision

[…]

Considerations

[…]

2. The relevant legal situation is as follows:

2.1. The second subsection of the section on the protection of personality rights contains the rules on counter statements and announcement of the outcome of criminal proceedings after the fact (Sec 9ff Media Act (*MedienG*)). Any natural or legal person who is not merely generally affected by a statement of fact that has been disseminated in a periodical medium is entitled to the free publication of a counter statement in that medium, unless the counter statement is untrue or its publication is excluded for other reasons (Sec 9(1) Media Act (*MedienG*)). The counter statement must explain briefly that and to what extent the statement of facts is incorrect or incomplete and why that is the case. The counter statement can be worded as the person wishes. It must either state facts that are correct in contrast to the statement of fact or supplement the latter in a significant way or otherwise directly refer to the statement of fact and its incorrectness or misleading incompleteness (Sec 9(3) Media Act (*MedienG*)).

2.2 The claim is first to be asserted through a written request for publication. This request, which demands the counter statement, is to be addressed to the media owner or the editorial office, together with the text of the publication requested (see Sec 12 Media Act (*MedienG*)). If the counter statement is not received within two months of the end of the day on which the statement of fact was published or made available, there is no obligation to publish it (Sec 11(1) No 10 Media Act (*MedienG*)). The media owner is obliged to comply with a request submitted in due time and form. If the periodical medium appears at least five times a week, the counter statement must be published no later than the fifth working day after the day of receipt (Sec 13(1) No 1 Media Act (*MedienG*)). If published on a website, the counter statement must be made available for one month […].

The court shall immediately serve the application on the defendant, requesting them to submit written objections and evidence within five working days. […] The judgment may in principle be appealed. However, this has no suspensive effect, if the publication of the counter statement has been ordered […] The counter statement is therefore to be published regardless of the success of the appeal, and the reply is to be quickly communicated to the media audience [..].

If the court orders the publication of the counter statement in the time-limited proceedings on counter statements (Sec 14f Media Act (*MedienG*)), the judgment can only be contested with an appeal if it does not concern the decision on the objection of the untruthfulness of the counter statement (Sec 11 (1) No 4 Media Act (*MedienG*); Sec 15 (5) Media Act (*MedienG*)). If the media owner has argued that the content of the requested counter statement is untrue, even if only in individual parts (Sec 11(1) (4) Media Act (*MedienG*)), the proceedings (in first instance) in this regard shall be continued at the request of the applicant or the defendant pursuant to Sec 16 Media Act (*MedienG*) […]. In these continued proceedings, the Court may issue a decision, similar to the decision of the court of appeal under Sec 17(4) Media Act (*MedienG*), authorizing those parts of the judgment, necessary to inform the public (Sec 16(2) Media Act (*MedienG*)), and an obligation on the applicant to pay 'reasonable costs' for this publication of the judgment and for the publication made on the basis of the earlier judgment,; Sec 17(4) Media Act (*MedienG*), the amount of these costs again being decided by order upon application of the defendant, comparable to Sec 17(5) Media Act (*MedienG*) (whereby the publication fee can again be reduced in cases of hardship However, these provisions are not the subject of the present judicial review proceedings.

2.3. The court must make a decision ordering publication of the counter statement, if it has been wrongfully not published or not properly (voluntarily) published […]. If the request for publication proves to be (partially) unjustified, Sec 17(4) and (5) Media Act (*MedienG*) provide that the applicant carries liability for the risk with regard to the claim for publication of the judgment and the obligation to pay the insertion fee for this, as well as for the unjustified counter statement […].

If a counter statement has been published on the basis of a judgment of the court of first instance and an appeal against the judgment is upheld in whole or in part, the defendant shall, upon request, be authorised to publish within a reasonable period of time those parts of the judgment on appeal which are necessary to inform the public (Sec 17(4) Media Act (*MedienG*)). The defendant is granted the right to publication of the relevant parts of the judgment as compensation for the fact that the appeal has no suspensive effect, and that publication must be carried out within the deadlines of Sec 13(1) Media Act (*MedienG*) […].

Furthermore, the court of appeal shall order the claimant to pay a fee for the publication of the counter statement obtained by unlawful means and for the publication of the appeal judgment, provided that the respective publication was actually made […].

2.4. The amount of these costs is to be decided upon request with a decision pursuant to Sec 17(5) Media Act (*MedienG*). The reason for this decision on costs, which is separate from the decision in the judgment itself, is that the court of appeal is often unable to set the amount of the placement fee in figures in the appeal judgment, as the media owner will not have disclosed the amount of the fee […]. According to prevailing opinion and the case law of the Austrian

Supreme Court, the placement fee is the amount that results from the usual tariff for advertisements and advertising placements for the specific medium at the time of the respective publication […]. 'The insertion fee not only covers the costs incurred by the media owner for publication; rather, it is intended to fully indemnify the media owner, in other words, to provide effective compensation for the fact that they were initially wrongfully held liable in the first place – from an *ex post* perspective' (Supreme Court of 15 September 2024, 15 Os 45/10x) […].

In cases of hardship, *i.e.* if the economic existence is endangered […], the court may moderate the intervention fee at its reasonable discretion (in doing so, the economic situation of the applicant must be weighed against the interests of the medium, '*i.e.* the economic situation of the applicant must not be considered one-sidedly', […]) and set a longer performance period not exceeding one year.

3. The concerns of the applicant are justified:

3.1. The basic idea of the counter statement is to allow the person who has become the subject of public debate in the media and who is affected by an incorrect or misleadingly incomplete statement of fact, the right, arising from their personal rights, to have its own corrective or supplementary presentation promptly in the same place and, where possible, at the same level pf publicity directed at the same public audience […]. In this respect, the counter statement also serves to ensure that the media audience is provided with correct and complete information […]. To this end, the counter statement must be made in such a way that it is sufficiently certain that the media audience that has become aware of the media claim which, according to the person concerned, is incorrect or misleading, will also learn of the counter statement. The counter statement must therefore have the same publication value as the original publication to which it refers (Sec 13(3) Media Act (*MedienG*)) and must be published within a recognisable time frame (*cf.* Sec 13(1) Media Act (*MedienG*)).

When regulating the right of reply, the legislator is constrained by fundamental rights in several respects. First of all, a statutory right of reply constitutes a restriction of the media owner's freedom of the media and of communication, which – in view of the importance of freedom of the media in a democratic society (*cf.* only ECtHR of 8 July 1986 [GC], App No 9815/82, *Lingens*, and Constitutional Court of 14 December 2022, G287/2022 ua) – must meet the requirements of Art 10(2) ECHR (*cf* with relevance for the present context ECHR of 12 July 1989, App No 13.010/87, *Ediciones Tiempo S.A.*, para 1; further ECtHR of 24 October 2017, App No 24.016/05, *Eker*, para 43). For an individual affected by a statement of fact in the media, the right of reply serves, on one hand, to protect their personal sphere, as it is also covered by the scope of protection of Art 8 ECHR (see ECtHR of 17 January 2023, App No 8964/18, *Axel Springer SE*, para 34), but also ensures their right, as recognised by Art

10(1) ECHR, to be able to counter incorrect or misleading reporting on facts concerning them in a manner that is comparably visible in public discourse in the media (see ECtHR of 5 July 2005, App No 28.743/03, *Melnychuk*), whereby the aspect of correct and complete information of the media audience, which is also covered by Art 10(1) ECHR, is taken into account in order to ensure the viability of public discourse […].

3.2 The statutory provisions that provide for the (modalities of the) obligation to publish the counter statement and, consequently, an authorisation to publish the appeal judgment for the initially obligated media owner and an obligation to pay on the part of person who has initiated a publication order of the counter statement that ultimately proves to be unlawful, therefore provide for a legal balance of interests and, in doing so, (also) substantiate the requirements of Arts 10 and 8 of the ECHR.

This balancing function is, on the one hand, effected through regulations that effectively uphold the right of reply of anyone who believes they have been affected by untrue or misleading facts in a periodical medium. For example, Sec 15(5) Media Act (*MedienG*), which does not recognise any suspensive effect on the appeal against the obligation of the media owner to publish a counter statement as ordered in a judgment in a time-limited procedure, ensures the necessary temporal connection between the media statement of fact and the counter statement. The provisions of Sec 13(3) and (3a) Media Act (*MedienG*) in particular are intended to ensure the same publication value of the counter statement with regard to informing the target audience. On the other hand, the provisions of media law seek to protect the media owner from an unreasonable obligation to publish counter statements by making them dependent on content-related or temporal conditions (see Sec 11(1) Media Act (*MedienG*)), subjecting them to judicial review and providing for compensatory mechanisms in favour of the media owner if they are burdened by the obligation to publish a counter statement that ultimately turns out to be illegal. The latter is particularly served by the provisions of Sec 17(4) and (5) Media Act (*MedienG*), in that they provide for a possibility of publication of the appeal judgment from which the unlawfulness of the counter statement to which the media owner was nevertheless obligated can be derived, and obliges the person who initiated the counter statement to pay a fee for the publication of the counter statement, which was obtained unlawfully, and for the publication of (parts of) the appeal judgment.

According to the case law of the Supreme Court, this insertion fee within the meaning of Sec 17(5) Media Act (*MedienG*) not only covers the costs incurred by the media owner as a result of the publication, but also includes the fee (as per the applicable rates) that would have been payable by the media owner for advertisements based exclusively on a private agreement and exclusively serves the private interests of the advertiser […].

4.1. In the light of Art 8 and Art 10 ECHR, which establish the right of reply of a person affected by an untrue or misleading statement of fact, the intervention fee under Sec 17(5) Media Act (*MedienG*) must not reach a level that – in the sense of a 'chilling effect' (see ECHR of 3 December 2013, App No 64.520/10, *Ungváry and Irodalom Kft.*, para 68) – discourages those affected by media reporting from exercising their right to reply in the first place.

4.2 The amount of the intervention fee is determined by a number of factors: These include, in particular, the rates that the media owner can otherwise demand for advertising in a specific medium, so that the market position of the medium is crucial. Furthermore, it follows from Sec 13(3a) Media Act (*MedienG*) that, in the case of counter statements on a website, the minimum publication period of one month provided for by law means that the relevant publication fee can reach a considerable amount, as the initial proceedings show.

The person entitled to the counter statement cannot influence these factors. They must decide – in the sense of an either/or decision – in favour of the publication of the counter statement to the extent prescribed by law and at a point in time at which the outcome of the court proceedings deciding on the lawfulness of the counter statement is still pending. Even if the relevant regulations regarding the time of publication in connection with the exclusion of the suspensive effect in Sec 15(5) Media Act (*MedienG*), like the aforementioned regulations to ensure an equal publication value, also serve the purpose of providing the public with complete information, the statutory regulations do not leave any room for the individual affected, who is initially protected by the right of reply, to limit their risk of payment in the event that the their reply ultimately turns out to be unlawful. With the reporting triggering the counter statement, the media owner has predetermined a certain media field – and thus certain specifications for the pricing of the publication fee […] – in which the person entitled to the counter statement must operate. They can influence neither the temporal context of the publication (even if it is to await the judgment of the court of appeal) nor the duration of publication on a website. On the other hand, the media owner's obligation to publish the counter statement is based on a court order (and thus a corresponding legal review). It should also be taken into account that a high fee resulting from a corresponding market position of the periodical medium usually goes hand in hand with a corresponding economic position of the medium and thus of the media owner, which will in many cases be superior to the 'other side' of the communication process opened by the periodical medium itself.

This means that the amount of the placement fee stipulated in Sec 17(5) Media Act (*MedienG*), which the person who has arranged for a counter statement that ultimately turns out to be unlawful, is obliged to pay, proves to be disproportionate: it exposes the person concerned to an economic risk (or forces them to completely refrain from making a counter statement) that can no longer be sustainable for them. Above all, the regulation of Sec 17(5) Media Act (*MedienG*) entails the risk of deterring those affected from asserting a counter statement from the outset and thus also of restricting the general information function of the counter statement right. On the other hand, the protection of the media owner against undue coercion to publish third-party content, which is equally essential from the point of view of Art 10 ECHR, can also be ensured in the proceedings for the enforcement of a counter statement if the payment obligation of the person entitled to a counter statement for a counter statement that is ultimately unlawful and the publication of the judgment relating to it does not reach a level that potentially deters persons entitled to a counter statement from the outset. In this respect, Sec 17(5) Media Act (*MedienG*), with the costs of the intervention fee to be determined in the system of the media law design of the right of reply, does not achieve a proportionate balance that takes into account the fundamental rights requirements of Art 8 ECHR and Art 10 ECHR with regard to the person affected by a report of facts considered to be untrue or misleading on the one hand, and the media owner (in the words of the ECtHR: the legislature fails to 'strike a fair balance' [see ECtHR of 17 December 2004, App No 33.348/96, *Cumpănă and Mazăre*, para 91] between the rights of the media owner and the person entitled to a counter statement).

[…]

6. The concerns of the applicant are therefore justified. Sec 17(5) Media Act (*MedienG*) is to be repealed (due to the inextricable connection between its individual sentences as a whole) for violating the constitutionally guaranteed rights under Art 10 and Art 8 ECHR.

FF.VIII.-2

Supreme Administrative Court, Judgment Ra 2022/10/0110-10 of 23 March 2023, ECLI:AT:VWGH:2023:RA2022100110.L00

Verwaltungsgerichtshof, Erkenntnis Ra 2022/10/0110-10 vom 23. März 2023, ECLI:AT:VWGH:2023:RA2022100110.L00

Keywords

European Union – free movement of people – European Convention on Human Rights (ECHR) – right to a fair trial – right to be heard – Art 6(1) EHCR – union citizenship – social assistance

Europäische Union – Personenfreizügigkeit – Europäische Menschenrechtskonvention (EMRK) – Recht auf ein faires Verfahren – Recht auf Gehör – Art 6(1) EMRK – Unionsbürgerschaft – Sozialhilfe

Facts and procedural history (summary)

The appellant, an Italian national, applied for social assistance benefits under the Upper Austrian Social Assistance Implementation Act (*Oö SOHAG*) on 7 February 2022. The application was rejected by the Mayor of Linz on 26 April 2022, on the grounds that she had not resided permanently in Austria for at least five years, as required by Sec 5(1) Upper Austrian Social Assistance Implementation Act (*Oö SOHAG*).

The appellant appealed that decision to the Regional Administrative Court Upper Austria, requesting an oral hearing and arguing that the authority had wrongly assumed that the five-year residency requirement applied to EU citizens. She based herself on Sec 5(4) Upper Austrian Social Assistance Implementation Act (*Oö SOHAG*), which allows EU citizens entitled to reside to be treated like Austrian citizens in certain cases. She also referenced Art 24(1) of EU Directive 2004/38/EC, which mandates equal treatment of EU citizens and Austrian citizens, particularly for workers or those who retain worker status when involuntarily unemployed. The appellant had worked until January 2022 and, having registered with the Austrian Public Employment Service, argued that her status as an employee was maintained, thus entitling her to social assistance.

However, on 10 June 2022, the Regional Administrative Court Upper Austria dismissed her appeal as unfounded, without holding a hearing. The court also declared that an appeal to the Supreme Administrative Court was inadmissible under Art 133(4) Federal Constitutional Law (*B-VG*). In its reasoning, the court stated that while the appellant had resided in Austria since May 2021 and had been employed until 15 January 2022, she was not currently employed. As a Union citizen, her right to stay in Austria for more than three months under Sec 51 Settlement and Residence Act (*NAG*) depended on either being employed, self-employed, or having sufficient resources and comprehensive health insurance to avoid reliance on social assistance or the equalization supplement. The court noted that the appellant had worked for only a few months, lacked sufficient means of subsistence, comprehensive health insurance, and was not entitled to a pension in Italy. Since she was claiming social assistance, it was concluded that her livelihood was not sufficiently secured, disqualifying her from extended residency and social assistance benefits.

The appellant filed an extraordinary appeal against this decision, and the Regional Administrative Court Upper Austria submitted the case files, while the authority involved submitted a response to the appeal.

The Supreme Administrative Court found (in excerpts):

Decision

The contested decision is set aside on the grounds of illegality due to a breach of procedural rules.

[…]

Legal reasoning

[…]

[9] Sec 5 Upper Austrian Social Assistance Implementation Act (*Oö. SOHAG*), State Law Gazette No 107/2019, reads in excerpts:

'*Sec 5 Personal requirements for the provision of social assistance*

(1) Without prejudice to mandatory obligations under international or EU law, social assistance benefits are obligations under international or European Union law, only Austrian citizens and persons entitled to asylum, and otherwise only to foreigners who are permanently resident aliens who have been living in Austria for at least five years of permanent, actual and legal residence in the federal territory.

(2) Unless otherwise provided for in this provincial law, social assistance may only be provided to persons who have their main residence and actual residence in the province of Upper Austria.

...

(4) Prior to the expiry of the period specified in (1), EU/EEA citizens entitled to reside, Swiss citizens and third-country nationals shall only be treated in the same way as Austrian citizens insofar as the granting of social assistance benefits is mandatory on the basis of international or EU law provisions and this has been determined in individual cases after consultation with the competent immigration authority.

…'

[10] Sec 51 Settlement and Residence Act (*NAG*), Federal Law Gazette I No 100/2005 as amended by Federal Law Gazette I No 56/2018, reads in excerpts:

'*Right of residence under Union law of EEA citizens for more than three months*

Sec 51 (1) On the basis of the Free Movement of Persons Directive, EEA citizens are entitled to stay for more than three months if they

1. are employed or self-employed in Austria;

2. have sufficient means of subsistence and comprehensive health insurance cover for themselves and their family members so that they do not have to claim social assistance benefits or the equalization supplement during their stay, or

3 ...

(2) The gainful employment status as an employee or self-employed person pursuant to (1)(1) shall remain with the EEA citizen who no longer pursues this gainful employment if he/she

1. is temporarily unable to work due to illness or accident;

2. makes himself/herself available to the competent regional office of the Public Employment Service as an employee in the case of duly confirmed involuntary unemployment after more than one year of employment;

3. makes himself/herself available to the competent regional office of the Public Employment Service as an employee in the event of duly confirmed involuntary unemployment after the expiry of his/her employment contract for a period of less than one year or in the event of involuntary unemployment occurring during the first twelve months, in which case the status of gainful employment is maintained for at least six months, or

...'

[11] Art 7 of Directive 2004/38/EC of the European Parliament and of the Council of April 29, 2004 on the right of citizens of the Union and their family members to move and reside freely within the territory of the Member States (Directive 2004/38/EC; Free Movement Directive) reads in excerpts:

'Article 7 Right of residence for more than three months

(1) All Union citizens shall have the right of residence on the territory of another Member State for a period of longer than three months if they:

(a) are workers or self-employed persons in the host Member State; or

(b) have sufficient resources for themselves and their family members not to become a burden on the social assistance system of the host Member State during their period of residence and have comprehensive sickness insurance cover in the host Member State; or

...

(3) For the purposes of (1)(a), a Union citizen who is no longer a worker or self-employed person shall retain the status of worker or self-employed person in the following circumstances:

(a) he/she is temporarily unable to work as the result of an illness or accident;

(b) he/she is in duly recorded involuntary unemployment after having been employed for more than one year and has registered as a job-seeker with the relevant employment office;

(c) he/she is in duly recorded involuntary unemployment after completing a fixed-term employment contract of less than a year or after having become involuntarily unemployed during the first twelve months and has registered as a job-seeker with the relevant employment office. In this case, the status of worker shall be retained for no less than six months;

...'

[12] In the grounds for admissibility of the present extraordinary appeal, it is argued (among other things) that 'since a public oral hearing was not held, [...] a legal question of fundamental importance exists' within the meaning of Art

133(4) Federal Constitutional Law (*B-VG*). A fundamental procedural principle is violated if the court, incorrectly assuming that the conditions for the omission of an oral hearing were met, failed to schedule such a hearing and to deal with the complaint of fact (see Supreme Administrative Court of 20 November 2014, Ra 2014/07/0052, VwSlg 18973 A).

[13] The appeal proves to be admissible and well-founded:

[14] Pursuant to Sec 24(4) Proceedings of Administrative Courts Act (*VwGVG*), the administrative court may, unless otherwise stipulated by federal or provincial law, refrain from holding a hearing regardless of the request by a party if the files indicate that the oral discussion cannot be expected to clarify the case further and neither Art 6(1) ECHR nor Art 47 CFR preclude the omission of a hearing.

[15] A hearing before an administrative court must therefore generally be held if it concerns 'civil rights' or 'criminal charges' within the meaning of Art 6 ECHR or the possibility of a violation of Union rights granted to a person (Art 47 CFR) and a substantive decision is made on the merits of the case. As the Supreme Administrative Court has already repeatedly stated with regard to Sec 24(4) Proceedings of Administrative Courts Act (*VwGVG*), the legislator intended that the purpose of an oral hearing was to clarify the facts of the case and to allow the parties to be heard, as well as the oral discussion of a disputed legal issue between the parties and the court. Art 6(1) ECHR and Art 47 CFR do not preclude that the administrative court refrain from holding a hearing in accordance with the Proceedings of Administrative Courts Act (*VwGVG*), in particular if the facts relevant to the decision are established and no questions regarding the assessment of evidence can arise, meaning that a hearing is not necessary. According to the case law of the ECtHR, the existence of exceptional circumstances can also justify dispensing with a public hearing. Accordingly, the waiver of an oral hearing within the scope of the Proceedings of Administrative Courts Act (*VwGVG*) may be justified, for example, in cases in which only legal issues of a limited nature or of no particular complexity are raised. If the obligation to hold a hearing is disregarded within the scope of application of Art 6 ECHR and Art 47 CFR, no relevance test is to be carried out with regard to the procedural defect (see Supreme Administrative Court of 21 December 2021, Ra 2020/10/0077, with reference to Supreme Administrative Court of 1 June 2021, Ro 2020/10/0002, with further references). According to the case law of the ECtHR, disputes about social welfare benefits concern civil rights within the meaning of Art 6 ECHR (see again Supreme Administrative Court of 21 December 2021, Ra 2020/10/0077, with reference to Supreme Administrative Court of 30 January 2014, 2012/10/0193; of 27 March 2012, 2009/10/0084; of 12 August 2010, 2008/10/0315).

[16] There is no explanation in the contested decision as to why the administrative court assumed that the requirements of Sec 24(4) Proceedings of Administrative Courts Act (*VwGVG*) were met. There is therefore no comprehensible justification for not holding the oral hearing. It is also not apparent that the requirements for not holding an oral hearing would have been met in any case. There can be no question that the facts relevant to the decision with regard to the question of whether the appellant, as a citizen of the Union, is equal to Austrian citizens on the basis of Sec 5(4) Upper Austrian Social Assistance Implementation Act (*Oö SOHAG*), the authority concerned based the rejection of the application on the fact that the appellant had not resided permanently in the federal territory for at least five years and failed to address the requirements of Sec 5(4) Upper Austrian Social Assistance Implementation Act (*Oö SOHAG*).

[17] The contested decision therefore had to be set aside as unlawful pursuant to Sec 42(2)(3)(b) and (c) Supreme Administrative Court Act (*VwGG*) as a result of a violation of procedural provisions, without the need to address the further appeal submissions.

[18] Apart from this, the following should be noted:

[19] According to the statement of reasons reproduced above, the administrative court based its assumption that the appellant did not have a right of residence under EU law for more than three months on the fact that this required the fulfilment of the conditions pursuant to Sec 51(1)(1) *and* (2) Settlement and Residence Act (*NAG*). Furthermore, the administrative court assumes that the requirements pursuant to Sec 51(1)(2) Settlement and Residence Act (*NAG*) are not met without addressing the issue raised in the complaint of the applicant's status as a worker within the meaning of Sec 51(2) Settlement and Residence Act (*NAG*).

[20] However, this fails to recognize that, according to the clear wording of both Sec 51(1) Settlement and Residence Act (*NAG*) and Art 7(1)(a) and (b) of Directive 2004/38/EC (*arguendo*: 'or'), it is not necessary for the requirements of Sec 51(1) Settlement and Residence Act (*NAG*) to be cumulatively fulfilled in order for the conditions of Sec 51(1) and (2) Settlement and Residence Act (*NAG*) to be met. Directive 2004/38/EC distinguishes between employed and non-employed persons with regard to the requirement of having sufficient resources. The former group of EU citizens who are in the host Member State are entitled to the right of residence under Art 7(1)(a) of Directive 2004/38/EC without having to fulfil any further requirements. In contrast, Art 7(1)(b) of this Directive requires persons who are not gainfully employed to have sufficient resources of their own (see Supreme Administrative Court of 14 November 2017, Ra 2017/21/0130, with reference to CJEU of 11 November 2014, C-333/13,

Dano; see also on Sec 5 Vienna Minimum Benefits Act (*WMG*) the Supreme Administrative Court of 16 March 2016, Ra 2015/10/0022, VwSlg. 19331 A). The administrative court should therefore have dealt with the question of whether the applicant is a gainfully employed person within the meaning of Sec 51(2) Settlement and Residence Act (*NAG*) with regard to Sec 5(4) Upper Austrian Social Assistance Implementation Act (*Oö SOHAG*).

[…]

FF.VIII.-3

Supreme Court, Decision 1 Ob 199/22d of 15 May 2023, ECLI:AT:OGH0002:2023:0010OB00199.22D.0515.000

Oberster Gerichtshof, Entscheidung 1 Ob 199/22d vom 15 Mai 2023, ECLI:AT:OGH0002:2023:0010OB00199.22D.0515.000

Keywords

Public liability – infectious diseases – COVID-19 – claims for damages for COVID-19 infection – European Convention on Human Rights (ECHR) – Art 2 ECHR – Art 8 ECHR – obligation to protect the life and health of individuals during a pandemic – duty to inform

Amtshaftung – Infektionskrankheiten – COVID-19 – Entschädigungsansprüche für COVID-19 – Europäische Menschenrechtskonvention (EMRK) – Art 2 EMRK – Art 8 EMRK – Schutzpflichten für Leben und Gesundheit von Individuen während einer Pandemie –Informationspflichten

Facts and procedural history (summary)

The plaintiff is a German national with a permanent residence in Germany. He travelled to Ischgl in Tyrol (Austria) on 7 March 2020 for leisure and stayed at a hotel. During his stay, he visited four après-ski bars. On 13 March 2020, he learned of the planned closure of the Paznaun Valley due to COVID-19 restrictions and travelled home the same day, immediately after which the first symptoms of an illness appeared. He tested positive for SARS-CoV-2 on 15 March 2020, was admitted to a hospital on 19 March 2020 and treated there until 31 March 2020. He was in considerable pain, had a high fever and massive, medically relevant anxiety, including fear of death. The plaintiff sought compensation from the Republic of Austria for pain and suffering, costs of medical care and loss of earnings totalling EUR 63,853, as well as a declaration that the Federal Government of Austria is liable for all further damages that he might suffer. He alleged that he had become infected with the coronavirus 'as a result of the catastrophic mismanagement of the responsible authorities'. If the authorities had acted lawfully and promptly, he would not have fallen ill. He alleged that the authorities were aware by 4 March 2020 at the latest that the SARS-CoV-2 virus was 'rampant' in Ischgl. They should therefore have taken the indispensable measures required by law at latest from 5 March 2020 onwards to identify the source of the infections and contain the further spread of the virus. The state authorities had thereby allegedly violated their obligation derived from Arts 2, 8 and (partly) 3 ECHR to take appropriate measures to protect the life and health of persons and to inform the public about life-threatening emergencies.

In summary, the defendant (the Republic of Austria) argued that the plaintiff's illness was in no way caused by its organs or was otherwise responsible for it. In particular, the plaintiff would have to prove that he had contracted the disease in Ischgl in the first place; there was no prima facie evidence for this. Furthermore, the health authorities had immediately taken all necessary measures in accordance with the information available at the time and in accordance with the existing legal framework. There could be no question of any unlawful and culpable action or omission on the part of these authorities, which were forced to make rapid decisions, in a special, crisis-ridden situation.

The court of first instance rejected the claim in a judgment. In essence, it justified the rejection of the action by stating that the legal basis for official action in the present case was the Law on Epidemics (*EpiG*). Its goal was to protect the public from the spread of communicable diseases, but not to prevent the infection of individuals, notwithstanding that the actions of authorities may reduce the risk of infection overall and thus (incidentally) for the individual as well. While the duty to protect under Art 2 and Art 8 ECHR requires that the state must take measures to avert danger in the event of an outbreak of an epidemic, and thus may not stay passive, that duty is directed at the legislator. This does not give rise to an individual right for the plaintiff. A claim based directly on a violation of fundamental rights, namely Art 2 ECHR, is therefore not given.

The court of appeal set aside this judgment and instructed the court of first instance to decide again after collecting additional evidence. In legal terms, it assumed that the legal protection of life and health required by fundamental rights in the event of an epidemic or pandemic had been ensured by the Law on Epidemic (*EpiG*) at the time of the plaintiff's illness. The law, according to the court of appeal, when interpreted in accordance with the constitution and fundamental rights, provides for a reasonable defence by the state against danger. The court considered that the plaintiff did not claim that the measures provided for in the Law on Epidemics (*EpiG*) were insufficient at the time and that this would have resulted in a violation of fundamental rights due to the lack of a legal basis. He merely criticised the inadequate implementation of the Law on Epidemics (*EpiG*). The plaintiff, who lives abroad, invokes the (passive) freedom to provide services, which in principle makes the Charter of the Fundamental

Rights of the EU applicable. However, the relevant Austrian legal provisions (Arts 2 and 8 ECHR, Sec 16 Civil Code (*ABGB*) and the provisions of the Criminal Code (*StGB*)) grant the same protection. To establish a possible liability of the state for violations of fundamental rights in connection with the fight against the pandemic there needed to be a causal connection between omissions of the state and the infection. The success of the action therefore only depended on whether the plaintiff could prove that state bodies had caused his COVID-19 infection by unjustifiably violating a protective law, which was intended to protect him from infection. Which protective purpose a law served – in this case the Law on Epidemics (*EpiG*) – was not to be determined in the context of the entire law, but rather in relation to each specific legal provision whose violation was in question.

The court of appeal further held that on 5 March 2020, the authorities had neither a duty to inform under statutory legislation nor derived directly from Art 2 ECHR, because at that time there was no 'clearly recognisable danger' to the general public. Such a duty to inform did not arise until the evening of 7 March 2020 at the earliest, when the positive test of the employee in one of the après-ski bars was available. The authorities would have taken this as the reason for the publication of a press release of 8 March 2020 anyway. Thus, a claim for compensation due to the omission of information at an earlier point in time had to fail as the conduct of the state authorities was not illegal. A 'travel warning' was a matter for the home countries of foreign travellers. The press conference on 13 March 2020 had served to inform the population about the measures taken based on Sec 24 Law on Epidemics (*EpiG*). However, the plaintiff could not derive any claims from the press conference or the 'exit chaos' caused by it because he was not directly affected by it, and it had not been proven that his infection was caused by it. Furthermore, it was not discernible in what way the – correct and complete – announcement of the closure of the Paznaun Valley made at the press conference might have been unlawful.

However, even where there is no duty to inform, the right to life (Art 2 ECHR) and to physical integrity (Art 8 ECHR) obliged the state to only provide information that is correct and complete with regard to imminent dangers, to protect all recipients of said information. This was not the case with the press release published 'against better knowledge' by the Office of the Tyrolean Provincial Government on 5 March 2020. Thus, liability of the Federal Government is only conceivable for the consequences of the misleading information of 5 March 2020. Whether the plaintiff suffered any damage at all because of this information depends on whether he was aware of this 'country information' and took the trip to Ischgl because of this information. If not, his damage could not have been caused by the misinformation, which would exclude a claim for damages. He had not yet made sufficient assertions in this regard, so that the court of first instance had not been able to gather any evidence on this. To make up for this, the contested judgment had to be set aside and the proceedings at first instance supplemented. However, for the first step of the causality test – infection of the plaintiff during his stay in Ischgl – the requirements for the application of prima facie evidence were met and this evidence had also been provided because the plaintiff had been at a 'hotspot' of the infection and had developed COVID-19 symptoms within the usual incubation period. The court of appeal declared the appeal to the Supreme Court admissible because there was a lack of jurisprudence on the protective purpose of Secs 5, 20 and 24 Law on Epidemics (*EpiG*), official media information and press conferences and the obligation derived from Arts 2 and 8 ECHR not to disseminate false or misleading information about imminent dangers.

The plaintiff and the defendant both filed an appeal against the decision of the court of appeal. The Supreme Court then had to decide if there was any public liability of the Republic of Austria based on the ECHR.

The Supreme Court held (in excerpts):

Decision

I. The appeals are upheld.

The contested order is set aside, and it is recognised in the matter that the judgment of the court of first instance is restored.

The plaintiff is ordered to reimburse the defendant for the costs of the appeal proceedings, determined at EUR 12,757.50 (including a flat fee of EUR 6,104), within 14 days.

II. The plaintiff's appeal on points of law is referred to the decision on its appeal. The defendant's application for an award of costs for the defence on appeal is dismissed.

Legal findings:

[…]

C. Liability for alleged violations of duties to protect under Art 2 and Art 8 ECHR:

1. Position of the plaintiff:

[81] The plaintiff further derives public liability claims (directly) from Art 2 and Art 8 ECHR. He claims that these provisions impose a legal duty on the authorities to inform the population quickly, completely and truthfully about imminent health risks. The competent bodies should have published an up-to-date, complete and truthful overview of the infection situation and the official countermeasures. The publication should have been in the form of a 'government travel warning' from 5 March 2020 to all those planning a stay in the Paznaun valley. The media information of 5 March and 8 March 2020 from the Office of

the Tyrolean Provincial Government was incomplete and incorrect and violated duties to inform derived from fundamental rights. On 9 March 2020, information should have been provided about further positive test results. The defendant should have taken 'measures required by fundamental rights' and 'clear steps' to protect the persons staying in the Paznaun valley and to protect him, as he was about to travel to the Paznaun valley.

[82] The defendant argued that a warning against travelling to Austria or to a certain Austrian region was not required by fundamental rights. The information of the Provincial Government of 5 March and 8 March 2020 had not been issued in their sovereign function, but in the context of private-sector administration. Art 2 ECHR could not be used as a legal basis to require the Provincial Government to provide information.

2. Duties of the state to inform based on Art 2 and Art 8 ECHR:

[83] 2.1 According to Art 2(1) first sentence ECHR, the right to life of every human being is protected by law. Under Art 8(1) ECHR, everyone has the right to respect for his private and family life, his home and his correspondence.

[84] 2.2 According to the case law of the European Court of Human Rights (ECtHR), both Art 2 and Art 8 ECHR establish positive obligations on states (parties).

[85] According to Art 2 ECHR, states are obliged to take reasonable steps to protect the lives of persons under its jurisdiction (ECtHR, *Budayeva and Others v Russia*, App No 15339/02; further references in RS0126701). Under Art 8 ECHR, the requirement of effective respect for private and family life imposes a positive obligation on the state to guarantee the right of its citizens to respect for their mental and physical integrity, which may give rise to positive obligations (ECtHR, *Tysiac v Poland*, App No 5410/03; further references in RS0126416; also, ECtHR, *Guerra and Others v Italy*, App No 14967/89; further references in RS0125035).

[86] In particular, the ECtHR derives duties to inform of the states parties from these provisions under certain conditions. It affirmed such obligations, for example

- to test subjects who took part in experiments with mustard and nerve gas as part of their employment in the army (ECtHR, *Roche v United Kingdom*, App No 32555/96),

- to inhabitants of an affected town after an ecological disaster about its consequences and the measures taken (ECtHR, *Tatar v Romania*, App No 67021/01, see also RS0127283),

- to the population about the increased risk of accidents in the event of a landslide (flooding of parts of a town because of a debris and mudslide, where a protective dam had already been severely damaged beforehand; ECtHR, *Budayeva and Others v Russia*, App No 15339/02), and
- *vis-à-vis* deep-sea divers about the decompression tables used by oil companies, which would have been decisive for the assessment of the danger and health during their diving operations (ECtHR, *Vilnes and Others v Norway*, App No 52806/09).

[87] 2.3 On the basis of this case law, Art 2 ECHR and Art 8 ECHR could also give rise to duties on the part of the state to provide information about imminent health risks, which may also include a risk to health associated with the COVID-19 pandemic. However, whether the authorities in the present case have sufficiently complied with any duties to inform required by fundamental rights and whether they may have violated such duties does not need to be examined in connection with the alleged violation of Art 2 and Art 8 ECHR for the following reasons.

3. Art 2 and Art 8 ECHR do not impose any specific duties for the executive of the state:

[88] 3.1 According to Art 18(1) Federal Constitutional Law (*B-VG*), the entire state administration may only be exercised based on the law. According to Art 17 Federal Constitutional Law (*B-VG*), the provisions of Art 10 to 15 on legislative and executive competences do not affect the position of the Federation and the Provinces as holders of private rights in any way (private sector administration).

[89] 3.2 The addressee of the obligations to protect under Art 2 and Art 8 ECHR is – in terms of international law – the state party to the ECHR.

[90] The state is responsible for providing effective protection of the right to health and life (*Kopetzki* in *Korinek/Holoubek/Bezemek/Fuchs/Martin/Zellenberg*, Österreichisches Bundesverfassungsrecht Art 2 EMRK [2002] para 68; *Kneihs*, Art 2 EMRK, in *Kneihs/Lienbacher, Rill-Schäffer*-Kommentar Bundesverfassungsrecht [2006] MN 16). From a domestic perspective, the state's obligation derived from Art 2 and Art 8 ECHR to protect its citizens from threats to their lives and health within the framework of a state organisation based on the principle of the separation of powers and the principle of legality in administration (Art 18 Federal Constitutional Law (*B-VG*)) is primarily addressed to the legislator. In the Austrian constitutional system, the legislator must define the specific duty of administrative bodies to inform the population in more detail (*Öhlinger*, Sind staatliche Organe überhaupt – und wenn ja: In welchem Umfang – zur Information der Bevölkerung über Unfallgefahren verpflichtet? ZVR 1995, 282 [284 f]; *Kneihs*, Das Recht auf Leben in Österreich, JBl 1999, 76 [82 f]; *Kneihs*,

Art 2 EMRK, in *Kneihs/Lienbacher*, *Rill-Schäffer*-Kommentar Bundesverfassungsrecht [2006] para 20; *Holoubek*, Grundrechtliche Gewährleistungspflichten [1997] 282; *Kopetzki* in *Korinek/Holoubek/Bezemek/Fuchs/Martin/Zellenberg*, Österreichisches Bundesverfassungsrecht Art 2 EMRK [2002] Art 2 EMRK MN 68, 72; *Berka*, Vorbemerkungen zum StGG, in *Kneihs/Lienbacher, Rill-Schäffer*-Kommentar Bundesverfassungsrecht [2001] MN 26, 28).

[91] The statutory protective provisions must enable law enforcement to adequately fulfil its so-called secondary/administrative duties of protection. In a system in which the principle of legality binds all executive action to the law, this means that the legislator must also provide appropriate powers to the executive for an efficient defence against dangers (*Kneihs*, Art 2 EMRK, in *Kneihs/Lienbacher, Rill-Schäffer*-Kommentar Bundesverfassungsrecht [2006] para 20; *Kopetzki* in *Korinek/Holoubek/Bezemek/Fuchs/Martin/Zellenberg*, Österreichisches Bundesverfassungsrecht Art 2 EMRK [2002] para 68).

[92] Accordingly, a legal duty of administrative bodies to provide information cannot be derived directly from the constitution (Art 2 and Art 8 ECHR). Rather, such an duty of administrative authorities to provide information about (accident) hazards would require a basis in law. An attempt to derive duties to inform of administrative bodies (in the form of warnings, recommendations and notices) directly from the state's duty to protect based on fundamental rights (including 'state liability' for inadequate or omitted information) certainly does not find any consensus in light of the current state of Austrian constitutional doctrine (*Öhlinger*, ZVR 1995, 285; *Holoubek*, Grundrechtliche Gewährleistungspflichten [1997] 282 f; *Bußjäger/Egger*, ÖJZ 2021, 67 FN 61). Just as no duties to act can be derived directly from the fundamental rights of the ECHR for the state executive, no subjective claim of the individual that can be directly enforced in court or through administrative channels may be derived directly from fundamental rights duties to protect under the ECHR. This is also dependent on 'legal mediation' (*Holoubek*, Grundrechtliche Gewährleistungspflichten [1997] 283).

[93] 3.3 In contrast to the completely uniform prevailing doctrine, the expert opinion of *Fister* (Öffentlich-rechtliche Betrachtungen zum Fall Ischgl, AnwBl 2022, 21 [26]) (acting on behalf of the Association for the Protection of Consumer Interests) considers that the Landeck district authority would have had to publish a travel warning on 5 March 2020 even without a special legal basis, but already 'in direct fulfilment of its duty to protect fundamental rights'. However, *Fister* cites neither a reference nor a legal basis for this and thus ignores the principle of legality (Art 18(1) Federal Constitutional Law (*B-VG*)). A direct 'fundamental right' obligation to act would also affect the democratic principle, as the legislator would not be required if the executive – according to its own judgment – could

be subject to specific legal obligations directly on the basis of Art 2 and Art 8 ECHR. *Fister's* view (which has remained isolated) must therefore be rejected.

4. In summary, it follows:

[94] Given that Art 2 and Art 8 ECHR have no direct effect on the executive, as well as on the specific official action, a purported violation of obligations to protect under Art 2 and Art 8 ECHR alleged by the plaintiff due to insufficient information cannot give rise to official liability claims.

[…]

FF.VIII.-4

Constitutional Court, Judgment E3489/2022 of 16. June 2023, ECLI:AT: VFGH:2023:E3489.2022

Verfassungsgerichtshof, Erkenntnis E3489/2022 vom 16. Juni 2023, ECLI:AT: VFGH:2023:E3489.2022

Keywords

Geneva Refugee Convention – European Convention of Human Rights (ECHR) – Art 2 Fourth Additional Protocol ECHR – right to freedom of movement – issuance of an alien's passport

Genfer Flüchtlingskonvention – Europäische Menschenrechtskonvention (EMRK) – Art 2 4. Zusatzprotokoll zur EMRK – Recht auf Bewegungsfreiheit – Ausstellung eines Fremdenpasses

Facts and procedural history (summary)

The complainant is an Afghan national who applied for asylum in 2015. In April 2021, his requests for asylum and subsidiary protection were rejected, and he was subsequently ordered to leave Austria. In November 2021, however, the Federal Office for Immigration and Asylum granted a residence permit for reasons particularly worthy of consideration in accordance with Sec 56(1) Asylum Act (*AsylG*) and after obtaining a business license for 'trade with the exception of regulated trades and commercial agents' was granted a 'Red-White-Red Card plus' pursuant to Sec 41a(9) Settlement and Residence Act (*NAG*). In July 2022, the applicant applied for the issuance of an alien's passport, which was rejected by the Federal Office for Immigration and Asylum.

The appeal of the complainant against this decision was similarly rejected by the Federal Administrative Court. It held that an essential prerequisite for the fulfilment of the criteria of the provision under Austrian law regulating the issuance of alien's passports, Sec 88 Aliens Police Act (*FPG*), was that the issuance of the alien's passport needs to be in the interest of the Republic of Austria. By issuing the passport, Austria enables its holder to travel and thus also assumes an obligation towards host countries. The Federal Administrative Court also argued that the complainant could not show how the non-issuance of the passport violated his freedom of movement.

The complainant subsequently filed a complaint with the Constitutional Court against this decision of the Federal Administrative Court. The complainant alleges that the requirement that a public interest for the Republic needs to be demonstrated for the issuance violates his right to freedom of movement under Art 2 Fourth Add Protocol ECHR.

The Constitutional Court held (in excerpts)

Decision

I. The complainant's constitutionally guaranteed right to freedom of exit (Art 2 Fourth Add Protocol ECHR) has been violated by the contested decision.

The decision is annulled.

[…]

Reasons for Decision

[…]

Considerations

1. The complaint is admissible and well-founded.

2. A violation of the constitutionally guaranteed right to freedom of exit under Art 2 Fourth Add Protocol ECHR occurs, *inter alia,* if an administrative court erroneously interpreted the norms applied in a manner that would make be contrary to the aforementioned provision.

3. According to Art 2(2) Fourth Add Protocol ECHR, everyone has the right to leave any country (including his or her own). The exercise of this right may not be subject to any restrictions other than such as are in accordance with law and are necessary in a democratic society in the interests of national security or public safety, for the maintenance of *ordre public*, for the prevention of crime, for the protection of health or morals, or for the protection of the rights and freedoms of others.

4. In its judgment of 14 June 2022, App No 38.121/20, *L.B.*, the ECtHR emphasised, *inter alia*, that the right to leave a country would not be practical and effective without the issuance of some form of travel document (para 60). Any measure by which a person is denied the use of a document that would have allowed him or her to leave a country – if he or she had wished to – constitutes an interference

with the right guaranteed by Art 2 Fourth Add Protocol ECHR (para 79, with further references). Finally, in the aforementioned judgment, the ECtHR found a violation of Art 2 Fourth Add Protocol ECHR, because the national authorities had refused to issue an alien's passport without having weighed the matter in the individual case and having ensured that such a measure was justified and proportionate in the specific individual case (para 96).

5. The Constitutional Service of Federal Chancellery correctly points out that in the aforementioned judgment the ECtHR also held that Art 2(2) Fourth Add Protocol ECHR does not impose a general obligation on the Contracting States to issue a specific document to foreign nationals residing in their territory, enabling them to travel abroad (para 59). Nevertheless, the ECtHR has ruled that Art 2(2) Fourth Add Protocol ECHR applies to situations in which a Contracting State, in its legal system, entitles lawfully resident foreign nationals to obtain an alien's passport, provided that they meet the relevant conditions; the scope of protection of Art 2(2) Fourth Add Protocol ECHR thus extends to such constellations (see paras 61f).

6. Against this background, the following should be noted:

7. Pursuant to Sec 88(1)(3) Aliens Police Act (*FPG*), foreign nationals who are unable to procure a valid travel document from their home country and who otherwise fulfil the requirements for the granting of a 'long-term resident – EU' residence title (*cf.* Art 45 of the Settlement and Residence Act (*NAG*)) may, upon application, be issued with alien passports, if this is in the interest of the Republic with regard to the person concerned.

8. The procedure for issuing passports to aliens under Sec 88(1) Aliens Police Act (*FPG*) is now of fundamental importance in that the authority can and must examine the consequences of a refusal for its proportionality with regard to Art 2 Fourth Add Protocol ECHR (see ECtHR, L.B., Z96).

9. In view of this, the condition 'if this is in the interest of the Republic with regard to the person concerned' in Sec 88(1) Aliens Police Act (*FPG*) is also fulfilled if the refusal to issue an alien's passport would mean a violation of the right to freedom of exit guaranteed by Art 2 Fourth Add Protocol ECHR [...].

10. Since the Federal Administrative Court refused to issue an alien's passport requested by the complainant (for the purpose of travelling abroad [including for professional reasons]), without carrying out a weighing of interests, and thus a proportionality test, it has interpreted Sec 88(1) Aliens Police Act (*FPG*) in a manner that is contrary to Art 2 Fourth Add Protocol ECHR.

Result

1. The complainant has thus been violated by the contested decision in his constitutionally guaranteed right to freedom of exit (Art 2 Fourth Add Protocol ECHR).

2. The finding must therefore be set aside without the need to address the further submissions in the complaint.

[…]

FF.VIII.-5

Constitutional Court, Decision E1008/2023 of 5 October 2023, ECLI:AT:VFGH:2023:E1008.2023

Verfassungsgerichtshof, Entscheidung E1008/2023 vom 5. Oktober 2023, ECLI:AT:VFGH:2023:E1008.2023

Keywords

Freedom of expression – European Convention on Human Rights (ECHR) – Art 10 ECHR – hate speech – audiovisual media – attribution of statements of a third person

Recht auf freie Meinungsäußerung – Europäische Menschenrechtskonvention (EMRK) – Art 10 EMRK – Verhetzung – Audiovisuelle Mediendienste – Zurechenbarkeit der Äußerung von dritten Personen

Facts and procedural history (summary)

On 26 May 2020, the complainant broadcasted a television program on its channel, featuring a live conversation between the presenter and a studio guest. The discussion covered the studio guest's personal life and activities during the COVID-19 pandemic. However, the conversation soon shifted to controversial statements regarding the COVID-19 virus and China, leading to the following exchange: The studio guest expressed frustration with the pandemic and voiced support for a petition named 'Stop the Corona madness'. The guest then blamed China for the pandemic, using derogatory terms such as 'gook virus' for the virus and 'slit eyes' for Chinese people. He called Chinese people 'dirty, filthy people who have no manners', likening them to pigs and accused them of various negative behaviors such as spitting and smacking their lips while eating. The guest proposed that China should be held financially responsible for the pandemic and face severe economic and diplomatic sanctions. The presenter mostly allowed these statements without significant interruption or disapproval, only briefly noting that these views were personal opinions of the guest.

The studio guest was subsequently found guilty of incitement to hatred under the Austrian Criminal Code (*StGB*) by the Vienna Regional Criminal Court on 20 December 2020. This decision was upheld by the Vienna Higher Regional Court on 14 October 2021. On 11 February 2021, the Communications Authority Austria (hereinafter: KommAustria) determined that the complainant violated

Sec 30(2) No 1 Audiovisual Media Services Act (*AMD-G*) by airing the program, which incited hatred based on race and nationality. KommAustria argued that the presenter, representing the complainant, should have adequately distanced himself from the studio guest's statements. The failure to do so meant the statements were attributable to the complainant. As a result, KommAustria mandated the complainant to broadcast a text detailing this violation on three working days between 21:00 and 22:00 and include it in their on-demand service.

The complainant's appeal against KommAustria's decision was dismissed by the Federal Administrative Court on 16 February 2023. The court held that the studio guest's language clearly aimed to incite hostility against a specific group, fulfilling the criteria of Sec 30(2)(1) Audiovisual Media Services Act (*AMD-G*). The court considered that the complainant had a duty to react appropriately to such statements in line with public service broadcasting norms. The presenter's minimal response, briefly pointing out once during the approximately five-minute interview passage that the studio guest was expressing his own personal opinion, was insufficient, leading to the statements being attributable to the complainant.

The complainant filed a complaint under Art 144 Federal Constitutional Law (*B-VG*), alleging a violation of the constitutionally guaranteed right to freedom of expression (Art 10 ECHR, Art 13 Basic Law on the General Rights of Nationals (*StGG*) and Art 11 CFR). The complainant sought to annul the contested decision with costs, arguing that the obligation to immediately distance oneself from third-party statements in an interview infringes on the complainant's freedom of expression and media freedom. The complainant contended that, as an independent medium, it should be allowed to feature provocative opinions without the risk of liability for third-party statements unless these are adopted as the medium's own views. The presenter did note the opinions were personal, negating the attribution of these statements to the complainant. The finding of a serious legal violation was disproportionate in view of the severe potential consequences.

The Federal Administrative Court submitted the administrative and court files but did not issue a rebuttal.

The Constitutional Court found (in excerpts):

I. The complainant's rights have neither been violated by the contested decision in a constitutionally guaranteed right nor due to the application of an unlawful general rule.

II. The appeal is dismissed and referred to the Administrative Court for a decision on whether the complainant's rights have been infringed by the contested decision.

Reasons for decision

[...]

II. Legal situation

The relevant legal situation in the present case is as follows:

1. The relevant provisions of the Federal Act on Audiovisual Media Services (*AMD-G*), Federal Law Gazette I 84/2001, as amended by Federal Law Gazette I 55/2022, read in excerpts as follows:

'*Scope of Application*

Sec 1. (1) This Federal Act shall regulate

1. the provision of television services by means of wireless terrestrial transmission (terrestrial and mobile terrestrial television), via satellite (satellite television) and in electronic communications networks;

2. the provision of other audiovisual media services;

3. the operation of multiplex platforms.

(2) [...]

Definitions

Sec 2. The following definitions shall apply to this Act:

1. [...]

3. audiovisual media service: A service as defined by Articles 56 and 57 of the Treaty on the Functioning of the European Union, where the principal purpose or a dissociable section of the service is devoted to providing programmes, under the editorial responsibility of a media service provider, in order to inform, entertain or educate, to the general public by electronic communications networks (point (1) of Art 2 of Directive (EU) 2018/1972 establishing the European Electronic Communications Code, OJ No. L 321 of 17 December 2018, page 36); audiovisual media services include television channels and on-demand audiovisual media services;

4. [...]

20. media service provider: The natural or legal person who has editorial responsibility for the choice of the audiovisual content of the audiovisual media service and determines the manner in which it is designed;

21. [...]

[...]

General Requirements Regarding Audiovisual Media Services

Sec 30. (1) Audiovisual media services shall respect the human dignity and fundamental rights of others with regard to the presentation and content of those services.

(2) Content in an audiovisual media services

1. shall not incite others to hatred or violence directed against a group of persons or a member of a group based on any ground such as sex, race, colour, ethnic or social origin, genetic features, language, religion or belief, political or any other

opinion, membership of a national minority, property, birth, disability, age or sexual orientation;

2. shall not contain an incitement to commit terrorist offences or approval of terrorist offences (Sec 282a Criminal Code (*StGB*)).

[…]

Determining the Infringement of the Law

Sec 62. (1) The decision by the regulatory authority shall consist of the determination of whether and by what facts a provision of this Federal Act has been violated. If the regulatory authority establishes that this Federal Act has been infringed, which continues to prevail at the time of the determination, the media service provider shall immediately create a situation that correlates with the legal view held by the regulatory authority.

(2) The regulatory authority shall make a decision on complaints without unreasonable delay, but not later than within six months of the date when the complaint is received. In the case of complaints filed with the regulatory authority, the days taken for postal delivery shall not be included.

(3) The regulatory authority may decide that its decision be published, and instruct the media service provider as to when, in what form and on which channel or media service this publication needs to be made.

(4) If the regulatory authority finds that a law has been violated, it shall include in its decree a finding on whether the infringement was a serious infringement of a provision of this Federal Act.

[…]

Penal Provisions under Administrative Law

Sec 64. (1) […]

(2) Any person who fails to comply with

1. the general content requirements pursuant to Sec 30(1) or (2),

2. […]'

2. The relevant provisions of Directive 2010/13/EU on the coordination of certain provisions laid down by law, regulation or administrative action in Member States concerning the provision of audiovisual media services (Audiovisual Media Services Directive), OJ 2010 L 95, 1, as amended by Directive (EU) 2018/1808 amending Directive 2010/13/EU (Audiovisual Media Services Directive) in view of changing market realities, OJ 2018 L 303, 69, read in extract as follows:

'Article 1

1. For the purposes of this Directive, the following definitions shall apply:

(a) 'audiovisual media service' means:

(i) a service as defined by Articles 56 and 57 of the Treaty on the Functioning of the European Union, where the principal purpose of the service or a dissociable section thereof is devoted to providing programmes, under the editorial responsibility of a media service provider, to the general public, in order to inform, entertain or educate, by means of electronic communications networks within the meaning of point (a) of Article 2 of Directive 2002/21/EC; such an audiovisual media service is either a television broadcast as defined in point (e) of this paragraph or an on-demand audiovisual media service as defined in point (g) of this paragraph;

(ii) audiovisual commercial communication;

(b) […]

(d) 'media service provider' means the natural or legal person who has editorial responsibility for the choice of the audiovisual content of the audiovisual media service and determines the manner in which it is organised;

(da) […]

Article 6

1. Without prejudice to the obligation of Member States to respect and protect human dignity, Member States shall ensure by appropriate means that audiovisual media services provided by media service providers under their jurisdiction do not contain any:

(a) incitement to violence or hatred directed against a group of persons or a member of a group based on any of the grounds referred to in Article 21 of the Charter;

b) public provocation to commit a terrorist offence as set out in Article 5 of Directive (EU) 2017/541.

2. The measures taken for the purposes of this Article shall be necessary and proportionate and shall respect the rights and observe principles set out in the Charter.'

3. Sec 10 of the Federal Act on the Austrian Broadcasting Corporation (ORF Act, ORF-G), Federal Law Gazette 379/1984, as amended by Federal Law Gazette I 150/2020, reads as follows:

'Principles concerning content

Sec 10. (1) All programmes of the Austrian Broadcasting Corporation must respect the human dignity and fundamental rights of others with regard to presentation and content.

(2) The programmes and online services shall not incite others to hatred or violence directed against a group of persons or a member of a group based on any grounds such as sex, race, colour, ethnic or social origin, genetic features, language, religion or belief, political or any other opinion, membership of a national minority, property, birth, disability, age or sexual orientation and shall not contain an incitement to commit terrorist offences (Sec 278c Criminal Code (*StGB*)).

(3) […]

(5) Information shall be comprehensive, independent, impartial and objective. Any newscasts and reports shall be examined carefully as to their truth and origin, and there shall be a clear distinction between newscasts and commentary.

(6) The diversity of opinions held in public life shall appropriately be taken into account, the human dignity, personal rights and privacy of the individual shall be respected.

(7) Commentaries, analyses and presentations shall be objective and based on re-constructible facts.

(8) […]'

4. Sec 6 Federal Act of 12 June 1981 on the Press and Other Publication Media (Media Act - *MedienG*), Federal Law Gazette 314/1981, as amended by Federal Law Gazette I 148/2020, reads as follows:

'Criminal defamation, insult, ridicule and false accusation

Sec 6. (1) If the offence of criminal defamation, insult, ridicule or false accusation is committed in a medium, the person affected is entitled to claim from the media owner indemnity for the adverse personal effects suffered (Sec 8(1)).

(2) No claims under (1) may be raised

1. […]

2. in cases of criminal defamation

a) if the published statement is true or

b) if the public had a predominant interest in the publication and, also in application of the journalistic diligence required, there was sufficient reason to take the statement for true,

3. if it is a live broadcast and employees or agents of the broadcaster were not guilty of neglecting the journalistic diligence required,

3a. if it concerns the availability for download of a website, provided that the media owner or one of his employees or agents has not failed to use due care, or

4. if it is a case of a true quotation of the statement of a third party and the public had a predominant interest in obtaining knowledge of the statement quoted.

(3) If the publication is related to the strictly private sphere, a claim under (1) is excluded only for reasons of (2)(1), (2)(2)(a), (2)(3) or (2)(3a), however in cases of (2)(2)(a) only in such cases, if the facts made public are directly related with public life.'

III. Considerations

1. The complaint is admissible, but not well-founded:

2. According to Art 10(1) ECHR, everyone has the right to freedom of expression. The fundamental right to freedom of expression also protects in particular 'news'

or 'ideas' that provoke, shock or disturb. This arises from the requirements of pluralism, tolerance and generosity, without which a democratic society cannot exist (ECtHR of 7 December 1976 [GC], 5493/72, *Handyside*; of 23 May 1991 [GC], 11.662/85, *Oberschlick*; VfSlg 13.694/1994). Freedom of political debate is essential to the concept of a democratic society (ECtHR of 8 July 1986 [GC], 9815/82, *Lingens*), and provocative speech (*inter alia* ECtHR of 6 December 2007, 19.331/05, *Katrami*, paras 39 ff) is a central component of political speech (*inter alia* ECtHR of 28 September 2000, 37.698/97, *Lopes Gomes da Silva*, para 35; of 14 March 2013, 26.118/10, *EON*, para 61 – on satirical speech). In view of the special importance and function of freedom of expression in a democratic society, the necessity of restricting freedom of expression – which Art 10(2) ECHR allows the legislator to do in individual cases, in particular in cases of political speech, in view of the fact that the exercise of this freedom entails duties and responsibilities, subject to the conditions set out therein – must be beyond doubt (see VfSlg 10.700/1985, 13.694/1994).The freedoms of Art 10(1) ECHR are of particular importance for the mass media. Although they too may not exceed the limits set by Art 10(2) ECHR in a democratic society, it is nevertheless their task to disseminate information and ideas on political issues and other matters of public interest. Not only do they have the task of disseminating such information and ideas, but the public also has a right to receive them (see, *mutatis mutandis*, ECtHR, *Lingens*, para 41; ECtHR of 26 April 1979 [GC], 6538/74, *Sunday Times*, para 65; for electronic mass media, for example, ECtHR of 23 September 1994 [GC], 15.890/89, *Jersild*, para 31; 22 April 2013 [GC], 48.876/08, *Animal Defenders International*, para 119).

3. Pursuant to Sec 30(1) Audiovisual Media Services Act (*AMD-G*), audiovisual media services must respect human dignity and the fundamental rights of others with regard to their presentation and content. According to Sec 30(2)(1) Audiovisual Media Services Act (*AMD-G*), content in audiovisual media services may not incite hatred or violence against a group of persons or a member of a group on the basis of gender, race, skin colour, ethnic or social origin, genetic characteristics, language, religion or belief, political or other opinion, membership of a national minority, property, birth, disability, age or sexual orientation.

This 'hate speech ban' (Constitutional Court of 23 June 2022, E 2977/2021) in (electronic) mass media takes into account the fact of their special importance as a 'medium and factor' in the formation of public opinion and thus the 'duties and responsibilities' that the mass media, which disseminate their news and ideas under editorial responsibility and decide who and what is made public in their programmes, have for public discourse in a democratic society.

In this context, the Constitutional Court has also pointed out that requirements for restrictions as enshrined in Art 10(2) ECHR show that limits can and should be placed on tendencies that endanger democracy and are directed against fundamental principles of the rule of law, such as racist expressions of opinion in particular, especially in order to prevent persons or groups from abusing the rights guaranteed in the European Convention on Human Rights precisely to abolish or restrict the rights of others (see with reference also to the prohibition of abuse in Art 17 ECHR Constitutional Court of 8 Marc 2022, E 3120/2021 with further references). The handling of restrictions, as set out in Sec 30(2)(1) Audiovisual Media Services Act (*AMD-G*), must therefore take into account both the responsibility of the mass medium and its particularly protected freedom in individual cases.

4. The Federal Administrative Court is correct when it considers the relevant statements of the studio guest to be suitable for inciting hatred on the basis of race and nationality. The complaining party does not dispute this assessment either.

5.1 The complainant considers (not the studio guest's freedom of expression, but) her freedom of the media protected by Art 10 ECHR to have been violated because the Federal Administrative Court attributes the statements of the studio guest to the complaining party due to a lack of sufficient distancing by the moderator and thus holds the complaining party responsible for the violation of Sec 30(2)(1) Audiovisual Media Services Act (*AMD-G*). This interpretation of the law would restrict the freedom of the complaining party to also invite people who hold critical, unpopular or even disturbing views as interview partners in its programmes and in this way to make the diversity of opinions visible in public discourse. This is an essential part of their journalistic media freedom, as particularly protected by Art 10 ECHR for media organisations such as the complaining party.

5.2 In principle, one of the main tasks of the mass media is to make opinions held in a democratic society visible in public discourse by enabling people to express their relevant opinions directly in the programmes of an audiovisual media service. As has been emphasised several times, this also applies to critical, offensive or shocking opinions. These are generally attributable to the persons who express themselves in this or that way, for example in an interview, in a live conversation or in a discussion round, and are the responsibility of these persons (VfSlg 20.427/2020).

5.3 A media organisation, such as the complaining party in the present case, is only responsible for such expressions of opinion in special constellations (which may differ from those in which the objectivity requirement for public service broadcasting updates its relevant responsibility, see VfSlg 20.427/2020). Such a constellation exists in the present case, as the Federal Administrative Court rightly assumes, if the expression of opinion of a third party reproduced in a programme of the audiovisual media service seriously calls into question the rights of others guaranteed in the ECHR, *i.e.* fulfils the elements of hate speech, as in this case, because it incites hatred against a group on the basis of ethnic origin. There is no doubt that the statements made by the studio guest in the present case would have to be sanctioned under Sec 30(2)(1) Audiovisual Media Services Act (*AMD-G*) if the audiovisual media service had distributed them under its editorial responsibility, for example as its own commentary.

However, because it is part of the complaining party's media freedom protected by Art 10(1) ECHR to also allow third parties who hold such opinions to have their say as part of the spectrum of opinions represented in democratic society, the complaining party can only be held responsible for the statement if it does not fulfil its editorial responsibility in a way that (expectably) makes clear the special democratic, constitutional and human rights threat potential of such statements.

This editorial responsibility, which is an expression of the special responsibility of the mass media for public discourse and the reason for the special protection of the mass media under Art 10 ECHR, can be exercised in different ways, for example by placing such interviews in the overall context of a programme (see ECtHR, *Jersild*, para 33) or by making the relevant potential threat posed by the opinion expressed by a person participating in the discussion clear in other statements by means of an appropriately clear composition of a discussion panel.

5.4 In the present constellation, the complaining party has invited only one studio guest to a longer studio interview. The presenter is therefore the only interlocutor and the programme consists only of this interview. In the programme, the presenter, who assumes editorial responsibility, expressly aims to ensure that the studio guest expresses corresponding opinions by asking him to 'speak plainly' and also motivating him to repeat or even exaggerate his statements that are derogatory to a certain group of people based on nationality or ethnicity (see the presenter's question: '[O]n purpose? Because they deliberately wanted to harm the Americans and Europeans, or simply because they are crazy people when it comes to health checks?'). In contrast, the moderator's relativisation of the statements made by the studio guest with regard to the rest of the democratic spectrum of opinion and, in particular, the protection of the group attacked in a special way, is only very restrained (when he follows the statement, 'They are dirty, filthy people who have no manners' with 'In your opinion'), whereupon the studio guest continues the disparagement in an intensified form.

If the Federal Administrative Court assumes – particularly in view of the moderator's comments that (once again) prompted relevant statements by the studio guest – that the moderator did not adequately fulfil his editorial responsibility in the specific interview situation in view of the content of the studio guest's statements, it cannot be contradicted from the constitutional perspective of Art 10 ECHR. If, for reasons of freedom of public debate in a democratic society, the complaining party also has the freedom to disseminate opinions such as those at issue here, this freedom can be permissibly restricted under Art 10(2) ECHR to the extent that the complaining party also fulfils its editorial responsibility accordingly. If the complaining party failed to do so in the present case, thereby being charged with a violation of Sec 30(2)(1) Audiovisual Media Services Act (*AMD-G*) with regard to the statements made by the studio guest, this constitutes a necessary barrier to media freedom in a democratic society with regard to the protection of ethnic groups from hate speech disseminated by the mass media in an audiovisual media service (see in a comparable context ECtHR, *Jersild*, para 30, 35; of 4 November 2008, 72.596/01, *Balsytė-Lideikienė*, paras 79 ff; of 24 February 2015, 21.830/09, *Haldimann*, paras 46 ff; of 15 October 2015 [GC], 27.510/08, *Perinçek*, paras 204 ff with further references; of 16 February 2021, 12.567/13, *Budinova and Chaprazov*, para 90).

6 The Constitutional Court also has no constitutional objections to the Federal Administrative Court qualifying violations of Sec 30(2)(1) Audiovisual Media Services Act (*AMD-G*) as a 'serious violation' of this law and imposing a corresponding publication obligation (see Constitutional Court 23 June 2022, E2977/2021).

IV. Result

1. The alleged violation of constitutionally guaranteed rights has therefore not occurred.

The proceedings also did not show that the complainant's constitutionally guaranteed rights, which she did not assert, were violated. In view of the harmlessness of the legal bases applied, it is also ruled out that her rights were violated due to the application of an unlawful general standard.

The complaint must therefore be dismissed and assigned to the Administrative Court in accordance with Art 144(3) Federal Constitutional Law (*B-VG*) [...].

2. This decision could be made without an oral hearing in a closed session in accordance with Sec 19(4) Constitutional Court Act (*VfGG*).

HH. Jurisdiction of the state/Jurisdiktion (Hoheitsgewalt)

III. Extra-territorial exercise of jurisdiction/ Extraterritoriale Ausübung von Hoheitsgewalt

1. General/Im allgemeinen

See *SS. VIII.*

OO. Coercive measures short of the use of force/ Zwangsmaßnahmen unter der Schwelle der Gewaltanwendung

II. Collective measures/Kollektivmaßnahmen

1. United Nations/Vereinte Nationen

See *EE.II.1.c.*

2. Collective measures outside the United Nations/ Kollektivmaßnahmen außerhalb der Vereinten Nationen

See *EE.II.1.c.*

SS. Legal aspects of international relations and cooperation in particular matters/Rechtliche Aspekte der internationalen Beziehungen und Zusammenarbeit in bestimmten Bereichen

VIII. Legal matters (*e.g.*, judicial assistance and crime control etc.)/Rechtliche Angelegenheiten (z.B. Rechtshilfe und Verbrechensbekämpfung etc.)

SS. VIII.

Regional Administrative Court Styria, Judgment LVwG 30.4-8656/2022 of 24 March 2023, ECLI:AT:LVWGST:2023:LVwG.30.4.8656.2022

Landesverwaltungsgericht Steiermark, Erkenntnis LVwG 30.4-8656/2022 vom 24. März 2023, ECLI:AT:LVWGST:2023:LVwG.30.4.8656.2022

Keywords

Service of documents of Austrian authorities abroad – service of documents as a sovereign act – administrative (penal) proceedings – driver identification request – Convention of 29 May 2000 on Mutual Assistance in Criminal Matters between the Member States of the European Union – international practice not amounting to customary international law – tacit consent – impermissibility of fictious service through deposit of documents

Zustellung von Schriftstücken von österreichischen Behörden im Ausland – Zustellung als hoheitliches Handeln – Verwaltungs(straf)verfahren – Lenkererhebung – Übereinkommen vom 29.05.2000 über die Rechtshilfe in Strafsachen zwischen den Mitgliedsstaaten der Europäischen Union – internationale Übung unter der Schwelle des Gewohnheitsrechts – stillschweigende Zustimmung – Unzulässigkeit der Zustellfiktion durch Hinterlegung der Schriftstücke

Facts and procedural history (summary)

The complainant is resident in Slovenia and is the registered owner of a motor vehicle with a Slovenian license plate. The district authority Deutschlandsberg (*Bezirkshauptmannschaft*) as the district authority sent the complainant a driver identification request on 14 June 2021, concerning the use of her vehicle on 22 May 2021. That request was sent in the original alongside a Slovenian translation through the postal service. The enveloped was returned unopened with the annotation 'unclaimed' by the Slovenian postal service on 13 July 2021, with further annotations indicating that apparently an unsuccessful delivery attempt was made on 17 June 2021. There is no indication whether and, if so where, the delivery had been deposited somewhere, nor that the complainant had been informed of such a deposit.

Without taking any further procedural steps, the district authority then issued a penalty notice (*Strafbescheid*) against the complainant on 14 July 2021, due to their alleged failure to identify the driver. A first attempt to serve this penalty notice through the postal service was unsuccessful. The second attempt, where service occurred through the District Court of Maribor (Slovenia) in accordance with Art 3 and 5 Convention on Mutual Assistance in Criminal Matters, then led to effective service on 17 September 2021. The complainant then contested the penalty notice, ultimately leading the district authority to open administrative penal proceedings. In the course of those proceedings, the district authority informed the complainant of the 'results of the gathering of evidence' and gave them an opportunity to be heard, which the complainant used to transmit the completed driver identification request.

The district authority issued an administrative penal decision (*Straferkenntnis*) on 23 November 2022. The complainant appealed that decision to the Regional Administrative Court Styria.

The Regional Administrative Court Styria held (in excerpts):

[…]

On the service of the driver identification request:

2. However, the lawful punishment under Sec 103(2) Motor Vehicles Act (*KFG*) requires that a *valid service of the identification request* has taken place (*cf* Supreme Administrative Court of 6 September 1989, 89/02/0034), since the time period to identify the driver only starts following the valid service of

the driver identification request. Without valid service, however, the two-week period stipulated in Sec 103(2) Motor Vehicles Act (*KFG*) is not triggered, so that a punishment for not providing the driver identification (in time) cannot be legally imposed.

3.1. The service of documents of any kind is subject to the rules of international treaties and the regulatory competence of the state on whose territory the service is to take place. The application of Austrian law abroad when it comes to the service of documents abroad is therefore out of the question. The regulation and execution of the service of documents of Austrian authorities abroad is, as a sovereign act of the state, in principle a matter of the foreign state, according to the principle of territoriality under international law, which, as a 'generally recognized rule of international law' within the meaning of Art 9(1) Federal Constitutional Law (*B-VG*), is also part of the Austrian legal system. If the state in question has legal provisions for the service of documents from foreign authorities, then – subject to international agreements – solely these are decisive.

3.2. Accordingly, Sec 11(1) Service of Documents Act (*ZustG*) stipulates that service of documents abroad shall be carried out in accordance with international agreements or, alternatively, in a manner permitted by the law or other legal provisions of the state in which service is to be effected, or in accordance with international practice, if necessary with the assistance of the Austrian diplomatic and consular missions. The Supreme Administrative Court has also ruled that Sec 11(1) Service of Documents Act (*ZustG*) – which forms part of Section I 'General Provisions' – stipulates derogations from the provisions of Section II of the Service of Documents Act (*ZustG*) with regard to 'physical service' in the event that 'physical' service is to be carried out abroad, and not in Austria (*cf* Supreme Administrative Court of 21 November 2017, Ro 2015/12/0017; of 2 May 2016, Ra 2015/08/0142; of 16 May 2011, 2009/17/0185, VwSlg. 18.129 A/2011).

3.3. Thus, before assuming a legally valid service of the driver identification request, the defendant authority, in accordance with Sec 11(1) Service of Documents Act (*ZustG*), should have ascertained which legal regulations apply in Slovenia with regard to the service of official documents of Austrian authorities, as well as in the case of the absence of international agreements or Slovenian legal provisions on the service of documents from foreign authorities, whether and to what extent an international practice can be presumed to exist with regard to the service of administrative documents (*cf* Supreme Administrative Court of 20 January 2015, Ro 2014/09/0059, VwSlg. 19.018 A/2015; of 29 February 2008, 2007/02/0315).

4.1. In the context of administrative penal cases, the Convention of 29 May 2000 on Mutual Assistance in Criminal Matters between the Member States of the European Union (OJ C 197 of 12 July 2000), Federal Law Gazette III No 62/2005 as amended by Federal Law Gazette III No 32/2015, includes provisions on the service of documents in the contracting parties to this Convention, which, apart from Austria, also includes Slovenia. Thus, Art 5(1) of this Convention provides for the service of procedural documents directly by post, and Art 5(3) provides, for example, an obligation to translate the essential elements of a procedural document issued in another Member State – an obligation that was also observed by the defendant authority in the administrative penal proceedings. However, this Convention is only applicable to administrative penal cases (*cf* Art 3(1) of this Convention; *cf* Supreme Administrative Court of 1 March 2016, Ra 2015/11/0097), and not to administrative proceedings.

4.2. The driver identification itself is not yet part of the administrative penal proceedings; the proceedings in which the request for information pursuant to Sec 103(2) Motor Vehicles Act (*KFG*) (driver identification request) is made are administrative proceedings (*cf* the settled case law of the Supreme Administrative Court: *e.g.* Supreme Administrative Court of 22 February 2018, Ra 2017/11/0313; of 11 November 1992, 92/92/0303). Only the proceedings subsequently initiated on suspicion of failure to provide the driver identification are administrative penal proceedings (Supreme Administrative Court of 21 June 2013, 2013/02/0097). Consequently, the Convention of 29 May 2000 on Mutual Assistance in Criminal Matters is not applicable to the service of the driver identification request.

4.3. Since Slovenia is also not a party to the European Convention on the Service Abroad of Documents relating to Administrative Matters, Federal Law Gazette No 67/1983 as amended by Federal Law Gazette III No 53/2005, and no relevant bilateral treaty exists (the Exchange of Notes between Republic of Austria and the Republic of Slovenia concerning the Continued Application of Certain Austrian-Yugoslavian Treaties, Federal Law Gazette No 714/1993, contains individual provisions on the requests for service and mutual legal assistance, however no provisions on the service of documents from Austrian authorities in Slovenia), the next step, according to Sec 11(1) Service of Documents Act (*ZustG*), is to examine whether national legislation on the permissibility and the form of the service of documents from foreign authorities in administrative matters exist (*cf* Supreme Administrative Court of 21 November 2017, Ro 2015/12/0017) and thus are applicable to the service of a driver identification request, which is part of administrative proceedings. According to the principles of international law, sovereign acts of the state, which also include the service of official documents, in particular those that trigger legally relevant effects for the addressee, such as in the present case the obligation (enforced by penalty) to identify the driver (Supreme Administrative Court of 27 October 1997, 96/17/0348, VwSlg. 7.231 F/1997), may not be carried out on foreign territory without the consent of the respective territorial state [...], foreign regulations within the meaning of Sec 11(1) Service of Documents Act (*ZustG*) can only be assumed to exist if they are explicitly applicable to the service of foreign documents, and therefore also those of Austrian authorities (see *Wessely*, Zur verwaltungsstrafrechtlichen Verfolgung ausländischer Täter, ZfV 2000, 391 [397]; *Raschauer* in *Frauenberger-Pfeiler/Raschauer/Sander/Wessely* (eds), Österreichisches Zustellrecht [2nd edn] (2011) on § 11 ZustG, MN 4f).

5. There are no such regulations on the permissibility and form of service of foreign documents applicable to administrative proceedings: Sec 34 of the Act on General Administrative Procedure of the Republic of Slovenia (*cf.* [...] Zakon o splošnem upravnem postopku (ZUP), Official Gazette of the Republic of Slovenia, No 80/99 as amended by No 3/22) only provides for regulations on legal assistance in its paragraphs 5 to 7, which – in the absence of international agreements – is coordinated by the Ministry responsible for foreign affairs, however, there is no regulation on the service of documents from foreign authorities on the territory of the Republic of Slovenia (*cf.* the judgment of the Supreme Administrative Court of 20 January 2015, Ro 2014/09/0059, VwSlg. 19.018 A/2015, which also reproduced a statement of the Slovenian Ministry of Justice, according to which there is neither a treaty between the Republic of Slovenia and Austria nor a Slovenian domestic legal basis for the service of foreign documents in administrative proceedings; see also the Administrative Wiki of the Federal Chancellery – Internationale Rechtshilfe – Slowenien, ÖEGV-Wiki).

6.1. If there is neither an international agreement nor national legislation of the state on the requirements of service on its territory, the case law of the Supreme Administrative Court considers that the permissibility and form of service of documents from Austrian authorities abroad is determined by international practice. According to prevailing doctrine, international practice is the regular behavior of states in certain matters, without it amounting to customary international law. Service of documents is deemed permissible, if it is knowingly tolerated by the respective state on its territory or can actually be effected without protest, whereby practice depends on the one hand in which state or with regard to which procedure service is to be effected out, and on the other hand on the content or legal significance of the documents (*cf. Wessely*, Probleme der Verfolgung ausländischer Täter im Straßenverkehr, ZVR 2008, 79 [80]; *Raschauer* in *FrauenbergerPfeiler/Raschauer/Sander/Wessely* (Hrsg), Österreichisches Zustellrecht [2nd edn] (2011) on § 11 ZustG, MN 5, each with further references). Thus, the permissibility and form of service of documents from Austrian authorities abroad is determined by whether and, if so, which form of service the foreign state in question usually allows on its territory without protest, thereby tacitly giving its consent to this practice (*cf.* Supreme Administrative Court of 20 January 2015, Ro 2014/09/0059, VwSlg. 19.018 A/2015; of 19 March 2003, 2001/03/0045).

6.2. It follows from international practice that direct postal service by Austrian authorities in Slovenia is permissible (*cf.* Supreme Administrative Court of 23 October 2002, 2001/16/0341; specifically for Slovenia the Administrative Wiki of the Federal Chancellery – Internationale Rechtshilfe – Slowenien, ÖEGV-Wiki). However, the international practice does not provide for a fiction of service in case of deposit, as is foreseen for domestic service in Sec 17(3) Service of Documents Act (*ZustG*), since this neither concerns the permissibility and form of service of documents of Austrian authorities *per se*, nor about the legal effects of service in accordance with international practice – pursuant to Sec 11(1) Service of Documents Act (*ZustG*) – but about the legal effects of the mere deposit of the document in case of non-delivery. The fiction of service through the deposit of a document cannot be based on the regular behavior of states of tolerating acts of service on their territory, but only from a legal norm that attributes the effect of service to the deposit of a document in the event of unsuccessful service. The fiction of service through deposition is not factual conduct that could be tolerated by states or protested by states.

7.1. Since there is no agreement with Slovenia regarding administrative proceedings, which for example provides that the Slovenian law applicable to domestic service is also applicable to service by foreign authorities, and there is also no provision under Slovenian law for the service of documents from foreign authorities, a deposit cannot give rise to the fiction of service in the event that service has not been effected. As explained above, the application of the fiction of service in case of deposit under Sec 17(3) Service of Documents Act (*ZustG*), which is only applicable to domestic service, is excluded in case of service abroad (*cf.* Supreme Administrative Court of 21 November 2017, Ro 2015/12/0017; of 2 May 2016, Ra 2015/08/0142; of 16 May 2011, 2009/17/0185, VwSlg. 18.129 A/2011; of 29 January 2003, 2000/03/0320).

7.2. In the present case, it is not even clear whether the driver identification request was deposited and whether the complainant was notified of this, as neither the deposit for a certain period of time nor the notification of the recipient is documented on the envelope on file, which was returned with the annotation 'unclaimed' by the Slovenian postal service. But even if the driver identification request had been deposited for collection and the complainant had been informed of the deposit, this deposit could not – in the absence of a legal provision on the fiction of service – have the effect of service.

8. Therefore, any potential deposit of the driver identification request had not have effected service. In addition, the letter was returned unopened by the

Slovenian postal service, which makes it clear that there was no cure within the meaning of Sec 7 Service of Documents Act (*ZustG*) (*cf.* on the applicability of Sec 7 Service of Documents Act (*ZustG*): Supreme Administrative Court of 21 November 2017, Ro 2015/12/0017; of 2 May 2016, Ra 2015/08/0142; of 16 May 2011, 2009/17/0185; of 27 October 1997, 96/17/034815.1.1986, 85/01/0244; of 23 June 2003, 2002/17/0182 ua).

9. This is not altered by the fact that the complainant became aware of the driver identification request through its transmission as the 'results of the gathering of evidence' on 17 May 2022. It can be left open whether this even constitutes a valid service of documents (*cf.* Supreme Administrative Court of 24 November 1987, 87/11/0154, according to which service of an administrative penal decision merely as an 'attachment' to a decision of withdrawal did not result in a legally effective issuance). On the one hand, it follows from the alleged date of the offence that the failure to provide driver identification was punished after two weeks of the first unsuccessful attempt of service and the Regional Administrative Court Styria would be prevented from replacing the alleged date of the offence [...], on the other hand, the driver identification request was in any case returned fully completed within two weeks of the date on which the notification of the results of the gathering of evidence was served.

10. In the absence of fictious service through a potential deposit of the identification request, no legally effective service was made that could initiate the time limit for providing the driver identification, so that the punishment according to Sec 103(2) Motor Vehicles Act (*KFG*) is unlawful (*cf.* Supreme Administrative Court of 6 September 1989, 89/02/0034). The administrative penal decision must therefore be quashed and the administrative penal proceedings discontinued pursuant to Sec 42(1) No 2 Administrative Penal Act 1991 (*VStG*) in conjunction with Sec 38 Proceedings of Administrative Courts Act (*VwGVG*), because the complainant did not commit the administrative offense of failing to provide the driver identification in due time pursuant to Sec 103(2) Motor Vehicles Act (*KFG*).

PART II – Austrian Diplomatic and Parliamentary Practice in International Law/Österreichische Diplomatische und Parlamentarische Praxis zum Internationalen Recht

Markus P Beham | Professor, Chair of Public International Law, European University Viadrina

Gerhard Hafner | Professor ret. of International and European Law, Department for European, International and Comparative Law, Section for International Law and International Relations, University of Vienna

Johannes Tropper | Researcher and lecturer (post doc), Department for European, International and Comparative Law, Section for International Law and International Relations, University of Vienna

Index of Documents*

* The digest covers the period from 1 January 2023 to 31 December 2023.

Austrian Review of International and European Law **28**: 339-468, 2023
 | DOI:10.1163/15736512-02801013

SS. Legal aspects of international relations and cooperation in particular matters/Rechtliche Aspekte der internationalen Beziehungen und Zusammenarbeit in bestimmten Bereichen

SS.I.3. – See *CC.II.2.-1* and *GG.VI.-2*.

SS.I.4. – See *CC.IV.3.-1*.

SS.III. – See *KK.XI.-1*.

SS.IV. – See *KK.XI.-1*.

SS.VIII. – See *FF.XI.-1*.

AA. International law in general/Völkerrecht – allgemein

I. Nature, basis, purpose/Natur, Grundlage, Funktionen

1. In general/Allgemeines

AA.I.1.-1

The rule of law at the national and international levels

Innerstaatliche und internationale Rechtsstaatlichkeit

On 16 October 2023, in the capacity of coordinator of the 'Group of Friends of the Rule of Law', the Austrian representative delivered the following statement to the Sixth Committee during the 78th Session of the General Assembly regarding Agenda Item 83 on 'The rule of law at the national and international levels':

> […] [O]ur discussions on this topic have been guided by the yearly report of the Secretary-General on 'Strengthening and coordinating United Nations rule of law activities'. The latest report contained in document A/78/184 saw a 'global decline in the rule of law and a backsliding of democracy and women's rights'. This is particularly worrying because the rule of law forms the basis for multilateral cooperation and political dialogue. In this regard, we welcome the Secretary-General's launch of the New Vision for the rule of law. It builds upon the declaration of the 2012 high-level meeting of the General Assembly on the rule of law at the national and international levels and is firmly grounded in the Charter of the UN. We fully agree that justice systems must put people at the center to address their needs and the rule of law is a key enabler of just, peaceful and inclusive societies with strong institutions and sustainable development.
>
> An important component in this regard is equal access to justice for all. It is also underscored as a sub target of SDG16. Access to justice can be hindered due to lack of awareness of the existence of certain services but also due to geographical realities. New technologies can remedy this situation. Therefore, today's topic 'Using technology to advance access to justice' is timely and appropriate. Key components of access to justice such as the right to legal aid or legal empowerment can be strengthened through means of technology. Digitalization can make legal services more accessible and affordable. At the same time, it must be ensured that human rights, including the right to a fair trial and data privacy are not jeopardized by the use of technology. Also, the challenges such as the digital divide, particularly for women and girls and people living in poverty, and risks associated with the use of AI must be addressed to enhance access to justice while safeguarding individuals' rights.
>
> Let us look at some examples of how technology is already advancing access to justice: E-Filing and E-Court systems allow parties to file cases and submit docu-

ments online. This reduces the need for physical visits to the courthouse, making processes more efficient and accessible to individuals who may have transportation or mobility challenges. […] Mobile apps, legal aid chatbots and virtual assistance can not only reduce the inhibition threshold for victims to get in touch with legal experts but also meet communication preferences of younger generations. This includes the dissemination of information via mobile apps. Answers to common legal questions and information on court procedures can be made available easily. Marginalized groups can also be made aware of their fundamental rights and the possibilities of the legal systems and get crucial support online. Certain low-value civil cases or small claims disputes could be settled via online dispute resolution. […] It is indisputable that AI offers many possibilities to enhance access to justice. This includes language translation tools to provide real-time translations during multilingual proceedings or machine learning which can make predictions by evaluating case files. Equally, the use of AI in judiciaries is a good example of how certain new technologies need proper control and accountability in order to be advantageous. […]

3. Soft law

See *CC.-1* and *EE.I.5.-2.*

BB. Sources of international law/Völkerrechtsquellen

III. General principles of law/Allgemeine Rechtsgrundsätze

BB.III.-1

Work of the International Law Commission on General Principles of Law

Arbeit der Völkerrechtskommission der Vereinten Nationen betreffend allgemeine Rechtsgrundsätze

On 23 October 2023, the Austrian representative to the 78th Session of the General Assembly delivered the following statement to the Sixth Committee on Report of the International Law Commission on the Work of its 73rd and 74th Session concerning the topic of 'General principles of law':

> Austria congratulates the Commission, and in particular Special Rapporteur Marcelo Vázquez-Bermúdez, on the adoption of the draft conclusions on 'General principles of international law' on first reading. Austria welcomes the inclusion of this topic in the work of the ILC, as this category of sources of international law is subject to highly divergent interpretations and, therefore, urgently requires clarification.

From the very beginning, Austria has been sceptical regarding general principles formed within the *international* legal system, referred to as a category distinct from principles derived from national legal systems in draft conclusion 3 on categories of general principles of law. In practice, it seems very difficult to distinguish between general principles formed within the international legal system and rules of customary international law.

Draft conclusion 7 on the identification of general principles of law formed within the international legal system contains a more detailed definition with examples in the commentary, which, in our view, are not very convincing. For instance, the nature of the *uti possidetis* principle is controversial: while the Commission suggests that it is a principle formed within the international legal system, it definitely has also roots in national legal systems and is considered by many as part of customary international law. Also, the freedom of maritime communication is often considered as too vague to have received normative force. Moreover, the different understanding of the term 'principles of international law' can also be seen in the title of the 1970 'Friendly Relations Declaration' of the General Assembly entitled 'Principles of *International* Law concerning Friendly Relations and Cooperation among States in accordance with the Charter of the United Nations'.

As the International Court of Justice has confirmed, the principles listed in this resolution belong to customary international law. Austria would be interested to be provided with other examples that might demonstrate the independent normative character of general principles of law formed within the international legal system.

The wording of draft conclusion 2 on recognition leaves it open as what exactly general principles of law must be recognized. We therefore propose to add that they must be recognized 'as such' by the international community. Austria wonders, if such a recognition can take place instantly or would have to evolve over a certain time. Furthermore, we prefer the term 'international community' to 'community of nations' since the term 'nation' has different meanings and is disputed and politically sensitive. In addition, the term 'community of nations' would exclude international organizations and other subjects of international law.

With regard to draft conclusion 4 on the identification of general principles of law derived from national legal systems, we support the view that the transposition of such principles to the international legal system does not require a 'formal or express act', as stated in paragraph 5 of the commentary. As far as the drafting of subparagraph (a) is concerned, we would prefer to speak about 'various *national* legal systems of the world' as in the title of this draft conclusion. The provision would otherwise also include international law.

Draft conclusion 6 on the determination of transposition to the international legal system raises many questions. In particular, the meaning of the phrase 'may be transposed' contains many elements of uncertainty. The compatibility with the international legal system pursuant to draft conclusion 6 seems to be a condition for the recognition as general principle of law as addressed in draft conclusion 2. Since both draft conclusions are closely connected, we suggest to integrate the compatibility test in draft conclusion 2.

With regard to draft conclusion 8 on decisions of courts and tribunals we suggest to use the term 'jurisprudence' instead of 'decisions', since the word 'decision' in general refers to binding acts of courts and tribunals as can be seen inter alia in Article 59 of the Statute of the International Court of Justice. We support that advisory opinions should be covered by that draft conclusion, which is also the intention of the Commission. In the present drafting, however, this is not sufficiently reflected and can only be deduced from the commentary. Furthermore, we suggest that the Commission considers whether bodies other than courts and tribunals empowered to decide disputes, interpret the law authoritatively or render advisory opinions, should also be covered by this draft conclusion.

With regard to draft conclusion 10 on functions of general principles of law, Austria notes that paragraph 1 is phrased as a statement of fact and not as a rule. We are aware of the explanation given in paragraph 3 of the commentary, but question the usefulness of statements of fact in draft conclusions and would rather prefer this conclusion to be drafted in a normative way.

We appreciate the examples given in paragraph 14 of the commentary to draft conclusion 10, however we are not sure to what extent all of these examples amount to general principles of law. Some, like the principle that no one can be judge in his or her own cause or the right to be heard, directly stem from the rule of law and could be regarded as general principles of law. Other examples, however, appear to be dependent on either the context or the applicable procedural rules. In any case, we do not accept *trial in absentia* as a general principle of law, as it is in conflict with the *ordre public* of a number of states.

Draft conclusion 11 on the relationship between general principles of law and treaties and customary international law denies the existence of a hierarchy between the general principles of law and the other sources of international law. However, draft conclusion 10 paragraph 1 creates a different picture as it states that general principles of law are mainly resorted to when other rules of international law do not resolve a particular issue.

This concept seems to exclude the existence of a general principle not in conformity with treaties and customary international law,so that, at least to that extent, some sort of hierarchy seems to exist. On the other hand, the 2006 Report of the Study Group on Fragmentation in International Law stated that '[t]he rules and principles of international law are not in a hierarchical relationship to each other. Nor are the different sources (treaty, custom, general principles of law) ranked in any general order of priority.' It would be helpful if the Commission could further look into this issue.

IV. Judicial decisions/Gerichtsentscheidungen

See also *BB.V.-1.*

V. Opinions of writers/Lehrmeinungen

BB.V.-1.

Work of the International Law Commission on Subsidiary Means for the Determination of Rules of International Law

Arbeit der Völkerrechtskommission der Vereinten Nationen betreffend Hilfsmittel zur Feststellung der völkerrechtlichen Rechtsnormen

On 31 October 2023, the Austrian representative to the 78th Session of the General Assembly delivered the following statement to the Sixth Committee on Report of the International Law Commission on the Work of its 73rd and 74th Session concerning the topic of 'Subsidiary means for the determination of rules of international law':

> […] With regard to the topic 'Subsidiary means for the determination of rules of international law' Austria congratulates Special Rapporteur Charles Jalloh on his first report. […]
>
> As regards draft conclusion 2 on categories of subsidiary means for the determination of rules of international law, Austria remains sceptical about the existence of additional types of subsidiary means as paragraph 5 of the general commentary appears to suggest and as is explicitly mentioned in draft conclusion 2 subparagraph (c) referring to 'any other means generally used to assist in determining international law.' Austria continues to support the view mentioned in the commentary that the existing list of subsidiary means contained in Article 38 paragraph 1 subparagraph (d) of the Statute of the International Court of Justice is sufficiently broad. In any event, we consider that the Special Rapporteur and the Commission would have to make a very cogent case for the existence of additional subsidiary means.
>
> We wonder whether the works of expert bodies and resolutions/decisions of international organizations would be useful candidates for such a third category of subsidiary means. Since the work of expert bodies is usually non-binding, it could be better subsumed under the concept of teachings. As a matter of drafting, we have the impression that subparagraph (c) of draft conclusion 2 is circular and we wonder whether this definition could not be refined.
>
> With regard to subparagraph (a) of draft conclusion 2, we appreciate the idea to cover the entire jurisprudence of courts and tribunals under this provision, but we are uncertain whether the change from 'judicial decisions' to 'decisions of courts and tribunals' achieves this goal in a satisfactory manner. In our view, a

decisive criterion should be whether any third-party dispute settlement institution is empowered to decide disputes, interpret the law authoritatively or render advisory opinions. However, even other bodies not qualifying as courts or tribunals might be empowered to do so, and should thus be included which could be easier achieved by referring to 'jurisprudence of courts and tribunals and other bodies'.

In this context, we should consider the reference in paragraph 6 of the comment to draft conclusion 2 to the views of the UN Human Rights Committee. As is generally known, the UN Human Rights Committee is not a court or tribunal empowered to decide cases, but can only issue legally non-binding views.

Austria agrees in substance with paragraph 14 of the comment to draft conclusion 2, i.e. that the representativeness of teachings is an important aspect. We wonder though why paragraph 14 refers to draft conclusion 5. It seems that the question of representativeness is addressed much more prominently in the current draft conclusion 3.

Let me turn to the suggested draft conclusion 3 on general criteria for the assessment of subsidiary means for the determination of rules of international law, containing a list of criteria relevant for the assessment of the value of subsidiary means for the determination of rules of international law. While Austria generally agrees with the criteria mentioned therein, it considers that subparagraph (b) on 'the quality of the reasoning' should be regarded as the paramount aspect that should be mentioned first. As much as Austria appreciates a reference to the reception by states, it doubts whether this is really a crucial aspect in assessing the weight of subsidiary means. At least it seems that like in subparagraph (f) the introductory phrase 'where applicable' should be inserted as well.

CC. The law of treaties/Recht der Verträge

CC.-1

Inclusion of the topic of Non-Legally Binding International Agreements in the Work of the International Law Commission

Aufnahme des Themas nicht rechtsverbindlicher internationaler Abkommen in die Arbeit der Völkerrechtskommission

On 23 October 2023, the Austrian representative to the 78th Session of the General Assembly delivered the following statement to the Sixth Committee on Report of the International Law Commission on the Work of its 73rd and 74th Session concerning the inclusion of the topic of 'Non-legally binding international agreements' in the Work of the International Law Commission:

Austria welcomes the decision of the Commission to address the issue of non-legally binding international instruments. We propose, however, not to refer to 'non-legally binding international *agreements*' as the title of the topic currently reads, but to 'non-legally binding international *instruments*' as the term 'agreement' should be reserved exclusively for legally binding documents. A similar decision to change the title from 'agreements' to 'instruments' has been taken by the Committee of Legal Advisers on Public International Law (CAHDI) of the Council of Europe.

I. Conclusion and entry into force of treaties/Abschluß und Inkrafttreten völkerrechtlicher Verträge

2. Reservations and declarations/Vorbehalte und Erklärungen

CC.I.2.-1

Objection to the declaration of Ukraine to the Convention on Preventing and Combating Violence against Women and Domestic Violence

Protest gegen die Erklärung Ukraines zum Übereinkommen des Europarats zur Verhütung und Bekämpfung von Gewalt gegen Frauen und häuslicher Gewalt

On 20 July 2023, Austria submitted to the Secretariat of the Council of Europe a *note verbale* containing an objection to the declaration of Ukraine to the Convention on Preventing and Combating Violence against Women and Domestic Violence made upon ratifying the Convention on 18 July 2022:[1]

> The Government of Austria has carefully examined the declaration made by Ukraine upon ratification of the Council of Europe Convention on preventing and combating violence against women and domestic violence on 18 July 2022.
>
> Austria considers the declaration to amount to a reservation, because it aims to apply the obligations of the Convention as determined by the Constitution of Ukraine and the Family Code of Ukraine.
>
> This reservation is not permissible in accordance with Article 78, paragraph 1, of the Convention that permits reservations to this Convention only with regard to a limited and specified number of articles.

---

[1] The relevant part of the declaration reads as follows: 'Ukraine declares that it will apply the Convention in accordance with the values, principles and norms within the limits determined by the Constitution of Ukraine, in particular with regard to the protection of human rights and fundamental freedoms, equality of the rights and opportunities of women and men, gender identity, the formation of responsible motherhood and fatherhood, the support of family and the protection of childhood.', available at <www.coe.int/en/web/conventions/full-list?module=declarations-by-treaty&numSte=210&codeNature=0> accessed on 2 March 2025.

> Furthermore, Austria also considers that by referring to the principles and provisions of the Constitution of Ukraine and the Ukrainian Family Code, Ukraine has made a reservation of a general and indeterminate scope. This reservation does not clearly define for the other States Parties to the Convention the extent to which the reserving State has accepted the obligations of the Convention.
>
> Austria therefore considers the reservation incompatible with the object and purpose of the Convention and objects to it. This objection does not preclude the entry into force of the Convention between the Republic of Austria and Ukraine.

II. Observance, application and interpretation of treaties/ Einhaltung, Anwendung und Auslegung von Verträgen

2. Application of treaties/Anwendung von Verträgen

CC.II.2-1

Austrian note verbale on the territorial application of the bilateral investment treaty between Austria and the Russian Federation

Österreichische Verbalnote zur territorialen Anwendung des bilateralen Investitionsabkommens zwischen Österreich und der Russischen Föderation

On 21 August 2023 the Austrian Embassy in Moscow received a *note verbale* from the Russian Federation, which stated that the Austria-Russia BIT (1990)[2] applied to the annexed territories of Ukraine, including Crimea, Luhansk and Donetsk. In response a *note verbale* was addressed to the Russian Foreign Ministry:

> The Republic of Austria considers that as regards the territorial scope of the Agreement between the Republic of Austria and the Union of Socialist Soviet Republics on the promotion and mutual protection of investments, signed on 8 February 1990 in Moscow, the territory of the Russian Federation corresponds to the one as recognised internationally in line with UNGA Resolution 68/262 of 27 March 2014 on the territorial integrity of Ukraine and UNGA Resolution ES 11/4 of 12 October 2022 on Territorial integrity of Ukraine: defending the principles of the Charter of the United Nations.[3]

---

[2] Abkommen zwischen der Republik Österreich und der Union der Sozialistischen Sowjetrepubliken über die Förderung und den gegenseitigen Schutz von Investitionen samt Notenwechsel, Federal Law Gazette III No 387/1991 as amended by Federal Law Gazette III No 257/1994.

[3] Reproduced in Helmut Tichy *et al*, 'Recent Austrian Practice in the Field of International Law Report for 2023' (2024) 78(1) Zeitschrift für öffentliches Recht 169, 177.

3. Interpretation of treaties/Auslegung von Verträgen

See *NN.II.7.a.-2.*

IV. Invalidity, termination and suspension of operation of treaties/ Ungültigkeit, Beendigung und Suspendierung von Verträgen

3. Termination and suspension of operation of treaties including denunciation and withdrawal/Beendigung und Suspendierung von Verträgen, einschließlich der Kündigung von Verträgen und des Rücktritts vom Vertrag

CC.IV.3.-1

Enquiry concerning the suspension of the double taxation agreement by the Russian Federation

Anfrage betreffend der Aussetzung Doppelbesteuerungsabkommen durch die Russische Föderation

On 4 October 2023, a number of representatives of the Austrian National Assembly raised a parliamentary enquiry to the Federal Minister concerning the unilateral suspension of double taxation agreements by the Russian Federation,[4] to which the Minister gave, *inter alia*, the following response on 3 December 2023:[5]

> [...] On the basis of a decree, various provisions of the [Austrian-Russian] double taxation agreement (DTA) were suspended by way of a Russian note verbale, since Austria – along with numerous other states – was considered an 'unfriendly state' by Russia. Accordingly, the application of the following provisions is suspended: Art. 5-22, 24, 26.1 and 26.2 of the DTA and also point 1, the provision 'In addition to Art. 5', the provision 'In addition to Art. 6', the provision 'In addition to Art. 7', the provision 'In addition to Art. 7 and 9', and the provision 'In addition to Art. 25' of the protocol of the DTA.
>
> The DTA itself does not provide for the suspension of individual provisions of the DTA. Termination in accordance with Art. 29 DTA can only be made by 30 June of each calendar year at the latest for it to take effect from 1 January of the following calendar year. The DTA has not yet been terminated. [...]
>
> Since the DTA itself does not contain any provisions on the suspension of individual or all provisions of the treaty, the lawfulness of the suspension must be assessed in accordance with the Vienna Convention on the Law of Treaties (VCLT)

4 Parliamentary Materials, 16438/J (XXVII. GP).

5 Parliamentary Materials, 15903/AB (XXVII. GP).

applicable here (Federal Law Gazette III No. 40/1980; Austria and Russia are parties to the treaty).

According to the principles of international law, a treaty can be suspended if, for example, there is a material breach of the treaty by the other contracting party or in the event of a fundamental change of circumstances existing at the time the treaty was concluded that was not foreseen by the treaty parties. In the absence of a material breach, the suspension of individual provisions of the DTA by Russia can be regarded as contrary to the treaty and international law of the DTA by Austria.

After Russia unlawfully ceased to apply the above-mentioned parts of the DTA with immediate effect, the decision was made that the suspended provisions of the agreement will also no longer be applied by Austria in the future following expiry of the relevant deadlines under the law of treaties. […]

The relevant parts of the German original read as follows:

[...] Auf Basis eines Dekrets wurden im Wege einer russischen Verbalnote diverse Bestimmungen des Doppelbesteuerungsabkommens (DBA) suspendiert, da Österreich – neben zahlreichen anderen Staaten – auf russischer Seite als „unfreundlicher Staat“ gewertet wurde. Demgemäß wird die Anwendung folgender Bestimmungen ausgesetzt: Art. 5-22, 24, 26.1 und 26.2 des DBA und ebenso Punkt 1, die Bestimmung „In Ergänzung zu Art. 5“, die Bestimmung „In Ergänzung zu Art. 6“, die Bestimmung „In Ergänzung zu Art. 7“, die Bestimmung „In Ergänzung zu den Art. 7 und 9“, und die Bestimmung „In Ergänzung zu Art. 25“ des Protokolls des DBA.

Eine Aussetzung einzelner Bestimmungen des DBA ist im DBA selbst nicht vorgesehen. Eine Kündigung gemäß Art. 29 DBA kann immer nur bis spätestens 30. Juni jedes Kalenderjahres erfolgen, um ab 1. Jänner des darauffolgenden Kalenderjahres wirksam zu werden. Das DBA wurde bisher nicht gekündigt. […]

Da das DBA selbst keine Bestimmungen über die Suspendierung einzelner oder aller Bestimmungen des Vertrags enthält, ist die Rechtmäßigkeit der Suspendierung nach der hier anwendbaren Wiener Vertragsrechtskonvention (WVK) zu beurteilen (BGBl. III Nr. 40/1980; Österreich und Russland sind Vertragsparteien). Nach den Grundsätzen des Völkerrechts kann ein Vertrag suspendiert werden, wenn etwa eine erhebliche Vertragsverletzung durch die andere Vertragspartei erfolgt oder im Fall einer grundlegenden Änderung der beim Vertragsabschluss gegebenen Umstände, die von den Vertragsparteien nicht vorausgesehen wurde. Die Suspendierung einzelner Bestimmungen des DBA durch Russland kann mangels erheblicher Verletzung des DBA durch Österreich als vertrags- und völkerrechtswidrig angesehen werden.

Nachdem Russland die oben genannten Teile des DBA in rechtswidriger Weise mit sofortiger Wirkung nicht mehr angewandt hat, wurde die Entscheidung getroffen, dass die suspendierten Bestimmungen des Abkommens nach Ablauf der maßgeblichen Fristen des Völkervertragsrechts auch von österreichischer Seite künftig nicht mehr angewandt werden. [...]

V. Depositaries, notifications, corrections and registration/Depositär, Notifikationen, Berichtigungen und Registrierung

CC.V.1

Austrian Statement on the Role of Depositaries

Österreichische Erklärung zur Rolle der Depositäre

On behalf of Austria, Brazil, Italy and Singapore, Argentina delivered a joint statement at the Session of the General Assembly Sixth Committee on Agenda Item 87 'Strengthening and Promoting the International Treaty Framework' on 18 October 2023 addressing the role of depositaries:

> […] 5. The practice of designating a 'depositary' of multilateral treaties came into being as a result of the increasing number of parties to multilateral agreements. In the past, only States were depositaries. However, with the establishment first of the League of Nations and later of the United Nations and its specialized agencies, these and other organizations have been increasingly entrusted with depositary functions.
>
> 6. The depositary is required to act impartially in the performance of its functions. The functions of the depositary are in principle related to the reception, formal review, transmission and storage of communications and acts of current or future States parties. The depositary may also examine the compliance with the formal requirements that States have to meet about a particular act. However, it is not for the depositary to adjudicate on the validity of the acts submitted to it. This competency lies exclusively with the States Parties. It is important to highlight the apolitical role ascribed to depositaries under established international treaty law.
>
> 7. While each organisation that performs the duty of depositary of multilateral treaties has developed a certain practice, depositaries should always be guided by the relevant provisions of the 1969 Vienna Convention on the Law of Treaties reflecting customary international law.
>
> 8. The UN Secretary-General is – by far – the most important depositary of multilateral treaties. Over six hundred multilateral treaties are deposited with the Secretary-General. The complex requirements relating to these treaties and the interaction with the many states that may undertake treaty actions with regard to them have significantly influenced and enriched his practice.
>
> We acknowledge – and value – that the UN Secretary-General, apart from performing the core depositary functions, engages in tasks that have modernized and expanded the traditional depositary role. The UN Secretary-General, through the Office of Legal Affairs, advises Member States on questions of treaty law and participation in the elaboration of new treaties, and promotes dissemination of UN treaties, including through treaty events. All these activities strengthen the international treaty framework. […]

VI. Consensual arrangements, other than in treaty-form/ Willensübereinkünfte in anderer Form

See *EE.I.5.-2.*

DD. Relationship between international law and internal law/ Völkerrecht und innerstaatliches Recht

See *EE.I.5.-2.*

EE. Subjects of International law/Völkerrechtssubjekte

I. States/Staaten

1. Status and powers/Status und Befugnisse

b. Sovereignty and independence/Souveränität und Unabhängigkeit

See *CC.II.2.-1*, *PP.I.-1*, *PP.I.-2*, and *PP.I.-3.*

2. Recognition/Anerkennung

b. Recognition of governments/Anerkennung von Regierungen

See *FF.VIII.-2, FF.VIII.-6, and GG.VI.-1.*

4. Formation, continuity, succession and extinction of States/ Entstehung von Staaten, Kontinuität, Staatennachfolge und Untergang von Staaten

d. Extinctions/Untergang von Staaten

bb. Effects of State succession/Rechtliche Folgen der Staatennachfolge

vii. Responsibility/Staatenverantwortlichkeit

EE.I.4.d.bb.vii.-1

International Law Commission Report on Succession of States in Respect of State Responsibility

Völkerrechtskommissionsbericht betreffend Nachfolge von Staaten in Bezug auf Staatenverantwortlichkeit

On 31 October 2023, the Austrian representative to the 78th Session of the General Assembly delivered the following statement to the Sixth Committee on Report of the International Law Commission on the Work of its 73rd and 74th Session concerning the topic of 'Succession of states in respect of state responsibility':

> […] Before addressing the substance of this topic, Austria wishes to express its appreciation to the former Special Rapporteur, Professor Pavel Šturma, for his dedication and hard work on this topic, which was clearly one where it was very difficult to reach consensus.
>
> With regard to the consideration of the topic during the last session, Austria welcomes the idea expressed in the Commission to produce a report on the topic. In our opinion, it would be most valuable to have a report outlining the scarce but important practice in this field and analysing the legal problems involved. We therefore agree with the decision of the Commission to establish a working group considering the next steps. Austria would very much welcome if the work on this topic could be speedily finalised next year by a report of the Commission.
>
> […]

5. Self-determination/Selbstbestimmung

EE.I.5.-1

Enquiry concerning the autonomy of South Tyrol

Anfrage betreffend die Autonomie Südtirols

On 2 November 2022, a number of representatives of the Austrian National Assembly raised a parliamentary enquiry to the Federal Minister for European and International Affairs concerning a joint declaration by Austria and Morocco on migration and asylum policy,[6] to which the Minister replied on 2 January 2023:[7]

> The increase in South Tyrol's competences since 1992 arises from the implementation of provisions of the Second Autonomy Statute of 1972, on ordinary legislative provisions at the state and regional level, and on the reorganisation

6 Parliamentary Materials, 12804/J (XXVII. GP).

7 Parliamentary Materials, 14000/AB (XXVII. GP).

of the distribution of competences between the state, regions, and provinces as a result of the Italian constitutional reform of 2001. The loss or restriction of South Tyrolean autonomy competences since 1992, on the other hand, is largely due to a line of jurisprudence developed by the Italian Constitutional Court on the basis of the revision of the Italian constitution in 2001 regarding state 'cross-cutting competences'. […]

The relevant parts of the German original read as follows:

[…] Der Zuwachs an Kompetenzen Südtirols seit dem Jahr 1992 beruht auf Durchführungsbestimmungen auf Basis des 2. Autonomiestatuts von 1972, auf einfachgesetzlichen Bestimmungen auf Staats- und Regionsebene sowie auf der Neuordnung der Kompetenzverteilung zwischen Staat, Regionen und Provinzen durch die italienische Verfassungsreform 2001. Der Verlust beziehungsweise die Einschränkung von Südtiroler Autonomiekompetenzen seit 1992 hingegen ist in einem erheblichen Ausmaß auf eine Rechtssprechungslinie zurückzuführen, die der italienische Verfassungsgerichtshof auf Basis der Revision der italienischen Verfassung im Jahr 2001 zu staatlichen „Querschnittskompetenzen“ entwickelt hat. […]

EE.I.5.-2

Enquiry concerning the joint declaration by Austria and Morocco on migration and asylum policy

Anfrage betreffend die gemeinsame Erklärung von Österreich und Marokko zur Migrations- und Asylpolitik

On 8 March 2023, a number of representatives of the Austrian National Assembly raised a parliamentary enquiry to the Federal Minister for European and International Affairs concerning a joint declaration by Austria and Morocco on migration and asylum policy,[8] to which the Minister replied on 8 May 2023:[9]

[…] The document is a joint declaration by the Federal Chancellor of the Republic of Austria and the Prime Minister of the Kingdom of Morocco, which was published at a joint press conference during the working visit to Morocco. [...] Parliament was not consulted, as this is not provided for in cases of a joint declaration that is not legally binding. […]

Austria's position on the Western Sahara conflict remains unchanged. Austria continues to support a just, lasting, and mutually acceptable political solution within the framework of the United Nations (UN) and on the basis of international law, including all UN Security Council resolutions on the issue. Austria supports the mandate of the Special Envoy for Western Sahara, Staffan de Mistura, and has

8 Parliamentary Materials, 14484/J (XXVII. GP).

9 Parliamentary Materials, 12561/AB (XXVII. GP).

been contributing to the UN mission for the preparation of a referendum on the status of Western Sahara (MINURSO) for years. In this context, Austria regards the autonomy plan presented by Morocco in 2007 as a serious and credible contribution to the UN-led political process and as a possible basis for a solution agreed by the parties themselves. The last meeting between the Head of the BMEIA's 'Middle East and North Africa Division; EU Southern Neighbourhood Policy' and representatives of the Frente Polisario took place on 8 November 2022.

The relevant parts of the German original read as follows:

Bei dem Dokument handelt es sich um eine gemeinsame Erklärung des Bundeskanzlers der Republik Österreich und des Premierministers des Königsreichs Marokko, welche im Rahmen einer gemeinsamen Pressekonferenz während des Arbeitsbesuches in Marokko veröffentlicht wurde. […] Das Parlament wurde nicht befasst, da bei einer nicht rechtsverbindlichen gemeinsamen Erklärung dies nicht vorgesehen ist. […]

Die Position Österreichs zum Westsahara-Konflikt ist unverändert. Österreich unterstützt weiterhin eine gerechte, dauerhafte und für beide Seiten akzeptable politische Lösung im Rahmen der Vereinten Nationen (VN) und auf Basis des Völkerrechts inklusive aller Resolutionen des VN-Sicherheitsrats zum Thema. Österreich unterstützt das Mandat des Sondergesandten für die Westsahara, Staffan de Mistura, und leistet seit Jahren einen Beitrag durch Entsendungen an die VN-Mission zur Vorbereitung eines Referendums über den Status der Westsahara (MINURSO). In diesem Kontext betrachtet Österreich den 2007 von Marokko vorgelegten Autonomieplan als einen ernsthaften und glaubwürdigen Beitrag zum VN-geführten politischen Prozess und als eine mögliche Grundlage für eine von den Parteien selbst vereinbarte Lösung. Das letzte Gespräch zwischen dem Leiter der Abteilung „Naher und Mittlerer Osten und Nordafrika; Südliche Nachbarschaftspolitik der EU" des BMEIA und Vertreterinnen und Vertretern der Frente Polisario fand am 8. November 2022 statt.

[…]

II. International organisations/Internationale Organisationen

EE.II.-1

Agreement between the Austrian Federal Government and the International Vaccine Institute on the Legal Status of the International Vaccine Institute in Austria

Abkommen zwischen der Österreichischen Bundesregierung und dem Internationalen Impfstoffinstitut über die Rechtsstellung des Internationalen Impfstoffinstituts in Österreich

On 14 December 2022, the Austrian Federal Government and the International Vaccine Institute signed an Agreement on the Legal Status of the International Vaccine Institute in Austria which entered into force on 1 April 2023:[10]

PREAMBLE

The Austrian Federal Government (hereinafter referred to as the 'Government') and the International Vaccine Institute (hereinafter referred to as 'the Institute')

CONSIDERING that cooperative efforts in the area of research and development of vaccines needed in developing countries will contribute to the goals of promoting the wide availability of safe, effective, and affordable vaccines for infants and young children and to the public sector of developing countries;

NOTING that the Institute has established an office in Vienna;

CONVINCED that the establishment of such an office will facilitate collaboration between Austrian partners and the Institute in the research and development of vaccines for global health;

DESIRING to define the status, privileges and immunities of such office in the Republic of Austria and to enable the office and its officials to fulfil its purposes and functions;

HAVE AGREED as follows:

Article 1

DEFINITIONS

For the purpose of this Agreement:

(a) 'Authorities' means such federal, regional, municipal or other authorities in the Republic of Austria as may be appropriate in the context, and in accordance with the laws and customs applicable in the Republic of Austria;

(b) 'Head of the Office' means the head of the office of the Institute in Vienna;

(c) 'Officials of the Institute' means all members of the staff of the office of the Institute in Vienna, except those who are both locally recruited and assigned to hourly rates;

(d) 'Official Visitor' means members of the Board of Trustees of the Institute, representatives of the Institute´s Member States and international organizations co-operating with the Institute as well as participants in the Institute's programs and other persons invited to the Institute on official business.

Article 2

LEGAL CAPACITY

The Government recognizes the legal personality of the Institute as an international organization. The Institute shall possess the legal capacity to conclude treaties, to contract, to acquire and dispose of immovable and movable property, to

---

10 Federal Law Gazette III No 54/2023.

institute and respond to legal proceedings and to take such other action as may be necessary or useful for its purpose and activities.

Article 3

PREMISES

(1) The premises of the office of the Institute in Vienna shall comprise the land, installations and offices that the Institute occupies for its activities. Its area shall be defined by common understanding between the Government and the Institute.

(2) Any further office and conference premises in or outside of Vienna used with the agreement of the Government for meetings convened by the Institute shall be deemed temporarily to form part of the premises.

(3) The Authorities shall exercise due diligence to ensure that the tranquillity of the premises is not disturbed by any person or group of persons attempting unauthorized entry.

Article 4

INVIOLABILITY OF PREMISES

(1) The premises of the Institute shall be inviolable. No officer or official of the Republic of Austria, or other person exercising any public authority within the Republic of Austria, may enter the premises to perform any duties except with the consent of, and under conditions approved by, the Head of the Office. However, in the event of fire or other such emergency, such consent shall be deemed to have been given if immediate protective measures are required. (2) Except as otherwise provided in this Agreement and subject to the power of the Institute to make regulations, the laws and regulations of the Republic of Austria shall apply within the premises.

(3) Instruments issued by Authorities may be served at the premises.

(4) The Institute shall be entitled to display its flag and emblem on the premises of the Institute when possible.

Article 5

IMMUNITY FROM JURISDICTION AND OTHER ACTIONS

(1) The Institute shall enjoy immunity from jurisdiction and enforcement, except:

(a) to the extent that the Institute shall have expressly waived such immunity in a particular case;

(b) in the case of civil action brought by a third party for damage resulting from an accident caused by a motor vehicle belonging to, or operated on behalf of, the Institute, or in respect of any infringement of laws and regulations governing the keeping, operation and use of motor vehicles;

(c) in the case of attachment, pursuant to a decision by the judicial authorities, of the salary, emoluments or indemnities owed by the Institute to an employee of the Institute, unless the Institute informs the Authorities within 14 days of the date on which it is notified of said decision by the Authorities that it does not waive its immunity.

(2) Without prejudice to paragraph 1, the property and assets of the Institute, wherever situated, shall be immune from any form of seizure, confiscation, expropriation and sequestration or any other form of judicial or administrative restraint.

(3) Any dispute between the Institute and a private party shall be finally settled by a tribunal composed of a single arbitrator appointed by the Secretary General of the Permanent Court of Arbitration in accordance with the relevant Optional Rules for Arbitration Involving International Organizations and Private Parties. The tribunal shall decide a dispute in accordance with such rules of law as may be agreed by the parties. In the absence of such agreement, the tribunal shall apply such rules of international law and general principles of law as may be applicable. Matters concerning the interpretation of the Agreement on the Establishment of the International Vaccine Institute, including the Constitution appended thereto, shall not be within the competence of the tribunal. Employment disputes between the Institute and its employees shall be settled by an effective dispute resolution mechanism that protects the rights of the employees in accordance with the European Convention on Human Rights, pursuant to the Institute´s internal regulations.

Article 6

INVIOLABILITY OF ARCHIVES

All the correspondence, documents, computer data, manuscripts, still and motion pictures, films and sound recordings, belonging to or held by the Institute in furtherance of its constitutional aims shall be inviolable, wherever located.

Article 7

COMMUNICATIONS

(1) The Government shall ensure that the Institute is able to send and receive communications in connection with its official activities without censorship or other interference.

(2) The Institute shall enjoy in the Republic of Austria, for its official communications and the transfer of all its documents, treatment not less advantageous to the Institute than the most favourable treatment accorded by the Republic of Austria to any international organization, in the matter of priorities, rates and surcharges on all forms of communication.

Article 8

FREEDOM FROM TAXATION AND CUSTOMS DUTIES

The Institute, its assets, income and other property shall be exempt:

(a) from all direct taxes; it is understood, however, that the Institute shall not claim exemption from taxes which are in fact no more than charges for public utility services;

(b) from all indirect taxes included in the prices of goods or services supplied to the Institute; these taxes shall be refunded to the Institute insofar as Austrian law makes provision to that effect for foreign diplomatic missions;

(c) from customs duties and other charges provided these are not simply charges for public utility services and prohibitions and restrictions on imports and exports in respect of articles, including motor vehicles and spare parts thereof, imported or exported by the Institute for its official use; it is understood, however, that articles imported under such exemption shall not be ceded or transferred by the Institute to third parties in the Republic of Austria within two years of their importation or acquisition;

(d) from all customs duties and quantitative restrictions on imports and exports in respect of its publications;

(e) from all taxes, recording charges and court fees in respect of all transactions to which the Institute is a party and all documents recording such transactions;

(f) from the obligation to pay employer's contributions to the Family Burden Equalization Fund or an instrument with equivalent objectives.

Article 9

FINANCIAL FACILITIES

Without being restricted by financial controls, regulations or moratoria of any kind, the

Institute may:

(a) purchase and receive through authorized channels, hold and dispose of any currencies or securities;

(b) open and operate bank accounts in any currency;

(c) transfer its funds, securities and currencies to, from or within the Republic of Austria.

Article 10

SOCIAL SECURITY

(1) The Institute and Officials of the Institute shall be exempt from all compulsory contributions to any social security scheme in the Republic of Austria.

(2) Officials of the Institute shall have the right to participate in any branch of the social insurance (health, accident and pension insurance) as well as in the unemployment insurance. This insurance shall have the same legal effect as a compulsory insurance.

(3) Officials of the Institute may avail themselves of the right under paragraph 2 by submitting a written declaration within three months after entry into force of this Agreement or within three months after taking up their assignment with the Institute.

(4) Insurance under paragraph 2 in the selected branch shall take effect with the date of taking up the assignment with the Institute, provided the declaration is submitted within seven business days after entry into force of this Agreement or after the date of taking up the assignment, otherwise on the day following the day of submission of the declaration.

(5) Insurance shall cease on the date on which the assignment with the Institute terminates.

(6) Throughout the duration of the insurance, Officials of the Institute shall be responsible for the payment of the entire contributions to Österreichische Gesundheitskasse.

(7) The declarations required to be made by an Official of the Institute under paragraph 3 shall be transmitted by the Institute on behalf of the Official of the Institute to Österreichische Gesundheitskasse. Upon request, the Institute shall provide Österreichische Gesundheitskasse with the information necessary for the implementation of the insurance.

Article 11

TRANSIT AND RESIDENCE

(1) The Government, in accordance with Austrian law, shall take all necessary measures to facilitate the entry into, and sojourn in, the Republic of Austria of the persons listed below, shall allow them to leave the Republic of Austria without interference and shall ensure that they can travel unimpeded to or from the premises, affording them any necessary protection when so travelling:

(a) Officials of the Institute and members of their family forming part of their household;

(b) Official Visitors.

(2) Visas which may be required by persons referred to in paragraph 1 shall be granted free of charge and as promptly as possible, in accordance with Austrian law.

(3) No activity performed by any person referred to in paragraph 1 in their official capacity with respect to the Institute shall constitute a reason for preventing their entry into, or departure from, the Republic of Austria.

(4) The Republic of Austria shall be entitled to require reasonable evidence to establish that persons claiming the rights granted by this Article fall within the categories described in paragraph 1, and to require compliance in a reasonable manner with quarantine and health regulations.

Article 12

OFFICIALS OF THE INSTITUTE

(1) Officials of the Institute shall enjoy, within and with respect to the Republic of Austria, the following privileges and immunities:

(a) immunity from jurisdiction in respect of words spoken or written and all acts performed by them in their official capacity; this immunity shall continue to apply even after the persons concerned have ceased to be Officials of the Institute;

(b) immunity from the seizure of their personal and official baggage;

(c) inviolability of all official documents, data and other material;

(d) exemption from taxation in respect of the salaries, emoluments including allowances, remunerations, indemnities and pensions paid to them by the Institute in connection with their service with it. This exemption shall extend also to assistance given to the families of Officials of the Institute;

(e) exemption from any form of taxation on income derived by them and by members of their families forming part of their household from sources outside the Republic of Austria;

(f) exemption from inheritance and gift taxes, except with respect to immovable property located in the Republic of Austria, insofar as such arise solely from the fact that Officials of the Institute or members of their families forming part of their household reside or maintain their usual domicile in the Republic of Austria;

(g) exemption from immigration restrictions and from registration formalities for themselves and members of their families forming part of their household;

(h) freedom to acquire or maintain within the Republic of Austria foreign securities, foreign currency accounts, other movable property and, under the same conditions as Austrian nationals, immovable property;

(i) the right to import for personal use, free of duty and other charges, provided these are not simply charges for public utility services, and exempt from economic import prohibitions and restrictions on imports and exports:

(i) their furniture and effects in one or more separate consignments when taking up their assignment, and necessary additions to the same within six months thereafter;

(ii) one motor vehicle every four years;

(j) the same protection and repatriation facilities with respect to themselves and members of their families forming part of their household as are accorded in time of international crises to members, having comparable rank, of the staffs of chiefs of diplomatic missions accredited to the Republic of Austria;

(k) access to the labour market for members of their families forming part of their household in accordance with Austrian law.

(2) Officials of the Institute and members of their families forming part of their household to whom this agreement applies shall not be entitled to payments out of the Family Burden Equalization Fund or an instrument with equivalent objectives. This provision shall not apply to Austrian nationals, to persons of other nationality granted equivalent status by European Union legislation, or to stateless persons with permanent residence in Austria.

Article 13

HEAD OF THE OFFICE

In addition to the privileges and immunities specified in Article 12, the Head of the Office as well as, during his or her absence from duty, the Official of the Institute acting on behalf of the Head of the Office, shall be accorded the privileges and immunities, exemptions and facilities accorded to heads of diplomatic missions, provided they are not Austrian nationals or permanent residents of the Republic of Austria.

Article 14

OFFICIAL VISITORS

(1) Official Visitors shall enjoy the following privileges and immunities:

(a) immunity from jurisdiction in respect of words spoken or written and all acts performed by them in their official capacity; this immunity shall continue to apply even after the persons concerned have ceased to be Official Visitors;

(b) immunity from the seizure of their personal and official baggage;

(c) inviolability of all official documents, data and other material;

(d) the exchange facilities necessary for the transfer of their emoluments and expenses.

(2) Where the incidence of any form of taxation depends upon residence, periods during which Official Visitors may be present in the Republic of Austria for the discharge of their duties shall not be considered as periods of residence. In particular, Official Visitors shall be exempt from taxation on their emoluments and expenses paid by the Institute during such periods of duty.

Article 15

NOTIFICATION AND IDENTITY CARDS

(1) The Institute shall communicate to the Authorities a list of the Officials of the Institute and shall revise such list from time to time as may be necessary.

(2) The Government shall issue to the Officials of the Institute and members of their families forming part of their household an identity card bearing the photograph of the holder in accordance with Austrian law. This card shall serve to identify the holder vis-à-vis the Authorities.

Article 16

AUSTRIAN NATIONALS AND PERMANENT RESIDENTS OF THE REPUBLIC OF AUSTRIA

Austrian nationals and persons who are permanently resident in Austria shall enjoy only the privileges and immunities specified in Article 10, Article 12 (1) (a), (b), (c) and (d) and Article 14 (1) (a), (b) and (c).

Article 17

PURPOSE OF PRIVILEGES AND IMMUNITIES

(1) The privileges and immunities provided for in this Agreement are not designed to give personal advantages to the persons to whom they are accorded. They are granted solely to ensure that the Institute is able to perform its official activities unimpeded at all times and that the persons to whom they are accorded have complete independence. The Institute shall engage to encourage its officials to comply with their legal obligations.

(2) The Institute shall waive immunity where it considers that such immunity would impede the normal course of justice and that it can be waived without prejudicing the interests of the Institute.

Article 18

SETTLEMENT OF DISPUTES

Unless the Parties decide otherwise, any dispute concerning the interpretation or application of the present Agreement which cannot be settled by negotiation shall be submitted to arbitration by a tribunal composed of a single arbitrator appointed by the Secretary General of the Permanent Court of Arbitration in accordance with the relevant Optional Rules for Arbitration Involving International Organizations and States, as in force on the date of signature of this Agreement. Such arbitration shall be final and binding. Each Party may however request the Secretary General of the Permanent Court of Arbitration to immediately appoint such an arbitrator to examine a request for provisional measures to protect its rights under the present Agreement. The place of arbitration shall be Vienna and the language to be used in the proceedings of the tribunal shall be English.

Article 19

MOST-FAVOURED ORGANIZATION

If and to the extent that the Government shall enter into any agreement with a comparable intergovernmental organization having its seat in Austria containing terms or conditions more favourable to that organization than similar terms or conditions of this Agreement, the Government shall extend such more favourable terms or conditions to the Institute, by means of a supplemental agreement.

Article 20

ENTRY INTO FORCE AND DURATION OF THE AGREEMENT

(1) This Agreement shall be concluded for an indefinite period. It shall enter into force on the first day of the month after the Government and the Institute have informed each other of the completion of the procedures required, for each of them, to be bound by it.

(2) The provisions of the present Agreement shall take effect as of 1 November 2022.

(3) This Agreement may be terminated by either Party by giving written notice to the other. It shall cease to be in force six months after the date of receipt of such notice.

EE.II.-2

Agreement between the Austrian Federal Government and the Permanent Court of Arbitration on the Legal Status of the Permanent Court of Arbitration in Austria

Abkommen zwischen der Österreichischen Bundesregierung und dem Ständigen Schiedshof über die Rechtsstellung des Ständigen Schiedshofs in Österreich

On 22 December 2022, the Austrian Federal Government and the Permanent Court of Arbitration signed an Agreement on the Legal Status of Permanent Court of Arbitration in Austria which entered into force on 1 June 2023:[11]

PREAMBLE

The Austrian Federal Government (hereinafter referred to as the 'Government') and the Permanent Court of Arbitration (hereinafter referred to as the 'PCA')

CONSIDERING that

International arbitration is a preferred means for the peaceful resolution of international disputes;

The PCA was established by the 1899 Convention for the Pacific Settlement of International Disputes (the '1899 Convention') at the first Hague Peace Conference, which was convened 'with the object of seeking the most objective means of ensuring to all peoples the benefits of a real and lasting peace';

The 1899 Convention was revised by the 1907 Convention for the Pacific Settlement of International Disputes (the '1907 Convention'), adopted at the second Hague Peace Conference;

In the 1899 and 1907 Conventions, the Contracting Parties undertook to maintain the PCA accessible at all times, as a global institution for the settlement of international disputes through third-party intervention;

To further the objectives of the 1899 and 1907 Conventions, it is material that Member States in all regions of the world enjoy access to international dispute resolution services provided by the PCA;

The Republic of Austria is a Contracting Party to the 1899 and 1907 Conventions, and the Secretary-General of the PCA has invited the Republic of Austria to become a host country for arbitration, mediation, conciliation, and fact-finding commissions of inquiry administered by the PCA and of an office of the PCA in Vienna; and

11 Federal Law Gazette III No 57/2023.

The Government has accepted the invitation of the Secretary-General of the PCA;

HAVE AGREED as follows:

Article 1

DEFINITIONS

For the purpose of this Agreement:

(a) 'Authorities' means such federal, regional, municipal or other authorities in the Republic of Austria as may be appropriate in the context, and in accordance with the laws and customs applicable in the Republic of Austria;

(b) 'Head of the Office' means the head of the office of the PCA in Vienna;

(c) 'Officials of the PCA' means all members of the staff of the PCA, except those who are both locally recruited and assigned to hourly rates;

(d) 'PCA Adjudicator' means any arbitrator, mediator, conciliator, or member of a commission of inquiry taking part in a hearing, meeting, or other activity in relation to PCA Proceedings;

(e) 'PCA Proceedings' means any dispute resolution proceedings administered by or under the auspices of the PCA, whether or not pursuant to the 1899 or 1907 Convention or any of the PCA's optional rules of procedure;

(f) 'Participant in Proceedings' means any person (whether natural or legal person) taking part in a hearing, meeting, or other activity in relation to PCA Proceedings, including but not limited to a witness, expert, counsel, party, agent or other party representative, interpreter, translator, court reporter or any person appointed to assist PCA Adjudicators such as tribunal assistant, secretary or registrar.

Article 2

LEGAL CAPACITY

The Government recognizes the legal capacity of the PCA, in particular its capacity to contract, to acquire and dispose of immovable and movable property, to institute and respond to legal proceedings and to take such other action as may be necessary or useful for its purpose and activities.

Article 3

PREMISES

(1) The premises of the office of the PCA in Vienna shall comprise the land, installations and offices that the PCA occupies for its activities. Its area shall be defined by common understanding between the Government and the PCA.

(2) Any further office and conference premises in or outside of Vienna used with the agreement of the Government for meetings convened by the PCA shall be deemed temporarily to form part of the premises.

(3) The Authorities shall exercise due diligence to ensure that the security of the PCA office is not impaired by any person or group of persons attempting unauthorised entry.

Article 4

INVIOLABILITY OF THE PREMISES

(1) The premises of the PCA shall be inviolable. No officer or official of the Republic of Austria, or other person exercising any public authority within the Republic of Austria, may enter the premises to perform any duties except with the consent of, and under conditions approved by, the Head of the Office. However, in the event of fire or other such emergency, such consent shall be deemed to have been given if immediate protective measures are required.

(2) Except as otherwise provided in this Agreement and subject to the power of the PCA to make regulations, the laws and regulations of the Republic of Austria shall apply within the premises.

(3) Instruments issued by Authorities may be served at the premises.

Article 5

IMMUNITY FROM JURISDICTION AND OTHER ACTIONS

(1) The PCA shall enjoy immunity from jurisdiction and enforcement, except:

(a) to the extent that the PCA shall have expressly waived such immunity in a particular case;

(b) in the case of civil action brought by a third party for damage resulting from an accident caused by a motor vehicle belonging to, or operated on behalf of, the PCA, or in respect of any infringement of laws and regulations governing the keeping, operation and use of motor vehicles;

(c) in the case of attachment, pursuant to a decision by the judicial authorities, of the salary, emoluments or indemnities owed by the PCA to an employee of the PCA, unless the PCA informs the Authorities within 14 days of the date on which it is notified of said decision by the Authorities that it does not waive its immunity.

(2) Without prejudice to paragraph 1, the property and assets of the PCA, wherever located and by whomsoever held, shall be immune from search, requisition, confiscation, expropriation and any other form of interference, whether by executive, administrative, judicial or legislative action.

(3) Unless an alternative dispute settlement mechanism has been agreed, any dispute between the PCA and a private party that might otherwise be brought before Austrian courts shall be settled by final and binding arbitration in accordance with the PCA Optional Rules for Arbitration Involving International Organizations and Private Parties, as in force on the date of

signature of this Agreement. The number of arbitrators shall be one. The Vienna International

Arbitral Centre of the Austrian Federal Economic Chamber shall act as appointing authority. The tribunal shall decide a dispute in accordance with such rules of law as may be agreed by the parties. In the absence of such agreement, the tribunal shall apply such rules of international law and general principles of law as may be applicable. Employment disputes shall not be within the competence of the tribunal. Employment disputes between the PCA and its employees shall be settled by an effective dispute resolution mechanism that protects the rights of the employees in accordance with the European Convention on Human Rights, pursuant to the PCA's internal regulations.

Article 6

INVIOLABILITY OF ARCHIVES

The archives of the PCA, and in general all documents belonging to it or held by it, shall be inviolable, wherever located.

Article 7

COMMUNICATIONS

(1) The Government shall ensure that the PCA is able to send and receive communications in connection with its official activities without censorship or other interference.

(2) The PCA shall enjoy in the Republic of Austria, for its official communications and the transfer of all its documents, treatment not less advantageous to the PCA than the most favourable treatment accorded by the Republic of Austria to any international organization, in the matter of priorities, rates and surcharges on all forms of communication.

(3) The PCA shall have the right to use codes and to dispatch and receive correspondence by courier or in sealed bags, which shall have the same immunities and privileges as diplomatic couriers and bags.

Article 8

FREEDOM FROM TAXATION AND CUSTOMS DUTIES

The PCA, its assets, income and other property shall be exempt:

(a) from all direct taxes; it is understood, however, that the Office shall not claim exemption from taxes which are in fact no more than charges for public utility services;

(b) from all indirect taxes included in the prices of goods or services supplied to the PCA; these taxes shall be refunded to the PCA insofar as Austrian law makes provision to that effect for foreign diplomatic missions;

(c) from customs duties and other charges provided these are not simply charges for public utility services and prohibitions and restrictions on imports and exports in respect of articles, including motor vehicles and spare parts thereof, imported or exported by the PCA for its official use; it is understood, however, that articles imported under such exemption shall not be ceded or transferred by the PCA to third parties in the Republic of Austria within two years of their importation or acquisition;

(d) from all customs duties and quantitative restrictions on imports and exports in respect of its publications;

(e) from all taxes, recording charges and court fees in respect of all transactions to which the PCA is a party and all documents recording such transactions;

(f) from the obligation to pay employer's contributions to the Family Burden Equalization Fund or an instrument with equivalent objectives.

Article 9

FINANCIAL FACILITIES

Without being restricted by financial controls, regulations or moratoria of any kind:

(a) the PCA may hold funds, currency of any kind, or other assets and operate accounts in any currency;

(b) the PCA shall be free to transfer its funds, currency, and assets to, from, or within the Republic of Austria and to convert any currency held by it into any other currency.

Article 10

SOCIAL SECURITY

(1) The PCA and Officials of the PCA who are members of the staff of the office of the PCA in Vienna shall be exempt from all compulsory contributions to any social security scheme in the Republic of Austria.

(2) The Officials of the Office shall be exempt from the application of Austrian social security laws.

(3) Officials of the PCA under paragraph 1 may avail themselves of the right under paragraph 2 by submitting a written declaration within three months after entry into force of this Agreement or within three months after taking up their assignment with the PCA.

(4) Insurance under paragraph 2 in the selected branch shall take effect with the date of taking up the assignment with the PCA, provided the declaration is submitted within seven business days after entry into force of this Agreement or after the date of taking up the assignment, otherwise on the day following the day of submission of the declaration.

(5) Insurance shall cease on the date on which the assignment with the PCA terminates.

(6) Throughout the duration of the insurance, Officials of the PCA shall be responsible for the payment of the entire contributions to Österreichische Gesundheitskasse.

(7) The declarations required to be made by an Official of the PCA under paragraph 3 shall be transmitted by the PCA on behalf of the Official of the PCA to Österreichische Gesundheitskasse. Upon request, the PCA shall provide Österreichische Gesundheitskasse with the information necessary for the implementation of the insurance.

Article 11

TRANSIT AND RESIDENCE

(1) The Government shall take all necessary measures in accordance with Austrian law to facilitate the entry into, and sojourn in, the Republic of Austria of the persons listed below, shall allow them to leave the Republic of Austria without interference and shall ensure that they can travel unimpeded to or from the premises, affording them any necessary protection when so travelling:

(a) Officials of the PCA and members of their family forming part of their household;

(b) PCA Adjudicators in proceedings that take place in the Republic of Austria;

(c) Participants in Proceedings that take place in the Republic of Austria.

(2) Visas which may be required by persons referred to in paragraph 1 shall be granted free of charge and as promptly as possible, in accordance with Austrian law.

(3) No activity performed by any person referred to in paragraph 1 in their official capacity with respect to the PCA shall constitute a reason for preventing their entry into, or departure from, the Republic of Austria.

(4) The Republic of Austria shall be entitled to require reasonable evidence to establish that persons claiming the rights granted by this Article fall within the categories described in paragraph 1, and to require compliance in a reasonable manner with quarantine and health regulations.

Article 12

OFFICIALS OF THE PCA

(1) Officials of the PCA who are members of the staff of the office of the PCA in Vienna shall enjoy the following privileges and immunities:

(a) in respect of words spoken or written and acts done by them in the course of the discharge of their duties, immunity from legal process of every kind. This immunity from legal process shall continue to be accorded, even after the person has ceased to exercise his or her functions in connection with the PCA;

(b) immunity from the seizure of their personal and official baggage;

(c) inviolability of all official documents, data and other material;

(d) exemption from taxation in respect of salaries and emoluments including allowances, remunerations, indemnities and pensions paid to them by the PCA in connection with their service with it. This exemption shall extend also to assistance given to the families of Officials of the PCA;

(e) exemption from any form of taxation on income derived by them and by members of their families forming part of their household from sources outside the Republic of Austria;

(f) exemption from inheritance and gift taxes, except with respect to immovable property located in the Republic of Austria, insofar as such arise solely from the fact that Officials of the PCA or members of their families forming part of their household reside or maintain their usual domicile in the Republic of Austria;

(g) exemption from immigration restrictions and from registration formalities for themselves and members of their families forming part of their household;

(h) freedom to acquire or maintain within the Republic of Austria foreign securities, foreign currency accounts, other movable property and, under the same conditions as Austrian nationals, immovable property;

(i) the right to import for personal use, free of duty and other charges, provided these are not simply charges for public utility services, and exempt from economic import prohibitions and restrictions on imports and exports:

(i) their furniture and personal effects in one or more separate consignments when taking up their assignment, and necessary additions to the same within six months thereafter;

(ii) one motor vehicle every four years;

(j) the same protection and repatriation facilities with respect to themselves and members of their families forming part of their household as are accorded in time of international crises to members, having comparable rank, of the staffs of chiefs of diplomatic missions accredited to the Republic of Austria.

(2) Officials of the PCA and the members of their families living in the same household to whom this agreement applies shall not be entitled to payments out of the Family Burden Equalization Fund or an instrument of the Republic of Austria with equivalent objectives. This provision shall not apply to Austrian nationals, to persons of other nationality granted equivalent status by European Union legislation, or to stateless persons with permanent residence in the Republic of Austria.

(3) Other Officials of the PCA shall enjoy with regard to the discharge of their duties the privileges and immunities specified under Article 15 paragraphs 1, 2 and 5.

Article 13

HEAD OF OFFICE

In addition to the privileges and immunities specified in Article 12, the Head of the Office as well as, during his or her absence from duty, the Official of the PCA acting on behalf of the Head of the Office, shall be accorded the privileges and immunities, exemptions and facilities accorded to heads of diplomatic missions, provided they are not Austrian nationals or permanent residents of the Republic of Austria.

Article 14

SECRETARY-GENERAL OF THE PCA

For the duration of his or her official business, the Secretary-General of the PCA shall be accorded the privileges and immunities, exemptions and facilities accorded to heads of diplomatic missions, provided they are not Austrian nationals or permanent residents of the Republic of Austria.

Article 15

PCA ADJUDICATORS AND PARTICIPANTS IN PROCEEDINGS

(1) PCA Adjudicators and Participants in Proceedings shall enjoy immunity from legal process of every kind in respect of words spoken or written and all acts performed by them in the course of their participation in PCA Proceedings. This immunity shall continue in perpetuity.

(2) Furthermore, PCA Adjudicators and Participants in Proceedings shall enjoy the following privileges and immunities if the proceedings take place in the Republic of Austria:

(a) immunity from personal arrest or detention;

(b) immunity from the seizure of their personal and official baggage;

(c) inviolability of all official documents, data and other material;

(d) the exchange facilities necessary for the transfer of their emoluments and expenses;

(e) for purposes of their communications in relation to PCA Proceedings, the right to receive and send papers and documents in whatever form by courier or in sealed bags;

(f) exemption from immigration restrictions or alien registration when they travel for purposes of their participation in PCA Proceedings.

(3) With regard to proceedings that take place in the Republic of Austria, the PCA shall provide PCA Adjudicators and Participants in Proceedings with a document certifying that their participation is required by the PCA and specifying a time period during which such participation is necessary. This document shall be withdrawn prior to its expiry if their appearance in PCA Proceedings or their presence within the Republic of Austria is no longer required.

(4) Except where specified otherwise in a document under paragraph (3), the privileges and immunities referred to in paragraphs (1) and (2) shall cease to apply after fifteen consecutive days following the date on which the presence of the PCA Adjudicator or Participant in Proceedings concerned is no longer required by the PCA, provided he or she had an opportunity to leave the Republic of Austria during that period.

(5) Except where specified otherwise in a document under paragraph (3), the privileges and immunities referred to in paragraphs (1) and (2) shall cease to apply after fifteen consecutive days following the date on which the presence of the PCA Adjudicator or Participant in Proceedings concerned is no longer required by the PCA, provided he or she had an opportunity to leave the Republic of Austria during that period.

Article 16

NOTIFICATION ND, IDENTITY CARDS

(1) The PCA shall communicate to the Authorities a list of the Officials of the PCA who are members of the staff of the office of the PCA in Vienna and shall revise such list from time to time as may be necessary.

(2) The Government shall issue to such Officials of the PCA and members of their families forming part of their household an identity card bearing the photograph of the holder in accordance with Austrian law. This card shall serve to identify the holder vis-à-vis the Authorities.

Article 17

AUSTRIAN NATIONALS AND PERMANENT RESIDENTS OF THE REPUBLIC OF AUSTRIA

Austrian nationals and persons who are permanently resident in the Republic of Austria shall enjoy only the privileges and immunities specified in Article 10, Article 12 (1) (a), (b), (c), (d) and Article 15 (1), (2) (a), (b), (c) and (e).

Article 18

PURPOSE OF PRIVILEGES AND IMMUNITIES

(1) The privileges and immunities provided for in this Agreement are not designed to give personal advantages to the persons to whom they are accorded. They are granted solely to ensure that the PCA is able to perform its official activities unimpeded at all times and that the persons to whom they are accorded have complete independence. The PCA engages to encourage its officials to comply with their legal obligations.

(2) The PCA shall waive immunity where it considers that such immunity would impede the normal course of justice and that it can be waived without prejudicing the interests of the PCA.

Article 19

SETTLEMENT OF DISPUTES

(1) Any dispute among the Parties to the present Agreement that is not settled by negotiation shall be settled by final and binding arbitration in accordance with the PCA Optional Rules for Arbitration Involving International Organizations and States as in force on the date of signature of this Agreement. The number of arbitrators shall be one. The Vienna International Arbitral Centre of the Austrian Federal Economic Chamber shall be the appointing authority. Each Party may however request the Vienna International Arbitral Centre of the Austrian Federal Economic Chamber to immediately appoint such an arbitrator to examine a request for provisional measures to protect its rights under the present Agreement. The place of arbitration shall be Vienna and the language to be used in the proceedings of the tribunal shall be English. (2) In any such arbitration proceedings, the registry, archive, and secretariat services of the PCA, referred to in Article 1,

paragraph 3, and Article 25, paragraph 3, of the Rules, will not be available, and the PCA shall not be empowered to request, hold, or disburse deposits of costs as provided for in Article 41, paragraph 1, of the Rules.

Article 20

MOST-FAVOURED ORGANIZATION

If and to the extent that the Government shall enter into any agreement with a comparable intergovernmental organization having its seat in the Republic of Austria containing terms or conditions more favourable to that organization than similar terms or conditions of this Agreement, the Government shall extend such more favourable terms or conditions to the PCA, by means of a supplemental agreement.

Article 21

ENTRY INTO FORCE, MODIFICATION AND DURATION OF THE AGREEMENT

(1) This Agreement shall be concluded for an indefinite period. It shall enter into force on the first day of the third month after the Government and the PCA have informed each other of the completion of the procedures required, for each of them, to be bound by it.

(2) The provisions of the present Agreement shall take effect as of 1 January 2023.

(3) This Agreement may be terminated by either Party by giving notice to the other. It shall cease to be in force one year after the date of receipt of such notice.

(4) With the entry into force of this Agreement, the Regulation of the Federal Government on the Status of the Permanent Court of Arbitration in Austria, Federal Law Gazette II No. 273/2014, shall cease to be in force.

EE.II.-3

Agreement between the Austrian Federal Government and the International Criminal Police Organization – Interpol (ICPO – Interpol) on the Privileges and Immunities of ICPO – Interpol for the 91st General Assembly Session and the Executive Committee Meetings to be Held in Vienna in 2023

Abkommen zwischen der Österreichischen Bundesregierung und der Internationalen Kriminalpolizeilichen Organisation-INTERPOL (ICPO-INTERPOL) über die Vorrechte und Befreiungen von ICPO-INTERPOL während der Sitzung der 91. Generalversammlung und der Treffen des Exekutivkomitees in Wien im Jahr 2023

On 13 November 2023, the Austrian Federal Government and the International Criminal Police Organization (ICPO)-INTERPOL signed an Agreement on the on the Privileges and Immunities of ICPO-Interpol for the 91st General Assembly Session and the Executive Committee Meetings held in Vienna from 23 November to 1 December 2023, which entered into force on 16 November 2023:[12]

PREAMBLE

The Austrian Federal Government (hereinafter referred to as the 'Host Country') and the International Criminal Police Organization-INTERPOL (hereinafter referred to as the 'ICPO-INTERPOL' or the 'Organization'),

In anticipation of the 91st General Assembly session and the Executive Committee meetings, which will be held in Vienna, Austria, from 23rd November to 1st December 2023, International arbitration is a preferred means for the peaceful resolution of international disputes,

Considering that ICPO-INTERPOL is an international organization governed by public

international law whose aims, under the terms of its Constitution, are to ensure the promotion of the widest possible mutual assistance between all criminal police authorities within the limits of the laws existing in the different countries and in the spirit of the Universal Declaration of Human Rights, and to establish and develop all institutions likely to contribute effectively to the prevention and suppression of ordinary law crimes,

Considering that, under the terms of Article 3 of ICPO-INTERPOL's Constitution, it is strictly forbidden for the Organization to undertake any intervention or activities of a political, military, religious or racial character,

Considering that, under the terms of Article 31 of ICPO-INTERPOL's Constitution, the

Organization needs the constant and active cooperation of its Members, who should do all within their power, which is compatible with the legislations of their countries to participate diligently in its activities,

Considering also that, under the terms of Article 30 of ICPO-INTERPOL's Constitution, all Members of the Organization shall do their best to assist the Secretary General and the staff in the discharge of their functions,

Convinced that for international police cooperation to be carried out successfully, solid guarantees are required, and that under international custom, guarantees are provided for international organizations governed by public international law,

Considering that on the territory of each of its member countries, the Organization must enjoy the guarantees it requires to carry out its mission for the benefit of all those countries,

Considering also that the representatives of the member countries and the staff of the Organization's General Secretariat must enjoy the privileges and immunities they require to discharge their functions on behalf of the Organization with complete independence,

---

12 Federal Law Gazette III No 177/2023.

Convinced that granting such privileges and immunities will contribute to strengthening and developing international police cooperation,

Bearing in mind Article 3 of the ICPO-INTERPOL General Regulations, which provides that any Member may, on behalf of its country, invite the Assembly to meet on the territory of that country,

Bearing in mind Article 17 on the 'Obligations incumbent upon countries hosting General Assembly sessions' of the Rules of Procedure of the ICPO-INTERPOL General Assembly and Article 4(5) of the Rules concerning the organization of General Assembly sessions which provides that the host country shall complete and execute a legally binding agreement on privileges and immunities for the General Assembly session and the Executive Committee meetings,

HAVE AGREED as follows:

Article 1

PURPOSE OF THE AGREEMENT AND OBJECTIVES OF THE COOPERATION

To enable the ICPO-INTERPOL to discharge the missions defined in its Constitution, and in particular to facilitate international police cooperation and the operation of the bodies listed in Article 5 thereof, the immunities and privileges defined in the present Agreement shall be granted to it on the territory of the Republic of Austria, for the time required to organize, hold and complete the 91st General Assembly session and the Executive Committee meetings to be held in Vienna, Republic of Austria, from 23rd November to 1st December 2023.

Article 2

ENTRY INTO THE HOST COUNTRY TERRITORY

(1) The competent government authorities of the Host Country shall allow to enter and leave their territory, for the duration of the 91st General Assembly session and the Executive Committee meetings:

(a) representatives of Member Countries attending the 91st General Assembly session and their delegations;

(b) members of the Executive Committee of the ICPO-INTERPOL and their delegations;

(c) members of the ICPO-INTERPOL General Secretariat staff;

(d) members of the Commission for the Control of INTERPOL's Files and the persons carrying out official duties on its behalf;

(e) interpreters and minute writers hired by the ICPO-INTERPOL General Secretariat;

(f) the Organization's Advisers;

(g) observers, experts and other persons who have been invited to attend the 91st General Assembly session and/or the Executive Committee meetings; and

(h) accompanying staff of the foregoing.

(2) The competent government authorities of the Republic of Austria shall issue free of charge and without delay any visas or entry or exit permits required for persons participating in the 91st General Assembly session and/or the Executive Committee meetings in accordance with European Union and national law.

(3) No person referred to in paragraph 1 shall be required by the Government of Austria to leave the territory of the Republic of Austria save in the event of an abuse of the privileges and immunities granted under this Agreement.

Article 3

ADDITIONAL GUARANTEES RELATED TO PUBLIC HEALTH AND SAFETY MEASURES

(1) All participants listed in Article 2 above shall enjoy the same exemptions of quarantine measures and other measures implemented to address public health and safety concerns as are enjoyed by persons visiting or working for international organizations in the Republic of Austria in accordance with national law.

(2) The Host Country and the General Secretariat of the ICPO-INTERPOL shall hold consultations and determine jointly any other measures that may be necessary to safeguard the health and safety of the participants and the general public taking into account the rights of the participants and the need for the General Assembly and the Executive Committee to function smoothly and efficiently.

Article 4

PRIVILEGES AND IMMUNITIES OF THE ORGANIZATION

(1) The ICPO-INTERPOL shall enjoy immunity from jurisdiction and enforcement, except:

(a) to the extent that the Secretary General shall have expressly waived such immunity in a particular case;

(b) in the case of civil action brought by a third party for damage resulting from an accident caused by a motor vehicle belonging to, or operated on behalf of, the ICPO-INTERPOL, or in respect of any infringement of laws and regulations governing the keeping, operation and use of motor vehicles.

(2) Without prejudice to paragraph 1, the property and assets of the ICPO-INTERPOL, wherever situated, shall be immune from any form of seizure, confiscation, expropriation and sequestration or any other form of judicial or administrative restraint.

(3) The Organization shall take appropriate measures for the satisfactory settlement of disputes:

(a) arising from written contracts to which the Organization is a party. The Organization shall include in its written contracts, other than those concluded with its officials, a clause whereby any dispute arising from the interpretation or performance of the contract shall be settled by consultation or mediation, or in the absence of an amicable settlement of the dispute between the two parties, by an arbitration procedure agreed between them;

(b) concerning data processing in the INTERPOL Information System, which may be brought before the Commission for the Control of INTERPOL's Files;

(c) between the Organization and its officials, which may be submitted to the Administrative Tribunal of the International Labour Organization.

(4) Tort claims arising from the wrongful or negligent act or omission of the ICPOINTERPOL in connection with the organization of the 91st General Assembly session and Executive Committee meetings in Vienna, Republic of Austria, from 23rd November to 1st December 2023, shall be settled using any method of settlement deemed appropriate by the ICPO-INTERPOL, and guaranteeing the independent and impartial settlement of the disputes within a reasonable time.

Article 5

INVIOLABILITY OF ARCHIVES AND CORRESPONDENCE

(1) All documents belonging to the ICPO-INTERPOL or held by it in whatever form and, *inter alia*, its archives and accounts, shall be inviolable wherever they are located.

(2) The inviolability of the ICPO-INTERPOL's official correspondence shall be guaranteed. Its official communications shall not be subject to censorship and it may make use of codes.

Article 6

FOREIGN EXCHANGE

The ICPO-INTERPOL may, without being subject to any financial controls, regulations or moratoria:

a) receive and hold funds and foreign exchange of all kinds, and operate accounts in all currencies on the territory of the Host Country;

(b) freely transfer its funds and foreign exchange within the territory of the Host Country, and from its Headquarters or one of its Sub-Regional Bureaus to the Host Country and vice versa.

Article 7

EXEMPTION FROM CUSTOMS DUTIES

Administrative, technical and scientific material provided by the ICPO-INTERPOL for the 91st General Assembly session and the Executive Committee meetings, as well as publications of the ICPO-INTERPOL and other official documents required for its work, and the usual gifts presented by or to the ICPO-INTERPOL Secretary General and officials of the Organization as well as promotional material of small value and limited quantity sold to participants during the 91st General Assembly session and the Executive Committee meetings shall be exempt from payment of import duties and all other taxes. The ICPO-INTERPOL undertakes to reexport all such material, publications and gifts that remain unused or undistributed at the end of the 91st General Assembly session and the Executive Committee meetings.

Article 8

PRIVILEGES AND IMMUNITIES OF PARTICIPANTS

The Host Country shall take appropriate measures to ensure that all participants listed in Article 2 shall be granted the following privileges and immunities in connection with their official duties and the missions assigned to them on the territory of the Host Country during the 91st General Assembly session and the Executive Committee meetings and during their journeys to and from the location where the meeting or session is being held:

(a) immunity from arrest, detention and seizure of personal baggage;

(b) immunity from legal process, even after the 91st General Assembly session and the Executive Committee meetings, for acts performed in the exercise of their official functions;

(c) inviolability of all official papers and documents;

(d) the same facilities with regard to foreign exchange as are granted to diplomatic agents.

Article 9

DIPLOMATIC PRIVILEGES

In addition to the privileges and immunities granted by Article 8 above, the Secretary General, the members of the Executive Committee and the family members accompanying them shall be accorded the privileges, immunities, and facilities as are granted, in accordance with international law, to diplomatic agents.

Article 10

USE OF IMMUNITIES

(1) The privileges and immunities provided for in Articles 8 and 9 of the present Agreement are granted to those concerned not for their personal benefit but in the interest of the smooth functioning of the institutions of the ICPO-INTERPOL.

(2) The ICPO-INTERPOL and the competent authorities in the Organization's Member Countries exercise the right and duty of waiving the immunity of those who enjoy it whenever such immunity would impede the course of justice and when the immunity can be waived without prejudice to the interests of ICPO-INTERPOL.

Article 11

SETTLEMENT OF DISPUTES

(1) Any dispute arising out of the interpretation or application of the present Agreement shall be settled by negotiation.

(2) Unless the parties decide otherwise, any dispute concerning the interpretation or application of the present Agreement which cannot be settled by negotiation shall be submitted to an arbitral tribunal composed of one or three arbitrators, as determined by the parties, in accordance with the 'Optional Rules of Arbitration

of the Permanent Court of Arbitration for International Organizations and States', as in force on the date of signature of this Agreement. The sole arbitrator shall be appointed by mutual agreement of the parties or, failing that, by the Secretary General of the Permanent Court of Arbitration. When the arbitral tribunal is composed of three members, one is appointed by the Austrian Federal Government, the other is appointed by the Organization and the third, presiding over the arbitral tribunal, by mutual agreement between the two arbitrators or, failing that, by the Secretary General of the Permanent Court of Arbitration. Such arbitration shall be final and binding.

(3) Each Party may however request the Secretary General of the Permanent Court of Arbitration to immediately set up such an arbitral tribunal to examine a request for provisional measures to protect its rights under the present Agreement.

(4) The language to be used in the proceedings of the arbitral tribunal shall be English.

(5) The arbitrations proceedings, including the existence of the arbitration, all oral and written submissions and all decisions and awards of the arbitral tribunal, shall be confidential, except where such information must be disclosed pursuant to a statutory or other legal obligation placed upon the Host Country or the Organization. In such a case, the party required to disclose the information shall consult the other party prior to disclosure.

Article 12

ENTRY INTO FORCE

The present Agreement shall enter into force three days after signature by both Parties.

EE.II.-4

Work of the International Law Commission on Settlement of disputes to which international organizations are parties

Arbeit der Völkerrechtskommission der Vereinten Nationen betreffend Beilegung von Streitigkeiten, an denen internationale Organisationen beteiligt

On 31 October 2023, the Austrian representative to the 78th Session of the General Assembly delivered the following statement to the Sixth Committee on Report of the International Law Commission on the Work of its 73rd and 74th Session concerning the topic of 'Settlement of disputes to which international organizations are parties':

> [...] Allow me to turn to chapter V, dealing with the topic 'Settlement of disputes to which international organizations are parties' and to congratulate Special Rapporteur August Reinisch for his first report.

Austria welcomes that the Commission has started working on this topic, which it considers to be of great practical value. This is particularly true for host states of international organizations, but equally for member states in international organizations. As a host country Austria has witnessed a number of cases were disputes of a private law character were brought before its domestic courts, raising complex issues of jurisdictional immunity and access to justice, both at a national constitutional as well as at an international human rights law level. Particularly these disputes with private parties are of practical importance. We therefore welcome the Commission's decision to clarify that any disputes to which international organizations are parties are covered by the topic - as has been made evident by changing the title of the topic, now generally referring to 'disputes' and not only to 'international disputes'.

As a host country, Austria is often faced with potentially conflicting obligations: On the one hand, it has to respect the broad jurisdictional immunity of international organizations under general immunity agreements and headquarters agreements. On the other hand, it is under an obligation pursuant to Article 6 of the European Convention on Human Rights to grant access to its courts in cases where civil rights are claimed by individual litigants. The European Court of Human Rights has clarified in its 1999 *Waite and Kennedy* judgment that this obligation in principle also extends to contractual and other private law claims of individuals against international organizations.

Therefore, Austria has constantly worked with international organizations headquartered in Austria to provide effective alternative forms of dispute settlement, including access to international bodies or independent internal mechanisms.

The collision of norms between the obligations of Austria as host country granting immunity from jurisdiction to international organizations and access to courts for individuals in case of human rights violations was a recent issue before the Austrian Constitutional Court regarding the headquarters agreement between OPEC and Austria.

[…] Austria welcomes the Commission's plan to produce a set of draft guidelines based on actual practice that will provide guidance for settling disputes to which international organizations are parties.

Austria appreciates the conceptual clarity brought into the core elements defining the scope of this topic in guideline 1 'scope' and guideline 2 'use of terms'. Austria is glad to see that the definition of international organizations in guideline 2 subparagraph (a), building on the one contained in the draft articles on the responsibility of international organizations adopted by the Commission in 2011, has been refined. Austria particularly welcomes that the possession of at least one organ capable of expressing a will distinct from that of its members has been included in this definition. Austria regards this a crucially important element, distinguishing international organizations from mere cooperation based on a treaty.

Austria also concurs with the idea that international organizations are created on the basis of a treaty or other instrument governed by international law. Austria would like to add that an 'instrument governed by international law' need not necessarily be a legally binding instrument. This implies that, under certain circumstances, permanent arrangements between states such as the Organisation for Security and Cooperation in Europe (OSCE) may also be regarded as international organizations.

Concerning the proposed definition of dispute in guideline 2 subparagraph (b), Austria concurs with the approach to build on the *Mavrommatis* definition, and to ensure that this definition would also be applicable to disputes of a private law character.

Austria also wants to point out that the fact that disputes at the international level may have political aspects does not change their character as legal disputes.

Furthermore, Austria is eager to learn from the Commission about the potential role of the International Court of Justice in regard to the settlement of disputes between international organizations and states through advisory opinions or, possibly in the future, through extending its contentious jurisdiction. [...]

1. In general/Allgemeines

a. Status and Powers/Status und Befugnisse

cc. Privileges and immunities of the organisation/Privilegien und Immunitäten der Organisation

See *EE.II.-1*, *EE.II.-2* and *EE.II.-3*.

b. Participation of States in international organisations and in their activities/Mitgliedschaft in internationalen Organisationen, Teilnahme an ihren Aktivitäten

EE.II.1.b.-1

Austrian statement at the Open Debate of the Security Council on 'The Promotion and Strengthening of the Rule of Law in the Maintenance of International Peace and Security: the Rule of Law among Nations'

Österreichische Erklärung bei der offenen Debatte des Sicherheitsrates zur Frage der Förderung und Stärkung der Rechtsstaatlichkeit bei der Erhaltung des Weltfriedens und des internationalen Friedens und der Sicherheit: die Rechtsstaatlichkeit unter den Nationen

On 12 January 2023, the Austrian permanent representative delivered the following statement at the Open Debate of the Security Council on 'The Promotion and Strengthening of the Rule of Law in the Maintenance of International Peace and Security: the Rule of Law among Nations':

> [...] The United Nations Charter is at the core of how Nations should co-exist peacefully. Through our ratification all Member States agreed to be legally bound by the Charter.
>
> The key difference between a political commitment and a norm of international law is the binding, obligatory nature of the latter.
>
> If a State breaches an obligation under international law, it must bear the legal consequences of State responsibility, as elaborated in detail by the International Law Commission in its Articles on State Responsibility.
>
> Adherence to the rule of law is intended to ensure that the principles and norms we agreed on are respected and implemented by all in good faith. This is in the interest of all States, large and small.
>
> By means of the UN Charter – a legally-binding treaty – the Member States agreed to the principle of sovereign equality and to refrain from the threat or use of force against the territorial integrity or political independence of any State.
>
> Several GA resolutions from last year reaffirmed the validity of these principles, for example when they underlined the sovereignty and territorial integrity of Ukraine and rejected attempts to acquire territories by force, called for an end to violations of international law in Myanmar, reaffirmed the right of the Palestinian people to self-determination and recalled the obligations of Afghanistan under international law. Clearly, UN Member States continue to value these fundamental principles, and the obligation to act in accordance with them.
>
> [...] Adherence to international law serves our collective security and guarantees the safety of our citizens. Many conflicts could be avoided if States showed respect for the rule of law and complied with their obligations under international law, especially the UN Charter. This includes the obligation to settle international disputes by peaceful means, an obligation that was complied with in several instances, for example by Italy and Austria with regard to the German-speaking minority 30 years ago or more recently by Canada and the Kingdom of Denmark together with Greenland regarding their maritime and land border dispute in the Arctic.
>
> If States do not resolve a conflict peacefully, the Security Council has the responsibility to maintain or restore international peace and security, including through restoring compliance with the law. In this context the misuse of the veto and the non-observance of Art. 27 (3) of the UN Charter is a grave concern. We welcome ideas to limit the use of the veto in certain cases, such as the French/Mexican initiative on suspension of the veto in cases of mass atrocities or the ACT code of conduct, as well as Liechtenstein's Veto Initiative, now GA resolution 76/262.
>
> At the same time, the UN must not give up if the Security Council cannot deliver. We saw this in the GA's Uniting for Peace resolution – as last resorted to in

February 2022. Perhaps the time is right to consider further means to strengthen adherence to the Charter reflecting its legally binding nature. Perhaps we could explore possible ways to more effectively, consistently and directly respond to grave violations of the Charter when the Security Council does not act.

[…] Probably no other international institution embodies the principle of the rule of law among States better than the International Court of Justice. We emphasize our appreciation for the Court's work and reiterate the need for all States to fulfil their obligation to respect and implement the Court's judgements and other binding measures. Similarly, we have the highest regard for other international courts and tribunals, such as the Permanent Court of Arbitration, the International Tribunal for the Law of the Sea and the International Criminal Court. The Security Council should continue to draw upon expertise of these institutions. When considering situations constituting a threat to international peace and security, the Council should consider whether the ICJ or any other court or tribunal could be seized of the matter to enable a peaceful settlement of a dispute

[…] The number of challenges the international community faces remains high. The rule of law must be part of the foundation on which we build our relationships and allow us to face those challenges together.

Over the past years, many have complained about a lack of trust, a lack of confidence among UN Member States. Compliance with international law is an excellent way to establish trust. If we can rely on each other to adhere to the law, we have an excellent foundation for peaceful international relations.

Let us not succumb to the temptations of power and force. Let us build on the power of law.

[…] Please allow me to add a few words in my national capacity: Austria has been a member of the UN since 1955. Our contribution has always been guided by the purposes of the Charter and the interests of the UN as a whole. We also proved our commitment to today's topic when we finalized a report with the title 'The UN Security Council and the Rule of Law' ahead of our last membership in the Council in 2009/2010.

Austria is fully committed to acting on these principles when it next will have the honor to serve as a member of the Security Council. We will continue to focus the discussions on strengthening the rule of law and international law, especially adherence to the UN Charter.

EE.II.1.b.-2

Austrian statement at the 77th Session of the General Assembly on Agenda Item 'Use of the Veto'

Österreichische Erklärung bei 77ten Sitzung der Generalversammlung zum Tagesordnungspunkt „Ausübung des Vetorechts"

On 26 April 2023, the Austrian deputy permanent representative delivered the following statement on 'Use of the Veto' in the UN General Assembly:

> […] Exactly one year ago, we gathered here to demonstrate that inaction or the deliberate prevention of action in times of crisis and emerging threats to international peace and security is unacceptable to the wider membership of the UN.
>
> By adopting Resolution 76/262 entitled '*Standing mandate for a GA debate when a veto is cast in the SC*' without a vote, the GA further pursued the aim of improving the accountability and transparency of the Security Council vis-à-vis the wider membership. This is of particular importance since Art. 24 of the Charter mandates the Security Council to act on behalf of all of us.
>
> Austria commends Liechtenstein for its efforts in this regard. We supported this initiative from the beginning and co-sponsored the resolution 76/262.
>
> [Relationship of the GA and the UNSC]
>
> We have always understood Resolution 76/262 as a contribution to strengthening the effectiveness of the Security Council, while enhancing the role of the General Assembly. And it is no overstatement to say that the 'veto initiative' has proven necessary and useful over the past year and will continue to do so.
>
> The veto will continue to present our multilateral system with challenges, especially in times of disagreement and overwhelming national interests. The misuse of the veto remains a grave concern. We acknowledge initiatives by some Permanent Members to voluntarily limit the use of the veto, such as the French-Mexican initiative on the suspension of veto powers in cases of mass atrocities, and fully support the ACT Code of Conduct and encourage all delegations to do the same.
>
> We also call on Council members to consistently implement and observe the provisions of Art. 27 (3) of the UN Charter regarding the participation of Council members when they are parties to a dispute.
>
> [Responsibility of UNSC members]
>
> For that reason, let me reiterate that the wider membership expects – especially in light of Article 24 (1) – that the Members of the Security Council act in concert towards peace and cooperation. There is no place for national interests. They should demand compliance with the purposes, principles and norms of the UN Charter and international law. Speak out against violations. Condemn wrongdoing and take a leading role. It is their duty to ensure an effective Security Council for the maintenance of international peace and security and not to veto actions against clear breaches of international law and the UN Charter to protect national interests.
>
> [Full implementation of the veto initiative]
>
> Colleagues,
>
> Since the adoption of Resolution 76/262, the mechanism envisaged in it has already been triggered three times. Each time, there was no doubt that the vast majority of this Assembly disagreed with the Permanent Member which cast the

veto. That is exactly the reason why sometimes, when the Security Council is unable to act, this Assembly has to put itself in the driver seat and take over responsibility in accordance with Article 11(2) of the Charter.

To this end, the passing and implementation of the 'veto initiative' can be regarded as a milestone. Austria underlines once more the importance of submitting a special report on the use of the veto in question to the General Assembly. It is crucial for a successful work of this Assembly as well as a core element for improving the accountability of the UNSC vis-à-vis the UNGA.

[Possible next steps]

But what now – what is the next step? In our opinion, we have to ensure the full implementation of this resolution and leverage the momentum, especially in areas, where we see the Security Council paralyzed. It is crucial that we come to a mutual agreement in this Assembly that we do not limit ourselves to mere condemnations and finger-pointing as soon as a crisis emerges. As we have seen in Ukraine, there will be times, when the Security Council is unable to fulfil its duties, in such cases, we as the wider membership have to take an operational role in crisis management.

[GA's role in crisis management]

Colleagues,

Let me be clear, we have the tools to do so! A quick look to the past can help us to better tackle challenges of the future. Our toolbox is well-equipped, including the possibility to send mediators or political missions to areas of conflict. Let me remind you of Resolution 48/267, where the General Assembly decided to send a peace verification mission to Guatemala. Or Resolution 66/253, where we requested the Secretary-General to appoint a Special Envoy for Syria in consultation with the Arab League. Thus, it is not a question of how we could act, but if we act. In order to refresh the institutional knowledge to be better prepared for potential action in the future, it would be useful to map

• precedents for the UNGA authorizing, requesting and recommending specific conflict prevention/management tools;

• the relevant language from past resolutions that could be adapted to address current challenges;

• possible monitoring mechanisms for implemented decisions.

[Conclusion]

Colleagues,

To sum up, the 'veto initiative', the FR/MX initiative on veto restraint in case of mass atrocities as well as the ACT code of conduct are fundamental steps towards a responsible use of the veto and accountability within the UN system. In addition, Art. 27 (3) set a clear normative boundary to the use of the veto in certain cases. Nevertheless, we have to avoid the abuse of the veto to protect national interests or mitigate the effects of such abuses. That is why the General Assembly has to step up by using its own broad mandate and demonstrate responsibility in times of urgent crisis.

Let us use this occasion today to remind ourselves that we do not have to accept inaction. In the challenging times we live in, we need a UN that is effective – we should remind ourselves that the General Assembly has the tools to act. We have demonstrated that in the past and we will do so in the future. […]

EE.II.1.b.-3

Austrian statement at the 77th Session of the General Assembly on Agenda Item 'Draft resolution: Request for an advisory opinion of the International Court of Justice on the obligations of States in respect of climate change'

Österreichische Erklärung bei 77ten Sitzung der Generalversammlung zum Tagesordnungspunkt „Entwurf einer Resolution: Ersuchen um ein Gutachten des Internationalen Gerichtshofs zu den Verpflichtungen der Staaten in Bezug auf den Klimawandel"

On 29 March 2023, the Austria delivered the following statement on the 'Request for an advisory opinion of the International Court of Justice on the obligations of States in respect of climate change' in General Assembly:

> […] Austria aligns itself with the statement delivered by the European Union.
>
> […] First, let me join others in congratulating Vanuatu for starting and leading this successful initiative. We appreciate that Vanuatu together with a core group of states conducted an extensive and inclusive consultation process, resulting in today's resolution. For Austria, the involvement of all interested parties is essential to the success of such an initiative
>
> As you know, Austria is a traditional and steadfast supporter of both multilateralism and international law. The resolution before us aims at strengthening both of these with regard to the overarching objective of countering climate change together. Climate change is the prime example of a challenge that cannot be addressed alone. Here we need concerted global action and multilateral coordination. And we need international legal clarity.
>
> As a small, independent country, Austria relies on the adherence to international law by all states. Our security depends on it.
>
> Similarly, we understand that the existential security of many states depends on global efforts to address climate change. And that they need also the power of law to make their population safe and life in their territories sustainable.
>
> Austria has been and will remain a steadfast supporter of strong global action on climate change and the environment. Last year we supported the landmark GA-resolution that recognized the right to a safe, healthy and sustainable environment. The resolution before us today will help to gain further legal clarity with regard to States' obligations on climate change.

> Our commitment to international law and the rule of law includes observance of existing rules and continuous development of international law. We are convinced that advisory opinions of the ICJ can be a useful instrument and can make a substantial contribution in this specific case. Consistent and equal application of laws and rules is a core rule of law principle. Principles we agreed on must be respected and implemented by all States, large and small, developed and developing states. We hope that this advisory opinion will help clarify obligations of all states in respect of climate change and that this will us all them [*sic*] to meet those obligations. […]

2. Particular types/Arten internationaler Organisationen

a. Universal organisations/Universelle Organisationen

See also *EE.II.1.b.-1*, *EE.II.1.b.-2*, and *EE.II.1.b.-3*.

EE.II.2.a.-1

Enquiry concerning the Vienna International School

Anfrage betreffend die Vienna International School

On 2 November 2022, a number of representatives of the Austrian National Assembly raised a parliamentary enquiry to the Federal Minister for European and International Affairs concerning the Vienna International School,[13] to which the Minister replied on 2 January 2023:[14]

> Austria's support for the financing of school places for children of employees of international organisations working in Vienna is one of many elements in strengthening the attractiveness of Vienna as a headquarter.
>
> There is no international treaty between the Republic of Austria and the Vienna International School (VIS). No financial contributions are currently being paid to VIS by the Republic of Austria. The Federal Ministry for European and International Affairs (BMEIA) is not aware of any financial contributions made by it to VIS in the past.
>
> The so-called Education Amount Agreement (Federal Law Gazette III No. 151/2016)[15] was concluded between the Republic of Austria and four international

[13] Parliamentary Materials, 12813/J (XXVII. GP).

[14] Parliamentary Materials, 12572/AB (XXVII. GP).

[15] Agreement between the Republic of Austria, the United Nations, the International Atomic Energy Agency, the United Nations Industrial Development Organization and the Preparatory Commission for the Comprehensive Nuclear-Test-Ban Treaty Organization, Federal Law Gazette III No 151/2016.

organisations based in Vienna – the United Nations (UNOV), the International Atomic Energy Agency (IAEA), the United Nations Industrial Development Organisation (UNIDO) and the Preparatory Commission for the Comprehensive Nuclear-Test-Ban Treaty Organisation (CTBTO). Art. 1 para. 1 of the agreement stipulates that the Republic of Austria shall make an annual educational contribution to these organisations. The amount of this contribution is regulated in Art. 1 and has totalled EUR 2 million per school year since 2019. The education contribution is transferred to the CTBTO at the request of the Federal Ministry of Finance by way of administrative assistance by the BMEIA. The agreement and the contribution are unlimited in time; rules on the termination of the agreement are regulated in Art. 5 of the agreement.

In accordance with Art. 1 para. 5 of the agreement, the international organisations select a suitable educational institution to which the education amount is transferred. The international organisations have selected VIS as the educational institution that will therefore receive the education grant from the international organisations. Art. 3 of the Agreement provides that the Republic of Austria – with the aim of ensuring the location of an educational institution within reasonable proximity to the Vienna International Centre – shall provide a property including buildings and equipment for the exclusive use for educational activities of the institution at least until July 2024. The ownership structure of the VIS buildings is not known to the BMEIA. Questions concerning the implementation of this provision do not fall within the remit of the BMEIA. The continued existence of the VIS is not linked to the UN headquarters in Vienna. [...]

The relevant parts of the German original read as follows:

[...] Die Unterstützung der Finanzierung von Schulplätzen für Kinder von in Wien tätigen Angestellten der internationalen Organisationen durch Österreich ist dabei einer von vielen Bestandteilen, um die Attraktivität des Amtssitzes Wien zu stärken.

Zwischen der Republik Österreich und der Vienna International School (VIS) gibt es keinen völkerrechtlichen Vertrag. Es werden derzeit auch keine finanziellen Zuwendungen vonseiten der Republik Österreich an die VIS geleistet. Finanzielle Zuwendungen des Bundesministeriums für europäische und internationale Angelegenheiten (BMEIA) an die VIS in der Vergangenheit sind nicht bekannt.

Das sogenannte Bildungsbeitragsabkommen (BGBl. III Nr. 151/2016) wurde zwischen der Republik Österreich und vier internationalen Organisationen am Amtssitz Wien – den Vereinten Nationen (UNOV), der Internationalen Atomenergie-Organisation (IAEO), der Organisation der Vereinten Nationen für industrielle Entwicklung (UNIDO) und der Vorbereitenden Kommission für die Organisation des Vertrages über das umfassende Verbot von Nuklearversuchen (CTBTO) – abgeschlossen. Art. 1 Abs. 1 des Abkommens sieht vor, dass die Republik Österreich einen jährlichen Bildungsbetrag an diese Organisationen leistet. Die Höhe dieses Beitrags ist in Art. 1 geregelt und beträgt seit dem Jahr 2019 2 Millionen Euro pro

Schuljahr. Der Bildungsbetrag wird auf Ersuchen des Bundesministeriums für Finanzen im Wege der Amtshilfe durch das BMEIA an die CTBTO überwiesen. Das Abkommen und der Beitrag sind zeitlich unbefristet, Regelungen zur Beendigung des Abkommens werden in Art. 5 des Abkommens geregelt.

Gemäß Art. 1 Abs. 5 des Abkommens wählen die internationalen Organisationen eine geeignete Bildungseinrichtung aus, an die der Bildungsbetrag übermittelt wird. Die internationalen Organisationen haben die VIS als Bildungseinrichtung ausgewählt, die daher von den internationalen Organisationen den Bildungsbetrag erhält. Art. 3 des Abkommens sieht vor, dass die Republik Österreich – mit dem Ziel, den Standort einer Bildungseinrichtung innerhalb angemessener Nähe zum Wiener Internationalen Zentrum sicherzustellen – zumindest bis Juli 2024 eine Liegenschaft einschließlich Gebäude und Ausstattung für die ausschließliche Nutzung für Bildungsaktivitäten der Einrichtung zur Verfügung stellt. Die Eigentumsverhältnisse an den Gebäuden der VIS sind dem BMEIA nicht bekannt. Fragen betreffend die Umsetzung dieser Bestimmung fallen nicht in die Vollziehung des BMEIA. Der Fortbestand der VIS ist nicht mit dem UNO Amtssitz Wien verknüpft. […]

b. Regional organisations/Regionalorganisationen

EE.II.2.b.-1

Enquiry concerning EU accession to the European Convention on Human Rights

Anfrage betreffend EU-Beitritt zur Europäischen Menschenrechtskonvention

On 29 March 2023, a number of representatives of the Austrian National Assembly raised a parliamentary enquiry to the Federal Minister for European and International Affairs concerning EU accession to the European Convention on Human Rights,[16] to which the Minister gave, *inter alia*, the following response on 26 May 2023:[17]

Since the resumption of negotiations in 2020, the ad hoc negotiating group of the Council of Europe's Steering Committee for Human Rights ('47+1' or, since the exclusion of Russia, '46+1') has met 14 times. The Austrian delegation, led by the Permanent Representative of Austria to the Council of Europe and with the participation of representatives of the Constitutional Office of the Federal Chancellery and the Office of the Legal Adviser of the Federal Ministry for European and International Affairs (BMEIA), was actively involved in all negotiations. In March 2023, the ad hoc negotiating group successfully concluded the negotiations on the instruments for accession of the European Union (EU) to the European

[16] Parliamentary Materials, 14708/J (XXVII. GP).

[17] Parliamentary Materials, 14196/AB (XXVII. GP).

Convention on Human Rights (ECHR) on a provisional basis. The instruments of accession consist of the draft accession agreement including an explanatory report, the draft EU declaration, the draft amendment to the Rules of Procedure of the Committee of Ministers and the draft *Memorandum of Understanding (MoU)* and are publicly available on the Council of Europe website.

The incompatibilities with Union law of the draft agreement from 2013 as set out by the European Court of Justice (ECJ) in its Opinion 2/13 were resolved in the revised accession instruments with one exception. An internal EU solution is being developed for the incompatibility of purely external judicial review of fundamental rights in areas beyond the jurisdiction of the ECJ, namely the Common Security and Defence Policy (CFSP) [*sic*]. This area has therefore been removed from the negotiations.

The relevant parts of the German original read as follows:

Seit der Wiederaufnahme der Verhandlungen im Jahr 2020 tagte die ad-hoc-Verhandlungsgruppe des Leitungskomitees für Menschenrechte des Europarates („47+1" bzw. seit dem Ausschluss Russlands „46+1") 14 Mal. Die österreichische Delegation unter Leitung der Ständigen Vertreterin Österreichs beim Europarat und unter Beteiligung von Vertreterinnen und Vertretern des Verfassungsdienstes des Bundeskanzleramts und des Völkerrechtsbüros im Bundesministerium für europäische und internationale Angelegenheiten (BMEIA) war an allen Verhandlungen aktiv beteiligt. Die ad-hoc-Verhandlungsgruppe konnte im März 2023 die Verhandlungen über die Instrumente für einen Beitritt der Europäischen Union (EU) zur Europäischen Menschenrechtskonvention (EMRK) erfolgreich vorläufig abschließen. Die Beitrittsinstrumente bestehen aus dem Entwurf des Beitrittsabkommens samt erläuterndem Bericht, dem Entwurf einer Erklärung der EU, dem Entwurf einer Novelle der Verfahrensordnung des Ministerkomitees sowie dem Entwurf eines *Memorandum of Understanding* (MoU) und sind auf der Internetseite des Europarates öffentlich zugänglich.

Die vom Europäischen Gerichtshof (EuGH) in seinem Gutachten 2/13 dargelegten Unionsrechtsunvereinbarkeiten des Abkommensentwurfes aus dem Jahr 2013 konnten in den revidierten Beitrittsinstrumenten mit einer Ausnahme gelöst werden. Zu der vom EuGH festgestellten Unvereinbarkeit einer rein externen gerichtlichen Grundrechtskontrolle in Bereichen, die der Jurisdiktion des EuGH entzogen sind, namentlich der Gemeinsamen Sicherheits- und Verteidigungspolitik (GASP) [*sic*], wird eine unionsinterne Lösung erarbeitet. Dieser Bereich wurde somit aus den Verhandlungen herausgelöst.

III. Other subjects of international law and entities and groups/ Andere Völkerrechtssubjekte, Einheiten und Gruppen

7. Others (indigenous people, minorities, national liberation movements, etc.)/Sonstige (indigene Völker, Minderheiten, Nationale Befreiungsbewegungen)

See *EE.I.5.-1* and *EE.I.5.-2*.

FF. The position of the individual (including the corporation) in international law/Die Stellung der Einzelperson (einschließlich der juristischen Person) im Völkerrecht

VI. Refugees/Flüchtlinge

FF.VI.-1

Austrian statement at the Online Global Commemoration – 25th Anniversary of the Guiding Principles on Internal Displacement

Österreichische Erklärung bei der Online Global Commemoration – 25. Jahrestag der Leitlinien zu Binnenvertreibung

On 17 April 2023, the Austrian representative made the following statement at the online commemoration of the 25th Anniversary of the Guiding Principles on Internal Displacement:

> […] I want to thank you for organizing this important event marking the 25th Anniversary of the Guiding Principles on Internal Displacement.
>
> […] The Guiding Principles on Internal Displacement were developed in 1998 as a set of international standards that provide a framework for the protection and assistance of IDPs. These principles are critical to ensuring that the human rights and fundamental freedoms of IDPs are respected and upheld during times of conflict, violence, and other forms of internal displacement.
>
> On the occasion of this anniversary, Austria reaffirms its commitment to the protecting the rights and dignity of IDPs in accordance with these principles. As one of Austria's priorities at the Human Rights Council, our efforts aim to improve the legal, institutional, and practical protection of internally displaced persons worldwide, with the mandate of the Special Rapporteur on the human rights of IDPs at the center of our efforts. […]

VII. Immigration and emigration, extradition, expulsion, asylum/Einwanderung und Auswanderung, Auslieferung, Ausweisung, Asyl

2. Extradition/Auslieferung

See *FF.X.-1.*

VIII. Human rights and fundamental freedoms/Menschenrechte und Grundfreiheiten

See also *EE.II.2.b.-1, FF.VI.-1, QQ.I.2.g.-2, QQ.I.2.g.-3, QQ.I.2.f.-1*, and *PP.I.-1*.

FF.VIII.-1

Austrian statement in the 52nd Session of the Human Rights Council: Interactive Dialogue with Special Rapporteur on human rights and the environment

Österreichische Erklärung in der 52. Sitzung des Menschenrechtsrates: Interaktiver Dialog mit dem Sonderberichterstatter für Menschenrechte und Umwelt

During the 52nd Session of the Human Rights Council on 9 March 2023, the Austrian representative made the following statement in relation to the 'Interactive Dialogue with Special Rapporteur on human rights and the environment':

> […] I would like to thank you for your work on further clarifying the human rights' impacts of the climate crisis. We highly appreciate the focus of your latest report, which outlines the links between gender equality and ecological sustainability.
>
> […] You rightly outline how a human-rights based approach to environmental protection includes procedural rights, such as the right to information, to public participation and to effective remedies. You only briefly touch upon the right to non-discrimination and to the equal access to education which is fundamental for the women's participation in decision-making. […]

FF.VIII.-2

Austrian statement in the 53rd Session of the Human Rights Council on the topic of 'Enhanced Interactive Dialogue on the situation of women and girls in Afghanistan'

Österreichische Erklärung in der 53. Sitzung des Menschenrechtsrates zum Thema „Verstärkter interaktiver Dialog über die Situation von Frauen und Mädchen in Afghanistan"

On 19 June 2023, the Austrian representative made a statement in the 53rd Session of the Human Rights Council on the topic of 'Enhanced Interactive Dialogue on the situation of women and girls in Afghanistan':

> [...] Austria aligns itself with the EU statement.
>
> Austria is extremely alarmed at the continuing deterioration of the human rights situation in Afghanistan, plagued by decades of conflict and human rights viola-

tions affecting all members of society, in particular women and girls, as well as minorities.

Since the collapse of the Republic, the *de facto* authorities have dismantled the legal and institutional framework and have been ruling through the most extreme forms of misogyny, destroying the relative progress towards gender equality achieved in the past two decades.

The Decrees of the Taliban, which effectively ban women and girls from public life through prohibiting them from working in humanitarian NGOs and from secondary and higher education, are unacceptable. This extreme situation of institutionalized gender-based discrimination in Afghanistan is unparalleled anywhere in the world. [...]

We call upon the *de facto* authorities to immediately reverse policies and directives that negatively impact women and girls as well as to prioritize womens' [*sic*] and girls' rights to equal participation in education, employment, and all other aspects of public life.

FF.VIII.-3

Austrian statement in the 53rd Session of the Human Rights Council: Interactive Dialogue with the Independent Expert on Sexual Orientation and Gender Identity

Österreichische Stellungnahme in der 53. Sitzung des Menschenrechtsrates: Interaktiver Dialog mit dem Unabhängigen Experten für sexuelle Orientierung und Geschlechtsidentität

During the 53rd Session of the Human Rights Council on 21 June 2023, the Austrian representative made the following statement in relation to the 'Interactive Dialogue with the Independent Expert on Sexual Orientation and Gender Identity'(SOGI):

[…] Austria aligns itself with the EU Statement and supports the Statement of the Group of Friends on SOGI.

[…] We all have committed to international obligations regarding anti-discrimination and they include ensuring that people are not subjected to discrimination or even physical and mental violence because of who they are or who they love.

We call on all countries to take a close look at their legislation and dismantle laws and policies that criminalize same-sex intimacy or gender identity and repeal laws criminalizing them as blasphemy.

We are particularly concerned about the continued criminalization – or even worse – the application of the death penalty for homosexual acts and fully agree with your assessment that this is a form of State-sponsored discrimination contrary to international human rights law. We call on all States to urgently and immediately change such legislation. […]

F. VIII.-4

Enquiry concerning a sanction mechanism against human rights violators

Anfrage betreffend einen Sanktionsmechanismus gegen Menschenrechtsverletzer:innen

On 11 July 2023, a number of representatives of the Austrian National Assembly raised a parliamentary enquiry to the Federal Minister for European and International Affairs concerning a sanction mechanism against human rights violators,[18] to which the Minister gave, *inter alia*, the following response on 11 September 2023:[19]

> [...] The listing criteria are contained in Art. 2 para. 1 and Art. 3 para. 1 in conjunction with Art. 1 para. 1 of Decision (CFSP) 2020/1999 concerning restrictive measures against serious human rights violations and abuses, OJ L No. 410I of 7.12.2020 p. 13 as amended. Accordingly, natural or legal persons, entities or bodies may be listed if they a) are responsible for serious human rights violations, or b) provide financial, technical, or material support for them or are otherwise involved, including by planning, directing, ordering, assisting, preparing, facilitating or promoting such acts, or c) are associated with the aforementioned natural or legal persons, entities, or bodies. Art. 1 para. 1 of the decision contains a list of the serious human rights violations covered by the decision. If a listed natural or legal person, organisation or entity no longer meets the listing criteria, it must be removed from the list. [...]
>
> Austria is in favour of the inclusion of a new listing criterion for corruption in the EU human rights sanctions regime. In the meantime, the EU High Representative for Foreign Affairs and Security Policy has also submitted a proposal for a separate EU sanctions regime against corruption, which Austria supports. [...]
>
> [...] In its judgement in the joined case C-402/05 P and C-415/05 P (*Kadi I*), the ECJ stated in para. 230 that national sanctions would impair the internal market. It follows from this that a purely national sanctions regime comparable to the EU human rights sanctions regime would not be compatible with EU law. [...]

The relevant parts of the German original read as follows:

> [...] Die Listungskriterien sind in Art. 2 Abs. 1 und Art. 3 Abs. 1 in Verbindung mit Art. 1 Abs. 1 des Beschlusses (GASP) 2020/1999 über restriktive Maßnahmen gegen schwere Menschenrechtsverletzungen und -verstöße, ABl. L Nr. 410I vom 7.12.2020 S. 13 idgF, enthalten. Demnach können natürliche oder juristische Personen, Organisationen oder Einrichtungen gelistet werden, die a) für schwerwiegende Menschenrechtsverletzungen verantwortlich sind, oder b) diese finanziell, technisch oder materiell unterstützen oder anderweitig daran beteiligt sind, u.a.

[18] Parliamentary Materials, 15782/J (XXVII. GP).

[19] Parliamentary Materials, 15277/AB (XXVII. GP).

durch Planung, Leitung, Anordnung, Unterstützung, Vorbereitung, Erleichterung oder Förderung solcher Handlungen, oder c) mit den vorgenannten natürlichen oder juristischen Personen, Organisationen oder Einrichtungen in Verbindung stehen. Art. 1 Abs. 1 des Beschlusses enthält eine Aufzählung jener schwerwiegenden Menschenrechtsverletzungen, die unter den Beschluss fallen. Erfüllt eine gelistete natürliche oder juristische Person, Organisation oder Einrichtung nicht mehr die Listungskriterien, ist sie von der Liste zu streichen. […]

Österreich spricht sich für die Aufnahme eines neuen Listungskriteriums betreffend Korruption in das EU-Menschenrechtssanktionsregime aus. Mittlerweile hat auch der Hohe Vertreter für Außen- und Sicherheitspolitik der EU einen Vorschlag für ein eigenes EU Sanktionsregime gegen Korruption vorgelegt, den Österreich unterstützt. […]

[…] In seinem Urteil in der verbundenen Rechtssache C-402/05 P und C-415/05 P (*Kadi I*) hielt der EuGH in Rz 230 fest, dass nationale Sanktionen den Binnenmarkt beeinträchtigen würden. Daraus ergibt sich, dass ein dem EU-Menschenrechtssanktionsregime vergleichbares, aber rein nationales Sanktionsregime mit dem Unionsrecht nicht vereinbar wäre. […]

FF.VIII.-5

Enquiry concerning the National Action Plan for Human Rights in Austria

Anfrage betreffend „Nationaler Aktionsplan für Menschenrechte in Österreich"

On 18 August 2023, a number of representatives of the Austrian National Assembly raised a parliamentary enquiry to the Federal Minister for the EU and Constitution concerning the National Action Plan for Human Rights in Austria,[20] to which the Minister gave, *inter alia*, the following response on 18 October 2023:[21]

[...] Austria already has a number of specific thematic national action plans, in particular on people with disabilities, human trafficking, the implementation of UN Security Council Resolution 1325 and integration, as well as a strategy for the prevention of extremism and deradicalisation and a national strategy against anti-Semitism, which are also regularly evaluated and updated. Further national action plans, e.g. to combat racism and discrimination, are planned. A draft National Action Plan for the implementation of the EU Child Guarantee is currently being prepared. Progress on these projects must be awaited before a comprehensive National Action Plan for Human Rights can be envisaged. [...]

---

[20] Parliamentary Materials, 15959/J (XXVII. GP). See also Parliamentary Materials, 15958/J (XXVII. GP).

[21] Parliamentary Materials, 15447/AB (XXVII. GP). See also Parliamentary Materials, 15462/AB (XXVII. GP).

The relevant parts of the German original read as follows:

> [...] Österreich verfügt bereits über eine Reihe spezifischer thematischer nationaler Aktionspläne, insbesondere zu Menschen mit Behinderung, zu Menschenhandel, zur Umsetzung der Resolution 1325 des UN Sicherheitsrates und zur Integration, zudem über eine Strategie zur Prävention von Extremismus und Deradikalisierung sowie eine Nationale Strategie gegen Antisemitismus, welche auch regelmäßig evaluiert und aktualisiert werden. Weitere Nationale Aktionspläne, z.B. zur Bekämpfung von Rassismus und Diskriminierung, sind geplant. Der Entwurf eines Nationalen Aktionsplans zur Umsetzung der EU-Kindergarantie wird gerade ausgearbeitet. Die Fortschritte bei diesen Projekten müssen zunächst abgewartet werden, bevor ein umfassender Nationaler Aktionsplan für Menschenrechte ins Auge gefasst werden kann. […]

FF.VIII.-6

Austrian statement in the 54th Session of the Human Rights Council: Interactive Dialogue with the Special Rapporteur on Afghanistan

Österreichische Erklärung in der 54. Sitzung des Menschenrechtsrates: Interaktiver Dialog mit dem Sonderberichterstatter für Afghanistan

On 11 September 2023, the Austrian representative made a statement in the in the 54th Session of the Human Rights Council dedicated to an Interactive Dialogue with the Special Rapporteur on Afghanistan:

> […] Austria aligns itself with the EU statement.
>
> Despite reassurances by the Taliban *de facto* authorities that any restrictions, would be temporary, the facts on the ground have demonstrated an accelerated system of segregation, marginalization and persecution.
>
> […]
>
> Afghanistan today is the most repressive country in the world regarding women's rights. We urge the *de facto* authorities to immediately reverse course on the treatment of women and girls, to enforce strict measures to prevent discrimination against ethnic and religious minorities, and to reverse actions that have resulted in the shrinking of civic space and ensure that civil society organisations, journalists and other media workers can function without undue hindrance.

FF.VIII.-7

Parliamentary resolution on respect for human rights, especially of women and girls, in Afghanistan

Parlamentarische Entschließung betreffend Wahrung der Menschenrechte, insbesondere von Frauen und Mädchen, in Afghanistan

On 19 October 2023, the National Assembly adopted a parliamentary resolution on respect for human rights, especially of women and girls, in Afghanistan:[22]

> The Federal Government, in particular the Federal Minister for European and International Affairs, is requested to continue to work at all levels to ensure that the rule of law, human rights, fundamental rights and freedoms as well as the opportunities for a self-determined life, especially for women and girls, are fully respected and ensured in Afghanistan.
>
> In this context, the Federal Minister for European and International Affairs is requested to advocate a more active role for the EU.
>
> In addition, the Federal Minister for European and International Affairs is requested to support the people in Afghanistan, and in particular women and girls, by issuing corresponding declarations, resolutions and restrictive measures in the relevant European and international organisations and bodies.
>
> The Federal Minister for European and International Affairs is requested to advocate in international bodies for the release of people who have become political prisoners because of their commitment to human and women's rights.

The German original reads as follows:

> Die Bundesregierung, insbesondere der Bundesminister für europäische und internationale Angelegenheiten, wird ersucht, sich weiterhin auf allen Ebenen dafür einzusetzen, dass die Rechtsstaatlichkeit, die Menschen-, Grund- und Freiheitsrechte sowie die Möglichkeiten für ein selbstbestimmtes Leben, insbesondere von Frauen und Mädchen, in Afghanistan vollumfänglich geachtet und gesichert wird.
>
> In diesem Zusammenhang wird der Bundesminister für europäische und internationale Angelegenheiten ersucht, sich für eine aktivere Rolle der EU einzusetzen.
>
> Zudem wird der Bundesminister für europäische und internationale Angelegenheiten zur Unterstützung der Menschen in Afghanistan und insbesondere der Frauen und Mädchen ersucht, entsprechende Erklärungen, Resolutionen sowie restriktive Maßnahmen in den zuständigen europäischen und internationalen Organisationen und Gremien weiterhin zu unterstützen.
>
> Der Bundesminister für europäische und internationale Angelegenheiten wird ersucht, sich für die Freilassung von Menschen, die aufgrund ihres Einsatzes für Menschen- und Frauenrechte politische Gefangene wurden, in internationalen Gremien einzusetzen.

X. Crimes under international law/Völkerrechtliche Verbrechen

See also *HH.I.4.-2* and *QQ.I.2.g.-3*.

---

[22] Parliamentary Materials, 342/E(XXVII. GP).

FF.X.-1

Written comments by Austria on the ILC Draft Articles on the Prevention and Punishment of Crimes against Humanity

Schriftliche Kommentare zum ILC-Artikelentwurf über die Verhütung und Bestrafung von Verbrechen gegen die Menschlichkeit

In response to the letter by the Office of Legal Affairs of the Secretariat of the United Nations of 20 January 2023, Austria submitted observations on the Draft Articles on the Prevention and Punishment of Crimes against Humanity prepared by the ILC:

> Austria re-emphasizes the importance of the ILC's work in particular with regard to a future convention on the prevention and punishment of crimes against humanity. Such a convention is needed both for humanitarian as well as systematic reasons. It would be a necessary first step for a complete and effective international criminal justice system to hold perpetrators accountable. While many aspects, such as the definition of crimes against humanity, constitute customary international law, a convention on this topic would not only fill an existing gap in international treaty law but would also be a strong signal that international crimes cannot go unpunished.
>
> Regarding the preambular paragraphs, we fully concur with the ILC's view that the prohibition of crimes against humanity already constitutes a peremptory norm of general international law.
>
> As to the scope of a future convention (as stated in Article 1), the Convention would apply to the prevention and the punishment of crimes against humanity. Nevertheless, matters that may not be covered by a future convention would still – to a large extent – be regulated by customary international law. Other grave international crimes such as genocide or war crimes should remain regulated in dedicated conventions and not be touched upon by the convention in question.
>
> The definition of crimes against humanity in Article 2 of the proposed convention codifies customary international law. Thus, from a legal point of view, the definition is not 'based' on Article 7 of the Rome Statute of the International Criminal Court as a matter of treaty law. It is evident that the Rome Statute and the proposed Convention are two individual and separate legal instruments with a different purpose and possibly different parties. The commonality is the definition of crimes against humanity under customary international law, which is important to avoid fragmentation and to ensure consistency in the international legal system. The ILC Draft Articles, however, do not have a direct connection with the Rome Statue and being a State party to the Rome Statute is neither a precondition nor a consequence for the application of the definition.
>
> Although prior conventions, such as the 1948 Convention on the Prevention and Punishment of the Crime of Genocide, have not expressly provided that States

shall not commit the acts in question in those conventions, we see merit in explicitly mentioning the obligation of states 'not to engage in acts that constitute crimes against humanity' in Article 3 (1). This obligation is two-fold and applies to state organs as well as persons acting on the instructions or under the direction or control of the state. We also welcome the addition of the explicit obligation to prevent crimes against humanity in Article 3 (2), as it is also stipulated in the Genocide Convention. Additionally, we welcome the explicit clarification in Article 3 (3) that no exceptional circumstances may be invoked as a justification for the commission of crimes against humanity.

The obligation of prevention in Article 4 includes 'effective legislative, administrative, judicial or other appropriate preventive measures', which was inspired by the wording of the Convention against Torture. Since torture is one of the acts listed in the draft definition of crimes against humanity, a similar approach on the prevention of crimes against humanity is only consequential. At the same time, the explicit requirement of preventive measures to be 'in conformity with international law' is in line with the jurisprudence of the International Court of Justice.

Crimes against humanity shall not be subject to any statute of limitations as drafted in Article 6 (6), although we would prefer a clear prohibition without states having to take respective measures. As foreseen in Article 6 (7), Austria has already criminalized crimes against humanity with appropriate penalties in Section 321a of the Austrian Criminal Code. We consider the emphasis on national criminal laws providing for appropriate penalties in the draft articles useful and would like to accentuate that existing national laws on the subject matter do not preclude states from engaging in a future convention.

Regarding the frequently discussed rules on the establishment of national jurisdiction in Article 7, we would like to underline that these rules are well established bases of criminal jurisdiction under customary and treaty law, which can be found in many international conventions on combating international crimes. In this context, it should be stressed that Article 7, as the ILC has pointed out in its commentary, only requires states to *establish* jurisdiction by adopting the necessary national legislation but *not to exercise* such jurisdiction unless the alleged perpetrator is present in the territory under the State's jurisdiction. Thus, in fact, the convention does not require States to exercise universal jurisdiction, since based on Articles 8, 9 and 10, States may only exercise jurisdiction when the perpetrator is present in their territory, thus requiring a connection between the perpetrator and the forum State which is based on the territoriality principle.

Austria welcomes the inclusion of the duty of investigation in Article 8 similar to the obligation in the Convention against Torture, which is key for effective prosecution and punishment. A broader obligation for a state to investigate acts committed outside its territory but still under its jurisdiction (in cases of a ship flying its flag or on board of an aircraft having the nationality of the State in which it is registered) could be discussed.

With regard to the principle of 'Aut dedere aut judicare' in Article 10, it is Austria's understanding that the reference to a competent international criminal court or tribunal also comprises hybrid courts or tribunals that combine both national and international elements. Should any court or international tribunal not have jurisdiction, the obligations of Article 10 remain binding on the State on whose territory the alleged offender is present.

FF.X.-2

Statement on Crimes Against Humanity before the Sixth Committee

Erklärung zu Verbrechen gegen die Menschlichkeit vor dem Sechsten Komitee

On 11 October 2023, the Austrian representative delivered the following statement to the Sixth Committee of the 78th Session of the General Assembly regarding Agenda Item 80 on 'Crimes Against Humanity':

> [...] My delegation fully aligns itself with the statement made by the European Union and we would like to reiterate the following points in our national capacity regarding the 'Draft articles on prevention and punishment of crimes against humanity' elaborated by the International Law Commission.
>
> At the outset, it is worthwhile recalling the preamble of the draft articles: Throughout history, millions of children, women and men have been victims of crimes that deeply shock the conscience of humanity. And this continues to happen as we recently witnessed in various regions of the world. Therefore, we are again reminded of the need, or even moral obligation, to work together towards effective prevention of crimes against humanity. While crimes against humanity are already established crimes under customary international law, there exists a gap in international treaty law on its criminalization and legal cooperation. A future convention would also be a strong signal that these international crimes cannot go unpunished.
>
> While criminalization does not always prevent crimes from happening in the first place, it still means a change of awareness. Codifying the criminalization of widespread or systematic attacks directed against civilian population would complement the Genocide Convention of 1948 and the Geneva Conventions of 1949. A dedicated convention based on the ILC-draft articles would ensure consistency in the international criminal justice system. It will strengthen prevention and offer a new legal basis for inter-state cooperation.
>
> For these reasons, Austria, like many other states, supports the early convening of a diplomatic conference to finalize and adopt an international convention on the basis of the 'Draft articles on prevention and punishment of crimes against humanity', as recommend by the International Law Commission. [...]

FF.X.-3

Statement in the General Debate of the Assembly of State Parties of the International Criminal Court

Erklärung in der Hauptversammlung der Versammlung der Vertragsstaaten des Internationalen Strafgerichtshofs

During the General Debate of the 22nd Session of the Assembly of State Parties of the International Criminal Court in The Hague which took place from 4 to 14 December 2023, Austria delivered a statement, the relevant parts of which read as follows:

> [...] Over the last year, important progress has been made in strengthening the Rome Statute system.
>
> Austria commends the Court for the advances it has made over the past year in relation to the Ukraine investigations.
>
> The arrest warrants against President Putin and Ms. Lvova Belova are an important first step towards justice for the thousands of children that became victims of the illegal aggression of Russia against Ukraine.
>
> The Commission of Inquiry on Ukraine with its seat in Vienna has collected ample evidence of horrendous crimes committed by Russian forces in Ukraine. The Court's work is indispensable in holding accountable the persons responsible for those crimes.
>
> Austria also welcomes Armenia's ratification of the Rome Statute. With soon 124 States parties, the Rome Statute is growing again. We should use this momentum to reinforce our efforts in advocating for universality.
>
> Looking ahead, in the course of this ASP, we are also set to accomplish important milestones for the Court.
>
> Austria is pleased that the ASP will adopt the permanent due diligence process and a new legal aid policy. These instruments are important tools for the Court and we wish to thank all those who worked hard on preparing them.
>
> [...]
>
> Austria strongly condemns any threats or attacks against the Court and its staff. The cyber operation against the Court, as well as the arrest warrants against Court officials are unacceptable. Our commitment to the Court remains unwavering and, together with other States Parties, we will defend it and stand firmly with its officials and personnel.
>
> Moreover, with four ongoing trials and 17 situations spanning over four continents, the Court's workload is heavy. Yet, this is likely to further increase in the coming months and years.
>
> [...] To fulfil its mission, the Court needs the support of all States Parties and the international community at large – now more than ever.

In particular, it is paramount that States Parties honour their obligations to fully cooperate with the Court, including by executing arrest warrants and observing the non-essential contacts policy.

Equally, given the threats against the Court, States should show their support by ratifying the Agreement on the Privileges and Immunities of the Court.

Moreover, States need to provide the Court and the Trust Fund for Victims with sufficient resources to carry out their invaluable work. In this regard, we call on all States Parties to pay their contributions to the regular budget in time.

Austria, on its part, has stepped up its support for the Court.

Since the beginning of Russia's war of aggression against Ukraine, Austria has made voluntary financial contributions to the trust fund of the Office of the Prosecutor amounting to € 400.000 and has seconded a legal expert. In 2024, we are planning to pay a further voluntary contribution and second another legal expert.

Moreover, in 2023, Austria increased its contribution to the Trust Fund for Victims, and contributed to the Trust Fund for Family Visits.

[…] This year marked the 25th anniversary of the Rome Statute. In order to commemorate this anniversary, but also to prepare for the review of the Kampala amendments on the crime of aggression in 2025, the University of Vienna, with the support of the Austrian Foreign Ministry, organized the Vienna Conference on Amendments on 6 and 7 October 2023, which reflected on possible options to amend the Rome Statute to harmonize the Court's exercise of jurisdiction over the crime of aggression.

Austria strongly supports the continuation of these discussions during next year in order to prepare for the review in 2025.

Today, as our international order based on international law is increasingly challenged, the Court remains a beacon of hope for maintaining the rule of law.

[…]

XI. Criminal responsibility of the individual (see MM.)/ Strafrechtliche Verantwortlichkeit des Einzelmenschen (siehe MM.)

See also *FF.X.-3* and *QQ.I.2.g.-3*.

FF.XI.-1

Enquiry concerning the collection and transmission of evidence on war crimes in Ukraine

Anfrage betreffend die Ermittlung und Weiterleitung von Beweisen in Bezug auf Kriegsverbrechen in der Ukraine

On 4 August 2023, a number of representatives of the Austrian National Assembly raised a parliamentary enquiry to the Federal Minister of Justice concerning the collection and transmission of evidence on war crimes in Ukraine,[23] to which the Minister gave, *inter alia*, the following response on 4 October 2023:[24]

> [...] Under Austrian law, the securing of evidence of war crimes in Ukraine by the judiciary requires the initiation of domestic proceedings or the submission of a request for legal assistance from another state or the International Criminal Court. [...]
>
> The transmission of evidence by Austrian judicial authorities to EUROJUST also requires pending investigative proceedings; as of 1 August 2023, no such proceedings are pending in connection with war crimes in Ukraine resulting from the Russian war of aggression that began on 24 February 2022. [...]
>
> As regards cooperation with the International Criminal Court, requests for mutual legal assistance within the scope of its jurisdiction are regularly executed on the basis of the Federal Act on Cooperation with the International Criminal Court, Federal Law Gazette I No. 135/2002 as amended. In the course of such legal assistance, evidence is also transmitted or independently collected by the International Criminal Court in accordance with § 13 leg.cit.

The relevant parts of the German original read as follows:

> […] Die Sicherung von Beweisen wegen Kriegsverbrechen in der Ukraine durch die Justiz setzt nach österreichischer Rechtslage die Einleitung eines Inlandsverfahrens oder das Vorliege eines Rechtshilfeersuchens eines anderen Staates oder des Internationalen Strafgerichtshofes voraus. [...]
>
> Die Übermittlung von Beweisen durch österreichische Justizbehörden an EUROJUST setzt ebenfalls ein anhängiges Ermittlungsverfahren voraus; mit Stand 1. August 2023 ist ein solches in Zusammenhang mit Kriegsverbrechen in der Ukraine auf Grund des am 24. Februar 2022 begonnenen russischen Angriffskriegs noch nicht anhängig. […]
>
> Was die Zusammenarbeit mit dem Internationalen Strafgerichtshof angeht, werden Rechtshilfeersuchen des Internationalen Strafgerichtshofes im Rahmen seiner Zuständigkeit auf der Grundlage des Bundesgesetzes über die Zusammenarbeit mit dem Internationalen Strafgerichtshof, BGBl I Nr. 135/2002 idgF, laufend erledigt. Im Rahmen solcher Rechtshilfeerledigungen werden auch Beweismittel übermittelt oder vom Internationalen Strafgerichtshof nach § 13 leg. cit. selbständig erhoben.

---

[23] Parliamentary Materials, 15875/J (XXVII. GP).

[24] Parliamentary Materials, 15373/AB (XXVII. GP).

FF.XI.-2

Enquiry concerning criminal proceedings against Syrian war criminal in Austria

Anfrage betreffend Strafverfahren gegen syrische Kriegsverbrecher in Österreich

On 13 September 2023, a number of representatives of the Austrian National Assembly raised a parliamentary enquiry to the Federal Minister of Justice concerning criminal proceedings against Syrian war criminals in Austria,[25] to which the Minister gave, *inter alia*, the following response on 13 November 2023:[26]

> [...] First of all, it should be clarified that according to the decree of 5 July 2022 on domestic jurisdiction for war crimes committed abroad and other offences under Chapter 25 of the Criminal Code and on the immunity of supreme organs of foreign states in Austrian criminal proceedings, in the opinion of the Federal Ministry of Justice – without prejudice to independent jurisprudence – Austrian interests within the meaning of Section 64 para. 1 no. 4c lit. b of the Criminal Code can be violated if persons flee to Austria due to a crime under Chapter 25 of the Criminal Code. The violation of Austrian interests must be caused by the (specific) offence. This causal link will have to be examined in each individual case according to the specific circumstances. It therefore always remains a case-by-case assessment. [...]

The relevant parts of the German original read as follows:

> [...] Zunächst ist klarzustellen, dass laut Erlass vom 5. Juli 2022 zur inländischen Gerichtsbarkeit bei im Ausland begangenen Kriegsverbrechen und anderen Straftaten nach dem 25. Abschnitt des StGB und zur Immunität oberster Organe fremder Staaten in österreichischen Strafverfahren nach Ansicht des BMJ – unvorgreiflich der unabhängigen Rechtsprechung – österreichische Interessen iSd § 64 Abs. 1 Z 4c lit. b StGB verletzt werden können, wenn Personen aufgrund eines Verbrechens nach dem 25. Abschnitt des StGB nach Österreich flüchten. Die Verletzung österreichischer Interessen muss dabei durch die (konkrete) Tat herbeigeführt werden. Dieser Kausalzusammenhang wird jeweils nach den konkreten Umständen im Einzelfall zu prüfen sein. Es bleibt sohin immer eine Beurteilung im Einzelfall. […]

---

[25] Parliamentary Materials, 16109/J (XXVII. GP).

[26] Parliamentary Materials, 15604/AB (XXVII. GP).

GG. Organs of the State and their legal status/Die Staatsorgane und ihr rechtlicher Status

GG.-1

Work of the International Law Commission on Immunity of State Officials from Criminal Jurisdiction

Arbeit der Völkerrechtskommission betreffend die Immunität von Staatsorgangen von strafrechtlicher Gerichtsbarkeit

On 23 October 2023, the Austrian representative to the 78th Session of the General Assembly delivered the following statement to the Sixth Committee on Report of the International Law Commission on the Work of its 73rd and 74th Session concerning the topic of 'Immunity of State Officials from Criminal Jurisdiction':

> Austria also intends to submit written comments on the 'Draft articles on immunity of State officials from foreign criminal jurisdiction' by 1 December of this year, in particular on draft article 7 on crimes under international law in respect of which immunity *ratione materiae* shall not apply. While we support article 7 as a central provision of the draft articles and as a contribution to the fight against impunity, we reiterate Austria's position that the list of exceptions to functional immunity in draft article 7 is incomplete and should also contain a reference to the crime of aggression.
>
> According to Austrian practice and *opinio iuris* no functional immunity exists for international crimes, including the crime of aggression. We therefore call on the Commission and the newly appointed Special Rapporteur Claudio Grossman Guiloff, whom we thank for taking over this very important topic, to revisit this matter and amend draft article 7 accordingly.
>
> In this context, we would like to express our support for the balanced approach of the draft articles containing important procedural safeguards, which should make the whole project acceptable to the international community. We encourage the Special Rapporteur to pursue work on the finalisation of the draft articles in this spirit.

IV. Diplomatic missions and their members/Diplomatische Vertretungen und ihre Mitglieder

GG.IV.-1

Enquiry concerning the reception of the 'ambassador' of Myanmar by representatives of Medical University of Vienna

Anfrage betreffend Empfang des „Botschafters" Myanmars durch Vertreter der MedUni Wien

On 14 February 2023, a number of representatives of the Austrian National Assembly raised a parliamentary enquiry to the Federal Minister for European and International Affairs concerning reception of Myanmar's 'ambassador' by representatives of the Medical University of Vienna,[27] to which the Minister replied 14 April 2023:[28]

> Austria, together with the EU Member States and the Secretary-General of the United Nations, has clearly condemned the violent military coup in Myanmar against the democratically elected government under Aung San Suu Kyi and supports the respective positions and all measures taken by the European Union towards Myanmar. […]
>
> Austria recognises neither governments nor regimes, but only states. In this sense, diplomatic relations between Myanmar and Austria continue to exist. Since the military coup, the Federal Ministry for European and International Affairs (BMEIA) has remained in contact with the Embassy of Myanmar in Vienna on administrative and protocol issues. On 10 December 2020, while Aung San Suu Kyi's government was still in power, Mr Min Thein presented the *copie d'usage* of his credentials to the BMEIA. A few weeks later, on 1 February 2021, when there was a violent takeover in Myanmar, he was denied the opportunity to officially present his credentials. Mr Min Thein is therefore only considered a designated ambassador and chargé d'affaires.
>
> It goes without saying that there is no co-operation with the military junta in Myanmar within the area of responsibility of the BMEIA. […]
>
> […] Austria, together with EU Member States, co-initiated Human Rights Council Resolution 39/2, adopted in September 2018, which established an open-ended accountability mechanism (IIMM[29]) to prepare investigations for fair and independent criminal proceedings for the worst international crimes committed in Myanmar since 2011.
>
> At the suggestion of the BMEIA, the Federal Law on Cooperation with International Courts (IG-ZG, Federal Law Gazette No. 263/1996) was amended in 2020 and supplemented by a provision that enables cooperation under criminal law with United Nations bodies entrusted with the investigation or preservation of evidence in relation to serious criminal offences. This also includes the commission of investigation on Myanmar. Austria supports the activities of the commission of investigation by providing financial support and exchanging information, among other things. My ministry is in contact with representatives of the 'Committee Representing Pyidaungsu Hluttaw/National Unity Government' (CRPH/NUG) in order to exchange information on current developments and the human rights situation in Myanmar, in particular with regard to the Rohingya.

---

27 Parliamentary Materials, 14133/J (XXVII. GP).

28 Parliamentary Materials, 13689/AB (XXVII. GP).

29 Independent Investigative Mechanism for Myanmar.

The relevant parts of the German original read as follows:

Österreich hat den gewaltsamen Militärputsch in Myanmar gegen die demokratisch gewählte Regierung unter Aung San Suu Kyi, gemeinsam mit den EU-Mitgliedstaaten und dem Generalsekretär der Vereinten Nationen, klar verurteilt und unterstützt die einschlägigen Positionen und alle Maßnahmen der Europäischen Union gegenüber Myanmar. [...]

Österreich erkennt weder Regierungen noch Regime an, sondern ausschließlich Staaten. In diesem Sinne bestehen zwischen Myanmar und Österreich auch weiterhin diplomatische Beziehungen. Seit dem Militärputsch steht das Bundesministerium für europäische und internationale Angelegenheiten (BMEIA) zur Botschaft Myanmars in Wien zu administrativen und protokollarischen Fragen weiterhin in Kontakt. Herr Min Thein überreichte am 10. Dezember 2020, noch zu Zeiten der Regierung Aung San Suu Kyis, im BMEIA die *copie d'usage* seines Beglaubigungsschreibens. Als wenige Wochen später, am 1. Februar 2021, in Myanmar die gewaltsame Machtübernahme erfolgte, wurde ihm die Möglichkeit verwehrt, sein Beglaubigungsschreiben offiziell zu überreichen. Somit gilt Herr Min Thein nur als designierter Botschafter und Geschäftsträger.

Im Zuständigkeitsbereich des BMEIA gibt es selbstverständlich keine Kooperationen mit der Militärjunta in Myanmar. [...]

[...] Österreich [hat] gemeinsam mit EU-Mitgliedstaaten, die im September 2018 verabschiedete Resolution 39/2 des Menschenrechtsrats mitinitiiert, mit der ein unbefristeter Rechenschaftspflichtmechanismus geschaffen wurde (IIMM), um Untersuchungen für faire und unabhängige Strafverfahren für die schlimmsten internationalen Verbrechen, die seit 2011 in Myanmar begangen wurden, vorzubereiten.

Auf Anregung des BMEIA wurde im Jahr 2020 das Bundesgesetz über die Zusammenarbeit mit den internationalen Gerichten (IG-ZG, BGBl. Nr. 263/1996) novelliert und um eine Bestimmung ergänzt, die eine strafrechtliche Zusammenarbeit mit Einrichtungen der Vereinten Nationen ermöglicht, die mit der Ermittlung oder Beweissicherung in Bezug auf schwere Straftaten betraut sind. Dies umfasst auch die Untersuchungskommission zu Myanmar. Österreich unterstützt die Aktivitäten der Untersuchungskommission unter anderem durch finanzielle Unterstützung und Informationsaustausch. Mein Ressort steht in Kontakt mit Vertretern des „Committee Representing Pyidaungsu Hluttaw/National Unity Government" (CRPH/NUG), um sich über die aktuellen Entwicklungen und die Menschenrechtslage in Myanmar, insbesondere auch der Rohingya, auszutauschen.

GG.IV.-2

Enquiry concerning an intervention by the Austrian ambassador in North Macedonia in the interests of Austrian corporations

Anfrage betreffend eine Intervention des österreichischen Botschafters in Nordmazedonien im Interesse österreichischer Unternehmen

On 7 July 2023, a number of representatives of the Austrian National Assembly raised a parliamentary enquiry to the Federal Minister for European and International Affairs an intervention by the Austrian ambassador in North Macedonia in the interests of Austrian corporations,[30] to which the Minister replied on 7 September 2023:[31]

> […] Irrespective of this, supporting Austrian exports abroad and promoting the country and the brand 'Austria' worldwide is one of the core tasks of the Austrian representations abroad. The aim is to open doors for Austrian business and facilitate access to difficult markets. In this way, the BMEIA contributes to strengthening Austria as a business and investment location, and ultimately to safeguarding jobs at home. The basis for these activities are the provisions of the two Vienna Conventions on Diplomatic and Consular Relations, the Consular Act, and the Federal Ministries Act, whereby activities abroad must always be carried out within the framework of international law and are also subject to the law of the receiving state. […]

The relevant parts of the German original read as follows:

> […] Davon unabhängig ist die Unterstützung der österreichischen Exportwirtschaft im Ausland sowie der weltweite Einsatz für den Standort und die Marke Österreich eine der Kernaufgaben der österreichischen Vertretungen im Ausland. Dabei geht es darum, für die österreichische Wirtschaft Türen zu öffnen und den Zugang auch in schwierige Märkte zu ermöglichen. Damit leistet das BMEIA einen Beitrag zur Stärkung des Wirtschafts- und Investitionsstandortes Österreich, und damit letztlich auch zur Sicherung von Arbeitsplätzen im Inland. Grundlage für diese Aktivitäten sind die Bestimmungen der beiden Wiener Übereinkommen über diplomatische bzw. konsularische Beziehungen, das Konsulargesetz und das Bundesministeriengesetz, wobei die Aktivitäten im Ausland stets im Rahmen des Völkerrechts erfolgen müssen und auch den Rechtsvorschriften des Empfangsstaats unterliegen. […]

30 Parliamentary Materials, 15760/J (XXVII. GP).

31 Parliamentary Materials, 15258/AB (XXVII. GP).

GG.IV.-3

Enquiry concerning the possibility of closing the Russian Culture Institute in Vienna

Anfrage betreffend die Möglichkeit der Schließung des Russischen Kulturinstitutes in Wien

On 2 August 2023, a number of representatives of the Austrian National Assembly raised a parliamentary enquiry to the Federal Minister for European and International Affairs concerning the possibility of closing the Russian Culture Institute in Vienna,[32] to which the Minister replied on 2 October 2023:[33]

> The Russian Culture Institute in Vienna has been notified as part of the Russian Embassy in Vienna for more than 30 years and is therefore protected by the Vienna Convention on Diplomatic Relations (VCDR; Federal Law Gazette No. 66/1966). The activities of the Cultural Institute in the fulfilment of diplomatic and consular tasks, including the development of cultural relations, are not subject to EU sanctions. In some other states, the Russian Cultural Institute is not notified as part of the Russian Embassy, which may have other legal consequences.
>
> Notwithstanding this, the Federal Ministry for European and International Affairs (BMEIA) has the right to declare Russian diplomats as unwelcome persons ('persona non grata') in the event of abuse of their special status. The BMEIA has exercised this right in such cases not only since the beginning of the Russian aggression against Ukraine on 24 February 2022, but also before.
>
> Pursuant to Art. 41 para. 1 VCDR, all persons enjoying privileges and immunities are, without prejudice to them, obliged to observe the laws and other legal provisions of the receiving state. They are also obliged not to interfere in the internal affairs of the receiving state. In accordance with Art. 41 para. 3 VCDR, the premises of the Mission may not be used in a manner that is incompatible with the tasks of the Mission as laid down in Art. 3 VCDR. The BMEIA is not aware of any activities of the Russian Cultural Institute in Vienna or its staff that violate Austrian criminal law (e.g. incitement to hatred pursuant to Section 283 of the Austrian Criminal Code or prohibited support of parties to armed conflicts pursuant to Section 320 of the Austrian Criminal Code) or are incompatible with the tasks of a diplomatic mission pursuant to Article 3 of the VCDR.
>
> It should be noted that, according to the VCDR, it is permissible for representatives of the Russian Embassy in Austria to communicate the current position of the Russian government in public. Just because it is legally permitted does not mean that this position is left unchallenged. [...]

32 Parliamentary Materials, 15854/J (XXVII.GP).

33 Parliamentary Materials, 15356/AB (XXVII. GP).

The relevant parts of the German original read as follows:

Das Russische Kulturinstitut in Wien ist seit mehr als 30 Jahren als Teil der Russischen Botschaft in Wien notifiziert und fällt somit unter den Schutz des Wiener Übereinkommens über diplomatische Beziehungen (WDK; BGBl. Nr. 66/1966). Die Tätigkeiten des Kulturinstituts in Wahrnehmung diplomatischer und konsularischer Aufgaben, wozu auch der Ausbau der kulturellen Beziehungen zählt, fallen nicht unter die EU-Sanktionen. In einigen anderen Staaten ist das Russische Kulturinstitut nicht als Teil der Russischen Botschaft notifiziert, was andere Rechtsfolgen nach sich ziehen kann. Ungeachtet dessen hat das Bundesministerium für europäische und internationale Angelegenheiten (BMEIA) das Recht, russische Diplomatinnen und Diplomaten im Falle eines Missbrauchs ihrer Sonderstellung zur unerwünschten Person („persona non grata“) zu erklären. Von diesem Recht hat das BMEIA im Anlassfall nicht nur seit Beginn der russischen Aggression gegen die Ukraine am 24. Februar 2022, sondern auch schon davor Gebrauch gemacht.

[...]

Gemäß Art. 41 Abs. 1 WDK sind alle Personen, die Vorrechte und Immunitäten genießen, unbeschadet derselben verpflichtet, die Gesetze und anderen Rechtsvorschriften des Empfangsstaats zu beachten. Sie sind ferner verpflichtet, sich nicht in dessen innere Angelegenheiten einzumischen. Gemäß Art. 41 Abs. 3 WDK dürfen die Räumlichkeiten der Mission nicht in einer Weise benutzt werden, die mit den Aufgaben der Mission gem. Art. 3 WDK unvereinbar ist. Aktivitäten des Russischen Kulturinstituts in Wien oder seines Personals, die z.B. gegen österreichische Strafgesetze verstoßen (z.B. Verhetzung gem. § 283 StGB oder Verbotene Unterstützung von Parteien bewaffneter Konflikte gem. § 320 StGB) oder mit den Aufgaben einer diplomatischen Mission gem. Art. 3 WDK unvereinbar sind, sind dem BMEIA nicht bekannt.

Dabei ist zu berücksichtigen, dass es gemäß der WDK zulässig ist, dass Vertreterinnen oder Vertreter der Russischen Botschaft in Österreich die aktuelle Haltung der Russischen Regierung auch im öffentlichen Auftritt kundtun. Nur weil es rechtlich zulässig ist, bedeutet das nicht, dass diese Haltung unwidersprochen im Raum stehen gelassen wird. [...]

GG.IV.-4

Statement by an Austrian embassy on the usage of the rainbow flag

Erklärung einer österreichischen Botschaft zur Verwendung der Regenbogenfahne

In 2023, a receiving State notified all diplomatic mission that the applicable law of the receiving state outlawed ‘the propagation of non-traditional sexual relationships'[34] and, *inter alia*, requested diplomatic missions not to use 'the rainbow flag on the grounds of diplomatic missions and consular facilities'.[35] The Austrian diplomatic mission notified the receiving State:

> [...] advertising policy positions of the sending state and protecting the interests of the sending State in the receiving State was in line with the diplomatic functions of an embassy and did not constitute any 'interference' with the domestic affairs of the receiving State in the meaning of Art 41(1) VCDR.[36]

VII. Trade delegations, information centres, etc./ Handelsvertretungen, Informationseinrichtungen etc.

GG.VII.-1

Enquiry concerning a networking event for Austrian business in the Russian Federation and its compatibility with the sanctions regime

Anfrage betreffend ein Netzwerktreffen für österreichische Unternehmen in der Russischen Föderation und deren Vereinbarkeit mit dem Sanktionsregime

On 25 January 2023, a number of representatives of the Austrian National Assembly raised a parliamentary enquiry to the Federal Minister for European and International Affairs concerning a networking event for Austrian business in the Russian Federation and its compatibility with the sanctions regime,[37] to which the Minister replied on 2 October 2023:[38]

> [...] The planned activity was undoubtedly inappropriate, but did not violate the international economic sanctions regime. Maintaining contact with representatives of Austrian companies in Russia is one of the key tasks of the representation authority, in particular the delegation of the Austrian Economic Chambers, even in times of Russia's war of aggression against Ukraine. [...]

The relevant parts of the German original read as follows:

> [...] Die geplante Aktivität war zweifellos unpassend, stand jedoch nicht im Widerspruch zum internationalen Wirtschaftssanktionsregime. Der laufende Kontakt zu Vertreterinnen und Vertretern österreichischer Unternehmen in Russland gehört zu den wesentlichen Aufgaben der Vertretungsbehörde, insbesondere des

---

34 Reproduced in Helmut Tichy *et al*, 'Recent Austrian Practice in the Field of International Law. Report for 2023' (2024) 78(1) Zeitschrift für öffentliches Recht 169, 184.

35 *Ibid.*

36 *Ibid.*

37 Parliamentary Materials, 13629/J (XXVII. GP).

38 Parliamentary Materials, 13289/AB (XXVII. GP).

AußenwirtschaftsCenters (AC) Moskau, auch in Zeiten des russischen Angriffskrieges gegen die Ukraine. […]

HH. Jurisdiction of the State/Jurisdiktion (Hoheitsgewalt)

I. Basis of jurisdiction/Grundlage der Jurisdiktion

4. Universality principle/Universalitätsprinzip

See also *FF.X.-1.*

HH.I.4.-1

The Scope and Application of the Principle of Universal Jurisdiction

Umfang und Anwendung des Grundsatzes des Weltrechtsprinzip

On 12 October 2023, the Czech Republic delivered a statement in the 78th Session of the General Assembly Sixth Committee on behalf of the Slavkov trilateral format (S3), which includes Austria, the Czech Republic and Slovakia on 'The scope and application of the principle of universal jurisdiction':

> […] Our delegations have stated, over the past years, that universal jurisdiction is an important jurisdictional basis for the prosecution of the most serious crimes under international law in cases where jurisdiction based on the principle of territoriality or personality cannot or will not be exercised. At the same time, universal jurisdiction is distinct from the jurisdiction of international courts and tribunals. Our understanding has not changed. The most serious crimes under international law must not go unpunished irrespective of who committed them or where they are perpetrated. Universal jurisdiction is a tool that can help deliver justice to victims, prevent further crimes and close the impunity gap in keeping with the guarantees of a fair trial, due process and other applicable norms of international law.
>
> […] [T]he delegations of the Slavkov trilateral format believe that the expert analysis of the International Law Commission would be of much needed added value in order to iron out differences on the three elements – definition, scope and application, and mostly to strip this topic of political sensitivities. This analysis would be without prejudice to the final decision on the topic, which would, as with any other ILC outputs, remain with States and this Committee. The S3 delegations find it difficult to understand, how such contribution of the ILC could be detrimental to our discussions. On the contrary, it could bring about legal clarity and certainty. It is in this context that we invite the ILC again to include the topic of universal jurisdiction in its short-term programme of work.

HH.I.4.-2

Information and Observations by Austria on the Principle of Universal Jurisdiction

Informationen und Anmerkungen Österreichs zum Grundsatz Grundsatzes des Weltrechtsprinzips

Austria submitted information and observations on the scope and application of universal jurisdiction pursuant to General Assembly Resolution 77/111,[39] which was included in a report of the Secretary-General.[40] The Austrian information included recent judicial practice:

> […] In two final judgments by Austrian criminal courts against non-Austrian nationals for terrorism-related acts committed abroad, the Austrian jurisdiction was based on Section 64 (1) (9) (b) of the Austrian Penal Code. In both cases, the perpetrators were domiciled or habitually resident in Austria at the time of the institution of criminal proceedings.
>
> a) Judgment of the Regional Court Eisenstadt, 23 March 2022, AZ 50 Hv 15/21w
>
> The perpetrator was a Syrian national who committed crimes in several locations in Syria, which were punishable as terrorism-related acts under Sections 278a, 278b (2) and 15 in combination with 75 and 278c (1) (1) of the Austrian Penal Code. The accused was sentenced to two years of imprisonment.
>
> b) Judgment of the Regional Court Wels, 19 December 2022, AZ 15 Hv 75/22f
>
> The two perpetrators were Syrian nationals and accused of having committed crimes in Syria and Turkey, which were punishable as terrorism-related acts under Sections 278a and 278 (3) of the Austrian Penal Code. The two accused were acquitted due to lack of sufficient evidence beyond reasonable doubt.

II. State territory/Das Staatsgebiet

I. Territory/Das Gebiet

See also *CC.II.2.-1.*

II.I.-1

Work of the International Law Commission on Sea-level rise in relation to international law

---

[39] UNGA A/RES/77/111 (20 December 2022) para 4.

[40] UNGA Res A/78/130 (6 July 2023).

Arbeit der Völkerrechtskommission betreffend steigende Meeresspiegel in Bezug auf das Völkerrecht

On 23 October 2023, the Austrian representative to the 78th Session of the General Assembly delivered the following statement to the Sixth Committee on Report of the International Law Commission on the Work of its 73rd and 74th Session concerning the topic of 'Sea-level rise in relation to international law':

> Turning now to the topic of 'Sea-level rise in relation to international law', Austria is grateful for the work of the Study Group presented by Professor Bogdan Aurescu and Professor Nilüfer Oral. Although Austria is a land-locked country and therefore not directly affected by sea-level rise, we attach utmost importance to this most urgent topic, which is of great practical relevance for all states either directly or indirectly.
>
> This year's report deals with a number of fundamental questions of international law relating to legal stability, in particular the question of the immutability of boundaries, fundamental change of circumstances, historical titles and rights, equity and permanent sovereignty over natural resources, to name only some of them. We welcome that the Study Group will continue its work next year, focusing on the subtopics of statehood and the protection of persons affected by sea-level rise. Progress on the topic of sea-level rise is very much needed and urgent in view of the increasing effects of the man-made climate crisis.
>
> The effects of climate change on borders are not just an issue for coastal and island states, but also for landlocked countries. For instance, Austria witnesses massive melting of its glaciers, which may lead to questions in cases where a treaty establishes the watershed as the boundary when the watershed was covered by glaciers, but now becomes visible and obviously differs from the boundaries legally fixed by bilateral border commissions based on the watershed when it was still covered. In such cases, Austria has accepted the stability of boundaries fixed by the bilateral commissions.
>
> As to the *uti possidetis* principle, the report of the Commission shows an inconsistency: Whereas the discussion of the Commission on general principles of law includes *uti possidetis* as a general principle formed within the international legal system, under the topic of sea-level rise, it is also regarded by the ILC as a rule of customary international law. In any case, we share the opinion that *uti possidetis* only applies in cases of state succession and would not contribute to a solution of the issue of sea-level rise.
>
> Austria agrees with the view expressed in the report that historic considerations do not create legal rights per se, but have primarily evidentiary value, as stated in by the International Court of Justice in the case concerning the Territorial and Maritime Dispute between Nicaragua and Colombia.
>
> Austria shares the view that any future outcome of the discussion on sea-level rise should not lead to a change of UNCLOS. We are open to achieving legal stability, certainty and predictability through an interpretation of the Convention.

II. Boundaries and frontiers/Grenzen

See *II.I.-1.*

KK. Seas/Meere

See also *II.I.-1.*

VIII. High seas/Die Hohe See

4. Piracy/Piraterie

KK. VIII. 4.-1

Work of the International Law Commission on Prevention and Repression of Piracy and Armed Robbery at Sea

Arbeit der Völkerrechtskommission der Vereinten Nationen betreffend die Verhütung und Bekämpfung von Seeräuberei und bewaffneten Raubüberfällen auf See

On 31 October 2023, the Austrian representative to the 78th Session of the General Assembly delivered the following statement to the Sixth Committee on Report of the International Law Commission on the Work of its 73rd and 74th Session concerning the topic of 'Prevention and repression of piracy and armed robbery at sea':

> Austria welcomes the inclusion of the topic 'Prevention and repression of piracy and armed robbery at sea' in the ILC's work program, given the continuing threat to international shipping, which negatively affects global trade. While UNCLOS establishes the general legal framework for this topic, there are still some gaps, since, for instance, the crime of piracy does not apply in the area of the territorial sea.
>
> We thank the Secretariat for preparing a memorandum, which gives a good overview of the existing legal situation and the discussions that have taken place so far. We are also grateful to the Special Rapporteur Yacouba Cissé for his first report, which already contains proposals for draft articles.
>
> Draft article 1 'scope' establishes the fundamental distinction between piracy and armed robbery. Such a distinction is necessary, since the basis of this definition of piracy is UNCLOS that deals with piracy only in the area of the high seas. We do not object to the distinction, although the Austrian legislation includes both crimes in one term, that of maritime robbery, which is geographically not restricted.

Concerning draft article 2 on the 'definition of piracy', the reference to the 'private ends' as a necessary element of piracy is to be understood as precluding any governmental acts. However, Austria wonders why the definition is restricted to private ships and aircrafts, since piracy could also be committed by the crews of government ships in case of mutiny as provided for in article 102 UNCLOS.

In addition, we suggest that the Commission also considers the extension of the definition of piracy to acts for private ends committed by government officials on government ships and aircraft.

The renunciation of the reference to land as the starting point of piracy, as paragraph 13 of the commentary to draft article 2 explains, is probably justified, if only in view of the fact that the territorial sea is already excluded there.

In our opinion the wording of draft article 2 paragraph 1 subparagraph (a) (ii) mentioning 'a place outside the jurisdiction of any state' where the rules on privacy do not apply, and draft article 2 paragraph 2 referring to article 58 paragraph 2 UNCLOS require further clarification.

These provisions raise some doubt whether the rules on piracy also apply to exclusive economic zones and should therefore be redrafted. In particular, paragraph 2 raises the question of the extent to which the reference to UNCLOS also obliges non-parties to comply with article 58 paragraph 2 UNCLOS.

As to draft article 3 'definition of armed robbery at sea', we are wondering whether the reference to acts of violence comprises all the acts, committed unlawfully and intentionally, which are listed in article 3 of the Convention for the Suppression of Unlawful Acts of Violence Against the Safety of Maritime Navigation (SUA Convention), or only the acts of violence explicitly referred to in paragraph 1 subparagraph (b) of article 3 of the SUA Convention. It might be useful to think about including also the other crimes listed in article 3 of the SUA Convention in the definition of the robbery at sea, such as, for instance, seizing or exercising control over a ship by force or destroying a ship or causing damage to a ship or to its cargo, which is likely to endanger the safe navigation of that ship. The present wording of draft article 3 creates an uncertainty regarding the precise definition of robbery at sea insofar, as it could be argued that, in view of a systematic interpretation, all the acts listed in the SUA Convention in addition to acts of violence are excluded from the definition in draft article 3. […]

XI. International sea-bed area/Internationaler Meeresboden

KK.XI.-1

Enquiry concerning a moratorium on the extraction of raw materials in the deep sea

Anfrage betreffend ein Moratorium zum Rohstoffabbau in der Tiefsee

On 26 July 2023, a number of representatives of the Austrian National Assembly raised a parliamentary enquiry to the Federal Minister for European and International Affairs concerning a moratorium on the extraction of raw materials in the deep sea,[41] to which the Minister replied on 26 September 2023:[42]

> Austria takes the view that commercial deep-sea mining should only be carried out once the effects on the marine environment, biodiversity, and human activities have been sufficiently explored in line with the precautionary principle and the ecosystem approach, the risks are known, and it is ensured that the technologies and operating practices used minimise the impact on the deep seabed environment. Austria has already expressed this view within the European Union, the Assembly of the International Seabed Authority, and the United Nations General Assembly and will continue to do so on appropriate occasions.

The relevant parts of the German original read as follows:

> […] Österreich [vertritt] die Ansicht, dass kommerzieller Tiefseebergbau erst dann betrieben werden sollte, wenn im Sinne des Vorsorgeprinzips und des Ökosystemansatzes die Auswirkungen auf die Meeresumwelt, die biologische Vielfalt und die menschlichen Aktivitäten ausreichend erforscht sind, die Risiken bekannt sind und sichergestellt ist, dass durch die angewandten Technologien und Betriebspraktiken die Auswirkungen auf die Umwelt des Tiefseebodens möglichst gering gehalten werden. Österreich hat diese Ansicht bereits im Rahmen der Europäischen Union, der Versammlung der Meeresbodenbehörde sowie der Generalversammlung der Vereinten Nationen vertreten und wird diese auch weiterhin bei entsprechender Gelegenheit vertreten.

XIII. Protection of the maritime environment/Schutz der Meeresumwelt

See *KK.XI.-1.*

LL. Air Space, outer space and Antarctica/Luftraum, Weltraum, Antarktis

II. Outer space/Weltraum

LL.II.-1

Activities in the Exploration, Exploitation and Utilization of Space Resources

Aktivitäten zur Erforschung, Erschließung und Nutzung von Weltraumressourcen

---

41 Parliamentary Materials, 15841/J (XXVII. GP).

42 Parliamentary Materials, 15337/AB (XXVII. GP).

On 20 March 2023, the Austrian representative delivered the following statement during the 62nd Session of the Legal Subcommittee of the Committee on the Peaceful Uses of Outer Space regarding Agenda Item 10 on 'General Exchange of Views on potential legal Models for Activities in the Exploration, Exploitation and Utilization of Space Resources':

> [...] While it is uncontended that the national appropriation of outer space, including the Moon and other celestial bodies, is prohibited under international law, it is still to be discussed if non-renewable space resources, such as minerals and water, can be subjected to an ownership regime.
>
> While a smaller group of technologically advanced States and non-governmental entities will lead the way in the exploration, exploitation and utilization of space resources, Austria submits that the guiding principles of the Outer Space Treaty safeguard the effective right of access to space resource activities and its benefits for all States. While recognizing the efforts made by those leading the way and rewarding their investment, we submit that the prevention of monopolization to the detriment of other legitimate interests is key for the sustainable and peaceful management of scarce space resources. Any new governance framework the Working Group develops must therefore carefully ensure the legitimate interests of emerging space-faring nations as well as the comprehensive protection the Outer Space Treaty and customary international law afford to scientific investigation and exploration of outer space. [...]
>
> Austria is of the view that, in order to implement the principles enshrined in the UN space treaties and affirmed by UN General Assembly resolutions, a multilateral approach is necessary. Such a multilateral approach should facilitate to the greatest extent possible the exploration, exploitation and use of the natural resources of the Moon and other celestial bodies, while respecting international law.
>
> Austria believes that the Legal Subcommittee of COPUOS, as the prime multilateral body with the mandate to promote the development of international space law, is the forum in which the potential legal models for activities in exploration, exploitation and utilization of space resources should be discussed and developed.
>
> To avoid conflict arising from competing interests, the Legal Subcommittee should develop a multilateral mechanism or instrument within the framework of the United Nations that provides a forum for coordination, cooperation and the deconfliction of space resource activities. Such a multilateral approach would give legal certainty to states as well as commercial actors and investors in space resource activities. [...]
>
> Austria is a Party to the 'Agreement Governing the Activities of States on the Moon and Other Celestial Bodies' – the 'Moon Treaty' – and we would like to encourage States, which have not done so, to become Parties to the Moon Treaty. We remain convinced that participation in the Moon Treaty offers substantial benefits and guarantees in addition to participation in the other four UN treaties on outer space. [...]

LL.II.-2

Space traffic management

Weltraumverkehrsmanagement

On 22 March 2023, the Austrian representative delivered the following statement during the 62nd Session of the Legal Subcommittee of the Committee on the Peaceful Uses of Outer Space regarding Agenda Item 13 on 'General exchange of views on the legal aspects of space traffic management':

> [...] Existing international space law already contains provisions that are of relevance for the management of space traffic, including the principles set forth in the 1967 Outer Space Treaty, such as the principle of non-appropriation of outer space and the use of outer space for peaceful purposes only. Moreover, the regimes on liability and registration contained in the respective Conventions of 1972 and 1975 are also relevant in the context of space traffic management.
>
> Of importance in this regard are also the international regulations of the ITU regarding the allocation of radio frequencies and satellite orbits, which are essential to allow a conduct of space activities free from harmful interference. Moreover, a number of issues related to space traffic management are covered by non-binding international instruments, such as the UNCOPUOS Space Debris Mitigation Guidelines adopted in 2007 or UNGA Resolution 62/101 of 2007 on enhancing the practice of States and international intergovernmental organisations in registering space objects.
>
> However, for an effective management of space traffic a more rapid progress of the work of the Working Group on Long-term Sustainability under the Scientific and Technical Subcommittee towards an international governance regime is needed. A multilateral, comprehensive approach is essential for enhancing the safety and sustainability of the use of outer space. Austria stands ready to support the efforts of the Working Group also regarding the development of new guidelines for the long-term sustainability of outer space activities and recommendations for their further practical implementation, taking into particular consideration the requirements of emerging space nations and developing countries. [...]
>
> On this occasion, Austria would like to highlight the situation with uncontrolled re-entries of space objects and their implications for aircraft in flight. Due to the enormous growth of space activities and especially mega-constellations, there are thousands of objects in orbit and more to come, many of which will at one point re-enter the Earth's atmosphere.
>
> Already several reports of close calls have been reported, and just last November part of the European airspace had been temporarily closed to reduce risks from a re-entry. This risk poses not only a severe disruption, but also unforeseen economic damage to airlines, as well as knock-on damage to entire economies. Thus, Austria urges to see progress in these areas and clarification of related aspects of

governance in the area of Air and Space Traffic Management and enforced cooperation and interoperability to reduce safety risks for aviation, as well as space operators and related infrastructures.

The time to act is now to address space debris holistically and to develop a comprehensive approach to space debris by incorporating the avoidance of predictable collisions, orbital debris mitigation and remediation as a first step towards the sustainable use of space. States should establish a strong safety culture in recognizing and defining the limits to the space-Earth system, such as carrying capacities, maximum tolerable re-entry rates. As another step, Austria emphasizes the global development of standards for issuing and responding to precautionary safety warnings related to uncontrolled re-entries which requires a transparent sharing of relevant data to enable rapid decision-making. [...]

MM. International responsibility/Völkerrechtliche Verantwortlichkeit

III. Responsible entities/Träger der Verantwortlichkeit

1. States/Staaten

See *EE.I.4.d.bb.vii.-1* and *EE.II.1.b.-1*.

NN. Pacific settlement of disputes/Friedliche Streitbelegung

II. Means of settlement/Methoden zur Streitbelegung

See also *EE.II.-1*, *EE.II.-2*, *EE.II.-3*, and *EE.II.-4*.

1. Negotiations and consultations/Verhandlungen und Konsultationen

See *PP.I.-1*, *PP.I.-2*, and *QQ.I.2.g.-4*.

6. Arbitration/Schiedsgerichtsbarkeit

b. Permanent Court of Arbitration/Ständiger Schiedshof

See *EE.II.-2*.

7. Judicial settlement/Gerichtliche Streitbelegung

a. International Court of Justice/Der Internationale Gerichtshof

See also *EE.II.1.b.-3*, and *QQ.I.2.g.-3*.

NN.II.7.a.-1

*Austrian observation on the admissibility of Austria's Declaration of Intervention in the Allegations of Genocide under the Convention on the Prevention and Punishment of the Crime of Genocide (*Ukraine v Russian Federation*) case*

Österreichische Anmerkungen zu der Zulässigkeit zur österreichischen Intervention im Allegations of Genocide under the Convention on the Prevention and Punishment of the Crime of Genocide (Ukraine v Russische Föderation)-Fall

On 15 November 2022, the Russian Federation objected[43] to Austria's right to intervene in the *Allegations of Genocide under the Convention on the Prevention and Punishment of the Crime of Genocide* (Ukraine *v.* Russian Federation) case[44]. In the light of these objections, Austria submitted observations on the admissibility of its declaration of intervention from 12 October 2022 on the right to intervene to the court on 13 February 2023.

To the Registrar of the International Court of Justice, the undersigned being duly authorized by the Republic of Austria:

1. On behalf of the Republic of Austria, I have the honour to refer to the Registrar's Letter No. 158444 of 31 January 2023 and submit to the Court the following Observations on the admissibility of Austria's Declaration of Intervention filed on 12 October 2022 ("Declaration") pursuant Article 63, paragraph 2, of the Statute of the International Court of Justice ("Statute"), in the case concerning *Allegations of Genocide under the Convention on the Prevention and Punishment of the Crime of Genocide (Ukraine v. Russian Federation).*

2. On 15 November 2022, the Russian Federation filed objections to the admissibility of the Declarations of Intervention submitted by Austria and nine other Parties to the 1948 Convention on the Prevention and Punishment of the Crime

---

[43] Written Observations of the Russian Federation on the admissibility of the Declarations of Intervention of the intervening parties (retrieved on 24 February 2025)

[44] Footnotes reproduced from original, therefore not in going with the style guide of the Austrian Review of International and European Law. The original numbering of the footnotes is followed in square brackets.

of Genocide ('Genocide Convention' or 'Convention').[45] [1] The Russian Federation's objections to the admissibility of Austria's Declaration are addressed below.

I. Article 63 of the Statute provides for a *Right* to Intervene

3. At the outset, it is worthwhile to reiterate that Article 63 of the Statute provides for the possibility of interventions by other Parties of a convention *as of right*.[46] [2] As long as the prerequisites of an intervention under Article 63 of the Statute are fulfilled, which is for the Court to determine, the intervention is admissible.[47] [3] Unlike Article 62 of the Statute, the decision on admissibility under Article 63 does not entail an element of discretion.[48] [4]

4. Notably, an intervention under Article 63 of the Statute does not require the intervening State to show any 'interest of a legal nature which may be affected by the decision in the case',[49] [5] a core requirement of interventions under Article 62. Under Article 63, such interest is presupposed: every Party of a convention *ipso facto* has an interest in the proper construction of the convention, which also determines the other Parties' own rights and obligations under intonational law. This is especially true with regard to a convention of such importance as the Genocide Convention. For this reason, Article 63 of the Statute vests every State Party, such as Austria, with a right to express its views on the construction of the Genocide Convention.

---

45 [1] *Allegations of Genocide under the Convention on the Prevention and Punishment of the Crime of Genocide* (Ukraine v. Russian Federation), The Russian Federation's Written Observations on Admissibility of the Declarations of Intervention submitted by Australia, Austria, Denmark, Estonia, Finland, Greece, Ireland, Luxembourg, Portugal and Spain of 15 November 2022 ('Written Observations of the Russian Federation').

46 [2] See also *Haya de la Torre* (Colombia v. Peru), Judgment of 13 June 1951, I.C.J. Reports 1951, p. 71, at p. 76; *Continental Shelf* (Tunisia/Libyan Arab Jamahiriya), Application by Malta for Permission to Intervene, Judgment of 14 April 1981, I.C.J. Reports 1981, p. 3, at pp. 13, 15, paras. 21, 26; *Territorial and Maritime Dispute* (Nicaragua v. Colombia), Application by Honduras for Permission to Intervene, Judgment of 4 May 2011, I.C.J. Reports 2011, p. 420, at p. 433, para. 35.

47 [3] See *Whaling in the Antarctic* (Australia v. Japan), Declaration of Intervention by New Zealand, Order of 6 February 2013, I.C.J. Reports 2013, p. 3, at pp. 5-6, paras. 7-8; *S.S. 'Wimbledon'* (Britain et al. v. Germany), Question of Intervention by Poland, Judgment of 28 June 1923, P.C.I.J. Series A, No. I, p. 12, at p. 13; *Continental Shelf* (Libyan Arab Jamahiriya/Malta), Application for Permission to Intervene of Italy, Judgment of 21 March 1984, Dissenting Opinion of Sir Robert Jennings, I.C.J. Reports 1984, p. 148, at pp. 156-157, paras. 25-26.

48 [4] J. Quintana, 'Intervention under Article 63 of the Statute', in J. Quintana (ed.), *International Litigation in Practice*, Vol. 10 (2015), p. 941

49 [5] Article 62, paragraph 1, Statute of the International Court of Justice.

5. The prerequisites for the admissibility of interventions under Article 63 are limited to those stated in the Statute and the Rules of Court. In addition to certain procedural requirements, all of which Austria has satisfied and none of which were put into question by the Russian Federation, there are only few substantive requirements to be determined by the Court.

6. First and foremost, the Court must determine whether a *convention*, to which the intervening State is a Party, is in question in the relevant case.[50] [6] The Russian Federation has neither denied that the Genocide Convention is in question, nor that Austria is a State Party to the Convention.

7. Second, an intervention under Article 63 must be limited to the *construction* of the convention in question. The Russian Federation claims that the existence of a dispute - a notion addressed in detail in Austria's Declaration - is not a question of construction of the Genocide Convention.[51] [7] However, this argument disregards the fact that the term 'dispute' is a central term in Article IX of the Genocide Convention, the provision which Austria wishes to construe in its intervention.[52] [8]

8. Article IX hinges on the question of what does or does not constitute a dispute. It would be virtually impossible to formulate a construction of Article IX without assessing the scope of the term 'dispute'. In the same vein, Austria invokes the question of good faith and abuse of rights only as tools of treaty interpretation that form part of its statement on the construction of Article IX. More specifically, the notions of good faith interpretation and abuse of rights inform Austria's view that the abusive interpretation of the Genocide Convention may result in a dispute under Article IX.

8. [*sic*] Contrary to what the Russian Federation claims,[53] [9] Austria's Declaration does not discuss the factual question as to whether a genocide has been or may be committed in Ukraine.

9. None of the other objections of the Russian Federation pertain to prerequisites for the admissibility of interventions under Article 63. It is not a prerequisite that only a certain number of States may intervene in a given case. It is also not a prerequisite that intervening States may not share the legal views of one of the disputing Parties, as confirmed in the PCIJ's *Wimbledon*[54] [10] and the Court's *Haya*

---

50 [6] J. Quintana, 'Intervention under Article 63 of the Statute', in J. Quintana (ed.), *International Litigation in Practice*, Vol. 10 (2015), pp. 932-933.

51 [7] Written Observations of the Russian Federation, para. 106(b).

52 [8] See Austria's Declaration, paras. 29 *et seq.*

53 [9] Written Observations of the Russian Federation, para. 106(b).

54 [10] *S.S. 'Wimbledon'* (Britain et al. v. Germany), Application to Intervene by Poland, 22 May 1923, P.C.LJ. Series A, No. 1, p. 9; *S.S. 'Wimbledon'* (Britain et al. v. Germany), Question of Intervention by Poland, Judgment of 28 June 1923, P.C.I.J. Series A, No. l, p. 12.

de la Torre[55] [11] and *Whaling* cases.[56] [12] Nor does the principle of equality of arms or the requirement of good administration abrogate the right of other Parties to the Convention to intervene, as the Statute and the Rules of Court vest the Court with appropriate tools to ensure procedural fairness and efficiency.[57] [13]

10. Accordingly, it is submitted that Austria's Declaration complies with all prerequisites for the admissibility of its intervention under Article 63 of the Statute. For the avoidance of doubt, the following sections of Austria's Observations will rebut the objections raised by the Russian Federation, even though the purported additional conditions invoked by the Russian Federation have no legal basis in the prerequisites prescribed by the Statute, the Rules of Court, and the Court's case law.

II. The Intervention is 'genuine'

11. The Russian Federation claims that Austria effectively seeks to become a *de facto* co-applicant by virtue of its intervention.[58] [14] Austria explicitly stated in its Declaration that it does not wish to become a Party to the proceedings.[59] [15] Contrary to how the Russian Federation interprets Austria's Declaration, the objective of Austria's Declaration is for the Court to take note of Austria's views on the proper construction of the Convention, as the Court's construction of the Convention affects Austria's rights and obligations as a Party. These rights and obligations also entail the compromissory clause in Article IX of the Convention.

12. As the Russian Federation points out itself, 'the only point which it is necessary to ascertain is whether the object of the intervention of [the intervening government] is in fact the interpretation of the treaty in question] ...'.[60] [16] Austria solely requests to intervene with respect to the construction of Article IX of the Convention, the interpretation of which forms part of the present dispute; Austria's Declaration addresses no other points.

---

55 [11] *Haya de la Torre* (Colombia v. Peru), Judgment of 13 June 1951, I.C.J. Reports 1951, p. 71; *Haya de la Torre* (Colombia v. Peru), Declaration of intervention by the Government of Cuba, 13 March 1951, p. 117.

56 [12] *Whaling in the Antarctic* (Australia v. Japan), Written observations of Japan on the Declaration of Intervention by New Zealand, 21 December 2012; *Whaling in the Antarctic* (Australia v. Japan), Declaration of Intervention by New Zealand, Order of 6 February 2013, I.C.J . Reports 2013, p. 3, at p. 9, para. 21.

57 [13] See *Whaling in the Antarctic* (Australia v. Japan), Declaration of Intervention by New Zealand, Order of 6 February 2013, I.C.J. Reports 2013, p. 3, at p. 9, para. 18.

58 [14] Written Observations of the Russian Federation, paras. 22, 24, 34, 48.

59 [15] Austria's Declaration, para. 7.

60 [16] *Haya de la Torre* (Colombia v. Peru), Judgment of 13 June 1951, IC.J. Reports 1951, p. 71, at p. 77.

13. Whether an intervention concerns the subject-matter of the respective case is to be determined by reference to the text of the Declaration of Intervention. The political context of an intervention is immaterial to determining the subject-matter of the intervention as well as the dispute.[61] [17] The Court confirmed this in its *Continental Shelf* case between Tunisia and Libya, where it '... emphasize[d] that it does not [have] any general discretion to accept or reject a request for permission to intervene for reasons simply of policy. On the contrary, in the view of the Court the task entrusted to it ... is to determine the admissibility or otherwise of the request by reference to the relevant provisions of the Statute.'[62] [18] Although this quotation stems from a judgment on an intervention under Article 62 of the Statute, it applies *a fortiori* for the admissibility of interventions *as of right* under Article 63, in contrast to discretionary interventions under Article 62.

14. It is thus immaterial that Austria had publicly expressed its intention to intervene prior to filing its Declaration. Yet, if the Russian Federation insists on probing Austria's 'true intentions',[63] [19] Austria reiterates that its 'true' and stated[64] [20] intention is the proper construction of the Genocide Convention by all member States and that the rule of law be upheld.

15. Therefore, Austria's Declaration must be distinguished from the intervention lodged in the Court's *Haya de la Torre* case, where the Court limited the admissibility of Cuba's intervention to arguments that concerned the subject-matter of the proceedings. In *Haya de la Torre*, Cuba aimed to intervene on matters that were not the subject-matter of the case but had already been decided by the Court in a previous judgment, making them *res judicata*. These matters were declared inadmissible, whereas Cuba's other submissions, which the Parties' submissions had not even addressed, were admitted, as they concerned the construction of a relevant Convention.[65] [21] Austria's Declaration, by contrast, concerns the same

61 [17] *Alleged Violations of the 1955 Treaty of Amity, Economic Relations, and Consular Rights* (Islamic Republic of Iran v. United States of America), Preliminary Objections, Judgment of 3 February 2021, I.C.J. Reports 2021, p. 9, at pp. 27-28, para. 59; *Whaling in the Antarctic* (Australia v. Japan), Written observations of Japan on The Declaration of Intervention by New Zealand, 21 December 2012; *Waling in the Antarctic* (Australia v. Japan), Declaration of Intervention by New Zealand, Order of 6 February 2013, I.C.J. Reports 2013, p. 3, at p. 9, paras. 18-21.

62 [18] *Continental Shelf* (Tunisia/Libyan Arab Jamahiriya), Application by Malta for Permission to Intervene, Judgment of 14 April 1981, I.C.J. Reports 1981, p. 3, at p. 12, para. 17.

63 [19] Written Observations of the Russian Federation, para. 23.

64 [20] Statement by the Austrian Minister of Foreign Affairs of 23 August 2022, available at http://www.eza.gv.atlen/the-ministry/press/speeches/2022l08/statment-of-foreign-minister-schallenbere-at-the-krim-plattform/.

65 [21] *Haya de la Torre* (Colombia v.Peru), Judgment of 13June 195l, I.C.J. Reports 195l, p. 7l, at pp. 76-77.

subject-matter on which both Parties to the present case have already presented their legal views.[66] [22] As a result, the Russian Federation's invocation of *Haya de la Torre* to argue that Austria's intervention is not 'genuine' is inapposite.

16. Further, it is possible and has indeed been a common occurrence that an intervening State's views on the proper construction of a convention overlap with the views of one of the disputing Parties[67] [23] – this does not tum the intervening State into a 'co-applicant'.[68] [24] The intervening State enjoys a distinct, statutory right to have its legal position heard, irrespective of what the other States may choose to argue.

17. Finally, Austria's openness to its intervention being grouped together by the Court with like-minded intervening States[69] [25] is meant to assist the Court in the good administration of justice, not to confer its right to intervene to another State.

III. Austria's Declaration of Intervention is in Line with the Principle of Equality of the Parties and the Requirement of Good Administration of Justice

18. Article 63 Statute creates a distinct right for intervening States, which exists in parallel to the principles of equality of the Parties and the requirement of good administration.

19. The Court has the requisite procedural tools and flexibility to reconcile the good administration of justice with multiple interventions. Consequently, denying States the right to intervene is *not necessary* to ensure the requirement of good administration of justice and would be contrary to the right enshrined in Article 63 of the Statute.

---

66 [22] *Allegations of Genocide under the Convention on the Prevention and Punishment of the Crime of Genocide* (Ukraine v. Russian Federation), Application instituting proceedings of 26 February 2022, pp. 4-8; *Allegations of Genocide under the Convention on the Prevention and Punishment of the Crime of Genocide* (Ukraine v. Russian Federation), Request for the indication of provisional measures, 26 February 2022, pp. 2-4; *Allegations of Genocide under the Convention on the Prevention and Punishment of the Crime of Genocide* (Ukraine v. Russian Federation), Document (with annexes) from the Russian Federation setting out its position regarding the alleged 'lack of jurisdiction' of the Court in the case, 7 March 2022, pp. 1-6.

67 [23] *Whaling in the Antarctic* (Australia v. Japan), Written observations of Japan on the Declaration of Intervention by New Zealand, 21 December 2012, paras. 2-5; *Whaling in the Antarctic* (Australia v. Japan), Written Observations of Japan on the written observations submitted by New Zealand, 31 May 2013, pp. 5-6, para. 9.

68 [24] Written Observations of the Russian Federation, para. 22; *Whaling in the Antarctic* (Australia v. Japan), Declaration of Intervention by New Zealand, Order of 6 February 2013, I.C.J. Reports 2013, p. 3, at p. 9, paras. 18-21.

69 [25] Written Observations of the Russian Federation, para. 28.

20. This was confirmed by the Court in the *Whaling* case: as long as an intervention under Article 63 of the Statute only concerns the construction of a convention, the equality of the parties is not at issue.[70] [26]

21. Russia's argument on the nationality of the Judges on the bench puts their impartiality and independence unduly into question.[71] [27] The Judges' nationality is immaterial for the admissibility of interventions and is thus not a consideration under the Statute and the Rules of Court. The Court's case law confirms this, most recently in the *Whaling* case, where the fact that Judge Keith shared the nationality of the intervening State did not affect the admissibility of the intervention.[72] [28]

IV. Austria's Declaration of Intervention is Admissible in the Jurisdictional Phase of these Proceedings

22. Austria's Declaration focuses entirely on jurisdictional questions, namely the compromissory clause of the Genocide Convention. Therefore, the jurisdictional phase is the only phase of the proceedings when Austria can exercise its right to intervene on the construction of Article IX of the Convention in an effective and meaningful manner. If Austria's Declaration was only admitted in the merits phase, its intervention would be moot. In turn, this would amount to a *de facto* denial of Austria's right to intervene as provided for under Article 63 of the Statute. It must also be borne in mind that Rule 82(1) of the Rules of Court states unequivocally that '(s)uch a declaration shall be filed as soon as possible, and not later than the date fixed for the opening of the oral proceedings.' If Article 63 were to only allow for interventions on substantive provisions, Rule 82(1) would have tied the time limit for Declarations to the 'opening of the oral proceedings *on the merits*', which it does not.

23.The reason for the lack of case law on interventions in the jurisdictional phase is that so far none of the interventions under Article 63 of the Statute presented views on the construction of a jurisdictional clause.[73] [29] Consequently, and contrary to what the Russian Federation would like the Court to draw from this, nothing can be derived from the absence of case law on interventions in the jurisdictional phase. The case at hand is the first time the Court is called upon to decide on this matter.

---

70 [26] *Whaling in the Antarctic* (Australia v. Japan), Declaration of Intervention by New Zealand, Order of 6 February 2013, I.C.J. Reports 2013, p. 3, at p. 9, para. 18.

71 [27] Written Observations of the Russian Federation, para. 5l.

72 [28] *Whaling in the Antarctic* (Australia v. Japan), Declaration of Intervention by New Zealand, Order of 6 February 2013, I.C.J. Reports 2013, p. 3, at p. 9, para. 21.

73 [29] J. Quintana, 'Intervention under Article 63 of the Statute', in J. Quintana (ed.), *International Litigation in Practice*, Vol. l0 (2015), pp. 929-93.

V. Austria's Declaration of Intervention does not presuppose the Court's Jurisdiction

24. The Russian Federation claims that Austria's Declaration presupposes the Court's jurisdiction, when in fact, the Declaration does the exact opposite: it revolves entirely around the Court's jurisdiction under the Genocide Convention.

25.The Court's decision on El Salvador's Declaration in *Nicaragua* cannot serve as a precedent for Austria's Declaration. Not even one of El Salvador's points was related to the jurisdictional clause of the case. Conversely, Austria's Declaration concerns only the compromissory clause of the Genocide Convention and does not construe any substantive provisions. Accordingly, and in distinction to El Salvador's Declaration, Austria's Declaration does not touch upon the merits of the case. Rather than presupposing the Court's jurisdiction, the question of jurisdiction takes centre stage in Austria's Declaration.

VI. Article IX can be the Subject of Interventions per se

26. The Russian Federation claims that Article IX of the Genocide Convention cannot be the subject of construction in interventions under Article 63 of the Statute.[74] [30] The Russian Federation's Written Observations do not, however, state any valid reasons why Article IX - an integral part of the Genocide Convention - should be treated differently from the substantive provisions of the Convention.

27. The fact that the dissenting Judge *ad hoc* Kreća in the Court's *Bosnian Genocide* case called Article IX a 'standard' compromissory clause does not explain why it should be impermissible for Austria to express its views on the proper construction of that provision.

28. Further, and contrary to what the Russian Federation claims,[75] [31] the *travaux préparatoires* of Article 63 of the Statute and its predecessor, Article 63 in the PCIJ Statute, do *not* exclude the construction of compromissory clauses from the purview of interventions under Article 63.[76] [32] That the intervention must relate to the 'subject-matter' of the case is in no way equivalent to a condition that the intervention relate to substantive provisions of the convention in question.[77] [33] Such a limitation to substantive provisions is neither stated in the Statute and Rules of Court nor would this align with their context or object and purpose.[78] [34]

74 [30] Written Observations of the Russian Federation, para. 93.

75 [31] *Ibid.*

76 [32] *Military and Paramilitary Activities in and against Nicaragua* (Nicaragua v. United States of America), Declaration of Intervention of the Republic of El Salvador, Order of 4 October 1984, Dissenting Opinion of Judge Schwebel, 223, at pp. 234-236; A. Miron/C. Chinkin, 'Article 63', in Zimmermann *et al.* (eds.), *The Statute of the International Court of Justice: A Commentary* (2019), p. 1741, at p. 1758, para. 46.

77 [33] *Cf.* Written Observations of the Russian Federation, para. 95.

78 [34] M. Shaw (ed.), *Rosenne's Law and Practice of the International Court 1920-2015* (5th edn., Vol III, 2016), p. 1533; H. Thirlway, *The Law and*

29. In fact, the subject-matter currently litigated in the present proceedings is of a non-substantive nature, as Russia opposes the Court's jurisdiction with Preliminary Objections. The Russian Federation contends, in a single sentence, that '[t]he mere fact that the Preliminary Objections were filed does not attest to the existence of a dispute on interpretation of this Article.'[79] [35] It remains unclear what the Russian Federation's manifest opposition to Ukraine's invocation of the Court's jurisdiction could be, other than a dispute on the subject-matter of jurisdiction.

VIII. Conclusion

30. For the reasons set out above, Austria respectfully requests the Court to decide that the Declaration of Intervention filed by Austria on 12 October 2022 is admissible. [...]

NN.II.7.a.-2

*Joint written observations of Austria, the Czech Republic and the Slovak Republic on the subject-matter of its intervention in the Allegations of Genocide under the Convention on the Prevention and Punishment of the Crime of Genocide (*Ukraine v Russian Federation*) case*

Gemeinsame schriftliche Stellungnahme Österreichs, der Tschechischen Republik und der Slowakei zum Gegenstand ihrer Intervention im Allegations of Genocide under the Convention on the Prevention and Punishment of the Crime of Genocide (Ukraine v Russische Föderation)-Fall

After the Court of Justice had declared the interventions of the three States admissible on 5 June 2023, Austria, together with the Czech Republic and the Slovak Republic, submitted joint written observations[80] in relation to the subject-matter of its intervention in the *Allegations of Genocide under the Convention on the Prevention and Punishment of the Crime of Genocide* (Ukraine *v.* Russian Federation) case of 5 July 2023:[81]

To the Registrar, International Court of Justice, the undersigned, being duly authorized by the Governments of the Republic of Austria ('Austria'), the Czech Republic ('Czechia') and the Slovak Republic ('Slovakia'):

Procedure of the International Court of Justice: Fifty Years of Jurisprudence (Vol I, 2013), p. 1031; A. Miron/C. Chinkin, 'Article 63', in Zimmermann *et al.* (eds.), *The Statute of the International Court of Justice: A Commentary* (2019), p. 1741, at p. 1763, para. 46.

79 [35] Written Observations of the Russian Federation, para. 92.

80 Joint written observations of Austria, Czechia and Slovakia on the subject-matter of their intervention (retrieved on 24 February 2025)

81 Footnotes reproduced from original, therefore not in going with the style guide of the Austrian Review of International and European Law. The original numbering of the footnotes is followed in square brackets.

1. On behalf of the Governments of Austria, Czechia and Slovakia ('the intervening States'), we have the honour to submit to the International Court of Justice ('the Court') the following Joint Written Observations in the Case concerning *Allegations of Genocide under the Convention on the Prevention and Punishment of the Crime of Genocide (Ukraine v. Russian Federation)* ('the Proceedings') in accordance with the Court's Order of 5 June 2023 on the admissibility of the declarations of intervention ('the Order').[82] [1]

I. Introduction

2. On 5 June 2023, the Court decided that the declarations of intervention under Article 63 of the Statute of the Court ('the Statute') submitted by, among others, Austria, Czechia and Slovakia in the Proceedings were admissible.[83] [2] The Court fixed 5 July 2023 as the time limit for the filing of the Written Observations referred to in Article 86, paragraph 1, of the Rules of Court ('the Rules').

3. The intervention by Austria, Czechia and Slovakia under Article 63 of the Statute involves the exercise of a right by a State Party to a convention the construction of which is in question before the Court. As determined by the Court in its Order, the construction of Article IX and of other provisions of the Convention on the Prevention and Punishment of the Crime of Genocide ('Genocide Convention' or 'Convention') concerning the Court's jurisdiction *ratione materiae* is in question at the present stage of the Proceedings. In accordance with the Court's Order, the Joint Written Observations will solely concern the construction of Article IX and other provisions of the Genocide Convention that are relevant for the determination of the Court's jurisdiction *ratione materiae* in the Proceedings. References to other rules and principles of international law outside the Genocide Convention in the Joint Written Observations will only concern the construction of the Genocide Convention's provisions, in accordance with the customary rule of interpretation reflected in Article 31 of the 1969 Vienna Convention on the Law of Treaties ('VCLT'). The intervening States will not address other matters, such as the existence of a dispute between the Parties, the evidence, the facts or the application of the Genocide Convention in the present case.

4. In its Order, the Court considered that there is nothing in the Statute or the Rules preventing States from filing a joint declaration of intervention.[84] [3] In addition, the Registrar noted in his letter of 6 June 2023 that the joint presentation of shared views can advance the good administration of justice.[85] [4] Moreover,

---

82 [1] *Allegations of Genocide under the Convention on the Prevention and Punishment of the Crime of Genocide* (Ukraine v. Russian Federation), Admissibility of the Declarations of Intervention, Order of 5 June 2023.

83 [2] Order, para. 102

84 [3] Order, para. 88.

85 [4] Letters from the Registrar of the International Court of Justice n° 159463, 159481 and 159468, 6 June 2023.

in his communication of 23 June 2023, the Registrar reiterated that he 'strongly encourages the intervening States to present joint written and oral observations to the extent possible.'[86] [5] Having in mind these concerns, Austria, Czechia and Slovakia hereby submit their Joint Written Observations.

II. The Construction of Article IX of the Genocide Convention

5. Article IX of the Genocide Convention reads as follows:

> 'Disputes between the Contracting Parties relating to the interpretation, application or fulfilment of the present Convention, including those relating to the responsibility of a State for genocide or for any of the other acts enumerated in article III, shall be submitted to the International Court of Justice at the request of any of the parties to the dispute.'

6. Article IX of the Genocide Convention is a broad jurisdictional clause, allowing the Court to adjudicate upon disputes between Contracting States relating to all aspects of interpretation, application or fulfilment of a Party's obligations under the Genocide Convention. In particular, Article IX vests the Court with the jurisdiction *ratione materiae* to adjudge and declare (a) the absence of acts of genocide, i.e. a non-violation of the Genocide Convention, as well as (b) a violation of the Genocide Convention through false or abusive allegations of genocide that contradict the letter and spirit of the Convention and are used to justify acts that negate the object and purpose of the Genocide Convention. 7. 'Negative declarations' establishing the non-violation of international obligations are as much part of the Court's competence as declaratory relief for the violation of obligations. For instance, in the case concerning *Rights of Nationals of the United States of America in Morocco*, the applicant requested the Court to declare that it had acted 'in conformity with the treaty provisions which are ... binding on France and the United States'.[87] [6] The Court, which has to verify its jurisdiction *proprio motu*,[88] [7] did not see any jurisdictional issues with France's request for a negative declaration and went on to consider the merits of the claim. Likewise, in its *Lockerbie* judgment, the Court confirmed its jurisdiction over the applicant's request for a negative declaration establishing that it had *not* violated the Montreal Convention.[89] [8]

---

86 [5] Letters from the Registrar of the International Court of Justice n° 159655, 159636 and 159642, 23 June 2023.

87 [6] R*ights of Nationals of the United States of America in Morocco* (France v. United States of America), Judgment of 27 August 1952, I.C.J. Reports 1952, p. 176, at p. 182.

88 [7] *Appeal Relating to the Jurisdiction of the ICAO Council* (India v. Pakistan), Judgment of 18 August 1972, I.C.J. Reports 1972, p. 46, at p. 52, para. 13.

89 [8] *Questions of Interpretation and Application of the 1971 Montreal Convention arising from the Aerial Incident at Lockerbie* (Libyan Arab Jamahiriya v. United Kingdom), Preliminary Objections, Judgment of 27 February 1998, I.C.J. Reports 1998, p. 8, at p. 13, para. 12 and p. 18, at p. 23, para. 38.

8. Consequently, the intervening States conclude from the Court's case law that the Court is competent to grant declaratory relief concerning the non-violation of international obligations.

1. The Rules of Interpretation applied to Article IX of the Convention

9. As a preliminary matter, the construction of Article IX of the Genocide Convention is governed by the customary international law of treaty interpretation, as reflected in the VCLT.[90] [9]

The general rule of interpretation, reflected in Article 31 of VCLT, provides that:

1. A treaty shall be interpreted in good faith in accordance with the ordinary meaning to be given to the terms of the treaty in their context and in the light of its object and purpose.

2. The context for the purpose of the interpretation of a treaty shall comprise, in addition to the text, including its preamble and annexes:

(a) any agreement relating to the treaty which was made between all the parties in connection with the conclusion of the treaty;

(b) any instrument which was made by one or more parties in connection with the conclusion of the treaty and accepted by the other parties as an instrument related to the treaty.

3. There shall be taken into account, together with the context:

(a) any subsequent agreement between the parties regarding the interpretation of the treaty or the application of its provisions;

(b) any subsequent practice in 'the application of the treaty which establishes the agreement of the parties regarding its interpretation;

(c) any relevant rules of international law applicable in the relations between the parties.

4. [...]

2. Ordinary Meaning of the Terms of Article IX

10. The point of departure of the general rule of interpretation is an interpretation of the terms of the treaty by their ordinary meaning.[91] [10]

11. According to the plain wording of Article IX of the Genocide Convention, the Court has jurisdiction over 'disputes' that relate to the interpretation, application or fulfilment of the Convention. This notion of a dispute – 'a disagreement on a

---

90 [9] See, *e.g.*, *Arbitral Award of 3 October 1899* (Guyana v. Venezuela), Jurisdiction of the Court, Judgment of 18 December 2020, I.C.J. Reports 2020, p. 455, at p. 475, para. 70.

91 [10] *E.g. Territorial Dispute* (Libyan Arab Jamahiriya/Chad), Judgment of 3 February 1994, I.C.J. Reports 1994, p. 6, at p. 22, para. 41.

point of law or fact, a conflict of legal views or of interests'[92] [11] – takes centre stage in the construction of Article IX.

12. A dispute exists if the two Parties 'hold clearly opposite views concerning the question of the performance or non-performance of certain international obligations.'[93] [12] In this connection, 'the positive opposition ... need not necessarily be stated *expressis verbis*',[94] [13] or formally declared,[95] [14] as long as 'the respondent was aware, or could not have been unaware, that its views were 'positively opposed' by the applicant.'[96] [15] Likewise, the Court has emphasized that a dispute under a specific treaty may exist despite the absence of 'a specific reference to the treaty or to its provisions in public statements by the parties, provided that those statements refer to the subject-matter of the treaty with sufficient clarity to enable the State against which a claim is made to identify that there is, or may be, a dispute with regard to that subject-matter.'[97] [16]

13. Moreover, the existence of a dispute must be determined objectively. One Party's unilateral denial that a dispute has arisen is not determinative of whether or not a dispute for the purposes of Article IX of the Genocide Convention.[98] [17]

---

92 [11] *Mavrommatis Palestine Concessions* (Greece v. United Kingdom), Preliminary Objections, Judgment of 30 August 1924, P.C.I.J. Series A, No. 2, at p. 11.

93 [12] *Alleged Violations of Sovereign Rights and Maritime Spaces in the Caribbean Sea* (Nicaragua v. Colombia), Preliminary Objections; Judgment of 17 March-2016, I.C.J. Reports 2016, p. 3, at p. 26, para. 50.

94 [13] *Land and Maritime Boundary between Cameroon and Nigeria* (Cameroon v. Nigeria), Preliminary Objections, Judgment of 11 June 1998, I.C.J. Reports 1998, p. 275, at p. 315, para. 89.

95 [14] *Alleged Violations of Sovereign Rights and Maritime Space in the Caribbean Sea* (Nicaragua v. Colombia), Preliminary Objections, Judgment of 17 March 2016, I.C.J. Reports 2016, p. 3, at p. 32, para. 72.

96 [15] See, *e.g. Obligations concerning Negotiations relating to Cessation of the Nuclear Arms Race and to Nuclear Disarmament* (Marshall Islands v. United Kingdom), Preliminary Objections, Judgment of 5 October 2016, I.C.J. Reports 2016, p. 833, at p. 850, para. 41; concerning the Court's observation that *conduct* of the Parties may suffice to establish the existence of a dispute, 'especially when there have been no diplomatic exchanges' between the Parties or in the context of an ongoing armed conflict, see also *ibid*, paras. 40, 54.

97 [16] *Application of the Convention on the Prevention and Punishment of the Crime of Genocide* (The Gambia v. Myanmar), Judgment of 22 July 2022, p. 27, para. 72, citing *Application of the International Convention on* the Elimination of All Forms of Racial Discrimination (Georgia v. Russian Federation), Preliminary Objections, Judgment, I.C.J. Reports 2011(1,), p. 85, para. 30.

98 [17] *See, e.g., Obligations concerning Negotiations relating to Cessation of the Nuclear Arms Race and to Nuclear Disarmament (Marshall Islands v. United Kingdom)* [*sic*], Preliminary Objections, Judgment of 5 October 2016, I.C.J. Reports 2016, pp. 849-851, paragraphs 39-43.

14. Evidence of a dispute derives from opposing positions attributable to the relevant States. The State' positions may not only originate from the highest State organs but could also emanate from other sources; it suffices that the conduct is attributable to the State and that it reflects the position of the State.[99] [18] Such conduct also includes statements of organs that enjoy independence such as domestic courts or quasi-judicial organs.[100] [19]

15. Accordingly, acts by independent State entities[101] [20] are attributable to the State. Therefore, if such entities make statements that are opposed to another State's legal position concerning the interpretation, application or fulfilment of the Genocide Convention, such statements are relevant to determine whether a dispute exists.

16. The dispute must in principle exist on the date on which the application is submitted to the Court.[102] [21] However, '[c]onduct subsequent to the application (or the application itself)' can also be used 'to confirm the existence of a dispute [or] to clarify its subject-matter'.[103] [22]

17. Following this construction of the term 'dispute', the ensuing paragraphs construe the ordinary meaning of the remaining terms of Article IX of the Convention.

18. The ordinary meaning of the phrase 'relating to the interpretation, application or fulfilment of the Convention' may be divided into two parts. The first part 'relating to' establishes a link between the dispute and the Genocide Convention. The subject matter of the dispute thus must concern the Genocide Convention itself. As for the second part 'interpretation, application or fulfilment', the wording is

---

99 [18] ILC, Draft Articles on the Responsibility of States for Internationally Wrongful Acts with commentaries (2001) p. 41, para. 4.

100 [19] *Jurisdictional Immunities of the State* (Germany v. Italy: Greece intervening), Judgment of 3 February 2012, I.C.J. Reports 2012, p. 99, at p. 118, para. 44. ('The "facts or situations" which have given rise to the dispute before the Court are constituted by Italian judicial decisions that denied Germany the jurisdictional immunity which it claimed, and by measures of constraint applied to property belonging to Germany.')

101 [20] Which include committees established by the State for the investigation for the purpose of criminal prosecution and deriving their authority from and answering to the Head of State.

102 [21] *Obligations concerning Negotiations relating to Cessation of the Nuclear Arms Race and to Nuclear Disarmament* (Marshall Islands v. United Kingdom), Preliminary Objections, Judgment of 5 October 2016, I.C.J . Reports 2016, p. 833, at p. 851, paras. 42-43.

103 [22] *Obligations concerning Negotiations relating to Cessation of the Nuclear Arms Race and to Nuclear Disarmament* (Marshall Islands v. United Kingdom), Preliminary Objections, Judgment of 5 October 2016, I.C.J . Reports 2016, p. 833, at p. 851, para. 43.

intentionally broad, 'opening the seizing of the Court as largely as possible'.[104] [23] In particular, the inclusion of the word 'fulfilment', in addition to 'interpretation and application' which are commonplace in compromissory clauses, manifests that the scope of Article IX must be construed broadly. Where one State Party to the Genocide Convention accuses another of genocidal acts, the 'fulfilment' of the Genocide Convention is clearly at stake. This also includes situations where the Court is asked to make 'negative declarations' after false or abusive allegations of violations of the Genocide Convention to justify unilateral acts that negate. the object and purpose of the Genocide Convention.

19. This interpretation is confirmed by the fact that the wording of Article IX expressly provides that the Court has jurisdiction 'at the request of any of the parties to the dispute'.[105] [24] This language suggests that a State accused of committing genocide has the same rights to have the dispute heard by the Court as the State making the accusation. Indeed, there is no reason why State facing what it considers to be an unfounded allegation of a breach of the Genocide Convention cannot, on its own accord, bring the matter before the Court. Such a State may thus bring a 'non-violation' complaint and seek a 'negative declaration' from the Court.

20. Moreover, disputes under Article IX 'includ[e] those relating to the responsibility of a State for genocide or for any of the acts enumerated in article III'. The use of the word 'include' signifies that such disputes 'are comprised within a broader group of disputes relating to the interpretation, application or fulfilment of the Convention'.[106] [25] There is nothing in this clause that limits the Court' s jurisdiction to the determination of the responsibility of a respondent State, as opposed to the responsibility of an applicant State.

21. Further, as the Court has noted, this clause 'does not exclude any form of State responsibility'.[107] [26] Thus, the Court's jurisdiction under the Convention covers State responsibility for any form of conduct, including false or abusive allegations of genocide to justify unilateral acts that negate the object and purpose of the Convention. In the same vein, the Court has confirmed that Article IX also pertains to disputes concerning obligations that are 'not expressly imposed by the

---

104 [23] R. Kolb, 'The Compromissory Clause of the Convention', in: Paola Gaeta (ed.), The UN Genocide Convention: A Commentary (OUP), p. 420.

105 [24] Emphasis added.

106 [25] *Application of the Convention of the Prevention and Punishment of the Crime of Genocide (Bosnia and Herzegovina v. Serbia and Montenegro)* [*sic*], Judgment of 26 February 2007, I.C.J. Reports 2007, p. 114, paragraph 169.

107 [26] *Application of the Convention on the Prevention and Punishment of the Crime of Genocide* (Bosnia and Herzegovina v. Yugoslavia), Preliminary Objections, Judgment of 11 July 1996, I.C.J. Reports 1996, p. 595, at p. 616, para. 32.

actual terms of the Convention.'[108] [27] Accordingly, the subject of the dispute may concern Article IX itself, as well as the good faith performance of the Convention read as a whole.[109] [28]

22. The ordinary meaning of Article IX thus establishes that the Court has jurisdiction *ratione materiae* to adjudge and declare the absence of genocide and the violation of the Genocide Convention due to a failure to fulfil the Convention in good faith, resulting in an abuse of law.

3. Good Faith Interpretation of the Genocide Convention

23. The Court has observed that the principle of good faith, reflected in Article 31 of the VCLT, 'obliges the Parties to apply [a treaty] in a reasonable way and in such a manner that its purpose can be realized'.[110] [29] Put differently, the obligation to interpret in good faith serves as a safeguard against any misuse of the terms of the treaty. In this sense, the principle of good faith constitutes the positive side of the prohibition of abuse of rights, so that a bad faith interpretation amounts to an abusive interpretation.[111] [30]

24. In light of the above, a State Party fails to interpret, apply or fulfil the Genocide Convention in good faith if its accusations of genocide, and any ensuing actions with the stated purpose of preventing and punishing such genocide, are not objectively supported by any factual and legal foundation.

25. A dispute as to whether a State Party has disregarded the principle of good faith and has thereby engaged in an abusive interpretation and application of the Genocide Convention falls under the purview of Article IX.

4. Context of the Genocide Convention

26. Pursuant to Article 31, paragraph 3 (c) of the VCLT, Article IX of the Genocide Convention has to be interpreted in the context of 'any relevant rules of

---

108 [27] *Application of the Convention on the Prevention and Punishment of the Crime of Genocide* (Bosnia and Herzegovina v. Serbia and Montenegro), Judgment of 26 February 2007, I.C.J. Reports 2007, p. 4, at p. 113, para. 166.

109 [28] *Application of the Convention on the Prevention and Punishment of the Crime of Genocide* (Bosnia and Herzegovina v. Yugoslavia), Preliminary Objections, Judgment of 11 July 1996, I.C.J. Reports 1996, p. 595, at p. 616, para. 33 ('[The Court] would moreover observe that it is sufficiently apparent from the very terms of [Yugoslavia's preliminary] objection that the Parties not only differ with respect to the facts of the case, their imputability and the applicability to them of the provisions of the Genocide Convention, but are moreover in disagreement with respect to the meaning and legal scope of several of those provisions, including Article IX.')

110 [29] *Gabcikovo-Nagymaros Project* (Hungary/Slovakia), Judgment of 25 September 1997, I.C.J. Reports 1997, p. 7, at p. 79, para. 142 .

111 [30] WTO, *United States-Import Prohibition of Certain Shrimp and Shrimp Products*, WT/DS58/AB/R, Report of the Appellate Body of 12 October 1998, para. 158.

international law applicable in the relations between the parties'. The Charter of the United Nations ('UN Charter') constitutes such international law that applies between the Contracting States of the Genocide Convention.[112] [31] The Genocide Convention must thus be interpreted in the context of the Parties' obligations under the UN Charter.

27. According to Article 1, paragraph 1, of the UN Charter, one of the purposes of the United Nations is 'to bring about by peaceful means, and in confo1mity with the principles of justice and international law, adjustment or settlement of international disputes or situations which might lead to a breach of the peace'.

28. Article 2, paragraph 3, of the UN Charter sets forth the principle according to which, in pursuit of the purposes stated in Article 1, the Member States of the United Nations 'shall settle their international disputes by peaceful means in such a manner that international peace and security, and justice, are not endangered'. This principle is further specified in Article 33 of the UN Charter, which provides that

> 'parties to any dispute, the continuance of which is likely to endanger the maintenance of international peace and security, shall, first of all, seek a solution by negotiation, enquiry, mediation, conciliation, arbitration, judicial settlement, resort to regional agencies or arrangements, or other peaceful means of their own choice.'

29. Article IX of the Genocide Convention reflects and specifies the principle of peaceful settlement of disputes, enshrined m the UN Charter, for the purposes of the Genocide Convention.

30. The Court has held that the obligation to seek the peaceful settlement of disputes must be implemented in good faith in accordance with Article 2, paragraph 2, of the UN Charter.[113] [32] The principle of peaceful dispute settlement is 'complementary to the . . . principle prohibiting recourse to the threat or use of force in international relations or the principle of nonintervention'.[114] [33]

31. The principle that international disputes shall be settled peacefully is binding upon all Member States of the United Nations. Consequently, a contextual interpretation confirms that Article IX of the Genocide Convention vests the Court with the jurisdiction to determine whether a Party violated the Genocide

---

112 [31] Relevant obligations constitute customary international law as confirmed in *Case concerning Military and Paramilitary Activities in and against Nicaragua*, Nicaragua v. United States of America, Judgment of 27 June 1986, para. 290.

113 [32] *Case Concerning the Aerial Incident of 10 August 1999* (Pakistan v. India), Jurisdiction of the Court, Judgment of 21 June 2000, at p. 25, para. 53.

114 [33] *Case concerning Military and Paramilitary Activities in and against Nicaragua, Nicaragua v. United States of America*, Judgment of 27 June 1986, para. 290.

Convention by failing to interpret, apply or fulfil the Convention in accordance with its obligations under the UN Charter.

32. In addition, the context of the phrase 'relating to the interpretation, application or fulfilment of the Convention, including those relating to the responsibility of a State for genocide or for any of the other acts enumerated in article III' reinforces this reading. In particular, the unusual feature of the word 'including' in the intermediate sentence of Article IX indicates an all-encompassing nature of Article IX. The provision expressly indicates that disputes 'relating to the responsibility of a State for genocide or for any of the other acts enumerated in article III' are 'included' in the wider phrase of disputes 'relating to the interpretation, application and fulfilment' of the Genocide Convention and they may thus be referred to the Court. There is nothing in this text which limits the Court's jurisdiction to the determination of the responsibility of a respondent State, as opposed to the responsibility of an applicant State.

5. Object and Purpose of the Genocide Convention

33. Article 31 of the VCLT requires a treaty to be interpreted in the light of its object and purpose, which may be reflected in its preamble.[115] [34] The preamble of the Genocide Convention indicates the object and purpose to further 'the spirit and aims of the United Nations'. This object and purpose entails that in their efforts to interpret, apply and fulfil the Convention, Contracting States may not act in a manner that contradicts the spirit and aims of the UN Charter. In the same vein, the Court has already affirmed that 'it is clear that every State may only act within the limits permitted by international law'.[116] [35]

34. The Court has emphasized in its 1951 Advisory Opinion that:

> 'The objects of such a convention must also be considered. The Convention was manifestly adopted for a purely humanitarian and civilizing purpose. It is indeed difficult to imagine a convention that might have this dual character to a greater degree, since its object on the one hand is to safeguard the very existence of certain human groups and on the other to confirm and endorse the most elementary principles of morality. In such a convention the contracting States do not have any interests of their own; they merely have, one and all, a common interest, namely, the accomplishment of those high purposes which are the *raison d'etre* of the convention. Consequently, in a convention of this type one cannot speak of individual advantages or disadvantages to States, or of the maintenance of a perfect contractual balance between rights and duties. The high ideals which

---

115 [34] *E.g. Question of the Delimitation of the Continental Shelf between Nicaragua and Colombia beyond 200 Nautical Miles from the Nicaraguan Coast* (Nicaragua v. Colombia), Preliminary Objections, Judgment of 17 March 2016, I.C.J. Reports 2016, p. 100, at p. 118, para. 39.

116 [35] *Application of the Convention on the Prevention and Punishment of the Crime of Genocide* (Bosnia and Herzegovina v. Serbia and Montenegro), Judgment of 26 February 2007, I.C.J. Reports 2007, p.435 [*sic*], at p. 221, para. 430.

inspired the Convention provide, by virtue of the common will of the parties, the foundation and measure of all its provisions.'[117] [36]

35. Since Article IX of the Convention provides a mandatory dispute settlement procedure – which aligns with the spirit and aims of the UN Charter – it corroborates the object and purpose of the Convention to ensure the peaceful settlement of disputes concerning the Genocide Convention. In this connection, this Court held:

'The Court thus finds that it has jurisdiction in this case to give effect to the Genocide Convention ... This finding is, moreover, in accordance with the object and purpose of the Convention as defined by the Court in [its Advisory Opinion of] 1951.'[118] [37]

36. It follows that denying a Party its right to dispute settlement under Article IX of the Convention would run counter to the object and purpose of the Convention, in particular since the State would have no other judicial instrument available to protect itself against any false or abusive allegation of genocide. The result would be to deny legal recourse to Contracting States that wish to be exonerated for allegations of violations of the Genocide Convention fabricated by another Contracting State. Such interpretation of Article IX could lead to serious abuses of the Genocide Convention.

37. Further, the Court recently held that

'[c]ertain acts may fall within the ambit of more than one instrument and a dispute relating to those acts may relate to the 'interpretation or application' of more than one treaty or other instrument.'[119] [38]

38. In other words, the fact that a Party's claims may simultaneously relate to other legal or political questions in addition to the 'interpretation, application or fulfilment' of the Genocide Convention does in no way abrogate Article IX. Even if the larger dispute gives rise to questions under the UN Charter or customary international law *in parallel* to questions under the Genocide Convention, the Court 'cannot infer the subject-matter of a dispute from the political Context' but must 'bas[e] itself on what the applicant has requested of it'[120] [39] under the Genocide Convention.

---

117 [36] *Reservations to the Convention on the Prevention and Punishment of the Crime of Genocide*, Advisory Opinion of 28 May 1951, I.C.J. Reports 195, page 23.

118 [37] *Application of the Convention on the Prevention and Punishment of the Crime of Genocide, Preliminary Objections,* Preliminary Objections, 1. C.J. [*sic*] Reports 1996, p. 595, para. 34.

119 [38] *Alleged Violations of the 1955 Treaty of Amity, Economic Relations, and Consular Rights* (Islamic Republic of Iran v. United States of America), Preliminary Objections, Judgment of 3 February 2021, I.C.J. Reports 2021, p. 9, at p. 27, para. 56.

120 [39] *Ibid*, para. 59.

39. A State cannot escape its obligations under the Genocide Convention by picking and choosing whether it applies the definitions and obligations under the Convention or customary

international law in a given situation. Rather, obligations under a treaty take precedence over customary international law in accordance with the interpretive maxim of *lex specialis*.[121] [40] If the reverse was the case – i.e. if respondent States could vitiate the application of a treaty's compromissory clause by claiming that the UN Charter or customary international law simultaneously apply to the conduct in question – the inclusion of compromissory clauses would be devoid of any practical value for the peaceful settlement of treaty disputes. In turn, this would negate the object and purpose of the Genocide Convention, which encompasses the peaceful dispute settlement as enshrined in Article IX.

40. In conclusion, the object and purpose of the Convention strongly militates in favour of an interpretation of Article IX according to which disputes relating to the interpretation, application or fulfilment include disputes about false or abusive allegations of genocide contradicting the letter and spirit of the Convention.

III. Conclusion

41. For the reasons given in these Joint Written Observations, the intervening States submit that the proper construction of Article IX of the Genocide Convention vests the Court with the jurisdiction to adjudge and declare (a) an applicant State's non-violation of the Convention and (b) a violation of the Convention due to the failure to interpret, apply or fulfil the Convention in good faith. […]

NN.II.7.a.-3

*Joint oral statement by Austria, the Czech Republic, Principality of Liechtenstein and the Slovak Republic in the Allegations of Genocide under the Convention on the Prevention and Punishment of the Crime of Genocide (*Ukraine v Russian Federation*) case*

Gemeinsame mündliche Stellungnahme Österreichs, der Tschechischen Republik, des Fürstentums Liechtenstein und der Slowakei im Allegations of Genocide under the Convention on the Prevention and Punishment of the Crime of Genocide (Ukraine v Russische Föderation)-Fall

On 20 September 2023, Austria submitted a joint oral statement together with the Czech Republic, the Principality of Liechtenstein and the Slovak Republic,

[121] [40] *Military and Paramilitary Activities in and against Nicaragua* (Nicaragua v. United States of America), Judgment of 27 June 1986, I.C.J. Reports 1986, p. 14, at p. 137, para. 274 ('In general, treaty rules being *lex specialis*, it would not be appropriate that a State should bring a claim based on a customary law rule if it has by treaty already provided means for settlement of a such a claim.')

before the International Court of Justice, which was delivered by the Czech agent:

> 'Madam President, Members of the Court, it is a great honour and privilege to appear before the Court on behalf of the Governments of the Republic of Austria, the Czech Republic, the Principality of Liechtenstein and the Slovak Republic. Our Governments presented joint written observations in the current dispute between Ukraine and the Russian Federation. The Convention on the Prevention and Punishment of the Crime of Genocide is a universal treaty acknowledging the inherent importance of and granting protection to some of the basic values of the international community as a whole.
>
> Therefore, we have a legal interest in and attach fundamental importance to its correct interpretation. As Contracting Parties to the Convention, we wish to present to the Court our views on the correct interpretation of relevant obligations under the Convention. In accordance with the Court's Order, our observations solely concern the construction of Art IX of the Convention, which is relevant for the determination of the Court's jurisdiction. We accept that, in accordance with Art 63, para 2, of the Court's Statute, we will be bound by the Court's construction of the Convention in this case. My task today is to address the salient elements of the interpretation of Art IX of the Convention, which we regard as relevant in the present dispute. In the interest of time, I will focus my observations on the following three points: First, Art IX of the Convention is a broad jurisdictional clause, allowing the Court to decide on 'negative declarations' establishing the non-violation of the Genocide Convention by an applicant State; Second, Art IX also vests the Court with the jurisdiction to adjudicate upon disputes relating to a violation of the Convention through false or abusive allegations of genocide; and Third, the Genocide Convention, including its Art IX, must be interpreted in the context of the obligations of State parties under the United Nations Charter.
>
> Madam President, Members of the Court, with your permission, I would now like to turn to our first point that Art IX allows the Court to decide on 'negative declarations' establishing the non-violation of the Genocide Convention by an applicant State. This means that the Court has jurisdiction over disputes concerning the request of an applicant State for a declaration that it had not violated the Genocide Convention. We would like to highlight that Art IX expressly allows the Court to adjudicate upon disputes relating to all aspects of interpretation, application or fulfilment of the Genocide Convention, including disputes 'relating to the responsibility of a State for genocide or for any of the other acts enumerated in Art III' of the Convention. Thus, we submit that when a State is accused by another State of being responsible for committing genocide, it has the same right to initiate proceedings before the Court, just as the State making such accusation. In both cases, the responsibility of a State for genocide, or the absence of such responsibility, is at stake and forms the subject-matter of the dispute. This interpretation of Art IX is confirmed by the Court's jurisprudence. The Court accepted jurisdiction in cases regarding claims of non-violation of conventional obligations, as referenced

in our written observations, such as the dispute between France and the United States of America concerning Rights of Nationals of the United States of America in Morocco or the dispute between Libya and the United Kingdom concerning the Aerial Incident at Lockerbie. Therefore, we submit that, under Art IX, the Court is competent to adjudge and declare the absence of responsibility for genocide, that is the non-violation of the Genocide Convention by an applicant State.

The second point of our observations concerns disputes about a violation of the Convention through false or abusive allegations of genocide. The customary rule reflected in Art 31 of the Vienna Convention on the Law of Treaties obliges States to interpret a treaty in good faith. As this Court held, in the Gabčíkovo-Nagymaros case, the principle of good faith 'obliges the Parties to apply [a treaty] in a reasonable way and in such a manner that its purpose can be realized'. The principle of good faith constitutes the positive side of the prohibition of abuse of rights. As such, the principle of good faith prohibits an abusive interpretation and/or application of the treaty. We submit that the subject-matter of the dispute under Art IX may concern the good faith interpretation, application or fulfilment of any right and obligation under the Convention, as well as the good faith performance of the Convention as a whole. For instance, in a situation where a Contracting Party accuses another Party of committing genocide, without any factual and legal foundations, and acts in contravention of international law for the alleged purpose of preventing such genocide, the Contracting Party fails to interpret, apply or fulfil the Convention in good faith and thus violates the Convention. For these reasons, it is our position that Art IX of the Convention covers disputes concerning false or abusive allegations of genocide made with the aim of justifying illegal unilateral acts and disregarding the principle of good faith interpretation and application of the Convention.

Third, we would like to point to the requirement of a contextual interpretation of Art IX of the Convention. Under the customary rule reflected in Art 31, para 3 (c), of the Vienna Convention, the Genocide Convention, including its Art IX, has to be interpreted in the context of 'any relevant rules of international law applicable in the relations between the parties'. The Charter of the United Nations constitutes such relevant international law applicable between the Contracting Parties of the Convention. One of the fundamental principles of the Charter stipulates that States shall settle their international disputes by peaceful means in such a manner that international peace, security and justice, are not endangered. In the words of the Court in the Nicaragua case, this principle is complementary to the 'principle prohibiting recourse to the threat or use of force in international relations' or the 'principle of non-intervention'. Art IX of the Convention reflects and specifies the principle of peaceful settlement of disputes for the purposes of the Convention. Any dispute among Contracting Parties concerning the interpretation, application or fulfilment of the Genocide Convention has to be settled peacefully in accordance with Art IX. Consequently, we submit that Art IX of the Convention also covers disputes whether a Contracting Party violated the Convention by failing to interpret, apply or fulfil the Convention in accordance with its obligations regarding the peaceful settlement of disputes under the UN Charter.

To conclude, we would like to emphasize that Art IX of the Convention establishes a mandatory procedure for the peaceful settlement of disputes, which aligns with the aims of the UN Charter and allows the effective fulfilment of the object and purpose of the Convention.

We submit that Art IX, interpreted in good faith in accordance with the ordinary meaning of its terms in their context and in light of the object and purpose of the Convention, covers disputes regarding the non-violation of the Genocide Convention by an applicant State and disputes relating to a violation of the Convention through false or abusive allegations of genocide, as we described in our joint written observations and outlined in this presentation.'[122]

b. Courts or tribunals, other than the ICJ/Sonstige Gerichte und Gerichtshöfe

See QQ.I.2.g.-3.

8. Settlement within international organisations/Streitbeilegung innerhalb der internationalen Organisationen

See *EE.II.-4.*

a. United Nations/Vereinte Nationen

See *EE.II.1.b.-1* and *EE.II.1.b.-2.*

OO. Coercive measures short of the use of force/Zwangsmaßnahmen unter der Schwelle der Gewaltanwendung

II. Collective measures/Kollektivmaßnahmen

2. Collective measures outside the United Nations/Kollektivmaßnahmen außerhalb der Vereinten Nationen

See *FF.VIII.-4*, *FF.VIII.-7*, and *GG.VII.-1.*

---

[122] Reproduced in Helmut Tichy *et al*, 'Recent Austrian Practice in the Field of International Law. Report for 2023' (2024) 78(1) Zeitschrift für öffentliches Recht 169, 192-194.

PP. Use of force/Gewaltanwendung

I. Prohibition of use of force/Gewaltverbot

See also *EE.II.1.b.-1.*

PP.I.-1

Parliamentary Resolution concerning support for Ukraine against the Russian aggression

Parlamentarische Entschließung betreffend Unterstützung der Ukraine gegen die russische Aggression

On 31 January 2023, the National Assembly adopted a parliamentary resolution concerning support for Ukraine against Russian aggression:[123]

> The Federal Government, in particular the Federal Minister for European Affairs, is requested to continue to strongly advocate for the immediate cessation of Russia's attacks and the immediate and complete withdrawal of Russian troops from Ukrainian territory, as well as the complete restoration of Ukraine's territorial integrity and full sovereignty and Russia's respect for the fundamental norms of international law and the United Nations Charter;
>
> to support all bilateral and multilateral initiatives, such as those within the framework of the UN and the OSCE, which can lead to a de-escalation of the war and the start of genuine peace negotiations between Moscow and Ukraine with the aim of a just peace and taking into account the 10-point formula drawn up by Ukraine.
>
> to continue to advocate vigorously at all levels for compliance with and implementation of the norms of international law, in particular international humanitarian law and human rights law, and in particular to advocate for compliance with international legal obligations under the Geneva Conventions and Additional Protocols concerning the protection of the civilian population and the treatment of prisoners of war;
>
> continue to provide humanitarian assistance to Ukraine and those affected by the humanitarian consequences of the conflict.

The German original reads as follows:

> Die Bundesregierung, insbesondere der Bundesminister für europäische Angelegenheiten, wird ersucht,
>
> sich weiterhin mit Nachdruck für die sofortige Einstellung der Angriffe Russlands und den unverzüglichen und vollständigen Abzug der russischen Truppen

123 Parliamentary Materials, 298/E(XXVII. GP).

vom ukrainischen Territorium, sowie die vollkommene Wiederherstellung der territorialen Integrität und der vollen Souveränität der Ukraine sowie die Achtung der Grundnormen des Völkerrechts und der Charta der Vereinten Nationen durch Russland einzusetzen;

alle bilateralen und multilateralen Initiativen wie jene im Rahmen der UN und der OSZE zu unterstützen, die zu einer Deeskalation des Krieges und zur Aufnahme seriöser Friedensverhandlungen zwischen Moskau und der Ukraine führen können mit dem Ziel eines gerechten Friedens und unter Berücksichtigung der von der Ukraine ausgearbeiteten 10-Punkte Formel. [*sic*]

weiterhin auf allen Ebenen mit Nachdruck für die Einhaltung und Durchsetzung der Normen des Völkerrechts, insbesondere des humanitären Völkerrechts und der Menschenrechte einzutreten, und sich dabei insbesondere für die Einhaltung der völkerrechtlichen Verpflichtungen aufgrund der Genfer Abkommen und Zusatzprotokolle betreffend den Schutz der Zivilbevölkerung und die Behandlung Kriegsgefangener einzusetzen;

weitere humanitäre Unterstützung für die Ukraine und die von den humanitären Auswirkungen des Krieges unmittelbar am stärksten betroffenen Nachbarstaaten bereitzustellen.

PP.I.-2

Parliamentary Resolution concerning the anniversary of the start of the Russian war of aggression against Ukraine

Parlamentarische Entschließung betreffend Jahrestag des Beginns des russischen Angriffskrieges gegen die Ukraine

On 24 February 2023, the National Assembly adopted a parliamentary resolution concerning on the anniversary of the start of the Russian war of aggression against Ukraine:[124]

The Federal Government, in particular the Federal Minister for European and International Affairs, is requested

- to continue to advocate vigorously, particularly in association with the EU and in close coordination with international partners, for the immediate cessation of Russia's attacks and the restoration of Ukraine's territorial integrity and full sovereignty, compliance with international law and human rights;

- to work to ensure that perpetrators and commanders of war crimes and crimes against humanity in Ukraine are swiftly held accountable,

- continue bilateral efforts and strongly support multilateral efforts, such as those within the United Nations and the OSCE, to de-escalate the war while keeping

[124] Parliamentary Materials, 303/E(XXVII. GP).

channels of dialogue open to promote a political peace process to establish a just and lasting peace, and

- provide further humanitarian support to Ukraine and the neighbouring countries in the region most affected by the negative effects of the war.

The German original reads as follows:

Die Bundesregierung, insbesondere der Bundesminister für europäische und internationale Angelegenheiten, wird ersucht,

- weiterhin mit Nachdruck insbesondere im Verband mit der EU und in enger Abstimmung mit internationalen Partnern wie bisher für die unverzügliche Einstellung der Angriffe Russlands und die Wiederherstellung der territorialen Integrität und vollen Souveränität der Ukraine, der Einhaltung des Völkerrechts und der Menschenrechte einzutreten,

- sich dafür einzusetzen, dass Täter und Befehlshaber für Kriegsverbrechen und Verbrechen gegen die Menschlichkeit in der Ukraine rasch zur Verantwortung gezogen werden,

- bilaterale Bemühungen fortzuführen und multilaterale Bemühungen wie jene im Rahmen der Vereinten Nationen und der OSZE mit Nachdruck zu unterstützen, um eine Deeskalation des Krieges bei gleichzeitigem Offenhalten von Gesprächskanälen zur Förderung eines politischen Friedensprozesses zur Herstellung eines gerechten und dauerhaften Friedens zu erreichen und

- weitere humanitäre Unterstützung für die Ukraine und den am meisten von den negativen Auswirkungen des Krieges betroffenen Nachbarländern in der Region bereitzustellen.

PP.I.-3

Austrian statement at Third Summit of the International Crimea Platform

Österreichische Erklärung beim dritten Gipfel der Internationalen Krim-Plattform

On 23 August 2023, the Austrian Foreign Minister delivered a speech at the Summit of the Crimea Platform in Prague:

[…] Tomorrow, we will mark 18 months since Russia has broken peace on our continent with its brutal invasion of Ukraine, a sovereign and independent neighbour.

Since then, this war of aggression has been causing unimaginable destruction and despair.

But we will not let Russia get away with this crime.

Austria is at the forefront of pushing for the establishment of a Special Tribunal.

Let me be clear: Russia's invasion of Ukraine on 24th February 2022 was not its first breach of international law.

> The roots of this evil reach back to the illegal annexation of Crimea and the City of Sevastopol.
>
> But its intentions remain the same: to redraw international borders in blatant violation of the UN Charter. […]
>
> We will not waver in our commitment to an independent, free and prosperous Ukraine.
>
> Nor will we forget about Crimea and the city of Sevastopol.
>
> Austria will continue to keep up pressure against the grave violations of human rights, in particular against Crimean Tatars, the ongoing militarization of Crimea, and its impact on the security in the Black Sea region, including on food exports. […]

II. Legitimate use of force/Rechtmäßiger Gewaltgebrauch

1. Self-defense/Selbstverteidigung

PP.II.1.-1

Enquiry concerning the Turkish military offensive in north-east Syria and northern Iraq

Anfrage betreffend die türkische Militäroffensive in Nordostsyrien und im Nordirak

On 13 December 2022, a number of representatives of the Austrian National Assembly raised a parliamentary enquiry to the Federal Minister for European and International Affairs (BMEIA) concerning the 'Turkish military offensive in north-east Syria and northern Iraq in violation of international law and the associated danger of the rise of IS terrorism',[125] to which the Minister replied on 13 February 2023:[126]

> [...] The question of whether Turkish military operations in north-east Syria and northern Iraq can be justified as measures of self-defence within the meaning of Article 51 of the UN Charter would have to be examined in each individual case on the basis of all relevant elements of the facts and therefore cannot be answered in general terms. In principle, it should be noted that the EU and Austria consistently condemn unilateral actions by Turkey in northern Syria and northern Iraq and warn against further destabilisation in the region. It goes without saying that this issue is regularly debated at the EU level. There are also diplomatic efforts at the European level in direct talks to persuade Turkey to exercise restraint. The

[125] Parliamentary Materials, 13226/J (XXVII. GP).

[126] Parliamentary Materials, 12888/AB (XXVII. GP).

EU is firmly opposed to a possible Turkish ground offensive in northern Syria. In this context, I would also like to refer to the conclusions on Turkey adopted by the European Council in December 2020 and in March and June 2021. This EU position remains unchanged. [...]

[…] Turkey is a contracting party to the Chemical Weapons Convention (CWC) and declared that it does not possess any stocks of chemical weapons when the convention came into force. With regard to armed conflicts, the CWC prohibits the use of toxic chemicals as weapons. Tear gas is not included in the CWC's list of chemicals and therefore does not fall under the definition of a chemical weapon under Art. II para. 1 of the CWC. The OPCW (Organisation for the Prohibition of Chemical Weapons) is responsible for ensuring the implementation of the CWC provisions, including the international verification of compliance with the Convention, and examines compliance with the treaty obligations by the states parties. At the 27th Meeting of States Parties to the CWC from 28 November to 1 December 2022, the OPCW did not raise any issues concerning Turkey. The BMEIA has no independent information on any violations of the CWC by Turkey on the territory of Syria or Iraq. […]

The relevant parts of the German original read as follows:

[...] Die Frage, ob türkische Militäroperationen in Nordostsyrien und im Nordirak als Maßnahmen zur Selbstverteidigung im Sinne des Art. 51 der VN-Satzung gerechtfertigt werden können, wäre in jedem Einzelfall anhand aller relevanten Sachverhaltselemente zu prüfen und kann daher nicht allgemein beantwortet werden. Grundsätzlich ist festzuhalten, dass die EU und Österreich unilaterale Handlungen von Seiten der Türkei in Nordsyrien und im Nordirak konsequent verurteilen und vor einer weiteren Destabilisierung in der Region warnen. Selbstverständlich wird dieses Thema regelmäßig auf EU-Ebene debattiert. Zudem gibt es auf europäischer Ebene in direkten Gesprächen diplomatische Bemühungen, die Türkei zur Zurückhaltung zu bewegen. Die EU steht einer möglichen Bodenoffensive der Türkei in Nordsyrien entschieden ablehnend gegenüber. Ich darf in diesem Zusammenhang auch auf die Schlussfolgerungen hinweisen, die der Europäische Rat im Dezember 2020 sowie im März und Juni 2021 zur Türkei beschlossen hat. Diese Position der EU gilt unverändert. [...]

[…] Die Türkei ist Vertragsstaat der Chemiewaffenkonvention (CWK) und hat bei Inkrafttreten der Konvention erklärt, keine Bestände an Chemiewaffen zu besitzen. In Hinblick auf bewaffnete Konflikte verbietet die CWK den Einsatz von toxischen Chemikalien als Waffen. Tränengas ist nicht in den Chemikalienlisten der CWK angeführt und fällt damit nicht unter die Definition von chemischen Waffe nach Art. II Abs. 1 der CWK. Die OPCW (Organisation for the Prohibition of Chemical Weapons) ist zur Gewährleistung der Durchführung der CWK Bestimmungen, einschließlich der internationalen Verifikation der Einhaltung der

> Konvention verantwortlich und prüft die Einhaltung der Vertragsverpflichtungen durch die Vertragsstaaten. Beim 27. Vertragsstaatentreffen der CWK von 28. November bis 1. Dezember 2022 wurde seitens der OPCW kein Sachverhalt betreffend die Türkei aufgebracht. Das BMEIA verfügt über keine eigenständigen Informationen über allfällige Verstöße der Türkei gegen die CWK auf dem Staatsgebiet Syriens bzw. des Iraks. [...]

QQ. The law of armed conflict and international humanitarian law/Recht des bewaffneten Konfliktes und internationales humanitäres Recht

I. International armed conflict/Der internationale bewaffnete Konflikt

2. The laws of international armed conflict/Das Recht des internationalen bewaffneten Konflikts

f. Distinction between combatants and non-combatants/Kombattanten - Nicht-Kombattanten

See also *QQ.I.2.g.-1.*

QQ.I.2.f.-1

Parliamentary resolution on the protection of the civilian population and compliance with human rights in Northern Syria and Northern Iraq

Parlamentarische Entschließung betreffend Schutz der Zivilbevölkerung und Einhaltung der Menschenrechte in Nordsyrien und im Nordirak

On 23 May 2023, the National Assembly adopted a parliamentary resolution on the protection of civilians and respect for human rights in northern Syria and northern Iraq:[127]

> The Federal Government, in particular the Federal Minister for European and International Affairs, is requested to continue its efforts at all levels to ensure that Turkey fully fulfils its obligations under international law.
>
> The Federal Government, in particular the Federal Minister for European and International Affairs, is also requested to continue to advocate at all levels vis-à-vis Turkey for comprehensive protection of the civilian population, civilian

[127] Parliamentary Materials, 312/E(XXVII. GP).

objects, and critical infrastructure in the region of northern Syria and northern Iraq as well as for full compliance with human and fundamental rights in the region, including the Kurdish population, and to continue to clearly identify violations of international law and human rights as such.

Furthermore, the Federal Government, in particular the Federal Minister for European and International Affairs, is requested to continue its efforts at all levels to provide humanitarian support for the civilian population in Syria, Iraq, and Turkey, including the Kurdish population.

The German original reads as follows:

Die Bundesregierung, insbesondere der Bundesminister für europäische und internationale Angelegenheiten, wird ersucht, sich auf allen Ebenen weiterhin dafür einzusetzen, dass die Türkei ihren völkerrechtlichen Verpflichtungen in vollem Umfang nachkommt.

Die Bundesregierung, insbesondere der Bundesminister für europäische und internationale Angelegenheiten, wird zudem ersucht, sich weiterhin auf allen Ebenen gegenüber der Türkei für einen umfassenden Schutz der Zivilbevölkerung, ziviler Objekte und kritischer Infrastruktur in der Region Nordsyriens und im Nordirak sowie für die vollumfängliche Einhaltung der Menschen- und Grundrechte in der Region, einschließlich der kurdischen Bevölkerung, einzusetzen, sowie Verletzungen des Völkerrechts und der Menschenrechte weiterhin klar als solche zu benennen.

Des Weiteren wird die Bundesregierung, insbesondere der Bundesminister für europäische und internationale Angelegenheiten, ersucht, sich auf allen Ebenen weiter für humanitäre Unterstützung für die Zivilbevölkerung in Syrien, dem Irak und der Türkei, einschließlich der kurdischen Bevölkerung, einzusetzen.

g. International humanitarian law (droit humanitaire international)/ Internationales humanitäres Recht

See *PP.I.-1.*

QQ.I.2.g.-1

Enquiry concerning the Austrian position regarding the United States' drone warfare

Anfrage betreffend der österreichischen Position zum Drohnenkrieg der USA

On 27 January 2023, a number of representatives of the Austrian National Assembly raised a parliamentary enquiry to the Federal Minister for European and International Affairs concerning the position regarding the drone warfare of the

United States of America,[128] to which the Minister gave, *inter alia*, the following response on 27 March 2023:[129]

> From the perspective of international law, the use of drones must be assessed differently depending on whether they are used in an armed conflict or outside an armed conflict: In armed conflicts, drones may only attack military targets in accordance with international humanitarian law. In doing so, the fundamental principles of international humanitarian law – proportionality, distinction, military necessity, protection of the civilian population, and avoidance of unnecessary suffering – must be observed. Since a drone is controlled and instructed by an individual, responsibility for compliance with these principles is generally guaranteed. The use of drones outside of armed conflicts, where drones are used, among other things, to combat terrorists, must be assessed differently. Austria regularly expresses its criticism at various diplomatic levels of problematic incidents if there is evidence of practices that are questionable under international law. The sometimes controversial question of whether or not an armed conflict exists, must be examined and assessed on a case-by-case basis. Austria does not differentiate between different states when it comes to the question of the assessment of the use of (combat) drones under international law and compliance with existing international law.

The German original reads as follows:

> Aus völkerrechtlicher Sicht muss für eine Bewertung des Einsatzes von Drohnen danach unterschieden werden, ob Drohnen in bewaffneten Konflikten oder außerhalb von bewaffneten Konflikten eingesetzt werden: In bewaffneten Konflikten dürfen Drohnen im Einklang mit dem humanitären Völkerrecht nur militärische Ziele angreifen. Dabei sind die im humanitären Völkerrecht geltenden Grundprinzipien – Verhältnismäßigkeit, Unterscheidung, militärische Notwendigkeit sowie Schutz der Zivilbevölkerung und Vermeidung unnötiger Leiden – zu beachten. Da ein Individuum die Drohne steuert und Instruktionen sendet, ist die Verantwortlichkeit für die Einhaltung dieser Grundprinzipien grundsätzlich gewährleistet. Anders ist der Einsatz von Drohnen außerhalb von bewaffneten Konflikten zu beurteilen, wo Drohnen unter anderem zur Bekämpfung von Terroristen eingesetzt werden. Österreich äußert sich regelmäßig auf unterschiedlichen diplomatischen Ebenen kritisch zu problematischen Vorkommnissen, sofern Belege für völkerrechtlich fragwürdige Praktiken vorliegen. Die manchmal strittige Frage, ob ein bewaffneter Konflikt vorliegt oder nicht, muss im Einzelfall geprüft und beurteilt werden. In der Frage der völkerrechtlichen Beurteilung des Einsatzes von (Kampf-)Drohnen und der Einhaltung der bestehenden völkerrechtlichen Regeln macht Österreich keinen Unterschied zwischen verschiedenen Staaten.

---

[128] Parliamentary Materials, 13771/J (XXVII. GP.).

[129] Parliamentary Materials, 13375/AB (XXVII. GP).

QQ.I.2.g.-2

Enquiry concerning the ban on autonomous weapons systems without human control

Anfrage betreffend das Verbot von autonomen Waffensystemen ohne menschliche Kontrolle

On 29 March 2023, a number of representatives of the Austrian National Assembly raised a parliamentary enquiry to the Federal Minister for European and International Affairs concerning the ban on autonomous weapons systems without human control,[130] to which the Minister gave, *inter alia*, the following response on 26 May 2023:[131]

> Austria is committed to so-called 'humanitarian disarmament', which focuses primarily on the impact of weapons on the civilian population and the strengthening of and compliance with international humanitarian law. […]
>
> With regard to autonomous weapons systems, my ministry has consistently upheld the position set out in National Council Resolution 136/E 'Prohibition of autonomous weapons systems without human control ('killer robots')'of 24 February 2021 and has actively advocated for international legal regulation of autonomous weapons systems, including a ban on autonomous weapons systems without significant human control, within the First Committee of the United Nations General Assembly (UNGA) as well as in the various bodies of the Conventional Weapons Convention (CCW) and in other relevant forums. Austria has regularly issued statements to this effect in the UN General Assembly (High-Level Debate, First Committee) and in the bodies of the Conventional Weapons Convention (CCW) as well as in the Conference on Disarmament, at relevant conferences and in other forums.
>
> In March 2023, my ministry presented a working paper to the CCW government expert group with concrete elements for the international legal regulation of autonomous weapons systems, including bans. Austria is in favour of international legal regulation of autonomous weapon systems and, like the majority of states, supports a two-pronged approach in which certain autonomous weapon systems must be banned per se for legal or ethical reasons and others are legally regulated to ensure meaningful human control.
>
> At the First Committee of the 77th UN General Assembly in 2022, the BMEIA initiated, drafted, coordinated and presented a cross-regional statement by 70 states, which represents the common ground of this broad group of states with regard to the need for rules and restrictions on autonomous weapons systems at the international level and the centrality of the human being in the use of force. In 2021, Austria, together with a cross-regional group of seven states, had already

---

130 Parliamentary Materials, 14634/J (XXVII. GP).

131 Parliamentary Materials, 14216/AB (XXVII. GP).

submitted a working paper on ethical considerations regarding the regulation of autonomous weapons systems to the CCW Governmental Group of Experts, and in 2022, together with a cross-regional group of 23 states, a working paper on 'Emerging Technologies in the Area of Lethal Autonomous Weapons Systems', which also elaborated elements for the prohibition and regulation of autonomous weapon systems and addressed the urgency of making progress in the international process.

Austria continues to advocate for an enhancement of the mandate of the Group of Governmental Experts established under the CCW with the aim of commencing negotiations on an international instrument to regulate autonomous weapons systems. My ministry also actively participated in the international conferences held in The Hague on 15-16 February 2023 and in San José, Costa Rica, on 23-24 February 2023. The aforementioned meetings of states parties and international conferences have contributed to awareness at the international level through their media coverage. […]

Within the framework of the traditional Austrian rule of law focus, Austria pursues a rules-based order for the digital space and actively advocates compliance with human rights standards in the development and application of new technologies and in the digital space in general. With this goal in mind, Austria is involved in international bodies in the development and implementation of human rights-based frameworks and international standards. At the EU level, the BMEIA has been particularly active since 2021 in promoting a more coherent, active and coordinated approach by the EU and its member states (EU MS) to advance a human rights-based approach to the digital space and digital technologies in all relevant international forums.

Austria is also playing a leading role in relevant initiatives within the UN. In the UN Human Rights Council (UNHRC), Austria, together with a core group, is introducing resolution initiatives on 'Human Rights and New Digital Technologies' and the 'Right to Privacy in the Digital Age'. The UN HRC resolution on new technologies and human rights (initiated by Austria, Brazil, Denmark, the Republic of Korea, Morocco and Singapore) focuses on the need for a better exchange between tech- and human rights experts, among others, and on the translation of human rights standards for the tech industry. The next resolution on this topic in the UN HRC will be presented by Austria in June 2023. In September 2022, Austria, together with Panama, introduced a resolution initiative on 'New and emerging technologies in the military sector' for the first time in the UN HRC, which mandates the submission of a report to the UN HRC on the 'human rights implications of new and emerging technologies in the military sector'. The text explicitly stipulates that a human being must always make the decision to use force.

At the conference 'REAIM 2023 – Summit on Responsible Artificial Intelligence in the Military Domain' organised by the Netherlands and the Republic of Korea on 15-16 February 2023, Austria emphasised the need for international regulation of autonomous weapons systems and the broad global consensus-building on this.

This should build on the work of the Group of Governmental Experts in Geneva and other UN bodies that are examining the military, legal, technical and ethical aspects of autonomous weapons.

In addition to the above-mentioned multilateral initiatives and activities of my ministry in the field of disarmament, in which questions of human rights, ethics, and morals were always part of the consideration, the topic of banning/regulating autonomous weapons systems was also included in the Austrian input for the UN Secretary-General's 'A New Agenda for Peace' and in the Austrian statement on the 'UN Global Digital Compact' with the aim of placing the topic high on the political agenda of the United Nations, to emphasise the urgency of the issue, and to achieve progress towards an international legal regulation of autonomous weapons systems.

The relevant parts of the German original read as follows:

Österreich setzt sich thematisch für die sogenannte „humanitäre Abrüstung" ein, die vor allem auf die Auswirkungen von Waffengattungen auf die zivile Bevölkerung und eine Stärkung und Einhaltung des humanitären Völkerrechts abstellt. […]

Betreffend autonome Waffensysteme hat mein Ressort konsequent die in der Entschließung des Nationalrates 136/E „Verbot von autonomen Waffensystemen ohne menschliche Kontrolle („Killer-Robotern")" vom 24.02.2021 dargelegte Position vertreten und sich aktiv im Rahmen des Ersten Ausschusses der Generalversammlung der Vereinten Nationen (VN-GV) wie auch der Konventionellen Waffenkonvention (CCW) und darüber hinaus in allen relevanten Foren für eine internationale rechtliche Regulierung von autonomen Waffensystemen, welches ein Verbot von autonomen Waffensystemen ohne bedeutende menschliche Kontrolle umfasst, eingesetzt. Österreich hat in der VN-GV (Hochrangige Debatte, Erster Ausschuss) und in den Gremien der Konventionellen Waffenkonvention (CCW) sowie in der Abrüstungskonferenz, bei einschlägigen Konferenzen und in anderen Foren regelmäßig Stellungnahmen in diesem Sinne abgegeben.

Im März 2023 hat mein Ressort ein Arbeitspapier in der CCW Regierungsexpertengruppe vorgelegt mit konkreten Elementen für eine international rechtliche Regulierung von autonomen Waffensystemen einschließlich von Verboten. Österreich setzt sich darin für eine internationale rechtliche Regulierung von autonomen Waffensystemen ein und unterstützt wie die Staatenmehrheit einen zweigliedrigen Ansatz, bei dem bestimmte autonome Waffensysteme aus rechtlichen oder ethischen Gründen per se verboten werden müssen und andere rechtlich reguliert werden, um bedeutende menschliche Kontrolle („meaningful human control") sicherzustellen.

Im Ersten Ausschuss der 77. VN-GV 2022 hat das BMEIA eine überregionale Erklärung von 70 Staaten initiiert, ausgearbeitet, koordiniert und präsentiert, welche die Gemeinsamkeiten dieser breiten Staatengruppe in Hinblick auf die Notwendigkeit von Regeln und Beschränkungen von autonomen Waffensystemen auf internationaler Ebene und die Zentralität des Menschen in der Gewaltanwendung darstellt. Im Jahr 2021 hatte Österreich bereits gemeinsam mit einer überregionalen Gruppe von sieben Staaten ein Arbeitspapier zu ethischen Überlegungen betreffend der Regulierung autonomer Waffensysteme in der CCW Regierungsexpertengruppe vorgelegt sowie 2022 gemeinsam mit einer überregionalen Gruppe von 23 Staaten ein Arbeitspapier zu „Emerging Technologies in the Area of Lethal Autonomous Weapons Systems", in welchem ebenfalls Elemente für Verbot und Regulierung von autonomen Waffensystemen herausgearbeitet wurden und die Dringlichkeit von Fortschritten im internationalen Prozess angesprochen wurde.

Österreich setzt sich weiterhin für eine Aufwertung des Mandats der Regierungsexpertengruppe im Rahmen der CCW ein, mit dem Ziel, Verhandlungen zu einem internationalen Rechtsinstrument zur Regulierung von autonomen Waffensystemen zu beginnen. Mein Ressort nahm weiters aktiv an den internationalen Konferenzen am 15.-16. Februar 2023 in Den Haag und am 23.-24. Februar 2023 in San José, Costa Rica, teil. Die erwähnten Vertragsstaatentreffen und internationalen Konferenzen haben durch ihren medialen Niederschlag zum Bewusstsein auf internationaler Ebene beigetragen. […]

Österreich verfolgt im Rahmen des traditionellen österreichischen Rechtsstaatlichkeitsschwerpunkts eine regelbasierte Ordnung des digitalen Raums und setzt sich aktiv für die Einhaltung menschenrechtlicher Standards bei der Entwicklung und Anwendung von neuen Technologien und generell im digitalen Raum ein. Mit diesem Ziel engagiert sich Österreich in internationalen Gremien bei der Entwicklung und Umsetzung menschenrechtsbasierter Rahmenwerke und internationaler Standards. Auf EU Ebene tritt das BMEIA seit 2021 insbesondere verstärkt für ein kohärenteres, aktiveres und besser koordiniertes Vorgehen der EU und ihrer Mitgliedstaaten (EU-MS) ein, um einen auf Menschenrechten basierenden Ansatz für den digitalen Raum und für digitale Technologien in allen relevanten internationalen Foren zu befördern.

Auch im Rahmen der VN beteiligt sich Österreich federführend an entsprechenden Initiativen. Im VN-Menschenrechtsrat (VN-MRR) bringt Österreich zusammen mit einer Kerngruppe Resolutionsinitiativen zu „Menschenrechten und neuen digitalen Technologien" und dem „Recht auf Privatsphäre im digitalen Zeitalter" ein. Die VN-MRR Resolution zu neuen Technologien und Menschenrechten (initiiert von Österreich, Brasilien, Dänemark, Republik Korea, Marokko und Singapur) legt den Fokus auf die Notwendigkeit besseren Austauschs zwischen unter anderem Tech- und Menschenrechtsexpertinnen und -experten, sowie auf die Übersetzung menschenrechtlicher Standards für die Tech-Industrie. Die nächste Resolution zu diesem Thema im VN-MRR wird von Österreich im Juni 2023 präsentiert. Österreich brachte, im September 2022 zusammen mit Panama zum ersten Mal im VN-MRR eine Resolutionsinitiative zu „Neue und aufkommenden Technologien im militärischen Bereich" ein, mit der der Auftrag erteilt wird, dem VN-MRR einen Bericht über die „Auswirkungen neuer und aufkommender Technologien im militärischen Bereich auf die Menschenrechte" vorzulegen. Der Text schreibt explizit fest, dass, stets ein Mensch die Entscheidung über Gewaltanwendung treffen müsse.

Österreich hat bei der von den Niederlanden und der Republik Korea am 15.-16. Februar 2023 organisierten Konferenz „REAIM 2023 – Summit on Responsible Artificial Intelligence in the Military Domain" die Notwendigkeit einer internationalen Regulierung autonomer Waffensysteme und der breiten globalen Konsensbildung dazu betont. Dabei sollte auf den Arbeiten der Gruppe von Regierungsexpertinnen und Regierungsexperten in Genf und anderer VN-Gremien aufgebaut werden, die militärische, rechtliche, technische und ethische Aspekte autonomer Waffensysteme prüfen.

Zusätzlich zu den oben genannten multilateralen Initiativen und Aktivitäten meines Ressorts im Abrüstungsbereich, in denen Fragen von Menschenrechten, der Ethik und Moral immer berücksichtigt wurden, wurde das Thema Verbot/Regulierung autonomer Waffensysteme auch in den österreichischen Input für „A New Agenda for Peace" des VN-Generalsekretärs und in die österreichische Stellungnahme zum „UN Global Digital Compact" aufgenommen mit dem Ziel, das Thema hoch auf die politische Agenda der Vereinten Nationen zu setzen, auf dessen Dringlichkeit zu verweisen und Fortschritte in Richtung einer internationalen rechtlichen Regulierung von autonomen Waffensystemen zu erzielen.

QQ.I.2.g.-3

Enquiry concerning respect for human rights and international humanitarian law in Ukraine

Anfrage betreffend Einhaltung der Menschenrechte und des humanitären Völkerrechts in der Ukraine

On 30 March 2023, a number of representatives of the Austrian National Assembly raised a parliamentary enquiry to the Federal Minister for the EU and Constitution concerning respect for human rights and international humanitarian law in Ukraine,[132] to which the Minister gave, *inter alia*, the following response on 30 May 2023:[133]

> [...] a few days after Russia's aggression against Ukraine began, Austria, together with 38 other states parties to the Rome Statute, referred the situation in Ukraine to the International Criminal Court (ICC). I welcome and support the investigations of the ICC's prosecutor, Karim Khan, regarding Ukraine. I strongly reject the Russian attempts to intimidate the chief prosecutor and other representatives of the ICC with coercive measures. Austria has complete confidence in the impartiality and independence of the court.

---

[132] Parliamentary Materials, 14713/J (XXVII. GP).

[133] Parliamentary Materials, 14302/AB (XXVII. GP).

Due to the limited jurisdiction of the ICC to crimes of genocide, crimes against humanity, and war crimes, the Ukrainian government called for the establishment of a special tribunal to prosecute Russian aggression against Ukraine. To implement this demand, the so-called core group for the establishment of a special tribunal for the crime of aggression against Ukraine was set up at the beginning of the year. At my instigation, Austria joined the core group in March 2023. Austria advocates closing the gap in jurisdiction with regard to the crime of aggression and is constructively participating in the core group's deliberations on the establishment of a special tribunal.

In the proceedings brought by Ukraine against the Russian Federation before the International Court of Justice (ICJ) on the basis of the Genocide Convention, I arranged for Austria to make statements in October 2022 and February 2023 in support of Ukraine as an intervener. In addition, Austria applied in September 2022 to be admitted as a third party in the state complaint of Ukraine against Russia before the European Court of Human Rights (ECtHR). In March 2023, the ECtHR confirmed a total of 31 third-party interventions, including that of Austria.

As a host state, Austria also makes extensive use of the OSCE, where all participants regularly come together to hold Russia and Belarus accountable for their role in the war of aggression and human rights violations. This is done in particular in the usually weekly debates in the Permanent Council and the Forum for Security Co-operation. Together with the overwhelming majority of participating States, Austria has twice invoked the OSCE's Moscow Mechanism to investigate human rights violations, including war crimes, in the context of Russia's war of aggression against Ukraine. On 30 March 2023, 45 OSCE states, including Austria, triggered the Moscow Mechanism again. The aim is to investigate allegations of serious human rights violations in connection with the forced relocation of Ukrainian children from occupied territories of Ukraine and the deportation of Ukrainian children to Russia. […]

The relevant parts of the German original read as follows:

[...] wenige Tage nach Beginn der russischen Aggression gegen die Ukraine, hat Österreich gemeinsam mit 38 weiteren Vertragsstaaten des Römer Statuts die Situation in der Ukraine an den Internationalen Strafgerichtshof (IStGH) verwiesen. Ich begrüße und unterstütze die Ermittlungen des Anklägers des IStGH, Karim Khan, zur Ukraine. Die russischen Versuche, den Chefankläger und andere Vertreterinnen und Vertreter des IStGH durch Zwangsmaßnahmen einzuschüchtern, weise ich aufs Schärfste zurück. Österreich hat vollstes Vertrauen in die Unparteilichkeit und Unabhängigkeit des Gerichtshofes. […]

Auf Grund der auf Völkermord, Verbrechen gegen die Menschlichkeit und Kriegsverbrechen beschränkten Zuständigkeit des IStGH wurde von der ukrainischen Regierung die Einrichtung eines Sondertribunals zur Verfolgung der russischen Aggression gegen die Ukraine gefordert. Zur Umsetzung dieser Forderung wurde Anfang des Jahres die sogenannte Kerngruppe zur Errichtung eines Sondertribunals zum Verbrechen der Aggression gegen die Ukraine ins Leben gerufen. Auf meine Veranlassung hin trat Österreich im März 2023 der Kerngruppe bei. Österreich tritt für die Schließung der Zuständigkeitslücke im Hinblick auf das Verbrechen der Aggression ein und beteiligt sich konstruktiv an den Beratungen der Kerngruppe zur Errichtung eines Sondertribunals.

In der Klage der Ukraine gegen die Russische Föderation vor dem Internationalen Gerichtshof (IGH) auf Grundlage der Völkermordkonvention habe ich veranlasst, dass Österreich im Oktober 2022 und Februar 2023 Erklärungen abgegeben hat, um die Ukraine als Streithelfer zu unterstützen. Es ist vollkommen inakzeptabel, dass Russland die Völkermordkonvention auf zynische Art und Weise missbraucht, um seinen brutalen und durch nichts zu rechtfertigenden Angriffskrieg gegen die Ukraine zu rechtfertigen. Außerdem hat Österreich im September 2022 um Zulassung als Drittintervenient in der Staatenklage der Ukraine gegen Russland vor dem Europäischen Gerichtshof für Menschenrechte (EGMR) angesucht. Im März 2023 bestätigte der EGMR insgesamt 31 Drittparteieninterventionen, darunter auch jene Österreichs.

Als Gaststaat nützt Österreich auch intensiv die OSZE, wo alle Beteiligten regelmäßig zusammenkommen, um Russland und auch Belarus für ihre Rolle im Angriffskrieg und bei Menschenrechtsverletzungen zur Verantwortung zu ziehen. Dies geschieht insbesondere in den in der Regel wöchentlichen Debatten im Ständigen Rat und im Forum für Sicherheitszusammenarbeit. Österreich hat gemeinsam mit der überwältigenden Mehrheit der teilnehmenden Staaten zwei Mal den Moskauer Mechanismus der OSZE zur Untersuchung von Menschenrechtsverletzungen einschließlich Kriegsverbrechen im Rahmen des russischen Angriffskrieges gegen die Ukraine angerufen. Am 30. März 2023 haben 45 Staaten der OSZE, darunter auch Österreich, den Moskauer Mechanismus noch einmal ausgelöst. Ziel ist es, die Vorwürfe schwerer Menschenrechtsverletzungen im Zusammenhang mit der erzwungenen Umsiedlung ukrainischer Kinder aus besetzten Gebiete der Ukraine sowie die Deportation ukrainischer Kinder nach Russland zu untersuchen. […]

QQ.I.2.g.-4

Parliamentary resolution concerning the Hamas terrorist attack on Israel

Parlamentarische Entschließung betreffend Terrorangriff der Hamas auf Israel

On 24 November 2023, the National Assembly adopted a parliamentary resolution concerning the Hamas terrorist attack on Israel:[134]

In view of the fact that the members of the presidential conferences of the Austrian National Council and the Federal Council condemn the terror against Israel in the strongest terms, demand the unconditional release of all hostages, above all

[134] Parliamentary Materials, 348/E(XXVII. GP).

to end the suffering of Israeli civilians, and that the Austrian Parliament expresses its unreserved solidarity with Israel and its people and expresses its deepest sympathy to the victims and their families, the Federal Government, in particular the Federal Minister for European and International Affairs, the Federal Minister for Arts, Culture, Civil Service and Sport, the Federal Minister for the EU and Constitution and the Federal Minister for Women, Family, Integration and the Media are requested,

- to continue to intensively support all political and diplomatic efforts, both bilaterally and in cooperation with the EU and international partners, to prevent a possible further spread of the war and to use all diplomatic levers to support an end to the violence against the civilian population;

- to work to ensure that the hostages abducted by Hamas and other terrorist groups in the Gaza Strip are released as soon as possible and unconditionally;

- to demand that international humanitarian law be respected by all parties involved in the course of hostilities, that humanitarian corridors be established and that safe and unrestricted access be guaranteed;

- to continue to work more intensively bilaterally and in harmony with the EU and international partners for compliance with international law and for a lasting and sustainable peace solution in the Middle East based on a two-state solution;

- to intensively and consistently continue the ongoing efforts in the fight against anti-Semitism, all forms of racism and extremism, hate speech and hate propaganda in Austria and throughout Europe;

- and to continue to vehemently support all international measures against terrorism and violent extremism.

The German original reads as follows:

Vor dem Hintergrund, dass die Mitglieder der Präsidialkonferenzen des österreichischen Nationalrats und des Bundesrates den Terror gegen Israel aufs Schärfste verurteilen, die bedingungslose Freilassung aller Geiseln fordern, vor allem, um das Leid der israelischen Zivilistinnen und Zivilisten zu beenden, und dass das österreichische Parlament seine uneingeschränkte Solidarität mit Israel und dessen Bevölkerung bekundet und den Opfern und deren Angehörigen sein tiefes Mitgefühl ausspricht, wird die Bundesregierung, insbesondere der Bundesminister für europäische und internationale Angelegenheiten, der Bundesminister für Kunst, Kultur, öffentlichen Dienst und Sport, die Bundesministerin für EU und Verfassung sowie die Bundesministerin für Frauen, Familie, Integration und Medien ersucht,

- weiterhin intensiv bilateral sowie im Verbund mit der EU und internationalen Partnern, alle politischen und diplomatischen Bemühungen zu unterstützen, um eine mögliche weitere Ausbreitung des Krieges zu unterbinden und alle diplomatischen Hebel zu nutzen, um ein Ende der Gewalt gegen die Zivilbevölkerung zu unterstützen;

- sich dafür einzusetzen, dass die durch die Hamas und andere Terrorgruppen in den Gazastreifen verschleppten Geiseln ehestmöglich und bedingungslos freigelassen werden;

- einzufordern, dass das humanitäre Völkerrecht im Zuge von Kampfhandlungen durch alle Beteiligten eingehalten, humanitäre Korridore eingerichtet und ein sicherer und uneingeschränkter Zugang gewährleistet werden;

- sich weiterhin verstärkt bilateral und im Einklang mit der EU und internationalen Partnern für die Einhaltung des Völkerrechts sowie für eine dauerhafte und nachhaltige Friedenslösung im Nahen Osten auf der Grundlage einer Zwei-Staaten-Lösung einzusetzen;

- die laufenden Bemühungen im Kampf gegen Antisemitismus, jegliche Form des Rassismus und Extremismus, der Hetze und Hasspropaganda in Österreich und in ganz Europa intensiv und konsequent fortzusetzen;

- sowie alle internationalen Maßnahmen gegen Terrorismus und gewalttätigen Extremismus weiter mit Vehemenz zu unterstützen.

i. Conventional, nuclear, bacteriological and chemical weapons/ Konventionelle, nukleare, bakteriologische und chemische Waffen

See *PP.II.1.-1* and *QQ.I.2.g.-2*.

II. Non-international armed conflict/Nicht-internationaler bewaffneter Konflikt

QQ.II.1

Parliamentary resolution on the immediate cessation of armed conflict in Sudan

Parlamentarische Entschließung betreffend die sofortige Einstellung der bewaffneten Auseinandersetzung im Sudan

On 23 May 2023, the National Assembly adopted a parliamentary resolution on the immediate cessation of armed conflict in Sudan:[135]

The Federal Government, in particular the Federal Minister for European and International Affairs, is requested

1. to work together with its EU partners and the United Nations in favour of an immediate end to the fighting in Sudan and for the observance of a sustainable ceasefire.

2. to work with EU partners to ensure the comprehensive protection of the civilian population and civilian infrastructure and compliance with international

---

[135] Parliamentary Materials, 323/E (XXVII.GP).

humanitarian law and to call for unhindered humanitarian access and an improvement in the humanitarian situation.

3. to maintain all efforts to provide assistance on the ground in order to alleviate the humanitarian emergency in Sudan and neighbouring countries.

4. to continue to work for the stabilisation of Sudan, a sustainable internal Sudanese political process and the establishment of democratic structures, and to provide Sudan with adequate instruments to overcome the socio-economic challenges in the country in the long term and continuously.

The German original reads as follows:

Die Bundesregierung, insbesondere der Bundesminister für europäische und internationale Angelegenheiten, wird ersucht,

1. sich im Verbund mit den EU-Partnern und den Vereinten Nationen für eine sofortige Einstellung der Kämpfe im Sudan und für die Einhaltung eines nachhaltigen Waffenstillstandes einzusetzen.

2. im Verbund mit den EU-Partnern für den umfassenden Schutz der Zivilbevölkerung und der zivilen Infrastruktur sowie die Einhaltung des humanitären Völkerrechts einzutreten und auf einen ungehinderten humanitären Zugang und eine Verbesserung der humanitären Lage hinzuwirken.

3. alle Bemühungen zur Hilfe vor Ort weiterhin aufrechtzuerhalten, um die humanitäre Notlage im Sudan und in den Nachbarländern zu mindern.

4. weiterhin für eine Stabilisierung des Sudan, einen nachhaltigen innersudanesischen politischen Prozess und die Etablierung demokratischer Strukturen einzutreten, sowie den Sudan mit adäquaten Instrumenten bei der Bewältigung der sozioökonomischen Herausforderungen im Land langfristig und kontinuierlich zu unterstützen.

SS. Legal aspects of international relations and cooperation in particular matters/Rechtliche Aspekte der internationalen Beziehungen und Zusammenarbeit in bestimmten Bereichen

I. General economic and financial matters/Wirtschaftliche und Finanzwirtschaftliche Angelegenheiten

3. Investments/Investitionen

See *CC.II.2-1.* and *GG.VI.-2.*

4. Taxes/Steuern

See *CC.IV.3.-1.*

III. Environment/Umwelt

See *KK.XI.-1.*

IV. Natural Resources/Natürliche Ressourcen

See *KK.XI.-1.*

VIII. Legal matters (*e.g.* judicial assistance and crime control etc.)/Rechtliche Angelegenheiten (z.B. Rechtshilfe und Verbrechensbekämpfung etc.)

See *FF.XI.-1.*

Book Reviews

Charles Proctor, *Mann and Proctor on the Law of Money*. Eighth Edition. Oxford University Press, Oxford, 2023. ISBN 9780198804925, lxxi + 845 pp., GBP 315.00 (Hardback)

What is money? How does it work? To what degree is its regulation, exchange, and cross-border traffic a topic of public international law? Is it even international law?

I have no clue. Until this day, I have not understood how money really works. Yes, I have heard about the differences between fiat money and currencies pegged against, most prominently, commodities like gold, about floating exchange rates or fixed ones, the US dollar as the global reserve currency, the end of the Bretton Woods system, and much more.

But I have not understood money and its legal rules, even more, I did not know them at all. So I did what people do nowadays, I googled and found the first edition from 1938, written by Mann himself, legally available for free,[1] an attempt, as he put it, to treat 'the legal aspects of money in a systematic and comprehensive manner' – exactly what I needed. Yet, Mann proceeded, directly in the opening sentences, to emphasize the obstacles he faced during the process of writing and compiling materials like court decisions. Furthermore, the book focused on English law and was obviously written before (albeit not that long) the establishment of the International Monetary Fund in 1944, the abolition of the Bretton Woods system in 1973, or the euro.

I then moved to the most recent – eighth – edition which surely does not lack resources, some 60 pages are dedicated to cases, legislation, and abbreviations. So does it provide what I was looking for – an explanation of what money is and how it is regulated?

If not in Mann's and – now Proctor's Law of Money, then probably nowhere. The book is as extensive as it gets: Chapter 1 defines money (including virtual and central bank digital currencies), Chapter 2 deals with the Organization of the Monetary system – albeit with a focus on the Sterling and the UK (there is also a short subchapter on France). Part II (Chapters 3-8) is dedicated to the private law of monetary obligations, Part III (Chapters 9-13) to nominalism, *i.e.*, to put it in general terms, the organizing principle that 'the State establishes a currency and its units of account represent their own independent value in terms of the

[1] <https://archive.org/details/mann-legal-aspect-money> accessed 6 December 2024.

Austrian Review of International and European Law **28**: 469-474, 2023.
© 2025 Koninklijke Brill BV | DOI:10.1163/15736512-02801014

domestic legal system, regardless of any external factors which may have an economic impact upon that currency'.[2] Part IV is focused on exchange controls, rates, and sanctions – again with a focus on the UK (which is dealt with in a distinct chapter (14)), but also includes chapters on the International Monetary Fund Agreement (Chapter 15), private international law of exchange control (Chapter 16), and a subchapter (17 E.) on EU sanctions. Part V moves to Public International Law of Money, with the final part dedicated to Monetary unions (the European Monetary Union is covered with two chapters here, 25 and 26), and other forms of monetary organizations. Here, we also find chapters on the Euro regulations (29), the Euro and monetary sovereignty (31) and, leaving us guessing why, withdrawal from the Eurozone (32).

The result is the most comprehensive book on the various legal frameworks dealing with money as such. While Proctor, like Mann, certainly does not read like a beginner's guide (I guess I still do not know what money is, but, having read Proctor himself, that is ok, in particular for lawyers, since no one really does[3]), he can take pride in continuing the standard work on this topic. Non-British readers should be particularly happy about Part V – monetary sovereignty, the protection of foreign currency systems and institutions, international rules of monetary conduct, and the monetary law of interstate obligations –, EU law people with Part VI and the chapters I just mentioned.

Those who are looking for a 'law of money for dummies'-book will not be happy as Proctor clearly does not address those who are at the very beginning of learning more about this topic. The international law-layman (me!) is being left alone to wonder who the target audience is ('What a book for bankers!', one of the reviewers wrote, '... a favourite for practitioners' another[4]) but happy about the part on public international money law – there is nothing comparable out there. *Iudex* apparently not only *non calculat*, but also seems unhappy to deal with money as such. That alone gives Proctor's continuance of the Mann tradition the status of an academic unicorn.

Ralph Janik

---

2 Charles Proctor, *Mann and Proctor on the Law of Money* (OUP 2022) 246.

3 'The troublesome question, "what is money?" has so frequently engaged the minds of economists that a lawyer might hesitate to join in the attempt to solve it'. *Ibid.*, 3.

4 See the OUP website, <https://global.oup.com/academic/product/mann-and-proctor-on-the-law-of-money-9780198804925?cc=at&lang=en&#> accessed 6 December 2024.

Martti Koskenniemi, *To the Uttermost Parts of the Earth. Legal Imagination and International Power*, 1300-1870. Cambridge University Press, Cambridge, 2021. ISBN 9780521745345, xviii + 1108 pp., GBP 78.99 (Paperback), GBP 165.00 (Hardback)

Martti Koskenniemi's rock star status in the world of international law means that the nerd community (to put it colloquially) has to read every word he writes. Or, at the very least, his books. *To the Uttermost Parts of the Earth* is obviously no exception.

With it, he travels back in history once again, but now way further than to the 'Men of 1873'[5], *i.e.* to those from the early 14th century – the beginning of the rule of law in France – to the German philosophical world of 1821 (Koskenniemi does not say whether he set this date because of the publication of Martens' third edition of his *Précis de droit des gens de l'Europe* or because of the publication of Hegel's *Grundlinien der Philosophie des Rechts*; the latter is, however, more likely).

At the same time, and as he himself makes clear at the very beginning, *To the Uttermost Parts of the Earth* is '*not* [own emphasis] a history of international law' as such but 'of the legal imagination as it operates in relationship to the use of power in contexts that we would today call international'[6] – that sounds similar but is fundamentally different. By legal imagination he means using a distinct vocabulary to persuade those with power and to find legal answers for new, albeit not-purely legal questions such as financing of medieval realms (international tax law?), the 'discovery' (my quotation marks fulfill the obvious purpose of making sure that no one accuses me of suggesting that one can really discover what others already 'found') of the 'new World' and how to treat its peoples, or a solution to the problem of two sides fighting a – subjectively or perhaps even objectively – just war. The men (and, as he again critically emphasized, these times were dominated by male philosophers) Koskenniemi describes were not hyper-objective and -rational individuals detached from real events. On the contrary, their thoughts were products of their time (paraphrazing the German '*ein Kind seiner Zeit*'-idiom) and surroundings, they wrote in specific contexts and (academic or other) settings. Koskenniemi thus went beyond merely reading texts and looked at their authors themselves, the times they lived in, and the interests they tried to defend (if they did). He both translates and takes the reader back in time and transplants their thoughts into the present.

---

5 Martti Koskenniemi, *The Gentle Civilizer of Nations: The Rise and Fall of International Law 1870–1960* (CUP 2009).

6 Martti Koskenniemi, To *the Uttermost Parts of the Earth. Legal Imagination and International Power, 1300-1870* (CUP 2021) 1.

To the Uttermost Parts of the Earth is also not a book that, like so many (interesting!) others that have been published recently, solely focuses on empire and colonialism (colonialism is hardly mentioned in the index, for example, as he views such politically, historically, and, more generally, emotionally charged words as more of a hindrance than those with explanatory value), but rather how pre-1870 philosophers 'used the legal vocabularies available to them in order to react to important events in the surrounding world'[7] in the 500 or so years before international law began to emerge as an intercommunal, European and US academic project. Legal imagination as the capacity of legal thinkers to create and conceptualize legal frameworks can be a form of political power and power language. Koskenniemi argues that the law was and is not simply a set of pre-existing rules that states follow, but a dynamic and evolving system shaped by individuals. Legal thought has always been intimately tied to political interests and the creation of legal concepts has been a way for powerful states or emperors to secure and consolidate their dominance.

Koskenniemi proceeds chronologically, by focusing on specific legal regions and institutions (*e.g.* Bologna, Montpellier, Orleans), and decisive events like the revolution in Haiti. Yet, by using legal imagination as the *Leitmotiv*, he once again adds to the fundamental and nowadays basic insight that international law and its legal-philosophical precursors have obviously always been shaped by political interests and power dynamics. Through a meticulous, Koskenniemi-style analysis of legal writings, treaties, and imperial expansion, we discover the numerous the ways in which legal imagination — the creation of legal concepts and frameworks — was instrumental in justifying and legitimizing the expansion of European empires, if not 'the' European empire (as a set of distinct power dynamics). Through the development and application of international law, European powers, flanked with philosophers of all sorts, justified their conquest of distant lands and the subjugation of indigenous peoples. Francisco de Vitoria and Hugo Grotius, to name just two examples, provided intellectual cover for the expansionist agendas of European empires by constructing legal arguments that rationalized colonialism as part of a divine or natural order. As it is now (hopefully!) well-known, international law was not merely a neutral framework for resolving disputes between states here, but an instrument of imperialism. From the late Middle Ages through the early modern period, legal doctrines were used to legitimize colonial expansion by framing European conquests as part of a civilizing mission. The doctrine of discovery, for example, provided a legal basis for European powers to claim sovereignty over lands occupied by indigenous populations. In this way, the legal imagination was not just a tool for governance; it was actively involved in constructing and reinforcing the power structures of empire.

---

[7] *Ibid.*

Overall, *To the Uttermost Parts of the Earth* is yet another Koskenniemi contribution to reading the history of international law, the relationship between law and power and how legal language adapted to new sociological, economic, or political trends. In line with Koskenniemi's reputation as one of the most influential figures in the field, the book offers an essential perspective on the way legal imagination has shaped – and continues to shape, but that is for the reader to discover – the global order. As implied at the beginning, this book is a must-read for anyone who seeks to understand not just the history of international law, but its ongoing implications for global politics and justice. Not because Koskenniemi's name is on the cover, but because the book itself is simply great.

Ralph Janik

David Schneiderman, *Investment Law's Alibis. Colonialism, Imperialism, Debt and Development*. Cambridge University Press: Cambridge, 2022. ISBN 9781009153492, x + 246 pp., GBP 22.99 (Softcover, published 2023), GBP 85.00 (Hardback)

Investment law has been heavily scrutinized and criticized in recent years,[8] with many of its conventional wisdoms constantly being challenged: did it fulfill its promises, are investment treaties really a prerequisite or even a guarantee for foreign direct investment, are arbitrators biased towards investors, are they really independent, do they take non-economic interests sufficiently into account, are their decisions sufficiently coherent, is there a chilling effect, and so on. The list is long and so are the arguments in favour and, even more so, against investment law as a whole or, at least, investor-state dispute settlement (ISDS).

As its very title already suggests, Schneiderman's book is no exception. He begins by revisiting the *very* origins of investment law – not the *Abs-Shawcross Draft Convention*[9] or the establishment of the International Centre for Settlement of Investment Disputes (ICSID) –,but 19th century European colonialism, to draw 'out resemblances, but also differences, between colonialism and the newer [implying that colonialism was its predecessor!] regime to protect foreign

8 See my review essay of Perrone, *Investment Treaties & The Legal Imagination. How Foreign Investors Play By Their Own Rules*, Salacuse, *The Law of Investment Treaties*, and Van Harten, *The Trouble with Foreign Investor Protection* published under the title 'The Twilight of Investor State Dispute Settlement (ISDS)' (2022) 26 ARIEL 643-647.

9 For further information and a discussion that aged well, see Georg Schwarzenberger, 'The Abs-Shawcross Draft Convention on Investments abroad: a critical commentary' (1960) 9 *Journal of Public Law* 147.

investors abroad'.[10] Chapter 2, then, treads the well-known path of the New International Economic Order (NIEO), followed by a discussion of the lasting impact of the late 19th/early 20th century 'discourse of civilized justice' (thus, the book does not follow a chronological order but rather tries to knit old with more recent or current debates, from the 'civilization' standard all the way to the self-assumed special status of liberal, market-based democracies (the new 'civilization' yardstick).

The fourth and fifth chapters go beyond core investment law-debates by critically assessing the role of the International Monetary Fund from the debt crisis of the 1980s onwards and how the concept of 'property' disregarded the rights of indigenous peoples. The final chapter, and this is one of the main strengths of this book, builds on these analyses and suggests alternatives and improvements of the investment law regime: 'divesting for development' and 'trimming the process', divestment instead of ISDS, engagement with local communities, and non-'Western' solutions. Personally, this chapter would certainly have deserved some more pages. Critiques of the investment regime have done their part in outlining the problems. For the real work to begin, the world, be it states or investors, needs implementable, realistic, and sufficiently promising alternatives – between apology and Utopia, not either-or.

For this reason alone (and many others), Schneiderman has managed to write a book that adds new perspectives and ideas to the many perspectives and ideas we already know when it comes to this popular genre of international law-related academic writing. If you thought *everything has been said, but not by everyone* applies to investment law-critique, Schneiderman's book will show you that it does not.

Ralph Janik

10 David Schneiderman, *Investment Law's Alibis. Colonialism, Imperialism, Debt and Development* (CUP 2022), 1.